EXPAND
STUDENT'S BOOK & WORKBOOK

Combo Edition

Carla Maurício Vianna
Charis Hannah - CSC India
Gisele Aga
Henrick Oprea
João Gabriel Schenferd
Luciana Santos Pinheiro
Megha Ramesh - CSC India
Simara H. Dal'Alba

Dados Internacionais de Catalogação na Publicação (CIP)
(Câmara Brasileira do Livro, SP, Brasil)

Expand: Student's Book: Combo Edition /
Carla Mauricio Vianna...[et al.]. -- São Paulo:
Pearson Education do Brasil, 2019.

Outros autores: Charis Hannah, Gisele Aga,
Henrick Oprea, João Gabriel Schenferd, Megha Ramesh.

ISBN 978-85-88317-84-0

1. Inglês (Ensino Médio) I. Vianna, Carla Mauricio.
II. Hannah, Charis. III. Aga, Gisele.
IV. Oprea, Henrick. V. Schenferd, João Gabriel.
VI. Ramesh, Megah.

19-25475   CDD-420.7

Índices para catálogo sistemático:
1. Inglês: Ensino Médio 420.7
Maria Alice Ferreira - Bibliotecária - CRB-8/7964

ISBN 978-85-88317-84-0 (Student's Book & Workbook)

2019

STUDENT'S BOOK & WORKBOOK

Carla Maurício Vianna
Charis Hannah
Gisele Aga
Henrick Oprea
João Gabriel Schenferd
Megha Ramesh

Head of Product - Pearson Brasil	Juliano de Melo Costa
Product Manager - Pearson Brasil	Marjorie Robles
Product Coordinator - ELT	Mônica Bicalho
Authors	Carla Maurício Vianna Gisele Aga Henrick Oprea
Teacher's Guide	Carla Maurício Vianna Gisele Aga
Workbook	Charis Hannah Gisele Aga Megha Ramesh João Gabriel Schenferd
Editor - ELT	Gisele Aga Renata S. C. Victor
Editor (Teacher's Book)	Simara H. Dal'Alba (Allya Assessoria Linguística)
Editorial Assistant - ELT	Simara H. Dal'Alba (Allya Assessoria Linguística)
Proofreader (English)	Silva Serviços de Educação
Proofreader (Portuguese)	Fernanda R. Braga Simon
Copyeditor	Maria Estela Alcântara
Pedagogical Reviewer	Najin Lima
Quality Control	Viviane Kirmeliene
Art and Design Coordinator	Rafael Lino
Art Editor - ELT	Emily Andrade
Acquisitions and permissions Manager	Maiti Salla
Acquisitions and permissions team	Cristiane Gameiro Heraldo Colon Maricy Queiroz Sandra Sebastião Shirlei Sebastião
Graphic design	Mirella Della Maggiore Armentano MRS Consultoria Editorial
Graphic design (cover)	Mirella Della Maggiore Armentano MRS Consultoria Editorial
Media Development	Estação Gráfica
Audio	Maximal Studio
Audiovisual Editor	Tatiane Almeida
Audiovisual	Desenrolados

The publisher would like to thank the following for their kind permission to reproduce their photographs:

123RF: p. 73. **ACPE**: p. 57. **Baldo**: p. 41. **Bridgeman**: p. 47. **Calvin & Hobbes**: p. 41, 116. **Cartoonstock**: p. 23. **Cathy Guisewite**: p. 40, 80. **Drable, Kevin Fagan**: p. 40. **Dreamstime**: p. 20, 56. **Food and Agriculture Organization of United Nations (FAO)**: p. 24. **Harvard T.H. Chan - School of Public Health**: p. 20 (Healthy eating plate). **iStock**: capa, p. 12, 13, 15, 18, 25, 27, 28, 32, 35, 53, 55, 56 (skateboarding), 61, 63, 71, 73, 106, 107, 108, 120. **Jump Start**: p. 40, 44. **King Features Syndication**: p. 116. **Met Museum**: p. 50. **Ministério da Saúde**: p. 109. **Paws**: p. 69. **Penguin Modern Classics**: p. 72, 78. **Shutterstock**: p. 9, 11, 17, 45, 46, 47, 59. **Stuart Carlson**: p. 80. **The Diana Award**: p.42. **Wonder Plugin**: p. 60

Every effort has been made to trace the copyright holders and we apologize in advance for any unintentional omissions. We would be pleased to insert the appropriate acknowledgement in any subsequent edition of this publication.

Dados Internacionais de Catalogação na Publicação (CIP)
(Câmara Brasileira do Livro, SP, Brasil)

Expand 1: Student's Book / Carla Maurício Vianna... [et al.]. -- São Paulo: Pearson Education do Brasil, 2019.

Outros autores: Charis Hannah, Gisele Aga, Henrick Oprea, João Gabriel Schenferd, Megha Ramesh.

ISBN 978-65-5011-028-4

1. Inglês (Ensino Médio) I. Vianna, Carla Maurício. II. Hannah, Charis. III. Aga, Gisele. IV. Oprea, Henrick. V. Schenferd, João Gabriel. VI. Ramesh, Megha.

19-25472　　　　　　　　　　　　　　　CDD-420.7

Índices para catálogo sistemático:
1. Inglês: Ensino Médio 420.7
Maria Alice Ferreira - Bibliotecária - CRB-8/7964

ISBN 978-65-50110-28-4 (Student's Book & Workbook)
ISBN 978-65-50110-29-1 (Teacher's Book)

2019

EXPAND 1

- Unit 1 9
- Unit 2 17
- Review 1 25
- Unit 3 27
- Unit 4 35
- Review 2 43
- Unit 5 45
- Unit 6 53
- Review 3 61
- Unit 7 63
- Unit 8 71
- Review 4 79

- Grammar Overview 81
- Language Reference 85
- Reading Strategies 93
- Irregular Verbs 94
- Common Mistakes 96
- False Friends 97
- Glossary 98
- Workbook 103
- Audio Scripts 136

CONTENTS

	READING	VOCABULARY IN USE	LANGUAGE IN USE 1	EXPAND YOUR READING	LANGUAGE IN USE 2	LISTENING COMPREHENSION
UNIT 1 Migration Trends — page 9	Article: What are the pull and push factors of migration?	Suffixes used to form adjectives	Simple present	Ad campaigns about immigration	Imperative form	Opinions about immigration
UNIT 2 "The First Wealth is Health" — page 17	Quiz: Healthy eating	Food items and nutrition	Simple present: interrogative form and frequency adverbs	Tips for making healthy eating decisions	Subject and object pronouns	Dietary guidelines around the world
Review 1 (Units 1-2) Page 25						
UNIT 3 Your Digital Self — page 27	Social media posts	False friends	Present simple vs. present continuous	Pros and cons of social media	Possessive adjectives	Social media extracts
UNIT 4 Establishing and Keeping Relationships — page 35	Magazine article: How the teen brain transforms relationships	Phrasal verbs related to relationships	Simple past	Comic strips about different kinds of relationship	Modal verbs: *can* and *should*	Bullying advice: an anti-bullying campaign
Review 2 (Units 3-4) Page 43						

Grammar Review page 81

Language Reference page 85

Reading Strategies page 93

Irregular Verbs page 94

	READING	VOCABULARY IN USE	LANGUAGE IN USE 1	EXPAND YOUR READING	LANGUAGE IN USE 2	LISTENING COMPREHENSION
UNIT 5 Art: The Language of Emotions ▶ page 45	Article: The most relevant art today is taking place outside the art world	Prefixes	Plural of nouns	Museum artifact descriptions	Order of adjectives	An artist talking about his work
UNIT 6 Sport is No Longer Just Sport ▶ page 53	Seminar series calendar: Power and politics of sports	Suffixes used to form nouns	Comparative adjectives	News report about the Olympic Games Tokyo 2020	Superlative adjectives	A talk about millennials' impact on the sports industry

Review 3 (Units 5-6)
▶ page 61

	READING	VOCABULARY IN USE	LANGUAGE IN USE 1	EXPAND YOUR READING	LANGUAGE IN USE 2	LISTENING COMPREHENSION
UNIT 7 Globish: Fad or Fact? ▶ page 63	Newspaper article: So, what's this Globish revolution?	Idioms	The 's for possession: the genitive case	Book summary: *The Future of English?*	Possessive pronouns	A talk about English being a global language
UNIT 8 Hit the Road ▶ page 71	Book excerpt: *The Great Railway Bazaar*	Packing for a trip and means of transportation	*Used to*	Tips on how to travel with only a carry-on bag	Modal verb: *must*	An interview about traveling on a radio show

Review 4 (Units 7-8)
▶ page 79

Common Mistakes
▶ page 96

False Friends
▶ page 97

Glossary
▶ page 98

Workbook
▶ page 103

Audio Scripts
▶ page 136

PRESENTATION

STUDENT'S BOOK

Welcome to the *Expand* collection! *Expand* prepares students for the English part of Brazilian exams ENEM and vestibular, which are aimed at testing students' ability to read a wide variety of authentic texts of different genres. *Expand* provides students with listening, speaking, and writing activities that help them to develop their overall knowledge of the language. Each thematic unit contains two reading sections that introduce grammar and vocabulary topics, as well as listening comprehension activities that give students contact with oral text genres.

OPENING PAGE

Each unit starts with an opening page containing:

IN THIS UNIT YOU WILL…

This shows the main objectives for the unit.

LEAD OFF

This section presents three to four questions for content contextualization.

> ▶ IN THIS UNIT YOU WILL…
> - talk about migration and its causes and results;
> - use the simple present to describe facts and routines;
> - use the imperative form to make requests and provide directions.

- What documents can you see in the picture?
- What does the word *immigration* mean to you?
- Why do people migrate?

READING PAGES

This two-page section contains the first reading text and activities of the unit. It develops reading strategies and is subdivided into the following stages:

BEFORE READING

This section contains one or two activities that help students to prepare for the text topic, which is presented in the section WHILE READING.

>> **BEFORE READING** — Bridging and relating to the topic

1. Not everything you read about nutrition is true. Read the statements and guess the ones that are not true. Then, check with your teacher.

WHILE READING

In this section students read a text and answer a question related to it. Texts are a variety of different genres and aimed at developing several reading strategies.

>> **WHILE READING** — Scanning

Read part of an article about the Globish revolution. According to the writer, is it easier or harder to communicate with business people using Globish?

So, what's this Globish revolution?

I say tomato… you say red, round fruit. Increasingly, people across the world use some sort of English, but it is not the Queen's. Robert McCrum, Observer Literary Editor, reports on why Globish - English-lite - is becoming the universal language of the **boardroom**,…

AFTER READING

This section has comprehension activities to help develop different after-reading strategies related to reading comprehension. These strategies are presented next to the instruction for each reading activity.

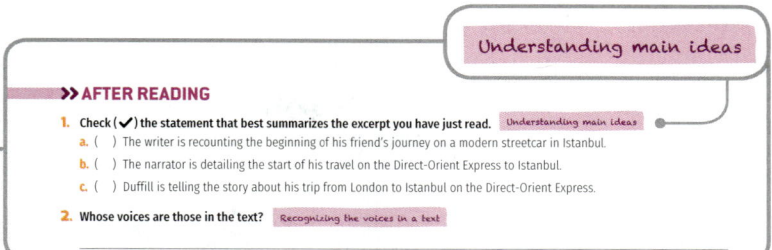

VOCABULARY PAGES

This stage develops students' vocabulary through activities containing vocabulary from the text and related to the topic of the unit.

EXPAND YOUR VOCABULARY

This section contains one to three activities related to the vocabulary presented in the text. It also prompts students to engage in conversational topics based on the text they have read.

VOCABULARY IN USE

Here students are presented with an example of target vocabulary taken from the main reading text and do activities to develop their vocabulary knowledge.

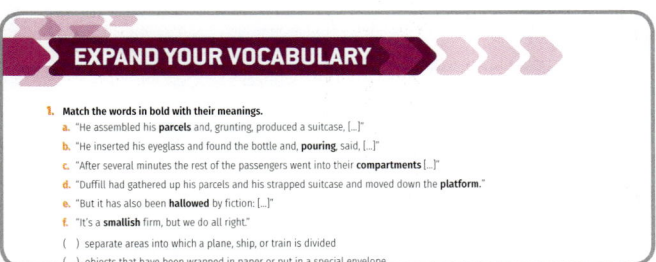

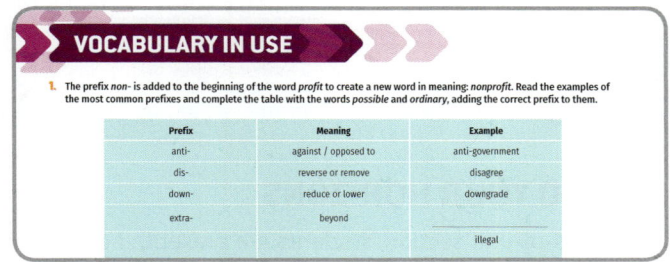

LANGUAGE IN USE 1

This page presents the first grammar topic of the unit. It contains examples from the text and activities that develop students' grammar knowledge in the target language.

EXPAND YOUR READING

This section contains another text for students to work on both the text genre and comprehension.

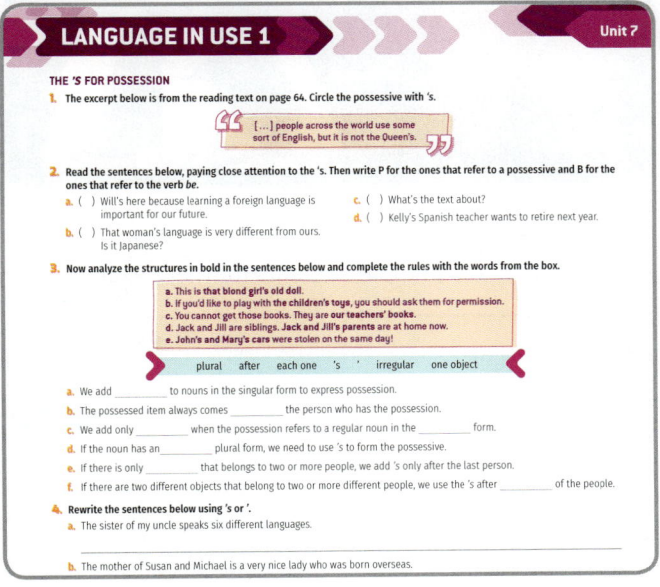

PRESENTATION

LANGUAGE IN USE 2

This page presents the second grammar topic of the unit. It contains examples from the text in *Expand your reading* and activities that develop students' grammar knowledge in the target language.

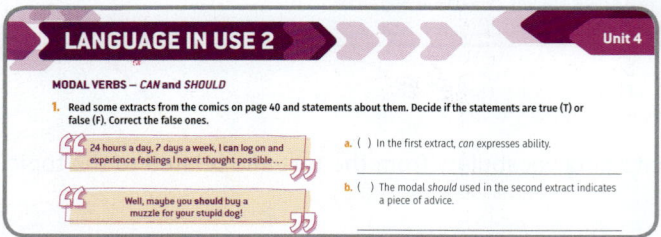

LISTENING COMPREHENSION

This section contains listening activities with authentic texts aimed at developing students' listening skills.

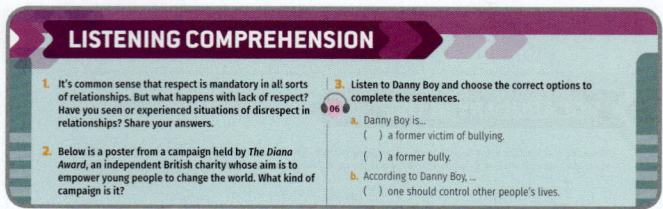

EXPAND YOUR HORIZONS

In this end-of-unit section, students are presented with three statements that allow them to discuss the topic in the listening comprehension section and think critically about it while using the target language.

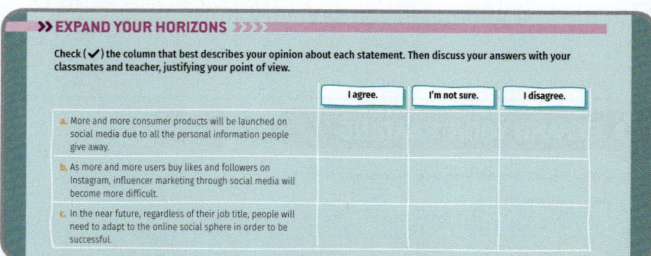

REVIEW

Every two units there is a two-page section for students to review and practice the language they have learned so far.

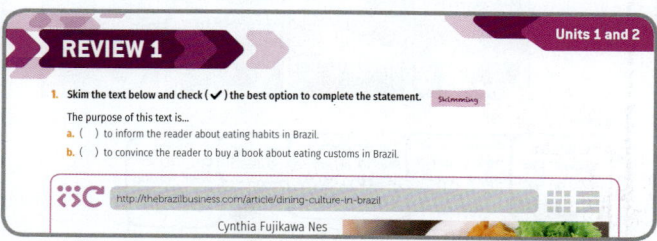

WORKBOOK

Each unit has four pages of reading, vocabulary, and grammar activities. It also has an ENEM or vestibular question in the section AN EYE ON ENEM / VESTIBULAR.

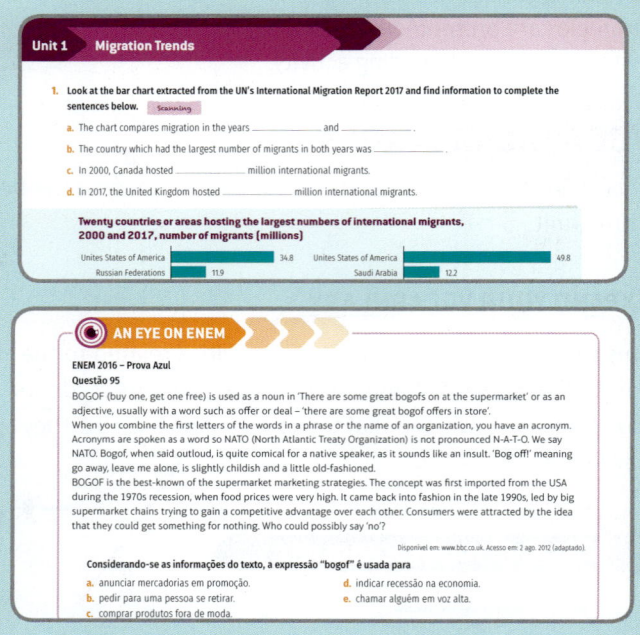

DIGITAL COMPONENTS

Video lessons for all *Language in Use* and *Vocabulary in Use* sections and for exam practice.

Mock test generator with major Brazilian *Vestibular* and ENEM questions to prepare students for these exams.

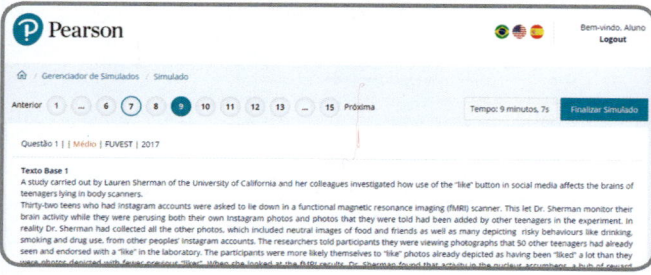

UNIT 1

Migration Trends

▶ IN THIS UNIT YOU WILL...

- talk about migration and its causes and results;
- use the simple present to describe facts and routines;
- learn how to form adjectives using suffixes;
- use the imperative form to make requests and provide directions.

LEAD OFF

- What documents can you see in the picture?
- What does the word *immigration* mean to you?
- Why do people migrate?

READING

›› BEFORE READING — Relating to the topic

There are several reasons why people migrate. Number the reasons from 1 (the most common) to 4 (the least common) in your opinion.

_____ environmental   _____ economic   _____ cultural   _____ socio-political

> **migrate** [intransitive + *from/to*] if people migrate, they go to live in another area or country, especially in order to find work
>
> Extracted from www.ldoceonline.com/dictionary/migrate. Accessed on May 4, 2018.

›› WHILE READING — Skimming

Skim the text to find out its main objective. Then check (✓).

a. ( ) To describe the writer's own experiences.
b. ( ) To inform the reader about why people migrate.

http://eschooltoday.com/migration/the-pull-and-push-factors-of-migration.html

What are the Pull and Push Factors of Migration?

People migrate for a number of reasons. These reasons may fall under these four areas: *Environmental, Economic, Cultural,* and *Socio-political*. Within these areas, the reasons may also be '*push*' or '*pull*' factors.

Push Factors

Push factors are those that force the individuals to move voluntarily, and in many cases, they are forced because they
5 risk something if they stay. Push factors may include *conflict, drought, famine,* or extreme religious activity.

Poor economic activity and
10 lack of job opportunities are also strong push factors for migration. Other strong push factors include race, discriminating cultures,
15 political *intolerance*, and *persecution* of people who question the **status quo**.

Pull Factors

Pull factors are those in the destination country that attract the individual or group to leave their home. Those factors are known
20 as "place utility", which is the **desirability** of a place that attracts people. Better economic opportunities, more jobs, and the promise of a better life often pull people into new locations.

Sometimes individuals have ideas and perceptions about places
25 that are not necessarily correct, but are strong pull factors for them. As people grow older and **retire**, many look for places with warm weather and peaceful and comfortable locations to spend their retirement after a lifetime of hard work and savings. Such ideal places are pull factors too.

Very often, people consider and prefer different opportunities closer
30 to their location than similar opportunities farther away. In the same vein, people often like to move to places with better cultural, political, climatic, and general terrain located closer to them. It is rare to find people who move very long distances to **settle** in places that they have little **knowledge** of.

Adapted from http://eschooltoday.com/migration/the-pull-and-push-factors-of-migration.html. Accessed on June 25, 2018.

Unit 1

»AFTER READING

1. Label the pictures according to the dictionary entries below. Can you exchange the labels of the pictures? Why (not?) *Understanding main ideas*

> **immigrant**
> someone who enters another country to live there permanently
>
> **refugee**
> someone who has been forced to leave their country, especially during a war, or for political or religious reasons
>
> Extracted from www.ldoceonline.com/dictionary/refugee. Accessed on June 26, 2018.

a.

b.

2. Underline the incorrect information in each statement. *Understanding details*

   a. Poor economic activity and a great number of job opportunities are also strong push factors for migration.

   b. Push factors do not include conflict, drought, famine, or extreme religious activity.

   c. Push factors are those in the destination country that attract the individual or group to leave their home.

   d. As people grow older and retire, some look for places with warm weather.

3. Rewrite the statements from activity 2 with the correct information.

   a. _____

   b. _____

   c. _____

   d. _____

EXPAND YOUR VOCABULARY

1. Find the words in *italics* in the reading. Then match each word with its meaning.

( ) conflict   **a.** unwillingness to accept ways of thinking and behaving that are different from your own

( ) drought   **b.** a long period of time when there is little or no rain

( ) famine   **c.** a state of disagreement or argument between people, groups, countries, etc.

( ) intolerance   **d.** a situation in which a large number of people have little or no food for a long time and many people die

( ) persecution   **e.** cruel or unfair treatment of someone over a period of time, especially because of their religious or political beliefs

2. What about your country or the area where you live? Does it have any of the issues mentioned above? Use some of the vocabulary from activity 1 to write a statement describing a similar issue where you live.

_____

_____

VOCABULARY IN USE

1. The suffix *-al* is used to form adjectives from nouns, with the meaning "relating to". The word *cultural* in the text means "relating to a particular society and its way of life". Go back to the text on page 10 and find other adjectives formed using the suffix *-al*.

_____

2. Use the following adjectives to complete the sentences.

> environmental   international   musical   political   presidential

a. They are a very _____ family.
b. Ocean pollution is a serious _____ issue.
c. This is an event organized by _____ activists.
d. A large crowd was in front of the _____ palace.
e. Immigration is an important _____ issue.

3. Use the suffixes in the columns to create new words from the words in the box.

> access   adventure   artist   attract   danger   economy
> harm   help   hope   invent   sleeve   understand

-able / -ible	-ful	-ic / -ical	-ive	-less	-ous

4. Complete the sentences below with some adjectives from the table in activity 3.

a. My brother is highly _____. He loves to create new things.

b. It's terribly hot here in the summer, so wear _____ shirts.

c. She is such an _____ girl that she is always looking for a new place to visit.

d. Susan is such a nice and _____ girl. She always offers help when needed.

e. The hotel is only _____ by boat as it is located on a island.

f. I love to watch the _____ in the synchronized swimming event in the Olympics.

5. Work with a partner. Describe one person and one thing in you classroom using adjectives with suffixes.

_____
_____

LANGUAGE IN USE 1

Unit 1

SIMPLE PRESENT

1. Read these excerpts from the text on page 10. Focus on the underlined words. Then decide if the statements are true (T) or false (F).

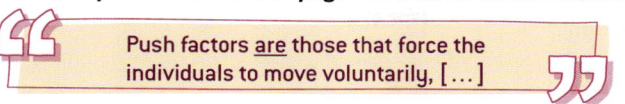
Push factors are those that force the individuals to move voluntarily, [...]

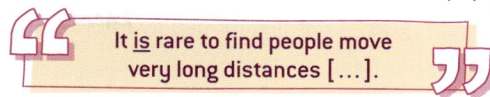
It is rare to find people move very long distances [...].

a. ( ) Based on the sentences we can say that *be* is a stative verb, that is, there is no action described.
b. ( ) Both sentences have the verb *be* as the main verb.
c. ( ) The verb *be* in the simple present has the same form for all subjects.

2. Now analyze the structures in bold in the excerpts below and check (✓) the option that corresponds to what they express.

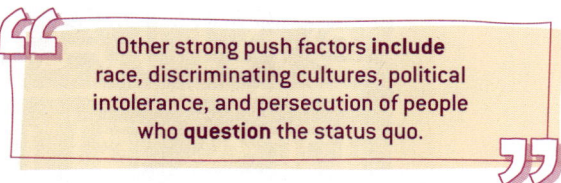
Other strong push factors **include** race, discriminating cultures, political intolerance, and persecution of people who **question** the status quo.

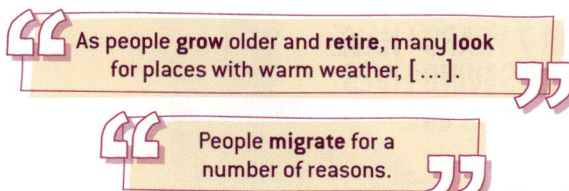
As people **grow** older and **retire**, many **look** for places with warm weather, [...].

People **migrate** for a number of reasons.

a. ( ) Something that is true in the present or something that happens again and again in the present.
b. ( ) Something that is happening at the moment of speaking.
c. ( ) Something which we think is temporary.

3. Complete the texts with the appropriate form of the verbs in parentheses.

a. Migration _____ (occur / occurs) primarily between countries that _____ (is / are) located within the same world region. In 2017, the majority of the international migrants originating from Europe (67%), Asia (60%), Oceania (60%) and Africa (53%) _____ (reside / resides) in a country located in their region of birth.
In contrast, international migrants from Latin America and the Caribbean (84%) and Northern America (72%) reside primarily outside their region of birth.

Extracted from www.un.org/en/development/desa/population/migration/publications/ migrationreport/docs/MigrationReport2017_Highlights.pdf. Accessed on March 6, 2018.

b. Globally, the twenty largest countries or areas of origin _____ (account / accounts) for almost half (49%) of all international migrants, while one-third (34%) of all international migrants _____ (originate / originates) in only ten countries. India _____ (is / are) now the country with the largest number of people living outside the country's borders ("diaspora"), followed by Mexico, the Russian Federation, and China.

Adapted from www.un.org/en/development/desa/population/migration/ publications/migrationreport/docs/MigrationReport2017_Highlights.pdf. Accessed on March 6, 2018.

4. Use the verbs from the box to complete the extract below.

| arrive | marks | sit | wait |

[...] The broken line snakes back 8 miles (13 km) to the border crossing at Paraguachon, where more than a hundred Venezuelans _____ in the heat outside the migration office.

Money changers _____ at tables stacked with wads of Venezuelan currency, made nearly worthless by hyperinflation under President Nicolas Maduro's socialist government.

The remote outpost on the arid La Guajira peninsula on Colombian's Caribbean coast _____ a frontline in Latin America's worst humanitarian crisis.

The Venezuelans _____ hungry, thirsty, and tired, often unsure where they will spend the night, but relieved to have escaped the calamitous situation in their homeland. [...]

Adapted from www.reuters.com/article/us-colombia-venezuela-migrants/ migrate-or-die-venezuelans-flood-into-colombia-despite-crackdown-idUSKCN1GA1K9. Accessed on March 7, 2018.

EXPAND YOUR READING

1. **Read these ad campaigns and complete the sentences with the corresponding letters.**

   a. Ads _____, _____, and _____ are for immigration and ad _____ is against immigration.

   b. Ad _____ gives a warning for people not to do something.

Extracted from us.iasservices.org.uk/I-Am-An-Immigrant-Poster-Campaign-Highlights-Positives-Of-Immigration. Accessed on May 6, 2018.

Extracted from weeklydialog.wordpress.com/2013/01/31/britain-0-vs-romania-1-ad-campaign-to-put-off-potential-immigrants/. Accessed on March 7, 2018.

Extracted from www.jigsaw-online.com/category/new/shop-the-campaign. Accessed on May 6, 2018.

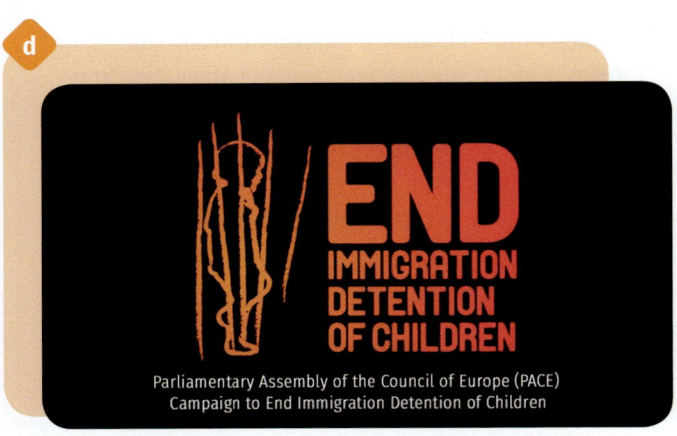

Extract from https://endchilddetention.org/. Acessed on November 11, 2018.

2. **Underline the correct option to complete the statements according to the ad campaigns you've just read.**

   a. The objective of the ads is to **encourage product sales** / **advertise an idea**.

   b. **All of them** / **Some of them** use appealing images.

   c. They **provoke** / **don't provoke** negative and positive social judgement.

LANGUAGE IN USE 2

Unit 1

IMPERATIVE FORM

1. Go back to the ads on the previous page and look at the verb *end*. It is in the affirmative imperative form. Why is this form of the verb used? Check (✓) the correct alternative.
   a. ( ) To give the target audience an instruction, a suggestion, or an order.
   b. ( ) To describe what is going on in each ad.

2. *Don't come* is in the negative imperative form. To form the negative imperative we use…

   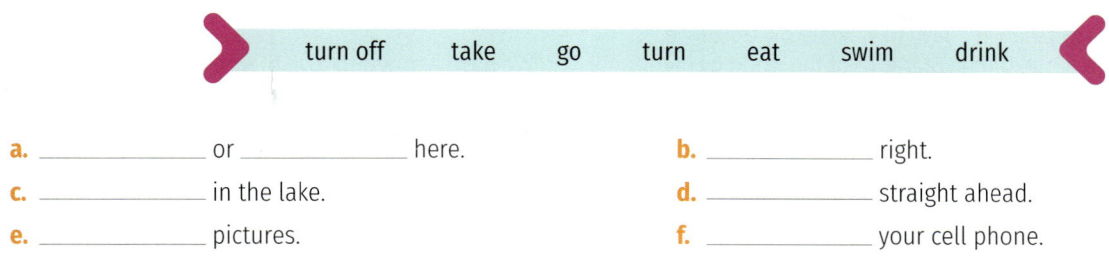
   _____ + the infinitive form of the verb without *to*

3. Complete the instructions with the correct imperative form of the verbs in the box. Then match the instructions with the signs.

   turn off   take   go   turn   eat   swim   drink

   a. _____ or _____ here.
   b. _____ right.
   c. _____ in the lake.
   d. _____ straight ahead.
   e. _____ pictures.
   f. _____ your cell phone.

LISTENING COMPREHENSION

1. Why are some people against immigration? Talk to a classmate and list some reasons. Then exchange ideas with your classmates and teacher.

_____
_____
_____

2. You are going to listen to some people talking about immigration. Label the excerpts a-e in the order you hear them.

02

( ) "Make us feel safe. We need to feel safe in this country. I think there's a great divide between the races."

Extracted from www.usatoday.com/pages/interactives/trump-nation/#/?_k=wi8jwl Accessed on May 7, 2018.

( ) "I don't feel as though I have to validate my existence as a citizen of the United States or of the world by my accomplishments but all of my accomplishments are driven by my family and where we're from."

Extracted from https://edition.cnn.com/videos/us/2018/01/12/ Accessed on March 7, 2018.

( ) "I believe that he will make America great again and that means a return of jobs. So, in that manner maybe I will find employment."

Extracted from www.usatoday.com/pages/interactives/trump-nation/#/?_k=wi8jwl Accessed on May 7, 2018.

( ) "When Mexico sends its people, they're not sending the best. They're sending people that have lots of problems and they're bringing those problems."

Extracted from www.cbsnews.com/pictures/wild-donald-trump-quotes/9. Accessed on May 6, 2018.

( ) "We have learned to love this country, Mr. President. This country does not belong to you only, but it belongs to all of us."

Extracted from https://edition.cnn.com/videos/us/2018/01/12/ Accessed on March 7, 2018.

( ) "We are able to move to these foreign countries where we don't know the language, we don't know the lifestyle, and adapt fairly quickly."

Extracted from https://edition.cnn.com/videos/us/2018/01/12/ Accessed on March 7, 2018.

3. Which testimonials do you think are said by immigrants? Why?

›› EXPAND YOUR HORIZONS ››››

Check (✓) the column that best describes your opinion about each statement. Then discuss your answers with your classmates and teacher, justifying your point of view.

	I agree.	I'm not sure.	I disagree.
a. Racism and xenophobia are feelings that local people may develop against immigrants.			
b. Immigration is a characteristic of our globalized world that has both positive and negative effects on the economy of a country.			
c. Cosmopolitan cities are multicultural because of their large immigrant population.			

STUDY THIS

xenophobia

strong fear or dislike of people from other countries

Extracted from www.ldoceonline.com/dictionary/xenophobia. Accessed on July 17, 2018.

UNIT 2
"The First Wealth is Health"
R. Emerson

▶ IN THIS UNIT YOU WILL...
- talk about nutritional information in Brazil and around the world;
- discuss healthy eating habits;
- use the simple present to ask and answer questions;
- use adverbs of frequency;
- learn how to use subject and object pronouns.

LEAD OFF

> What can you see in the picture?
> How does the picture relate to your eating habits?
> Read the title of the unit: do you agree with the quote by the American poet Ralph Waldo Emerson?
> What do you consider healthy eating?

READING

►► BEFORE READING — Bridging and relating to the topic

1. Not everything you read about nutrition is true. Read the statements and guess the ones that are <u>not</u> true. Then check with your teacher.
   - a. ( ) Lunch is the most important meal of the day.
   - b. ( ) People with diabetes don't need to give up sweets.
   - c. ( ) Carbohydrates aren't part of a healthy diet.
   - d. ( ) Milk is one of the best and cheapest calcium sources.
   - e. ( ) Egg yolks are unhealthy.

2. Work in small groups. Discuss the statements from activity 1. Relate the myths or facts to your reality at home and at school.

►► WHILE READING

1. Look at the text's layout and title. Then read the statements below and underline the one that best summarizes it. *Skimming*
   - a. The text persuades readers to buy a product.
   - b. The text invites readers to join an event.
   - c. The text measures readers' knowledge about a topic.

2. Take the Fruit Quiz below and test your knowledge.

---

https://www.choosemyplate.gov/quiz

Quiz Time!

QUESTION 1
Which of these nutrients can you get from eating whole fruit that is not usually found in juice?
( ) Vitamins   ( ) Minerals   ( ) Fiber   ( ) Sugar

QUESTION 2
Potassium is a nutrient that many Americans don't get enough of. Which of the following is a good fruit source of this mineral known to help regulate **blood pressure**?
( ) **Dried apricots**   ( ) Orange juice
( ) Bananas   ( ) All of the above

QUESTION 3
Which fruit is this?
( ) **Cantaloupe**   ( ) **Star fruit**
( ) Papaya   ( ) **Moon fruit**
( ) Mango

QUESTION 4
Eating a diet rich in fruits and vegetables as part of an overall healthy diet may protect against certain types of cancer.
( ) True   ( ) False

QUESTION 5
Which of the following counts as part of the Fruit Group?
( ) **Canned** peaches   ( ) Fresh strawberries
( ) Dried apricots   ( ) All of the above
( ) 100% orange juice

QUESTION 6
Fiber found in fruit is associated with which of the following health **outcomes**?
( ) **Strengthening** bones
( ) Maintaining proper **bowel** function
( ) Building muscle
( ) Making new blood cells

QUESTION 7
Fruits are sources of which of the following?
( ) Folate   ( ) Vitamin D   ( ) Calcium   ( ) Protein

QUESTION 8
Which of these foods is actually a fruit in plant biology?
( ) Onion   ( ) **Mushrooms**
( ) Pepper   ( ) All of the above

QUESTION 9
Which of these foods is a **source** of vitamin C?
( ) Pineapples   ( ) Oranges
( ) Strawberries   ( ) All of the above

QUESTION 10
What do fruits have that make them sweet?
( ) Vitamin C   ( ) Protein
( ) Fiber   ( ) **Pleasing** or **agreeable** personalities
( ) Fructose

Extracted from www.choosemyplate.gov/quiz. Accessed on May 11, 2018.

>> AFTER READING

1. Check the answers to the quiz. Compare your results to a classmate's.   *Understanding main ideas*

QUESTION 1

Correct Answer: Fiber

Fiber is found in the pulp of the fruit. When juice is made, the pulp is usually removed. Unfortunately, the fiber goes with it.

QUESTION 2

Correct Answer: All of the above

Potassium is a nutrient found in a wide variety of foods – from fruits to some beans (**white beans**, **soy beans**), vegetables (spinach, potatoes), fish (**halibut**, **tuna**), and low-fat yogurt and milk, too.

QUESTION 3

Correct Answer: Mango

Mango is a fruit that can be eaten **raw** or added to recipes, such as a **stir fry**, for added sweetness.

QUESTION 4

Correct Answer: True

As a part of an overall healthy diet, eating a diet rich in fruits and vegetables may reduce risk for heart disease, protect against certain types of cancer, and help **lower intake** of calories.

QUESTION 5

Correct Answer: All of the above

Any fruit or 100% fruit juice counts as part of the Fruit Group. Fruits may be fresh, canned, frozen, or dried, and may be whole, **cut-up**, or **pureed**.

QUESTION 6

Correct Answer: Maintaining proper bowel function

Eating foods that contain fiber – such as fruits, vegetables, and whole grains – may reduce risk for heart disease, protect against certain types of cancer, and help maintain proper bowel function.

QUESTION 7

Correct Answer: **Folate**

Folate is one of the B vitamins and is needed by all of our cells for **growth**. Although vitamin D and calcium are not typically found in high amounts in fruits, you can find some 100% orange juices that are fortified with calcium and vitamin D.

QUESTION 8

Correct Answer: Pepper

In plant biology, a fruit contains the seeds of a plant. Though it is botanically a fruit, a pepper counts toward the Vegetable Group because we eat peppers in a similar way to vegetables (on sandwiches, in soups, in pasta **sauces**). **Likewise**, tomatoes, **squash**, **cucumbers**, and pumpkins all contain the seeds of the plant and are therefore botanically fruits.

QUESTION 9

Correct Answer: All of the above

All fruits (and vegetables, too) contain some amount of vitamin C – an important nutrient that is needed for the growth and repair of **tissues** in all parts of your body.

QUESTION 10

Correct Answer: Fructose

Fructose is a natural sugar found in fruit that is responsible for the sweet flavor of many fruits.

Adapted from www.choosemyplate.gov/quiz. Accessed on June 29, 2018.

2. Read the quiz and its answers again. Then analyze the statements below and decide if they are true (T) or false (F).   *Understanding details*

a. (   ) All fruits have high amounts of vitamin D and calcium.

b. (   ) Tomatoes and pumpkins are considered botanically fruits because they contain some amount of vitamin C.

c. (   ) Potassium can be found in several foods such as spinach, white beans, bananas, and low-fat milk.

d. (   ) Eating foods rich in fiber helps reduce risk for heart disease.

e. (   ) Fructose and pepper are important nutrients for the growth and repair of our body tissues.

EXPAND YOUR VOCABULARY

1. Refer back to the quiz and look for words or expressions to fit the definitions below.

a. _____: the amount of food, drink, etc, that you take into your body

b. _____: the soft inside part of a fruit or vegetable

c. _____: an illness which affects a person, animal, or plant

d. _____: the particular taste of a food or drink

e. _____: a natural substance such as iron that is present in some foods and is important for good health

Adapted from www.ldoceonline.com/dictionary/. Accessed on June 29, 2018.

2. Discuss the questions below with a classmate.

a. How important is it to learn about good nutrition?

b. What role do financial circumstances play in healthy eating habits?

c. What is the basic food intake pattern in Brazil based on?

d. If you could change one thing about your nutrition habits, what would it be? Why?

VOCABULARY IN USE

1. The Healthy Eating Plate was designed by nutrition experts at Harvard School of Public Health and editors at Harvard Health Publications. Use the words from the box to complete it.

   colors   butter   healthy protein   vegetables   coffee   white bread

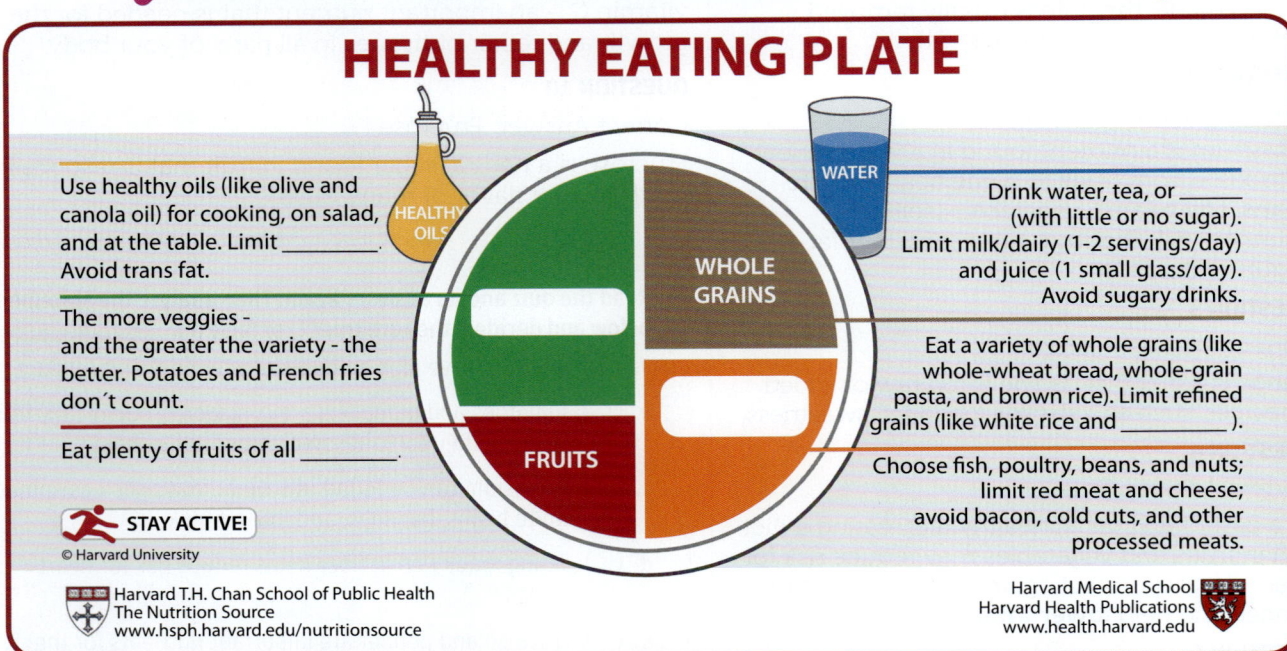

Extracted from www.hsph.harvard.edu/nutritionsource/healthy-eating-plate. Accessed on May 13, 2018.

2. Circle the best options to complete the statements about healthy eating according to the infographic in activity 1.
   a. One should restrict milk and dairy products such as **whole grain pasta and brown rice** / **cheese and butter** to one or two servings per day.
   b. **Olive and canola oils** / **Partially hydrogenated oils** are considered healthy oils.
   c. **Seafood and red meat** / **Bread and pasta**, mainly their wholegrain versions, are high in fiber, thus lowering one's risk of heart disease and constipation.
   d. **Lettuce, cabbage, and carrots** / **Fish, poultry, and beans** are examples of vegetables.
   e. Sodas, fruit juices, energy drinks, sugar-sweetened teas, and coffees are high in **added sugar and calories** / **carbohydrates** and refined oils and low in **fat** / **nutrients**.

3. Look at some other food items. Write their names under the correct headings.

Fruit & Vegetables	Proteins	Grains	Dairy

4. Compare your eating habits and the Healthy Eating Plate. Do you think the infographic reflects the reality of the region where you live? Justify your answer.

_____

_____

LANGUAGE IN USE 1

Unit 2

SIMPLE PRESENT – INTERROGATIVE FORM AND FREQUENCY ADVERBS

1. The questions below were extracted from the quiz on page 18. Read them and complete the statements about the simple present.

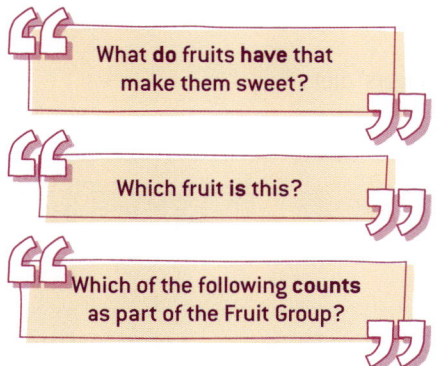

- "What **do** fruits **have** that make them sweet?"
- "Which fruit **is** this?"
- "Which of the following **counts** as part of the Fruit Group?"

a. The extracts on the left are in the _____ form.

b. To form interrogative sentences in the simple present, we use _____ when *I*, *you*, *we*, and *they* are the subject and *does* when *he*, *she*, and *it* are the subject.

c. For questions with the verb _____, we invert the position of the subject and the verb.

d. In subject questions, like the third one, there is no _____ verb and the word order is not inverted.

e. _____, *which*, *when*, *where*, and *how* are some question words that are used in information questions.

2. Now read the testimonials below carefully, paying attention to the words in bold, and choose the right alternative to complete the paragraph.

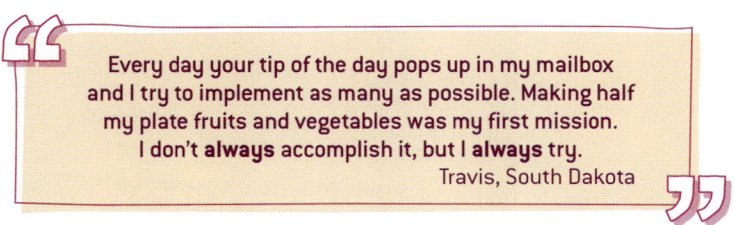

"Every day your tip of the day pops up in my mailbox and I try to implement as many as possible. Making half my plate fruits and vegetables was my first mission. I don't **always** accomplish it, but I **always** try."
Travis, South Dakota

"I **never** ate a lot of leafy green things before my nutrition class this semester. Our teacher brought in kale and spinach and a few others and we each took one home. My Mom used one of your recipes and made a kale salad that I have to admit was actually really good! #GoMom"
Kevin, New Hampshire

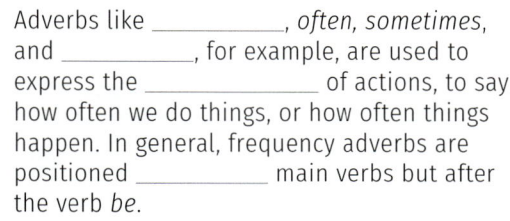

Adverbs like _____, *often*, *sometimes*, and _____, for example, are used to express the _____ of actions, to say how often we do things, or how often things happen. In general, frequency adverbs are positioned _____ main verbs but after the verb *be*.

a. ( ) always – far – frequency – after
b. ( ) always – never – frequency – before
c. ( ) often – always – time – before

Extracted from www.choosemyplate.gov/testimonials.
Accessed on June 29, 2018.

3. Use the correct form of the verbs from the box to complete the questions from the Brazilian Dietary Guidelines.

| affect | be | broaden | derive | refer |

a. Besides the intake of nutrients, what else _____ diet _____ to?
Diet also refers to nutritious foods and how they are combined and prepared in meals.

b. _____ cultural and social dimensions of food choices _____ health and well-being?
Yes, and so do food preparation and modes of eating.

c. Where _____ healthy diets _____ from?
They derive from socially and environmentally sustainable food systems.

d. What _____ people's autonomy in food choices?
The access to respectable dietary recommendations.

e. _____ dietary patterns different in most countries?
Yes, they are. Especially in economically emerging countries.

Based on www.bvsms.saude.gov.br/bvs/publicacoes/dietary_guidelines_brazilian_population.pdf. Accessed on June 29, 2018.

EXPAND YOUR READING

1. **Read the text and circle the correct option.**
   a. The objective of the text is to show healthy recipes for teenagers.
   b. The text shows healthy tips for teenagers.
   c. The text presents a list of fruits and vegetables that teenagers can't eat.
   d. The objective of the text is to talk about ads and how they influence teenagers' diets.

---

www.niddk.nih.gov/health-information/weight-management/take-charge-health-guide-teenagers

Take Charge of your Health: a Guide for Teenagers

Here are some helpful tips for making healthy eating decisions.

Many teens need more of these nutrients:

- Calcium, to build strong bones and teeth. Good sources of calcium are fat-free or low-fat milk, yogurt, and cheese.
- Vitamin D, to keep bones healthy. Good sources of vitamin D include orange juice, whole oranges, tuna, and fat-free or low-fat milk.
- Potassium, to help lower blood pressure. Try a banana, or **baked** potato with the skin, for a potassium boost.
- Fiber, to help you stay regular and feel full. Good sources of fiber include beans and **celery**.

- Protein, to power you up and help you grow strong. Peanut butter; eggs; tofu; legumes, such as lentils and peas; and chicken, fish, and low-fat meats are all good sources of protein.
- **Iron**, to help you grow. Red meat contains a form of iron that your body absorbs best. Spinach, beans, peas, and iron-fortified cereals are also sources of iron. You can help your body absorb the iron from these foods better when you also eat foods with vitamin C, like an orange.

Control your food portions

A portion is how much food or beverage you choose to consume at one time, whether in a restaurant, from a package, at school or a friend's, or at home. Many people consume larger portions than they need, especially when away from home.

Just one super-sized, fast food meal may have more calories than you need in a whole day. And when people are served more food, they may eat or drink more—even if they don't need it. This habit may lead to weight gain.

Adapted from www.niddk.nih.gov/health-information/weight-management/take-charge-health-guide-teenagers. Accessed on July 19, 2018.

---

2. **Read the text again and underline the correct options.**
   a. One of the main nutrients that teens need is **iron** / **vitamin E**.
   b. A good source of protein is **baked potato** / **fish**.
   c. Your body absorbs iron more easily if you eat foods with **vitamin C** / **vitamin D**.
   d. Eating one very large meal a day gives you **more** / **less** calories than you need in a whole day.
   e. **Spinach** / **Banana** is also a source of iron.
   f. **Protein** / **Calcium** helps to build strong teeth and bones.

LANGUAGE IN USE 2

Unit 2

OBJECT PRONOUNS

1. Below you will find some extracts from the text on page 22. Read them and answer the questions that follow.

> [...] protein, to power **you** up and help **you** grow strong

> **You** can help your body absorb the iron from these foods better when **you** also eat foods with vitamin C [...]

> And when people are served more food, **they** may eat or drink more—even if **they** don't need **it**.

a. In the first extract, is the pronoun *you* a subject or object of the sentence?

_____

b. How about in the second extract? Is the pronoun *you* the subject or the object of the sentence?

_____

c. In the third extract, what does the subject pronoun *they* refer to?

_____

d. In the third extract, is the pronoun *it* the subject or the object of the sentence? What does it refer to?

_____

2. Read the paragraph and complete the table below with the object pronouns in bold.

> My mom usually makes **me** lunch and she always makes sure that some of the food contains protein. She usually cooks red meat, because I love **it**! She also cooks some vegetables, like broccoli and carrots, but to be honest, I don't like **them** very much. Sometimes we have lunch together and I can tell **her** all about my day at school.

Subject pronouns	Object pronouns
I	
you	you
he	him
she	
it	
we	us
you	you
they	

3. Work in pairs. Circle the pronouns in the cartoon and discuss whether they are subject or object pronouns. Then share your opinions about the cartoon.

"Chocolate covered raisins, chocolate covered strawberries, chocolate covered cherries, and chocolate covered orange slices is not what I meant when I said that fruit is healthy for you."

Extracted from www.cartoonstock.com/cartoonview.asp?catref=aban1560. Accessed on May 14, 2018.

4 Read part of a news article called *Brazil has the best nutritional guidelines in the world* and choose the correct pronouns to complete it. Then work with a partner and discuss whether or not you agree with the idea it conveys.

> Yesterday, a US-government appointed scientific panel released a 600-page report that will inform America's new dietary guidelines. These guidelines only come out every five years, and they matter because _____ (they / them) truly set the tone for how Americans eat: they're used by doctors and nutritionists to guide patient care, by schools to plan kids' lunches, and to calculate nutrition information on every food package you pick up, to name just a few areas of impact.
>
> But this panel and their guidelines too often overcomplicate what _____ (it / we) know about healthy eating. They take a rather punitive approach to food, reducing _____ (it / us) to its nutrient parts and emphasizing its relationship to obesity. Food is removed from the context of family and society and taken into the lab or clinic.
>
> Brazil, on the other hand, does exactly the opposite. Their national guidelines don't dwell on nutrients, calories, or weight loss. _____ (They / Them) don't jam foods into pyramids or child-like plates. Instead, they focus on meals and encourage citizens to simply cook whole foods at home, and to be critical of the seductive marketing practices of Big Food.
>
> The approach is so refreshing that _____ (me / it) has attracted praise from critics like Marion Nestle and Yoni Freedhoff, and when _____ (you / him) contrast the Brazilian method with the American way it's not hard to understand why.

Adapted from www.vox.com/2015/2/20/8076961/brazil-food-guide. Accessed on June 29, 2018.

LISTENING COMPREHENSION

1. Work with a partner. Are nutritional guidelines different around the world? Exchange ideas and report your opinions to the class.

2. 🎧 03 Listen to the recording and check your answers to the question in activity 1. Were you right?

3. 🎧 04 Listen again and match the pictures with the nutritional guidelines they represent. Then go to the audio scripts on page 136 and check your answers.

| Germany | Guyana | Singapore | South Africa |

4. Based on the recording and on the discussions throughout the unit, come up with the ideal plate, considering all the possible variables for people your age. Then share your ideas with your classmates and teacher.

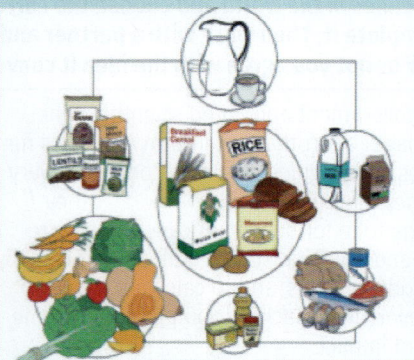

>> EXPAND YOUR HORIZONS >>>>

Check (✔) the column that best describes your opinion about each statement. Then discuss your answers with your classmates and teacher, justifying your point of view.

	I agree.	I'm not sure.	I disagree.
a. Learning about healthy nutrition habits concerns everyone as it relates to cultural, social, political, and environmental issues.			
b. Natural, whole grain, gluten-free and organic may not always mean healthy alternatives.			
c. Dietary Guidelines should always reflect the local culture, prevention of diseases, healthy food and lifestyle, besides the importance of physical activity and weight management.			

REVIEW 1

Unit 1 and 2

1. Skim the text below and check (✓) the best option to complete the statement.   *Skimming*

The purpose of this text is...

a. (   ) to inform the reader about eating habits in Brazil.

b. (   ) to convince the reader to buy a book about eating customs in Brazil.

---

http://thebrazilbusiness.com/article/dining-culture-in-brazil

Cynthia Fujikawa Nes
Co-Founder The Brazil Business

Updated
August 13, 2016

Dining Culture in Brazil

Brazilians are people who enjoy eating and like doing it a lot, even with only three meals. Here you will discover more about the Brazilian eating habits, such as tips on how to **behave** and cultural curiosities.

5 Lunch time is sacred for Brazilians. They may think you are kidding if you say that you often just have a cold sandwich for lunch. A few hours after a light breakfast early in the morning – usually French bread and some coffee – people stream out of buildings ready to **tuck**
10 **into** a large hot meal together with their coworkers.

As most Brazilians will suggest, go to a *churrascaria* to have lunch. It is paradise for meat lovers. For those who are not familiar with the concept: *churrascaria* is a typical Brazilian steak house. At *churrascarias* with *rodízio* you will have
15 waiters coming to your table with different types of meat on skewers which are carved at your table. There is usually salad and a buffet with hot dishes, so there is something for everybody in this type of restaurant. On your table you will find a disk: turn it green for a parade of meats to come
20 to your table and red to stop it.

Eating times in the afternoon are not a Brazilian habit, so do not expect to have a meal then. Some people drink coffee during this period, but since most Brazilians are working or doing some activity at this time of the
25 day, they do not have time to stop and eat something of quality. A cereal bar, a chocolate bar, some candies, or potato chips are normally found in a Brazilian's bag or backpack. These items can be found in small stores usually located around office buildings.

30 Dinner is the second main Brazilian meal and, more than lunch, is a family meal. Just like lunch, the Brazilian dinner is heavy and full of food, although it can be **obfuscated** by the goodies eaten in the afternoon.

In terms of etiquette, the ideal thing to do is to wait
35 until everybody has been served before starting eating, but it is accepted to start eating if the service is very slow. Brazilians use **cutlery** except for food like bread or boned chicken.

Adapted from www.thebrazilbusiness.com/article/dining-culture-in-brazil. Accessed on July 17, 2018.

---

2. Underline the incorrect part in each sentence, according to the text. Then rewrite the sentences correcting them.   *Understanding details*

a. Brazilians usually have only four meals.

_____

b. In Brazil, people usually have French bread and tea for breakfast.

_____

c. Churrascarias are typical Brazilian pasta houses.

_____

d. Brazilians have a meal in the afternoon.

_____

e. The Brazilian dinner is light.

_____

3. **Reread the text in activity 1 and find:**

   a. two frequency adverbs: _____ and _____.

   b. what the object pronoun *it* refers to in "turn *it* green for a parade of meats and red to stop", line 19: _____.

   c. what the subject pronoun *it* refers to in "*it* can be obfuscated by the goodies eaten in the afternoon", lines 31-32: _____.

   d. a suggestion in the affirmative form: _____.

   e. an instruction in the negative form: _____.

4. **Read part of the text "Brazil Should Do More for Venezuela's Refugees and Migrants" and fill in the blanks with the simple present of the verbs in parentheses.**

   ## Brazil Should Do More for Venezuela's Refugees and Migrants
   BY MARIA BEATRIZ BONNA NOGUEIRA AND MAIARA FOLLY | MARCH 20, 2017

   Over the past few months, thousands of Venezuelans have fled across the border to seek sanctuary in northern Brazil […] According to one recent arrival, Merlina Ferreira, "In Venezuela, I was a psychologist and my husband a lawyer. Here in Brazil, he _____ (unload) trucks and I _____ (look after) our small children since daycare _____ (be) too costly." Merlina _____ (join) at least 5,000 compatriots who recently applied for asylum in Boa Vista, a city in the state of Roraima. According to the Federal Police, the numbers **sky-rocketed** in the first few months of 2017, as compared to 2,230 applications in 2016, 234 in 2015, and just 9 in 2014. The spike in population displacement _____ (reflect) a dramatically deteriorating situation in Venezuela. Reports _____ (be) emerging of **spiraling** criminal violence, prolonged food shortages, and sustained unemployment. It _____ (be) still an open question whether these factors are legitimate grounds for refugee protection under international law. That hardly **matters** to people like Ferreira who _____ (feel) that their last resort to avoid starvation and homelessness is to cross an international border. Refugee specialist Alexander Betts _____ (describe) this phenomenon as "survival migration," and for good reason.

   Extracted from www.americasquarterly.org/content/brazil-should-do-more-venezuelas-refugees-and-migrants. Accessed on May 29, 2018.

5. **Complete the mind maps below with the words from the box.**

   citizenship   fiber   homeland   nutrition   fruit   persecution   policy   refugee   vegetables   whole grains

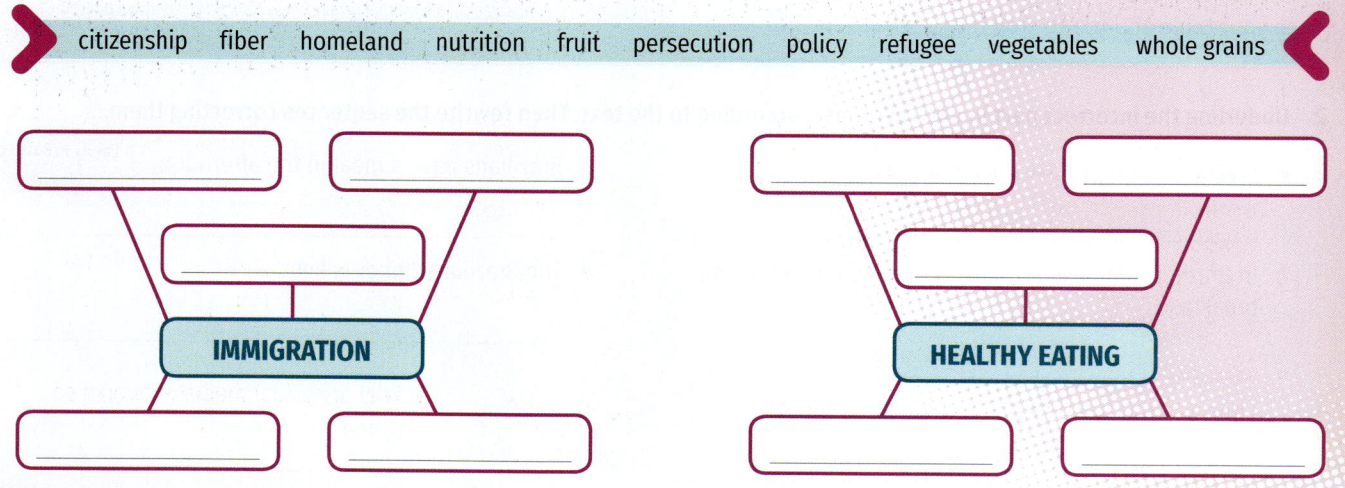

UNIT 3
Your Digital Self

IN THIS UNIT YOU WILL...
- talk about social media and big data;
- contrast the use of the present continuous and the simple present;
- learn how to use possessive adjectives;
- learn some common false cognates in English for Portuguese speakers.

LEAD OFF
- What social media services do you use?
- How much of your personal life do you usually share online?
- Why are social media networks so popular?

READING

>> BEFORE READING — Relating to the topic

1. Rank the social media networks below 1-5 (1 = most used; 5 = least used) according to how often you use them. How similar or different is your ranking compared to your friends'?

   ____ Facebook   ____ Snapchat   ____ Instagram   ____ Twitter   ____ YouTube

2. Which of the following quotes do you mostly agree with? Why?

   a. " Smartphones and social media expand our universe. We can connect with others or collect information easier and faster than ever.
   Daniel Goleman "

   Extracted from www.brainyquote.com/quotes/daniel_goleman_585902?src=t_social_media. Accessed on May 8, 2018.

   b. " It's so funny how social media was just this fun thing, and now it's this monster that consumes so many millennial lives.
   Cazzie David "

   Extracted from www.brainyquote.com/quotes/cazzie_david_822611. Accessed on May 8, 2018.

>> WHILE READING

Look at the snapshots of social media posts. What is each person doing? — Scanning

a. ( ) Sharing a disappointment.
b. ( ) Seeking advice from the community.
c. ( ) Celebrating an accomplishment.
d. ( ) Posting a recommendation.

1 RANDY SCHWARTZ [FOLLOW]
@randyscw Apr 7

I am studying for my English exams. I am *struggling* with a couple of things, but I have no time to study everything. Gee... is using *proper* grammar on Twitter considered studying?

2 YAY, Dude! BFF

I'm so happy!!! In a few hours we're all traveling to play in the finals of the tournament!

3

♥ 42 likes

bittersweet Sometimes those you *trust* the most *bring you down*. I'm not feeling very well at the moment, and I don't know why I'm always making the same mistakes. People say time heals all, but the truth is that more

joycejjj Don't worry about that! I'm sure you *deserve* a lot more than that. Just give yourself time to *heal*.

3 DAYS AGO

4

Diane W. B. Brown is at **The #1 Pizza Place** with **Amanda H.** and 4 others

OMG!!! I can't believe it's taken me this long to try this place! I'm having the best pizza EVER!!!! You guys should just stop whatever you're doing and try their pizza!! They aren't *kidding* about their name! It actually is the #1 pizza place on my list!! YUMMY!!

Unit 3

>> AFTER READING

1. Who would be likely to say the following sentences? Match the number of the text you read with each of the sentences below. *Understanding main ideas*

   a. ( ) Next time I go out with my friends to grab a bite, I'm definitely coming back here!

   b. ( ) My life is so messed up at the moment that I don't know how long it'll take for me to get back on my feet.

   c. ( ) Well, they do say that you should try things out in real life if you really want learning to stick, right?

   d. ( ) I'm sure we're going to do well tomorrow! Everyone is feeling great about the game!

2. Match the following replies with the texts you read.

   a. ( ) I've already bought my tickets! I'm looking forward to seeing you all!! Go get 'em!

   b. ( ) Hey! I thought we were going there together! I'm so dying to get to know this place!

   c. ( ) Not sure what your point is. Maybe the best option is to focus on one thing at a time, don't you think?

   d. ( ) Don't let that hit you so hard! You'll soon notice that this is a great learning opportunity for you!

STUDY THIS

going to there → going there

EXPAND YOUR VOCABULARY

1. Find the words or phrase in *italics* in the social media posts. Then match each of them with its meaning.

   a. joking   ( ) struggling

   b. make you feel bad   ( ) proper

   c. get what you should get because of your actions   ( ) yay

   d. having difficulties   ( ) trust

   e. an interjection of happiness and celebration   ( ) bring you down

   f. correct, accurate   ( ) heals

   g. believe, able to depend on   ( ) deserve

   h. helps in the recovery   ( ) kidding

2. Work in pairs. Discuss the questions below.

   a. Have you ever heard of "big data"?

   b. What do you understand by this term? What does big data know about you?

   c. Is it possible not to leave a digital trail every time we use a computer, access our phones, or open up an app on a tablet? If so, how?

VOCABULARY IN USE

1. Some words in English are very similar to words in Portuguese, but they have different meanings. Look at the following sentence from text 4 and circle one word that is similar to Portuguese.

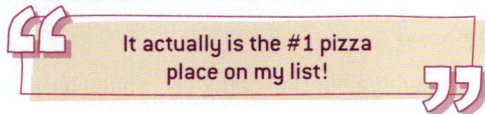
It actually is the #1 pizza place on my list!

   The word *actually* in the sentence above is used because the author wants to emphasize her belief that that is the best pizza place in town. It has no reference to time. Words that seem similar in two languages, but that have different meanings are commonly known as *false friends*.

2. Match the false friends below with their correct definition.

   a. parents

   b. library

   c. assume

   d. balcony

   e. pretend

   f. push

   g. support

   h. assist

   i. notice

   j. fabric

   ( ) to help someone to do something

   ( ) to make someone or something move by pressing them with your hands, arms, etc.

   ( ) the mother and father of a person or animal

   ( ) to behave as if something is true when in fact you know it is not, in order to deceive people or for fun

   ( ) cloth used for making clothes, curtains, etc.

   ( ) a room or building containing books that can be looked at or borrowed

   ( ) approval, encouragement, and perhaps help for a person, idea, plan, etc.

   ( ) to think that something is true, although you do not have definite proof

   ( ) a structure that you can stand on, that is attached to the outside wall of a building, above ground level

   ( ) to realize that something or someone exists, especially because you can see, hear, or feel them

3. Use the words from activity 2 to complete the sentences below.

   a. I don't want to go to the movies with them, so I'll just _____ I'm busy.

   b. Susan really needs the _____ of her friends to win the competition.

   c. Can you _____ your brother with his homework?

   d. Mark _____ his sister and she fell on the floor.

   e. I _____ Facebook keeps track of everything we post there.

   f. You don't go to a _____ to buy books! You go to a bookstore!

   g. Jack has a nice _____ in his house where he keeps a hammock.

   h. Did you _____ that Google knows what you have searched for and makes suggestions based on that?

   i. Yes, my _____ are coming to visit for the holidays, but my siblings aren't.

   j. You can't find a better_____ than this for running T-shirts.

4. Do you know any other false friends? Come up with at least two more examples and write down sentences to illustrate their correct use.

   _____

   _____

LANGUAGE IN USE 1

Unit 3

PRESENT SIMPLE vs. PRESENT CONTINUOUS

1. Read these excerpts from the social media posts on page 28. Focus on the underlined words. Match the numbers with the meaning they convey.

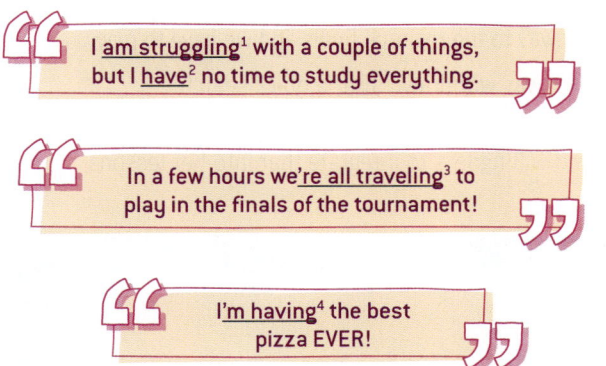

"I am struggling¹ with a couple of things, but I have² no time to study everything."

"In a few hours we're all traveling³ to play in the finals of the tournament!"

"I'm having⁴ the best pizza EVER!"

"I'm not feeling⁵ very well at the moment, and I don't know⁶ why I'm always making⁷ the same mistakes."

a. (   ) an action taking place at the moment of speech
b. (   ) a fact
c. (   ) an action that will happen in the future
d. (   ) an action that repeats itself constantly

2. Underline the correct option to complete each sentence.

a. I **don't usually share / am not usually sharing** lots of personal information on social media sites. However, today I **post / am posting** a picture of my birthday with my whole family.

b. Mark **enjoys / is enjoying** reading before going to bed, but he **doesn't do / isn't doing** that anymore because he **work / is working** a lot and he only **wants / is wanting** to sleep when he **gets / is getting** home.

c. Every time we **meet / are meeting** she **annoys / is annoying** me about getting a new hair cut.

d. Where **do you go / are you going** today after class? Can I come with you?

3. Complete the text with the appropriate verb form of the verbs in parentheses.

a. Tim _____ (wants / is wanting) to share what he _____ (does / is doing) right now with his friends from all over the world. He is a very popular boy, so he _____ (has / is having) many friends. Now he _____ (takes / is taking) pictures of his dog performing different tricks. However, he _____ (thinks / is thinking) about his privacy settings right now. Should he share the photos publicly or privately? He _____ (remembers / is remembering) what his parents told him: be careful with what you share online – it _____ (lives / is living) online forever!

b. Jane _____ (thinks / is thinking) about changing her phone, but she _____ (doesn't want / isn't wanting) to spend a lot of money. She _____ (likes / is liking) taking pictures, so it is important that the phone _____ (has / is having) a good camera. She also _____ (enjoys / is enjoying) spending hours on end talking to her friends on many messenger apps, so she _____ (needs / is needing) a phone with a good battery life. Actually, she _____ (has / is having) problems with her cell phone right now! She _____ (does / is doing) some research on what phone to buy, but the battery _____ (dies / is dying); she only has 15% left.

4. Rita is a teenager who uses social media a lot. In the extract below, she is explaining to her friend how she manages her Instagram account. Use the verbs from the box in the correct form to complete the passage. Use the negative form, if necessary.

> choose   edit (x2)   get   have
> photoshop   want   work

OK, so this is how it _____. You _____ to share everything you do with everybody online. Sometimes, I _____ photos that I only want to share with my close friends, like, it's my inner thoughts and my real self, and other times there are photos I want everyone to see. Let me show you... here... I _____ a photo to post to my *rinsta*, which is my real Instagram account, the one with all the edited photos and open to all. I _____ the photo because I really want it to look good so I _____ more likes. However, the photos that go onto my *finsta*, which is the account I share only with my closest friends, are a lot less edited. I mean, I usually _____ the photos that go there, but this one in particular I _____ because I want to blur the face of that woman behind me.

31

EXPAND YOUR READING

1. Read the passages below and decide if each person is talking about one of the pros (P) or cons (C) of social media.
   a. (   ) My sister's best friend is studying abroad. They hate the distance, but at least they can keep their communication up to date through the use of the Internet.
   b. (   ) I have a big test tomorrow, but my friends want me to join them in this online LOL competition. I think my grades are going to suffer a lot, but I can't help it! We are on our way to the regional finals and we have to play.
   c. (   ) Jack had been offered a great job from a company, but the offer was withdrawn after a quick search of his timeline.
   d. (   ) Mrs. Wilson is just the best! Her knowledge of social media and willingness to integrate that into her lessons makes it a lot easier for kids to focus on their tasks!

Raising a Teenager in the Digital Age

It seems like the Internet just came out of nowhere and changed everything, including childhood. Whether this change has been for the better or worse depends on how you look at it.

Teens today are the first generation that cannot imagine life without the Internet and the various devices that connect us to it. *Our* electronic gadgets have become extensions of our bodies, like crutches. On the other hand, you might also say that these powerful tools give us wings. Some people believe that the Internet and *its* various social networking options affect us negatively while others beg to differ. Parents who cling to their pre-Internet way of life are scrambling to make sure they have the right answers to guide *their* kids.

CONS
- Heavy social media use can possibly lead to depression, anxiety, and low self-esteem.
- It can prevent the development of some social and direct communication skills.
- Can **embolden** people to **harass** others online.
- Can be a major distraction for students and can lead to poor academic performance.
- Some inappropriate posts may hurt job opportunities down the line.

PROS
- Can **provide** a platform for shy people to express themselves and boost their confidence.
- Can facilitate communication between those that are marginalized.
- Can **strengthen** and maintain relationships to friends close and far.
- Classrooms can use social media to keep students engaged with study materials and lessons.
- A healthy social media presence can be beneficial in attracting employers.

Adapted from www.wehavekids.com/parenting/social-network-to-teens. Accessed on May 11, 2018.

2. Underline the correct option to complete the statements according to the text you have just read.
   a. Social media **can make it easier / make it harder** for people who are shy to express their thoughts.
   b. Bullies might feel **stronger / weaker** because of the anonymity that the Internet provides.
   c. If you use it correctly, social media can actually **hinder / help** with the chances of landing a new job.
   d. People who use social media a lot **may / may not** have difficulties dealing with real-life encounters.
   e. Social media is **only / also** great for people to keep in touch with their friends who live far away.

LANGUAGE IN USE 2

Unit 3

POSSESSIVE ADJECTIVES

1. Read the sentence below and check (✓) the correct sentence.

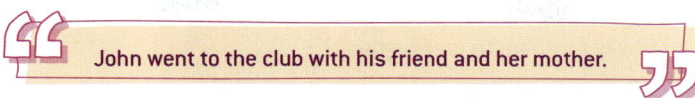
> John went to the club with his friend and her mother.

In the sentence above, we can say that the following people went to the club:

a. ( ) One man and two women.

b. ( ) One man, one woman, and one person who can be a man or a woman.

c. ( ) Two men and one woman.

2. Circle the correct option to complete the rules below.

a. The possessive adjective comes **before** / **after** the noun.

b. We **use** / **do not use** articles when we use a possessive adjective.

Go back to activity 1 on page 32 and complete the table with the possessive adjectives in italics.

Subject Pronouns	Possessive Adjective
I	my
you	your
he	his
she	her
it	
we	
you	your
they	

STUDY THIS

Even though the word *friend* can be used either for a man or a woman, in the sentence in activity 1, the possessive adjective before the word *mother* refers back to the word *friend*. In English, all possessive adjectives make reference to the possessor, not to the object or person that the they are describing. Consequently, when we say *her mother*, we know that the friend is a woman because of the possessive adjective that was used: HER.

3. Complete the sentences below with the correct possessive adjective.

a. I am playing *League of Legends* and I am talking to _____ friends online. We need to come up with _____ strategy to win the game.

b. Our friends asked _____ parents if they could come to the movie theater with us.

c. What social media site/network do you use the most to share _____ pictures?

d. Facebook has decided to change _____ privacy rules again.

e. What is _____ opinion about Snapchat? Do you think it is still the number one social media app for teenagers, or do they use Instagram for _____ stories now?

f. Jenny is going to ask_____ dad if _____ friends are also taking _____ children to the party so that she knows there'll be someone _____ age there as well.

g. My cousin Josh and _____ dad are taking cooking lessons and _____ teacher is a famous chef from London. How great is that?

h. Last week I posted _____ birthday pictures on Instagram. I love the fact that we can use social media as an online photo album.

LISTENING COMPREHENSION

1. **Work in pairs and discuss the questions below.**
   a. How concerned are you about your privacy online?
   b. How do social media platforms make money?
   c. Can you think of an alternative way for them to make money?

2. **You will hear five different extracts about social media networks and how people use them. Match each extract (1–5) with one of the opinions below.**

   05
   a. ( ) We need to think about both the pros and the cons of social media any time we log on to one of these sites.
   b. ( ) Some media sites are great tools and we don't need to feel guilty about using them.
   c. ( ) It is difficult for competitors to deal with social media giants these days.
   d. ( ) There is a lot of talk about innovation, but the social media landscape is not innovative at the moment.
   e. ( ) Just like it happened with cars and paint, social networks need to offer safety tools.

3. **Go to the audio script on page 136 and check your answers. Then do the activities that follow.**
   a. Choose three words or phrases from the audio scripts that you would like to learn.
   b. Ask your friends if they know the meaning of the words you have chosen.
   c. Write down one original sentence using each one of the words or phrases.

   _____
   _____
   _____
   _____
   _____
   _____

>> EXPAND YOUR HORIZONS >>>>

Check (✓) the column that best describes your opinion about each statement. Then discuss your answers with your classmates and teacher, justifying your point of view.

	I agree.	I'm not sure.	I disagree.
a. More and more consumer products will be launched on social media due to all the personal information people give away.			
b. As more and more users buy likes and followers on Instagram, influencer marketing through social media will become more difficult.			
c. In the near future, regardless of their job title, people will need to adapt to the online social sphere in order to be successful.			

UNIT 4
Establishing and Keeping Relationships

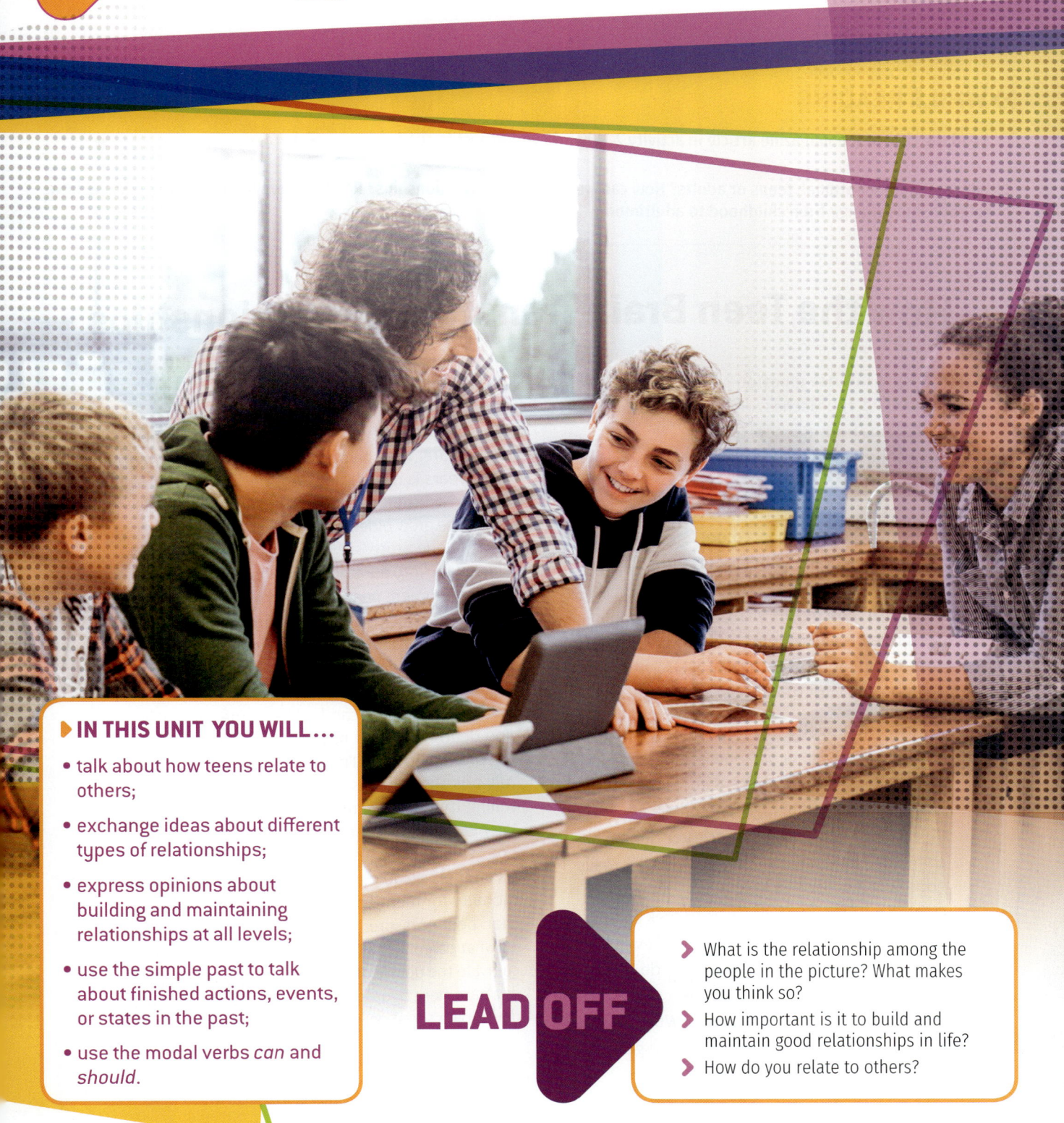

▶ IN THIS UNIT YOU WILL…

- talk about how teens relate to others;
- exchange ideas about different types of relationships;
- express opinions about building and maintaining relationships at all levels;
- use the simple past to talk about finished actions, events, or states in the past;
- use the modal verbs *can* and *should*.

LEAD OFF

- ▷ What is the relationship among the people in the picture? What makes you think so?
- ▷ How important is it to build and maintain good relationships in life?
- ▷ How do you relate to others?

READING

BEFORE READING

Discuss the quote below in pairs. Then report your opinions to the class.   *Bridging and relating to the topic*

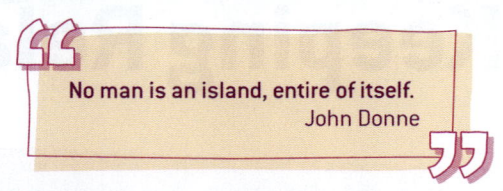

> "No man is an island, entire of itself."
> John Donne

Extracted from www.goodreads.com/work/quotes/6791114-no-man-is-an-island. Accessed on May 16, 2018.

WHILE READING

1. Read the title of the magazine article in activity 2. What do you expect to read about?   *Predicting*

2. Who are more emotional, teens or adults? How can we build better relationships? Read the text below and understand how relationships change from childhood to adulthood.

How the Teen Brain Transforms Relationships

BY DANIEL SIEGEL | AUGUST 12, 2014

1. More intense emotion

As a child approaches adolescence, his or her emotions become more intense.
One study, for example, put kids, adolescents, and adults into a brain scanner and showed them a picture of an emotionally expressive or neutral face. They found more intense emotional responses among adolescents, and a relatively mild response among both the kids and adults. The **downside** of this increased emotionality is that teens can become more easily irritated, upset, and moody—and they can have a relationship with themselves that's confusing.

2. Risk and novelty becomes more compelling

Compared to a kid or an adult, the baseline levels of dopamine in an adolescent are lower. But the **release** amounts are higher—and novelty is one of the major things that can **trigger** dopamine release. This means new things feel really, really good to a teenager. This is brilliant. Nature has created a system that drives us to seek change and novelty, a push for the unfamiliar and even the uncertain, which is what a teen must do if they're ever going to get out of the house. But there's a downside, of course: What happens when dopamine levels drop? The teen gets bored with the same old, same old.

3. We seek attachment in peers

We mammals have attachment, which is built on four childhood needs: to be seen, safe, **soothed**, and secure. What happens with attachment in the early years is really important because infants depend on their **caregivers** to survive.
But as we grow older, attachment doesn't go away—it's a lifelong process. What happens when you're a kid moving into adolescence? What do you do with your attachment needs? Instead of turning only toward your parents, you start turning to your peers more, which is a very healthy thing to do.
One really big downside is that membership in an adolescent **peer** group—even if it's just one other person—can feel like a matter of life and death: "If I don't have at least one peer that I'm connected with, I'm gonna die." That's what millions and millions of years of evolution are telling this adolescent.
We need that closeness for another reason that goes well beyond just one party, which is that, given the psychological stakes, teens can sacrifice morality for membership. We have a name for that: peer pressure.
So what parents and teens need to do, together, is cultivate the upside of this shift from parents to peers as attachment figures. If you spend your adolescence developing social skills, your adulthood is going to be so much better.

Adapted from www.greatergood.berkeley.edu/article/item/how_the_teen_brain_transforms_relationships. Accessed on May 16, 2018.

» AFTER READING

1. Refer back to the question in activity 1 on page 36. Were your predictions correct? Talk to a classmate and explain your answer. *Checking predictions*

2. Underline the correct statements according to the magazine article. *Understanding details*

   a. The study found more emotional responses among teenagers than adults and children.
   b. When dopamine levels drop, teenagers tend to stick to their safe old habits.
   c. Peer pressure is the pressure you feel to behave in the way that your family expects you to.
   d. Mammals feel that connecting with a peer group can be a matter of survival.

3. Work in groups to discuss the following questions.

   a. Are teens' relationships today different from past generations'?
   b. Has the Internet affected any sorts of relationships? How?
   c. To what extent do aspects such as finances, social level, affinities, and schooling interfere with the relationships you build?

EXPAND YOUR VOCABULARY

1. Go through the article on page 36 again and find:

   a. a synonym for *adolescent*: _____;
   b. three stages in one's existence: _____, _____, and _____;
   c. three adjectives often attributed to teens on increased emotionality: _____, _____, and _____;
   d. four childhood needs: _____;
   e. a neurotransmitter that is triggered by novelty, among other things: _____;
   f. an opposite of *aversion, disconnection*: _____.

2. Check (✓) the correct meaning of the words and expressions in bold in the extracts below according to the context.

   a. What happens when dopamine levels drop? The teen gets bored with the **same old, same old**.
      ( ) used to describe a fun, exciting event
      ( ) used to say that a situation has not changed, when this is boring or annoying

   b. "Nature has created a system that **drives** us to seek change and novelty, a push for the unfamiliar and even the uncertain, [...]"
      ( ) strongly influences
      ( ) makes a car move along

   c. "We need that closeness for another reason that goes well beyond just one party, which is that, given the psychological **stakes**, [...]"
      ( ) boundary marks such as sticks or posts pointed at one end
      ( ) risks or investments

   d. "So what parents and teens need to do, together, is cultivate the **upside** of this shift from parents to peers as attachment figures."
      ( ) the positive part of a usually bad situation
      ( ) the upper side or part of something

3. Use at least three words and expressions listed in activities 1 and 2 to finish the paragraph below.

   In my opinion, the role of relationships in teenage life...
   _____
   _____
   _____
   _____
   _____

VOCABULARY IN USE

1. Go back to the text on page 36 and search for the phrasal verb whose meaning is "leave a place or a person".

2. The phrasal verbs below refer to relationships at all levels. Match them with their definitions.

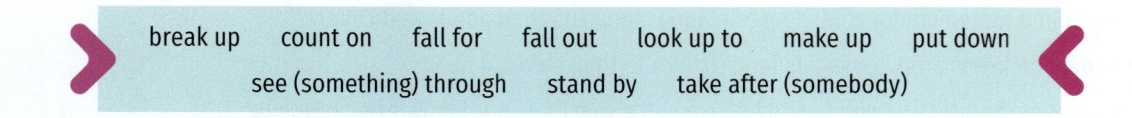

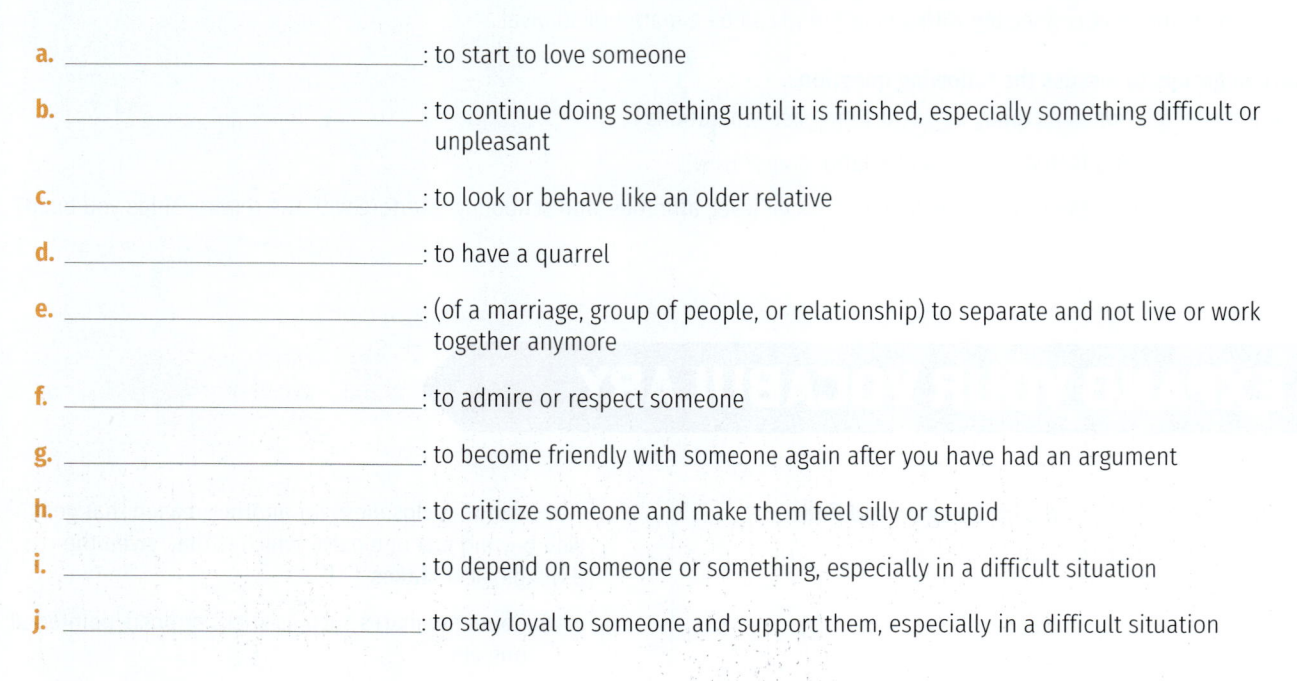

> break up   count on   fall for   fall out   look up to   make up   put down
> see (something) through   stand by   take after (somebody)

a. _____ : to start to love someone

b. _____ : to continue doing something until it is finished, especially something difficult or unpleasant

c. _____ : to look or behave like an older relative

d. _____ : to have a quarrel

e. _____ : (of a marriage, group of people, or relationship) to separate and not live or work together anymore

f. _____ : to admire or respect someone

g. _____ : to become friendly with someone again after you have had an argument

h. _____ : to criticize someone and make them feel silly or stupid

i. _____ : to depend on someone or something, especially in a difficult situation

j. _____ : to stay loyal to someone and support them, especially in a difficult situation

Extracted from www.ldoceonline.com/. Accessed on June 28, 2018.

3. Use some of the phrasal verbs from activity 2 to complete the quotes below. Then talk to a classmate about what they mean and say if you agree with them.

a. " I want to _____ my country, but I cannot vote for war.
   Jeannette Rankin "

b. " It hurts when people _____ you _____.
   Timbaland "

c. " It's good for kids to _____ sporting role models.
   Adam Peaty "

d. " When I get right down to it, my mother and father are two people I can _____ no matter what.
   Jack Wagner "

e. " Too many couples _____ without understanding the consequences for their families.
   Iain Duncan Smith "

Extracted from www.brainyquote.com. Accessed on July 16, 2018.

LANGUAGE IN USE 1

Unit 4

SIMPLE PAST

1. The excerpt below was extracted from the article on page 36. Read it and check (✓) the correct answer to the question that follows.

> One study, for example, **put** kids, adolescents, and adults into a brain scanner and **showed** them a picture of an emotionally expressive or neutral face. They **found** more intense emotional responses among adolescents, and a relatively mild response among both the kids and adults.

Why is the simple past used in this fragment of the article?

( ) Because it is about facts that are happening at the moment.

( ) Because this part of the text talks about completed actions in the past.

2. Reread the excerpt in activity 1 and complete the sentences about the simple past.

a. The _____ is used to talk about _____ actions, events, and states that happened at a specific time in the past.

b. _____ is an example of a regular verb in the past. In the simple past, regular verbs end in _____.

c. _____ and _____ are examples of irregular verbs in the past. Irregular verbs don't follow any specific spelling rules in the simple past.

3. Now read the questions and answers based on the extracts from activity 1 and make more deductions about the simple past.

> **Were** adults part of the study?
> Yes, they **were**.

> **Did** they **find** more intense emotional responses among the kids and adults?
> No, they **didn't**.

> What **did** the researchers **show** kids, adolescents, and adults in the study?
> They **showed** them a picture of an emotionally expressive or neutral face.

a. While in _____ sentences the past forms of the verb are used, in interrogative and negative forms we use the auxiliaries _____ and _____ respectively and the verb is in its base form.

b. The past forms of the verb *be* are *was* and _____. For short answers we use *Yes* / *No* followed by the _____ and *was*, *were* / *wasn't*, *weren't*.

4. Use the verbs in parentheses in the affirmative form of the simple past to complete the poem below.

Love And Friendship

A poem by George Bernard Shaw

Have you told your kids I love you?
Given them all a big hug today?
In my youth loving words _____ (be) few,
We were sent out to be out of the way.
Indoors we _____ (speak) when spoken to,
Silence _____ (rule) most of our day.
When breaking a rule we always _____ (know),
That punishment would come our way.
Each _____ (have) their jobs of work to be done,
We _____ (clean) and polished and _____ (shine).
Life believe me _____ (be) not much fun,
For breach of the rules we were fined.
In the orphanage no one _____ (say) I love you,
Never the time for a hug and a kiss,
Friendship _____ (be) for me something new,
It was the main thing that I did most miss.
So remember to hug and kiss your kids each day,
Show them that you love and care.
That they too will go on their way,
With love and friendship to share.

Extracted from www.poemhunter.com/poems/friendship/page-1/263674. Accessed on May 19, 2018.

EXPAND YOUR READING

1. Read the texts and check the correct option to complete the sentence.

   Cathy November 18, 2010

   Drabble November 16, 2012

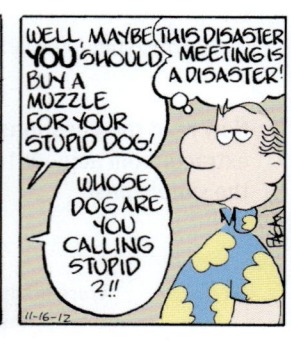

   JumpStart June 10, 2010

   Extracted from https://assets.amuniversal.com. Accessed on May 19, 2018.

   Comic strips…

   ( ) present words and are seen in books or newspapers. They describe the pictures and explain what they show.

   ( ) present a series of pictures, usually organized horizontally, designed as a narrative or a chronological sequence.

2. Circle the correct options to complete the characteristics of comic strips.
   Comic strips…
   a. are generally **humorous** / **serious** and sometimes have a moral.
   b. use graphic conventions such as **speech and thought bubbles** / **captions** and punctuation signs in the text.
   c. employ visual arrangements to tell a story and often reproduce **formal** / **oral** language.
   d. are written in **lower case** / **capital** letters most of the times.
   e. **never** / **usually** use facial expressions and gestures to show action and thoughts.

3. Work in pairs. What kinds of relationship do the comic strips present?

LANGUAGE IN USE 2

Unit 4

MODAL VERBS — *CAN* and *SHOULD*

1. Read some extracts from the comics on page 40 and statements about them. Decide if the statements are true (T) or false (F). Correct the false ones.

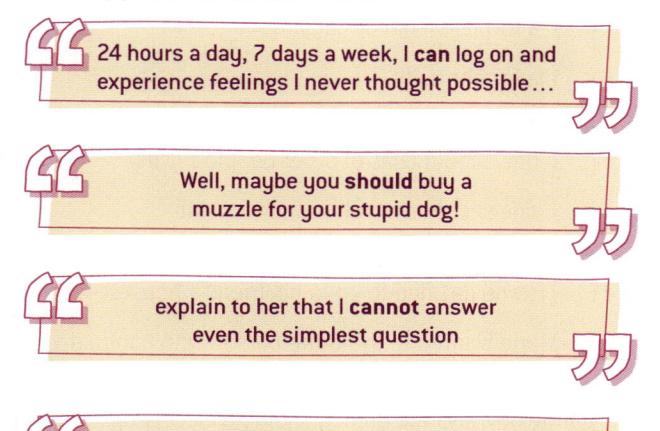

   > 24 hours a day, 7 days a week, I **can** log on and experience feelings I never thought possible…

   > Well, maybe you **should** buy a muzzle for your stupid dog!

   > explain to her that I **cannot** answer even the simplest question

   > **Can** you at least remind me what her name is?

   a. (   ) In the first extract, *can* expresses ability.
   _____

   b. (   ) The modal *should* used in the second extract indicates a piece of advice.
   _____

   c. (   ) In the third extract, *cannot* means *not able to*.
   _____

   d. (   ) In the fourth extract, *can* is used to ask what is probable to happen.
   _____

2. Read the comic strip below and answer the question in pairs. Then share your opinions about it. In the first and second panels of the strip, is *can* used for possibility or permission?

   Baldo   September 09, 2010

   Extracted from www.assets.amuniversal.com/7a5c2fa0ca650131604c005056a9545dw. Accessed on May 20, 2018.

3. Choose the correct option to complete the comics.

   Calvin and Hobbes   February 26, 1990

   Extracted from www.assets.amuniversal.com/6ac251f0dece013171ac005056a9545dw. Accessed on May 20, 2018.

   a. (   ) can I go / should I stay / can things be

   b. (   ) should I go / can't I stay / can't things be

41

LISTENING COMPREHENSION

1. It's common sense that respect is mandatory in all sorts of relationships. But what happens with lack of respect? Have you seen or experienced situations of disrespect in relationships? Share your answers.

2. Below is a poster from a campaign held by *The Diana Award*, an independent British charity whose aim is to empower young people to change the world. What kind of campaign is it?

BACK_2 SCHOOL

FROM THE DIANA AWARD
ANTI-BULLYING CAMPAIGN

Extracted from www.youtube.com/watch?v=F3kR5fwscg4.
Accessed on May 20, 2018.

3. Listen to Danny Boy and choose the correct options to complete the sentences.

   06

   a. Danny Boy is...
      ( ) a former victim of bullying.
      ( ) a former bully.
   b. According to Danny Boy, ...
      ( ) one should control other people's lives.
      ( ) one should control his/her own life.
   c. Danny Boy used to feel scared...
      ( ) so he decided to go to his friend's house.
      ( ) and wanted to avoid the person who habitually intimidated him.
   d. Danny Boy says the bullied should (select two)...
      ( ) call the police immediately.
      ( ) approach the ones who like them.
      ( ) open up and talk to people.
      ( ) join a therapy group.

4. Work in small groups. Discuss the questions below with your classmates. Then report your answers to the class.

   a. What other damages can be caused when people disrespect and violate the standards of good relationships?
   b. When you come across a conflict in a relationship, how do you usually cope with it?
   c. Do all countries have the same cultural values regarding relationships at all levels? Justify your answer.

>> EXPAND YOUR HORIZONS >>>>

Check (✔) the column that best describes your opinion about each statement. Then discuss your answers with your classmates and teacher, justifying your point of view.

	I agree.	I'm not sure.	I disagree.
a. Compromise is a crucial part of a relationship. Everyone should make sacrifices for the sake of relating to others effectively.			
b. Understanding the background of the people you relate to helps maintain healthy relationships at all levels.			
c. Communication, acceptance, and respect are inherited traits of any good relationship and the lack of those may bring about serious damage to people.			

REVIEW 2

Unit 3 and 4

1. Read the title of the text below. What do you expect to read about? *Predicting*

The problems of big data, and what to do about them

In the last 15 years, we have **witnessed** an explosion in the amount of digital data available – from the Internet, social media, scientific equipment, smart phones, surveillance cameras, and many other sources – and in the computer technologies used to process it. "Big Data," as it is known, will **undoubtedly** deliver important scientific, technological, and medical advances. But Big Data also poses serious risks if it is misused or abused.

5 Already, major innovations such as Internet search engines, machine translation, and image labeling have relied on applying machine-learning techniques to vast data sets. And, in the near future, Big Data could significantly improve government policymaking, social-welfare programs, and **scholarship**.

But having more data is no substitute for having high-quality data. For example, a recent article in *Nature* reports that election pollsters in the United States are struggling to obtain representative samples of the population, because they are
10 legally permitted to call only landline telephones, whereas Americans increasingly rely on cell phones. […]

In recent years, automated programs based on biased data sets have caused numerous scandals. For example, last April, when a college student searched Google images for "unprofessional hairstyles for work," the results showed mostly pictures of black people; when the student changed the first search term to "professional," Google returned mostly pictures of white people. […]

Another **hazard** of Big Data is that it can be gamed. When people know that a data set is being used to make important
15 decisions that will affect them, they have an incentive to tip the scales in their favor. […]

A third hazard is privacy violations, because so much of the data now available contains personal information. In recent years, enormous collections of confidential data have been stolen from commercial and government sites; and researchers have shown how people's political opinions or even sexual preferences can be accurately gleaned from seemingly innocuous online postings, such as movie reviews – even when they are published pseudonymously.

20 Finally, Big Data poses a challenge for **accountability**. Someone who feels that he or she has been treated **unfairly** by an algorithm's decision often has no way to appeal it, either because specific results cannot be interpreted, or because the people who have written the algorithm refuse to provide details about how it works. […]

The good news is that the hazards of Big Data can be largely avoided. But they won't be unless we **zealously** protect people's privacy, detect and correct unfairness, use algorithmic recommendations prudently, and maintain a rigorous understanding of algorithms' inner workings and the data that informs their decisions.

Extracted from www.weforum.org/agenda/2017/02/big-data-how-we-can-manage-the-risks. Accessed on June 04, 2018.

---

2. Read the text in activity 1 and check the most appropriate definition for Big Data. *Making inferences*

   a. ( ) a system of connecting computers to the Internet and moving information, such as messages or pictures, at a very high speed

   b. ( ) the very large amounts of information that can now be gathered, kept, and analyzed, especially information about people's interests or what they like, as a result of things such as social media use

Adapted from http://www.ldoceonline.com/. Accessed on June 28, 2018.

3. Mention two risks posed if Big Data is misused or abused, according to the text. *Understanding details*

_____

_____

4. Read an extract from the text. Circle the sentence that refers to a fact and underline the sentence that refers to an action taking place at the moment the text was written.

> "[…]
>
> But having more data is no substitute for having high-quality data. For example, a recent article in *Nature* reports that election pollsters in the United States are struggling to obtain representative samples of the population, because they are legally permitted to call only landline telephones, whereas Americans increasingly rely on cellphones.
>
> […]"

5. **Choose the correct option to complete the paragraph.**

We _____ in a digital age, so technology is definitely a part of our daily life. Teens _____ social media platforms such as Facebook, Instagram, and Twitter to express themselves and to look for information as well. In fact, teens _____ always _____ the virtual world to communicate with one another. It's also true that most teens _____ to one site; they often _____ and end up using multiple ones.

a. ( ) are living / are accessing / are… using / doesn't stick / are experimenting
b. ( ) live / access / are… using / don't stick / are experimenting
c. ( ) live / are accessing / are… using / don't stick / experiment

6. **Use the cues from the box to complete the quotes. There is an extra option which you do not need to use.**

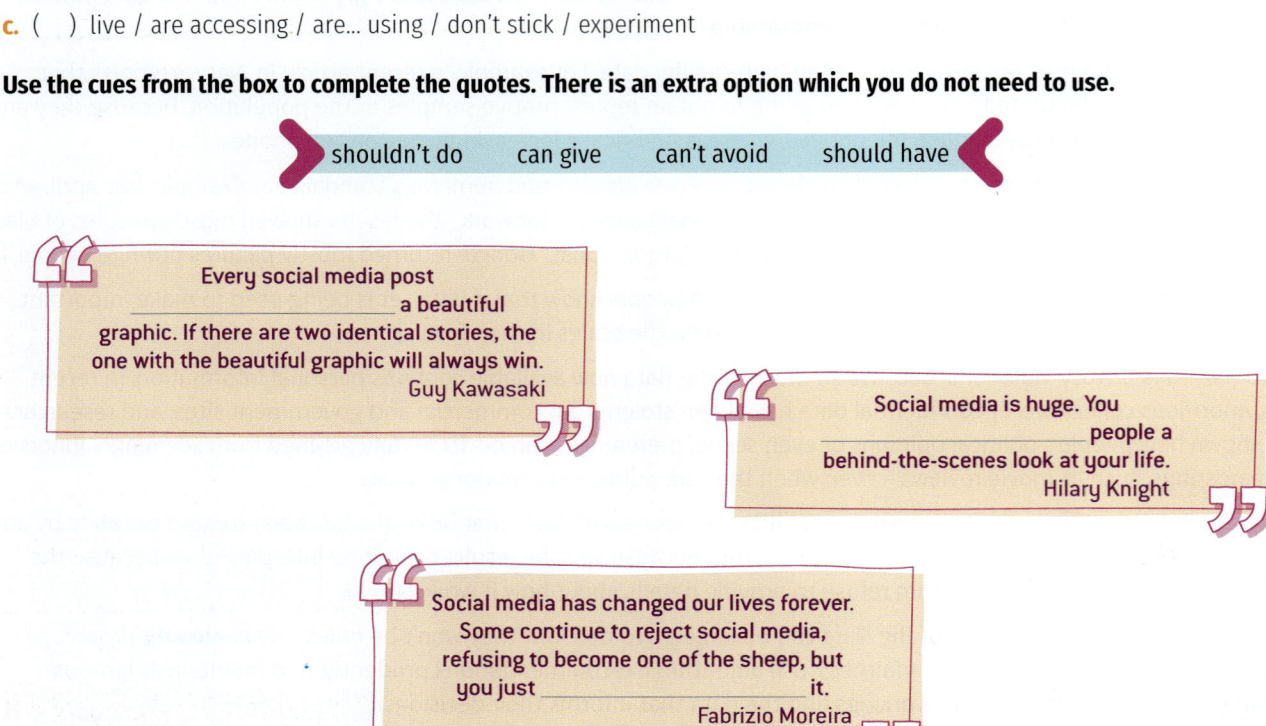

> shouldn't do   can give   can't avoid   should have

"Every social media post _____ a beautiful graphic. If there are two identical stories, the one with the beautiful graphic will always win."
Guy Kawasaki

"Social media is huge. You _____ people a behind-the-scenes look at your life."
Hilary Knight

"Social media has changed our lives forever. Some continue to reject social media, refusing to become one of the sheep, but you just _____ it."
Fabrizio Moreira

Extracted from www.brainyquote.com. Accessed on September 21, 2018.

7. **Fill in the blanks in the comic strip with the simple past of the verbs *be*, *transform*, and *turn*.**

JumpStart   February 24, 2011   ID: 283486

- Benny, you _____ absolutely right!
- I _____ all my "friends" into "followers"
- Which _____ me into a "leader"!
- Where are you leading us?
- You _____ followers can be awfully pushy!

Extracted from https://assets.amuniversal.com/01fb6fe01b37012ea5c900163e41dd5bw. Accessed on June 5, 2018.

UNIT 5
Art: The Language of Emotions

▶ IN THIS UNIT YOU WILL...
- talk about different forms of art;
- learn how to form words using prefixes;
- understand the formation of plural nouns;
- learn the correct order of adjectives when describing a noun.

LEAD OFF

> What comes to your mind when you think of art?
> What do you see in the picture?
> What do you think the author of this picture wanted to express? Which themes are depicted in the picture?

READING

BEFORE READING — Relating to the topic

1. Art comes in different forms and can be found in different places. Look at the pictures and identify where you would most likely find these examples of art.

a ( ) on the streets
b ( ) in a museum
c ( ) in an art gallery
d ( ) at an event

2. What do you think of the following quote? How much do you agree with it?

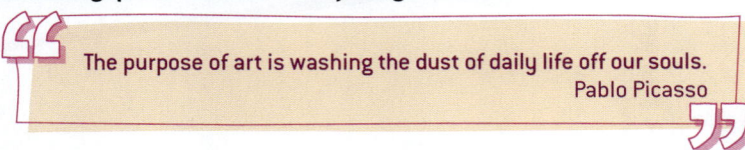

> "The purpose of art is washing the dust of daily life off our souls."
> Pablo Picasso

WHILE READING

Read the article and decide if the statements are true (T) or false (F). — Scanning

a. ( ) Art is only art if it is in a museum.
b. ( ) Any place can be a possible site for art.
c. ( ) One of the goals of art is to engage a community.
d. ( ) Creativity is not innate in human beings.

www.artsy.net/article/artsy-editorial-the-most-relevant-art-today-is-taking-place-outside-the-art-world

The Most Relevant Art Today Is Taking Place Outside the Art World

[…] If you walk east from Columbia's Butler Library, down the rocky hills of Morningside Park, and cross a few avenues, you will find a relatively *nondescript* **laundromat**, one of some 3,000 in New York. It's not a gallery, nor *a pop-up space*, nor the work of an artist who turned an abandoned building into a functioning laundromat. No, it's a laundromat, but *nonetheless* one *bursting* with creativity.

5 […] During the summer months, it *hosts* workshops by The Laundromat Project, a nonprofit officially started in 2005 that **seeks** to "amplify the creativity that already exists within communities" through residencies, development programs, and a host of other events, as its executive director Kemi Ilesanmi explained to me. The benefit of hosting public events in laundromats is engaging a diverse group of people. In New York, at least, they are "multi-generational, multi-race, and multi-class spaces," says Ilesanmi. The type of community engagement *fostered* by the
10 project isn't about painting a mural and walking away, but rather commissioning artists who think long and hard about how to engage the communities where the project operates: Harlem, Bedford Stuyvesant, and Hunts Point/Longwood, three neighborhoods primarily made up of people of color with modest incomes and rich histories. […]

"One of the things that makes us *stand out* is that we meet people where they are," said Ilesanmi. "It's not that museums can't or have never done that. But we actually do it all the time. It's not a special project. […] In our opinion everyone is
15 creative, and we remind them of that even when they don't think that about themselves," said Ilesanmi, adding, "creative expression is just a part of being human beings." As we spoke, she talked through the imagined voice of any given person: "I dance, I love music, I love "fill in the blank", as a human being in the world. However, I don't need that validated by, nor do I feel like I have to go into, a formal setting." Likely because of this inclusive approach, the Laundromat Project has been met with success. The organization was featured at the Creative Time **summit** and successfully raised $35,000
20 in 10 days this year. It's now thinking about how it will adapt and change its program in the future.

Extracted from www.artsy.net/article/artsy-editorial-the-most-relevant-art-today-is-taking-place-outside-the-art-world. Accessed on June 12, 2018.

AFTER READING

1. What are your interpretations for the pieces of art below? Match the numbers with the pictures.

a. to reflect about conflict

b. to reflect about conformity

c. to reflect about human identity

( )
Head in the Box, 1979-81, Peter Wilson

( )
Rage, the Flower Thrower, 2005, Banksy

( )
Cape Cod Evening, 1939, Edward Hopper

2. Underline the incorrect information in each statement according to the article. *Understanding details*

a. Most people are creative and the Laundromat Project accepts this as a universal truth.

b. The Laundromat project has certainly been successful because of its inclusive approach.

c. The Laundromat project reminds people of how creative they are only if they think that about themselves.

d. Only a specific group of people is engaged with art in the Laundromat project.

3. Rewrite the statements from activity 2 with the correct information.

a. _____

b. _____

c. _____

d. _____

EXPAND YOUR VOCABULARY

1. Find the words or expressions in *italics* in the reading. Then match each one with its meaning.

a. helped a skill, feeling, idea, etc, develop over a period of time

b. so full that nothing else can fit inside

c. opened somewhere for a short, limited period of time

d. looking very ordinary and not at all interesting

e. to be much better than other similar people or things

f. in spite of the fact that has just been mentioned

g. to provide the place and everything that is needed for an organized event

( ) nondescript

( ) a pop-up space

( ) nonetheless

( ) bursting

( ) host

( ) fostered

( ) stand out

2. Is there any space in your city that is used, or could be used, to host such an event? Are the people who live in your city creative? How do (or would) they benefit from such a space to express their art?

VOCABULARY IN USE

1. The prefix *non-* is added to the beginning of the word *profit* to create a new word in meaning: *nonprofit*. Read the examples of the most common prefixes and complete the table with the words *possible* and *ordinary*, adding the correct prefix to them.

Prefix	Meaning	Example
anti-	against / opposed to	anti-government
dis-	reverse or remove	disagree
down-	reduce or lower	downgrade
extra-	beyond	_____
il- / im- / in- / ir-	not	illegal _____ insecure irregular
mis-	incorrectly	misspelled
non-	not	nonpayment
re-	again	redo
co-	together, mutually	co-worker

2. Circle the prefix in the words below.

   a. dishonest
   b. redo
   c. illiterate
   d. extraterrestrial
   e. non-smoking
   f. irresponsible
   g. misbehave
   h. downhearted
   i. incapable
   j. anti-racist
   k. immigrate

3. Complete the sentences with a word from activity 2.
   a. My grade was extremely low, so my teacher told me to _____ my essay.
   b. Brian was _____ because his friend was moving away.
   c. It was _____ of you to leave her alone.
   d. The city's road system is _____ of handling such a volume of traffic.
   e. How do scientists search for _____ life?
   f. One of my principles is that we should never be _____. Honesty is extremely important for our character.

4. What do these sentences mean? Underline the correct alternative.

   I'm worried that they will **disappear** before they pay.

   a. I'm worried that they will appear again before they pay.
   b. I'm worried that they will not appear again before they pay.

   I think you **misunderstood** my instructions. I said you needed to complete it by Thursday, not Tuesday.

   a. I think you didn't understand my instructions correctly. It was Thursday, not Tuesday.
   b. I think you understood my instructions, but decided to complete it on Tuesday instead of Thursday.

LANGUAGE IN USE 1

Unit 5

PLURAL OF NOUNS

1. Read this excerpt from the text on page 46. Focus on the words in bold. Then read the statements and write true (T) or false (F).

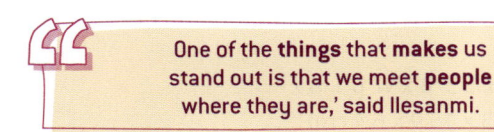

> "One of the **things** that **makes** us stand out is that we meet **people** where they are,' said Ilesanmi."

a. (   ) The letter *s* in English can be used to indicate the plural of a noun and the third person singular of a verb in the simple present.
b. (   ) All plural forms in English are formed with *-s* or *-es*.
c. (   ) Irregular plural forms in English have no rule.
d. (   ) All words in bold in the excerpt indicate a plural form.

2. Look at the table below and complete the rule with the words and letters from the box.

Singular	Plural	Singular	Plural	Singular	Plural
boy	boys	girl	girls	book	books
box	boxes	match	matches	class	classes
brush	brushes	hero	heroes	potato	potatoes
piano	pianos	photo	photos	baby	babies
city	cities	leaf	leaves	life	lives
belief	beliefs	roof	roofs / rooves	man	men
woman	women	child	children	person	people

> o   s   ies   y
> ves   irregular   es   es
> y   f   y   s

Many English nouns form their plural by adding _____ or _____. We usually add _____ to words that end in *s*, *x*, *ch*, *sh* and, sometimes, *o*. However, some words ending in _____ also have their plural form just by the addition of *-s*. When a word ends in a _____ that comes after a consonant, we substitute the _____ for _____ to form the plural. Words ending in a _____ that come after a vowel have their plural form created by adding _____ such as *play*. Some words ending in *f* or in *fe* require you to substitute the *f* or the *fe* for _____. However, other words ending in _____ are made plural by adding *s* only. Some words have _____ plural forms, and need to be memorized.

3. Rewrite these excerpts from the text on page 46 in the plural form. Pay attention to the other changes you need to make.

a. "It's not a gallery, nor a pop-up space, nor the work of an artist who turned an abandoned building into a functioning laundromat."

_____

b. "The type of community engagement fostered by the project isn't about painting a mural and walking away."

_____

4. Look at the new sentences you wrote in activity 3. Then check (✓) the sentences below that are true.

a. (   ) Some words don't have a plural form; they are uncountable nouns.
b. (   ) Don't use indefinite articles with nouns in the plural form. However, it's OK to use the definite article with either the singular or the plural.
c. (   ) Don't make any changes to the pronouns in your sentences.
d. (   ) Adjectives don't have a plural form.

EXPAND YOUR READING

1. Look at the pictures below. They show works of art. What do you think they represent?

https://www.metmuseum.org/toah/works-of-art/21.6.73/

Headrest
Date: 19th–20th century
Geography: Zimbabwe
Culture: Shona peoples
Medium: Wood
Dimensions: H. 5 5/8 x W. 6 1/4 x D. 2 1/2 in. (14.3 x 15.9 x 6.4 cm)
Classification: Wood-Furniture
Credit Line: Anonymous Gift, 1986
Accession Number: 1986.484.1

Description
The use of headrests in southern Africa has been traced back to the twelfth-century archaeological site of Mapungubwe, an urban center along the Limpopo River. There, evidence of gold **sheeting** believed to have adorned a long-disintegrated wooden headrest has been recovered.

The designs of such works, created to protect elaborate **coiffures**, reflect a range of regional styles. Among the Shona, headrests were exclusively carved and used by men. Since they also functioned as vehicles of communication with the ancestral **realm**, headrests and other personal articles were frequently **buried** with their owners, evidencing the intimate connection between the object and its owner. In other cases, they were passed along to male descendants.

Extracted from www.metmuseum.org/toah/works-of-art/1986.484.1/. Accessed on September 25, 2018.

Taweret amulet with double head
Period: New Kingdom
Dynasty: Dynasty 18, late–Dynasty 19
Date: ca. 1390–1213 B.C.
Geography: From Egypt
Medium: Blue faience
Dimensions: H. 2 cm (13/16 in.); W. 1.4 cm (9/16 in.); D. 0.4 cm (3/16 in.)
Credit Line: Gift of Lily S. Place, 1921
Accession Number: 21.6.73

Description
Double-headed amulets of the domestic **goddess** Taweret are rare forms and date to the 18th dynasty. Amarna is among the known **findspots** for these, although this particular example is without **provenance**.

Extracted from www.metmuseum.org/toah/works-of-art/21.6.73/. Accessed on November 7, 2018.

2. Check (✔) the correct alternative to complete the sentences below.

   a. The texts are...

   ( ) argumentative.
   ( ) narrative.
   ( ) descriptive.

   b. The purpose of the text "Headrest" is to...

   ( ) give information about and describe a headrest.
   ( ) discuss the pros and cons of headrests.
   ( ) inform readers about the technical features of a headrest.

   c. Both texts were probably taken from...

   ( ) a blog.
   ( ) a news website.
   ( ) a museum website.

3. Now answer the questions that follow.

   a. Which artwork is older?
   _____

   b. Which artwork could only be used by men?
   _____

   c. Why were headrests buried with their owners?
   _____

   d. What is Taweret?
   _____

LANGUAGE IN USE 2

Unit 5

ORDER OF ADJECTIVES

1. Read this excerpt from the text on page 50 again and pay attention to the words in bold.

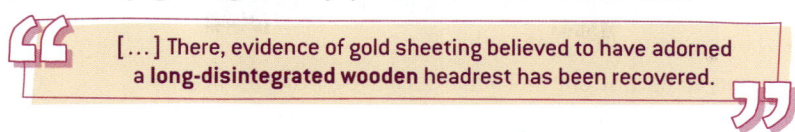

> [...] There, evidence of gold sheeting believed to have adorned a **long-disintegrated wooden** headrest has been recovered.

The words in bold describe and / or add information to the word *headrest*. In English, these words are positioned before the corresponding noun. However, there is a word order to follow.

The most usual sequence of adjectives is as follows (10th = farther from the noun; 1st = closer to the noun):

Order	Relating to	Examples
10th	opinion	interesting, pretty, funny
9th	size	large, small, short
8th	physical quality	organized, slim, messy
7th	shape	square, rectangular, oval
6th	age	old, young, ancient
5th	color	pink, blue, green
4th	origin	Brazilian, American, Australian
3rd	material	wooden, glass, plastic
2nd	type	technological, vegan, self-cleaning
1st	purpose	washing, decorative

2. Rewrite the following sentences. Use the adjectives in parentheses in the correct order.

a. All the boys were wearing shirts. (clean, flannel, new)

_____

b. Jessica's friends fell in love with her classmate. (handsome, Mexican, new)

_____

c. He gave his mother a vase. (black, Egyptian, small)

_____

d. She sat behind a desk. (big, brown, wooden)

_____

3. Describe two different objects that you have. Use at least three adjectives to describe each of them.

_____

_____

LISTENING COMPREHENSION

1. **You are going to listen to an artist called John McKenna talking about his work. As you listen, number the sentences below in the order the actions are mentioned.**

   ( ) He stopped studying art at college when his father's house was repossessed.
   ( ) Sometimes he thinks he chose the wrong job for his life.
   ( ) He says that it is necessary to have strong motivation to make a living as an artist.
   ( ) He saw a TV program about a sculpture school and knew he wanted to start studying there.
   ( ) He tried studying accountancy, but then he changed to art.
   ( ) He started painting signs and painted 60 signs a day for a supermarket.
   ( ) He was commissioned to sculpt a herd of bronze jersey cows.
   ( ) His mother died when he was very young.

2. **Go to the audio scripts on page 137 and read the personal account again. Then talk to a partner and retell the story.**

   _____
   _____
   _____
   _____
   _____

3. **Read the saying below taken from the audio script. Do you agree with it? Exchange ideas with your classmates.**

   > "What is meant for you doesn't pass by you."

›› EXPAND YOUR HORIZONS ››››

Check (✓) the column that best describes your opinion about each statement. Then discuss your answers with your classmates and teacher, justifying your point of view.

	I agree.	I'm not sure.	I disagree.
a. Art is not meant to transform society, but to represent it.			
b. It is possible to rank different forms of art in terms of their importance.			
c. Traditional art is losing its place and relevance in today's world.			

UNIT 6
Sport is No Longer Just Sport

▶ IN THIS UNIT YOU WILL...

- talk about how sports have become big business;
- learn how to form nouns using suffixes;
- exchange ideas about the inclusion of new sports in the 2020 Olympics;
- make comparisons using the comparative and the superlative forms.

LEAD OFF

- How are the title of this unit and the picture related?
- Has the commercialization of sport changed the behavior of players? How?
- How do sports help nations?

READING

BEFORE READING

Work in pairs. List some problems the sports industry faces nowadays.

Bridging and relating to the topic

WHILE READING

Scan the text and answer the question: what is it about? Circle at least two elements that justify your answer.

Finding organizational patterns

http://politics.uchicago.edu/pages/juliet-macur-seminar-series

THE UNIVERSITY OF CHICAGO INSTITUTE OF POLITICS | HOME ABOUT CAREER DEVELOPMENT CIVIC ENGAGEMENT SPEAKER SERIES FELLOWS PROGRAM MEDIA | Facebook Twitter Instagram Youtube

The Power and Politics of Sports: Why Games Aren't Just Games Anymore

Sports used to be simple. Go to games. Play games. Have fun. Be entertained. Now it's so much more. Every level of sports – from your local youth leagues straight up to the pros – has become big business that generates big money and big influence. For good and bad, the sports world is bigger and more powerful than ever, with athletes **wielding** more and more influence over our culture and our politics.

5 **RSVP for all of Juliet's seminars here**

January 12: The Power of the Athlete

Should athletes keep their focus on the playing field, or do they have a duty to speak out on social issues because so many people look up to them? When Muhammad Ali and Kareem Abdul-Jabbar spoke out about Donald Trump's idea to ban all Muslims from entry into the United States, why did it make an impact? Or, when Russia enacted an anti-gay law before the 2014 Sochi Winter Games, why did so many Olympic athletes refuse to talk about the politics of it, saying sports and politics
10 should **remain** separate? What, exactly, is the duty of the athlete in those situations?

January 19: The FIFA Takedown – Corruption in Soccer and International Sports

One morning last May in Zurich, Swiss law enforcement **raided** a five-star lakeside hotel and arrested some of the world's most powerful officials in worldwide soccer. Those arrests marked the beginning of perhaps the biggest takedown in the history of sports, with FIFA, soccer's global governing body, at the center of it all and United States federal **prosecutors**
15 leading the charge to clean up the sport. How did those FIFA officials reign with so much impunity for so many years? How did the International Olympic Committee allow global soccer to get to this point of such widespread corruption that, by the end of 2015, more than 40 officials in the sport pleaded **guilty** or were arrested for crimes that included receiving bribes and kickbacks? [...]

January 26: Fantasy Football Feud: The Debate over DraftKings & FanDuel

Fantasy-league betting has become a multibillion-dollar industry. But will it soon be extinct? Online daily fantasy sports sites, like DraftKings and FanDuel, are commanding attention now and it's nearly impossible to watch sports on television – or go to
20 a sporting event, for that matter – without seeing their ads. Yet those days might be coming to an end. Those sites and ones like them are at the center of an ongoing, **sizzling** public policy debate that pits whether internet fantasy league gambling is a game of chance or a game of skill. If it's a game of chance, then the government would have to step in to regulate it, or ban it outright. We discuss the future of fantasy leagues and whether they should be legal. Also, does that type of gambling dehumanize the athletes, who feel like disposable pawns in that money-making game? Should fans even care?

February 2: Former US Soccer Captain & Current ESPN Analyst Julie Foudy on Women in Sports

25 The United States women's national soccer team sued FIFA and the Canadian Soccer Association last year, claiming discrimination because the 2015 Women's World Cup had only artificial **turf** fields, instead of grass ones, which is the preferred surface for the game. The team asked: The men's World Cup is played on grass and will be for the foreseeable future, so why do the women have to play on an inferior surface? The women's team backed down from its case, as FIFA basically ran out the clock. Now do these women, whose World Cup-winning final game was the most watched soccer game in United States history, have the power to demand better fields? Or will women in sports always find themselves stuck behind men?

Adapted from http://politics.uchicago.edu/pages/juliet-macur-seminar-series. Accessed on May 25, 2018.

Unit 6

>> **AFTER READING**

1. Check (✔) the issues that are <u>not</u> discussed in the seminars mentioned in the text.   *Understanding main ideas*
   a. (   ) discrimination
   b. (   ) fantasy sports sites
   c. (   ) being a sportswriter
   d. (   ) doping
   e. (   ) widespread corruption

2. Answer these questions. If necessary, go back to the text.   *Understanding details*
   a. What event is considered the starting point of perhaps the biggest dishonor in the history of sports?
   _____
   b. Which online daily fantasy sports sites are mentioned in the text?
   _____
   c. Why did the United States women's national soccer team sue FIFA and the Canadian Soccer Association last year?
   _____
   _____

3. From your view, which seminar brings up the most controversial subject? Explain.

EXPAND YOUR VOCABULARY

1. Find in the text the words that correspond to these definitions. Write them in the blanks.
   a. _____ : *noun [uncountable]* when people risk money or possessions on the result of something which is not certain, such as a card game or a horse race → betting
   b. _____ : *noun [countable]* informal money that someone pays secretly and dishonestly in return for someone's help
   c. _____ : *adjective* too strong to be destroyed or defeated
   d. _____ : *noun [countable, uncountable]* something that you have to do because it is morally or legally right
   e. _____ : *noun [countable]* someone who is used by a more powerful person or group and has no control of the situation

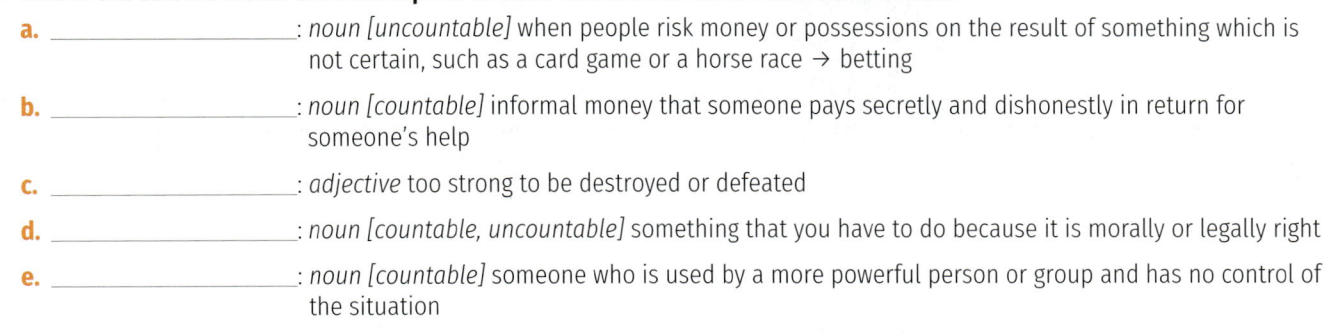

   Extracted from www.ldoceonline.com. Accessed on June 15, 2018.

2. Read this tweet about sports. Talk to a classmate about whether you agree with it or not.

> **Vallery Stevens** ✓
> @Vall_13
>
> I realize sport has turned into a business. That's why nowadays I don't get too high or low as far as emotions are concerned. It's a money grab!
>
> 4:50 pm – May 25, 2018
>
> ♡ 11   💬 21 people are talking about this

VOCABULARY IN USE

1. Read a subtitle extracted from another part of the text on page 54.

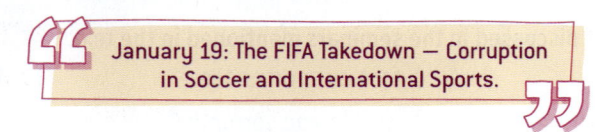

> "January 19: The FIFA Takedown — Corruption in Soccer and International Sports."

The suffix *-ion* has changed the verb *corrupt* to the noun *corruption*. Besides *-ion*, the suffixes *-tion*, *-sion*, and *-ation* refer to a state or process; for example, *corruption* is the process of corrupting.

Go back to the text and find other nouns formed by one of these suffixes.

_____

2. Form singular or plural nouns from the verbs in the box to complete the text below.

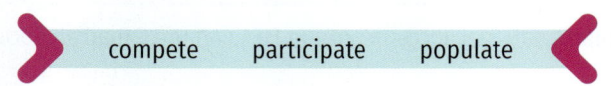

> compete   participate   populate

Sports in Brazil

Brazilian sports have a very strong heritage in the country. The majority of the _____ often follows and participates in various sports. Sports are considered a large part of the Brazilian culture rather than just being sporting events. Besides soccer being the most popular, Brazil has various other sports that the country is very proud of. They have progressed and earned medals in swimming, sailing, athletics, and judo.

Brazil in the Olympics

Since Brazil has a typically tropical and subtropical climate, it does not usually compete in the Winter Olympics. The country made its first appearance in the Winter Games in 1992, and most recently participated in 2006. Despite their minimal _____ in the Winter Olympics, Brazil has been competing in the Summer Olympics since 1920. Today, they come in at 33rd in the overall ranking of medals in the Summer Olympics.

Top Three Sports in Brazil

Soccer is the most popular sport in Brazil. It is taken very seriously where anything less than a win is, essentially, considered worthless. Volleyball is the second most popular sport in Brazil. Brazil is also the most successful country in this sport. Their men's national volleyball team is currently the champion in the 2 major _____ (Volleyball World Cup and Volleyball World Championship). [...] Brazilian athletes have also greatly succeeded worldwide in beach volleyball.

Adapted from www.thetranslationcompany.com/news/blog/language-news/portuguese/sports-brazil. Accessed on May 25, 2018.

3. Work with a partner. Write about two sports represented below. Use a noun formed by one of the suffixes studied in this section.

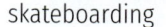

skateboarding    footvolley    surfing    judo

_____
_____

LANGUAGE IN USE 1

Unit 6

COMPARATIVE ADJECTIVES

1. Read this excerpt from the text on page 54 and underline the correct option to complete the sentences.

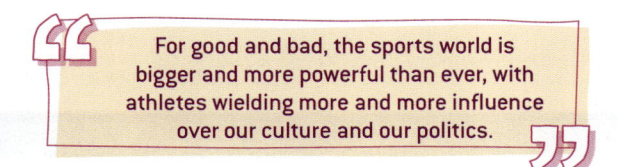

> "For good and bad, the sports world is bigger and more powerful than ever, with athletes wielding more and more influence over our culture and our politics."

a. The structures used to compare the world of sports are **good and bad / bigger and more powerful**.

b. The author compares the sports world today to **our culture and politics / the sports world in the past**.

c. In the author's opinion, the world of sports in the past was **smaller and less powerful than / as big and powerful as** it is now.

2. Complete the table according to what you have studied in activity 1.

	short adjectives	long adjectives
Comparative of superiority	small____ + _____	_____ + powerful + _____
Comparative of inferiority	short or long adjectives	
	_____ + famous + _____	
	_____ + competitive + _____	
Comparative of equality	short or long adjectives	
	____ + big + ____	
	____ + powerful + ____	

3. Read the infographic below and circle the adjectives in the comparative form. Then complete the sentences with the comparative form of the adjectives in parentheses.

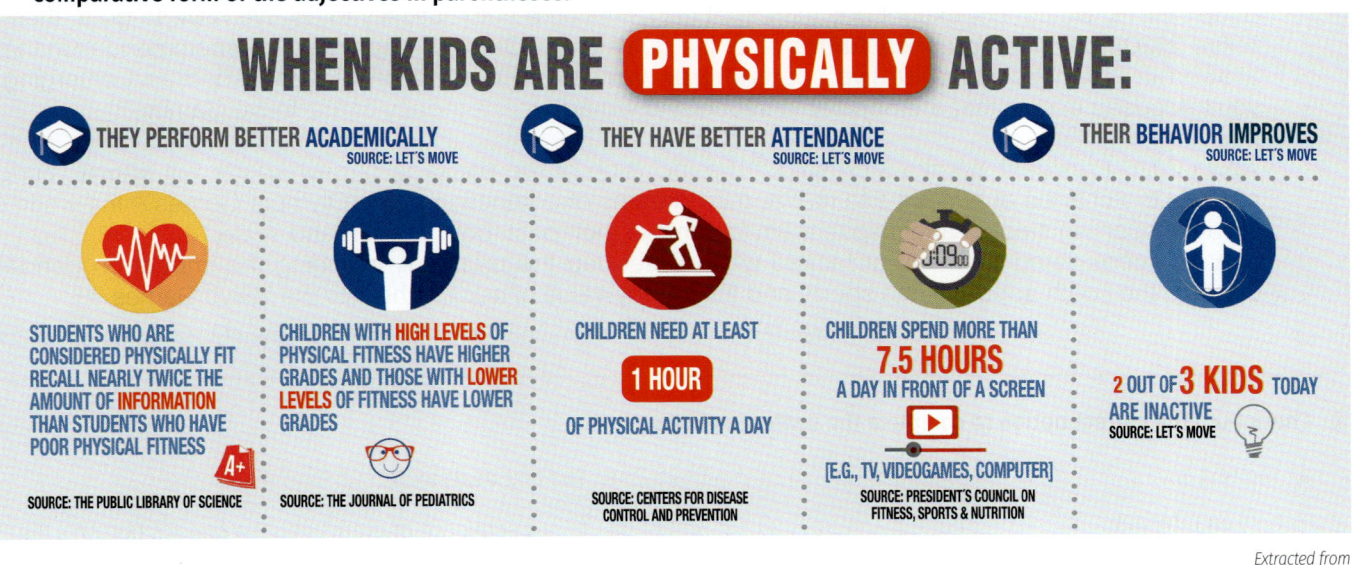

WHEN KIDS ARE PHYSICALLY ACTIVE:

THEY PERFORM BETTER ACADEMICALLY
SOURCE: LET'S MOVE

THEY HAVE BETTER ATTENDANCE
SOURCE: LET'S MOVE

THEIR BEHAVIOR IMPROVES
SOURCE: LET'S MOVE

STUDENTS WHO ARE CONSIDERED PHYSICALLY FIT RECALL NEARLY TWICE THE AMOUNT OF **INFORMATION** THAN STUDENTS WHO HAVE POOR PHYSICAL FITNESS
SOURCE: THE PUBLIC LIBRARY OF SCIENCE

CHILDREN WITH **HIGH LEVELS** OF PHYSICAL FITNESS HAVE HIGHER GRADES AND THOSE WITH **LOWER LEVELS** OF FITNESS HAVE LOWER GRADES
SOURCE: THE JOURNAL OF PEDIATRICS

CHILDREN NEED AT LEAST **1 HOUR** OF PHYSICAL ACTIVITY A DAY
SOURCE: CENTERS FOR DISEASE CONTROL AND PREVENTION

CHILDREN SPEND MORE THAN **7.5 HOURS** A DAY IN FRONT OF A SCREEN
[E.G., TV, VIDEOGAMES, COMPUTER]
SOURCE: PRESIDENT'S COUNCIL ON FITNESS, SPORTS & NUTRITION

2 OUT OF 3 KIDS TODAY ARE INACTIVE
SOURCE: LET'S MOVE

Extracted from https://sites.google.com/site/sportsinschoolarevery benficial/counterclaims. Accessed on May 25, 2018.

a. When kids are not physically active, they have _____ (bad) performance than when they are.

b. Kids' behavior is _____ (appropriate) when they practice sports.

c. Students who are physically fit are _____ (good) at recalling information than those who have poor physical fitness.

4. Work in pairs. Ask each other two questions about the infographic using adjectives in the comparative form.

STUDY THIS

Irregular Comparatives

good – better
bad – worse
far – farther / further

little – less
much – more

EXPAND YOUR READING

1. Read the text below and relate it to the one on page 54. In your opinion, how is the addition of five new sports events to the Tokyo Olympics in 2020 associated with the power and politics of sports? Share your opinion with your classmates.

https://www.olympic.org/news/ioc-approves-five-new-sports-for-olympic-games-tokyo-2020

IOC APPROVES FIVE NEW SPORTS FOR OLYMPIC GAMES TOKYO 2020

Updated 1658 GMT (0058 HKT) August 4, 2016

THE INTERNATIONAL OLYMPIC COMMITTEE (IOC) TODAY AGREED TO ADD BASEBALL/SOFTBALL, KARATE, SKATEBOARDING, SPORTS CLIMBING AND SURFING TO THE SPORTS PROGRAM FOR THE OLYMPIC GAMES TOKYO 2020.

The decision by the 129th IOC Session in Rio de Janeiro was the most comprehensive evolution of the Olympic program in modern history. Plans call for **staging** the skateboarding and sports climbing events in temporary **venues** installed in urban settings, marking a historic step in bringing the Games to young people and reflecting the trend of urbanization of sport.

5 The Organizing Committee for the Tokyo 2020 Games proposed the five new sports in response to the new flexibility provided by Olympic Agenda 2020.
[…]
Tokyo 2020, the first Organizing Committee able to take advantage of the change, submitted its proposal for the five new sports to the IOC in September 2015.

10 IOC President Thomas Bach said, "We want to take sport to the **youth**. With the many options that young people have, we cannot expect any more that they will come automatically to us. We have to go to them. Tokyo 2020's balanced proposal **fulfills** all of the goals of the Olympic Agenda 2020 recommendation that allowed it. Taken together, the five sports are an innovative combination of established and emerging, youth-focused events that are popular in Japan and will add to the legacy of the Tokyo Games."

15 […]
Tokyo 2020 President Yoshiro Mori said, "The inclusion of the package of new sports will **afford** young athletes the chance of a lifetime to realize their dreams of competing in the Olympic Games – the world's greatest sporting stage – and inspire them to achieve their best, both in sport and in life."

The IOC considered a variety of factors when assessing the proposal, including the impact on gender
20 equality, the youth appeal of the sports and the legacy value of adding them to the Tokyo Games.

Adapted from www.olympic.org/news/ioc-approves-five-new-sports-for-olympic-games-tokyo-2020. Accessed on July 25, 2018.

2. Check (✓) the correct option to complete the sentences below.

a. The text is...
   ( ) an interview.
   ( ) a scientific article.
   ( ) a news report.

b. The purpose of the text is to...
   ( ) inform readers about the inclusion of new sports in the 2020 Tokyo Olympic Games.
   ( ) discuss sports as social tools to be implemented in Tokyo in 2020.
   ( ) offer a critical perspective on urban sports in Tokyo in a humorous way.

c. The text deals with...
   ( ) a sequence of events about a famous person's life.
   ( ) a contemporary topic that interests a vast audience.
   ( ) a known fact described in the first person singular.

d. The number of sports being introduced in the 2020 Tokyo Olympic Games is...
   ( ) four.
   ( ) five.
   ( ) seven.

LANGUAGE IN USE 2

Unit 6

SUPERLATIVE ADJECTIVES

1. Below you will find some extracts from the news report on page 58. Read them and match the sentence halves to form meaningful statements about superlatives.

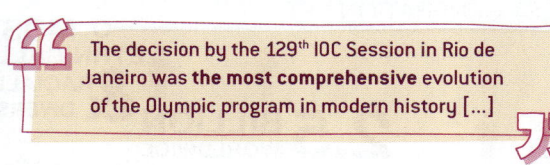

> "The decision by the 129th IOC Session in Rio de Janeiro was **the most comprehensive** evolution of the Olympic program in modern history [...]"

> "[...] the chance of a lifetime to realize their dreams of competing in the Olympic Games – the world's **greatest** sporting stage – and inspire them to achieve their **best**, both in sport and in life."

a. In the first extract, *the evolution* is compared to...
b. In the second extract, *the Olympic Games* are compared to...
c. The word *best* is...

( ) the superlative form of the adjective *good*.
( ) all the evolutions of the Olympics in modern history.
( ) all the sporting stages.

2. Now based on activity 1, complete the following statements.

a. To form the superlative of most long adjectives, we use _____ before them.

b. To form the superlative of most short adjectives, we add _____ to them.

c. In superlatives, it is common to use the definite article _____ before adjectives.

d. Some adjectives such as *good* and *bad*, for example, have irregular forms in their superlatives. Those are _____ and *the worst*, respectively.

STUDY THIS

Irregular Superlatives

good – best	little – least	far – farthest / furthest
bad – worst	much – most	

3. Use the superlative form of the adjectives from the box to complete the quotes below.

> bad   great   hard   high

a. "I always felt that my _____ asset was not my physical ability, it was my mental ability." – Caitlyn Jenner

b. "Make sure your _____ enemy doesn't live between your own two ears." – Laird Hamilton

c. "You are never really playing an opponent. You are playing yourself, your own _____ standards, and when you reach your limits, that is real joy." – Arthur Ashe

d. "The _____ skill to acquire in this sport is the one where you compete all out, give it all you have, and you are still getting beat no matter what you do. When you have the killer instinct to fight through that, it is very special." – Eddie Reese

Extracted from www.keepinspiring.me/100-most-inspirational-sports-quotes-of-all-time. Accessed on May 28, 2018.

4. Underline a superlative structure in the text fragment below. Then rewrite the whole sentence using a synonym.

Currently, there are an estimated 30 million people worldwide who skate at least once a week.

[...]
Chris Cole is a professional American skateboarder who is excited at the possible prospect of competing at the Olympic Games.
The 32-year-old is one of the most recognizable stars in the skateboarding community, winning numerous gold medals at the X-Games – an annual event for extreme sports.
[...]

Adapted from www.bbc.com/sport/olympics/27372110. Accessed on May 28, 2018.

_____

_____

LISTENING COMPREHENSION

1. Read the infographic below and answer: Who are millennials? In your opinion, do they influence the sports industry? Justify your answer.

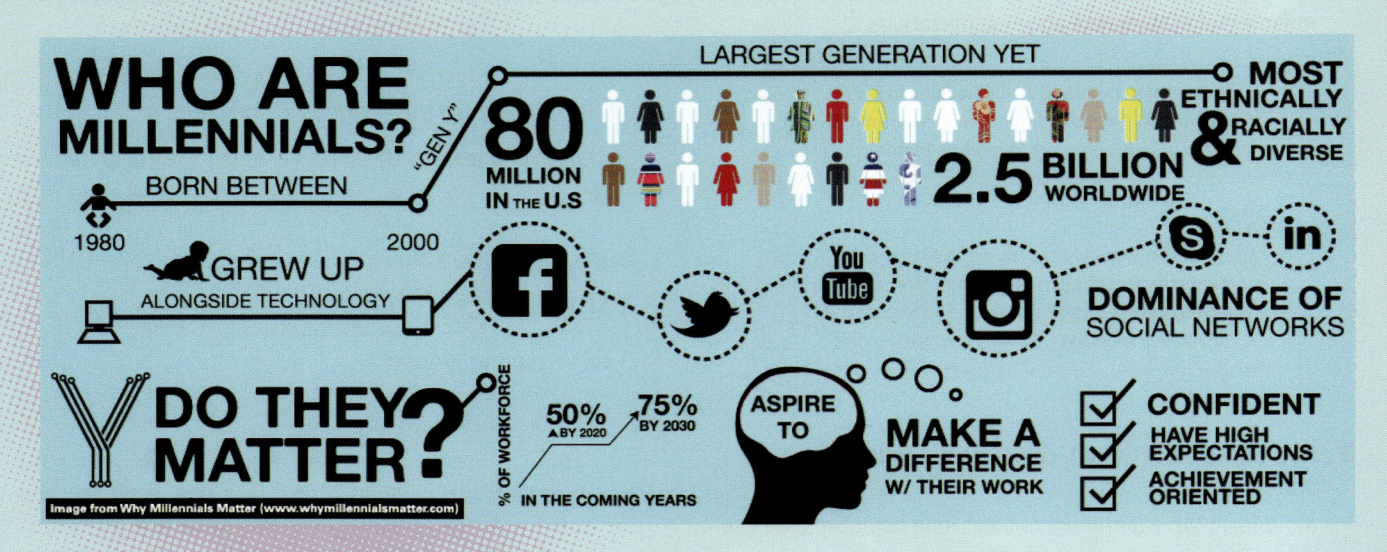

WHO ARE MILLENNIALS? "GEN Y"
BORN BETWEEN 1980 – 2000
GREW UP ALONGSIDE TECHNOLOGY
LARGEST GENERATION YET
80 MILLION IN THE U.S
2.5 BILLION WORLDWIDE
MOST ETHNICALLY & RACIALLY DIVERSE
DOMINANCE OF SOCIAL NETWORKS
DO THEY MATTER?
50% OF WORKFORCE BY 2020
75% BY 2030
% IN THE COMING YEARS
ASPIRE TO MAKE A DIFFERENCE W/ THEIR WORK
CONFIDENT
HAVE HIGH EXPECTATIONS
ACHIEVEMENT ORIENTED

Image from Why Millennials Matter (www.whymillennialsmatter.com)

Extracted from http://whymillennialsmatter.com. Accessed on May 27, 2018.

2. Listen to the conclusions of a study comparing the involvement in sports by millennials and non-millennials. Then complete the blanks with numbers. 🎧 08

   a. Non-millennials spend _____% of their media time watching sports on television.

   b. They spend _____% of that time on online TV.

   c. Millennials spend _____% of their time watching sports on television.

   d. They spend _____% of that time on online TV.

   e. The survey was conducted with more than _____ people.

   f. _____% of millennial sports fans say that they prefer e-sports to traditional sports.

   g. _____% of non-millennial sports fans say that they prefer e-sports to traditional sports.

3. Why do you think millenials are less involved in traditional sports than previous generations? Exchange ideas with your classmates.

›› EXPAND YOUR HORIZONS ››››

Check (✔) the column that best describes your opinion about each statement. Then discuss your answers with your classmates and teacher, justifying your point of view.

	I agree.	I'm not sure.	I disagree.
a. Commercialization of sports is definitely inevitable because it empowers players financially and keeps professional sports highly qualified and entertaining.			
b. As sports have become more professional and politicized in the past years, corrupting effects have also emerged.			
c. The inclusion of new sports in the Olympics certainly favors the younger generation of athletes.			

REVIEW 3

Unit 5 and 6

1. Read the text and check (✔) the picture that corresponds to the type of art it describes. *Relating to the topic*

a ( )   b ( )

What is Installation Art? | History and Top Art Installations Since 2013

By My Modern Met Team on April 15, 2018

Like most movements that make up modern and contemporary **art**, installation art exhibits an interest in innovating. **Though** similar to sculpture and related to a range of recent artistic **genres**, the immersive practice offers a unique way to experience art. In order to **grasp** the significance of such a movement, it is important to understand what makes it so special, from its distinctive qualities to its artistic influences.

[…]

What is Installation Art?

Installation art is a modern movement characterized by immersive, larger-than-life **works of art**. Usually, installation artists create these pieces for specific locations, enabling them to **expertly** transform any space into a customized, interactive **environment**.

[…]

A key attribute of installation art is its ability to physically interact with viewers. While all artistic mediums have the ability to engage individuals, most do not completely immerse them in interactive experiences.

In addition to facilitating dialogues between observers and works of art, this unique characteristic invites individuals to view art from new and different **perspectives**—literally!

[…]

PERFORMANCE ART

While performance art—a practice performed before an audience—may seem dissimilar to installation, a form of fine art, the two movements are linked by a key characteristic: a creative and conceptual **use** of space. In both cases, artists find innovative and inventive **ways** to reinterpret and reimagine everyday environments.

Extracted from www.mymodernmet.com/what-is-installation-art-history-artists. Accessed on June 15, 2018.

2. Underline the statement that is <u>not</u> true according to the text. *Understanding details*

   a. Installation art provides opportunities for observers to really interact with art.

   b. Installation art is modern, innovative, and often collaborative as well.

   c. Performance and installation arts are completely disassociated movements.

   d. Communication between spectators and works of art is easier with installations.

   e. Artistis are innovative when they reinterpret everyday environments.

3. Refer back to the text on page 61 and find the adjectives used to qualify the nouns in bold.

a. _____ art
b. _____ genres
c. _____ works of art
d. _____ environment
e. _____ perspectives
f. _____ use
g. _____ ways

4. Which nouns in the text follow the same plural spelling rule shown in *qualities* in "from its distinctive *qualities* to its artistic influences"?

a. (   ) way, ability
b. (   ) ability, history
c. (   ) history, way
d. (   ) exhibit, history

5. Read some headlines related to sports news. Then fill in the blanks with the adjectives from the box in the comparative or superlative form.

> fast   good   bad   old

a. **Kilian Jornet: inside the mind of the world's _____ mountain runner**
Kilian Jornet, 29, is widely considered the world's best ultra-distance and mountain runner. Last month, he conquered Mount Everest twice in one week without using supplemental oxygen or fixed ropes. [...]

Extracted from www.theguardian.com. Accessed on November 9, 2018.

b. **D-day veteran becomes world's _____ skydiver at 101 and 38 days**
Verdun Hayes breaks record by completing tandem skydive with three generations of his family in Devon

Extracted from www.theguardian.com. Accessed on November 9, 2018.

c. **French sailor François Gabart makes _____ solo circumnavigation**
Journey around world took 42 days and 16 hours – six days faster than previous record

Extracted from www.theguardian.com. Accessed on November 9, 2018.

d. **The decline of competitive sports days is a tragedy – but a lack of exercise is even _____**
Competitive sports are good – and fun

Extracted from www.telegraph.co.uk. Accessed on November 9, 2018.

6. Use the cues to write affirmative or negative sentences in the comparative form.

a. Verdun Hayes / be / much old / Kilian Jornet

_____

b. The previous fastest solo circumnavigation / be / six days / long / François Gabart's solo circumnavigation

_____

c. Mountain runners / be usually / well equipped / Kilian Jornet

_____

d. People / be / competitive / in the past / they / be / now

_____

UNIT 7
Globish: Fad or Fact?

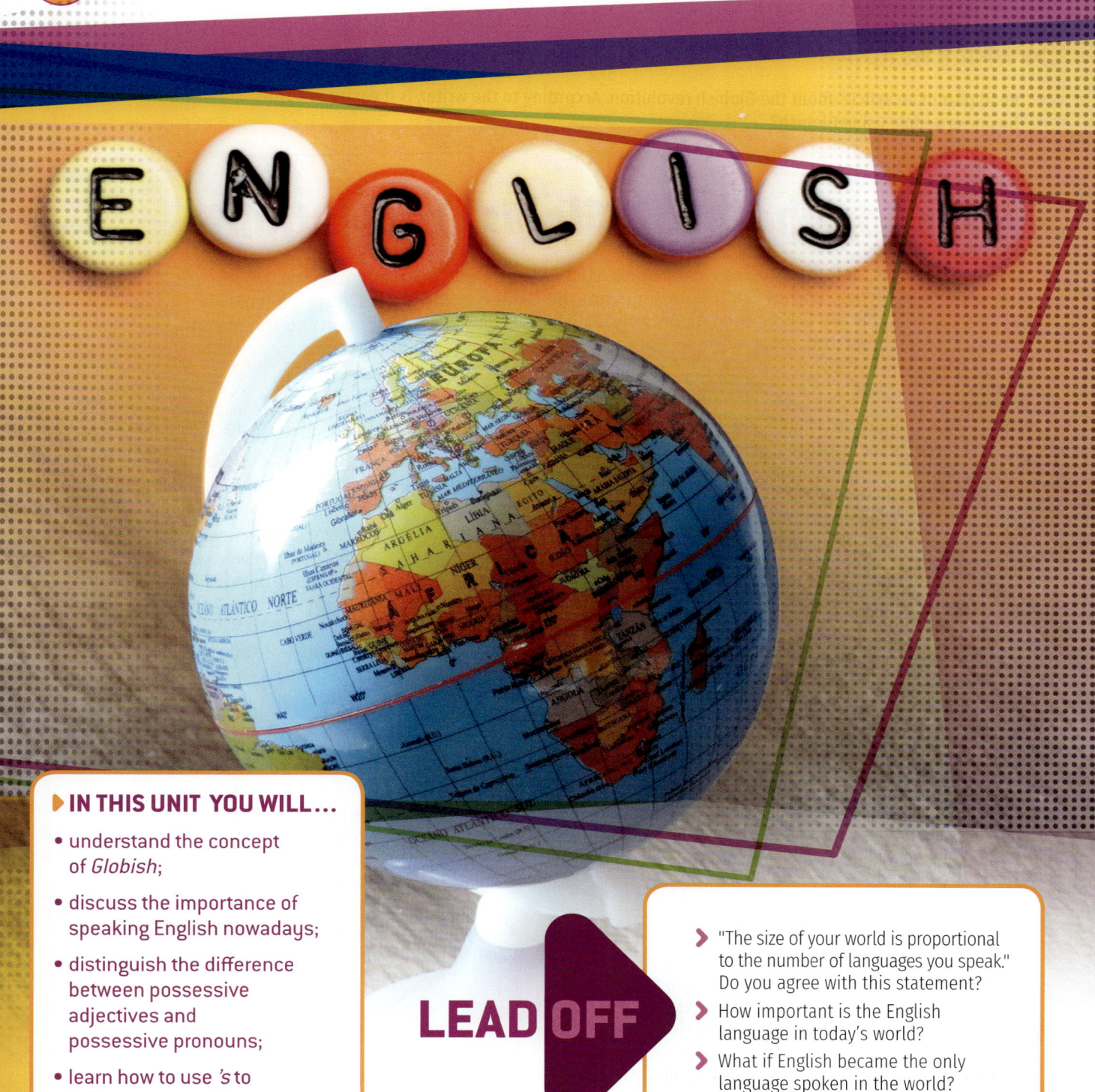

▶ IN THIS UNIT YOU WILL…

- understand the concept of *Globish*;
- discuss the importance of speaking English nowadays;
- distinguish the difference between possessive adjectives and possessive pronouns;
- learn how to use *'s* to indicate possession.

LEAD OFF

> "The size of your world is proportional to the number of languages you speak." Do you agree with this statement?
> How important is the English language in today's world?
> What if English became the only language spoken in the world?

READING

BEFORE READING

How much do you know about Globish? Check (✓) the statements that you think are true. Then read the text and check your answers. `Activating previous knowledge`

a. ( ) Globish is a sophisticated version of English used by native speakers.

b. ( ) The word *Globish* is a blend of the words *Globe* and *English*.

c. ( ) Globish is an international auxiliary language used by non-native speakers.

WHILE READING

Read part of an article about the Globish revolution. According to the writer, is it easier or harder to communicate with business people using Globish? `Scanning`

So, what's this Globish revolution?

I say tomato… you say red, round fruit. Increasingly, people across the world use some sort of English, but it is not the Queen's. Robert McCrum, Observer Literary Editor, reports on why Globish - English-lite - is becoming the universal language of the **boardroom**, the net and politics

Jean-Paul Nerriere is the kind of high-flying Frenchman at which the Grandes Ecoles excel: cosmopolitan, **witty**, voluble and insatiably
5 curious about the world around him. Formerly a naval commander, then a businessman, he is the proud holder of the Legion d'Honneur. In his blue blazer and **cravat**, twinkly Nerriere cuts a **dashing** figure, seems much younger than his 65 years
10 and occupies a surprising place in contemporary European culture.

In scenes reminiscent of Lost in Translation, Nerriere noted that his conversation with the Japanese and Koreans was 'much easier and more efficient than what could be observed
15 between them and the British and American (IBM) employees who came with me'. A thoughtful man, with a fascination for the exploits of Nelson, he noted that this observation of non-Anglophone English communication applied to
20 'all non-English-speaking countries'.

Then Nerriere came to his radical, perhaps revolutionary, conclusion: 'The language non-Anglophones spoke together,' he says, 'was not English, but something vaguely like it.'
25 In this language, he noted, 'we were better off than genuine Anglophones'. This language, he decided, 'was the worldwide dialect of the third millennium'. In a moment of pure inspiration he called it 'Globish' (pronounced 'globe-ish').

30 Globish is not '**pidgin**' or 'broken' English but it is highly simplified and unidiomatic. Nerriere observes that in Globish you could never say, 'This **erstwhile** buddy of yours is a weird duck who will probably **put the kibosh on** all our good
35 **deeds**.' That might make sense on Acacia Avenue but it will not play in Buenos Aires or Zurich. In Globish you would express this as: 'Your old friend is too strange. He would ruin all our efforts.' Globish, says Nerriere, is
40 'decaffeinated English, or English-lite'.

[…]

Nerriere himself is sometimes described as a remarkable man whose ambition is to promote global understanding between nationalities. He speaks passionately about his hopes for
45 Globish as 'an official language that would facilitate the life of everyone and put everyone on a par'. He hopes that 'some day it will be accepted as a viable alternative by the European Union or the United Nations'.

[…]

Extracted from www.theguardian.com/theobserver/2006/dec/03/features.review37. Accessed on August 08, 2018.

>> AFTER READING

Scan the text and find the information below. *Scanning*

a. What is this sort of English becoming a universal language called?
___

b. What is Jean-Paul Nerriere's nationality?
___

c. Was it easier for Jean-Paul Nerriere or the British and Americans with him to communicate with the Japanese and Koreans?
___

d. What was Nerriere's conclusion?
___

e. What characteristics does the writer give to Globish?
___

f. How does he simplify the statement: *'This erstwhile buddy of yours is a weird duck who will probably put the kibosh on all our good deeds.'*
___

EXPAND YOUR VOCABULARY

1. **Choose the correct synonym for each word in bold. If necessary, refer back to the text.**

   a. "Jean-Paul Nerriere is the kind of **high-flying** Frenchman […]"
      - ( ) failed
      - ( ) successful

   b. "[…] **twinkly** Nerriere cuts a dashing figure, seems much younger than his 65 years and occupies a surprising place in contemporary European culture."
      - ( ) friendly
      - ( ) unfriendly

   c. "We were **better off** than genuine Anglophones."
      - ( ) more fortunate
      - ( ) more helpless

   d. "Nerriere himself is sometimes described as a **remarkable** man […]"
      - ( ) extremely intelligent
      - ( ) positively surprising

   e. "[…] Globish as 'an official language that would facilitate the life of everyone and put everyone **on a par**'."
      - ( ) at different levels
      - ( ) at the same level

2. What do you think the author meant by "Globish […] is <u>decaffeinated</u> English, or <u>English-lite</u>"?
___
___

VOCABULARY IN USE

1. Reread this excerpt from the text on page 64 and choose the best option to complete the sentences.

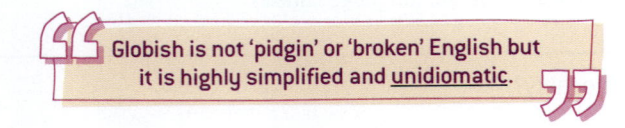

   > Globish is not 'pidgin' or 'broken' English but it is highly simplified and <u>unidiomatic</u>.

   a. By employing the underlined expression, the author means that people who speak Globish **use / do not use** idioms in their speech.

   b. Idioms are combinations of words whose meaning is **difficult / easy** to guess from the meaning of each individual word.

2. The idioms in bold in the sentences below are related to body parts. Read the sentences and infer the meaning of the idioms. Then match the columns.

   a. Susan always **has butterflies in her stomach** before she speaks in public.
   b. Jack is **the apple of his father's eye**.
   c. I was going to buy that new cell phone, but it costs **an arm and a leg**!

   ( ) loved and cherished by someone
   ( ) becomes nervous
   ( ) a lot of money

3. Complete the sentences below with the idioms from the box. Make all the necessary changes.

   > put your foot in your mouth   know your onions   apples and oranges   a piece of cake   cup of tea
   > have a finger in every pie   cold feet   give someone the cold shoulder   know something by heart

   a. I don't need you to remind me the lyrics of that song. I _____.
   b. That was probably the easiest game we've ever played! It was _____!
   c. I didn't mean to offend you, really! I guess I just _____.
   d. In all honesty, pop music is not my _____. I prefer rock.
   e. If you have any questions about language, you can ask James. He really _____.
   f. Mary doesn't like focusing on one thing only! She _____.
   g. You can't really compare riding a bike to traveling by plane. It's like _____! Two completely different things!
   h. I saw Judy at the party, but she _____. I don't know why she ignored me like that.
   i. I thought I'd be OK with it, but now I'm not sure I want to travel. I'm getting _____ about this trip.

4. Work with a partner. Think of three sentences with any idiom from the previous activity. Two sentences have to be true about you, and one has to be false. Guess which is your partner's false sentence.

_____

_____

_____

_____

LANGUAGE IN USE 1

Unit 7

THE 'S FOR POSSESSION

1. The excerpt below is from the reading text on page 64. Circle the possessive with 's.

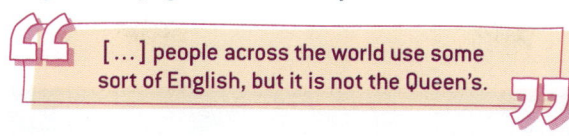

> [...] people across the world use some sort of English, but it is not the Queen's.

2. Read the sentences below, paying close attention to the 's. Then write P for the ones that refer to a possessive and B for the ones that refer to the verb *be*.

   a. ( ) Will's here because learning a foreign language is important for our future.

   b. ( ) That woman's language is very different from ours. Is it Japanese?

   c. ( ) What's the text about?

   d. ( ) Kelly's Spanish teacher wants to retire next year.

3. Now analyze the structures in bold in the sentences below and complete the rules with the words from the box.

> a. This is **that blond girl's old doll**.
> b. If you'd like to play with **the children's toys**, you should ask them for permission.
> c. You cannot get those books. They are **our teachers' books**.
> d. Jack and Jill are siblings. **Jack and Jill's parents** are at home now.
> e. **John's and Mary's cars** were stolen on the same day!

> plural   after   each one   's   '   irregular   one object

   a. We add _____ to nouns in the singular form to express possession.

   b. The possessed item always comes _____ the person who has the possession.

   c. We add only _____ when the possession refers to a regular noun in the _____ form.

   d. If the noun has an _____ plural form, we need to use 's to form the possessive.

   e. If there is only _____ that belongs to two or more people, we add 's only after the last person.

   f. If there are two different objects that belong to two or more different people, we use the 's after _____ of the people.

4. Rewrite the sentences below using 's or '.

   a. The sister of my uncle speaks six different languages.

   _____

   b. The mother of Susan and Michael is a very nice lady who was born overseas.

   _____

   c. This car belongs to those women.

   _____

   d. These T-shirts belong to the students.

   _____

5. Now rewrite these sentences with the verbs given also expressing possession.

   a. This is my sister's computer. (belongs)

   _____

   b. That is Jack's car. (owns)

   _____

   c. This is Lucas's bike. (has)

   _____

EXPAND YOUR READING

1. Read the text and answer: Is it a book summary or a book review?

The Future of English?

This book is about the English language in the 21st century: about who will speak it and for what **purposes**. It is a practical briefing document, written for educators, politicians, managers – any decision maker or planning team with a professional interest in the development of English worldwide.

5 The book explores the possible long-term impact on the English language from developments in communications technology, growing economic globalization and major demographic **shifts** at the end of the twentieth century and **beyond**. It uses existing linguistic research as a basis for examining new trends in globalization, popular culture, and economic development to see how these affect the future use of English.

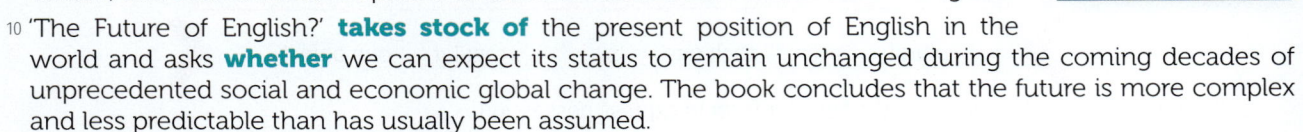

10 'The Future of English?' **takes stock of** the present position of English in the world and asks **whether** we can expect its status to remain unchanged during the coming decades of unprecedented social and economic global change. The book concludes that the future is more complex and less predictable than has usually been assumed.

First published in 1997, the book was commissioned by the British Council and was intended to stimulate
15 constructive debate about the future status of English at that time.

The book is divided into five main sections:
Section 1 – How English reached its position
Section 2 – Techniques of **forecasting** and identifying patterns of linguistic change
Section 3 – Significant global social and economic trends
20 Section 4 – The impact of such trends on language and communication
Section 5 – A summary of the impact for the English language

About the author
David Graddol is a British applied linguist, well known as a writer, **broadcaster**, **researcher**, and consultant on issues relating to global English.

Adapted from https://englishagenda.britishcouncil.org/continuing-professional-development/cpd-managers/future-english. Accessed on July 23, 2018. Reproduced with kind permission of the British Council.

2. Identify the incorrect information in the sentences below. Then rewrite them with the correct information.
   a. The book is recommended for students who are learning English.
   _____
   _____

   b. The book examines new trends in education to see how they affect the future use of English.
   _____
   _____

   c. The author did not have the intention of stimulating constructive debate about the future status of English when it was first published.
   _____
   _____

LANGUAGE IN USE 2

Unit 7

POSSESSIVE PRONOUNS

1. Based on the comic strip complete the examples.

> YOURS substitutes for **your weird dream**.
> MINE substitutes for **my weird dream**.
> THEIRS substitutes for **their weird dream**.

In English, we use a **possessive pronoun** when we replace both the noun and the possessive adjective or the 's for one single pronoun. For example:

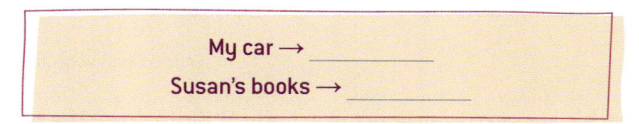

> My car → _____
> Susan's books → _____

Remember that it is important for your interlocutor to know what you are talking about when you use only a pronoun. For example:

> That is his dog, and this is **mine**. (my dog)

2. Possessive pronouns are used in reference to the possessor and, as such, are closely linked to subject pronouns. It's important not to confuse them with possessive adjectives. Complete the table below to visualize the differences between them.

Subject pronoun	Possessive adjective	Possessive pronoun
I	my	
You	your	
He	his	
She	her	
It	its	
We	our	
They	their	

3. Complete the sentences below with possessive adjectives or possessive pronouns.
   a. I have _____ books, and William has _____.
   b. David doesn't want to talk to _____ parents, but you can talk to _____.
   c. We are going to wait for _____ friends. Donna and Albert are going to wait for _____.
   d. Are you asking them to share _____ secrets without sharing _____ first?
   e. Jane and Sean are coming over to pick up _____ cat, Yaros… Yarosv… What is _____ name again?
   f. This is not Matthew's car, it's Anna's. _____ is older than Matthew's.

LISTENING COMPREHENSION

1. Will English always be the global language? What has made it the global language today? Discuss your thoughts with a classmate.

2. You will hear part of a talk given by Dr. David Crystal, one of the most renowned linguists of our times. He is answering the question, "Will English always be the global language?". Check (✓) the sentences below that correspond with David Crystal's views.

   a. (   ) It was easy to have predicted that Latin was no longer going to be spoken by the vast majority of the globe.
   b. (   ) We can't be sure if English will be the dominant language in 100 years' time.
   c. (   ) The future of language and the future of society are connected.
   d. (   ) There are many reasons why a language becomes global.
   e. (   ) People want to speak a foreign language because of power.
   f. (   ) Among the reasons why English became global, we can mention the Industrial Revolution.
   g. (   ) The Internet is still monolingual.
   h. (   ) It is very difficult to imagine a scenario in which English won't be the global language.
   i. (   ) Spanish is the fastest-growing language in the world.
   j. (   ) English will retain the title of global language for the short-term future.

   Extracted from www.youtube.com/watch?v=5Kvs8SxN8mc. Accessed on June 29, 2018.

3. How similar or how different were his answers from yours in activity 1? Write down the two most important things that David Crystal mentioned in his talk and compare them with a classmate.

   _____
   _____

›› EXPAND YOUR HORIZONS ››››

Check (✓) the column that best describes your opinion about each statement below. Then discuss your answers with your classmates and teacher, justifying your point of view.

	I agree.	I'm not sure.	I disagree.
a. If we speak Globish, we have access to a broader range of information, connections, and opportunities.			
b. It is possible that one day English will no longer be one of the world's most used languages.			
c. English should not be the leading language as it is not the most popular language.			

UNIT 8
Hit the Road

▶ IN THIS UNIT YOU WILL...
- talk about the means of transportation used for long-distance travels;
- exchange ideas about traveling smart and packing light;
- refer to past actions with *used to*;
- use the modal verb *must*.

LEAD OFF

- ❯ What does the picture represent? How is it related to the title of this unit?
- ❯ Have you ever heard the expression *travel smart*? What do you think it means?
- ❯ What are the means of transportation people often use for short trips? What about long trips?

READING

BEFORE READING
Predicting the theme and the literary genre

Look at the book cover below and read the synopsis that follows. What do you think the book is about? And what genre of book is it?

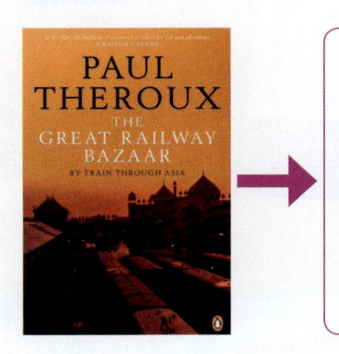

> Paul Theroux is a vocal **proponent** of rail travel over air travel, which he **likens** to traveling by submarine for all that goes unseen and not experienced by its adherents. *The Great Railway Bazaar*, his 1975 account of a four-month railroad journey through Europe and Asia begins, "I **sought** trains, I found passengers." It is certainly the individuals that Theroux meets along the way, rather than the cities, buildings, or sites of touristic import, to which he devotes his most generous descriptions.
>
> Adapted from THEROUX, Paul. The Great Railway Bazaar. PLACE: Penguin, YEAR, p. 2.

WHILE READING

Scan the text. Do you expect it to be narrative or argumentative? Mention the characteristics that support your answer.

Recognizing textual types

Chapter Two THE DIRECT-ORIENT EXPRESS

Duffill had put on a pair of glasses, wire-framed and with enough Scotch tape on the lenses to prevent his seeing the Blue **Mosque**. He assembled his parcels and, **grunting**, produced a suitcase, bound with a selection of leather and canvas belts as an added guarantee against it **bursting** open. A few cars down we met again to read the sign on the side of the wagon-lit: direct-orient and its itinerary, PARIS – LAUSANNE –
5   MILANO – TRIESTE – ZAGREB – BEOGRAD – SOFIYA – ISTANBUL. We stood there, staring at this sign; Duffill worked his glasses like binoculars. Finally he said, 'I took this train in nineteen twenty-nine.'

It seemed to call for a reply, but by the time a reply occurred to me ('Judging from its condition, it was probably this very train!') Duffill had gathered up his parcels and his **strapped** suitcase and moved down the platform. It was a great train in 1929, and it goes without saying that the Orient Express is the most famous train
10 in the world. Like the Trans-Siberian, it links Europe with Asia, which **accounts** for some of its romance. But it has also been hallowed by fiction: **restless** Lady Chatterley took it; so did Hercule Poirot and James Bond; […]

After several minutes the rest of the passengers went into their compartments – from my own I heard the smashing of paper parcels being stuffed into corners. This left the drinker, whom I had started to think of as the Captain, and me alone in the passage. He looked my way and said, 'Istanbul?'
15   'Yes.'
'Have a drink.'
[…]
His name was Molesworth, but he said it so distinctly that the first time I heard it I thought it was a **double-barreled** name. There was something military in his posture and the promptness of his speech, and at the same time this **flair** could have been an actor's. […]
20   'I'm an actors' agent,' he said. 'I've got my own firm in London. It's a smallish firm, but we do all right. We always have more than we can handle.'
'Any actors I might know?'
He named several famous actors.
I said, 'I thought you might be army.'
25   '*Did* you?' He said that he had been in the Indian army – Poona, Simla, Madras – and his duties there were of a theatrical nature, organizing shows for the troops. […]
We talked about Indian trains. Molesworth said they were magnificent. 'They have showers, and there's always a little man who brings you what you need. At mealtime they telegraph ahead to the next station for hampers. Oh, you'll like it.'
30   Duffill put his head out the door and said, 'I think I'll go to bed now.'
'He's your **chap**, is he?' said Molesworth. He surveyed the car. 'This train isn't what it was. Pity. It used to be one of the best, a *train de luxe* – royalty took it. Now, I'm not sure about this, but I don't think we have a dining car, which is going to be a terrible bore if it's true. Have you got a **hamper**?'
I said I hadn't, though I had been advised to bring one.
35   'That was good advice,' Molesworth said. 'I don't have a hamper myself, but then I don't eat much. I like the *thought* of food, but I much prefer drinking. How do you like your Chablis? Will you have more?' He inserted his eyeglass and found the bottle and, **pouring**, said, 'These French wines take an awful lot of **beating**.'

Adapted from THEROUX, Paul. **The Great Railway Bazaar**. Penguin, General UK, 2008, p. 14, 16, and 17.

Unit 8

» AFTER READING

1. **Check (✓) the statement that best summarizes the excerpt you have just read.** *Understanding main ideas*
   a. ( ) The writer is recounting the beginning of his friend's journey on a modern streetcar in Istanbul.
   b. ( ) The narrator is detailing the start of his travel on the Direct-Orient Express to Istanbul.
   c. ( ) Duffill is telling the story about his trip from London to Istanbul on the Direct-Orient Express.

2. **Whose voices are those in the text?** *Recognizing the voices in a text*
   _____
   _____

3. **Decide if the sentences are true (T) or false (F).** *Understanding details*
   a. ( ) In Molesworth's opinion, the Orient Express is better off these days than it was in the past.
   b. ( ) Duffill wasn't carrying any luggage.
   c. ( ) The Orient Express taken by the narrator ran between Paris and Istanbul.
   d. ( ) The narrator brought a hamper along because a friend had advised him to do so.
   e. ( ) Although he was not an actor, Molesworth's elegant style made him look like one.

EXPAND YOUR VOCABULARY

1. **Match the words in bold with their meanings.**
   a. "He assembled his **parcels** and, grunting, produced a suitcase, [...]"
   b. "He inserted his eyeglass and found the bottle and, **pouring**, said, [...]"
   c. "After several minutes the rest of the passengers went into their **compartments** [...]"
   d. "Duffill had gathered up his parcels and his strapped suitcase and moved down the **platform**."
   e. "But it has also been **hallowed** by fiction: [...]"
   f. "It's a **smallish** firm, but we do all right."

   ( ) separate areas into which a plane, ship, or train is divided
   ( ) objects that have been wrapped in paper or put in a special envelope
   ( ) respected or greatly admired
   ( ) an adjective to describe something fairly small
   ( ) making a liquid or other substance flow out of or into a container by holding it at an angle
   ( ) the raised place beside a railway track where you get on and off a train in a station

   Adapted from www.ldoceonline.com. Accessed on June 20, 2018.

2. **What are the most common means of transportation for long distances? What means of transportation do you use on long-distance trips? How can you compare ship to air travel in terms of speed, comfort, and luggage capacity? Exchange ideas with a classmate.**

VOCABULARY IN USE

1. In the extract "He assembled his parcels and, grunting, produced a suitcase, bound with a selection of leather and canvas belts as an added guarantee against it bursting open.", which words refer to travel packing or bag types?

2. Below you will find other travel packing or bag types. Work in pairs to match them with their corresponding pictures.

   a. suitcase
   b. duffel bag
   c. backpack
   d. toiletry bag
   e. messenger bag
   f. laptop case
   g. rolling suitcase
   h. garment bag

   ( ) ( ) ( ) ( )

   ( ) ( ) ( ) ( )

3. Insert the words from the box in the correct mind map. Then come up with one more item to fit each category.

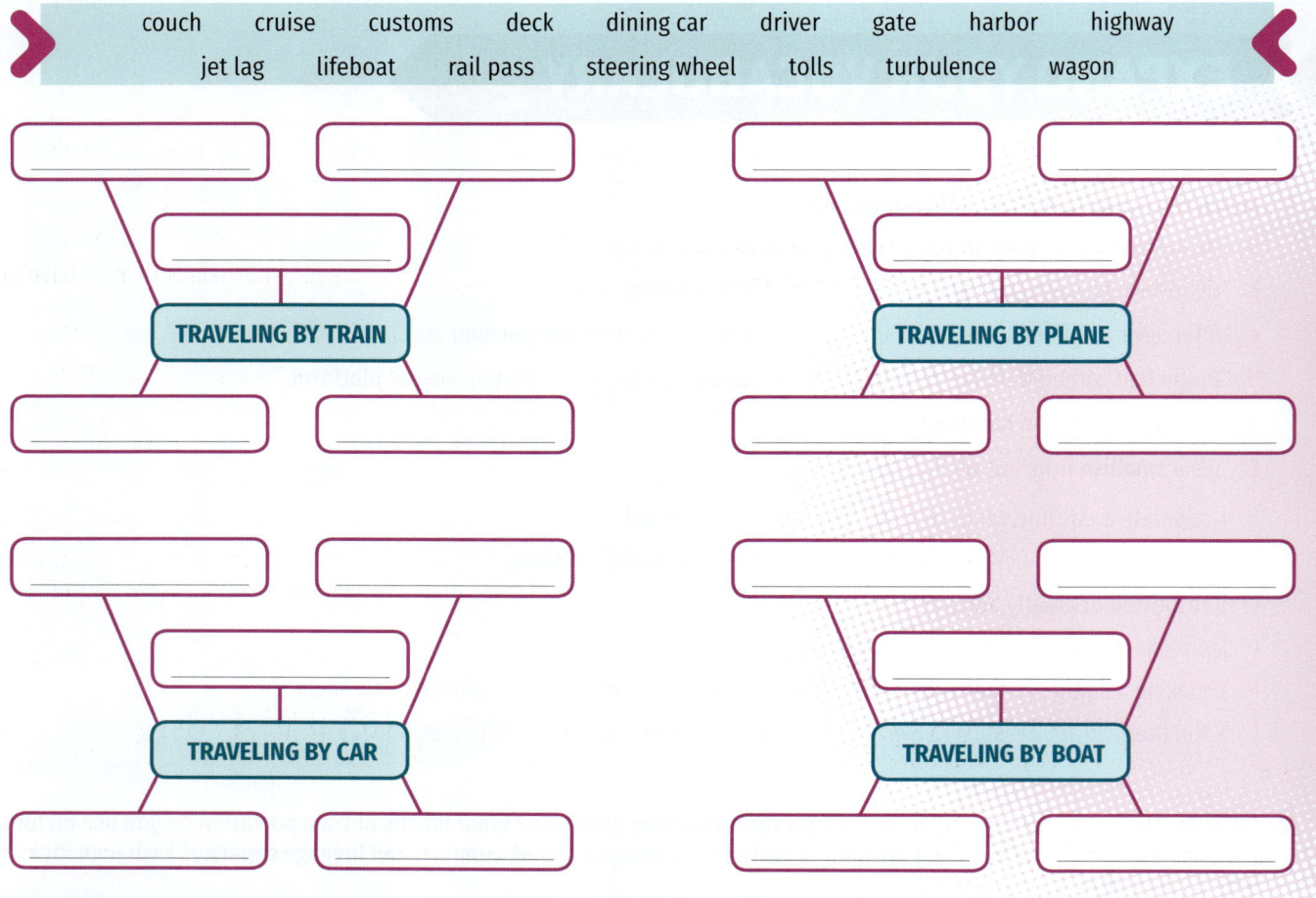

   | couch | cruise | customs | deck | dining car | driver | gate | harbor | highway |
   | jet lag | lifeboat | rail pass | steering wheel | tolls | turbulence | wagon |

   TRAVELING BY TRAIN

   TRAVELING BY PLANE

   TRAVELING BY CAR

   TRAVELING BY BOAT

4. Work with a partner. Describe your ideal type of travel using some words from the previous activities.

LANGUAGE IN USE 1

Unit 8

USED TO

1. The excerpt below was extracted from the text on page 72. Read it, pay special attention to the part in bold, and check (✓) the correct statement about it.

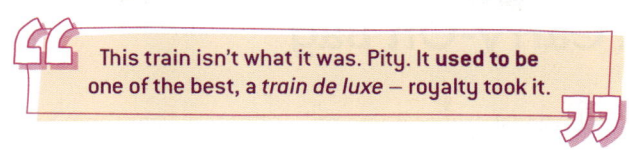

> This train isn't what it was. Pity. It **used to be** one of the best, a *train de luxe* – royalty took it.

( ) It refers to a regular past state or habit that is finished now.
( ) It refers to a regular past state or habit that is still happening now.

2. Read the text below and answer the questions accordingly.

How have our travel habits changed over the past 50 years?

October 21, 2015 9:58 A.M. EDT

We tend to assume that travel today is fundamentally different from what it was half a century ago. We have easier access to faster forms of transport, and we expect to be able to move quickly and easily whenever we wish. But a recent overview of travel behavior in England—celebrating 50 years of data from the National Travel Survey (NTS)—shows that while some things have certainly changed, much remains the same.

According to the authors of the report, the most striking change to our travel habits is that "we are traveling further but not more often". In other words, though the individual trips we take are longer in terms of distance, the number of times we travel has remained much the same over the past 50 years. What's more, there has been little change in the total time spent traveling, due to faster travel speeds. And the purposes of our trips have changed only slightly: the biggest change has been an increase in the number of journeys we take to escort others.

[…]

Adapted from www.theconversation.com/how-have-our-travel-habits-changed-over-the-past-50-years-49029. Accessed on June 10, 2018.

a. Do we have easy access to faster forms of transport nowadays?

_____

b. Did we **use to** have such an easy access to those quicker means of travel 50 years ago?

_____

c. According to the report of travel behavior in England, are they traveling more often these days?

_____

d. How far **did** they **use to** travel 50 years ago?

_____

3. Now reread the extract in activity 1 and the questions and answers in activity 2 to complete the sentences about *used to*.

a. We use _____ followed by the main verb in its base form to describe regular past habits or states that do not happen or are not true anymore.

b. In interrogative sentences, we use the structure _____ + subject + _____ + the main verb in its base form. In short answers, either *did* or *didn't* is used.

c. In _____ sentences, we use the structure _____ *use to* + the main verb in its base form.

4. Answer the questions with *used to* or *didn't use to*.

a. Do you think air travel used to be more pleasant in the past? Why (not)?

_____
_____

b. In your opinion, how did travelers use to plan their trips in the past? How do they plan their trips nowadays?

_____
_____

c. What did you use to do before and while traveling in the past that you don't do anymore?

_____
_____

EXPAND YOUR READING

1. **Read part of an article on packing and complete the infographic.**

How To Travel Anywhere With Nothing But A Carry-On Bag
Deborah L. Jacobs — Forbes Staff

Whether you are packing for a business trip or going on vacation, it pays to travel light.

The trade-off is that you must live with less, which involves what may seem like some tough choices about what stays and what goes. No matter how long you are away for, pack just one week's worth of clothing. Here's how to think–and pack–like a minimalist.

1. Put things in perspective.

To pack light, you must be willing to live with less. If that makes you uncomfortable, remember it's only temporary; consider it a vacation from your possessions.

2. Choose a capacious carry-on.

Whatever bag you choose sets the limit on how much you can take: if it doesn't fit, it doesn't go. On the other hand, don't feel you must fill every available crevice. You will welcome the extra space for those must-have souvenirs.

3. Bring ample footwear.

Figure out what's appropriate for the activities you have planned. When I need to bring hiking boots or winter boots, I wear them on trains and planes, and carry a pair of ballet slippers in my purse to change into once I'm on board. The only footwear that goes in my suitcase is a pair of sneakers or comfortable walking shoes, and a set of flip flops that I use as bedroom slippers, to pad around hotels, and when going to the beach or swimming pool.

4. Be a minimalist with toiletries.

Pare your list down to what you absolutely need.

5. Layer to change your look.

This approach gives you more outfits and the flexibility to adjust for weather changes–for example if your trip takes you to various climate zones, or you run into a heat wave or cold snap. For example, one long-sleeve button-down shirt, two camisoles, two tank tops and a cardigan can be combined in multiple ways.

Adapted from www.forbes.com/sites/deborahljacobs/2013/07/29/how-to-travel-anywhere-with-nothing-but-a-carry-on-bag/. Accessed on August 8, 2018.

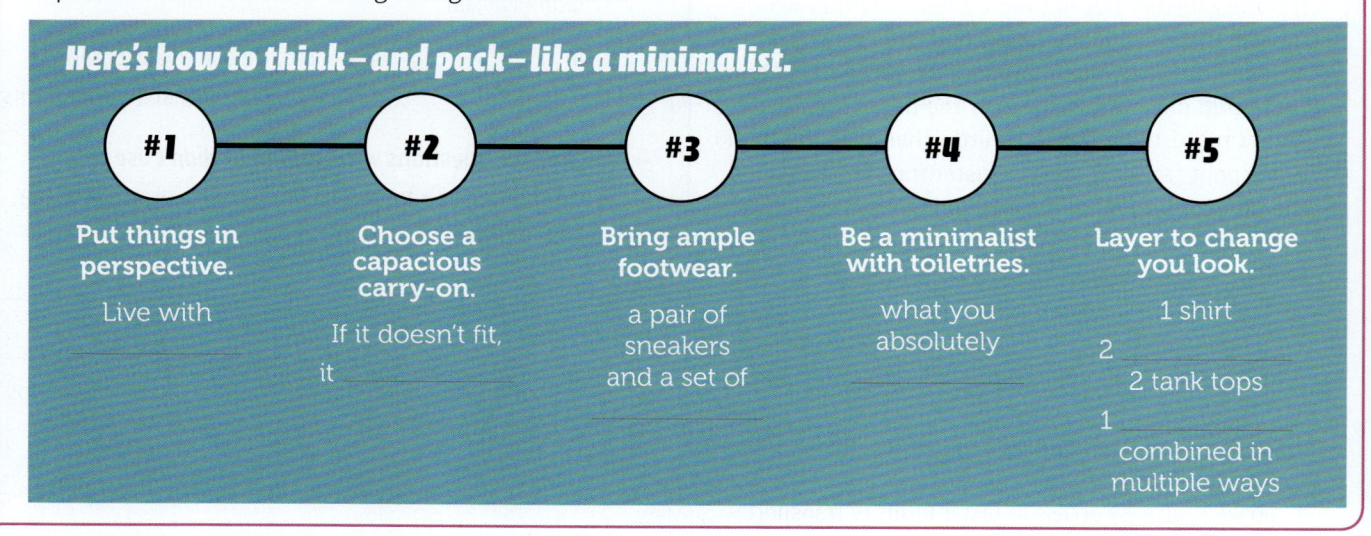

Here's how to think – and pack – like a minimalist.

#1 Put things in perspective.
Live with _____

#2 Choose a capacious carry-on.
If it doesn't fit, it _____

#3 Bring ample footwear.
a pair of sneakers and a set of _____

#4 Be a minimalist with toiletries.
what you absolutely _____

#5 Layer to change you look.
1 shirt
2 _____
2 tank tops
1 _____
combined in multiple ways

2. **Underline the option that best completes the description. Infographics…**

   a. are sets of drawings containing commentaries expressing the author's opinion about a topic often associated with politics or social issues.

   b. are visual representations of information in the forms of images and texts intended to provide readers with an easier comprehension of often complex subjects.

LANGUAGE IN USE 2

Unit 8

MODAL VERB – *MUST*

1. Check (✔) the sentence that has a similar meaning to this extract from the infographic on page 76.

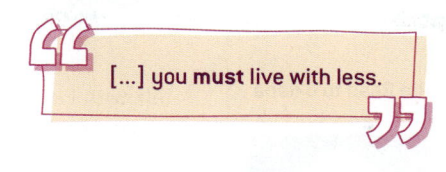

> [...] you **must** live with less.

( ) It's possible to live with less.
( ) It's necessary to live with less.
( ) It's correct to live with less.

2. Match the modal verbs in bold in the sentences below to the ideas they convey.

   a. Drivers and car passengers **must** wear a seatbelt.
   b. So you're a travel agent? That **must** be very interesting!
   c. One **must not** use a handheld cell phone while driving.

   ( ) prohibition
   ( ) obligation
   ( ) deduction

3. Read the text and use *must* or *mustn't* and the verbs from the box to fill in the blanks.

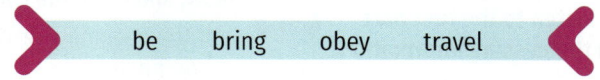

   be   bring   obey   travel

TRAVEL TIPS

Things you _____ with if you are leaving on a flight

Africa is an amazing place to be and exotic for those who want to spend their vacation here. However, it can be a nightmare for foreigners who end up on the wrong side of the law. Before you make your way to Africa, make sure that you have understood the local laws and abide by these rules and regulations.

African airports may not be as digitally advanced as airports in more developed countries. You may think that these airports are not strict or governed by rules you _____. However, you are expected to be on your best behavior and never find yourself in the line of fire of lawyers or the local police by running the risk of getting yourself arrested. These are some of the things you _____ to the airport.

Excessive Money

You may be a business person, but it is expected that you handle your business transactions online. Money laundering is a serious crime. There is a limit on the amount of money you are expected to carry with you.

Countries have different rules about receiving money in their airports.
[...]

Live Animals

No matter how much you love your kids, they will always grow and become independent. However, if you love your pets and you want to travel with them, you _____ sure the airport you are going to use does not have a restriction.

Fresh Food

You are not allowed to travel in or out with fresh products like fruits, vegetables, and eggs.

Precious Metals

Customs officers demand that you present to them for assessment any precious metals that you have bought. They would be the ones to talk to concerning the rules about those precious metals that may be imported and those that may be taken out.
[...]

Adapted from www.momoafrica.com/things-you-mustnt-travel-with-if-you-are-leaving-with-a-flight. Accessed on June 10, 2018.

4. Based on the discussions throughout this unit, write a new tip for packing wisely.

   In order to pack wisely, you must _____

LISTENING COMPREHENSION

1. **Look at the book covers below. What do all these books have in common?**

   _____

   Ghost Train to the Eastern Star

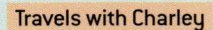

   Travels with Charley

   The Road to Oxiana

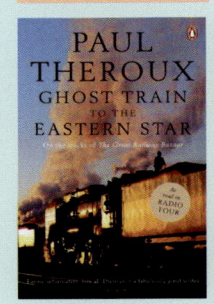

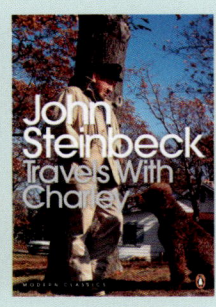

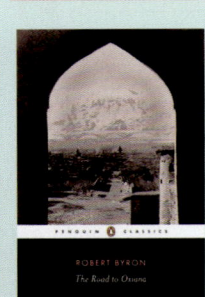

2. **You are going to listen to part of the radio program *Talk of the Nation*, in which the American journalist Neal Conan talks to and about Paul Theroux. Listen to the first part and complete the transcript with the missing information.**

   This is Talk of the Nation. I'm Neal Conan in Washington. In 1973, Paul Theroux said goodbye to his wife and children in London and set off on a _____ that would make his career and change his life. Theroux was a novelist then, out of ideas, and he hoped that a trip across Europe and Asia and back would inspire a new book. Theroux boarded the Golden Arrow, took the ferry to France, transferred to the _____, and rode the _____ east to Iran and Afghanistan, India, Burma, Vietnam, China, and Japan, then home again through the length of the Soviet Union. It took him four and a half months, and he then wrote a now classic book, "The Great Railway Bazaar," which many credit as the start of a new kind of travel _____.

   More than three decades later, Theroux retraced his steps as much as he could. There are new train routes, different landscapes, new borders, and different political realities, and he chronicles that trip in his new book, "Ghost _____ to the Eastern Star." If you'd like to talk with Paul Theroux about his _____, about what's changed, and what hasn't, along the way, our phone number is 800-989-8255. The email address is talk@npr.org, and you can join the conversation on our blog. That's at npr.org/blogofthenation. While you're there, you can go to our blog and read an excerpt from "Ghost Train to the Eastern Star." That's at npr.org/blogofthenation.

   [...]

   Extracted from www.npr.org/templates/story/story.php?storyId=93702596. Accessed on June 10, 2018.

3. **Listen to another part of the program, read the sentences below, and circle the correct alternatives to complete them.**

   a. At the beginning of Theroux's *Ghost Train to the Eastern Star*, he describes traveling as one of the **cheapest / easiest** ways of passing time.

   b. Conan tells Theroux that many of their listeners will remember him as a marvelous **travel agent / traveling companion** 35 years ago.

   c. In Theroux's opinion, travelers **must / must not** be optimistic and in a fairly good mood.

4. **Listen to the last part of the talk, in which Mr. Theroux explains why he thinks luxury is the enemy of observation in travels. Then work with a partner to answer the questions: Do you agree that someone can travel around quite cheaply if he / she gives up opulence? In your opinion, what really matters when it comes to traveling? Report your opinions to the class.**

›› EXPAND YOUR HORIZONS ››››

Check (✓) the column that best describes your opinion about each statement. Then discuss your answers with your classmates and teacher, justifying your point of view.

	I agree.	I'm not sure.	I disagree.
a. Packing wisely equals traveling happily, saving more time, money, and annoyance.			
b. Air travels in economy cabins will only get worse because airlines will keep opting to cram more and more travelers into a plane.			
c. One will never be the same again after going on a journey, be it a luxurious or a modest one.			

REVIEW 4

Unit 7 and 8

1. Read the dictionary entry and the title of the text below. What do you think the text is about? Exchange ideas with a classmate. *Predicting the theme*

peak
1 [usually singular] the time when something or someone is best, greatest, highest, most successful, etc.

Adapted from www.ldoceonline.com/dictionary/peak. Accessed on July 18, 2018.

www.theguardian.com/commentisfree/2018/feb/27/reached-peak-english-britain-china

News | Opinion | Sport | Culture | Lifestyle

Have we reached peak English in the world?
Nicholas Ostler

In China last month, Theresa May attended the **launch** of the British Council's English is Great campaign, intended to **boost** interest and fluency in our national language. This might sound like Donald Trump's notorious "Make America great again", but comes in fact from a stronger position. **Beyond doubt**, the use of English is greater than ever, and far more **widespread** than any other language in the world. All non-English-speaking powers of our globalized world
5 recognize it as the first foreign language to learn; it is also, uniquely, in practical use worldwide. The British Council **reckons** that English is spoken at a useful level by some 1.75 billion people, a quarter of the world's population. It is taught from primary level up in all China's schools; it is the working language of the whole European Union.

[…]

This global acceptance of English, now far beyond the zones of influence of the British Empire or the United States' backyard, has effectively grown up in just a century – **neatly**, and a little paradoxically, since the 1919 treaty of
10 Versailles. In deference to that of the U.S., this was the first international treaty written in English; but it also turned out to mark the incipient decline of the world's greatest English-speaking institution, the British Empire. From a language point of view, however, British power had the good fortune to be succeeded by its cousin in North America, so that the usual historic **lag**, as political command leads on to linguistic imitation, was disguised. Even as Britain began to decline economically, its established position was reflected by increased take-up of English as the language to learn.

15 But all this while, especially from the 1920s to the 1990s, the focus of U.S. expansion was changing, moving from North America to the world, leading to influence on trade, engineering, telecommunications, mining, media, science, and finance, as the dollar moved to replace sterling as the world's reserve currency. This was followed by the digital information revolution, creating new fortunes based in Silicon Valley at the turn of the 21st century. These were all positive for the world role of English (a role founded by Great Britain), but should have been
20 expected to peak later, in the growth of soft power and the increased popularity of American culture.

It is this lagged growth of English, reflecting U.S. influence **hitherto**, that we are now experiencing. Yet it is happening in a 21st century when other nations, particularly in Asia but also in South America and Africa, are far **outpacing** the USA (let alone Britain and the European Union) in economic growth rates. This is an amazing juncture in world history. And two questions arise. Is the position of English a real asset to the states that speak it natively? And is the language likely to hold this position in the **pecking order** indefinitely?

[…]

Adapted from www.theguardian.com/commentisfree/2018/feb/27/reached-peak-english-britain-china. Accessed on June 29, 2018.

2. Check (✓) the statements that are **not** true according to the text. *Understanding details*

a. (   ) When circumstances change, dominant languages fall.
b. (   ) Some nations still resist and choose not to accept English as the language to be learned.
c. (   ) The influence of English has risen immensely in just 100 years.
d. (   ) Britain's current economic power is the cause of success of English as the global language.
e. (   ) The economies of countries in South America, Africa, and Asia are growing more than that of the U.S.

3. Read the sentences below, extracted from the text on the previous page, and circle the possessive 's (or genitive case).
   a. "[...] Theresa May attended the launch of the British Council's English is Great campaign, [...]"
   b. "[...] This might sound like Donald Trump's notorious "Make America great again", [...]"
   c. "[...] It is taught from primary level up in all China's schools; it is the working language of the whole European Union. [...]"
   d. "[...] This global acceptance of English, now far beyond the zones of influence of the British Empire or the United States' backyard. [...]"

4. Complete the following sentences with the correct possessive pronouns.
   a. I need to fix my suitcase and you need to fix _____, too.
   b. She has already arrived at her final destination. He has arrived at _____, too.
   c. Our zipper tab is broken. Ann and Jeff told me _____ is broken, too.
   d. No, this is their baggage. Is this _____, honey?

5. Read the comic strips. Then complete them with the correct form of *used to* followed by the main verbs *come* or *be*.

6. Rewrite the following sentences with *must*.
   a. You have to have duct tape when you travel in case you need to fix your suitcase.

   _____
   _____

   b. It is very likely that one of the passengers will have duct tape.

   _____

GRAMMAR OVERVIEW

Verb tenses

Tense	Use(s)	Example(s) affirmative	Example(s) negative	Example(s) interrogative
Simple present	• Habits; • Routines; • Timeless events; • Narratives; • Scheduled events; • With frequency adverbs (e.g. *always*, *never*); • With stative verbs.	I **go** to school in the morning. Our class always **starts** at 8. I **am** very happy today.	I **do not / don't go** to school in the afternoon. Our class **does not / doesn't** usually **start** at 7. She **is not / isn't** very happy today.	When **do** you **go** to school? **Does** your class always **start** at 8? **Is** he always happy?
Present continuous	• Actions in progress in the present; • With action verbs.	They **are playing** basketball now. Daisy **is making** lunch.	They **are not / aren't playing** video games now. Daisy **is not / isn't making** a lot of food for lunch.	**Are** they **playing** sports now? **Is** Daisy **making** lunch for us?
Imperative form	• Ask for favors (informal); • Give commands.	**Open** the window (please).	**Do not / Don't close** the window (please). It's hot.	**Close** the window, will you?
Simple past	• Completed actions in the past; • Sequence of events in the past; • With past time expressions (e.g., *yesterday*, *last month*).	I **studied** in the morning. Then I **went** to the park. He **had** lunch at home yesterday.	Doug **did not / didn't study** with us. He **did not / didn't have** pizza for lunch.	**Did** you **study** for your test? Where **did** they **have** lunch?

Pronouns

Pronouns	Form	Use	Example(s)
Subject pronouns	I / you / he / she / it / we / they	Before the main verb to replace the subject	**I** am thankful for your help. **She** didn't work much last week.
Object pronouns	me / you / him / her / it / us / them	After the main verb to replace the object	I can't help **him**. I'm sorry. Can I go to the party with **them**?
Possessive adjectives	my / your / his / her / its / our / their	Before nouns to refer to possession	This is **my** car. Do you want a ride? When is **your** birthday?
Possessive pronouns	mine / yours / his / hers / its / ours / theirs	Before verbs; At the end of a clause.	This is my jacket. **Hers** is red, not blue. Your house is much bigger than **mine**.

GRAMMAR OVERVIEW

Modal verbs

Modal verb	Use(s)	Example(s) affirmative	Example(s) negative	Example(s) interrogative
Can	• Ability; • Permission; • Possibility; • Requests; • Offers; • Prohibition (*can't*).	I **can run** very fast. Of course she **can come** to visit us!	I **cannot / can't swim** well. You **cannot / can't drive** without a license.	**Can** he **run** fast, too? **Can** I **use** the restroom? **Can** I **help** you?
Could	• Ability in the past; • Formal requests; • Suggestions; • Possibility.	We **could go** to the movies.	She **could not / couldn't dance** before, but now she is a pro!	**Could** you **tell** me the way to the airport?
Should	• Advice; • Suggestions; • Ideal situations.	You **should take** an aspirin for your headache. People **should be** respectful toward nature.	You **should not / shouldn't eat** too much. He **should not / shouldn't spend** so much money on clothes.	**Should** I **call** her? What **should** we all **do** to take care of nature?
Must	• Obligation; • Prohibition; • Deduction (affirmative only); • Laws and rules.	We **must carry** an ID at all times. You **must be** very tired after all that exercise!	You **must not drink** and **drive**!	**Do** I have to **go**? I don't want to.
Used to	• A state in the past; • Habit or regular activity in the past.	They **used to see** each other every day. Now they never meet up	We **didn't use to be** friends, but now we get along.	**Did** John **use to** be a good student? How many hours **did** you **use to spend** in front of the TV?

Plural of nouns

Case	Plural form	Example(s)
Plural with *s*	Add *s* to the noun.	hous**es**, cat**s**, newspaper**s**
Plural with *es*	Add *es* to nouns ending in *s / sh / ch / x*.	bus**es**, dish**es**, match**es**, box**es**
Plural with *ies*	Remove *y* and add *ies* to nouns ending in consonant + *y*.	bab**ies**, cit**ies**
Irregular plurals	Use a different word to refer to plural; Some words finishing in *s* have the same word for plural.	child – children person – people man – men news – news gymnastics – gymnastics
Collective nouns	Use to refer to a group of a given noun.	musicians – band people – crowd students – class

's for possession (genitive case)

Case	Form and use	Example(s)
's	Add 's to singular nouns to refer to possession; Add 's to irregular plurals to refer to possession;	This is Lisa's book. The children's room is a mess!
'	Add only ' to regular plurals; Add only ' to names ending in s.	The students' grades are bad. They all need to review the content. I love James' new house! It's small and cozy.
of	Use the preposition *of* when the possession refers to inanimate beings (not people or animals).	The roof **of** the house is brown. The battery **of** the telephones last for a very short time nowadays.

Prefixes

Prefix	Meaning	Example(s)
auto-	self	**auto**biography
inter-	between	**inter**planetary
mid-	middle	**mid**day
out-	go beyond	**out**perform
over-	too much	**over**weight
post-	after	**post**-graduation
pre-	before	**pre**view
under-	less	**under**achieve

Suffixes

Suffix	Forms a(n)	Example(s)
-able	adjective	avail**able**
-ive	adjective	informat**ive**
-al	adjective / noun	classic**al** / surviv**al**
-ful	adjective	help**ful**
-ish	adjective	child**ish**
-less	adjective	use**less**
-ous	adjective	gener**ous**
-y	adjective	snow**y**
-ance	noun	appear**ance**
-ation / -tion	noun	applic**ation**
-sion	noun	illu**sion**
-ure	noun	proced**ure**
-ment	noun	argu**ment**
-age	noun	herit**age**

GRAMMAR OVERVIEW

Comparative and superlative forms

Structure	Form	Example(s)
Comparative of superiority: one or two-syllable adjectives	Add –er to the adjective (+ than)	My sister is taller than me. Math equations were easier in the past (than they are now).
Comparative of superiority: nouns, adverbs ending in –ly, and three- or four-syllable adjectives	Add more before the adjective / noun (+ than)	I eat more vegetables now than when I was a child. He walks more slowly than his mom. That leaflet is more informative than the one they had last year.
Comparative of superiority: irregular adjectives	good – better bad – worse far – farther / further little – less	I find this movie way better than the one we watched last night. We can go to that store, but it's farther than the one we usually go to.
Double comparatives	The (comparative)… the (comparative)	The more I try, the easier it gets. The more, the better!
Superlative of superiority: one or two-syllable adjectives	Add the or possessive adjective before the adjective and –est to the adjective	It is the largest pizza I have ever eaten! That was my fastest trip! It took only five minutes.
Superlative of superiority: three- or four-syllable adjectives	Add the most before the adjective	Wow! This is the most comfortable armchair I have sat on! They have the most delicious food in the city.

Word categories

Category	Form / Examples in words	Meaning	Examples in a sentence
Slang and informal terms about relationships	1. Dump 2. Have a crush on	1. To end a relationship with someone. 2. Someone you have romantic feelings for, but not are not in a relationship with.	Did you hear the last news? George dumped Amy! OK, I'll tell you the truth. I have a crush on your brother.
Idioms	1. It's all Greek to me. 2. Loaded language	1. Used to say that you cannot understand something. 2. Persuasive language	What's this new software? It's all Greek to me! Don't come to me with this loaded language. I know your true intentions.
Phrasal verbs	Verb + one or two prepositions / adverbs	The meaning of phrasal verbs can sometimes be literal, but it can also be very different from the meaning of the two or three words read separately.	I need to go the gym and work out. The hotel manager said that we can check in an hour earlier.

Adjectives – word order

Opinion	Size	Physical quality	Age	Shape	Color	Origin	Material	Type	Purpose
beautiful	small	unmarked	old	square	blue	Italian	paper	bilingual	dictionary

It's a **lovely old wooden** house.
I have two **square blue vintage** tables.

LANGUAGE REFERENCE

UNIT 1
SIMPLE PRESENT

Usage Notes

The simple present is often used to refer to:

- present facts or timeless events;

  Why **does** migration **occur**?

  Migration **occurs** because of economic, political, social, religious, and other different reasons.

- habits, routines, and repeated actions in the present.

  In some schools, English classes **don't take place** in regular classrooms. Students **attend** classes in language labs.

Forms

- Affirmative sentences use the verb in its base form unless the subject is the third person singular (*he*, *she*, *it*); in this case, *-s* or *-es* is added.

  A healthy life **includes** more than having a balanced diet and exercising. It **means** balance!

- Verbs in the third person singular (*he*, *she*, *it*) follow these spelling rules:

  – if the verb ends in *-ss*, *-x*, *-ch*, *-sh*, *-o* add *-es*;

  kiss – kisses
  fix – fixes
  watch – watches

  – if the verb ends with a *consonant* + *y*, remove the *-y* and add *-ies*.

  study – studies
  hurry – hurries

- Negative sentences use an auxiliary verb followed by the main verb in its base form. When the subject is *I, you, we*, or *they, do not* (*don't*) is used.
  When the subject is **he, she, or it**, *does not* (*doesn't*) is used.

  Globalization **doesn't increase** borders between nations. On the contrary, nations **don't seem** so distant these days, thanks to the Internet.

- Note that when the subject is *he, she, it*, the main verb is used in its base form:

  Globalization **doesn't increase** borders between nations.

NOT Globalization ~~doesn't increases~~ borders ~~between nations.~~

IMPERATIVE

Usage Notes

- When we make requests it's more polite to use a modal verb instead of the imperative.

  "Could you open the window?" is more polite than "**Open** the window, please."

- To make imperatives sound less direct we can use *please*, for example.

  "**Stop** talking, please." is less direct than "**Stop** talking."

- To add emphasis and be more direct, we may use subjects in imperatives.

  Everybody **look** at the board!

  Don't you **pretend** not to know me! We were classmates last year.

ADJECTIVE SUFFIXES

Suffixes are letters added to the end of a word to form new words. Below is a list of suffixes that change verbs and nouns into adjectives.

Verb + Suffix	Examples
rely + -able	reliable
create + -ive	creative
Noun + Suffix	**Examples**
misery + -able	miserable
music + -al	musical
pain + -ful	painful
hero + -ic	heroic
self + -ish	selfish
effect + -ive	effective
end + -less	endless
fame + -ous	famous
wind + -y	windy

Usage Notes

- Adjectives ending in *-ical* and *-ic* often have different meanings, for example:

LANGUAGE REFERENCE

- *classic* means typical, admired, very good, while *classical* means traditional;
- *economic* means relating to trade, industry, and the management of money, while *economical* means using money, time, goods, etc., carefully and without wasting any;
- *historic* can mean very important, while *historical* means related to the past.

▶ UNIT 2

SIMPLE PRESENT

Usage Notes

Besides the common usages listed on page 85, the simple present may also be used:

- in narratives or descriptions of past events.

  Next thing I **know**, I **slip** on a banana peel and **fall** to the ground. Then I **look** around, **pretend** nothing **bothers** me, **get** up, and **head** to the restroom.

- to talk about scheduled events.

  The field trip bus **leaves** at 7 A.M. next Tuesday.

Form

- Interrogative sentences use an auxiliary verb before the subject and the main verb in its base form. When the subject is *I, you, we,* or *they, do* is used. When the subject is *he, she,* or *it, does* is used.

  Do you **have** any questions?

  Does the teacher **need** our help with the classroom organization?

- However, in information questions, when the subject is the answer to the question, the main verb in the simple present form is used.

  Who **lives** with you?

  What **makes** your life happier?

- Note that when the subject is *he, she, it,* the main verb is used in its base form.

  Does the teacher **need** our help with the classroom organization?

  NOT ~~Does the teacher needs our help with the classroom organization?~~

FREQUENCY ADVERBS

Usage Notes

Frequency adverbs describe when or how often something is done. There are two types of frequency adverbs: definite frequency and indefinite frequency adverbs.

- Adverbs of definite frequency such as *last month, every day,* and *once a week,* often take the end position; they are not placed after the verb *be* and before regular verbs as indefinite frequency adverbs such as *always, never,* and *usually.*

  I have English classes **twice a week**.

  I **sometimes** visit my relatives in the country.

  Britney's parents pick her up at school **every day**.

  Cooks **often** refer to themselves as chefs.

  Lennon was the best student in class **last year**.

  I am **never** late for class.

IDIOMS ABOUT HEALTH

Idioms are a group of words that has a special meaning that is different from the ordinary meaning of each separate word.

Idiom	Meaning	Example
a bag of bones	someone who is much too thin	He's lost too much weight because of his illness. He's **a bag of bones** these days.
a clean bill of health	a report that says you are healthy or that a machine or building is safe	Inspectors gave our school **a clean bill of health**.
kick the bucket	to die – used humorously	Uncle Jerry was so appalled by what he saw that he almost **kicked the bucket**.
safe and sound	unharmed, especially after being in danger	The missing teens are back home **safe and sound**.
under the knife	having a medical operation	Men and women go **under the knife** to enhance their looks.

Based on from www.ldoceonline.com/dictionary. Accessed on August 20, 2018.

PHRASAL VERBS ABOUT HEALTH

Phrasal verbs are "a group of words that is used like a verb and consists of a verb with an adverb or preposition after it [...]"

Phrasal Verb	Meaning	Example
come down with	to get an illness	I've been sneezing all morning. I think I'm **coming down with** the flu.

Phrasal Verb	Meaning	Example
get over	to become well again after an illness	Dad can't seem to **get over** his cold.
pass away	to die	Sadly, Peter's uncle **passed away**.
throw up	to bring food or drink up from your stomach out through your mouth because you are ill	Just the thought of coffee makes me feel like **throwing up**.
work out	to make your body fit and strong by doing exercises	Bodybuilders **work out** for several hours a day.

Based on www.ldoceonline.com/dictionary. Accessed on August 20, 2018.

UNIT 3
PRESENT CONTINUOUS AND SIMPLE PRESENT: STATIVE VS. ACTION VERBS

Usage Notes

A few verbs are rarely used in the present continuous form because they describe states or situations that are not expected to change. They are called stative verbs as they do not describe actions. Stative verbs may indicate:

- feelings and emotions (*dislike, like, love, need, appreciate, want, hate, wish,* etc.);

  I dislike math but I **love** English.

- senses (*smell, hear, see, taste, seem,* etc.);

  I'm afraid that cake **doesn't smell** good.

- possessions (*have, belong, possess, own,* etc.);

  This house **belongs** to my grandma.

- opinions, knowledge, or beliefs (*mean, believe, doubt, imagine, think, guess, know, understand,* etc.).

  I **don't believe** that the manager is right this time.

Other common stative verbs are:

- be

  They**'re** physicians.

- concern

  That issue **concerns** all 9th grade students.

- consist

  The test **consists** of 5 open-ended questions.

- cost

  Those fancy shirts **cost** a fortune!

- depend

  Our decision about the trip **depends** on the weather.

- fit

  Your plans **don't fit** the family schedule.

- involve

  Being healthy **involves** real hard work.

- lack

  The teacher said my writing **lacks** cohesion.

- matter

  Does it really **matter** what he thinks about you?

Some verbs describe both a state and an action and are used in the simple present or in the present continuous, respectively.

- feel

  I **don't feel** I should try to call him again.

  I**'m feeling** terrible right now

- see

  I **see** your point.

  They**'re seeing** a marriage counselor.

- think

  He **thinks** they are better than us.

  He**'s thinking** about moving abroad.

- appear

  Your prediction **appears** to be true.

  That famous actress **is appearing** in a new commercial.

- look

  This **looks** amazing!

  We**'re looking** at the stars and making wishes.

- taste

  Her food **tastes** delicious!

  The chefs **are tasting** the contestants' dishes.

FALSE FRIENDS

Examples	Meaning
agenda	a list of the subjects to be discussed at a meeting
attend	to go to an event such as a meeting or a class
college	a large school where you can study after high school and get a degree

LANGUAGE REFERENCE

Examples	Meaning
costume	a set of clothes worn by an actor or by someone to make them look like something or someone else, such as an animal, famous person, etc.
curse	swear
eventually	after a long time, or after a lot of things have happened
intend	to have something in your mind as a plan or purpose
legend	an old well-known story, often about brave people, adventures, or magical events
particular	certain, specific
prescribe	to say what medicine or treatment a sick person should have
retired	having stopped working, usually because of your age
turn	to move your body so that you are looking in a different direction

Based on www.ldoceonline.com/dictionary. Accessed on August 20, 2018.

UNIT 4
SIMPLE PAST
Usage Notes

The simple past is used to refer to:
- completed actions in the past;
  Where **did** the family reunion **take place**?
  We **met** at Britany's.
  They **didn't remember** to call us.
- a series of completed actions in the past;
  I **woke up** at 6, **took** a shower, **had** breakfast, and then **left** for work.
- an action that started and finished in the past;
  We **spoke** for half an hour.
  They **didn't live** in Rome for very long.

Pronunciation of -ed endings

For regular verbs, -ed endings are pronounced:
- /d/ after all vowel sounds and after voiced consonants (except /d/)
  /m/ /n/ /ŋ/ /l/ /g/ /dʒ/ /z/ /b/ /v/;
  enjoyed, tried, smiled, lived
- /t/ after all voiceless consonants (except /t/)
  /k/ /p/ /f/ /s/ /ʃ/ /tʃ/;
  shopped, laughed, crossed, wished
- /ɪd/ after /d/ and /t/.
  needed, decided, hated, started

MODAL VERBS

Modal verbs are auxiliary verbs used to add to or change meanings of main verbs. *Can, should, must, may,* and *could* are examples of modal verbs. Modal verbs are different from regular verbs because:
- they are followed by an infinitive without "to" (except for *ought to*);
- they don't take *-s* in the third person singular;
- they are used like auxiliaries for questions and negatives.

MODAL VERB - CAN
Usage Notes

We use *can* or *cannot* (*can't*) for:
- permission;
  Can I talk to you for a second?
- prohibition;
  Students **can't** use dictionaries during tests.
- ability;
  Harry **can** speak four languages fluently.
- general truths;
  Leading a healthy life **can** be difficult, but the hard work will pay off in the future.
- possibility;
  Larry **can** help you with the interview because he has worked in PR.
- guessing and predicting;
  This awful test **can't** be mine! I'm sure I did a good job.
- requests;
  Can I see your passport, please?
- offers;
  Can I help you carry those bags?
- reproaches.
  Can't you stop making that noise? I'm trying to concentrate here!

We also use *can* with verbs of perception such as *see, hear, taste, smell,* and other verbs such as *imagine, guess,* and *follow* when they mean *understand*.

I **can** guess why you look so upset.
I **can** hear you.

MODAL VERB - *SHOULD*

Usage Notes

Some common uses of *should* are:

- for advice or suggestions;

  You **should** cut down on sugar if you have diabetes.

- to talk about what is ideal or desirable;

  There **should** be a dedicated entrance for the elderly in this stadium.

- to talk about what is likely to happen;

  Let's start our discussions. The other students **should** be here soon.

- for possibilities in hypothetical conditional sentences;

  Should you want to contact me, there's a private number you can call.

- to express gratitude.

  A: Lisa, I bought you a handmade scarf.

  B: Oh, you **shouldn't** have!

SLANG OR INFORMAL TERMS ABOUT RELATIONSHIPS

Examples	Meaning
catfish	someone who lies about themselves on the Internet in order to impress people, especially so that someone will start a relationship with them
dump	to end a relationship with someone
frenemy	someone you have a friendly relationship with, but who is really an enemy or competitor
have a crush on	someone you have a feeling of romantic love for, but who you do not know well
hit on somebody	to talk to someone in a way that shows you are sexually attracted to them
pop the question	to ask someone to marry you
top dog	the person who has the most power in a group, especially after a struggle

Based on www.ldoceonline.com/dictionary. Accessed on August 20, 2018.

UNIT 5
PLURAL NOUNS

Usage Notes

- Some nouns keep the same forms for singular or plural forms. Seeing them in context is the key to identifying them as singular or plural.

  fish, sheep, series, species, deer, etc.

- Some nouns only have a plural form.

  clothes, contents, dislikes, glasses, pants, jeans, pajamas, scissors, shorts, stairs, likes, etc.

- Some nouns are used only in the singular form, although they end in *-s*.

  classics, economics, physics, gymnastics, aerobics, measles, news, etc.

- Collective nouns name groups of people and may take a singular verb if they are considered a single unit or a plural verb if they are considered a collection of individuals. Some common collective nouns are:

  army, audience, committee, company, crew, family, government, jury, etc.

- Other collective nouns are:

band	musicians
board	directors
choir	singers
class	students
crowd	people
gang	thieves
team	players
bouquet	flowers
fleet	ships
forest	trees
galaxy	stars
pack	cards
range	mountains
army	ants
flock	birds
flock	sheep
hive	bees
pack	wolves

LANGUAGE REFERENCE

ADJECTIVES – WORD ORDER

Usage Notes

- When there is more than one adjective after a linking verb such as *be*, the last two adjectives are usually connected by *and*. However, *and* is less common when those adjectives come before the noun they qualify.

  Linda is **happy, young, and Greek**. You'll like her, for sure.

  Linda has always been **a happy, young, Greek** girl.

- The connector *and* can be used when there are two or more adjectives of the same type as well.

  That was a **lovely and unusual** dinner.

  Have you seen my **yellow and green** sneakers?

PREFIXES

Some other common prefixes in English.

Prefix	Meaning	Example
auto-	self	autoimmunity
inter-	between	international
mega-	very big, important	megapixel
mid-	middle	midnight
out-	go beyond	outbreak
over-	too much	overdose
post-	after	post-war
pre-	before	prehistoric
trans-	across	transformation
under-	less than, beneath	underestimate
up-	make or move higher	upstairs

▶ UNIT 6

COMPARATIVES AND SUPERLATIVES

Usage Note

- Some adjectives do not have a comparative or superlative form because they can't show a greater or lesser amount.
  These are called absolute adjectives. A few examples are: adequate, complete, dead, fatal, ideal, impossible, infinite, perfect, universal, round, and unique.

  She is a unique woman and I admire her a lot.

  NOT ~~She is the most unique woman I have ever met.~~

  These games are perfect for learning.

  NOT ~~They are the most perfect games for learning.~~

DOUBLE COMPARATIVES

- Double comparatives are used to express increasing or decreasing degrees.

  The more I work, **the more** I want to work.

  The less time I spend here, **the more** spare time I'll have.

  The harder the task, **the fiercer** I become.

  The more you explain, **the more** they learn.

  The older you get, **the more experienced** you get.

Usage Note

In spoken English, some double comparatives are usually shortened.

  The more the merrier.

  The sooner the better.

IRREGULAR COMPARATIVES AND SUPERLATIVES

Regular form	Comparative form	Superlative form
bad	worse	the worst
far (distance)	farther	the farthest
far (extent)	further	the furthest
good	better	the best
less	lesser	the least
little	less	the least
many / much	more	the most

VERB TO NOUN SUFFIXES

Verb + suffix	Examples
arrive + -al	arrival
accept + -ance	acceptance
declare + -ation / -tion	declaration
confuse + -sion	confusion
fail + -ure	failure
punish + -ment	punishment
marry + -age	marriage
bless + -ing	blessing
bake + -ery	bakery

▶ UNIT 7

'S FOR POSSESSION

Usage Notes

's and ' can also be used in the following situations:

- when it is not necessary to repeat a noun;
  She is not my sister. She is Anna's.
- when we are referring to somebody's home or store;
  We're spending the holidays at our grandma's.
- with places;
  Rio's levels of violence are increasing.
- with time expressions.
  Yesterday's episode was amazing.
  I'm sure we'll meet in two weeks' time!
- When the owner is a thing and not a person or an animal, we often use the structure noun + of + noun.
  The leg of the table is broken.
- In this case, it is also possible to use the structure noun + noun.
  The table leg is broken.
- When the owner is longer or when it's a descriptive fragment, we don't use 's. We use of.
  The father of the student who failed the finals is waiting in the hall.

POSSESSIVE PRONOUNS

Usage Note

- Possessive pronouns are also used in the construction a friend / neighbor / student / of mine, of yours, etc. In this structure, the friend, neighbor, or student is a little more general, distant, or non-specific than when possessive adjectives are used (my friend, my neighbor, my student).

(Non-specific)
A cousin of mine is coming to visit us on the weekend.

(Specific)
My cousin is coming to visit us on the weekend.

IDIOMS ABOUT LANGUAGE

Idiom	Meaning
beyond words	astonishing situation where a person can't find the right words to express his/her emotions
in plain English/language	in clear and simple words, without using technical language
it goes without saying	a thing that is so obvious that it is not necessary to mention
it's all Greek to me	used to say that you cannot understand something
loaded language	persuasive language
speak the same language	if two people or groups speak the same language, they have similar attitudes and opinions
talk a mile a minute	talk very fast
talk is cheap	used to say that you do not believe someone will do what they say

Based on www.ldoceonline.com/dictionary. Accessed on August 20, 2018.

LANGUAGE REFERENCE

UNIT 8
USED TO

Usage Notes

- We use *used to* + *infinitive* to talk about a habit, a regular activity, or state in the past.

  They **used to** live in the suburbs.
  (= They do not live in the suburbs anymore.)

- Besides *used to*, *would* can also be used to talk about repeated past actions. But *would* isn't used when we talk about past states.

  I **used to** ride my bike to school on weekdays.
  I **would** ride my bike to school on weekdays.
  I **used to** love field trips when I was in younger.
  NOT I would love field trips when I was in younger.

MODAL VERB - *MUST*

Usage Notes

We use *must* for:
- deductions and conclusions;

  Harry is late. He **must** be stuck in traffic.

- obligation and necessity;

  Policemen **must** wear a badge.

- laws and rules.

  Voters **must** present their voter card and a valid photo identification at the voting station.

- For invitations and encouragement, *have to* is more common than *must*.

  You **have to** try this carrot cake. It's pretty tasty!

- *Must not* and *don't have to* have different meanings. *Must not* means something is forbidden and *don't have to* means something is not necessary.

  You **must not** speak Portuguese in this class.
  You **don't have to** speak English all the time.

PHRASAL VERBS ABOUT TRAVELING

Phrasal Verb	Meaning	Example
check in / check out	if you check in or are checked in at a hotel or airport, you report that you have arrived; if you check out, you leave a hotel after paying the bill	We need to **check in** at least two hours before the fight.
drop off	take someone or something to a place by car and leave them there	Dad **dropped** me **off** on his way to the office.
get away	take a vacation away from the place you normally live	I'm really looking forward to **getting away** this weekend.
pack up	put things into cases, bags, etc. ready for a trip somewhere	Is there anyone to help me **pack up** for the trip?
see off	go to an airport, train station, etc. to say goodbye to someone	Claire has just left for the airport to **see** her boyfriend **off**.
set out	start a journey, especially a long journey	I'm **setting out** on a round-the-world tour next year.
stop over	stop somewhere and stay a short time before continuing a long journey	We are **stopping over** in São Paulo on the way to Lima.
take off	if an aircraft takes off, it rises into the air from the ground	I always get a bit anxious when the plane **takes off**.

Based on www.ldoceonline.com/dictionary. Accessed on August 20, 2018.

READING STRATEGIES

Ao longo da coleção, estamos sinalizando algumas estratégias de leitura voltadas à melhora na compreensão de textos. O principal objetivo dessas estratégias é fazer com que você, aluno, torne-se um aprendiz mais eficaz e alcance resultados positivos nos exames e vestibulares a serem realizados ao final do Ensino Médio.

A seguir você encontrará uma breve explicação sobre as estratégias mais comumente abordadas antes e durante a leitura dos textos.

Activating previous knowledge – Esta estratégia consiste em acionar, quando preciso, o conhecimento que você tem guardado em sua mente. Quando falamos em conhecimento prévio na leitura, estamos nos referindo às informações que você precisa ter para ler um texto sem muita dificuldade para compreendê-lo.

Brainstorming – O termo foi criado a partir da junção das palavras *brain* (cérebro) e *storm* (tempestade), portanto, significa "tempestade cerebral" ou "tempestade de ideias". A estratégia propõe que você e seus colegas de sala explorem sua capacidade criativa, na medida em que trocam ideias a respeito do assunto que será abordado no texto.

Bridging – O termo vem da palavra *bridge*, que significa "ponte". A estratégia consiste, então, em "fazer uma ponte", isto é, em estabelecer uma relação entre o seu conhecimento prévio sobre o assunto que será explorado no texto e o texto propriamente.

Finding organizational patterns or understanding text structure – A estrutura de um texto diz respeito à forma como as informações estão nele organizadas. Artigos, por exemplo, contam com uma introdução, um desenvolvimento e uma conclusão; as informações nas biografias são, em geral, organizadas em sequência cronológica; as receitas, na maioria das vezes, são divididas em duas partes – ingredientes e modo de preparo. Assim, estar atento aos padrões de organização de um texto ajuda-o a identificar seu gênero e, consequentemente, sua função social.

Predicting – A palavra *predict* significa "prever". Ao lermos o título de um texto ou observarmos as imagens que o acompanham, por exemplo, podemos prever ou deduzir seu conteúdo. Quanto mais conhecimento geral você tiver, mais facilmente vai prever o assunto de um texto. Em algumas atividades, você é convidado especificamente a prever o tema e o gênero do texto (*predicting the theme and the genre*).

Recognizing or identifying – Reconhecer significa identificar algo que se conhece. Portanto, reconhecer ou identificar o tipo textual (*textual type*), a voz, ou seja, quem está falando no texto (*voice in a text*), a perspectiva do autor (*the author's perspective*), a fonte do texto (*the source of the text*), o público ao qual o texto se destina (*the target audience*), o propósito principal do texto (*the main purpose*), etc. ajuda-o a antecipar o que está por vir no texto a ser lido.

Skimming – Consiste em observar o texto rapidamente para detectar o assunto geral ou o seu propósito geral (*skimming to identify the main purpose*), por exemplo. Nesse momento, não há nenhuma preocupação em se atentar aos detalhes. É importante que você observe o *layout* do texto, seu título e sub-títulos, cognatos, primeiras e últimas linhas de cada parágrafo, bem como as imagens, gráficos e tabelas que o acompanham.

Scanning – é uma técnica de leitura que consiste em correr rapidamente os olhos pelo texto até localizar a informação específica desejada. O *scanning* é prática rotineira na vida das pessoas. Alguns exemplos típicos pode. Alguns exemplos típicos são o uso do dicionário para obter informação sobre o significado de palavras ou a utilização do índice de um livro para encontrar um artigo ou capítulo de interesse.

Há, também, estratégias que são trabalhadas após a leitura dos textos. Observe:

Making inferences or inferring – A estratégia de inferência tem como objetivo fazê-lo capturar aquilo que não está dito no texto de forma explícita. Essas adivinhações podem ter como base as pistas dadas pelo próprio texto ou o seu próprio conhecimento. Trata-se de uma estratégia de leitura extremamente importante, pois um texto só terá sentido se você puder estabelecer relações entre as partes, ou seja, entre as palavras, frases, parágrafos etc.

Selecting a good title – Muitas vezes o título de um texto resume sua ideia central. Para selecionar o título mais apropriado para o texto que você acabou de ler, leia-o novamente e anote os pontos que mais chamaram sua atenção. O mesmo se aplica para quando você tiver que afirmar ou declarar a ideia ou o propósito principal do texto lido (*stating the main idea or the main purpose of the text*).

Understanding details – Para entender os detalhes de um texto é preciso fazer uma leitura lenta e concentrar-se durante essa leitura, isto é, ficar longe de qualquer coisa que possa distraí-lo. Recorrer a um dicionário para consultar as palavras e expressões desconhecidas e anotar seu significado, bem como fazer paráfrases durante a leitura, são algumas das ações que contribuem para a compreensão detalhada do texto. Podem contribuir, também, para as atividades que pedem que você resuma o texto lido (*summarizing*).

Understanding main ideas – Para realizar atividades que têm esta estratégia sinalizada, não é necessário fazer uma leitura tão detalhada, nem mesmo procurar todas as palavras desconhecidas em um dicionário. Basta fazer uma leitura geral do texto com atenção e compreender sua mensagem principal.

IRREGULAR VERBS

Base form	Past form	Past Participle	Translation
awake	awoke	awoken	acordar
be	was, were	been	ser, estar
become	became	become	tornar-se
begin	began	begun	começar
bend	bent	bent	dobrar
bet	bet	bet	apostar
bite	bit	bitten	morder
blow	blew	blown	soprar
break	broke	broken	quebrar
bring	brought	brought	trazer
build	built	built	construir
burn	burnt/burned	burnt/burned	queimar
buy	bought	bought	comprar
catch	caught	caught	pegar
choose	chose	chosen	escolher
come	came	come	vir
cut	cut	cut	cortar
do	did	done	fazer
draw	drew	drawn	desenhar
dream	dreamed/dreamt	dreamed/dreamt	sonhar
drink	drank	drunk	beber
drive	drove	driven	dirigir
eat	ate	eaten	comer
fall	fell	fallen	cair
feed	fed	fed	alimentar
feel	felt	felt	sentir
fight	fought	fought	lutar
find	found	found	achar
fly	flew	flown	voar
forget	forgot	forgotten	esquecer
forgive	forgave	forgiven	perdoar
get	got	got/gotten	conseguir
get up	got up	got up/gotten up	levantar-se
give	gave	given	dar
go	went	gone	ir
grow	grew	grown	crescer
hang out	hung out	hung out	passar tempo
have	had	had	ter
hear	heard	heard	ouvir
hide	hid	hidden	esconder
hit	hit	hit	atingir
hold	held	held	segurar
hurt	hurt	hurt	machucar
keep	kept	kept	manter

Base form	Past form	Past Participle	Translation
know	knew	known	saber, conhecer
lean	leant/leaned	leant/leaned	inclinar-se
learn	learnt/learned	learnt/learned	aprender
leave	left	left	deixar, sair
lend	lent	lent	emprestar
let	let	let	deixar
lose	lost	lost	perder
make	made	made	fazer
mean	meant	meant	significar
meet	met	met	encontrar, conhecer
overcome	overcame	overcome	superar
pay	paid	paid	pagar
put	put	put	colocar
read	read	read	ler
ride	rode	ridden	andar de
ring	rang	rung	tocar
rise	rose	risen	subir, aumentar
run	ran	run	correr
say	said	said	dizer
see	saw	seen	ver
sell	sold	sold	vender
send	sent	sent	enviar
set	set	set	estabelecer
show	showed	shown	mostrar
sing	sang	sung	cantar
sit	sat	sat	sentar
sleep	slept	slept	dormir
speak	spoke	spoken	falar
spell	spelled/spelt	spelled/spelt	soletrar
spend	spent	spent	gastar, passar tempo
split	split	split	dividir
stand up	stood up	stood up	ficar de pé
steal	stole	stolen	roubar
swim	swam	swum	nadar
take	took	taken	pegar, tomar
teach	taught	taught	ensinar
tell	told	told	contar
think	thought	thought	pensar
throw	threw	thrown	jogar
understand	understood	understood	entender
wake up	woke up	woken up	acordar
wear	wore	worn	vestir
win	won	won	ganhar
write	wrote	written	escrever

COMMON MISTAKES

Speakers of Portuguese are more likely to make certain mistakes in English because of interference from Portuguese. Let's take a look at some common mistakes:

TOPIC	COMMON MISTAKE	RIGHT FORM	SOME EXPLANATION
SAYING ONE'S AGE	I ~~have~~ sixteen years old.	I <u>am</u> sixteen years old.	In Portuguese, we use the verb *have* for saying one's age, but in English we use the verb *be*.
ASKING QUESTIONS	You study geography with Mr. Perry?	"<u>Do</u> you study geography with Mr. Perry?	In Portuguese, we ask questions changing the intonation of the sentence. The same does not work in English as we need an auxiliary to form questions.
USING -S FOR THIRD PERSON SINGULAR IN THE SIMPLE PRESENT	My little sister always ~~complain~~ when I can't give her attention.	My little sister always <u>complains</u> when I can't give her attention.	It may be confusing to use -*s* at the end of verbs for the third person singular when we immediately associate the -*s* with plural. Beware! The -*s* in this case is <u>not</u> plural, it is just the correct verb form.
YOUR vs. HIS/HER	Laura is very cute, ~~your~~ voice is sweet, and ~~your~~ smile is beautiful.	Laura is very cute, <u>her</u> voice is sweet, and <u>her</u> smile is beautiful.	Translating *your* (seu/sua/seus/suas) may be tricky because in Portuguese we say, for example: "Laura é muito fofa, <u>sua</u> voz é doce e <u>seu</u> sorriso largo". However, in this case we do not use *your voice* or *your smile*, we have to think of "voz dela", "sorriso dela".
NEGATIVE ORDERS AND INSTRUCTIONS	~~No~~ touch!	Don't touch!	In Portuguese, when we give negative orders or instructions we say, for example: "Não toque!" However, in English we need the auxiliary.
TALKING ABOUT POSSESSIONS	The house of John is huge!	John's house is huge!	In Portuguese, we do not have the use of 's for possessions because we usually use the possession before the person. In English, it is the opposite, so we use 's to identify that something belongs to someone else.
IRREGULAR PLURAL	More people ~~is~~ arriving soon.	More people are arriving soon.	Because irregular plural words do not always end with an -*s*, it can easily be mistaken with a singular word, but we need to use a plural verb.
HAVE vs. THERE + BE	~~Have~~ a spider on the wall.	There is a spider on the wall.	When we use "*ter*" meaning "*haver/existir*", we can't use *have*. We need to use *there + be*.

FALSE FRIENDS

False friends are words with similar sound and form, but with different meanings. When we look at the word *actually*, for example, we immediately associate it with the Portuguese word "*atualmente*", because of its similarity. However, *actually* means "*na realidade*" as in "It **actually** costs three thousand dollars, not three hundred." Let's take a look at some other examples.

English	Portuguese translation	Example	Don't get confused with…	Which in English is…
alias	pseudônimo, nome falso	He used to work under an **alias**.	aliás	by the way
anthem	hino	Are you able to sing the American national **anthem**?	antena	antenna
appoint	nomear	Tom Leary was **appointed** to a new position.	apontar	point
assist	ajudar	Who is going to **assist** the new judge?	assistir	watch
college	faculdade	I can't believe you are not excited about going to **college**!	colégio	school
comprehensive	abrangente, amplo	It was a very **comprehensive** report.	compreensível	understandable
convict	condenado(a)	The **convict** had to be handcuffed.	convicto(a)	certain
costume	fantasia	How much is the vampire **costume**?	costume	habit
data	dados	We have gathered a lot of **data** on the subject.	data	date
exit	saída	Where is the **exit** door?	êxito	success
fabric	tecido	Silk is a very expensive **fabric**.	fábrica	factory
hazard	risco	This medicine presents no **hazard** to your health.	azar	bad luck
inhabited	habitado(a)	It is an **inhabited** island.	inabitado(a)	uninhabited
journal	revista especializada, diário	Tom is the editor of a very important medical **journal**.	jornal	newspaper
lecture	palestra	The **lecture** had a very young audience.	leitura	reading
legend	lenda	Have you heard of the **legend** of Billy Jack?	legenda	subtitle
library	biblioteca	Is there a **library** around here where I can borrow some comics?	livraria	bookstore
novel	romance	*My Brilliant Friend* is a **novel** written by Elena Ferrante, a mysterious Italian writer.	novela	soap opera
notice	notar, observar	Have you **noticed** the new furniture in the study hall?	notícia	news
parents	pais	My **parents** got married in the early nineties.	parentes	relatives
physician	médico	He is a respected **physician** who is looking after the president's health.	físico	physicist
prejudice	preconceito	We must always fight against all kinds of **prejudice**.	prejuízo	harm
pretend	fingir	Stop **pretending**! I know you are not telling the truth.	pretender	intend
realize	perceber	Have you **realized** how far we are from our goal?	realizar	accomplish
resume	recomeçar	After a long break they **resumed** the session.	resumir	summarize
sensible	sensato(a)	Choosing to cross the river in such a small boat is not a **sensible** option.	sensível	sensitive
support	apoiar	The homeless shelter is **supported** by a group of volunteers.	suportar	bear

GLOSSARY

Unit 1

blending – mescla
desirability – desejabilidade
knowledge – conhecimento
retire – aposentar-se
settle – estabelecer-se
status quo – situação atual (latim)

Unit 2

agreeable – colaborativo (para uma pessoa)
approach – abordagem
baked – assado(a)
blood pressure – pressão sanguínea
bowel – intestino
canned – enlatado(a)
cantaloupe – melão-cantalupe
celery – aipo
cucumbers – pepinos
cut-up – cortado(a)
dried apricots – damascos secos
folate – folato, um tipo de vitamina B
growth – crescimento
halibut – peixe linguado
ingrained – enraizado
iron – ferro
lays out – dispõe (infinitivo: *lay out*)
likewise – da mesma forma
lower intake – baixo consumo
moon fruit – araçá-boi
mushrooms – cogumelos
outcomes – resultados
pleasing – agradável
pureed – pure

raw – cru
released – lançou (infinitivo: *release*)
rendering – representar (infinitivo: *render*)
sauces – molhos
set the tone – dar o tom
source – fonte
soy beans – soja
squash – abobrinha
star fruit – carambola
stir-fry – refogar
strengthening – fortalecer (infinitivo: *strengthen*)
tissues – tecidos
tuna – atum
white beans – feijões brancos

Review 1

behave – comportar-se
cutlery – cutelaria
matters – importa (infinitivo: *matter*)
obfuscated – ofuscado(a)
sky-rocketed – disparou (infinitivo: *sky-rocket*)
spiraling – rotativo(a)
tuck into – cair dentro

Unit 3

embolden – encorajar
harass – assediar
provide – oferecer
raw – puro, cru
shelf life – vida útil
strengthen – fortalecer
toward – em direção a

Unit 4

caregivers – cuidadores
downside – lado negativo
peer – igual
release – liberação
soothed – acalmado (infinitivo: *soothe*)
trigger – provocar

Review 2

accountability – prestação de contas
hazard – risco
scholarship – bolsa de estudos
undoubtedly – sem sombra de dúvida, indubitavelmente
unfairly – injustamente
witnessed – presenciamos (infinitivo: *witness*)
zealously – zelosamente, com cuidado

Unit 5

coiffure – cabeleireiro
enhance – aumentar
buried – enterrado (infinitvo: *burry*)
heightened – maior
laundromat – lavanderia automática
realm – reino
seeks – busca (infinitivo: *seek*)
sheeting – película
summit – cúpula, reunião de líderes
swapping – trocando (infinitivo: *swap*)

Unit 6

afford – proporcionar
apparel – vestimenta

appeal – agrado
fulfills – cumpre (infinitivo: *fulfill*)
guilty – culpado(a)
hubbas – oba!
prosecutors – promotores
raided – deu uma batida (policial)
remain – permanecer
scholarships – bolsas de estudos
seemingly – aparentemente
sizzling – quente, acalorado
sponsors – patrocinadores
staging – organizar, apresentar (infinitivo: *stage*)
stormed out – saiu irado(a) (infinitivo: *storm out*)
submitted – enviou (infinitivo: *submit*)
turf – relva, gramado
venues – locais
wielding – exercendo
youth – juventude

Review 3

expertly – habilmente
grasp – segurar
though – mas, apesar disso

Unit 7

beyond – além
boardroom – sala de reunião
broadcaster – locutor
claiming – alegando (infinitivo: *claim*)
contenders – competidores
cravat – peitilho (gravata)
dashing – elegante
deeds – atos, ações

GLOSSARY

erstwhile – antigo

forecasting – previsão

patois – dialeto, gíria

pidgin – simplificado

purposes – propósitos

put the kibosh on – destruir uma ideia

researcher – pesquisador

shifts – muda (infinitivo: *shift*)

spreading – espalhando-se

struggle – esforçar-se, ter dificuldade

takes stock of – avalia algo (infinitivo: *take stock of*)

turnout – comparecimento

whether – se

witty – sagaz

Unit 8

accounts – justifica (infinitivo: *account*)

beating – batida

belongings – pertences

bundle – embrulho

bursting – repentinamente e com impulso

chap – amigo

double-barreled – duplo

dual-purpose – com propósito duplo

flair – talento

grunting – grunhindo

hamper – cesto

likens – assemelha-se (infinitivo: *liken*)

mosque – mesquita

ounce – medida correspondente a 28,34 gramas

pouring – servindo

proponent – proponente, defensor

remained – permaneceu (infinitivo: *remain*)

restless – inquieto(a)

sought – buscou (infinitivo: *seek*)

strapped – quebrado(a)

striking – impressionante

wardrobe – guarda-roupa

wish – desejar

Review 4

beyond doubt – sem sombra de dúvida

boost – estimular

hitherto – até este ponto

lag – atraso

launch – lançamento

neatly – organizadamente

outpacing – ultrapassando (infinitivo: *outpace*)

pecking order – hierarquia

reckons – estima (infinitivo: *reckon*)

widespread – difundido(a)

NOTES

NOTES

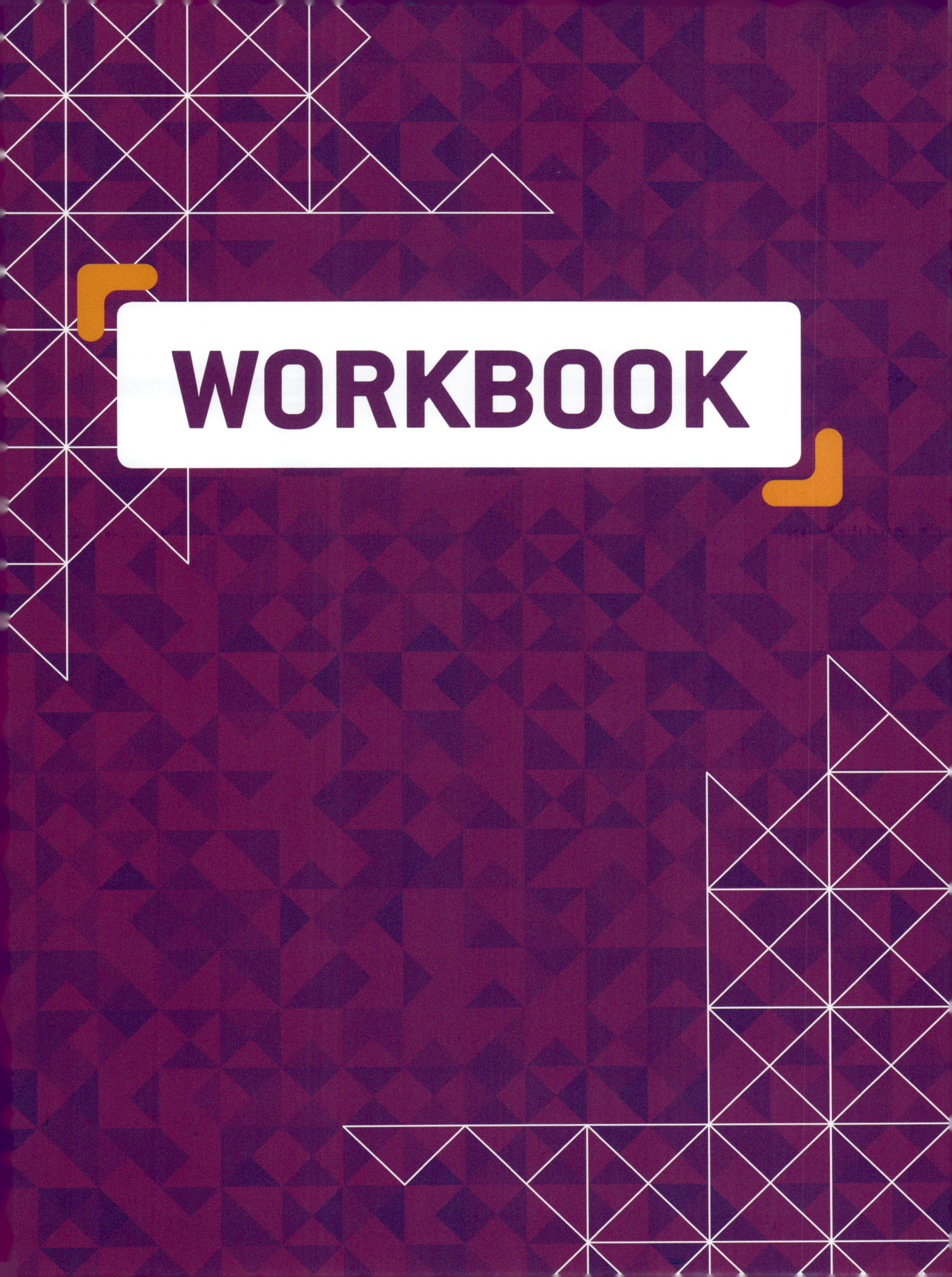

WORKBOOK

Unit 1 — Migration Trends

1. **Look at the bar chart extracted from the UN's International Migration Report 2017 and find information to complete the sentences below.** *Scanning*

   a. The chart compares migration in the years _____ and _____.

   b. The country which had the largest number of migrants in both years was _____.

   c. In 2000, Canada hosted _____ million international migrants.

   d. In 2017, the United Kingdom hosted _____ million international migrants.

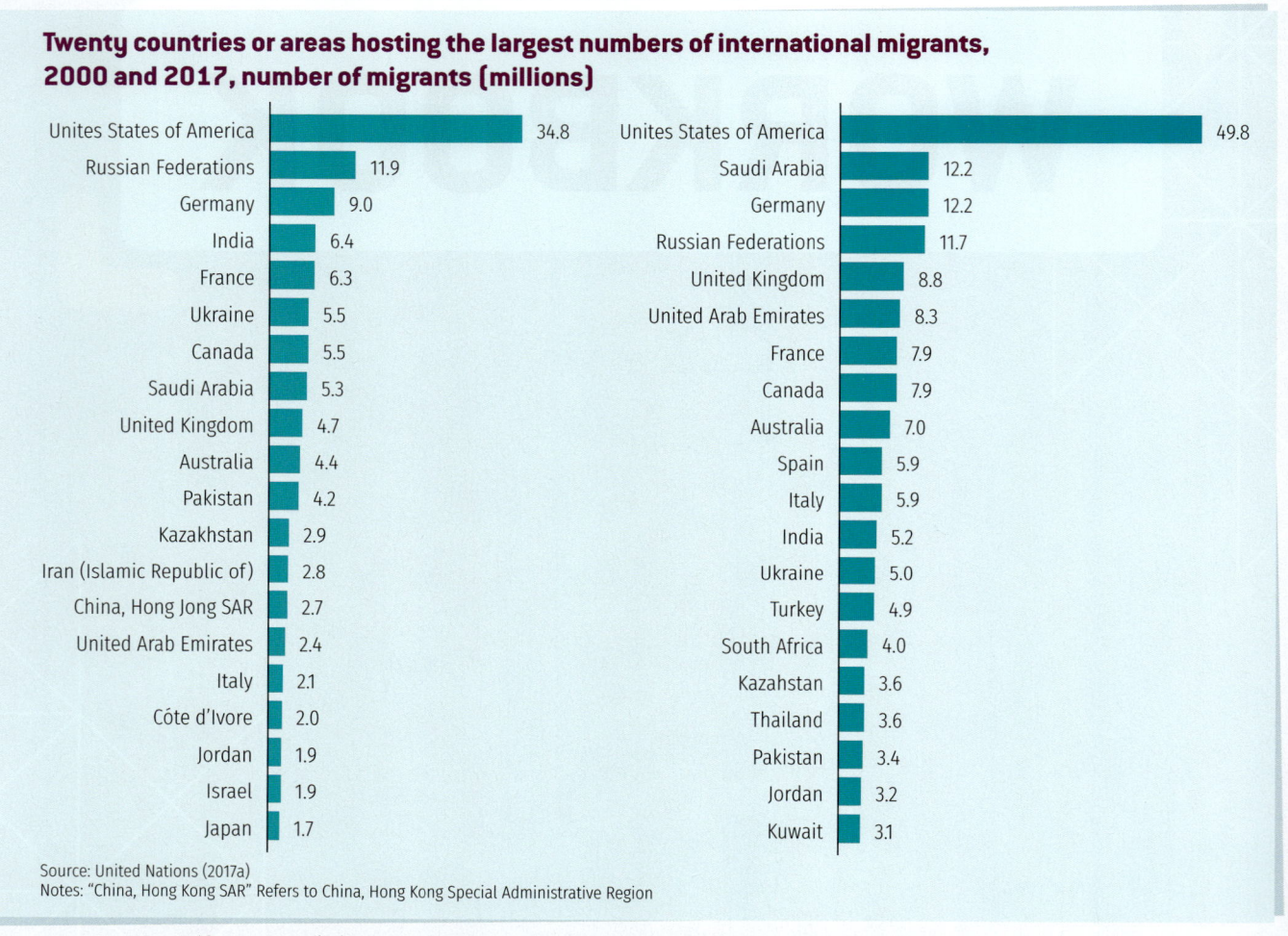

   Twenty countries or areas hosting the largest numbers of international migrants, 2000 and 2017, number of migrants (millions)

2000		2017	
Unites States of America	34.8	Unites States of America	49.8
Russian Federations	11.9	Saudi Arabia	12.2
Germany	9.0	Germany	12.2
India	6.4	Russian Federations	11.7
France	6.3	United Kingdom	8.8
Ukraine	5.5	United Arab Emirates	8.3
Canada	5.5	France	7.9
Saudi Arabia	5.3	Canada	7.9
United Kingdom	4.7	Australia	7.0
Australia	4.4	Spain	5.9
Pakistan	4.2	Italy	5.9
Kazakhstan	2.9	India	5.2
Iran (Islamic Republic of)	2.8	Ukraine	5.0
China, Hong Jong SAR	2.7	Turkey	4.9
United Arab Emirates	2.4	South Africa	4.0
Italy	2.1	Kazakhstan	3.6
Côte d'Ivore	2.0	Thailand	3.6
Jordan	1.9	Pakistan	3.4
Israel	1.9	Jordan	3.2
Japan	1.7	Kuwait	3.1

   Source: United Nations (2017a)
   Notes: "China, Hong Kong SAR" Refers to China, Hong Kong Special Administrative Region

   Extracted from www.un.org/en/development/desa/population/migration/publications/migrationreport/docs/MigrationReport2017_Highlights.pdf. Accessed on May 25, 2018.

2. **Complete these excerpts with the verb *be* in the affirmative or negative form.**

   a. "Immigration _____ the international movement of people into a destination country of which they are not natives […]"

   Extracted from www.wikipedia.org/wiki/Immigration. Accessed on March 10, 2018.

   b. "[…] As for economic effects, research suggests that migration _____ beneficial both to the receiving and sending countries. […]"

   Extracted from www.wikipedia.org/wiki/Immigration. Accessed on March 10, 2018.

   c. Launched in May 2016, *I _____ a refugee* is a digital platform that intends to humanize the discussions about refugees; to allow refugees to speak for themselves; and to fight growing populism, fears, stereotypes, and prejudice.

   Adapted from www.workshopx.org/im-not-refugee. Accessed on March 10, 2018.

3. Unscramble the words and write questions. Then match the questions with the answers.

a. the purpose / of your visit / is / business / ?

_____

b. here alone / are / you / ?

_____

c. these / your bags / are / ?

_____

d. a problem / migration / to another / from one country / is / ?

_____

e. migration / immigration / is / the same as / ?

_____

f. they / from / China / are / ?

_____

( ) No, they are different. Immigration means entering another country to live permanently.
( ) There are pros and cons. I cannot say it is a real problem.
( ) No. Those are my bags over there.
( ) Yes, they are. They're from Hong Kong.
( ) No, my wife and daughters are with me.
( ) No, I'm here on vacation.

4. Use the correct form of the verbs in the box to complete the following texts.

> happen   be (x2)   occur   spread

a. Cultural diffusion _____ via human migration, intercultural marriages, or cultural exchange via letters, books, or electronic media. It _____ a phenomenon in which specific cultural concepts, ideas, or technologies _____ from one culture to another.

Adapted from www.answers.com/Q/Does_migration_cause_cultural_diffusion. Accessed on March 10, 2018.

b. In a very simple definition, cultural diffusion is when different cultures are spread into different areas. It _____ the mixing or **blending** of different ideas, beliefs, and innovations from one group to another. Cultural diffusion _____ all over the world, from fast food restaurants to new technologies.

Adapted from http://bookbuilder.cast.org/view_print.php?book=63595. Accessed on March 10, 2018.

5. Transform these statements into negatives.

a. Cultural diffusion always leads to positive exchanges.

_____

b. Immigration plays an important role in cultural diffusion.

_____

c. Most refugees seek asylum in other countries.

_____

6. **Match the questions with the answers.**
   a. How does the Internet affect cultural diffusion in the world today?
   b. What does cultural diffusion mean?
   c. How does globalization lead to cultural exchange?
   ( ) Globalization provides both positive and negative influences on cultural diversity.
   ( ) The effect that it has on both local and global cultures is significant.
   ( ) The spreading out of culture, culture traits, or a cultural pattern from a central point.

7. **Look at the ads closely. Then use one of the imperative statements below to complete each message.**

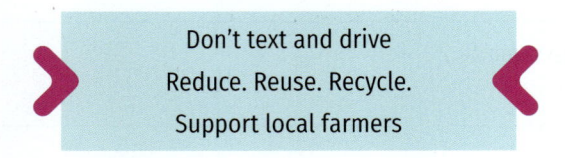

   > Don't text and drive
   > Reduce. Reuse. Recycle.
   > Support local farmers

8. **Form adjectives with the suffixes from the box. Then use the adjectives to complete the sentences below.**

   > -ful   -ive   -ous   -able / -ible   -less   -al

   a. use _____
   b. color _____
   c. comfort _____
   d. danger _____
   e. mathematics _____
   f. attract _____

   1. I love her new blouse; it's so _____ .
   2. Wear _____ shoes to walk around the city.
   3. They usually record changes with _____ precision.
   4. Don't text and drive because it's _____ .
   5. These old cell phones are _____ ; they can't be updated.
   6. I don't think he's _____ .

9. Complete the sentences with the correct word from the box.

> drought   employment
> flooding   hazards

a. Some push factors for immigration are natural _____ such as _____ or _____.

b. Some people also migrate to look for better _____ opportunities.

AN EYE ON ENEM

ENEM 2012 – Prova Amarela
Questão 92

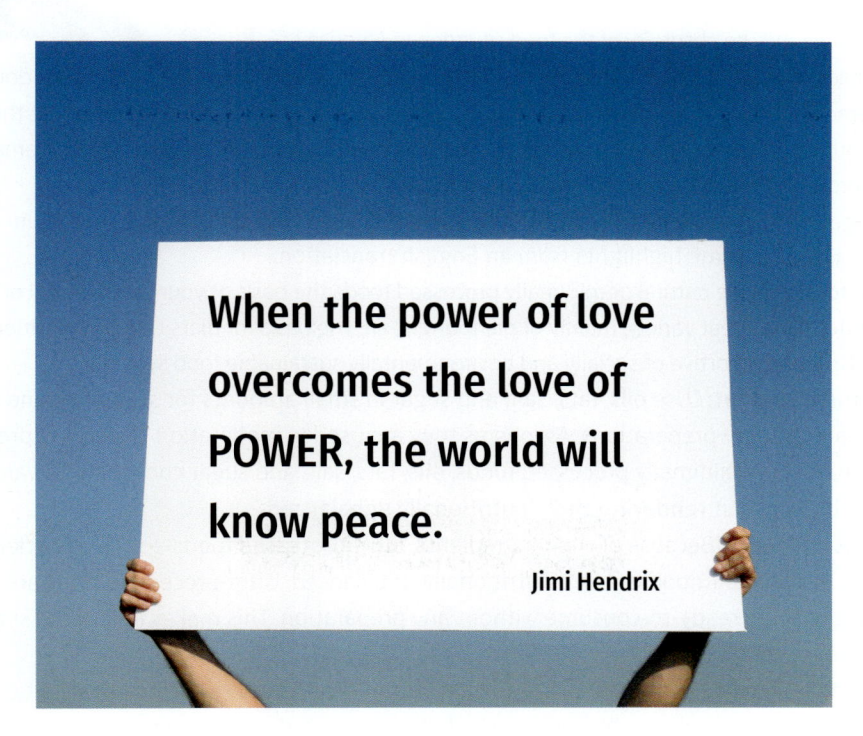

> When the power of love overcomes the love of POWER, the world will know peace.
> — Jimi Hendrix

Aproveitando-se de seu status social e da possível influência sobre seus fãs, o famoso músico Jimi Hendrix associa, em seu texto, os termos *love*, *power* e *peace* para justificar sua opinião de que

a. a paz tem o poder de aumentar o amor entre os homens.
b. o amor pelo poder deve ser menor do que o poder do amor.
c. o poder deve ser compartilhado entre aqueles que se amam.
d. o amor pelo poder é capaz de desunir cada vez mais as pessoas.
e. a paz será alcançada quando a busca pelo poder deixar de existir.

Unit 2 — "The First Wealth is Health"

1. **Read the text and choose the best title for it.** *Skimming*
   a. Nutritional guidelines around the world. ( )
   b. Brazil has the best nutritional guidelines in the world. ( )
   c. Brazil and the USA have the same nutritional guidelines. ( )

> The way we talk about nutrition in this country is absurd. And you only need to look as far as Brazil to understand why.
>
> Yesterday, a U.S. government-appointed scientific panel **released** a 600-page report that will inform America's new dietary guidelines. These guidelines only come out every five years, and they matter because they truly **set the tone** for how Americans eat. […]
>
> But this panel and their guidelines too often over complicate what we know about healthy eating. They take a rather punitive **approach** to food, reducing it to its nutrient parts and emphasizing its relationship to obesity. […]
>
> To fully understand the absurdity of the food situation in America, let's turn back to Brazil. Brazil is clearly a very different context than America. The country has only relatively recently emerged as a global economic force, and under-nutrition is still as much a concern as the rising obesity problem. But it's a fascinating country when it comes to health and it's probably exactly their emerging status that has forced them to be smarter about food and nutrition.
>
> In 143 pages, the Brazilian health ministry also **lays out** what may be the most intelligent food guide in the world. Here are some highlights from an English translation:
>
> **On whole foods:** "Make natural or minimally processed foods the basis of your diet. Natural or minimally processed foods, in great variety, mainly of plant origin, are the basis for diets that are nutritious, delicious, appropriate, and supportive of socially and environmentally sustainable food systems."
>
> **On salt, sugar and fat:** "Use oils, fats, salt, and sugar in small amounts for seasoning and cooking foods and to create culinary preparations. As long as they are used in moderation in culinary preparations based on natural or minimally processed foods, oils, fats, salt, and sugar contribute toward diverse and delicious diets without **rendering** them nutritionally unbalanced."
>
> **On processed foods:** "Because of their ingredients, ultra-processed foods—such as packaged snacks, soft drinks, and instant noodles—are nutritionally unbalanced. Ultra-processed foods are formulated and packaged to be ready-to-consume without any preparation. This makes meals and sharing of food at table unnecessary."
>
> **On eating as a social experience:** "Clean, quiet, and comfortable places encourage attention to the act of eating mindfully and slowly, enable meals to be fully appreciated, and decrease overeating… Humans are social beings. Eating together is **ingrained** in human history, as is the sharing and division of responsibility for finding, acquiring, preparing, and cooking food. Eating together is a natural, simple yet profound way to create and develop relationships between people. Thus, eating is a natural part of social life."
>
> Adapted from www.vox.com/2015/2/20/8076961/brazil-food-guide. Accessed on June 25, 2018.

2. **Number the recommendations 1-4 as they are mentioned in the text.** *Understanding details*
   a. Use oils, fats, salt, and sugar in small amounts for seasoning and cooking. ( )
   b. Eating together helps to develop relationships with people. ( )
   c. Avoid processed and ultra-processed foods. ( )
   d. Make natural or minimally processed foods the basis of your diet. ( )

Unit 2

3. Below are photos of lunches that follow the Brazilian dietary guidelines. Complete the captions with the food items that are missing.

a. Rice, beans, baked _____ leg, beetroot, and cornmeal with _____ .

b. Rice, _____, omelette, and sautéed jilo.

c. Feijoada, _____, onion and tomato vinagrette, cassava flower, sautéed cole, and _____ .

d. _____ salad, rice, beans, grilled beef, and fruit salad.

Source: Brazilian Dietary Guidelines. www.foodpolitics.com/wp-content/uploads/Brazilian-Dietary-Guidelines-2014.pdf. Accessed on June 26, 2018.

4. Complete the table with words from the previous activity.

Fruits and vegetables	Proteins	Grains	Dairy

5. Complete the following sentences using the simple present form of the verbs in paretheses.

a. Riley usually _____ (prefer) places that serve freshly-made meals.

b. The quality of fruit and vegetables that Steve _____ (buy) in supermarkets is not as good as at farms.

c. _____ you _____ (eat) fresh fruit and vegetables every day?

d. I _____ (not pay) attention to the type of milk I use; should I?

e. Susan _____ (not have) lunch at home, so she _____ (try) to have healthy snacks with her.

6. **Rewrite the sentences to include the adverb in parentheses in the correct place.**

   a. In Brazil, cow's milk is consumed with fruit or with coffee at the first meal of the day. (often)
   _____

   b. People think that it costs a lot to eat healthily. (often)
   _____

   c. Animal foods are good sources of proteins, vitamins, and minerals. (usually)
   _____

   d. I eat junk. It doesn't make me feel good. (rarely)
   _____

   e. Fresh fruit and vegetables are better for your health than processed foods. (always)
   _____

   f. People comment on my green drinks, but I love them! (always)
   _____

7. **Choose the best option to complete each sentence.**

   1. A processed food is _____ easily recognizable as a modified version of the original food.

   a. frequently   **b.** never   **c.** usually   **d.** daily

   2. _____ choose natural or minimally processed foods and freshly made dishes and meals over ultra-processed foods.

   a. Often   **b.** Always   **c.** Sometimes   **d.** Rarely

   3. Far too often, people go on extreme diets they can't maintain, which means they _____ actually develop long-term, healthy eating habits.

   a. always   **b.** sometimes   **c.** never   **d.** often

   4. _____ people need to accept and act on the fact that food, diet, and nutrition are vital to their health, and also to the health of others in their lives.

   a. Never   **b.** Sometimes   **c.** Frequently   **d.** Regularly

8. **Rewrite the sentences replacing the words in bold with the correct subject or object pronoun.**

   a. Susan borrowed some of my books, but **Susan** returned **the books** yesterday.
   _____

   b. Look at Rodrigo's new shoes! **The shoes** look very nice on **Rodrigo**.
   _____

   c. The Brazilian Dietary Guidelines state that oil, salt, and sugar should be used in moderation. **Oil, salt, and sugar** can be harmful when consumed in large amounts.
   _____

   d. My classmates and I love our cooking classes with Mr. Simmons. **Mr. Simmons** teaches **my classmates and me** a lot of new recipes.
   _____

9. Complete the article with the words from the box.

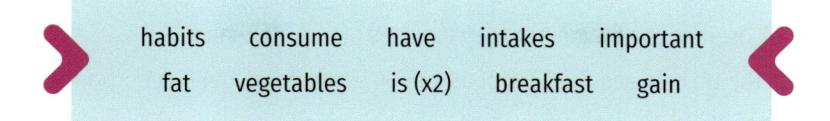

> habits   consume   have   intakes   important
> fat   vegetables   is (x2)   breakfast   gain

Breakfast eating among Brazilian adolescents: Analysis of the National Dietary Survey 2008-2009

Eating habits _____ a significant influence on the growth, development, and health of individuals. High consumption of _____ and sugar-rich foods and low consumption of fruit and _____ has been observed among Brazilian adolescents, resulting in nutritionally inadequate diets. Meal skipping and eating away from home have also been observed. Moreover, when compared to adults and older adults, Brazilian adolescents _____ more soft drinks, cookies, and sandwiches and fewer beans, salads, and vegetables.

Breakfast _____ considered the first and most _____ meal of the day. The quality of food at breakfast has been identified as essential for children and adolescents to achieve or maintain adequate health conditions since the consumption of cereal and fruit _____ important for the prevention of chronic non-communicable diseases.

In children and adolescents, _____ has been associated with improvement in attention, memory, and mood; it has also been possibly associated with improvements in motivation, cognitive function, and academic achievement, as well as with higher _____ of vitamin D and calcium. However, irregular breakfast _____ have been associated with unfavorable health outcomes and weight _____ among adolescents.

Adapted from www.scielo.br/scielo.php?script=sci_arttext&pid=S1415-52732017000400463. Accessed on June 26, 2018.

AN EYE ON ENEM

ENEM 2016 – Prova Azul
Questão 95

BOGOF (buy one, get one free) is used as a noun in 'There are some great bogofs on at the supermarket' or as an adjective, usually with a word such as offer or deal – 'there are some great bogof offers in store'.

When you combine the first letters of the words in a phrase or the name of an organization, you have an acronym. Acronyms are spoken as a word so NATO (North Atlantic Treaty Organization) is not pronounced N-A-T-O. We say NATO. Bogof, when said outloud, is quite comical for a native speaker, as it sounds like an insult. 'Bog off!' meaning go away, leave me alone, is slightly childish and a little old-fashioned.

BOGOF is the best-known of the supermarket marketing strategies. The concept was first imported from the USA during the 1970s recession, when food prices were very high. It came back into fashion in the late 1990s, led by big supermarket chains trying to gain a competitive advantage over each other. Consumers were attracted by the idea that they could get something for nothing. Who could possibly say 'no'?

Disponível em: www.bbc.co.uk. Acesso em: 2 ago. 2012 (adaptado).

Considerando-se as informações do texto, a expressão "bogof" é usada para

a. anunciar mercadorias em promoção.
b. pedir para uma pessoa se retirar.
c. comprar produtos fora de moda.
d. indicar recessão na economia.
e. chamar alguém em voz alta.

Unit 3 — Your Digital Self

1. **Look at the information below, extracted from research published in *The Guardian*, and complete the statements.** *Scanning*
   a. The number of people in the UK between the ages of 18 and 24 expected to stop using Facebook in 2018 is _____.
   b. As of 2017, most Facebook users in the UK are between the ages of _____ and _____.
   c. The number of people in the UK between the ages of 55 and 64 expected to join Facebook in 2018 is _____.
   d. As of 2017, 2.2 million Facebook users in the UK are between the ages of _____ and _____.

   > **Is Facebook for old people? Over-55s flock in as the young leave**
   > Facebook UK users 2017 vs. 2018
   > **Age 12 to 17** 2.2m, down 300,000
   > **Age 18 to 24** 4.5, down 400,000
   > **Age 25 to 34** 7.2m, flat
   > **Age 35 to 44** 5.9m, flat
   > **Age 45 to 54** 5.6m, up 100,000 users
   > **Age 55 to 64** 3.5m, up 200,000 users
   > **Age 65-plus** 2.9m, up 300,000 users
   >
   > Extracted from www.theguardian.com/technology/2018/feb/12/is-facebook-for-old-people-over-55s-flock-in-as-the-young-leave. Accessed on June 17, 2018.

2. **Complete the sentences with the correct possessive adjective.**
   a. Jason is always on _____ phone posting pictures of himself and _____ friends. Jason's friends also love posting pictures on _____ social networks – they even have a group only for that.
   b. This is _____ sister Maria. She is 5 years older than me, but we get along very well. We like to ride _____ bikes at the park in the afternoon when it's cool.
   c. Can I use _____ phone? _____ phone's battery is dead.
   d. Is this _____ backpack? Someone left it in the schoolyard.
   e. Brazil is famous for _____ beaches, but it should be famous for all _____ natural beauties.
   f. Tina forgot _____ jacket, can you return it to her?

3. **Match the false friends in the sentences below with their meanings.**
   a. Actually, I'm not afraid of traveling alone.
   b. Have you seen Bob lately?
   c. What is the most durable fabric for clothing?
   d. I work in a factory that manufactures decorative accessories.

   (   ) cloth produced especially by knitting, weaving, or felting fibers

   (   ) in fact, in reality

   (   ) not long ago, recently

   (   ) a building or group of buildings in which goods are manufactured

4. Fill in the blanks using the false friends from the box.

> newspapers   lately   actually   fabric   journal   factory

a. This _____ is very chic. It's made of cotton with details in silk.

b. Some people use Facebook as a personal _____ .

c. I haven't seen any of my friends _____ .

d. He is the HR manager at the _____ .

e. I don't buy _____ I read the news online.

f. This letter is _____ for you, not for me.

5. Underline the false friends in the excerpts below. Then underline the alternative that best summarizes the paragraph.

1.

> Social media platforms have become a dominant source of data used by governments, corporations, and academics to study human society. Yet, in the rush **towards** ever-more sophisticated algorithms and visualizations to analyze trends from social media, we are ignoring the critical questions of how well social media actually reflects societal trends and just how to use all of the analysis we produce.
>
> Extracted from www.forbes.com/sites/kalevleetaru/2016/02/16/does-social-media-actually-reflect-reality/#61e292cf4e43. Accessed on June 18, 2018.

a. Social media is an accurate data source for social trends.

b. Social trends are usually followed and displayed in social media, as research continues to demonstrate.

c. Social media never reflects social trends; therefore, one is not related to the other.

d. It's still uncertain how social media and social trends are related. One doesn't necessarily reflect the other.

e. The more people use social media, the more information will be accurate.

2.

> If kids are online, parents are usually more effective acting as mentors than as micromanagers. Having open-ended conversations rather than wielding authoritative control enables kids to build the critical-thinking skills needed to make smarter decisions online and in real life. For some kids, a finsta ("fake" Instagram) or a rinsta ("real" Instagram) might be where they feel they can share their **raw**, authentic feelings, even though they don't always realize that anything shared online has the potential for a greater audience, amplified consequences or longer **shelf life**. It's up to parents to find a way in, not through coercion, but through conversation.
>
> Extracted from www.washingtonpost.com/news/parenting/wp/2018/01/09/what-teens-wish-their-parents-knew-about-social-media/?noredirect=on&utm_term=.017d8dc1dead. Accessed on June 19, 2018.

a. Parents should keep track of their kids' life on social media in order to control their online interactions.

b. Micromanaging is important once children start hiding their online activities from their parents.

c. Critical-thinking skills are built on imposition and by modeling behavior with punishment.

d. Understanding how kids interact through social media involves micromanaging and authoritative control.

e. When dealing with kids, offering good advice and mentoring is usually more effective than being imposing and dictatorial.

6. Complete the sentences with the correct form of the verbs in the box.

> be   think   decide   help   spend

a. Kids usually _____ most of their time on social media and online games rather than studying or having face-to-face interactions.

b. Most parents _____ small children shouldn't be allowed to go online without supervision, because they might be exposed to harm and danger.

c. Teenagers _____ getting more and more resourceful as time goes by. They can solve most types of problems without asking their parents for support.

d. Children shouldn't be allowed to _____ how much time they spend on social media. Parents' supervision is important to help them develop awareness.

e. Cyberbullying is real, and parents must act as mentors and _____ kids navigate through social media the safest way possible.

7. Read the sentences below and note the verbs in bold. Then match them with their meaning.

a. Anthony **looks down on** anyone who doesn't have a Master's degree.

b. Sonja **looks after** her sister whenever their parents are out.

c. I've always **looked up to** my grandfather. He's accomplished a lot in his life.

d. The detectives are **looking into** the crime, but there are no suspects yet.

(   ) to respect something or someone, and to show respect

(   ) to try to find out information

(   ) to take care of something or someone

(   ) to not value something or someone

8. Fill in the blanks with the verbs in the box.

> look up to   look after   look into   look down on

a. "See, there's a difference between you and me. You _____ people because of what YOU THINK they can or can't afford. You clearly believe that a man's worth should be measured by the car he chooses to drive… but I think differently."

Adapted from www.pmnewsnigeria.com/2018/07/18/banky-w-replies-ladies-trolling-him/. Acessed on July 19, 2018.

b. "Danica Patrick, the first woman to win an IndyCar race, had simple advice for people who _____ her: know what you love."

Extracted from www.abc11.com/sports/danica-patrick-makes-espys-history-as-first-female-host/3777902/. Acessed on July 19, 2018.

c. "This means you have to keep in mind that there are loads of things that potentially pose a risk to your children. The more you can do to address these problems, the better the kids will be as a result. So, these are some of the best ideas you can come up with that are going to help you _____ your kids' well-being right now!"

Extracted from www.t2conline.com/look-after-your-kids-well-being-with-these-great-parenting-ideas/. Acessed on July 19, 2018.

d. "Two US senators, members of the Commerce, Science, and Transportation Committee, have asked the Federal Trade Commission (FTC) to _____ the private policies and practices of smart TV manufacturers."

Extracted from www.telecompaper.com/news/us-senators-call-on-ftc-to-look-into-smart-tv-privacy-practices--1252840. Acessed on July 19, 2018.

9. Choose the correct option to complete the sentences below.

a. _____ Tony _____ a message now?
   a. Does / write   b. Is / writing

b. Jude and Tom _____ their children anymore. They usually communicate through social media.
   a. don't call   b. are not calling

c. We sometimes _____ to the movies together.
   a. go   b. are going

d. First, I _____ dinner then I _____ my emails.
   a. have / read   b. am having / am reading

10. Fill in the blanks with the simple present or the present continuous using the information given.

a. Peter _____ (not like) playing soccer with his siblings.

b. _____ you _____ (call) your mother now?

c. _____ they _____ (go) to the same restaurant every week?

d. Mark _____ (not eat) meat. He's a vegetarian.

e. George and Peter _____ (walk) to the park every Sunday morning.

f. Sue _____ (not be) now. She _____ (watch) TV.

AN EYE ON ENEM

ENEM 2013 – Prova Cinza
Questão 93

STEVE JOBS: A LIFE REMEMBERED 1955-2011

Readersdigest.ca takes a look back at Steve Jobs, and his contribution to our digital world.

CEO. Tech-Guru. Artist. There are few corporate figures as famous and well regarded as former Apple CEO, Steve Jobs. His list of achievements is staggering, and his contribution to modern technology, digital media, and indeed the world as a whole, cannot be downplayed.

With his passing on October 5, 2011, readersdigest.ca looks back at some of his greatest achievements, and pays our respects to a digital pioneer who helped pave the way for a generation of technology and possibilities, few could have imagined.

Disponível em www.readersdigest.ca. Acesso em: 25 fev. 2012.

Informações sobre pessoas famosas são recorrentes na mídia, divulgadas de forma impressa ou virtualmente. Em relação a Steve Jobs, este texto propõe:

a. Expor as maiores conquistas da empresa.
b. Descrever suas criações na área da tecnologia.
c. Enaltecer sua contribuição para o mundo digital.
d. Lamentar sua ausência na criação de novas tecnologias.
e. Discutir o impacto de seu trabalho para a geração atual.

Unit 4   **Establishing and Keeping Relationships**

1. Read the comic strip below and choose the best answer to the question that follows. *Scanning*

   Extracted from www.arcticcirclecartoons.com/comics/august-26-2013. Accessed on July 2, 2018

   What message does the comic strip convey?
   a. The key to establishing and keeping true friendship is to monitor your friends' lives all the time.
   b. Friendship is not always about having extensive dialogues, but rather about understanding the needs and interests of each other.
   c. Ironically, eletronic gadgets prevent friends from talking to each other even when they are near each other.
   d. When making new friends, make sure you have a lot in common. You'll be frustrated otherwise.

2. The modal verb *can* is used by one of the characters from the comic strip in activity 1. In that context, the modal verb stands for…
   a. permission.
   b. ability.
   c. prohibition.
   d. suggestion.
   e. offering.

3. Circle the modal verb that completes all the blanks in this comic strip.

   Extracted from https://br.pinterest.com/pin/459859811945777037. Accessed on July 2, 2018.

   a. can
   b. should
   c. can't
   d. shouldn't
   e. may

4. Read the sentences. Then use the modal verbs in parentheses to reply to the situations presented.

   a. Suzanne doesn't have a driver's license. (can't)
   _____

   b. Peter is feeling sick. (should)
   _____

   c. Samantha studies English every day. (can)
   _____

   d. It's very cold outside. (shouldn't)
   _____

   e. This shirt is very old. (should)
   _____

5. Read the excerpt below and do the activities that follow.

"On paper, home sharing sounds perfect. It matches young people, like myself, who can't afford London's rocketing rents, with older people who are lonely.

As I was about to start a full-time master's course, I was only going to be able to work part-time, so renting a normal flat was out of the question. I searched for alternative options from being a property guardian to being an au pair. […]"

Extracted from www.theguardian.com/society/2015/mar/03/young-person-live-older-person-cheap-rent-live-in-care. Accessed on July 2, 2018.

   a. Circle the verbs in the simple past.
   b. Answer the question: What is the infinitive form of the verbs you circled in the text?

6. Write the simple past form of the following verbs.

   a. buy _____
   b. see _____
   c. eat _____
   d. look _____
   e. live _____
   f. go _____
   g. be _____
   h. cook _____
   i. do _____
   j. make _____
   k. study _____
   l. learn _____

7. Rewrite these sentences in the simple past. Make all the necessary changes.

   a. My father often makes furniture using discarded plastic bottles.
   _____

   b. My best friend studies English in Jamaica.
   _____

   c. I don't share an apartment with my classmates.
   _____

   d. My sister works at Google now.
   _____

   e. My brother doesn't live with his girlfriend.
   _____

8. Complete the excerpts below with the phrasal verbs from the box.

> back off   break up   stand by

a. "[...] Sometimes you don't have to question whether you have good reasons to _____ – you just know it's time. But other times you're not so sure. [...]

Extracted from www.eharmony.com/dating-advice/breaking-up/15-ways-to-know-its-time-to-break-up. Accessed on July 17, 2018.

b. "[...] Friends are supposed to love you no matter what, but what is important is that they also _____ you. [...]"

Extracted from www.theodysseyonline.com/the-importance-of-having-friends-who-stand-up-for-you. Accessed on July 17, 2018.

c. "[...] If you want to _____ in a relationship, then find the things that you love to do and let them distract you. If you are too wound up in a union, it is easy to make it the center point of your life. [...]"

Extracted from www.lovepanky.com/love-couch/better-love/how-to-pull-back-in-a-relationship. Accessed on July 17, 2018.

9. Choose the phrasal verb to substitute for the word(s) in bold in each sentence below. Then rewrite each sentence with the phrasal verb you have chosen.

a. I might be able to help you financially, but don't **depend on** it.
( ) take after   ( ) count on
_____

b. My father is someone I have always **admired**.
( ) looked up to   ( ) took after
_____

c. Can't you just stop **arguing** all the time?
( ) falling out   ( ) putting down
_____

d. I need one more week to **complete** the project.
( ) stand by   ( ) see (something) through
_____

e. Sean is a great friend of mine. He **is always loyal to** me.
( ) always stands by   ( ) always takes after
_____

f. Everyone says I **am a lot like** my dad, we both love soccer and reading novels.
( ) take after   ( ) put down
_____

g. I **stopped** dancing years ago. I wasn't any good at it.
( ) gave up   ( ) gave in
_____

10. **Complete the tasks below with your own information.**

a. Write three abilities you have using *can*.

_____
_____
_____

b. Write three prohibitions in your school using *can't*.

_____
_____
_____

c. Write three things friends should or shouldn't do.

_____
_____
_____

AN EYE ON ENEM

ENEM 2014 – Prova amarela

Questão 95

The Road Not Taken (by Robert Frost)

Two roads diverged in a wood, and I —
I took the one less traveled by,
And that has made all the difference.

Disponível em: www.poetryfoundation.org. Acesso em: 29 nov. 2011 (fragmento).

Estes são os versos finais do famoso poema *The Road Not Taken*, do poeta americano Robert Frost. Levando-se em consideração que a vida é comumente metaforizada como uma viagem, esses versos indicam que o autor

a. festeja o fato de ter sido ousado na escolha que fez em sua vida.
b. lamenta por ter sido um viajante que encontrou muitas bifurcações.
c. viaja muito pouco e que essa escolha fez toda a diferença em sua vida.
d. reconhece que as dificuldades em sua vida foram todas superadas.
e. percorre várias estradas durante as diferentes fases de sua vida.

Unit 5   Art: The Language of Emotions

1. Read the article below and choose the option that best summarizes the conclusions of the study. *Skimming*

THE UNEXPECTED, CREATIVE BENEFITS OF SHARING YOUR STUDIO

With the rise of trendy co-working spaces like The Wing and WeWork in recent years, the benefits of such environments have come to the fore. While these companies promise opportunities for networking, career advancement, and off-the-charts idea exchange (not to mention stylish digs), compelling research has found that the people frequenting co-working spaces – like freelancers, entrepreneurs, and remote employees – experience enhanced creativity.

But can the same creative benefits be felt when artists share a studio? You might think the answer is yes, but it's not always the case. Shared studios can help **enhance** creativity, but only if the artists are frequently interacting, **swapping** resources, and exchanging feedback.

Dr. Thalia R. Goldstein, assistant professor of applied developmental psychology at George Mason University, has noted that under the right circumstances, the benefits of co-working spaces can also be felt by artists sharing a studio, by virtue of the fact that it fosters collaboration, as well as the "freedom and time to engage with others," she said.

Multiple research findings back up this notion. At the University of Michigan's Stephen M. Ross School of Business, the first phase of an ongoing study on co-working spaces (chaired by Dr. Gretchen Speitzer, Dr. Peter Bacevice, and Lyndon Garrett) found that the freedom to think and create independently, with self-defined opportunities to join in community, led to a **heightened** sense of achievement.

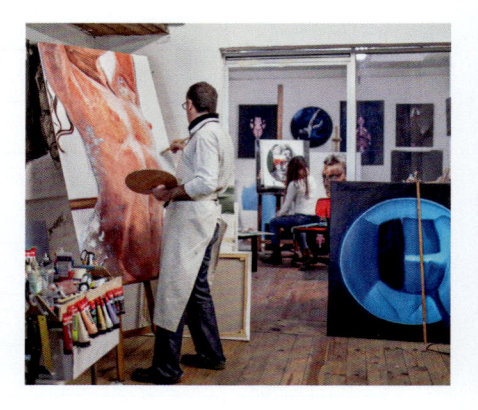

Extracted from www.artsy.net/article/artsy-editorial-unexpected-creative-benefits-sharing-studio. Accessed on July 19, 2018.

a. Although they are usually used as a cost-reducing alternative for companies and small businesses, co-working spaces are not considered a plausible alternative for artists.

b. Company employees who commonly use co-working spaces are looking for opportunities for networking, career advancement, and off-the-charts idea exchange.

c. According to a study conducted by Dr. Goldstein, shared studios are positive only for artists who are looking for collaboration and the freedom to engage with others.

d. The study concludes that, under the right circumstances, the benefits of co-working spaces can also be found with shared studios. They foster collaboration and also provide artists with the freedom and time to engage with each other.

e. According to Dr. Speitzer, Dr. Bacevice, and Garrett, the freedom to think enabled by co-working spaces makes artists more independent.

2. Read the article again and complete the tasks below.

a. Underline the words with prefixes.

b. Find a word that means *not expected, unforeseen*. _____

c. Find a word that means *talking to each other, working together*: _____

3. Match the prefixes on the left with a word on the right to form new words. Use these words to complete the sentences below.

PREFIX	BASE WORD
over-	biography
auto-	finished
im-	react
dis-	possible
self-	agree
un-	esteem

a. You always _____ to criticism, and it's not a good thing about you.

b. *Long Walk to Freedom* is the name of Nelson Mandela's _____.

c. It's _____ to visit the Sistine Chapel and not be mesmerized by its ceiling. It's wonderful!

d. You might _____, but I think *Guernica* is the most striking painting of all times.

e. *The Gran Cavallo* is one of Da Vinci's most famous _____ works.

f. Some artists have very low _____. They think their work is never good.

4. Read the excerpt below and answer the question that follows.

"Having established his genius as a sculptor and painter, Michelangelo **went on** to completely change the Roman skyline with his architectural designs."

Extracted from www.bbc.co.uk/pressoffice/pressreleases/stories/2004/02_february/05/divine_michelangelo_synopses.shtml. Accessed on July 06, 2018.

The phrasal verb *went on* in the excerpt, whose base form is *go on*, stands for:

a. pass
b. do something without planning or preparing
c. attack someone or argue with someone
d. experience a difficult or unpleasant situation
e. continue

5. Read the definitions for some phrasal verbs with *go*. Then complete the sentences using them.

go for
 choose or accept
go up
 increase in price or value
go over
 review or examine
go out
 feel sympathy or pity
go into
 start to do a particular type of job

a. I need to _____ a few documents before I sign the lease on my art gallery.
b. We need to buy our tickets to the concert before prices _____ again.
c. She plans to _____ teaching after college.
d. Since they are saving money, Mary and Pete decided to _____ the cheapest alternative.
e. Our hearts _____ to the people affected by the hurricane.

6. Complete the table below with the missing words.

SINGULAR	PLURAL
painting	_____
_____	sculptures
picture	_____
wife	_____
opportunity	_____
_____	countries
_____	responsibilities
kid	_____
wish	_____
kiss	_____
knife	_____
museum	_____

7. Complete the sentences below with the plural form of the nouns.

   a. Picasso is not only famous for his _____ (painting), but he's also famous for many other art _____ (form).

   b. The work of Andy Warhol, one of the most well-known _____ (name) from the pop art movement, has been the subject of multiple _____ (study) around the world.

   c. Gustav Mahler, an Austro-Bohemian composer, is mostly known for his _____ (symphony) from the late-Romantic period.

   d. _____ (family) are more and more attracted by art _____ (exhibit). Engaging art and technology is an effective way _____ (artist) have found to encourage _____ (parent) and _____ (kid) to visit _____ (museum) and art _____ (gallery).

   e. Although only active for about 10 _____ (year), Vincent Van Gogh created almost 900 _____ (work of art).

8. Read the sentence below and circle the option that describes the word order.

> This is a beautiful small round old blue French leather bag.

   a. opinion – size – shape – age – color – origin – material
   b. size – age – opinion – shape – origin – color – material
   c. size – shape – age – color – origin – material – opinion
   d. opinion – material – shape – age – size – color – origin
   e. color – opinion – size – shape – age – origin – material

9. Check (✔) the correct option to complete the sentences.

   a. The *Mona Lisa* is _____ by Leonardo da Vinci. You can find it in the Louvre Museum now.
   (   ) a world-famous portrait painting
   (   ) a portrait painting world-famous

   b. Vincent Van Gogh is _____. He was born in the 19th century.
   (   ) a European painter Post-Impressionist
   (   ) a European Post-Impressionist painter

   c. The Statue of Liberty is _____ situated on Liberty Island in New York City, USA.
   (   ) a famous neoclassical sculpture
   (   ) a neoclassical famous sculpture

   d. *Christ the Redeemer* is _____ of Jesus Christ located in Rio de Janeiro.
   (   ) a colossal Art Deco statue
   (   ) an Art Deco colossal statue

   e. The Egyptian pyramids are _____ located in Egypt.
   (   ) ancient pyramid-shaped structures
   (   ) ancient structures pyramid-shaped

   f. *Starry Night* is a _____ painting by Van Gogh. It was painted in 1889.
   (   ) fascinating, dark-colored
   (   ) dark-colored, fascinating

10. Describe the following using at least three adjectives each.

   a. A place you like going to.

   b. An item of clothing you like wearing.

   c. A monument in your city or country.

   d. A book you have read and liked.

AN EYE ON ENEM

ENEM 2017 – Prova Amarela
Questão 01

Israel Travel Guide

Israel has always been a standout destination. From the days of prophets to the modern-day nomad this tiny slice of land on the eastern Mediterranean has long attracted visitors. While some arrive in the 'Holy Land' on a spiritual quest, many others are on cultural tours, beach vacations, and ecotourism trips. Weeding through Israel's convoluted history is both exhilarating and exhausting. There are crumbling temples, ruined cities, abandoned forts, and hundreds of places associated with the Bible. And while a sense of adventure is required, most sites are safe and easily accessible. Most of all, Israel is about its incredibly diverse population. Jews come from all over the world to live here, while about 20% of the population is Muslim. Politics are hard to get away from in Israel as everyone has an opinion on how to move the country forward – with a ready ear you're sure to hear opinions from every side of the political spectrum.

Disponível em: www.worldtravelguide.net. Acesso em: 15 jun. 2012.

Antes de viajar, turistas geralmente buscam informações sobre o local para onde pretendem ir. O trecho do guia de viagens de Israel

a. descreve a história desse local para que turistas valorizem seus costumes milenares.
b. informa hábitos religiosos para auxiliar turistas a entenderem as diferenças culturais.
c. divulga os principais pontos turísticos para ajudar turistas a planejarem sua viagem.
d. recomenda medidas de segurança para alertar turistas sobre possíveis riscos locais.
e. apresenta aspectos gerais da cultura do país para continuar a atrair turistas estrangeiros.

Unit 6 — Sport Is No Longer Just Sport

1. Read part of an article and check (✓) the best title. *Skimming*
   - ( ) Skateboarding in Australia
   - ( ) Olympic Skateboarding: Tokyo 2020
   - ( ) Rio Olympics was different

www.boardworld.com.au/articles/olympic

1. PARK & STREET DISCIPLINES

If you're wondering which disciplines will be represented at Tokyo 2020, wonder no longer. The Olympic competition will be split into two distinct contests. One will cover street skateboarding – think Street League courses; rails, **hubbas**, ledges, stairs. The other will be a park discipline, which will target transition skaters – think Vans Park Series. [...]
As expected, the Olympics will feature both male and female skateboarders competing in each discipline. According to the ISF, the total number of competitors is expected to be around 80, with an equal split between genders. That means we can expect roughly 40 men and 40 women to compete at the Games, possibly split between 20 per discipline, although it's possible that some skaters will compete in both park and street. [...]

2. ROLLERBLADERS ARE IN CHARGE – SORT OF

Skateboarding will be governed, at least in part, by the Fédération Internationale de Roller Sports (FIRS). The International Skateboarding Federation was able to **strike** a deal with the Olympics to co-govern the sport alongside our rollerblading cousins, forming the Tokyo 2020 Skateboarding Commission, despite the best efforts of FIRS to take full control.

3. EVERYONE WILL WEAR NIKE

This one almost sounds untrue, but it's absolutely confirmed – at least for U.S. athletes. Part of the U.S. Olympic Commission's massive deal with Nike stipulates that all athletes must be dressed head-to-toe in Nike **apparel** and footwear during all official Olympic engagements. This includes press conferences, interviews, official appearances, and medal ceremonies, however it doesn't extend to appearances in the actual competition, as far as we understand. [...]

4. **SPONSORS** WILL BE SILENCED

At the Rio 2016 Olympics, the British Olympic Commission outlined a number of sponsor-related rules that athletes had to accept in order to be allowed to compete. The rules outlaw sponsors who aren't partnered with the BOA from congratulating athletes or even wishing them good luck in a public forum during the Olympic Games.
Any skate sponsor (besides Adidas) must pretend that their U.K. rider is not actually at the Olympics, completely ignoring the competition altogether, or said skateboarder will be disallowed from competing. It's unclear whether this extends to other nations, however considering that Adidas has partnered with numerous Olympic Commissions across the world – including Australia for the past 12 years – it seems likely. Welcome to corporate sports.

5. AUSTRALIA IS WAY AHEAD OF THE GAME

While some nations, namely the USA, have **seemingly** made little progress with their Olympic skateboarding program, Australia has **stormed out** of the blocks. The AOC became the first Olympic Commission to publicly support a skateboarder when they granted Shane O'Neill a $20,000 medal incentive bonus almost immediately after the sport was confirmed for Tokyo 2020. Two Australian skateboarders were recently granted full university **scholarships** as a direct result of skateboarding's inclusion in the Games, while the Australian Skateboarding Federation has already partnered with the AIS for several skate-related Olympic workshops across the country. [...]

6. THE OLYMPIC COURSE WILL BE OPEN TO THE PUBLIC

Skateboarding will be held at the Aomi Urban Sports Venue in Tokyo, where street and park courses will be purpose-built for the Olympic Games. Amazingly, the IOC has confirmed that the skateparks will be open to the general public to skate during the Olympics, even on the same day they're used for competition. [...]

Extracted from www.boardworld.com.au/articles/olympic-skateboarding-6-things-we-know. Accessed on July 30, 2018.

2. Unscramble the words and write questions. Then match the questions with the answers.

a. contests / the Olympic competition / how many / will / distinct / be split into / ?
_____

b. the skateboarding event / take place / 2020 Olympics / will / where / in the / ?
_____

c. country / has stormed out of / in skateboarding / which / the blocks / ?
_____

d. competitors / event / take part in / the / how many / are expected to / ?
_____

e. sponsoring / for / the / will be / competitors / who / the apparel / ?
_____

f. the skateparks / access / the public / will / to / have / ?
_____

(   ) Eighty competitors are expected to participate in the skateboarding event, with an equal split between genders.
(   ) The Olympic competition will be split into two distinct contests.
(   ) Australia has stormed out of the blocks in skateboarding by supporting its players from the beginning.
(   ) Yes, the public will be able to access the skateparks after the events have taken place.
(   ) Skateboarding will be held at the Aomi Urban Sports venue in Tokyo.
(   ) According to sources, Nike will definitely be sponsoring the U.S. team and maybe that of other countries as well.

3. Fill in the blanks with the comparative form of the adjectives in parentheses.

a. That cat is _____ (mean) than my dog.

b. That sports TV show is _____ (strange) than the one we watched last night.

c. Volleyball player Walsh Jennings's hair is _____ (light) than Logan Tom's hair.

d. Carson's television is _____ (big) than mine. Let's all watch the games there.

4. Read the sentences and check (✔) the options that complete them.

a. Samuel is _____ at sports than me.
(   ) good
(   ) better
(   ) best

b. George is _____ than Robert.
(   ) funnier
(   ) funniest
(   ) funny

c. Soccer is _____ than handball.
(   ) most popular
(   ) more popular
(   ) populous

d. I think baseball is _____ than rugby, but I don't like either of them.
(   ) bad
(   ) worst
(   ) worse

e. I think Serena Williams is still the _____ tennis player in the world.
(   ) good
(   ) better
(   ) best

f. Running is one of the _____ Olympic sports.
(   ) older
(   ) old
(   ) oldest

Unit 6

5. Select the underlined word or phrase that needs to be changed to correct the sentence.

1. The oldest of the triplets is the livelier one, perhaps because he intuitively knows that he is the big brother who needs to take care of everyone.
   a. oldest   b. who   c. livelier   d. big

2. Among the major newspapers in Los Angeles, the more popular one is *The Los Angeles Times*, outselling the four other large publications in the area.
   a. major   b. outselling   c. large   d. more

3. While I enjoy both swimming and running, I am fine at swimming, as I naturally have more upper body strength and feel very natural in the water.
   a. very   b. both   c. fine   d. more

4. The environmentalist isn't sure which is worst for the environment between Styrofoam and plastic.
   a. worst   b. and   c. isn't   d. which

6. Complete the sentences by changing the words in parentheses into a noun using suffixes.

a. The _____ (create) of an independent body to monitor violence on television might succeed in putting these concerns to rest.

b. The _____ (involve) of parents in elementary school classrooms has several benefits for the children's education.

c. The first step should be the _____ (identify) of students who cause trouble in the classroom so that appropriate action can be taken.

d. There is of course a striking _____ (similar) between what happens in the workplace and at home.

e. This is such a common _____ (occur) that the authorities need to take immediate action.

7. Read the quotes and complete them with the words from the box.

> creation   inspiration   evolution   ability   arguments   humanity

a. "Genius is one percent _____ and ninety-nine percent perspiration." - Thomas Edison

b. "Silence is one of the hardest _____ to refute." – Josh Billings

c. "Nature used human imagination to lift her work of _____ to even higher levels." – Luigi Pirandello

d. "For success, attitude is equally as important as _____." – Walter Scott

e. "To deny people their human rights is to challenge their very _____." – Nelson Mandela

f. "_____ is the fundamental idea in all of life science – in all of biology." – Bill Nye

Source: www.brainyquote.com. Accessed on August 24, 2018.

Unit 6

8. Complete the root word with the correct suffix to form an adjective. You can choose from *-ous*, *-able*, *-ful*, *-y*, or *-ly*. Then use the adjectives to fill in the blanks.

- **a.** danger_____
- **b.** fam_____
- **c.** pain_____
- **d.** help_____
- **e.** sun_____
- **f.** wind_____

- **a.** The way to the stadium was slippery and _____ for Edward to drive on a rainy day.
- **b.** I personally know some of the most _____ sports people in my country.
- **c.** It was supposed to be _____ today for the games, but it's raining. I think we need to cancel them.
- **d.** I tried wearing heels for a day, but it was _____. I wonder how women manage to run with heels on.
- **e.** The surfers were really excited about the big waves because it was _____.
- **f.** Anything you can tell us about the winners would be _____.

9. Underline the correct suffixes to complete the words.

- **a.** I am look_____ (ing / ed) for information about previous Olympic games, but there are too many book_____ (s / es) to choose from in the library.
- **b.** The player who substituted for our goalkeeper was young_____ (er / est) than me. In fact, he was the young_____ (er / est) player in the competition.
- **c.** It was really thought_____ (ful / less) of you to get me a ticket for the game, especially as my son had been so care_____ (ful / less) with the tickets we had bought before.
- **d.** Are you look_____ (ing / ed) for yesterday's paper? After I look_____ (ing / ed) at it, I put it in the recycl_____ (ing / ed) can.

AN EYE ON ENEM

ENEM 2016 – Prova Amarela

Questão 94

Global **Flu Pandemic**
9/11 **Terrorism**
Earthquake **Haiti**
Katrina **Hurricane**
Chernobyl **Nuclear**

Connecticut?
Would you know what to do if disaster struck here? Learn to live prepared.
To learn more about living prepared, go to
ct.gov/dph/prepare
Funded by the federal Centers for Disease Control and Prevention

Disponível em: www.ct.gov. Acesso em: 30 jul. 2012 (adaptado).

Orientações à população são encontradas também em sites oficiais. Ao clicar no endereço eletrônico mencionado no cartaz disponível na internet, o leitor tem acesso aos(às)

- **a.** ações do governo local referentes a calamidades.
- **b.** relatos de sobreviventes em tragédias marcantes.
- **c.** tipos de desastres naturais possíveis de acontecer.
- **d.** informações sobre acidentes ocorridos em Connecticut.
- **e.** medidas de emergência a serem tomadas em catástrofes.

Unit 7   Globish: Fad or Fact?

1. What do you remember about the meaning of *globish*? Read the text and answer the question: what is the European form of globish?   `Using previous knowledge`

_____

_____

---

www.economist.com/europe/2014/05/24/the-globish-speaking-union

Topics ⌄   Current edition ⌄   More ⌄   **Subscribe**

WHAT language does Europe speak? France has lost its battle for French. Europeans now overwhelmingly opt for English. The Eurovision song contest, won this month by an Austrian cross-dresser, is mostly English-speaking, even if the votes are translated into French. The European Union conducts ever more business in English. Interpreters sometimes feel they are speaking to themselves. Last year, Germany's President, Joachim Gauck, argued for an English-speaking Europe: national languages would be cherished for spirituality and poetry alongside "a workable English for all of life's situations and all age groups".

Some detect a European form of global English (globish): a **patois** with English physiognomy, cross-dressed with continental cadences and syntax, a train of EU institutional jargon and sequins of linguistic false friends (mostly French). In Brussels "to assist" means to be present, not to help; "to control" means to check, rather than to exercise power; "adequate" means appropriate or suitable, rather than (barely) sufficient; and mass nouns are countable, such as advice, informations, and aids. "Anglo-Saxon" is not a historical term referring to Germanic Tribes in Britain, but a political insult followed by "capitalism" or even "press".

Ordinary Europeans got a first taste of Euro-globish in the televised debates among leading **contenders** for the European election on May 22nd–25th. The idea of the main European political groups picking "*Spitzenkandidaten*" to become the president of the European Commission is a novelty (and has created Brussels's first German neologism in years). It is meant to close the democratic deficit, stir excitement, arrest the fall in **turnout** and check the rise of anti-EU parties.

Of the five *Spitzenkandidaten* debating in Brussels on May 15th, Alexis Tsipras, champion of a far-left alliance, insisted on speaking Greek. Jean-Claude Juncker, Luxembourg's standard-bearer for the Christian Democrats, chose French. The three others gamely abided by the request to speak English: two Germans, Martin Schulz and Ska Keller from the Social Democrats and Greens, respectively, and a Belgian, Guy Verhofstadt, for the Liberals.

[…]

Politics is surely best conducted in the vernacular. John Stuart Mill, for one, thought multilingual democracy a nonsense because "the united public opinion, necessary to the working of a representative government, cannot exist." Yet, as Switzerland shows, a country can have more than one vernacular. In theory that might work for Europe. Mr. Schulz and Mr. Juncker got more prime-time attention when they debated separately on French and German TV in the local tongue. However, even the finest polyglot would **struggle** to reach voters in 24 official languages.

Philippe Van Parijs, a professor at Louvain University, argues that European-level democracy does not require a homogenous culture, or ethnos; a common political community, or demos, needs only a lingua franca. Was Nelson Mandela less democratic for speaking English in multi-ethnic and multilingual South Africa? English is **spreading** fast, with more than 40% of young Europeans **claiming** to be able to speak it in some form. The answer to Europe's democratic deficit, says Mr. Van Parijs, is to accelerate the process so that English is not just the language of an elite but also the means for poorer Europeans to be heard. An approximate version of English, with a limited vocabulary of just a few hundred words, would suffice.

Extracted from www.economist.com/europe/2014/05/24/the-globish-speaking-union. Accessed on July 30, 2018.

---

2. Read the article and answer the following questions.   `Scanning`

  a. In which region does "adequate" mean "suitable"? What is the most common meaning of "adequate"? _____

  b. Can you guess from the article the meaning of "Spitzenkandidaten"? _____

  c. According to the passage, which country has more than one vernacular? _____

  d. What do you call a person who can speak many languages? _____

3. Read the statements and write true (T) or false (F).

Understanding details

a. (   ) "Anglo-Saxon" is a historical term referring to Germanic tribes in Britain, but in Brussels it is a political insult.

b. (   ) Ordinary Europeans witnessed the first use of Euro-globish in televised debates among leading contenders for the European election on May 22nd–25th.

c. (   ) During the debate in Brussels on May 15th, Jean-Claude, Luxembourg's standard-bearer for the Christian Democrats, spoke in English.

d. (   ) Mr. Schulz and Mr. Juncker got no prime-time attention when they debated separately on French and German TV in the local tongue.

e. (   ) English is not just the language of an elite, but also a way for poorer Europeans to be heard.

4. Unscramble the words to form questions. Answer them with your opinion.

a. meaning / of / is / Globish / the / what / ?
_____

b. language / official / does / one / Europe / have / ?
_____

c. become / did / world's / English / language / the / how / ?
_____

d. prefer / do / Globish / you / in / English / or / speaking / ?
_____

e. English / is / different / Globish / from / ?
_____

5. Write the correct form of the possessives in the blanks.

a. _____ (People) faith in their own capabilities grows when they see their friends having positive experiences with radical change.

b. Did you watch _____ (yesterday) game?

c. Where is the _____ (ladies) showroom?

d. The pudding would not be to _____ (everyone) taste.

e. _____ and _____ (Anna / Elle) mother invited us to her party.

f. These are our _____ (friends) in our garden.

g. I believe _____ (Ross) English dictionary app isn't the best one.

h. My _____ (parents) friend speaks four languages fluently.

6. Rewrite the noun phrases with the appropriate possessive pronouns replacing the underlined words.

a. Alejandro is your cousin, so is he my cousin, too?
_____

b. Whose umbrella is this? Is it your umbrella?
_____

c. Her eyes are blue; our eyes are brown.
_____

d. Is that your bottle? No, it's my bottle.
_____

e. Can you lend her your shoes? Her shoes are missing.
_____

7. Rewrite the sentences using 's or '.

a. David and Lucy are siblings.
_____

b. All the employees have put their cell phones in the locker.
_____

c. Mr. and Mrs. Rodrigues have a son, Miguel.
_____

d. Alice makes delicious salads.
_____

e. Juan was born on April 30th.
_____

f. The party was at the house of Maria, near the beach.
_____

g. My colleagues have a house next door to ours.
_____

h. That notebook belongs to Gloria.
_____

8. Complete the quote with a pronoun. Then check (✓) the correct option.

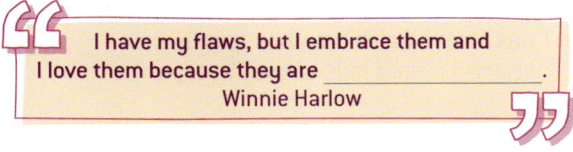

> " I have my flaws, but I embrace them and I love them because they are _____.
> Winnie Harlow "

Source: www.brainyquote.com. Accessed on August, 9, 2018.

The word you completed it with is a...

(   ) subject pronoun.
(   ) possessive adjective.
(   ) possessive pronoun.

Unit 7

129

9. **Complete the sentences with possessive adjectives and possessive pronouns.**

   a. Mary has _____ own closet and Mark has _____.
   b. She had created this problem and now it was _____ to face alone.
   c. Paul and Sabrina's work isn't finished yet, but Lara and Claire finished _____ yesterday.
   d. The article on the first page is _____. I wrote it last month.
   e. The money is _____, not _____. You and I worked for it, not only me.

10. **Identify if the word in bold is a possessive adjective (A) or a possessive pronoun (P).**

    a. ( ) These are Ana's books. **Mine** are at home.
    b. ( ) **Theirs** is the largest English-speaking country.
    c. ( ) When you travel, you can take **your** work with you.
    d. ( ) **Her** name is fancier than mine.
    e. ( ) A friend of **hers** who is a florist asks if she can advertise on the site.

11. **Complete the sentences below with the idioms in the box.**

    > the grass is always greener on the other side
    > know your onions
    > on cloud nine
    > know it by heart
    > have a finger in every pie
    > a piece of cake
    > give it your best shot
    > to hit the road
    > cold feet
    > every nook and cranny

    a. They always need to be involved in every project! They _____!
    b. I was able to finish the exam quickly because I always read about this topic. I _____.
    c. You should study a lot harder to make sure you _____.
    d. I looked in _____, but I couldn't find what I was looking for.
    e. I know the homework is difficult but _____.

    f. Whenever she complains about her town and wants to leave, I remind her that _____.
    g. When the bell rang, the teacher told the students _____.
    h. Juan was _____ when he discovered that he had been selected to the soccer team.
    i. I always get _____ when I have to speak in public, but I guess it is normal to feel nervous before it.
    j. This activity is really easy. It's _____!

12. **Check (✓) the option with the correct meaning of the idiom / phrase.**

    a. These two languages have no similarity whatsoever! They are **apples and oranges**.
       ( ) Both languages are like fruits.
       ( ) The languages are very different from each other.
       ( ) The languages have great similarities.
    b. José was accusing us of stealing his charger until he found it, and now he's trying **to sweep it under the rug**.
       ( ) José thinks that his charger will be safer if he hides it under the rug.
       ( ) José wants to do something to make up for his mistake.
       ( ) José wants to pretend that the incident never happened.
    c. You might think Elizabeth is a kid who has it easy, but if you saw the list of chores her parents give her, I guarantee that you wouldn't want to be **in her shoes**.
       ( ) You wouldn't want your shoes to get as dirty as Elizabeth's when she's doing her chores.
       ( ) If you had to do as many chores as Elizabeth, you'd want a pair of comfortable shoes.
       ( ) Elizabeth has so many chores to do that it is unpleasant to imagine being her.
    d. Look at Amanda! She seems to be drawn to painting, just like her father! Well, an **apple doesn't fall far from the tree**.
       ( ) Amanda looks just like her father.
       ( ) Amanda's painting and her father's painting look similar.
       ( ) Amanda's interest in painting is the same as her father's.
    e. Anna says she doesn't need any more practice for her piano concert. She **knows the song by heart**.
       ( ) She knows the song as much as she knows her heart.
       ( ) She knows the song very well and needs no extra practice.
       ( ) She sings the song about heart and love.

13. Complete the article with the words from the box.

> common   distinction   work permit   fluent   generation   vocabulary
> fill   eloquence   qualified   oblivious   mile   held

Sir,
As always in his take on Globish, Simon Kuper hits the nail right on the head (FT Magazine, January 13/14).
A _____ must be made between spoken and written Globish. Spoken Globish is fine – we are thankful that there is one _____ language in which conferences can be _____, even if the effortless _____ of speeches or the witty banter during coffee breaks remain the preserve of the Brits.
But written Globish doesn't cut it, ever. A European speaker of English, having learned it as a second language in school, may feel _____ to write entire articles or web texts in the language (ouch). But native English speakers can tell from a _____ away this is Globish, while the person _____ in Globish is _____ to any wrongdoing.
This is good news for subeditors – or (former) translators into English. Obviously, post-Brexit, British subeditors wanting to ply their trade in the EU will need a _____.
So, either the Irish will _____ these posts or Globish might become the new national language of the EU – just until the new _____ that speaks less Globish and more English […] have brushed up on their idioms (and use them correctly), lost their accent, and expanded their _____.

Extracted from www.economist.com/europe/2014/05/24/the-globish-speaking-union. Accessed on Jul 30, 2018.

AN EYE ON ENEM

ENEM 2016 – Prova azul
Questão 93

Italian university switches to English

By Sean Coughlan, BBC News education correspondent 16 May 2012 Last updated at 09:49 GMT

Milan is crowded with Italian icons, which makes it even more of a cultural earthquake that one of Italy's leading universities—the Politecnico di Milano—is going to switch to the English language. The university has announced that from 2014 most of its degree courses—including all its graduate courses—will be taught and assessed entirely in English rather than Italian.
The waters of globalization are rising around higher education—and the university believes that if it remains Italian-speaking it risks isolation and will be unable to compete as an international institution. "We strongly believe our classes should be international classes—and the only way to have international classes is to use the English language," says the university rector, Giovanni Azzone.

COUGHLAN, S. Disponível em: bbc.co.uk. Acesso em: 31 jul. 2012.

As línguas têm um papel importante na comunicação entre pessoas de diferentes culturas. Diante do movimento de internacionalização no ensino superior, a universidade Politecnico di Milano decidiu

a. elaborar exames em língua inglesa para o ingresso na universidade.
b. ampliar a oferta de vagas na graduação para alunos estrangeiros.
c. investir na divulgação da universidade no mercado internacional.
d. substituir a língua nacional para se inserir no contexto da globalização.
e. estabelecer metas para melhorar a qualidade do ensino de italiano.

Unit 8 — Hit the Road

1. Read the packing list below and answer the question: who is this text for? `Identifying the target audience`

Family vacation packing list: the ultimate guide

BY Sally Peck, FAMILY TRAVEL AND BEACHES EDITOR
20 JUNE 2017 · 12:30PM

My grandmother never goes anywhere without a bathing suit and a book – if things are going well, she reasons, she'll get to use both. Make this your policy.

There are, of course, a few other practical things to consider. Check the items below off of your packing list [...].

[...]

For any holiday...

- ( ) 1 **driver's** license, code for rental car; email a copy of both to yourself
- ( ) 2 **tickets** for plane, train or bus
- ( ) 3 **cell phone** and charger
- ( ) 4 **music** on your device of choice for playing in the car (and relevant cable)
- ( ) 5 **wallet** with credit and debit cards and some cash
- ( ) 6 **keys**
- ( ) 7 **camera** and charger
- ( ) 8 **backpack** or another hands-free bag for carrying around daily essentials
- ( ) 9 **clothes**: socks; shoes (at least two pairs); pants; bras; shorts; shirts; warm layers; bathing suit; rainy day gear; pajamas
- ( ) 10 **medication** (anything you regularly take plus Calpol) and a copy of your family's prescriptions
- ( ) 11 **first aid** kit

  [...]

- ( ) 12 **face wash** in a small container, if you're flying
- ( ) 13 **moisturizer**
- ( ) 14 **shampoo** and conditioner for all
- ( ) 15 **toothbrushes** and toothpaste
- ( ) 16 **glasses or contact lenses** plus case and lens solution
- ( ) 17 **sunglasses**
- ( ) 18 **hairbrushes** for young and old, plus hair clips
- ( ) 19 **books** and magazines for all ages
- ( ) 20 **tablet** loaded with programs viewable offline for planes or cars

  [...]

- ( ) 21 **playing** cards
- ( ) 22 **extra bag** for dirty laundry
- ( ) 23 **water bottle** to refill

Adapted from www.telegraph.co.uk/travel/family-holidays/family-holiday-packing-list-the-ultimate-guide/. Accessed on November 12, 2018.

2. Read the text and underline the correct statement(s) about checklists. `Identifying features of the genre`

   Checklists...
   a. contain long paragraphs explaining a subject.
   b. contain a set of items rather than long paragraphs.
   c. can be long or short.
   d. are always long.

Unit 8

3. Read the text again and check (✓) the correct alternative. *Scanning*

   a. Which of the following categories can you find most in the list?
      ( ) electronics
      ( ) hygiene items and medication
      ( ) food items

   b. Which of the following categories does not appear in the text?
      ( ) food items   ( ) documents   ( ) accessories

   c. Which of the following items from the list could you use on rainy days during your vacation?
      ( ) sunglasses   ( ) playing cards   ( ) bathing suit   ( ) passport

   d. Which of the following items will you need if you get sick?
      ( ) moisturizer
      ( ) a hairbrush
      ( ) medication

   e. Which of the following items are not used for entertainment purposes?
      ( ) books and magazines
      ( ) playing cards
      ( ) a backpack

4. Complete the sentences with *used to*, *didn't use to*, or *did... use to*.

   a. _____ be blond! I remember your hair being darker.
   b. _____ she _____ travel by train with you?
   c. They _____ like traveling by plane, but now they do it all the time.
   d. Carla _____ take lots of things in her hand luggage, but now she takes just the essentials.
   e. Joey _____ make a packing list before traveling, but now he always makes one.
   f. Security _____ be so strict in airports. It is much stricter nowadays.
   g. _____ Andy _____ take to the road every weekend before he met you?
   h. I _____ bring any snacks with me on my road trips, but now I always have something to eat.

5. Underline the correct options to complete the sentences.

   a. At first I _____ pay attention to the safety instructions at the beginning of a flight, but now I always do.
      a. used to   b. didn't use to   c. didn't used to

   b. He _____ several books a month, but he doesn't have time any more.
      a. used to reading   b. used to read   c. use to read

   c. Did Sarah _____ fasten her seatbelt during takeoff? She didn't fasten it this time.
      a. used to   b. use to   c. used

   d. Caroline _____ the bus, but now she walks to work.
      a. used to take   b. was used to taking   c. is used to take

   e. He _____ a lot of poems when he was younger.
      a. used to wrote   b. used to written   c. used to write

   f. When Pete Smith was the head of our office, everything _____ well organized. Now it's total chaos here.
      a. use to be   b. used to be   c. used to being

6. Complete the sentences with *must* or *must not* and the verbs in parentheses.
   a. Passengers _____ (talk) to the driver while the bus is in motion.
   b. I really loved your company. We _____ (meet) more often.
   c. I _____ (finish) this project today. It has to be handed in by tomorrow.
   d. We _____ (miss) the train, because it's the last one.
   e. I _____ (eat) too much or I'll get fat.
   f. He had been working for more than 11 hours. He _____ (be) tired after a long day.

7. Read the article and match the words in bold with their meanings.

> Back when the TSA first introduced its 3-1-1 rules for carry-on liquids, a traveler named Ashley **inadvertently** tried to bring a large, expensive bottle of shampoo through airport security. When the TSA officer threatened to **confiscate** the shampoo, Ashley returned to her airline's counter to check her bag. The line was long, and she was in danger of missing her flight. She **begged** a nearby airline staffer to let her skip to the front of the line; he refused. Only when Ashley started to cry did the **red-faced** airline worker **begrudgingly** allow her to bypass the line.
> She made her flight with minutes to spare – but the airline subsequently lost her checked bag. Says Ashley, "If I had known how much trouble the whole thing would be, I would have just forfeited the shampoo."
> When it comes to packing, a small mistake like putting a **prohibited** item in your carry-on bag can snowball into a messy chain of events. Fortunately, travelers faced with similar packing problems don't have to **rely** on tears to save their vacations. Whether you're dealing with a confiscated item in the security line, a **surplus** of **souvenirs**, a nasty spill, or a broken bag, a bit of packing emergency know-how can mean the difference between a disaster and a worry-free getaway.
> Many travelers forget to save a little extra space in their suitcase for souvenirs. Others only travel with a carry-on, which means that some souvenirs they might purchase, like liquid-filled snow globes, may be prohibited past the airport security checkpoint. [...]
> Many travelers ship souvenirs back home – especially large or **fragile** things like handmade Moroccan rugs or Waterford crystal. A **reputable** shop that caters largely to tourists (and sells big and expensive items like furniture) will likely ship your goods back home right from the store. However, without shipping insurance or a tracking number, you have little control over the fate of your purchase.
>
> *Extracted from www.smartertravel.com/2017/06/19/5-worst-packing-problems-solve. Accessed on July 31, 2018.*

   a. _____ : say that something is not permitted or allowed
   b. _____ : trust or depend on someone or something to do what you need or expect them to do
   c. _____ : respected for being honest or for doing good work
   d. _____ : officially take private property away from someone, usually as a punishment
   e. _____ : easily broken or damaged
   f. _____ : an amount of something that is more than what is needed or used; excess
   g. _____ : objects that you buy or keep to remind yourself of a special occasion or a place you have visited
   h. _____ : do something reluctantly because you feel angry, envious, or upset
   i. _____ : accidently, without realizing what you are doing
   j. _____ : asked for something in an anxious or urgent way, because you wanted it very much

8. Check (✓) the correct options.

a. What do you call the feeling of confusion and tiredness you have after flying a very long distance?

( ) toll ( ) jet lag ( ) turbulence ( ) deck

b. What do you call a large open container pulled by a train and used to carry goods?

( ) gate ( ) rail pass ( ) wagon ( ) cruise

c. What do you call the place at an airport through which people and goods arriving in a country must pass and where any tax owed must be paid?

( ) lifeboat ( ) customs ( ) rail pass ( ) gate

d. What do you call a vacation on a large ship?

( ) cruise ( ) toll ( ) lifeboat ( ) boat

e. What do you call the irregular and violent movements of air or water that are caused by the wind?

( ) toll ( ) lifeboat ( ) turbulence ( ) deck

AN EYE ON ENEM

ENEM 2013 - Prova Cinza

Questão 95

Do one thing for diversity and inclusion

The United Nations Alliance of Civilizations (UNAOC) is launching a campaign aimed at engaging people around the world to Do One Thing to support Cultural Diversity and Inclusion. Every one of us can do ONE thing for diversity and inclusion; even one very little thing can become a global action if we all take part in it.

Simple things YOU can do to celebrate the World Day for Cultural Diversity for Dialogue and Development on May 21.

1. Visit an art exhibit or a museum dedicated to other cultures.
2. Read about the great thinkers of other cultures.
3. Visit a place of worship other than yours and participate in the celebration.
4. Spread your own culture around the world and learn about other cultures.
5. Explore music of a different culture.

There are thousands of things that you can do, are you taking part in it?

UNITED NATIONS ALLIANCE OF CIVILIZATIONS. Disponível em: www.unaoc.org. Acesso em: 16 fev. 2013 (adaptado).

Internautas costumam manifestar suas opiniões sobre artigos on-line por meio da postagem de comentários. O comentário que exemplifica o engajamento proposto na quarta dica da campanha apresentada no texto é:

a. "Lá na minha escola, aprendi a jogar capoeira para uma apresentação no Dia da Consciência Negra."

b. "Outro dia assisti na TV uma reportagem sobre respeito à diversidade. Gente de todos os tipos, várias tribos. Curti bastante."

c. "Eu me inscrevi no Programa Jovens Embaixadores para mostrar o que tem de bom em meu país e conhecer outras formas de ser."

d. "Curto muito bater papo na internet. Meus amigos estrangeiros me ajudam a aperfeiçoar minha proficiência em língua estrangeira."

e. "Pesquisei em sites de culinária e preparei uma festa árabe para uns amigos da escola. Eles adoraram, principalmente, os doces!"

AUDIO SCRIPTS

Unit 1
Track 02 — Activity 3

a. "We are able to move to these foreign countries where we don't know the language, we don't know the lifestyle, and adapt fairly quickly."

Extracted from https://edition.cnn.com/videos/us/2018/01/12/ Accessed on March 7, 2018.

b. "When Mexico sends its people, they're not sending the best. They're sending people that have lots of problems and they're bringing those problems."

Extracted from www.cbsnews.com/pictures/wild-donald-trump-quotes/9. Accessed on May 6, 2018.

c. "I don't feel as though I have to validate my existence as a citizen of the United States or of the world by my accomplishments but all of my accomplishments are driven by my family and where we're from."

Extracted from https://edition.cnn.com/videos/us/2018/01/12/ Accessed on March 7, 2018.

d. "We have learned to love this country, Mr. President. This country does not belong to you only, but it belongs to all of us."

Extracted from https://edition.cnn.com/videos/us/2018/01/12/immigrants-respond-to-president-trump-orig-tc.cnn/video/playlists/trumps-shithole-comment-and-reaction Accessed on March 7, 2018.

e. "Make us feel safe. We need to feel safe in this country. I think there's a great divide between the races"

Extracted from www.usatoday.com/pages/interactives/trump-nation/#/?_k=wi8jwl Accessed on May 7, 2018.

f. "I believe that he will make America great again and that means a return of jobs. So, in that manner maybe I will find employment."

Extracted from www.usatoday.com/pages/interactives/trump-nation/#/?_k=wi8jwl. Accessed on May 7, 2018.

Unit 2
Tracks 03 and 04 — Activities 2 and 3

Join me as I travel the globe in search of nutrition guidelines!

We begin our journey in Antigua & Barbuda! Antigua & Barbuda have opted for a Food Guide Pineapple which divides foods into 7 groups: starchy foods; vegetables; fruits; food from animals; peas, beans & nuts; fats & oils; sugars and sweeteners.

Next stop is Guyana. Why not display dietary guidelines in a way that people can easily identify with such as a Stew Pot!? Include in your stew staples, vegetables, fruits, legumes, food from animals and fats.

Over we go to Germany. Here we find a German Nutrition Circle. The circle is divided into food groups with numbers representing the quantity to consume, 1 being eat most, 6 eat least, and 7 includes water which sits in the middle. An interesting message they promote is, "Do not overcook your meals" and they also note the importance of meal times by including, "Allow plenty of time for eating and enjoy mealtimes".

We now move continents to South Africa. South Africa only shows food groups that should be eaten that are necessary for health and do not include groups that should be limited such as salt and processed foods. They also encourage local and affordable foods.

While we are in Africa we will visit Namibia. The Namibia food guide shows only 4 groups – cereals and cereal products, vegetables and fruits, beans, and fats, oils, and sugar.

Now we make our stopover in Singapore. Singapore uses a My Healthy Plate model and reminds people to "Use My Healthy Plate to achieve a balanced diet that provides all the nutrients you need each day".

Adapted from https://thedietitianspantry.com/2015/04/01/dietary-guidelines-around-the-world/. Accessed on June 29, 2018.

Unit 3
Track 05 — Activity 2

1. "If you follow Facebook, you know that when they decide they want to enter a market, they can absolutely crush a competitor. Last year, they decided to copy Snapchat stories, introduce that feature. And now Snapchat is really struggling."

Extracted from www.npr.org/2018/05/02/607817969/facebook-to-join-the-dating-game-as-privacy-concerns-abound. Accessed on May 14, 2018.

2. "Well, I haven't quit Facebook. But I think a lot about what happens when I open the app – the good and bad about my complicated relationship with Facebook and social media in general."

Extracted from www.npr.org/2018/04/12/601951556/can-social-media-have-a-structure-that-does-more-good-than-harm. Accessed on May 14, 2018.

3. "How do we proceed so that – just like earlier technologies – we no longer have lead in paint. Our cars have seatbelts and emission controls and airbags, right? We need to put the safety and oversight to our digital tools so that they're not a surveillance machine."

Extracted from www.npr.org/2018/04/12/601951556/can-social-media-have-a-structure-that-does-more-good-than-harm. Accessed on May 14, 2018.

4. "A lot of people are feeling guilty that they're using Facebook, and my response is don't. It's a great product in many ways."

Extracted from www.npr.org/2018/04/12/601951556/can-social-media-have-a-structure-that-does-more-good-than-harm. Accessed on May 14, 2018.

5. "For all the talk of innovation, Silicon Valley right now is a very boring place. Everybody's trying to get purchased by Facebook or Google. That is not an innovative landscape.

Extracted from www.npr.org/2018/04/12/601951556/can-social-media-have-a-structure-that-does-more-good-than-harm. Accessed on May 14, 2018.

Unit 4

Track 06 – Activity 3

Don't let the bully control every day. Every day should be your day, every day should be something that you are in control of. Every day, if you feel like you can't leave the house so you feel like you can't go and play football or tennis or cricket or you feel like you can't go around your friend's house or you feel like you can't go to the shop because you're scared and you want to avoid this person like I felt every day, surround yourself with the people that love and care for you, find the courage somewhere, talk to people. That's what I wish I did.

Extracted from www.youtube.com/watch?v=BCABNJKoklU. Accessed on May 20, 2018.

Unit 5

Track 07 – Activity 1

Occasionally I wonder whether I chose the wrong path in life. If I'd put the same amount of work into an office job or a trade instead of sculpting I may have been much better off financially, but probably not spiritually.

I was one of five children of immigrant Irish parents and grew up hand-to-mouth, for my mother died when I was 10 and my father had to bring us up on his clerk's salary. My parents had that immigrant aspiration for us all and insisted we study for the 11-plus. We all got into grammar school where the expectation was that we'd join the professional upper middle class.

I tried accountancy but it nearly killed me with boredom and I dropped out of art college when my father's house was repossessed. I then got into sign-writing for a supermarket and painted about 60 signs a day for £5.50 an hour which was decent money in the 80s.

One night I saw a program on TV about the Sir Henry Doulton Sculpture School in Stoke where students were given funding for fees and living costs. I immediately knew that's where I wanted to go. [...]

Life changed when I was commissioned to sculpt a herd of bronze Jersey cows for the town square in St Helier. The fee was £220,000 for two years' work and that included the cost of the bronze and other expenses, but what was left over enabled me to self-certify for a massive mortgage and buy a £235,000 smallholding on the Scottish coast in 2002.

[...]

You need strong motivation to make a living as an artist, but if I'd stayed with accountancy I wouldn't have met my wife, had my three children, or lived in this glorious place. There's a saying up here, "What is meant for you doesn't pass by you", and for me that has always been true.

Adapted from www.theguardian.com/money/2018/oct/20/its-precarious-being-an-artist-you-have-lean-and-hectic-years. Accessed on December 13, 2018.

Unit 6

Track 08 – Activity 2

Millennial sports fans are bypassing cable television and abandoning traditional sports for online video game tournaments and other "eSports." Both developments spell a potential headache for professional sports teams, leagues, broadcast partners, and other stakeholders.

Sports fandom is marked by a sharp generational divide. [...] Non-millennial sports fans report spending 41 percent of their media time on TV, but only nine percent of it on online TV. Millennial sports fans report spending much less of their media time (33 percent) on TV - but 20 percent of that TV time is online. [...]

Based on a survey of more than 1,500 U.S. sports fans conducted in the third quarter of 2016, the study also shows that millennial sports fans with at least a "little bit" of interest in eSports significantly prefer their favorite eSports to traditional sports - 27 percent for millennials, versus 13 percent for non-millennial sports fans.

These changes are likely to have implications on viewership for professional sports leagues like the NFL, MLB, and NASCAR, and networks like ESPN, Fox Sports, and individual teams.

Extracted from www.prnewswire.com/news-releases/millennials-abandon-sports-on-tv-posing-threat-to-teams-leagues-broadcast-partners-finds-study-from-lek-consulting-300423351.html. Accessed on September 25, 2018.

Unit 7

Track 09 – Activity 2

Will English always be the global language?

Asking about the future of language is... that way madness lies. Who would have predicted, a thousand years ago, that Latin would no longer be used in a thousand years' time by hardly anybody? You know, I mean obviously Latin is still used in certain circumstances, but it would not be the normal education to be fluent in Latin. If you'd said that a thousand years ago people would have said you were mad. So, in a thousand years' time, will English still be a global language? We could all be speaking Martian, by then, if they land, and take over. You know who knows what's going to happen? To ask about the future of languages is to really ask about the future of... society. And futurologists are just as unclear about what will happen eventually as I am about language. Because language, you see, is global for one reason only, and that is the power of the people who speak it. Power always drives language. There is no other reason to speak somebody else's language other than you want to improve your quality of life, or you want to influence them in some way, or whatever it might be. I mean the tradition in English, of course, English became global for a whole variety of reasons. First of all, the power of the British Empire. Later, the power of American imperialism. Later, in the 17th century, the power of the Industrial Revolution, which meant that the language of science and technology became English, predominantly. In the 19th century, the power of money. Money talks. And the two most productive nations of the world were Britain and America, both using English. So, the language of international banking became the pound and the dollar. English, once again. And then, in the 20th century, cultural power, as you all know, because every aspect of culture you've encountered has some sort of history in the English language, like pop songs, for example, international advertising, air traffic control, the development of radio and television, the development of the internet. Internet, 100 percent an English-language medium when it started, but today, only a fraction of the Internet is English. Internet has become multilingual. So what's going to happen next? English will stay a global language as long as certain things happen. First of all, that the nations that are the recognized as the most powerful nations in the world continue to use English, and all the other nations want to be like them, or want to interact with them, or want to sell things to them, and so on. And so, English will stay like that for as long as those nations retain that kind of power. We're talking mainly America here, aren't we, predominantly? On the other hand, it doesn't take a… it isn't rocket science to think of scenarios where, for whatever reason, American power diminishes, the power of some other nations grow…eh… grows, and you get other parts of the world becoming more dominant and, you know, people say, well what about Chinese, for one day, may be. At the moment, there's no sign of China… China wanting Chinese to be a global language because they're all learning English in China, for the most part. But you could imagine a scenario where it was the other way around. You can imagine a scenario in Spanish, Spanish is the fastest-growing language in the world at the moment, population-wise. Because of South America and Central America, and increasingly in North America, Spanish is becoming very widely used. You can imagine a scenario where, one day, we might all end up speaking Spanish. In another scenario, you can imagine one day we might all end up speaking Arabic. For reasons that are perfectly obvious to anybody who looks at the world. So, all of these things could happen. At the moment, there's no sign of a diminution in the prestige of English. The desire to learn English. The figures are going up, and up, and up every year. At the moment, over 2 billion people speak English. There's never been so many people speaking one language before, and there's no sign of any slackening off in that progress. So, the long-term future, no idea. The short-term future, no change.

Extracted from https://www.youtube.com/watch?v=5Kvs8SxN8mc. Accessed on July 13, 2018.

Unit 8

Track 10 – Activity 2

CONAN: This is Talk of the Nation. I'm Neal Conan in Washington. In 1973, Paul Theroux said goodbye to his wife and children in London and set off on a journey that would make his career and change his life. Theroux was a novelist then, out of ideas, and he hoped that a trip across Europe and Asia and back would inspire a new book. Theroux boarded the Golden Arrow, took the ferry to France, transferred to the Orient Express, and rode the rails east to Iran and Afghanistan, India, Burma, Vietnam, China, and Japan, then home again through the length of the Soviet Union. It took him four and a half months, and he then wrote a now classic book, "The Great Railway Bazaar," which many credit as the start of a new kind of travel literature.

More than three decades later, Theroux retraced his steps as much as he could. There are new train routes, different landscapes, new borders, and different political realities, and he chronicles that trip in his new book, "Ghost Train to the Eastern Star." If you'd like to talk with Paul Theroux about his travels, about what's changed, and what hasn't, along the way, our phone number is 800-989-8255. The email address is talk@npr.org, and you can join the conversation on our blog. That's at npr.org/blogofthenation. While you're there, you can go to our blog and read an excerpt from "Ghost Train to the Eastern Star." That's at npr.org/blogofthenation.

Extracted from www.npr.org/templates/story/story.php?storyId=93702596. Accessed on June 10, 2018.

Track 11 – Activity 3

CONAN: And we're having some difficulty with the studio in Massachusetts where Paul Theroux is going to join us, some technical problems. He's there. We'll be ready to go in just a moment. But in the meantime, why don't we read some excerpts from the "Ghost Train to the Eastern Star"? And this is the beginning:

"You think of travelers as bold, but our guilty secret is that travel is one of the laziest ways on Earth of passing the time. Travel is not merely the business of being bone-idle, but also an elaborate bumming evasion allowing us to call attention to ourselves with our conspicuous absence while we intrude upon other people's privacy".

Well, Paul Theroux, the author of "The Great Railway Bazaar" and "Ghost Train to the Eastern Star", is now with us. He's at the studios of WCAI, the Cape and Islands' NPR station in Woods Hole, Massachusetts, and it's nice to have you with us today.

PAUL THEROUX: Hi. Neal, can you hear me?

C: Yes, you're on the air.

P: Ah, fine. (Soundbite of laughter)

C: I'm glad you made it.

P: No, I made it, but I'm using a common or garden-type telephone.

C: Well, we'll try to get the better connection up as soon as we can figure out the technical problems.

P: OK, that's great. I heard your introduction, anyway.

C: Well, many of our listeners will well remember you as a marvelous traveling companion 35 years ago. You described yourself in this book as jolly in those days.

P: I've always been jolly. You know, if you're a traveler, you need to be optimistic and be in a fairly good mood. I have a reputation for being cantankerous and gloomy, but actually, you can't travel in that mood. And I've always been, I think, in a good mood, thinking there's going to be something good around the corner, even if the corner happens to be Gori in western Georgia.

Extracted from www.npr.org/templates/story/story.php?storyId=93702596. Accessed on June 10, 2018.

Track 12 — Activity 4

C: You rode the Orient Express, but we should be clear, the Orient Express you took was the local, not the luxury, train. In fact, you write that luxury is the enemy of observation.

P: It is. Luxury is the enemy. With luxury, all you say is, I had a nice time. And I don't want to say I had an awful time, but I'd like to, you know, see something, do something. I took the train from Thailand, from Bangkok to the border, Aranyaprathet, but I took a bus because there was no train to Siem Reap. And when I got off the bus in Siem Reap to go to Angkor, I had the option of, you know, lots of hotels but — Siem Reap is a city now of a million people. So, they have five-star hotels and four-star hotels. They have casinos. They have girly shows. They have really everything you want if you're stupid.

But I stayed in a hotel called the Green Town Guest house for 10 dollars a night. And to do laundry was a dollar for two kilos. And I thought, I could stay here for the next two years, you know, at 10 dollars night. I saw some grizzled old men doing pretty much that, actually long-term residents. So, you don't — it wasn't that I was — I didn't want luxury. I thought, this is really pleasant, staying in a place with a courtyard. Eating noodles and paying 10 bucks a night was really pleasant.

I don't know what my total trip cost but some parts were incredibly expensive. Japan is an expensive country. The Trans-Siberian is expensive. But in general, you can get along quite cheaply if you put your mind to it and you don't mind a few cockroaches.

Extracted from www.npr.org/templates/story/story.php?storyId=93702596. Accessed on June 10, 2018.

NOTES

NOTES

NOTES

EXPAND 2

STUDENT'S BOOK & WORKBOOK

Carla Maurício Vianna
Gisele Aga
João Gabriel Schenferd
Simara H. Dal'Alba

Pearson

Pearson

Head of Product - Pearson Brasil	Juliano de Melo Costa
Product Manager - Pearson Brasil	Marjorie Robles
Product Coordinator - ELT	Mônica Bicalho
Authors	Carla Maurício Vianna Gisele Aga João Gabriel Schenferd Simara H. Dal'Alba
Teacher's Guide	Carla Maurício Vianna
Workbook	João Gabriel Schenferd Simara H. Dal'Alba
Extra content	Carla Maurício Vianna Luciana Santos Pinheiro (Allya Assessoria Linguística)
Editors - ELT	Gisele Aga Renata S. C. Victor Simara H. Dal'Alba (Allya Assessoria Linguística)
Editor (Teacher's Book)	Gisele Aga
Proofreader (English)	Silva Serviços de Educação
Proofreader (Portuguese)	Fernanda R. Braga Simon
Copyeditor	Maria Estela Alcântara
Pedagogical Reviewer	Najin Lima
Quality Control	Viviane Kirmeliene
Art and Design Coordinator	Rafael Lino
Art Editor - ELT	Emily Andrade
Acquisitions and permissions Manager	Maiti Salla
Acquisitions and permissions team	Andrea Bolanho Cristiane Gameiro Heraldo Colon Maricy Queiroz Paula Quirino Sandra Sebastião Shirlei Sebastião
Graphic design	Mirella Della Maggiore Armentano MRS Consultoria Editorial
Graphic design (cover)	Mirella Della Maggiore Armentano MRS Consultoria Editorial
Media Development	Estação Gráfica
Audio	Maximal Studio
Audiovisual Editor	Tatiane Almeida
Audiovisual	Desenrolados

The publisher would like to thank the following for their kind permission to reproduce their photographs:

Calvin & Hobbes: p. 21. **Cartoonstock:** p. 29. **CRITE, Rohan Allan:** p. 48. **FGV:** p. 25. **Garfield, Jim Davis:** p. 114. **Glasbergen:** p. 115. **iStock:** capa, p. 9, 10, 17, 27, 35, 45, 52, 53, 63, 71, 80, 128. **JumpStart:** p. 15. **Lynn Johnston:** p. 107. **Marketingland:** p. 79. **OECD:** p. 25. **Shutterstock:** p. 80.

Every effort has been made to trace the copyright holders and we apologize in advance for any unintentional omissions. We would be pleased to insert the appropriate acknowledgement in any subsequent edition of this publication.

Dados Internacionais de Catalogação na Publicação (CIP)
(Câmara Brasileira do Livro, SP, Brasil)

Expand 2: Student's Book / Carla Maurício Vianna, Henrick Oprea. -- São Paulo: Pearson Education do Brasil, 2019.

ISBN 978-65-50110-32-1

1. Inglês (Ensino médio) I. Oprea, Henrick. II. Título.

19-25482   CDD-420.7

Índices para catálogo sistemático:
1. Inglês: Ensino Médio 420.7
Maria Alice Ferreira - Bibliotecária - CRB-8/7964

ISBN 978-65-50110-32-1 (Student's Book & Workbook)
ISBN 978-65-50110-33-8 (Teacher's Book)

2019

EXPAND 2

- Unit 1 9
- Unit 2 17
- Review 1 25

- Unit 3 27
- Unit 4 35
- Review 2 43

- Unit 5 45
- Unit 6 53
- Review 3 61

- Unit 7 63
- Unit 8 71
- Review 4 79

Grammar Overview 81
Language Reference 85
Reading Strategies 93
Irregular Verbs 94
Common Mistakes 96
False Friends 98
Glossary 99
Workbook 104
Audio Scripts 136

CONTENTS

	READING	VOCABULARY IN USE	LANGUAGE IN USE 1	EXPAND YOUR READING	LANGUAGE IN USE 2	LISTENING COMPREHENSION
UNIT 1 **Hooked on Social Media** page 9	Informative article: Forget FOMO! We're now more likely to suffer from FOJI, MOMO and JOMO (and it's all social media's fault)	Phrasal verbs and adjectives + *to*	Present perfect	Blog post: How I Overcame Social Media Anxiety	Past continuous and simple past	A radio program about fighting social media addiction
UNIT 2 **The Rocky Road of Good Urban Transportation** page 17	News article: a competition between a driver and a bus passenger to cross London	Prefixes	Modal verbs *can* and *could*	News report: With bikes, transit, Uber unveils urban transportation vision	Zero and first conditionals	News about a self-driving car running over a pedestrian

Review 1 (Units 1-2) Page 25

	READING	VOCABULARY IN USE	LANGUAGE IN USE 1	EXPAND YOUR READING	LANGUAGE IN USE 2	LISTENING COMPREHENSION
UNIT 3 **Generation Z: Conservative or Liberal?** page 27	Informative article: Conservative or Liberal? For Generation Z, It's Not That Simple	Collocations with *make* and *do*	Relative clauses	Interview about Dr. Jean Twenge's book on the iGeneration	*So* for cause and result	A guide to generations
UNIT 4 **What's Going Abroad Like?** page 35	Informative article: Undiscovered destinations: Now that's what I call off the beaten track	Idioms related to travel	*Have to* and *need to*	Blog post: Why the tourism industry has to change and how you can help it do so	Tag questions	Jason Moore interviews Tim Leffel about the ins and outs of living abroad

Review 2 (Units 3-4) Page 43

Grammar Review page 81

Language Reference page 85

Reading Strategies page 93

Irregular Verbs page 94

	READING	VOCABULARY IN USE	LANGUAGE IN USE 1	EXPAND YOUR READING	LANGUAGE IN USE 2	LISTENING COMPREHENSION
UNIT 5 **What the Future Holds** page 45	Testimonials: Professors' opinions on what universities will be like 10 years from now	Adverbs: suffix -ly	*Will* vs. *be going to*	Survey: Workforce of the Future	*May, might, could*	A testimonial about taking a gap year
UNIT 6 **It's Time We Reforested the Agribusiness** page 53	Informative article, facts and figures: Agribusiness issue	Collocations with *get* and *set*	Passive voice	Encyclopedia entry: Agroforestry	Discourse markers	News about Brazil's position as an agricultural powerhouse

Review 3 (Units 5-6)
page 61

	READING	VOCABULARY IN USE	LANGUAGE IN USE 1	EXPAND YOUR READING	LANGUAGE IN USE 2	LISTENING COMPREHENSION
UNIT 7 **The Economic Effects of Globalization** page 63	Opinion article: The globalization counter-reaction	Vocabulary related to economy	Present perfect - *since* / *for*	Infographic: A tale of two economies	Present perfect vs. simple past	An interview about financial crisis
UNIT 8 **Spotting Fake News among the Real Stories** page 71	News report: Facebook has a fake news 'war room' – but is it really working?	Vocabulary related to fake news	Verb tense review	Narrative essay: Experience: I write fake news	Embedded questions	A teacher's talk about how to identify real news

Review 4 (Units 7-8)
page 79

Common Mistakes	False Friends	Glossary	Workbook	Audio Scripts
page 96	page 98	page 99	page 104	page 136

PRESENTATION

STUDENT'S BOOK

Welcome to the *Expand* collection! *Expand* prepares students for the English part of Brazilian exams ENEM and vestibular, which are aimed at testing students' ability to read a wide variety of authentic texts of different genres. *Expand* provides students with listening, speaking, and writing activities that help them to develop their overall knowledge of the language. Each thematic unit contains two reading sections that introduce grammar and vocabulary topics, as well as listening comprehension activities that give students contact with oral text genres.

OPENING PAGE

Each unit starts with an opening page containing:

IN THIS UNIT YOU WILL…

This shows the main objectives for the unit.

LEAD OFF

This section presents three to four questions for content contextualization.

> **IN THIS UNIT YOU WILL…**
> - talk about social media addiction;
> - exchange ideas about how one can overcome social media anxiety;
> - learn how to use the present perfect;
> - talk about completed actions in the past using the simple past;
> - describe actions in progress in the past using the past continuous.

LEAD OFF
- How can you relate the picture to the title of this unit?
- Why is there so much concern about the excessive use of social media nowadays?
- In your opinion, is social media addictive? Why (not)?
- Are you a social network addict? How can you tell?

READING PAGES

This two-page section contains the first reading text and activities of the unit. It develops reading strategies and is subdivided into the following stages:

BEFORE READING

This section contains one or two activities that help students to prepare for the text topic, which is presented in the section WHILE READING.

WHILE READING

In this section students read a text and answer a question related to it. Texts are in a variety of different genres and aimed at developing several reading strategies.

READING

» BEFORE READING *Relating to the topic*

Read the first paragraph of the online article "How owning a car might soon become as old-fashioned as owing a horse." Then exchange ideas with your classmates whether you agree with the message conveyed or not.

» WHILE READING — *Identifying the author's tone*

Read the text and classify the author's tone as mocking, apprehensive, vindictive, or humorous. Underline the fragments that support your answer. *Identifying the author's tone*

The 1914 effect
The globalization counter-reaction
*Globalization is a highly **disruptive** force. It provoked a reaction in the early 20th century. Are we seeing a repeat?*
Buttonwood's notebook
Jun 14th 2017 | by Buttonwood

AFTER READING

This section has comprehension activities to help develop different after-reading strategies related to reading comprehension. These strategies are presented next to the instruction for each reading activity.

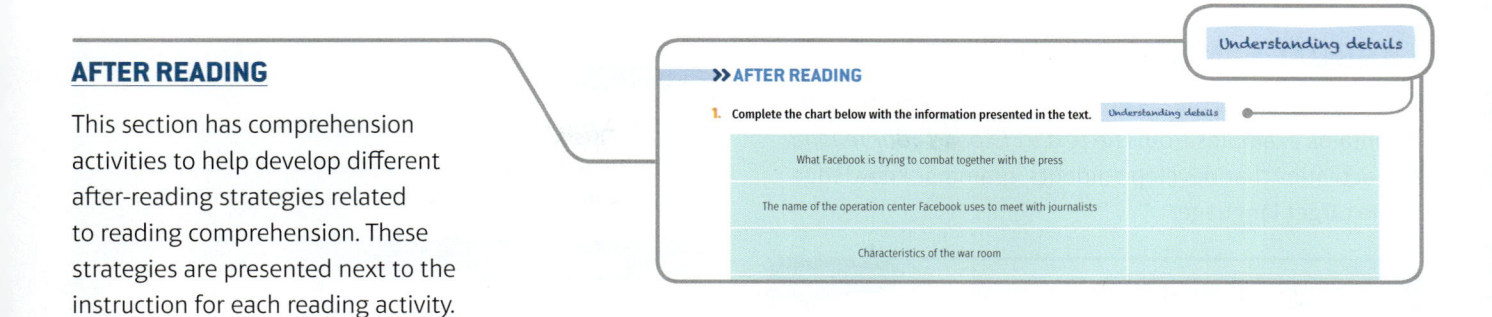

VOCABULARY PAGES

This stage develops students' vocabulary through activities containing vocabulary from the text and related to the topic of the unit.

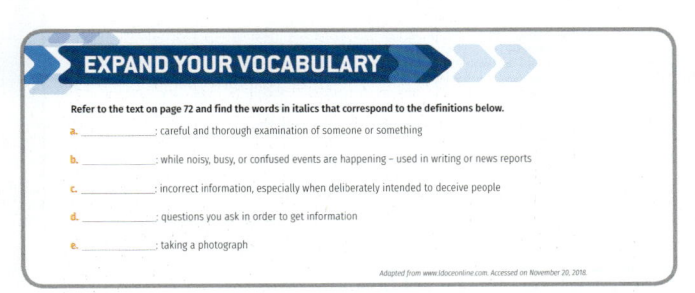

EXPAND YOUR VOCABULARY

This section contains one to three activities related to the vocabulary presented in the text. It also prompts students to engage in conversational topics based on the text they have read.

VOCABULARY IN USE

Here students are presented with an example of target vocabulary taken from the main reading text and do activities to develop their vocabulary knowledge.

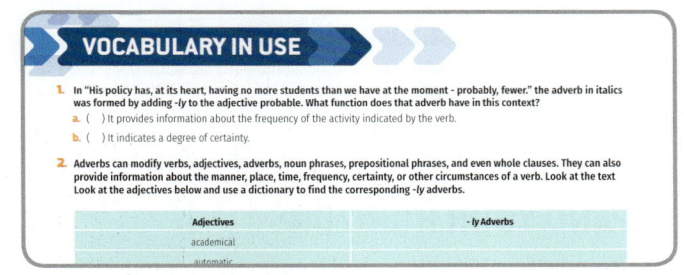

LANGUAGE IN USE 1

This page presents the first grammar topic of the unit. It contains examples from the text and activities that develop students' grammar knowledge in the target language.

EXPAND YOUR READING

This section contains another text for students to work on both the text genre and comprehension.

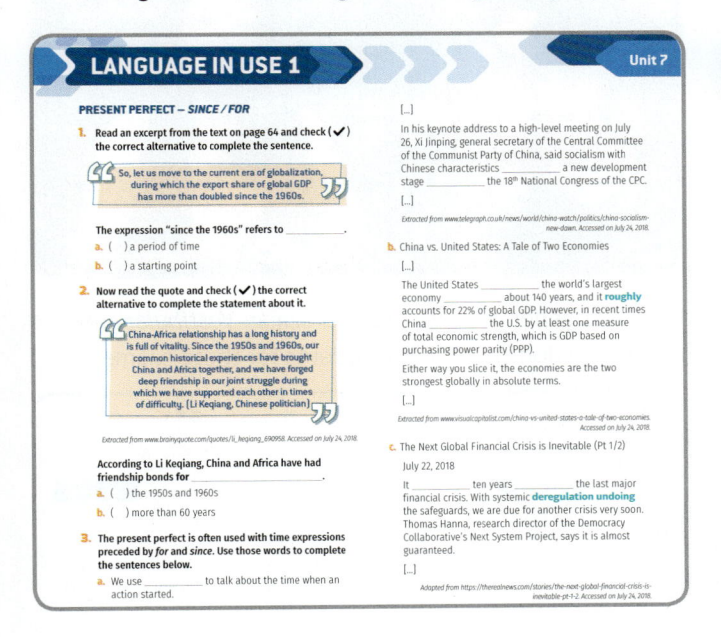

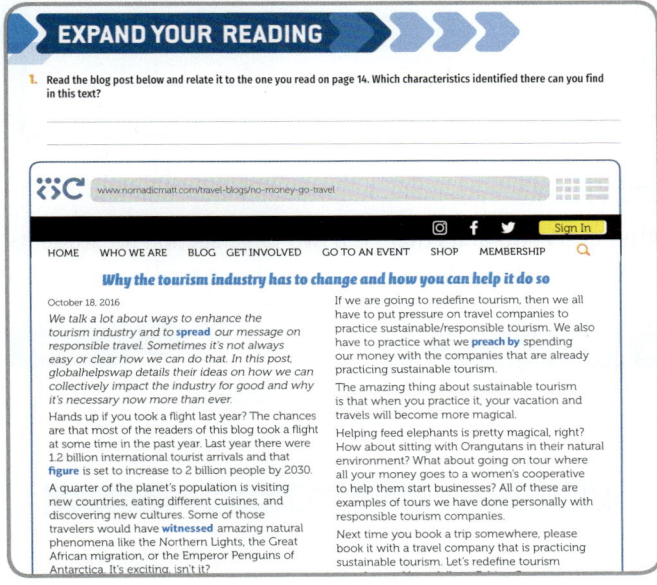

PRESENTATION

LANGUAGE IN USE 2

This page presents the second grammar topic of the unit. It contains examples from the text in *Expand your reading* and activities that develop students' grammar knowledge in the target language.

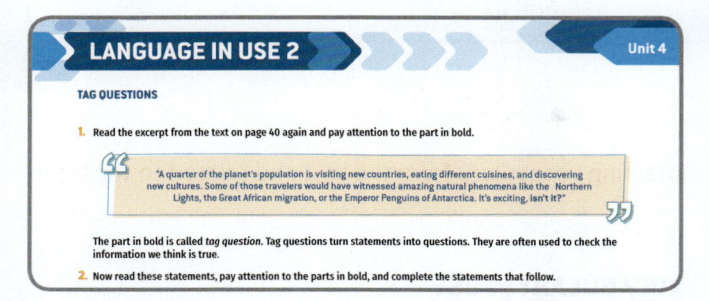

LISTENING COMPREHENSION

This section contains listening activities with authentic texts aimed at developing students' listening skills.

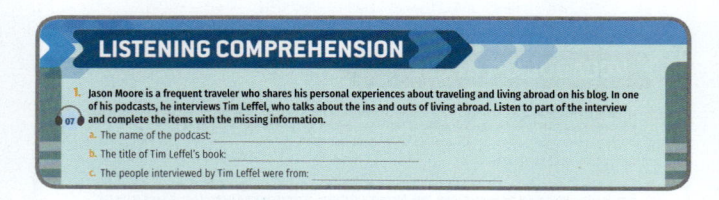

EXPAND YOUR HORIZONS

In this end-of-unit section, students are presented with three statements that allow them to discuss the topic in the listening comprehension section and think critically about it while using the target language.

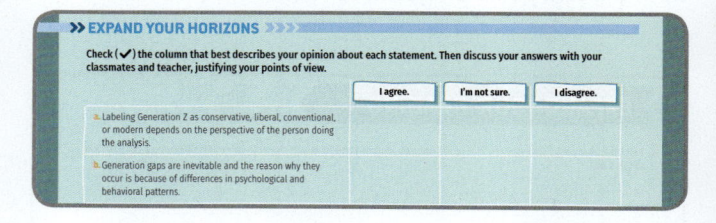

REVIEW

After every two units there is a two-page section for students to review and practice the language they have learned so far.

WORKBOOK

Each unit has four pages of reading, vocabulary, and grammar activities. It also has an ENEM or vestibular question in the section AN EYE ON ENEM / VESTIBULAR.

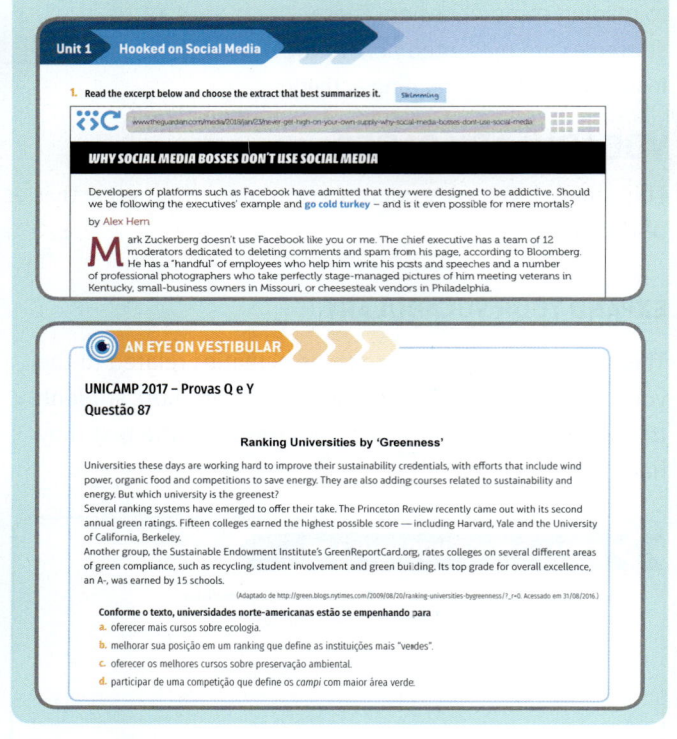

DIGITAL COMPONENTS

Video lessons for all *Language in Use* and *Vocabulary in Use* sections and for exam practice.

Mock test generator with major Brazilian *Vestibular* and ENEM questions to prepare students for these exams.

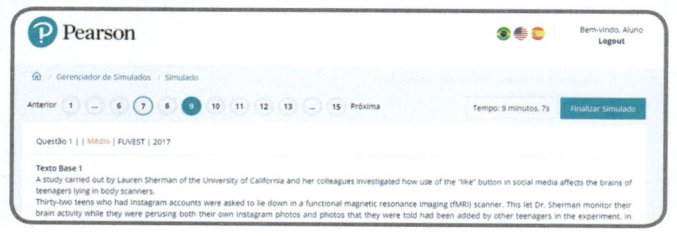

UNIT 1
Hooked on Social Media

IN THIS UNIT YOU WILL...

- talk about social media addiction;
- exchange ideas about how one can overcome social media anxiety;
- learn how to use the present perfect;
- learn some phrasal verbs and adjectives with *to*;
- talk about completed actions in the past using the simple past;
- describe actions in progress in the past using the past continuous.

LEAD OFF

> How can you relate the picture to the title of this unit?
> Why is there so much concern about the excessive use of social media nowadays?
> In your opinion, is social media addictive? Why (not)?
> Are you a social network addict? How can you tell?

READING

BEFORE READING

Look at the picture on the right, which shows some messaging platforms, some apps and brands, and social media, and name the social networks you once were or are a member of. What others would you add to this list?

Activating previous knowledge

WHILE READING

Skim the text and identify its probable target audience.

Skimming to identify target audience

Forget FOMO! We're now more likely to suffer from FOJI, MOMO and JOMO (and it's all social media's fault)

By UNITY BLOTT FOR MAILONLINE

PUBLISHED: 07:28 GMT, 22 JANUARY 2016 | UPDATED: 09:47 GMT, 22 JANUARY 2016

It was hailed as one of the biggest causes of social anxiety of our generation.

FOMO - shorthand for *fear* of missing out - which fell into our collective vocabulary in 2011, is the acute and often unjustified belief that everyone is having more fun than you, and that you're somehow being left out of all the fun.

But this affliction, thought to be caused by social media where you see endless status updates and photos of your friends showing off their (supposedly) happier, more exciting lives, is just the tip of the worry iceberg.

In fact, FOMO has become such a problem that recent studies suggest it can manifest as a genuine form of social anxiety and even lead to an increased risk of alcohol abuse and depression among certain age groups.

But now *commentators* are suggesting that FOMO is just the tip of the iceberg when it comes to social media-related acronyms.

There is now a whole *range* of afflictions caused by all the fun your friends are having on Facebook, Instagram, Twitter and Snapchat - and the chances are, you're suffering from at least one of them.

[...]

FOMOMO: Fear of the mystery of missing out

A more extreme case of FOMO that occurs only when your phone is broken or out of battery. According to the Guardian, it means you're afraid of missing out, but not because of what you see on social media - it's what you don't see that's causing you real angst.

[...]

MOMO: Mystery of missing out

This is the paranoia that *arises* when your friends don't post anything on social media at all. Instead, you're left with no option but to *scroll* obsessively through your Facebook and Twitter timelines searching for clues.

[...]

FOJI: Fear of joining in

The polar opposite to MOMO; if you suffer from FOJI, you're far less likely to keep your friends updated on Facebook and Instagram because you're not quite sure what to post and you're worried that nobody will like or comment on your photos.

BROMO: When your 'bros' (friends) protect you from missing out

An act of solidarity from your friends. If they've been out the night before, they'll deliberately refrain from posting photos of the fun they were having, for fear of making you feel left out.

SLOMO: Slow to missing out

In this case, your anxiety is probably justified. Everybody is having a better time than you, but you're asleep so you don't know it until the next morning when you log into Facebook and find your timeline littered with photos of the night before.

JOMO: The joy of missing out

Taking pleasure in 'missing out' by not feeling like you have to be everywhere at once. Instead, you're quite content with staying in bed with a cup of tea and a book.

Extracted from www.dailymail.co.uk/femail/article-3410074/Forget-FOMO-FOJI-MOMO-JOMO-new-anxieties-caused-social-media.html. Accessed on November 19, 2018.

Unit 1

» AFTER READING

1. Check (✓) the statement that defines FOMO.   *Understanding main ideas*
   a. ( ) Those who have FOMO are afraid of being without their phones and unable to contact their social media friends.
   b. ( ) Someone who has FOMO believes that other people's lives are more interesting than their own life.
   c. ( ) If someone has FOMO, this person is afraid that his/her friends are having fun, but they are not telling him/her.

2. The author mentions two severe consequences of FOMO. What are they?   *Understanding details*
   _____
   _____

3. Read the description of the afflictions caused by social media again. Then read the testimonials below and match them with one of the acronyms. In small groups, say how you think the people feel about the their affliction.   *Understanding details and evaluating a text critically*
   a. "When I woke up today, I saw my friends' post on Instagram about a party they went to last night. I'm glad they didn't invite me, because I really needed to stay at home and relax by myself."
   b. "I'm so mad today! My friends went to a concert without inviting me! I am being bombarded with all these pictures on my timeline showing them having a great time."
   c. "OMG! I left my phone at home! Now how will I know where my friends are and what they are doing?"
   d. "I'll post a picture of my healthy lunch. Wait, who wants to know what I eat? Nobody will like my picture. My friends don't care about it. Forget it, I won't post anything."

   ( ) SLOMO   ( ) FOMOMO   ( ) JOMO   ( ) FOJI

EXPAND YOUR VOCABULARY

1. Refer to the text on page 10 and find words in italics that match the definitions below. Then use one of them to complete both blanks in the quote.
   a. _____ : people who know a lot about a particular subject, and who write about it or discuss it on the television or radio
   b. _____ : a number of people or things that are all different, but are all of the same general type
   c. _____ : begins to happen
   d. _____ : the feeling you get when you are afraid or worried that something bad is going to happen
   e. _____ : to move information on a computer or phone screen up or down so that you can read it

   Adapted from www.ldoceonline.com. Accessed on November 19, 2018.

   > Internet freedom is not possible without freedom from _____, and users will not be free from _____ unless they are sufficiently protected from online **theft** and attack.
   > Rebecca MacKinnon

   Extracted from www.brainyquote.com. Accessed on November 19, 2018.

2. In pairs, read the quote again. Do you share Rebecca MacKinnon's opinion? Justify your view.
   _____
   _____

VOCABULARY IN USE

1. In the extract "But this affliction, thought to be caused by social media where you see endless status updates and photos of your friends showing off their (supposedly) happier, more exciting lives, is just the tip of the worry iceberg", *showing off* is a phrasal verb (or a multi word verb). Phrasal verbs are...

   a. ( ) made of two words. The first one is a particle (a preposition or an adverb) and the second one is a verb.

   b. ( ) made of two or more words. The first one is a verb and the second (and sometimes third) one is a particle (a preposition or an adverb).

2. Below you will find phrasal verbs with one or more particles. Complete the definitions and examples with the same phrasal verb from the box.

   > come up with   filter out   log off / out   log on
   > plug in   run out   sign up   walk out on

   a. _____: to do the necessary actions on a computer system that will allow you to begin using it

   You need to _____ before you start using this software.

   b. _____: to use all of something and not have any more left

   You can borrow my batteries in case you _____.

   c. _____: to connect a piece of electrical equipment to the main supply of electricity, or to another piece of electrical equipment

   I thought my printer wasn't working, but I had just forgotten to _____ it _____. What a relief!

   d. _____: to stop doing something you have agreed to do or that you are responsible for

   From our point of view, it's unethical to _____ a deal.

   e. _____: to do the actions that are necessary when you finish using a computer system

   Is it safe not to _____ of social media accounts on one's personal laptop?

   f. _____: to think of an idea, answer, etc.

   The students were asked to _____ ideas on how to protect themselves from internet addiction.

   g. _____: to put your name on a list for something because you want to take part in it

   They wanted to take an IT course, but it was necessary to _____ for it beforehand.

   h. _____: to remove words, information, etc. that you do not need or want

   I'm searching for a software program that might help me _____ unwanted emails.

   Extracted from www.ldoceonline.com. Accessed on July 6, 2018.

3. In English, some adjectives are usually followed by certain prepositions. Read the extract from the text on page 10 and circle the *adjective + preposition* combination.

   > "The polar opposite to MOMO; if you suffer from FOJI, you're far less likely to keep your friends updated on Facebook and Instagram because you're not quite sure what to post [...]."

4. Here are some other examples of adjectives that often go with the preposition *to*. Read them and complete the sentences.

   > addicted   generous   rude   similar

   a. Social networking has such a huge impact on the real world that its craving is considered _____ the cravings for cigarettes and alcohol.

   b. A great number of social media users don't follow netiquettes and are _____ other users.

   c. Ken is so _____ surfing the Net that he doesn't even stop doing that when he is having his meals.

   d. My virtual friends have been _____ me as far as attention is concerned. I could count on their support to listen to me every time I needed it.

5. Finish the paragraph below. Use at least one *phrasal verb* and one *adjective + preposition* combination you learned in this section.

   Some people turn to social media interactions...

   _____
   _____
   _____
   _____
   _____
   _____

LANGUAGE IN USE 1

Unit 1

PRESENT PERFECT

1. The excerpt below was extracted from the text on page 10. Read it, paying special attention to the part in bold, and check (✓) the correct answer to the question that follows.

> [...] FOMO **has become** such a problem that recent studies suggest it can manifest as a genuine form of social anxiety [...]

Why is the present perfect tense used in this extract?

a. (   ) To talk about something that had happened at a specific time in the past.

b. (   ) To talk about something that started in the past and continues up to now.

2. Read a fragment about teens and social media addiction and underline other examples of the present perfect tense. Then choose the correct alternative to complete the sentences.

> Teenage social media addiction can be described as a preoccupation and obsession. A teenager with a social media addiction has become so engrossed in the virtual world that it has impacted the real world, causing harmful effects. While many teens engage in social media through platforms such as Facebook, Twitter, YouTube, Snapchat, and others, teens who are addicted to social media see a negative impact on their real-life relationships and responsibilities. [...]

Adapted from www.shepherdshillacademy.org/resources/teens-social-media-addiction. Accessed on July 7, 2018.

a. In the extract above, the present perfect refers to actions that started at a / an _____ (specific / unspecific) time in the past and continue up to the present. They indicate changes that have happened over a period of time and have consequences in the _____ (present / future).

b. To form the present perfect, we use the auxiliary verb - _____ (does / have) or *has* - and the main verb in the past participle. In questions, the _____ (main / auxiliary) verb and the subject are inverted and in negative sentences, we use *not* after the auxiliary verb.

c. The particles *'ve* and *'s* are the contracted forms in _____ (affirmative / interrogative) sentences while *haven't* and *hasn't* are the contracted forms in negative sentences.

d. Some adverbs such as _____ (ever / now), *never*, *already*, *yet*, etc. are commonly used with the present perfect.

3. Use the verbs from the box in the present perfect to complete the text. Refer to the list of irregular verbs on pages 94 and 95 if necessary.

> come   find   see   spark   warn

Neurochemically, smartphone addiction is real - Now what?

We'_____ all _____ it: crowds of people walking with their heads bent, thumbs frantically scrolling, eyes **glazed**. Smartphones and social media take up hours of time in the average person's day.

Now, scientists _____ a connection between smartphone use and neurochemical imbalances in the brain. [...]

For years, scientists and researchers _____ about the possible negative effects of staring at screens for too many hours a day. From the very first video games to the latest virtual reality experiences, every new piece of technology _____ with **pundits** questioning their safety.

Yet, no smart device _____ the word "addiction" more than the smartphone. Many recent articles state that smartphone and social media addiction isn't just real, but that it's commonplace.

[...]

Extracted from https://fightaddictionnow.org/blog/smartphone-social-media-addiction-new-face-dependence. Accessed on July 7, 2018.

4. Work in pairs. Use the present perfect tense to answer the questions below. Then report your answers to the class.

a. Have you ever noticed any signs of social media addiction among your friends? If so, how have you tried to help him/her?

b. Have you ever received offensive or intimidating messages through social media? If so, why has that happened?

c. Some schools have used social media for informational and educational purposes. How has that happened at your school? Have you benefited from it?

EXPAND YOUR READING

1. Look at the text below briefly and check (✓) the elements you can see.

a. (   ) menu or navigation bar

b. (   ) publication date

c. (   ) latest update date

d. (   ) icons for network sharing

e. (   ) writer's credentials

---

https://www.belivingbelieving.com/2017/12/27/how-i-overcame-social-media-anxiety-part-1/

beliving & believing

How I Overcame Social Media Anxiety

[...] Susan 📅 December 27, 2017. 💬 No Comments

Instagram

I love pictures. I always took pictures growing up and when I discovered Instagram I'd post about my family, friends, and myself just living life because I wanted to share what God was doing in my life. I'd also ask people to snap a photo of me because we'd be at a cool monument or on vacation. And a lot of my feed was about highlighting peoples' qualities with a nice picture of them. Then passive aggressive **remarks** started coming: "You think you're pretty, huh?" [...] "Don't be fake." The comments and questions were unnecessary and in **hindsight** it was just a projection of themselves.

But, I had people-pleasing problems. I believed their words even though they weren't true. I didn't know how to navigate through it so the best thing I thought to do was delete all the photos that seemed to make everyone feel uncomfortable. I decided to post **landscapes** and food only. Though I loved sharing about my family, I didn't want others to think I was showing off, so I stopped.

The Problem

I had fear of peoples' opinions of what they believed I was doing while posting photos and sharing testimonies. Social media *exposed* the deep-rooted fear in me – how much I cared about others' negative opinions about me and my life. [...]

Adapted from www.belivingbelieving.com/2017/12/27/how-i-overcame-social-media-anxiety-part-1. Accessed on July 7, 2018.

---

2. Read the text carefully. Based on the layout clues, tone, and content of the text, where do you think it was published? Why do you think so?

_____

_____

_____

_____

3. Read the text once again and underline the correct statements about blog posts.

a. Blog posts often appear on the website in chronological order.

b. Readers can't write comments expressing their opinions about what they've read.

c. Blog posts might include images, hyperlinks, or links to other blogs.

d. Blog posts can be written in many genres such as testimonials, poems, travel diaries, etc.

e. They are very formal pieces of writing and must be arranged in justified alignment.

LANGUAGE IN USE 2

Unit 1

PAST CONTINUOUS and SIMPLE PAST

1. Read the extracts from the blog post on page 14 and check (✓) the correct endings to the sentences about the past continuous.

> I'd post about my family, friends, and myself just living life because I wanted to share what God **was doing** in my life.

> Though I loved sharing about my family, I didn't want others to think I **was showing off**, so I stopped.

a. In both extracts, the past continuous is used to talk about…

( ) finished actions in the past.

( ) actions in progress in the past.

b. To form the past continuous, we use…

( ) *was / were* + main verb in the *-ing* form.

( ) *did / didn't* + main verb in the *-ing* form.

c. The past continuous is frequently used with the simple past with *when* and *while*. In this case, the past continuous describes…

( ) a shorter action or event, while the simple past describes a longer action or situation.

( ) a longer action or situation, while the simple past describes a shorter action or event.

2. Circle the finished actions or states and underline the actions that were in progress in the past in the strips below. Then exchange ideas about the comic strips with a classmate.

Extracted from www.amureprints.com/reprints/results?terms=facebook&feature_codes%5B%5D=jt&release_date_from=&release_date_to=&commit=Search. Accessed on July 8, 2018.

3. Read part of a text by the entrepreneur Jason Zook about his 30-day social media detox and use the verbs from the box in the simple past or past continuous to fill in the blanks.

decide	do	feel	hit
roll down		stare	

Day One of living without social media:

All notifications were turned off. All apps were removed. And I _____ an immediate feeling of freedom living without social media.

I could feel myself wanting to go to Facebook, Twitter, and Instagram, especially on this day because I had just relaunched my personal website the day before (the timing was not only impeccable, it was planned).

After what felt like a few grueling hours, I had spent 30 minutes answering e-mails. One of my first realizations was just how much time can be wasted browsing social networks without knowing it. I could feel myself wanting to sneak a peek at Facebook, so I _____ to get up from my desk and run an errand.

Most of us don't even realize how much we're checking things while driving. I probably glanced down at my phone 20 times during the course of an eight-minute drive. Then I _____ a stoplight. Like a drug addict reaching for his/her fix, I scooped my phone up from the cupholder and swiped it open. It wasn't until I _____ at a barren Home screen, devoid of red notification icons, that I realized what I _____. I closed the phone and put it back in the cupholder. I took notice of how beautiful of a day it was. I _____ the windows and took the moment of beauty in, completely understanding how often I take for granted amazing weather and a moment of stillness.

Adapted from https://jasondoesstuff.com/social-media-detox-recap. Accessed on July 8, 2018.

4. Suppose you were having social media addiction problems and had to disconnect from all social networks for a week. How easy or hard would it be for you and why?

LISTENING COMPREHENSION

1. **Read the sentences below. What do those conditions have in common? What do you know about them? Exchange your opinions with a classmate.**

   _____ smartphone _____
   _____
   _____
   _____

   > **FOMO** (Fear Of Missing Out) is the compulsion to be constantly connected to social media so as not to miss anything.
   >
   > **Nomophobia** is the fear of leaving your phone at home.
   >
   > **Sleep texting** happens when people send text messages while they're sleeping.
   >
   > **Phantom vibration syndrome** occurs when people think their phones vibrate when in fact they do not.
   >
   > Based on mobileworldcapital.com/2013/09/25/180. Accessed on July 8, 2018.

2. **Listen to part of a radio program about fighting social media addiction. Which of the conditions in activity 1 does it talk about?** (02)

   _____
   _____

3. **Listen to the second part of the program and mark the statements true (T) or false (F).** (03)

   a. ( ) British teenagers spend more than twice the time they used to on social media.
   b. ( ) About 30% of teenagers are constantly online in the USA.
   c. ( ) According to a survey carried out by the Australian Psychological Society, most teenagers suffer from FOMO.
   d. ( ) Another study says that using social media at night can affect your sleep.
   e. ( ) Although most of the results of studies were negative, the Australian researchers found that using social media can also bring benefits to teens' lives.

4. **Read the transcript of both audios on page 136. Have you ever felt the symptoms described in the studies? Do you agree that social media has been affecting teens' lives negatively more than positively? Justify.**

   _____
   _____
   _____
   _____
   _____

❯❯ EXPAND YOUR HORIZONS ❯❯❯❯

Check (✔) the column that best describes your opinion about each statement. Then discuss your answers with your classmates and teacher, justifying your point of view.

	I agree.	I'm not sure.	I disagree.
a. Smartphone addiction, FOMO, and other disorders are a growing problem nowadays, especially for teenagers.			
b. Social media are, in fact, extensions of being social.			
c. Joining social media isn't necessarily a bad thing if one doesn't make it a priority and manages to spend time doing more important things.			

UNIT 2
The Rocky Road of Good Urban Transportation

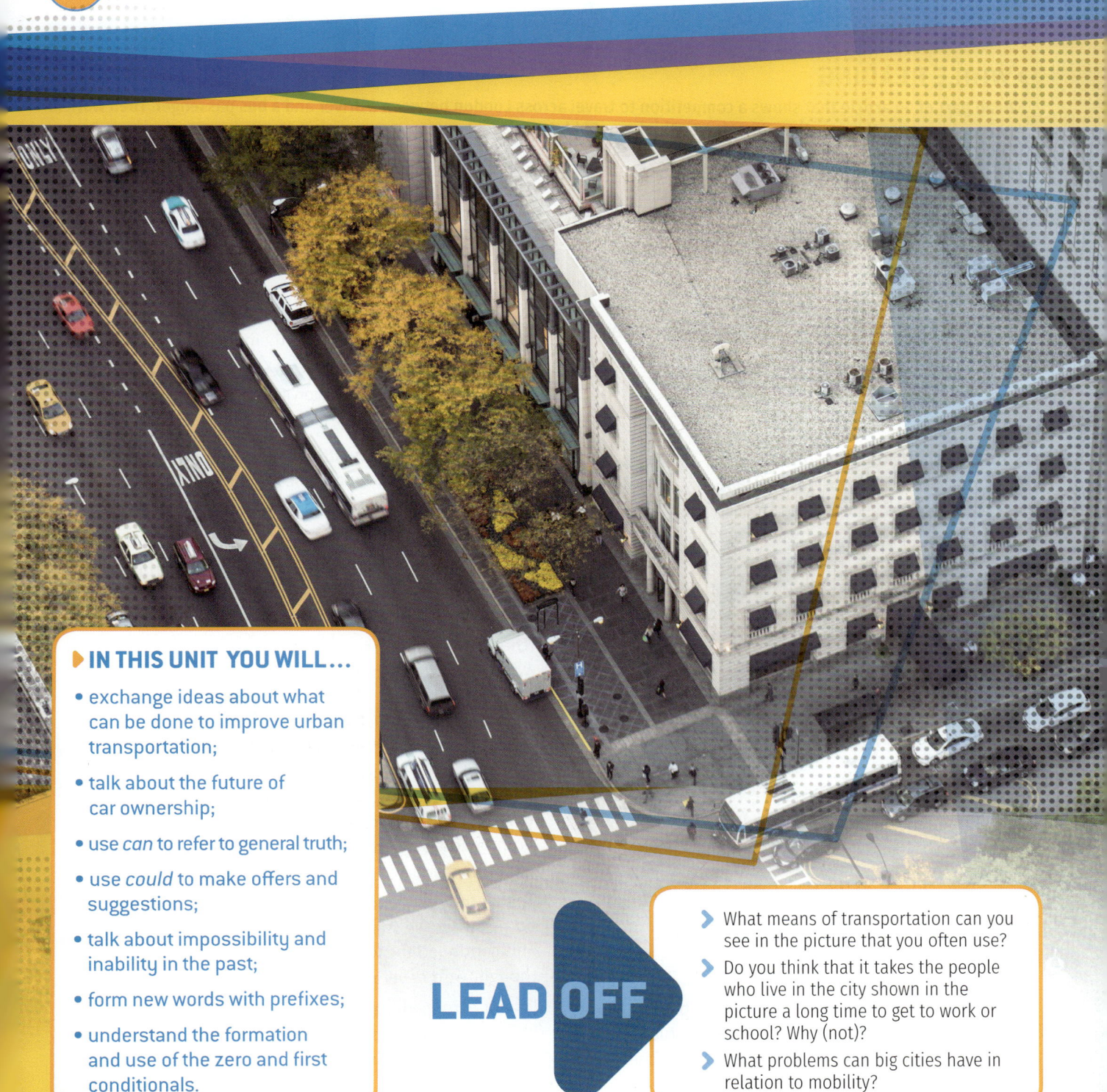

▶ IN THIS UNIT YOU WILL...

- exchange ideas about what can be done to improve urban transportation;
- talk about the future of car ownership;
- use *can* to refer to general truth;
- use *could* to make offers and suggestions;
- talk about impossibility and inability in the past;
- form new words with prefixes;
- understand the formation and use of the zero and first conditionals.

LEAD OFF

- What means of transportation can you see in the picture that you often use?
- Do you think that it takes the people who live in the city shown in the picture a long time to get to work or school? Why (not)?
- What problems can big cities have in relation to mobility?

READING

▸▸ BEFORE READING

Read the first paragraph of the online article "How owning a car might soon become as old-fashioned as owing a horse." Then discuss with your classmates whether you agree with the message conveyed or not.

Relating to the topic

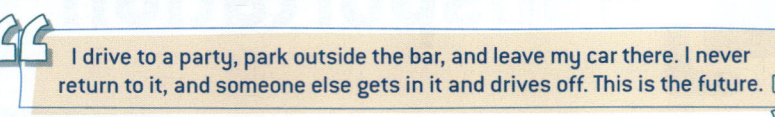

> " I drive to a party, park outside the bar, and leave my car there. I never return to it, and someone else gets in it and drives off. This is the future. "

Extracted from www.independent.co.uk/life-style/gadgets-and-tech/how-owning-a-car-might-soon-become-as-old-fashioned-as-owning-a-horse-a7195836.html. Accessed on September 18, 2018.

▸▸ WHILE READING

Read part of an article that shows a competition to travel across London between a driver and a bus passenger. Then work in pairs and answer the question: Who do you think would like to read it?

Identifying the target audience

DRIVER: 17 MINS 41 SECS

Two-and-a-half million Londoners own cars — but car ownership is declining.

With so many alternative ways of getting around, driving is reserved for those who don't have a choice
5 — such as the elderly or disabled, or those who do it for a living.

[...]

The challenger: Vittorio Frediani, 43, a security driver from South-West London.

10 I'm behind the wheel all day, every day. I see the best and worst of the city roads — and there are definitely more bad than good.

London is becoming impossible for motorists. Roads that used to flow freely have been **narrowed** so
15 much by cycle lanes that there's always solid traffic. London might be cyclist-friendly, but it's becoming car-unfriendly.

I started neck-and-neck with Dan's bike and we followed the same route past Buckingham Palace.
20 Then he veered off onto his (**rather** empty) cycle lane. I felt like my car was surrounded by a swarm of cyclists, cutting me off at every corner. You can't take your eyes off the road for a second, even to check the sat nav. Unlike them, I couldn't cut corners, and instead ended
25 up in gridlock on The Mall. Then I spent another ten minutes in search of a parking space before sprinting to the finish line. What a nightmare!

BUS PASSENGER: 18 MINS 20 SECS

London's public transport system is its beating heart,
30 so heavily do its residents rely on buses, Tubes and trains. But travelling this way doesn't come cheap — with a Tube journey costing £2.90 with an Oyster or contactless card, or £4.90 with cash.

For large families, those on a lower **income** or children
35 travelling alone — who only get free Tube travel until the age 11 — buses are the only way to get around, with a single fare costing just £1.50. However, cyclists can use bus lanes, too, slowing them down.

There are 8,000 buses on 700 different routes in London,
40 and commuters take 1.8 billion journeys every year.

[...]

**The challenger: Vicky Allen, 24, an office manager from South-East London. She's lived in the capital all her life but only started commuting, to a new
45 job in the City, last month.**

I used to work near where I live, so I'm new to this route — and that means I don't have the patience of someone who's done this for years.

There's nothing worse than having to stand the
50 whole way while a bus driver jerks around corners and stops abruptly — it makes me feel sick. The No. 38 bus goes from Victoria to Piccadilly, so my route was straightforward. Buses come every 20 minutes and I got lucky, with one pulling up minutes after
55 I had arrived at the stop. I even got a seat — a miracle in rush hour! — but it soon filled up with grumpy-looking commuters, many of whom were forced to stand.

The journey was smooth until we reached Hyde Park
60 Corner, when we started crawling at a snail's pace. This continued the whole way along Piccadilly — I thought we'd never get there!

I'm not surprised I came last. But it does seem unfair that bus routes are clogged with cyclists —
65 they should stick to their own lanes.

Adapted from www.dailymail.co.uk/news/article-5884743/Ready-steady-GRIDLOCK-SARAH-RAINEY-puts-public-transport-test.html. Accessed on January 4, 2019.

Unit 2

>> **AFTER READING**

1. Read the questions below and check (✓) the correct alternative. *Understanding main ideas*
Which commuter...

  a. was the last one to arrive?　　　　　　　　( ) Bus passenger　　　　( ) Driver
  b. says London is a difficult city to drive?　　( ) Bus passenger　　　　( ) Driver
  c. says London is cyclist-friendly?　　　　　　( ) Bus passenger　　　　( ) Driver
  d. refers to two different types of　　　　　　( ) Bus passenger　　　　( ) Driver
      transportation using the same lane?

2. Underline the statements that are correct according to the article. *Understanding details*

  a. More and more people are using cars in London.
  b. Because of the heavy traffic, it was difficult for the driver to take his eyes off the road.
  c. It can be expensive to use public transport in London, but buses are considered a quite cheap alternative.
  d. The bus passenger believes that the main problem in London is that cars and buses use the same lanes.

3. Discuss the following questions in pairs. Then report your answers to the class.

  a. Which commuter from the text on page 18 do you think has the most stressful journey? Why?
  b. Why do you think more and more people are looking for alternatives other than cars to commute in London?
  c. Which kind of transportation do you think would be the fastest in your city? Justify.

EXPAND YOUR VOCABULARY

1. Match the words in bold with their meanings.
  a. "I'm behind the **wheel** all day, every day."
  b. "[...] driving is reserved for those who don't have a choice — such as the elderly or **disabled** [...]."
  c. "Then I spent another ten minutes in search of a parking space before **sprinting** to the finish line."
  d. "Buses come every 20 minutes and I got lucky, with one **pulling up** minutes after I had arrived at the stop."
  e. The journey was **smooth** until we reached Hyde Park Corner, when we started crawling at a snail's pace."

  ( ) running fast for a short distance
  ( ) the round piece of equipment that you turn to make a car, ship etc. move in a particular direction
  ( ) happening or operating successfully, without any problems
  ( ) someone who cannot use a part of their body properly, or cannot learn easily
  ( ) stopping the vehicle that someone is driving

Adapted from www.ldoceonline.com. Accessed on January 4, 2019

2. Go back to the extract about the driver on page 18 and find a phrasal verb that has the following meaning:

> _____ : someone or something that was in a particular situation, state, or place after a series of events, especially when they did not plan it

Extracted from www.ldoceonline.com. Accessed on January 4 2019.

VOCABULARY IN USE

1. Read the following excerpt from the text on page 18 again and choose the best answer to the question.

> "London is becoming **impossible** for motorists. Roads that used to flow freely have been narrowed so much by cycle lanes that there's always solid traffic. London might be cyclist-friendly, but it's becoming car-**unfriendly**."

The prefixes *im-* and *un-* were added to the beginning of the words *possible* and *friendly* and formed new words with different meanings. For example, prefixes can create a new word opposite in meaning to the words they are attached to. They can also make words negative. In fact, every prefix has a meaning.

What are the prefixes *im-* and *un-* used for?
a. (   ) To show that someone does a job with someone else.
b. (   ) To show a negative, a lack, or an opposite.

2. Write the words below in the correct column according to their meaning. Then complete the chart with the corresponding prefix.

encourage	unimportant	amoral	enlarge	enable
uninterested	atypically	irresponsible	co-create	recreate
regroup	impolite	co-pilot	endanger	reclaim
insensitive	illegal	renew	inexperienced	

PREFIX(ES)					
MEANING	to make someone or something be in a particular state or have a particular quality	to do something with someone else as an equal or with less responsibility	the opposite or lack of something	again or back to a former state	not or without
EXAMPLES					

3. Read a shared mobility principle and underline three words formed by different prefixes from the ones in activity 2. Then match each prefix with its corresponding meaning.

"2. WE PRIORITIZE PEOPLE OVER VEHICLES.

The mobility of people and not vehicles shall be in the center of transportation planning and decision-making. Cities shall prioritize walking, cycling, public transportation, and other efficient shared mobility, as well as their interconnectivity. Cities shall discourage the use of cars, single-passenger taxis, and other oversized vehicles transporting one person."

Adapted from www.sharedmobilityprinciples.org. Accessed on September 20, 2018.

a. _____ : shows an opposite or negative

b. _____ : between or involving two or more different things, places, or people

c. _____ : too much

LANGUAGE IN USE 1

Unit 2

MODAL VERBS *CAN* and *COULD*

1. Work in pairs. Compare these excerpts from the article on page 18. Then complete the sentences with *can*, *can't*, *could*, and *couldn't*.

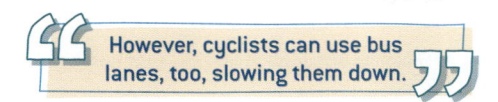

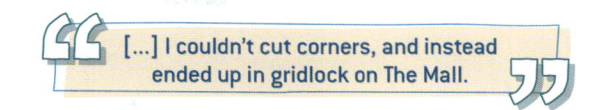

> "However, cyclists can use bus lanes, too, slowing them down."

> "[...] I couldn't cut corners, and instead ended up in gridlock on The Mall."

Can expresses what the speaker believes is a permission, a general truth or a strong possibility.
Could does not express a general truth. The speaker only wants to express a possibility or impossibility.

As seen in *Expand 1*, the modal verb *can* is used in the present. _____ is the past of _____. It is used to talk about an ability in the past or a possibility.

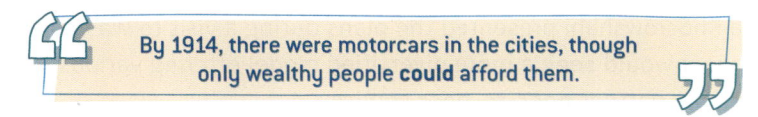

> "By 1914, there were motorcars in the cities, though only wealthy people **could** afford them."

_____ is the short form of *cannot*; _____ is the short form of *could not*. We use *couldn't* when we refer to a past impossibility, a past inability, or a polite present inability.

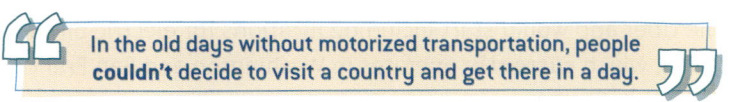

> "In the old days without motorized transportation, people **couldn't** decide to visit a country and get there in a day."

Could is also used to make suggestions and polite offers.

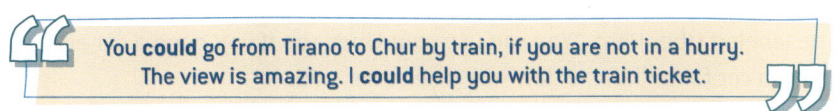

> "You **could** go from Tirano to Chur by train, if you are not in a hurry. The view is amazing. I **could** help you with the train ticket."

2. Read the comic strips below and complete them with the words from the box. There is an extra option.

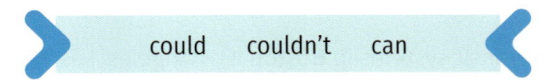

> could   couldn't   can

Panel 1: NOTHING MAKES ME MORE MAD THAN WASTING A GOOD HAIRCUT!
Panel 2: LAST SATURDAY I GOT A HAIRCUT SO I'D LOOK NICE FOR SCHOOL MONDAY MORNING..
Panel 3: THEN ON MONDAY I GOT SICK, AND I _____ GO TO SCHOOL FOR THREE DAYS.
Panel 4: I WASTED A GOOD HAIRCUT!

Extracted from www.gocomics.com/peanuts/1962/09/21. Accessed on September 20, 2018.

Panel 4: WELL, LEAST ONE OF US _____ GO HOME EARLY.

Extracted from http://www.bullspress.com/produkter-tjanster/produkter-tjanster/nemi/. Accessed on September 20, 2018.

EXPAND YOUR READING

1. Scan the text and answer: Where was it published? Is the full text presented here?

_____

www.dailymail.co.uk/wires/afp/article-5604689/With-bikes-transit-Uber-unveils-new-vision-urban-transport.html

With bikes, transit, Uber *unveils* urban transportation vision

By AFP   PUBLISHED: 18:57 BST, 11 April 2018 | UPDATED: 20:57 BST, 11 April 2018

Uber said Wednesday it plans to add mass transit, bike-sharing, and other options to its mobile app, as it unveiled a vision for urban transportation that goes well **beyond** its **core** ridesharing offer.

Chief executive Dara Khosrowshahi presented the plans during a visit to Washington, where he said the **ride-hailing** pioneer would **seek** a more diversified model offering various transportation options, including car rentals on a partner **peer-to-peer** service.

"More and more, Uber is not just going to be about taking a car, but is about moving from point A to point B in the best way," Khosrowshahi told an event in the newly launched Uber driver center in the US capital.

Khosrowshahi said the Uber app would start including locations for electric bikes from its newly **acquired** bike-sharing group Jump, which **currently** operates in Washington and San Francisco.

10 Uber also announced a partnership with the peer-to-peer car-sharing service Getaround to allow users to rent vehicles from individual owners, with a launch planned later this month in San Francisco.

The service will be labeled Uber Rent. "You can use your Uber app if you need a car and you want to drive yourself, if you need a car for an hour, a day," the Uber chief said.

For mass transit, the San Francisco startup said it would allow app users to see various options and would
15 **launch** a partnership with e-ticketing service Masabi that would eventually allow the Uber app to be used instead of tickets or passes.

Masabi has partnerships with transit systems in Boston, Los Angeles, Las Vegas, and New York, as well as train and transit operators in Europe.

Khosrowshahi said the new plans would help Uber offer solutions for an increasingly urban world population
20 and reduce the need for car ownership.
[…]

Extracted from www.dailymail.co.uk/wires/afp/article-5604689/With-bikes-transit-Uber-unveils-new-vision-urban-transport.html. Accessed on September 20, 2018.

2. Check (✓) the sentences that are true about the news report you have just read.
   a. (   ) It is clear, objective, and personal.
   b. (   ) Paragraphs are brief, and they often consist of a few sentences or a single sentence.
   c. (   ) It counts on quotations, which give the text strength and credibility.
   d. (   ) The headline is long, and it does not tell the reader what the story is about.
   e. (   ) It does not mention who wrote the article.

3. News reports aim at informing readers about daily facts or events. In pairs, summarize the main information provided in the piece of news above.

_____

_____

_____

LANGUAGE IN USE 2

Unit 2

ZERO and FIRST CONDITIONALS

1. Study the excerpts below. Then match the columns.

Zero conditional

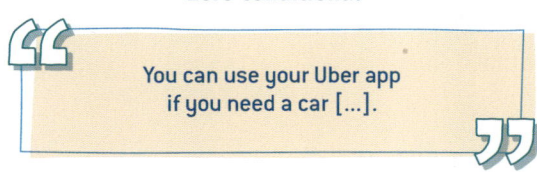

> You can use your Uber app if you need a car [...].

First conditional

> If Uber adds electric bikes to its services, users will have more options to get around.

a. These excerpts express...
b. They are known as...
c. They are often...
d. Conditional sentences consist of...
e. The zero conditional...
f. The first conditional...
g. The zero conditional is formed by...
h. The first conditional is formed by...

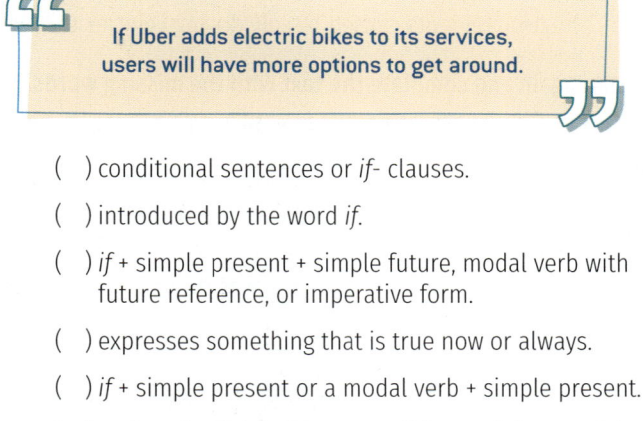

( ) conditional sentences or *if*- clauses.
( ) introduced by the word *if*.
( ) *if* + simple present + simple future, modal verb with future reference, or imperative form.
( ) expresses something that is true now or always.
( ) *if* + simple present or a modal verb + simple present.
( ) an imagined situation or condition and the possible result of that situation.
( ) reflects a realistic possibility.
( ) a main clause and a conditional dependent clause.

2. Complete the text with the verbs in parentheses. Use the appropriate conditional structure.

[...]

Choose the best option: cycling and walking

It's a no-brainer: burning our personal energy rather than **fossil fuels** is the most sustainable way to get around – and good for our health and **hip pockets**, too. But few Australians regularly choose active travel, like walking or cycling to work or study.

Again, the **sheer** size of our country is partly to blame. But if you _____ (live) close to work, active transportation is attractive when the math _____ (be) considered. "Owning and operating a car costs about $225 per week, not including parking," the Bicycle Queensland chief executive, Anne Savage, says. "If you _____ (ride) 10km to and from work regularly, it _____ (save) the average household at least $1,700 per year in transportation costs, and it _____ (reduce) **greenhouse gas** emissions by 1.5 tons annually." If you _____ (ride) a bike to work, it _____ dramatically _____ (modal verb for possibility, lower) the risk of heart disease and cancer, Savage says.

These days, one doesn't even need to own a bike. Sharing schemes such as Reddy Go, oBike, ofo, and mobike all operate via mobile phone apps, while many major cities also offer local sharing systems. And if going up hills _____ (discourage) you, _____ (consider) electric bikes (ideally if you have solar power at home for recharging).

Going carless won't always be possible, but if you _____ (consider) more sustainable modes of transportation, it _____ (modal verb for possibility, make) a big difference.

[...]

Adapted from www.theguardian.com/lifeandstyle/2018/mar/18/car-share-public-transport-and-walking-better-ways-to-get-from-a-to-b.
Accessed on September 20, 2018.

LISTENING COMPREHENSION

1. **Listen to a piece of news and check (✓) the alternative that best describes what it is about.**
   - a. (   ) The advances in self-driving vehicles.
   - b. (   ) The investments Uber has been making in self-driving vehicles.
   - c. (   ) An accident caused by a self-driving vehicle that made Uber stop using them.
   - d. (   ) A few accidents caused by self-driving vehicles that were under trial.

2. **Listen again and complete the text with the missing words.**

   A self-driving car has killed a pedestrian for the first time ever.

   The _____ car, operated by Uber, struck a pedestrian and killed them in what is thought to be the first death of its kind. The autonomous taxi was operating as part of a trial that Uber hoped would represent the future, but has now been suspended.

   At the time of the accident, the car was driving itself in autonomous mode, Tempe police said. There was a _____ operator behind the wheel, but they weren't in control of the car at the time of the crash.

   […]

   A spokesman for Uber Technologies Inc. said the company was _____ its North American tests. People have died in crashes involving vehicles that are driving themselves before. But this is thought to be the first time that a pedestrian has died after being hit by a self-driving vehicle.

   Uber's autonomous taxis, like the self-driving cars made by other companies, use a series of sensors built into the car to spot _____, cyclists, and other cars, feeding that into a computer that is able to steer and accelerate. Until recently, they have required a real person to be sat in the front of the car and ready to take over – but recently California officials approved the testing of such vehicles without humans in the front _____.

   […]

   The cars have also been involved in smaller issues, such as running red lights.

   Adapted from www.independent.co.uk/life-style/gadgets-and-tech/news/uber-self-driving-car-killed-pedestrian-death-tempe-arizona-autonomous-vehicle-a8263921.html.
   Accessed on October 5, 2018.

3. **Do you think self-driving cars should be given another try after safety adjustments? In your opinion, how will transportation and traffic change after self-driving vehicles? Discuss your ideas with your classmates and teacher.**

›› EXPAND YOUR HORIZONS ››››

Check (✓) the column that best describes your opinion about each statement. Then discuss your answers with your classmates and teacher, justifying your point of view.

	I agree.	I'm not sure.	I disagree.
a. Fast-moving trends have been influencing urban mobility.			
b. Advances in autonomous driving will definitely solve road-safety concerns.			
c. The first truly autonomous cars will probably cost a fortune, so not many people will buy them.			

REVIEW 1

Units 1 and 2

1. Skim the text and identify its target audience. *Skimming to identify target audience*

---

www.oecd.org/brazil/innovation-urban-mobility-brazil.htm

OECD

Business brief: Innovation and urban mobility in Brazil

"What is the city but the people?" asked Shakespeare in *Coriolanus*. All city planning focuses on people and the quality of life. The big cities in Brazil took shape from the 1950s, when the country's population **amounted** to approximately 52 million inhabitants, only 36.2% of whom lived in cities. The development focus during the post-war period, led by the modernist **canons** that guided the conception of Brasília, **spread** across numerous cities where the automobile was the leading actor, and was supported by investments all over the country to build roads and other infrastructure, such as ports, railroads, and electric power plants.

[...]

It is obvious that today's urban population of over 160 million, with the rate of urbanization **standing at** 84.4%, is stimulating massive expansion, with ever-increasing distances and extremely high costs to attend to for public transportation networks. The Brazilian government's policies **remain** quite unclear on this issue, and few of Brazil's cities have effective urban-mobility plans. On the other hand, the automobile industry delivers 200,000 vehicles to the market every month. This perpetuates the car/city combination, while forcing planners to find solutions for sustainable mobility that are compatible with the extending urban space.

[...]

The fundamental starting points for proper integrated city planning, and consequently mobility, are first, a deep familiarity with the clear social and economic profiles of the city's inhabitants (together with their expectations and demands regarding work, education, and health), and second, to know the origin and destination of their journeys. Sustainable planning of mobility depends basically on city planning, and this requires a social, participative approach that reaches beyond how to manage just the city itself.

[...]

Brazil was a pioneer in creating the BRT (Bus Rapid Transport), with exclusive corridors and boarding stations that reduce waiting times for commuters. Based on TOD (Transit-Oriented Development), a worldwide city planning approach that combines walking, cycling, and public transportation spaces with compact, well-serviced, population centers, this medium-size system is far less costly than building subway lines. **Nevertheless**, the BRT systems, which can use sustainable fuels like biodiesel or electric power, still need infrastructure work to guarantee large-scale **viability**.

[...]

Integrated planning, supported by clear public policies, new technologies, and ways to **safeguard** the environment, is the **path** towards sustainable mobility in cities in Brazil, as elsewhere.

Visit http://fgvprojetos.fgv.br/

Sponsored by **FGV PROJETOS**

Adapted from www.oecd.org/brazil/innovation-urban-mobility-brazil.htm. Accessed on July 25, 2018.

---

2. Read the text in activity 1 carefully and check (✓) the correct statements. *Understanding details*

   a. ( ) BRT systems first started in Brazil, but they lack the appropriate infrastructure to work efficiently.

   b. ( ) City planning and a social, participative approach are extremely important for sustainable mobility in Brazilian cities.

   c. ( ) The Brazilian government's policies have worked with well-structured and efficient urban-mobility plans.

3. Using your own words, explain the "car/city combination" mentioned in the second paragraph of the text.

4. In "Nevertheless, the BRT systems, which *can* use sustainable fuels like biodiesel or electric power, still need infrastructure work to guarantee large-scale viability," what does the modal verb in italics indicate?

_____

5. Read an extract that was omitted from the text on page 25 and fill in the blanks with the verbs *increase* and *help* in the present perfect tense.

> "[...]
> Meanwhile, the use of technologies to control and **oversee** transit _____ to improve the quality of city commuting. The centers for monitoring with cameras and GPS localization devices on collective vehicles, as well as collaborative applications that commuters use, such as Waze and Google Maps, on about 7 million smartphones _____ the efficiency of commuting. Not only smartphones, but also vehicles and objects that rely on **tiny** sensors to provide masses of data, can help make mobility more efficient.
> [...]"

Adapted from www.oecd.org/brazil/innovation-urban-mobility-brazil.htm. Accessed on July 26, 2018.

6. Read the comic strip below. Then circle the completed actions or states in the past and underline the past ongoing action.

Grand Avenue by Mike Thompson

Panel 1: KIDS, I TOOK A VIDEO OF ME LOUDLY SINGING CHRISTMAS CAROLS. WILL YOU POST IT ON YOUR SOCIAL MEDIA ACCOUNTS FOR ME?

Panel 2: UHHH... SORRY, GRANDMA, WE WERE JUST GETTING OFF THE COMPUTER.

Panel 3: THAT WAS TOO EASY.

Extracted from www.gocomics.com/grand-avenue/2013/12/03. Accessed on July 26, 2018.

7. Answer the questions about the comic strip above.

a. What **did** Grandma **say** she **was doing** in the video?

_____

b. Did Grandma really **want** to post the video?

_____

c. What **did** Gradma **want** to do?

_____

d. Why **did** the kids **say** that they **were getting off** the computer?

_____

8. Talk to a classmate about things you did last weekend. Then write two things that you both did last weekend.

_____
_____

UNIT 3
Generation Z: Conservative or Liberal?

technology

social

GENERATION Z

educated

visual

realist

▶ IN THIS UNIT YOU WILL...
- take part in discussions about Generation Z;
- exchange ideas about what characterizes Generation Z and other generations;
- learn how to use defining relative clauses;
- learn how to use the linking word *so*.

LEAD OFF

- What is the so-called Generation Z or iGeneration?
- What clear differences can you notice between your generation and your parents'?
- What influences the values, styles, and interests of a generation?
- Do you consider yourself conservative or liberal? Why?

READING

BEFORE READING

Read the title of the text below. List everything that comes to your mind about this theme.   *Brainstorming*

WHILE READING

Identifying the author's perspective

Read the text and examine how the author feels about the topic she is writing about. What opinions or beliefs are evident?

---

huffingtonpost.com/entry/conservative-or-liberal-its-not-that-simple-with_us_59ea34f7e4b034105edd4e32

Conservative or Liberal? For Generation Z, It's Not That Simple

10/20/2017 01:48 pm ET **Updated** Oct 20, 2017

Anne Loehr, Contributor
Expert in Preparing Leaders for the Workforce of the future

It might be time for the Millennial media obsession to wind down as a new generation inches up in age and takes their first baby steps into the workforce. I'm talking about Generation Z, the next demographic **cohort** after the Millennials. While there is no set consensus on when this generation begins, it is commonly believed that members of Generation Z were born between 1998 and 2001.

Is Generation Z Conservative?

- A 2016 American study found that while only 18% of Millennials attended church, church attendance was 41% among Generation Z.
- **Polls** found eight out of ten members of Gen Z considered themselves "fiscally conservative."
- In certain areas, Generation Z is more risk-averse than the Millennials. [...]
- A 2016 study done by the Annie E. Casey Foundation found that Generation Z had lower teen pregnancy rates, less substance abuse, and higher on-time high school graduation rates compared to Millennials.
- Business Insider describes Generation Z as more conservative, more money-oriented, more **entrepreneurial** and **pragmatic** about money compared to Millennials. [...]
- One British study conducted by global consultancy firm, The Gild, found Generation Z participants ten times more likely than Millennials to dislike tattoos and body piercings.

Is Generation Z Liberal?

- Gen Z is more diverse than any generation. Frank N. Magid estimates that Gen Z is 55% Caucasian, 24% Hispanic, 14% African American, 4% Asian, and 4% mixed race or other. He also states that Gen Z exhibits positive feelings about ethnic diversity in the U.S. and is more likely than older generations to have social circles that include different ethnic groups, races, and religions. [...]
- Generation Z is more liberal in areas like marijuana legalization, and transgender issues, according to a study done by The Gild. [...]
- 75% of Gen Z support same sex marriage. They're more likely to have grown up around same sex parents, and **therefore** don't see this as unusual—or illegal.
- 76% are concerned about global warming. [...]
- It has been reported that Generation Z is, "the least likely to believe that there is such a thing as the American Dream."

[...]

It's Time to Rethink What Divides Us

So, which is it? How do we categorize a generation that presents common ideals of both conservatives and liberals? Maybe we don't. Maybe we need to rethink what it is to be "conservative" and "liberal" and consider that in the future the distinction will be different. This generation just might **disrupt** the huge US bipartisan divide we are experiencing now. And maybe we would be better for it.

Adapted from www.huffingtonpost.com/entry/conservative-or-liberal-its-not-that-simple-with_us_59ea34f7e4b034105edd4e32. Accessed on July 13, 2018.

Unit 3

>> **AFTER READING**

1. **What clause best states the gist of the text?** *Understanding main ideas*
   a. ( ) To discredit theories about Generation Z and persuade the reader to believe Generation Z is complicated and pragmatic at the same time when it comes to Americans.
   b. ( ) To summarize the reasons why Generation Z might be considered conservative or liberal and advocate a reconsideration of what it is to be conservative and liberal in the US.

2. **Decide whether the excerpts below refer to conservative (C) or liberal (L) concepts, according to the text.** *Understanding details*
   a. ( ) "Over a third of Gen Z respondents also strongly agreed that gender did not define a person as much as it used to."
   b. ( ) "In 2013, 66% of teenagers had tried alcohol, down from 82% in 1991."
   c. ( ) "This makes sense considering the amount of environmental disasters they've **witnessed** so far, including the 2013 Colorado forest fires (most destructive wildfires in history,) tornado in Joplin, Missouri in 2011 (single deadliest tornado in U.S. history since the advent of modern weather forecasting), the flooding that devastated the Mississippi river valley (one of largest and most damaging **floods** recorded in the past century) and many more."

   Adapted from www.huffingtonpost.com/entry/conservative-or-liberal-its-not-that-simple-with_us_59ea34f7e4b034105edd4e32. Accessed on July 13, 2018.

3. In your opinion, can we categorize Generation Z as either conservative or liberal? Explain.

EXPAND YOUR VOCABULARY

1. **Find the alternative that best explains each word or expression in bold in the excerpts below.**
   a. "It might be time for the Millennial media obsession to **wind down** as a new generation inches up in age and takes their first baby steps into the workforce."
   b. "In certain areas, Generation Z is more **risk-averse** than the Millennials."
   c. "One British study conducted by global consultancy firm, The Gild, found Gen Z participants ten times more **likely** than Millennials to dislike tattoos and body piercings."
   d. "Generation Z is more liberal in areas like marijuana legalization, and transgender **issues**, according to a study done by The Gild."
   e. "76% are **concerned about** global warming."
   f. "This generation just might disrupt the huge U.S. **bipartisan** divide we are experiencing now."

   ( ) a subject or problem that is often discussed or argued about, especially a social or political matter that affects the interests of a lot of people
   ( ) involving two political parties, especially parties with opposing views
   ( ) to gradually reduce the work of a business or organization so that it can be closed down completely
   ( ) something that will probably happen or is probably true
   ( ) worried about something
   ( ) not willing to take risks

   Extracted from www.ldoceonline.com. Accessed on July 13, 2018.

2. **How does the cartoon below relate to the text on page 28? What are some themes that people from different generations disagree on? What changes in traditional values contribute to a generation gap? Work in pairs and write your answers.**

Cartoon: "UNFORTUNATELY, OUR DEFINITION OF 'JOB' DIFFERS." ©Jeff Stahler/Distributed by Universal Uclick for UFS via CartoonStock.com

VOCABULARY IN USE

1. **Pay attention to another excerpt from the text "Conservative or Liberal? For Generation Z, It's Not That Simple." Observe that the part in bold shows a collocation with the verb *make*. Check (✓) the correct meaning conveyed by that combination.**

> This **makes sense** considering members of Generation Z have watched their parents live through the second worst economic decline in American history (starting in 2008), and have witnessed the aftermath of mass layoffs and rampant foreclosures.

   a. (   ) find out if something is true or check that something has been done
   b. (   ) have a clear meaning and be easy to understand
   c. (   ) promise to do something or behave in a particular way

Extracted from www.ldoceonline.com. Accessed on July 13, 2018.

The verb *make* can be confusing in English because its meaning is similar to the meaning of the verb *do*, but they are combined with different words. These combinations are called *collocations*. They refer to words that often go together.

2. **Can you figure out new collocations with the verbs *make* and *do*? Complete the chart with the words from the box. Then use one collocation from each column to complete the texts.**

   a difference   a favor   an effort   an offer
   business   friends   good   harm   money
   noise   (my) nails   exercise

DO	MAKE

   a. **Millennials want job stability, Gen Z wants passion**

   [...]

   Generation Z is "The Change Generation," because all of the recent global events increase their desire to _____ in their future careers — and it also exacerbates their need for more "mental health support" from their employers, according to Lovell Corp.'s "2017 Change Generation Report: How Millennials and Generation Z Are Redefining Work."

   Extracted from www.benefitspro.com/2017/11/21/millennials-want-job-stability-gen-z-wants-passion/?slreturn=20180613095527. Accessed on July 13, 2018.

   b. **"iGen" author on how digital devices are slowing the development of today's kids**

   [...]

   "Anything that's done with a screen: texting, social media, TV, online, computer games — all of those are correlated with lower happiness," Twenge said. "The smartphone's one of the keys in explaining why they [iGen] are so different from Millennials. So, for example, their mental health has really trended downwards starting around 2012."

   Despite this correlation, Twenge said up to an hour and a half a day of screen time likely won't _____ , but that "two hours and beyond—that's when you start to see a link to these mental health issues."

   [...]

   Extracted from www.cbsnews.com/news/igen-author-effect-of-digital-devices-on-generation-born-1995-to-2012. Accessed on July 13, 2018.

3. **Answer the questions below. Use collocations with *make* and *do* in your answers. Compare your answers with a classmate's and explain your opinions.**

   a. Some define the super-connected iGens as less happy and more unprepared for adulthood. How would that affect their relationships at all levels?

   _____
   _____
   _____

   b. Assuming that today's teens are better behaved than in past generations, what factors contribute to this?

   _____
   _____
   _____

   c. In your opinion, what are iGens' worries? What pressures do they suffer? Do you share those same feelings?

   _____
   _____
   _____

LANGUAGE IN USE 1

Unit 3

RELATIVE CLAUSES

1. The excerpt below was extracted from the text on page 28. Read it and answer: what does the relative pronoun in bold refer to? Why was it used?

> " How do we categorize a generation **that** presents common ideals of both conservatives and liberals? "

2. Use the words from the box to complete the information about relative clauses.

> person   possession   relative   which   who

a. Relative clauses can be defining or non-defining. Defining relative clauses such as the one in activity 1 often begin with a _____ pronoun (*who, that, which, whose, where, when*) and provide specific information to identify or define the _____ or thing we are talking about.

b. In defining relative clauses, we can use _____ or *that* to talk about people, with no difference in meaning, although *who* is often preferred in more formal contexts.

c. *That* or _____ are used to talk about things and again *that* is mostly used in more informal contexts. The relative pronouns *where*, *when*, and *whose* refer to places, time, and _____, respectively.

3. Now read another excerpt from the text on page 28 and check (✓) the correct alternative to complete the sentence that follows.

> " This generation just might disrupt the huge U.S. bipartisan divide we are experiencing now. "

It is possible to reduce or simplify defining relative clauses in various forms, for example, omitting the relative pronoun. In the excerpt above, it is possible to omit the relative pronoun *that* or *which* after the word *divide* because…

a. (   ) it is the subject of the verb form *are experiencing*.

b. (   ) it is the object of the verb form *are experiencing*.

4. Match the relative clauses with their corresponding main clauses and learn more about the previous and present generations.

a. The Greatest Generation (1901—1924) grew up without modern conveniences…

b. The Silent Generation (1924—1945) was a period…

c. Baby Boomers (1946—1964) had rock and roll, miniskirts, and Barbie™ dolls. They were the ones…

d. Generation X (1965—1980) grew up street-smart but lonely because they're the kids…

e. Generation Y or Millennials (early 1980s—early 2000s) are those from a technological and globalized world…

f. Generation Z (1995—) has never known a world…

(   ) **where** price comparisons and product information are common.

(   ) **when** children had no voice. They were seen, but they were not heard.

(   ) **whose** parents often divorced or were more worried about their careers.

(   ) **which** make our lives much easier, such as refrigerators, air conditioning, TV etc.

(   ) **who** fought the Cold War and pulled the Berlin Wall down.

(   ) **that** doesn't depend on computers and cell phones.

Based on http://fourhooks.com/marketing/the-generation-guide-millennials-gen-x-y-z-and-baby-boomers-art5910718593. Accessed on July 14, 2018.

5. Work in pairs. Which generation from the ones listed in activity 4 do you find most interesting? Justify your choice. Then write two new sentences about it. Use relative clauses.

EXPAND YOUR READING

1. Read psychology professor Dr. Jean Twenge's interview about her book on the iGeneration (also known as Generation Z) and relate it to the text on page 28. Then underline the information that matches your reality and aspirations as an iGeneration teen.

> **Move Over, Millennials: How 'iGen' Is Different From Any Other Generation**
> By: Angie Marcos
> 8/22/2017
> [...]
> We sat down to ask Twenge what we should know about the iGen children, teens, and young adults — how they're different, what they care about, and how they'll make their mark on the world.
>
> **Q: How is iGen different from their Millennial predecessors and other generations before them?**
>
> **Dr. Jean Twenge:** iGen was born between 1995 and 2012, so they are the first generation to spend their entire adolescence with a smartphone; this has had ripple effects across many areas of their lives. As teens especially, they spend their time differently from any generation before them.
>
> iGen is more practical in their work attitudes than Millennials were at the same age. They are more **willing** to work overtime to do a good job and less likely to have **unrealistically** high expectations.
>
> However, due to their slow and protected **upbringing**, they are also less independent. iGen arrives at college with less experience with adult situations — including sex and alcohol — thus, they may not know how to handle them. Compared to previous generations, iGen high school seniors are less likely to drive, work, drink alcohol, date, have sex, or go out without their parents. This is part of a broader cultural **trend** toward growing up more slowly and taking longer to become an adult.
>
> **Q: What is the significance of iGen being the first generation to spend their entire adolescence on a smartphone?**
>
> **Dr. Twenge:** Around 2012, I started to notice big shifts in the large national surveys of the teens and young adults I use in my research. Depression and **loneliness** started to rise sharply and soon reached all-time highs.
> [...]
>
> **Q: According to your book, iGen is more interested in safety and tolerance than any other generation. You also write that they "have no patience for inequality." Where do this generation's values come from?**
>
> **Dr. Twenge:** iGen was born into a more individualistic culture than previous generations, one that favors the self more and social rules less. [This culture] treats people as individuals instead of as members of groups, and thus promotes equality for all. This is a central tenet of individualism and iGen reflects that.
> [...]
>
> **Q: How does iGen see higher education?**
>
> **Dr. Twenge:** iGen is more likely than previous generations to go to college to get a good job and less likely to go to get an "education." Although we have to bring students around to the idea of the importance of education for its own sake, we also have to keep their practical goals in mind when reaching out to them and teaching them.
>
> iGen brings unique experiences to the classroom. As just one example, they have spent much more time online and much less time reading books than previous generations. That alone means we have to think about teaching them differently.

Adapted from www2.calstate.edu/csu-system/news/Pages/Move-Over-Millennials-How-iGen-Is-Different-Than-Any-Other-Generation-.aspx. Accessed on July 13, 2018.

2. Choose the correct alternatives in parentheses to complete the statements about interviews.

   a. Interviews are very popular in _____ (the news / museum brochures), but they are also seen in other contexts such as research and entertainment, for instance.

   b. They are essentially _____ (a written / an oral) genre. Written interviews often derive from a transcription of an oral interaction.

   c. Interviews are organized with _____ (quotations / questions) and answers between one or more interviewers and interviewees.

   d. There may be a short passage before the interview to _____ (introduce / criticize) the interviewee and mention his/her credentials.

LANGUAGE IN USE 2

Unit 3

CAUSE AND RESULT — THE USE OF *SO*

1. Read an excerpt from the interview on page 32 and compare it to two other excerpts from the text on page 28. Which linking word / conjunction do they have in common?

_____

> iGen was born between 1995 and 2012, so they are the first generation to spend their entire adolescence with a smartphone.

> It's important to note that generational lines are not based on science, so clear definitions are not always available.

> So, which is it? How do we categorize a generation that presents common ideals of both conservatives and liberals?

2. What is the word you identified in the excerpts above commonly used for? Underline the correct alternatives.

a. To introduce clauses of result or decision.
b. To link contrasting ideas.
c. To connect sentences and make discourse more coherent.
d. To introduce a series of examples referring to previously stated ideas.
e. To express logical relations between ideas.

3. The linking word *so* was omitted once in the text below. Choose the sentence from which it was omitted and rewrite the sentence inserting it.

> Generation Z Under Academic Pressure
> [...]
> **(a)** We also learned from both African-American and Hispanic participants that getting a four-year degree has been preached to them as the "only option" to be successful — especially if they are to be the first in their families to graduate from college. **(b)** And at their high schools, tours were being organized to visit four-year degree-conferring colleges but no other options. **(c)** These kids weren't considering community college to hold education costs down nor were they exposed to trade schools. [...]
>
> Adapted from www.mediapost.com/publications/article/309010/generation-z-under-academic-pressure.html. Accessed on July 15, 2018.

_____
_____

4. Work in pairs. Now read these other sentences, paying attention to the structures in bold. Then answer the questions.

> Technology is **so essential** to iGens **that** we end up picturing them as the multi-screening and multi-tasking generation.

> There is **so much** pressure on teenagers nowadays **that** some of them might not be able to just stand, stare, and value simple aspects of their lives.

a. Does the structure *so + adjective* before the *that-clause* in the first sentence express concession or cause and effect?

_____

b. What does the structure *so + quantifier (much)* before the *that-clause* in the second sentence indicate?

_____

c. In this structure, the word *so* can be followed by either an adjective or an adverb. What kind of word is it in the first sentence? How about in the second sentence?

_____

5. Read the excerpt, paying attention to the sentence in italics, to identify cause and effect. In pairs, discuss whether it is true for you and your friends.

> [...] The desire for Gen Z to stay connected constantly has shaped the way they choose to communicate. For Gen Z, communication is fluid and continual, with online communication seamlessly flowing on from any face-to-face interaction and vice versa—there is no real barrier or demarcation between online and offline. *Social media is now so integrated into everyday life that it is no longer considered separate from other forms of interaction*, and many find it easier to communicate online with their peers and social network than they do face to face. [...]
>
> Adapted from https://clairemadden.com/10-reasons-generation-z-use-social-media-part-1. Accessed on July 15, 2018.

a. Cause: _____

b. Effect: _____

LISTENING COMPREHENSION

1. **Think of the name of different generations and list characteristics you think they have. Exchange ideas with a classmate.**

   _____
   _____
   _____

2. **Listen to part of a guide to generations. Are any of the generations you listed in activity 1 mentioned?**

   🎧 06

   _____

3. **Listen again carefully, underline the mistakes in the sentences below, and rewrite them according to the recording.**

   🎧 07

   a. Generation Z is smarter and more reckless than Gen Y.

   _____
   _____

   b. Gen Z likes to spend their money.

   _____
   _____

   c. Generation Z is described as the second tribe of digital natives.

   _____
   _____

   d. Generation Y, or Millenials, are those born until 1990.

   _____
   _____

   e. Generation X has spent too little of their adulthood sitting around in coffee shops.

   _____
   _____

4. **Work with a partner and discuss the questions below. Then share your opinions with your classmates.**

   a. Do you think the same generation labeling applies to generations throughout the world, in developed and developing countries, for example? Why (not)?

   b. What can we do to overcome generation gaps in different contexts, such as at home and at school?

   c. If you could record one important message for the generations to come, what would it be? Justify your answer.

›› EXPAND YOUR HORIZONS ››››

Check (✓) the column that best describes your opinion about each statement. Then discuss your answers with your classmates and teacher, justifying your point of view.

	I agree.	I'm not sure.	I disagree.
a. Labeling Generation Z as conservative, liberal, conventional, or modern depends on the perspective of the person doing the analysis.			
b. Generation gaps are inevitable and the reason why they occur is because of differences in psychological and behavioral patterns.			
c. All generations suffer different pressures throughout their lives. What really changes is the way that each generation deals with pressure.			

UNIT 4
What's Going Abroad Like?

IN THIS UNIT YOU WILL…
- exchange ideas about traveling to undiscovered destinations;
- talk about responsible travel;
- understand the difference between *need to* and *have to*;
- learn what tag questions are and how to use them.

LEAD OFF

- How can you relate the picture to the title of the unit?
- What feelings can a teenager in that situation have?
- In your opinion, what makes people leave their countries to go after opportunities overseas?

READING

BEFORE READING

Read the title of the blog post. What do you think the text is about? Exchange ideas with a classmate.

Predicting

WHILE READING

Skim the article to check your predictions. Then read the whole text and do the activities that follow.

Skimming to check predictions

| TRAVEL TIPS | ABOUT | BLOG | DESTINATIONS | RESOURCES | COMMUNITY | MEDIA SCHOOL |

Undiscovered destinations: Now *that's* what I call off the beaten track

By TOM CHESSYRE
UPDATED: 15:23 GMT, 25 March 2009

Do not expect the Costa del Sol, Florida or the French Riviera when you book a break with **perhaps** the most adventurous of all Britain's tour operators - Undiscovered Destinations.

This company's name does what it says, with no **messing** around. A list of a few of the countries **featured** in its holidays gives a **flavor** of what is offered: Burma, East Timor, Ethiopia, Sierra Leone, Papua New Guinea, Comoros and Sudan. It was set up two years ago by Jim Louth, a former employee of mass-market travel agent Trailfinders, who once lived in Brazil and has traveled to more than 80 countries. 'I wanted to do something a little bit different,' he says, in rather an **understatement**. 'People are incredibly well traveled these days and they're really looking to go off the beaten track.'

There are tour operators like Exodus and Explore that offer adventures but, with respect to them, they've become a bit mainstream and are not as challenging as they used to be.' One of his favorite trips is to Angola, on the west coast of southern Africa. Few tourists have visited the country, which was engaged in a bloody 27-year civil war until 2002, when a ceasefire brought an end to the violence and a chance for more than four million refugees to return home.

Undiscovered Destinations regards its 17-day expedition as 'pioneering', as it was the first to offer group holidays in the country. The tour is in four-wheel-drive, off-road vehicles - 'There is no road in most places so it has to be off-road,' says Louth - with most nights spent camping. The country is so unused to tourists that many people have never seen white faces before and visits to local Himba villages have to be spontaneous, as there are few phones to make contact in advance. This is all part of the appeal, says Louth. 'Sure, you can visit Himba tribes in Namibia [directly south of Angola], but everything there is a bit stage-managed. In Angola it's much more real.'

The scenery is a mixture of bush and desert - with the sands of the Skeleton Coast of Namibia extending into Angola. Trips are arranged to local markets, volcanic fissures, coffee-growing regions and **pristine** beaches (where great seafood is served at restaurants or cooked at night on camp fires). A highlight is the journey to Kalandula Falls, one of Africa's largest waterfalls. There is also a drive through Kissama National Park, where guides explain Operation Noah's Ark, a project to relocate elephants from overcrowded parts of Botswana and South Africa to Angola. It can get bumpy - there are 'boneshaking' rides across rugged **terrain**. But it is not exhausting; most of Undiscovered Destinations' customers are aged over 50 and many are retired. Angola, however, is not cheap. This is because there is a shortage of both vehicles and English-speaking guides, according to Louth. The country, a former Portuguese colony that gained independence in 1975, makes most of its money from diamonds and petroleum, not from tourists.

The Foreign Office says it is unsafe to visit the ironically named Democratic Republic of Congo, to the north, where Joseph Conrad set The Heart Of Darkness. But Angola is OK. 'For those who like their travel on the wild side, it has everything,' says Louth.

Adapted from www.dailymail.co.uk/travel/article-1163915/Undiscovered-destinations-Now-thats-I-beaten-track.html. Accessed on November 20, 2018.

>> AFTER READING

1 Check (✓) the statement that best describes the main purpose of the writer.

Determining the author's purpose

a. (   ) To present an unusual travel destination and a company that can take you there.

b. (   ) To discuss differences between travel destinations and how travel agencies feel about it.

2 Read the statements below and write true (T) or false (F) according to the information in the text.

Understanding details

a. (   ) The name of the agency which can take you to unusual destinations is *All Britain's Tour Operators*.

b. (   ) Jim Louth is the man who started *Undiscovered Destinations*.

c. (   ) Jim Louth has visited almost 80 countries.

d. (   ) The civil war in Angola ended in 2002.

e. (   ) Caucasians are very uncommon in Angola.

f. (   ) *Undiscovered Destinations* has only a few customers aged under 50.

g. (   ) There are many English-speaking guides in Angola.

3 Rewrite the false statements from the previous activity making the appropriate corrections.

___

EXPAND YOUR VOCABULARY

1 Find the words to the definitions below in the article on page 36. Then use two of these words to complete the extracts that follow. Make any necessary changes.

a. _____ : designed to be used on rough ground as well as on roads

b. _____ : to start a company, organization, committee etc.

c. _____ : accepted by or involving most people in a society

d. _____ : designed to be a public event, such as a meeting, in a way that will give you the result that you want – often used to show disapproval

e. _____ : filled with too many people or things

f. _____ : rough and uneven

Adapted from www.ldoceonline.com. Accessed on November 20, 2018.

> " [...] Not all _____ destinations are suitable for off-season travel (Machu Picchu in rainy season? No thanks). And some are far from ports. Going elsewhere, for now, may be the best option. [...] "

Extracted from http://time.com/4915745/crowded-tourist-cities-alternatives/. Accessed on November 20, 2018.

> " Hitting the open road is a distinctly American pastime, and no season calls for it more than summer. But might we suggest a little twist on the idea? We call it the _____ trip, for the folks with four-wheel-drive and a taste for adventure—not to mention dust. [...] "

Extracted from www.roadandtrack.com/car-culture/travel/g6375/america-10-best-off-road-trips-4x4/. Accessed on November 20, 2018.

2 Work in small groups. Answer the questions below and then report your answers to the class. Remember to support your answers.

a. Do you think the author is convincing when he defends Angola as a great tourist destination?

b. What do you think you would like about traveling to Angola? What wouldn't you like?

c. If you had to choose between traveling to a famous destination and to an unusual destination, which one would you choose? Why?

VOCABULARY IN USE

1. **Reread this extract from the text on page 36, paying attention to the idiom in bold. Then choose its most appropriate meaning.**

   > 'I wanted to do something a little bit different,' he says, in rather an understatement. 'People are incredibly well traveled these days and they're really looking to go **off the beaten track**.

   a. ( ) to approach, confront, or deal with a problem or difficult situation directly and with clear, confident action
   b. ( ) a place that is not well known and is far away from the places that people usually visit

   Extracted from https://idioms.thefreedictionary.com. Accessed on October 2, 2018.

2. **Read the following extracts, paying attention to the underlined idioms. Then match them with their most appropriate meanings.**

   a. "Tommy Hamilton's wife told him they would not <u>ride out the storm</u> at their house. He was stubborn at first, 'you don't want to leave your home. You want to stay.' She won the argument, and they rode the storm out at a different location."

   Extracted from www.southeastfarmpress.com/peanuts/storm-takes-homes-rattles-community-and-cripples-foundation. Accessed on October 2, 2018.

   b. "How do you <u>live out of a suitcase</u> for a year? Sounds like a **tall order**. You may think it is impossible. [...]

   To be honest, living out of a **carry-on sized backpack** was **freeing** but came with a few minor inconveniences. For example, when I walked into the luxurious Four Seasons Hotel Lion Palace in St. Petersburg, Russia with my backpack, no one took me seriously until I took out my passports and presented the confirmed reservation for two nights at the hotel. [...]"

   Extracted from www.gocollette.com/en/traveling-well/2017/6/how-to-live-out-of-a-suitcase. Accessed on October 2, 2018.

   c. "[...] So what do you do if you're **all geared up** with no one to travel with? Well, you have two options. Don't travel at all or go it alone. If you have a passion for travel and an **itch** to <u>hit the road</u> (or the beach, if it suits you), why not take off on a solo adventure and see the world with a whole new perspective? [...]"

   Extracted from www.uniglobephillipstravel.com/post/view/why-more-and-more-travellers-are-hitting-the-road-alone. Accessed on October 2, 2018.

   ( ) to begin a journey

   ( ) manage to survive a difficult period or situation

   ( ) spend a lot of time traveling

   Adapted from www.ldoceonline.com. Accessed on October 16, 2018.

3. **Now read some other idioms and their definitions. Then complete the paragraph with them.**

   at the wheel: in control of a vehicle's steering wheel
   the highways and byways: the important and less important parts
   a back seat driver: a passenger in the back of a car who gives unwanted advice to the driver about how to drive

   Adapted from www.ldoceonline.com. Accessed on October 16, 2018.

   I enjoy traveling with my cousin. When we travel together, I'm usually the one _____. The only thing I don't like is that he is sort of _____. He keeps telling me when to change lanes, where to turn left... it is so annoying! Anyway, last weekend we decided to travel to England and get to know the surroundings by car. We traveled _____ of Cambridge. That part was awesome! I'm glad we could save enough money to take this trip.

LANGUAGE IN USE 1

Unit 4

HAVE TO and NEED TO

1. The excerpt in A was extracted from "Undiscovered destinations: Now *that's* what I call off the beaten track" on page 36 and the extract in B was extracted from an article called "Why being broke is the best time to travel", by Nomadic Matt. Read them carefully, paying attention to the words in bold, and match them with the meaning conveyed.

   a.
   > The country is so unused to tourists that many people have never seen white faces before and visits to local Himba villages **have to** be spontaneous, as there are few phones to make contact in advance.

   b.
   > There's nothing like getting paid to have a conversation in the language you speak every day. These sites are hugely popular – and you **don't need to** be a teacher.

   (   ) something that's not necessary in order to achieve a goal or make something happen

   (   ) when there's no other option instead of doing things a certain way. It might be an obligation, something one's committed to, or a situation that cannot be postponed

2. Read the comic strips below and complete with the words from the box. There is an extra option.

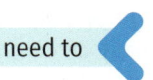

   > don't have to   have to   need to

   a.

   [Comic strip 1 - Luann]

   Panel 1: "Your brother's wedding was great, but it sure made me realize something" / "You're a lousy dancer?"

   Panel 2: "That I'm nowhere near ready to get married. There are so many things I really _____ do first"

   Panel 3: "Like get my degree, travel the world, visit important museums, tour historic sites, climb the Alps..."

   Panel 4: "Ride in a blimp, learn to speak French, take harp lessons..." / "Find a guy who wants to marry you..."

   Extracted from www.thecomicstrips.com/store/add.php?iid=152189. Accessed on October 2, 2018.

   b.

   [Comic strip 2 - Airport Security]

   "It takes longer getting through security, but by wearing all my clothes, I _____ pay to check a bag!"

   Extracted from www.thecomicstrips.com/store/add.php?iid=64137. Accessed on October 2, 2018.

39

EXPAND YOUR READING

1. Read the blog post below and relate it to the one you read on page 14. Which characteristics identified there can you find in this text?

www.nomadicmatt.com/travel-blogs/no-money-go-travel

HOME   WHO WE ARE   BLOG   GET INVOLVED   GO TO AN EVENT   SHOP   MEMBERSHIP   Sign In

Why the tourism industry has to change and how you can help it do so

October 18, 2016

We talk a lot about ways to enhance the tourism industry and to **spread** our message on responsible travel. Sometimes it's not always easy or clear how we can do that. In this post, Globalhelpswap details
5 their ideas on how we can collectively impact the industry for good and why it's necessary now more than ever.

Hands up if you took a flight last year? The chances are that most of the readers of this blog took a flight
10 at some time in the past year. Last year there were 1.2 billion international tourist arrivals and that **figure** is set to increase to 2 billion people by 2030.

A quarter of the planet's population is visiting new countries, eating different cuisines, and discovering
15 new cultures. Some of those travelers would have witnessed amazing natural phenomena like the Northern Lights, the Great African migration, or the Emperor Penguins of Antarctica. It's exciting, isn't it?

20 Travel breaks down barriers like no other industry and is responsible for 1 in 11 jobs around the world. If you ask most people what they are looking forward to most in the year, their answer will be a well-earned vacation. [...]

Can we change how we travel?

25 The good news is, yes we can. But, and this is a big but, it will take a collective effort from the tourism industry, governments, transportation as well as you and I. [...]

If we are going to redefine tourism, then we all have
30 to put pressure on travel companies to practice sustainable/responsible tourism. We also have to practice what we **preach** by spending our money with the companies that are already practicing sustainable tourism.

35 The amazing thing about sustainable tourism is that when you practice it, your vacation and travels will become more magical.

Helping feed elephants is pretty magical, right? How about sitting with orangutans in their natural
40 environment? What about going on tour where all your money goes to a women's cooperative to help them start businesses? All of these are examples of tours we have done personally with responsible tourism companies.

45 Next time you book a trip somewhere, please book it with a travel company that is practicing sustainable tourism. Let's redefine tourism together and hopefully as Fabien Cousteau said: *"I look forward to the day when there is no sustainable tourism, just*
50 *tourism".*

How would you redefine tourism? Please leave a comment below.

#RedefineTourism   #LoveYourTravels

This post was done in conjunction with The World Tourism Council.

Adapted from www.impacttravelalliance.org/2016/10/18/why-the-tourism-industry-has-to-change-and-how-you-can-help-it-do-so. Accessed on August 28, 2018.

2. In small groups, write a comment that answers the question in bold at the end of the text: "How would you redefine tourism?" Share your answer with your classmates.

LANGUAGE IN USE 2

Unit 4

TAG QUESTIONS

1. Read the excerpt from the text on page 40 again, paying attention to the part in bold. Then circle the pronoun and underline the auxiliary verb.

> A quarter of the planet's population is visiting new countries, eating different cuisines, and discovering new cultures. Some of those travelers would have witnessed amazing natural phenomena like the Northern Lights, the Great African migration, or the Emperor Penguins of Antarctica. It's exciting, **isn't it?**

The part in bold is called *tag question*. Tag questions turn statements into questions. They are often used to check the information we think is true.

2. Now read these statements, paying attention to the parts in bold, and complete the statements that follow with the words from the box.

- You **don't have** a frequent flyer discount, **do you**?
- You **are taking** a road trip with Emma, **aren't you**?
- He **didn't get** on that plane, **did he**?
- They **were coming** home by motorcycle, **weren't they**?
- **Come** to London after your wedding, **will you**?
- **Let's travel** on our next summer vacation, **shall we**?

> negative   tag question   auxiliary
> positive   Let's   main clause   imperative

a. Tag questions are usually made using an _____ verb, such as *be*, *do*, and *did* + a subject pronoun.

b. If the main clause has an auxiliary verb, you use the same verb in the _____.

c. If there is no auxiliary verb in the _____, use *do*, *does*, *did*, just like when you ask a normal question.

d. If the main clause is positive, the tag question is usually _____.

e. If the main clause is negative, the tag question is _____.

f. If there is an _____ in the main clause, the tag question is formed by *will* + the subject pronoun *you*.

g. If the main clause starts with _____, the tag question is formed by *shall* + the subject pronoun *we*.

3. Based on what you studied above, match the main clauses with the appropriate tag questions.

a. Traveling solo is not as difficult as you think,   ( ) will you?
b. Picture yourself in the middle of your ideal trip,   ( ) weren't they?
c. There aren't limitations on when you can go on your trip,   ( ) didn't she?
d. But some portions of your trip were spent on your own,   ( ) are there?
e. He was taking a short course overseas at that time,   ( ) is it?
f. She made friends with like-minded people when she visited the country,   ( ) shall we?
g. Let's plan a road trip across Latin America,   ( ) wasn't he?

4. Work in pairs. Talk to a classmate about things you know about them, their hobbies, what they did last weekend, and what they will do after class. Use a tag question at the end of your sentences to confirm the information.

41

LISTENING COMPREHENSION

1. Jason Moore is a frequent traveler who shares his personal experiences about traveling and living abroad on his blog. In one of his podcasts, he interviews Tim Leffel, who talks about the ins and outs of living abroad. Listen to part of the interview and complete the items with the missing information.

   a. The name of the podcast: _____
   b. The title of Tim Leffel's book: _____
   c. The people interviewed by Tim Leffel were from: _____
   d. The benefit from moving from a really expensive country to a much cheaper country: _____
   e. When people move from an expensive country to a cheap country, they might cut their expenses in: _____
   f. Places where Tim and his wife worked as English teachers: _____

2. Tim says, "[...] in general, if you move from a more developed country to a less developed country you're just going to be able to cut your expenses in half pretty easily if you do it right." In your opinion, what does "if you do it right" mean in this context? Explain. Then share your ideas with a classmate.

   _____
   _____
   _____
   _____

❯❯ EXPAND YOUR HORIZONS ❯❯❯❯

Check (✓) the column that best describes your opinion about each statement. Then discuss your answers with your classmates and teacher, justifying your point of view.

	I agree.	I'm not sure.	I disagree.
a. Picking up and leaving when we are struggling may seem quite scary.			
b. Besides taking us out of our comfort zone, traveling to new destinations usually helps us build self-confidence and be more independent.			
c. We need to change the way we travel and make sure all our choices are sustainable, even when this decision affects our personal goals during a trip.			

REVIEW 2

Units 3 and 4

1. Read the text and examine how the author feels about the topic. What opinions or beliefs are evident? *Identifying the author's perspective*

Generation Z's Rightward Drift

The data is consistent across the board: today's kids are more conservative than their parents were.

By TYLER ARNOLD • February 5, 2018

Blaming "kids these days" for society's shift towards social progressivism and libertinism is common within conservative circles. The right loves to **reminisce** about how previous generations walked uphill both ways to school and romanticize the values with which they grew up. I mean, they did have "Little House on the Prairie" while kids these days just spend all their time on smartphones, right?

5 But is this criticism really fair? Younger generations are actually **embracing** traditional conservative values more than people realize.

[…]

About 40 percent of Generation Z high school seniors disagreed that men should be **breadwinners** and women homemakers, compared to more than 60 percent in the mid-'90s. That study, led by sociologist David Cotter from Union College, shows that younger generations are turning back towards traditional
10 gender roles after a half century of going in the opposite direction.

Business Insider also points out that Gen Z has a stronger entrepreneurial spirit than previous cohorts, and shows signs of being more fiscally responsible. According to one study by a British brand consultancy called The Gild, Gen Z in the UK is exhibiting more socially conservative views than prior generations.

15 On the other hand, a study by Northwestern University shows that Gen Z is about as likely to support gay marriage and government involvement in health care as Millennials, and more likely to support transgender rights. Atheism rises by five percentage points among Gen Z, and despite promising signs of an increase in religiosity, teenagers are taking less traditional **approaches** to Christianity than previous generations, according to researchers at the Barna Group.

20 But while not everything is looking up, decision making and moral behavior definitely are. And while many don't see Millennials as very conservative, they are actually more conservative than Boomers and Gen Xers were when they were growing up. Considering that the latter two generations both got more conservative as they aged, if Millennials and Gen Z do the same, we could see a strong revival of conservative values.

[…]

Extracted from www.theamericanconservative.com/articles/generation-zs-rightward-drift/. Accessed on July 25, 2018.

2. Underline the clause that best explains the gist of the text. *Skimming*

   a. The youngest generations oppose a revival of conservative thoughts and values.

   b. Gen Z society is on an uncontrollable movement towards libertinism and progressivism.

   c. The younger generation is often more cautious and traditional than the previous ones.

3. Check (✔) the alternative that does **not** correspond to the new generation as described in the text. *Understanding main ideas*

   a. (   ) They are more inclined to approve of transgender rights and gay marriage.

   b. (   ) They follow less conventional approaches to Christianity.

   c. (   ) Most of them don't believe the roles of providers for men and housewives for women should be respected.

4. Read the conclusion of the previous text, paying attention to the verb in bold. What meaning does it convey?

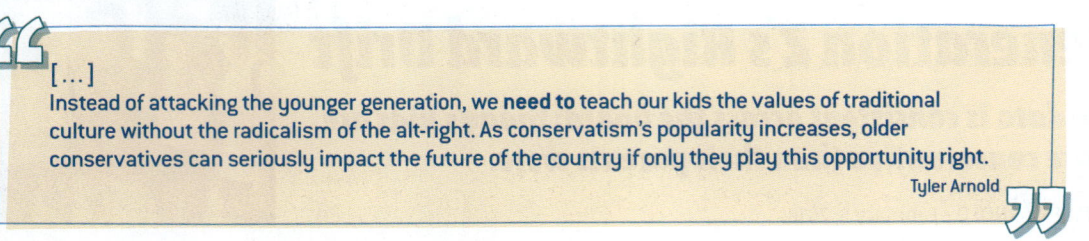

> [...]
> Instead of attacking the younger generation, we **need to** teach our kids the values of traditional culture without the radicalism of the alt-right. As conservatism's popularity increases, older conservatives can seriously impact the future of the country if only they play this opportunity right.
> Tyler Arnold

Extracted from www.theamericanconservative.com/articles/generation-zs-rightward-drift. Accessed on July 25, 2018.

5. Add tag questions to the statements below.

  a. Sustainable tourism requires constant monitoring of social and environmental impacts, _____

  b. Responsible tourism is related to any form of tourism that can be consumed in a more responsible way, _____

  c. Ecotourism trips shouldn't disturb natural areas, _____

6. Read the text and complete the relative clauses with the pronouns *who* or *which*. Then work in pairs. Exchange ideas about the question in the title of the text.

> **Do-gooders on vacation call it voluntourism. But is it doing anyone any good?**
> [...]
> Malawi is a landlocked nation in southern Africa. Its one claim to fame is that Madonna adopted one of its citizens—"Baby David" Banda—in 2006. Other than that, the country is known mainly to people _____ collect statistics on global misery. It's in a three-way tie for seventh place among countries with the lowest per capita income. It also ranks eleventh for overall death rate. By some estimates, the prevalence of HIV/AIDS in Malawi's cities is one person in three.
> One of the few funny things I've heard said about the place was a traveler's joke: "*Malawi*? I thought you said we were going to *Maui*!" It is indeed funny to imagine a tourist, expecting Hamoa Beach, instead being dropped on so-called Devil Street in Malawi's capital, Lilongwe. Not that there aren't any tourist attractions here. Most of the country's eastern edge spills into Lake Malawi, _____ has white-sand beaches and the widest variety of freshwater fish in the world. But the sunburn-and-souvenirs set has generally stayed away. Apparently even bargain destinations have to exceed a **threshold** of human suffering before they're accepted as **believably** fun. [...]
> All of which might suggest that Malawi is **off the beaten track**. Wrong. The place is swarming with visitors, and almost every single one is with an *organization*. They are volunteer tourists—or, if you're a fan of neologisms, *voluntourists*—and they are among the fastest-growing sectors in international adventure travel.[...]

Extracted from www.utne.com/politics/the-dark-side-of-volunteer-tourism-voluntourism. Accessed on July 25, 2018.

7. Rewrite the extract "One of the few funny things I've heard said about the place was a traveler's joke" inserting a relative pronoun where it fits. Then explain why it was omitted.

_____

_____

UNIT 5
What the Future Holds

▶ IN THIS UNIT YOU WILL…

- exchange ideas about what to do after high school is over;
- take part in discussions about what the future of work will look like;
- learn how to talk about the future using *be going to* and *will*;
- use modal verbs for assumption and speculation about the future.

LEAD OFF

- What does the picture represent?
- What feelings might the teenager in the picture be experiencing? Can you relate to those feelings?
- Have you decided about what to do after you finish high school?
- What do you think the job market will be like in ten years?

READING

BEFORE READING

Read the title of the text. In your opinion, what is its target audience?

Identifying the target audience

WHILE READING

Read some testimonials by professors presented on a text on the topic "What will universities be like 10 years from now?", presented in the Browne Review, a document about higher education in England. Then answer the question: What's the purpose of the text?

Identifying the main purpose of a text

What will universities be like 10 years from now?

The Browne review suggests drastic changes to the funding of higher education. We ask academics what the effect will be.

Gillian Evans, emeritus professor of medieval theology and intellectual history, University of Cambridge

There will be no more **block grant** for teaching, and the block grant has always provided the infrastructure. So if Browne succeeds in ending funding for all subjects that are not considered priority science and technology subjects, strategically important languages or ones that provide "significant social returns", presumably that means that history, politics, archeology, paleography and English literature will have to move out of the publicly funded buildings and into tents in the car park. Or departments of philosophy may have to go back to the Aristotelian peripatetic method in the streets and stay off-campus. This could widen access to no end. You could have Socratics vs. **hoodies** debates in the shopping mall.

How will library provisions work if in future only books on "priority subjects" may be purchased with public money and the rest put into storage to make space on the shelves? Or **pulped** to save public money being spent on the storage.

And there will be no more buffer body between government and universities. Despite what Browne says about this new Higher Education Council being independent, it is pretty obvious the government is going to decide what the priority subjects are this week. You thought you were studying French? No, sorry, the government's just axed that. It will be Mandarin Chinese.

Danny Dorling, professor of human geography at the University of Sheffield

We have a strange higher education system for historical reasons, and it will become stranger. The Americans will think we are going in the right direction. The Europeans will think we are **fools**.

In 10 years' time, there will be a lot of disappointed moms. Browne moves us away from the trend in the rest of the affluent world, in which a majority go to university and where student numbers are rising. His policy means, at its heart, having no more students than we have at the moment – probably, fewer. How do you get more students if you are charging them more?

[...]

David Colquhoun, research professor of pharmacology, University College London

The existing class divide between who gets to higher education and who doesn't will get wider. Vice-chancellors will make noises about providing **bursaries**, but that won't solve the problem. The problem is partly bursaries, but it's also about perception. Just the big headline fee is **off-putting**. It's like a return to the days of the scholarship boy at grammar school.

[...]

Deian Hopkin, former vice-chancellor of London South Bank University

In 10 years' time, geographically, provision might be **diminished**. The advantage of having a block grant, managed by the Higher Education Funding Council for England, was that it could support institutions in parts of the country where it felt it was appropriate to have them. The market won't necessarily do that. Unless we are careful, we may have larger **patches** of under-provision, or very different provision in different parts of the country. I also fear for the support for subjects that don't have an obvious function in the economy or utilitarian value – such as history. They could find themselves in difficulty, especially outside a small group of institutions, where there will always be demand.

Extracted from www.theguardian.com/education/2010/oct/19/browne-review-university-funding-future. Accessed on January 7, 2019.

>> AFTER READING

1. **Read the sentences below and check (✓) the one that does not relate to the overall content of the text on page 46.**

   Understanding main ideas

   a. ( ) Two of the professors believe that less socially or economically valued subjects, such as history, will stop receiving funds from the government in England.

   b. ( ) Even though students are paying less for university tuitions in England, the number of students is still low.

   c. ( ) More people won't be able to get higher education in England because of the fees.

   d. ( ) Some parts of England may receive fewer provisions for their universities.

2. **Write Evans, Dorling, Colquhoun, or Hopkin.**

   Understanding details

   a. _____ says it is necessary to be careful so as to make sure to have provisions in most parts of the country.

   b. _____ believes that the problem of higher tuitions can be solved in part by providing scholarships.

   c. _____ lists a number of subjects that may stop receiving a fund from the government for being considered less socially important.

   d. _____ believes that even some books will be less frequent in libraries to make room for those considered more important for society.

   e. _____ claims that students from other wealthy countries in the world enroll in university courses more than students in England.

3. **Which of the professors do you think seem to be more concerned about the changes expected for education in England? Refer to the text and underline fragments that support your answer.**

4. **Work in small groups. What changes do you expect to see in the universities in your country in the next few years? Do you think changes are going to be mostly positive? Why (not)?**

EXPAND YOUR VOCABULARY

1. **Read the sentences and decide how they are related to the text on page 46.**

   a. I'm changing my **major** to political science.
   b. Many college graduates are paying off huge **loans**.
   c. Languages are an essential part of the **school curriculum**.
   d. Justice says they should be allowed to attend the **public school**.

   Extracted from www.ldoceonline.com. Accessed on January 7, 2019.

2. **Now refer back to the text and find other words or expressions about the same topic to complete the chart below.**

	Definition
	amounts of money that you pay to do something or that you pay to a professional person for their work
	areas of knowledge that you study at a school or university
	college or university education as opposed to elementary school or high school
	an amount of money that is given to someone by an educational organization to help pay for their education
	a school in Britain for children over the age of 11 who have to pass a special examination to go there; (AmE) an elementary school
	someone who is responsible for a particular part of some universities in Britain

   Adapted from www.ldoceonline.com. Accessed on January 7, 2019.

3. **Discuss the following statements in pairs. Use as many words from the previous activities as possible. Then report and justify your opinions to the class.**

   a. If you plan early in life, paying for college tuitions and fees is easier.
   b. Getting a loan to pay for college or university has both positive and negative sides.
   c. In Brazil, most high school students know whether they are going to proceed to higher education, enter the job market, or do both.

VOCABULARY IN USE

1. In "His policy means, at its heart, having no more students than we have at the moment - *probably*, fewer." the adverb in italics was formed by adding *-ly* to the adjective *probable*. What function does that adverb have in this context?
   a. (   ) It provides information about the frequency of the activity indicated by the verb.
   b. (   ) It indicates a degree of certainty.

2. Adverbs can modify verbs, adjectives, adverbs, noun phrases, prepositional phrases, and even whole clauses. They can also provide information about the manner, place, time, frequency, certainty, or other circumstances of a verb. Look at the adjectives below and use a dictionary to find the corresponding -ly adverbs.

Adjectives	- ly Adverbs
a. academic	
b. automatic	
c. especial	
d. financial	
e. hopeful	
f. primary	
g. probable	
h. real	

3. Work in pairs. Choose two adverbs from the chart above and write sentences using them.

_____
_____

4. Look at the painting and read its exhibition label. Then find the *-ly* adverb and indicate its function. Keep in mind that not all words ending in *-ly* are adverbs.

_____

Exhibition Label

Crite thought of himself as an artist-reporter whose assignment was to capture the daily lives of ordinary people. His skill as an acute observer of American life is apparent in *School's Out*, which shows dozens of children leaving the annex of Everett elementary school in Boston's South End at a time when boys and girls were taught separately. Although Crite acknowledged that School's Out may reflect a romanticized view, it also presents a universal statement about community, stability, and the bonds of family life.

African American Art: Harlem Renaissance, Civil Rights Era, and Beyond, 2012

Extracted from americanart.si.edu/artwork/schools-out-5965. Accessed on July 20, 2018.

LANGUAGE IN USE 1

Unit 5

WILL vs. BE GOING TO

1. Read the extracts from the text on page 46 and underline the verb structures used to talk about the future.

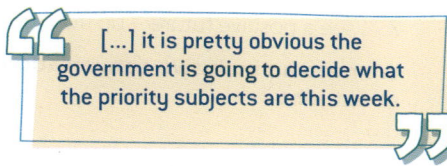

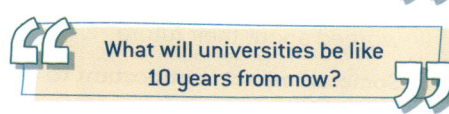

> [...] it is pretty obvious the government is going to decide what the priority subjects are this week.

> What will universities be like 10 years from now?

2. Read the extracts in activity 1 again and check (✓) the correct alternative to complete the paragraph about *will* vs. *be going to*.

We often use *will* and *be going to* to talk about the _____, although it is also possible to use tenses such as the simple present and the present continuous, for example. We use *will* to make _____, to mean *want to* or *be willing to*, to make or talk about offers and _____, and to refer to decisions made at the moment of speaking. *Be going to* is used to talk about _____ and intentions and to say that something is likely to happen, based on real evidence.

a. (   ) future / suggestions / plans / promises
b. (   ) past / requests / arrangements / plans
c. (   ) future / predictions / promises / plans

3. Refer back to the extracts in activity 1, identify the verb usages, and finish the sentences.

a. In the first extract, *be going to* is used because it refers to _____.

b. In the second extract, *will* indicates _____.

4. Use the verbs from the box to complete the text.

> 's going to be   will determine   won't define

Helping Teenagers Find Their Dreams
By Eilene Zimmerman

Some parents are apt to put pressure on their children about choosing a first career, thinking that it _____ the course of their lives. Yet as adults, we often reinvent ourselves more than once, moving among professions. So whatever your children choose now _____ necessarily _____ their future.

"I see many teens who jump on the first career track that someone recommends just to avoid being directionless, only to find themselves miserable a few years later," said Tamar E. Chansky, a child-and-adolescent psychologist in Plymouth Meeting, Pa., and author of "Freeing Your Child From Anxiety. [...]"
You may feel compelled to give career advice because you see particular talents in your child, but parents are more limited by their own experience than they think", said Steve Langerud, director of career services at DePauw University in Greencastle, Ind. As well-meaning as the advice might be, it "doesn't take into account what _____ available to your child in the future," he said.
"The market is changing so fast there may be careers that exist when a student gets out of college that simply didn't exist when they started," he added.

Extracted from www.nytimes.com/2009/10/25/jobs/25career.html. Accessed on July 20, 2018.

5. Answer the questions below. Remember to use *will* or *be going to* in your answers when possible.

a. Why are students often worried and afraid when it comes to choosing their path after high school?
_____
_____

b. What do you think should be taken into consideration when choosing a career?
_____
_____

c. Do you suffer any kind of pressure from family or friends, or even from people at your school, to decide what you want to study at college? Explain.
_____
_____

d. Do you think vocational or career aptitude tests can help teenagers decide on what kind of career they will follow? Explain.
_____
_____

EXPAND YOUR READING

1. **You are going to read part of a survey report by PwC entitled "Workforce of the future". What do you think it is about? Read the Foreword fragment and check your predictions.**

Foreword

We are in the **midst** of one of the most important periods of change in the workplace that we are likely to see in our lifetime. No one really knows how our world will be shaped by technology, what the future of work will look like, or whether work and employment as we know them will even exist. However, much of this debate focuses on what technology could do, and not around the choices we will have about how we will use it.

[...]
Carol Stubbings
Global Leader,
People and Organization

Those with fewer years of formal education are more worried

One in three of those educated to school leaver level are worried about their future – considerably more than those who are university graduates (13%) or post-graduate educated (11%). What does this mean for employers, governments, and society? We think it means a real need to open up a genuine and fully-
-inclusive conversation about the future of work.

[...]

Key findings

Excited about the future
[...]
73% see a positive future – up from 66% in 2014

We need an inclusive conversation about jobs
[...]
32% educated to **school leaver** level are worried about their future

Societal impact is important to people
[...]
70% want to work for an organization with a powerful social conscience

Trading liberties for good jobs
[...]
70% would use performance **enhancers** to improve employment prospects

Wildly different levels of confidence in skills
[...]
74% in India say they have **STEM skills** – only 33% in UK say the same

Giving CEOs the soft skills they want
[...]
85% say they have problem-solving skills

Conclusion

A deeper **dive** into the survey findings identifies some interesting trends and differences between countries and demographic groups in people's attitudes to the future of work and how it will impact them. PwC highlight some issues which will be of concern to governments. Notably a lack of confidence in skills in some countries and a clear need for an inclusive conversation about jobs to include all educational levels. But also some reasons to be **cheerful**. Three-quarters of people surveyed are positive about the future and have confidence in their soft skills. These are the skills that businesses will need in the future as human work becomes more collaborative with artificial intelligence. [...]

Extracted from www.pwc.com/gx/en/services/people-organisation/workforce-of-the-future/workforce-of-future-appendix.pdf. Accessed on July 20, 2018.

2. **Underline the only characteristic that <u>doesn't</u> refer to survey reports.**
   a. Survey reports present a summary of the data collected in a survey on a given subject.
   b. They present analyses based on the results of the survey, as well as some conclusions.
   c. Data may be summarized using visual representations such as graphics or boxes dividing content.
   d. Survey reports use informal language and never include recommendations.
   e. Statistics are often given by means of proportions and percentages.

3. **Read the whole text and decide if the sentences below are true (T) or false (F).**
   a. (   ) When people think about how affected their lives will be by the future world of work, most of them feel positive.
   b. (   ) More than 50% of people in the UK believe they have science, technology, engineering, and math skills.
   c. (   ) Less than half of people globally would like to improve their work performances.

LANGUAGE IN USE 2

Unit 5

MODAL VERBS - MAY, MIGHT, COULD

1. Read two extracts from the survey report on page 50 and one extract from the text on page 46 and answer the question that follows.

> However, much of this debate focuses on what technology **could** do, [...]

> PwC expands more on what work **might** look like in 2030 in our report 'Workforce of the future'.

> The market is changing so fast there **may** be careers that exist when a student gets out of college that simply didn't exist when they started.

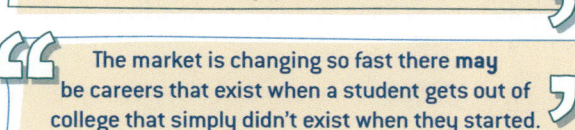

What do the modal verbs in bold have in common in these contexts?

a. (   ) They express ability and permission.
b. (   ) They give advice and indicate a strong belief.
c. (   ) They indicate assumptions or speculations for the future.

2. Match the columns to form complete statements.

a. We can use *may*, *might*, or *could* to say that...
b. *Might not* and *may not*...
c. In this context, *could not* (*couldn't*) is used...

(   ) are the forms used for talking about a negative possibility.
(   ) to talk about something that is completely impossible.
(   ) it is possible that something will happen in the future.

3. The fragments below were extracted from the survey report on page 50. Rewrite them substituting *will* for one of the modals used for assumption or speculation about the future.

a. "These are the skills that businesses will need in the future as human work becomes more collaborative with artificial intelligence."

_____
_____
_____

b. "PwC highlight some issues which will be of concern to governments."

_____
_____
_____

4. Work in pairs. Discuss the skills described by the author as "essential to your future success," come up with 2 others, and describe them on the lines below. Use the modals *may*, *might*, or *could* in your writing.

Top 10 Jobs in 2030: Skills You Need Now to Land the Jobs of the Future
[...]
1. Mental Elasticity and Complex Problem Solving:
[...] Luckily, this skill is highly **developable** and simply takes practice. The more difficult problems you **tackle**, the more **bendy** your brain will get!
2. Critical Thinking:
[...] You'll constantly need to be analyzing various situations, considering multiple solutions, and making decisions **on the fly** through logic and reasoning.
3. Creativity:
Worried about robots **stealing** your job? The more creative you are, the less likely you are to lose your job to a robot! [...]
4. People Skills:
[...] If you want to succeed in the future job market, you'll need to learn how to manage and work with people (and robots), which includes getting in touch with your emotions, having empathy, and listening,
5. STEM:
Even though science, technology, engineering, and math jobs are super hot right now, don't expect them to go away in the future. [...] Also **coding**. Learn how to code.
6. SMAC:
You've heard of STEM, but you probably haven't heard of SMAC (social, mobile, analytics, and cloud). **Catchy**, right? Learning all of these skills/platforms will make you **stand out** in the future job market!
7. Interdisciplinary Knowledge:
Your future career will require you to pull information from many different fields to come up with creative solutions to future problems. This skill's easy to work on as well. Start by reading as much as you can about anything and everything that interests you. [...]

Extracted from https://blog.crimsoneducation.org/blog/jobs-of-the-future. Accessed on July 20, 2018.

_____
_____
_____

LISTENING COMPREHENSION

1. **What is a gap year? Read the word cloud and come up with your own definition for the term.**

   STUDIES EXPLORE GAP YEAR EXPERIENCE EDUCATION CHOICE ADVENTURE GRADUATE EXCITING CULTURAL EXPOSURE UNIVERSITY TRIP CAREER TRAVELING OPPORTUNITY INTERNSHIP WORKING HOLIDAY BACKPACKING DISCOVER

   _____
   _____
   _____
   _____

2. **Listen to the first part of the recording. How does Josh describe a gap year? Is his definition close to yours? Compare your answer to a classmate's.**

   _____
   _____
   _____

3. **Listen to the second part of the recording, read the statements that follow, and decide if they are true (T) or false (F).**

   a. ( ) Josh was 18 when he finished school.
   b. ( ) Josh went away for a year. He worked in a school in England.
   c. ( ) Josh started his gap year teaching computer classes.
   d. ( ) When Josh returned to Macquarie University, he switched his degree into a Bachelor of Arts with the Diploma of Education.
   e. ( ) In Josh's opinion, a gap year is a waste of time and money that should be invested in paying for university.
   f. ( ) Josh felt that he was supported by Macquarie through his gap year.

4. **Listen to the last part of the recording and check (✓) the only thing not mentioned by Josh.**

   a. ( ) It teaches you more about yourself.
   b. ( ) You learn what your strengths are.
   c. ( ) You get homesick.
   d. ( ) You're able to figure out what you want to do with the rest of your life.

5. **Josh says that a gap year "teaches you more about yourself". How do you think a gap year can help you to learn more about yourself?**

6. **Do you think 17- or 18-year-old teens are too young to choose what they want to do for the rest of their lives? Is it common for Brazilian students to take a gap year? Would you like to have such an experience? Justify your answers.**

›› EXPAND YOUR HORIZONS ››››

Check (✓) the column that best describes your opinion about each statement. Then discuss your answers with your classmates and teacher, justifying your point of view.

	I agree.	I'm not sure.	I disagree.
a. Every year, a large number of teenagers graduate from high school without having a clear idea of what they are going to do next.			
b. In a near future, work and employment will be dictated by technology and the ones who lack those skills won't fit.			
c. Most students might benefit from a break right before college so that they can learn how to be responsible for themselves.			

UNIT 6

It's Time We Reforested the Agribusiness

IN THIS UNIT YOU WILL...

- understand the difference between agribusiness and agroforestry;
- talk about the benefits of agroforestry;
- exchange ideas about how farmers can be motivated to plant trees;
- get to know some collocations with the verbs *get* and *set*;
- learn how to use the passive voice;
- distinguish some discourse connectors.

LEAD OFF

> What kind of business can the pictures represent? What do you know about them?
> How can you relate the pictures to the title of the unit?
> "Farmers should use some of their land to plant more trees." Do you agree with this statement?

READING

BEFORE READING

Read the statements below. Do you think they are true (T) or false (F)? In small groups, exchange ideas with your classmates.

Activating previous knowledge

a. ( ) It is expected that people will eat less meat in the future.
b. ( ) Small farmers in a large part of the developing world provide most of the food in it.
c. ( ) More than half of the world's land is used for planting.

WHILE READING

Read the report below and check your answers to the activity above. *Scanning*

http://www.fao.org/home/en/

Food and Agriculture Organization of the United Nations

STATISTICS AT FAO

1. FAO (Food and Agriculture Organization) develops methods and **standards** for food and agriculture statistics, provides technical assistance services, and disseminates data for global monitoring. Statistical activities at FAO include the development and implementation of methodologies and standards for data collection, validation, processing and analysis. FAO also **plays** a vital part in the global compilation, processing and dissemination of food and agriculture statistics, and provides essential statistical capacity development to member countries.

2. Statistical activities at FAO cover the areas of agriculture, forestry and fisheries, land and water resources and use, climate, environment, population, gender, nutrition, **poverty**, rural development, education and health as well as many others.

3. Below you can find some recent facts and figures.

4.
FACTS AND FIGURES

- **60-70%** increase in food production is needed to feed more than 9 billion people by 2050.*

- **73%** is the expected increase in the demand for meat by 2050, driven from an emerging global middle class.*

- **80%** of the food consumed in a large part of the developing world is provided by small farmers. ***

- **79%** increase in productivity can be expected if smallholder farmers adopt sustainable agricultural practices.*

- **70%** of the world's freshwater withdrawals are used in agriculture this reaches 95% in developing countries.*

- **38.5%** of the world's land is dedicated to agriculture.*

- **1/4 TO 1/3** of all food produced for human consumption is lost or wasted. **

- **842 MILLION PEOPLE** experienced chronic hunger in 2011–2013.*

- **$3.5 TRILLION** is the cost to the global economy caused by lost productivity related to malnutrition and lack of direct healthcare.*

- **$450 BILLION** is the estimated global demand for small farmer agricultural finance.°

- **100-150 MILLION PEOPLE** could escape hunger if women farmers had the same access to productivity resources as men.*

* Food and Agriculture Organization of the United Nations (FAO)
** FAO and World Resources Institute – World Food Price Watch, February 2014
*** UN Report 2013, Smallholders, food security, and the environment
° Catalyzing Smallholder Agricultural Finance report, published by Dalberg in September 2012

Adapted from www.fao.org/home/en/. Accessed on September 23, 2018.

>> AFTER READING

Unit 6

1. Write the number of each part of the text next to what is presented in it. *Understanding main ideas*
   a. (   ) The areas that FAO statistics cover.
   b. (   ) An introduction to the figures presented on food production and consumption.
   c. (   ) An introduction to the organization.
   d. (   ) Data related to food consumption and production.

2. Rewrite these sentences correcting the information that is **not** true. *Understanding details*
   a. A high increase in the demand for meat is expected in the emerging developing countries.
   _____

   b. The estimated impact of malnutrition on the global economy is higher than US$3.5 trillion.
   _____

   c. By 2050 at least a 70% in food increase will be needed to feed the world's population.
   _____

   d. Women farmers have the same access to productivity resources as men.
   _____

3. Work in small groups. Read the excerpt below and answer: If tree-based farming provides all these benefits, why do you think every farmer isn't planting trees?

> "In communities around the world, agroforestry – which involves growing trees among or around food crops – has been a proven method for farmers to cultivate more diverse, productive, and profitable crops. What's more, it helps protect the environment by preventing soil erosion and reducing reliance on forests.
> As such, agroforestry can make a key contribution to the UN's Zero Hunger Challenge, which aims to end global hunger, eliminate malnutrition, and build sustainable food systems. [...]"
>
> *Extracted from https://forestsnews.cifor.org/55549/agroforestry-why-dont-farmers-plant-more-trees?fnl=en. Accessed on September 25, 2018.*

EXPAND YOUR VOCABULARY

1. Go back to the text and find the words and expressions below. Reread the sentences they are in. Then match them with their meanings.

   a. disseminate
   b. forestry
   c. increase
   d. withdrawal

   (   ) to make something become bigger in amount, number, or degree
   (   ) the science or skill of looking after large areas of trees
   (   ) to spread information or ideas to as many people as possible
   (   ) the removal or stopping of something such as support, an offer, or a service

   Adapted from www.ldoceonline.com/dictionary. Accessed on September 24, 2018.

2. Use one word from activity 1 to complete the excerpt below.

> "Agricultural intensification refers to interventions to _____ the outputs per hectare of crops or livestock. **Whilst** intensification can occur through local demand for innovation, it is increasingly imposed through policy interventions in forest-agriculture frontiers."
>
> *Extracted from www.espa.ac.uk/projects/ne-p008356-1. Accessed on November 13, 2018.*

55

VOCABULARY IN USE

1. Read the excerpts below, paying attention to the parts in bold. They show collocations with the verbs *get* and *set*. Check (✓) the correct meaning conveyed by those combinations.

   a. "This includes considering the particular space or **niche** the tree occupies in the farming system, as well as the total number of trees of that species that need to be planted. **Getting** this **right** is important to maximize the ecological and socioeconomic benefits from the tree itself and simultaneously to reduce the potential competition with other components of the system such as annual **crops**. [...]"

   Extracted from www.worldagroforestry.org/downloads/Publications/PDFS/B17460.pdf. Accessed on September 25, 2018.

   ( ) understanding something in the wrong way
   ( ) understanding something accurately

   b. "The current reform of the Common Agricultural Policy (CAP) has **set** new **rules** regarding the eligibility of agroforestry parcels for CAP first **pillar support**. The application of the new Basic Payment Scheme is creating concern for agroforesters, as some of the rules and regulations regarding the presence of trees, **shrubs**, or **hedges** in agricultural land are becoming more restrictive. [...]"

   Extracted from www.eurafagroforestry.eu/action/policy/Eligibility_of_agroforestry_parcels_for_CAP_basic_payments. Accessed on September 25, 2018.

   ( ) established rules
   ( ) change rules drastically

2. Can you make new collocations with the verbs *get* and *set*? Complete the mind maps with the words and expressions from the box. Then use one collocation from each mind map to write a statement related to the facts and figures showed in the text on page 54.

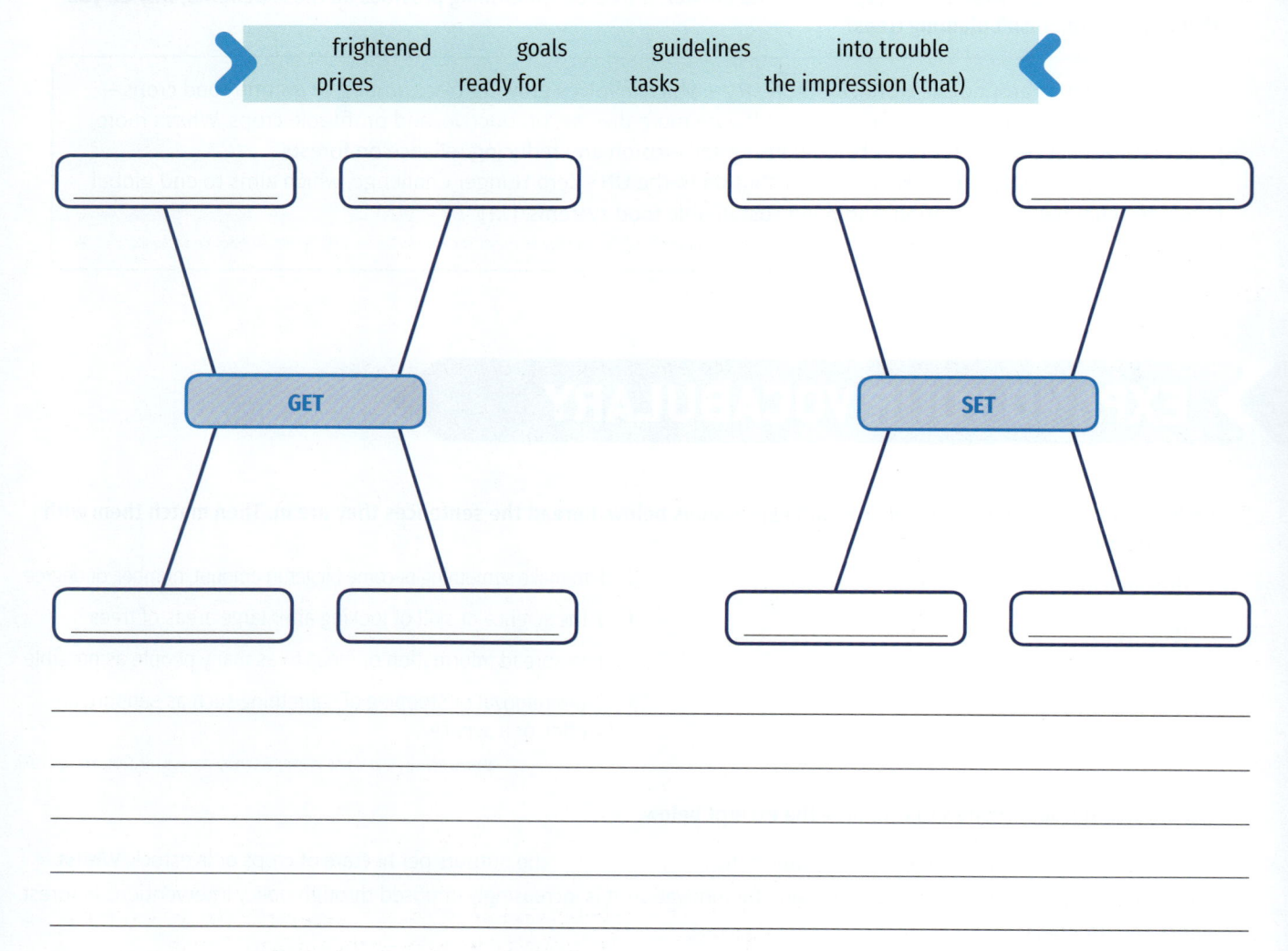

frightened	goals	guidelines	into trouble
prices	ready for	tasks	the impression (that)

GET

SET

_____
_____
_____
_____
_____

LANGUAGE IN USE 1

Unit 6

PASSIVE VOICE

1. Read these two excerpts from the report on page 54, circle the subjects, and underline all the verb forms. Then decide if the statements are true (T) or false (F) and correct the false one(s).

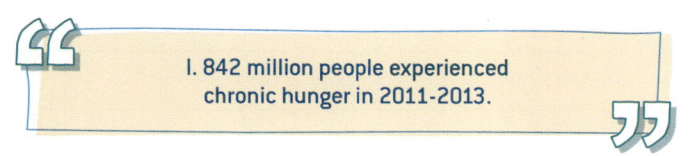

> I. 842 million people experienced chronic hunger in 2011-2013.

> II. 38.5% of the world land is dedicated to agriculture.

a. ( ) The subjects of both extracts I and II are the ones who perform the actions.
_____

b. ( ) In extract II the subject is the one who receives the action.
_____

c. ( ) Extract II focuses on the action itself and not on who or what performs the action. It shows a passive voice structure.
_____

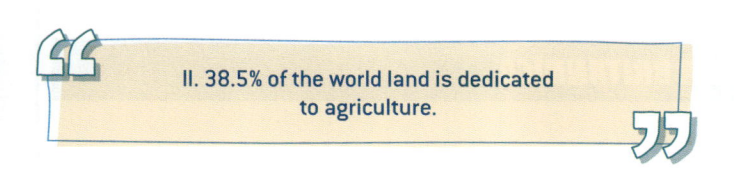

2. Read the statements below carefully and match the columns.

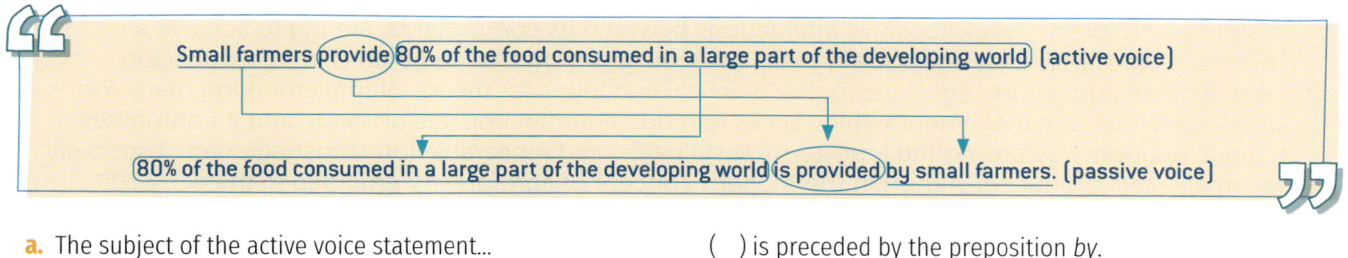

> Small farmers provide 80% of the food consumed in a large part of the developing world. (active voice)
>
> 80% of the food consumed in a large part of the developing world is provided by small farmers. (passive voice)

a. The subject of the active voice statement...
b. The agent of the passive voice statement...
c. The object of the active voice statement...
d. The passive form of the verb has as its basic structure...

( ) is preceded by the preposition *by*.
( ) *be* and a verb in the past participle.
( ) becomes the subject of the active voice statement.
( ) becomes the agent of the passive voice statement.

Keep in mind that:
- in most passive statements, the agent is not mentioned.
- in the passive voice statement, *be* is in the same tense of the main verb of the active voice.

3. Read part of the article "Pesticides Use and Exposure Extensive Worldwide" and complete it with the correct passive form of the verbs from the box.

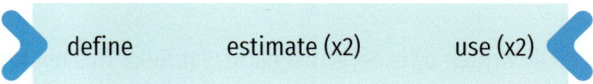

> define   estimate (x2)   use (x2)

"Worldwide it _____ that approximately 1.8 billion people engage in agriculture and most use pesticides to protect the food and commercial products that they produce. Others use pesticides occupationally for public health programs, and in commercial applications, while many others use pesticides for **lawn** and garden applications and in and around the home.

Pesticides _____ as 'chemical substances used to prevent, destroy, repel, or **mitigate** any pest ranging from insects (i.e., insecticides), **rodents** (i.e., rodenticides), and **weeds** (herbicides) to microorganisms (i.e., algicides, fungicides, or bactericides)'.

Over 1 billion pounds of pesticides _____ in the United State (US) each year and approximately 5.6 billion pounds _____ worldwide. In many developing countries programs to control exposures are limited or non-existent. As a consequence, it has been estimated that as many as 25 million agricultural workers worldwide experience unintentional pesticide **poisonings** each year. In a large prospective study of pesticide users in the United States, the Agricultural Health Study, it _____ that 16% of the cohort had at least one pesticide poisoning or an unusually high pesticide exposure episode in their lifetime. [...]"

Extracted from www.ncbi.nlm.nih.gov/pmc/articles/PMC2946087/. Accessed on September 26, 2018.

EXPAND YOUR READING

1. Read the encyclopedia entry below. Then refer to the text in activity 3 on page 55 and answer: What other benefits of agroforestry can you learn from this text?

_____

_____

_____

www.britannica.com/science/agroforestry

ENCYCLOPEDIA BRITANNICA

Agroforestry

WRITTEN BY: Michael A. Gold (co-editor of an agroforestry newsletter)

Agroforestry, cultivation, and use of trees and shrubs with crops and **livestock** in agricultural systems. Agroforestry **seeks** positive interactions between its components, aiming to achieve a more ecologically diverse and socially productive **output** from the land than is possible through conventional agriculture. Agroforestry is a practical and low-cost means of implementing many forms of integrated land management (which seeks to reduce human impacts on land), and it contributes to a green economy by promoting long-term, sustainable, and renewable forest management, especially for small-scale producers. Although the modern concept of agroforestry emerged in the early 20th century, the use of **woody perennials** in agricultural systems is ancient, with written descriptions of the practice dating back to Roman times. Indeed, integrating trees with crops and animals is a long-standing tradition throughout the world. In 2004 the World Bank estimated that agroforestry practices were being used by 1.2 billion people.

Extracted from www.britannica.com/science/agroforestry. Accessed on September 26, 2018.

2. Check (✓) the statements that are true about encyclopedia entries.
   a. (   ) People read encyclopedia entries because they want to go deeper into or learn more about a topic.
   b. (   ) Encyclopedia entries are rarely organized into alphabetical order.
   c. (   ) Encyclopedia entries need to present clearly articulated explanations that can help readers.
   d. (   ) Online and printed encyclopedia entries are always updated once a year or every other year to address changes since the last publication.
   e. (   ) Encyclopedia entries are usually written by experts in a particular field. This lends authority to the encyclopedia and strengthens it as a reference tool.

3. Scan the text and answer the questions that follow.
   a. What is the aim of agroforesty?

   _____

   b. How does it contribute to a green economy?

   _____

   c. When did the modern concept of agroforestry emerge?

   _____

   d. How many people are estimated to be using agroforestry practices?

   _____

LANGUAGE IN USE 2

Unit 6

DISCOURSE MARKERS

1. Read the sentence below, extracted from the encyclopedia entry on page 58, paying attention to the word in bold. Then read the definition and answer the questions that follow.

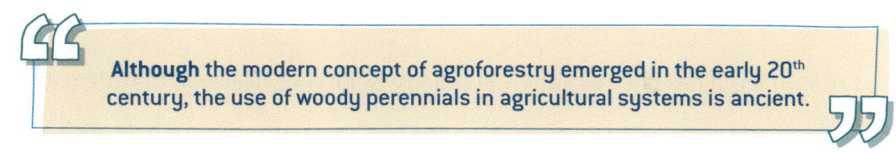

> **Although** the modern concept of agroforestry emerged in the early 20th century, the use of woody perennials in agricultural systems is ancient.

The word in bold is a discourse marker. Discourse markers, or connectors, are words and phrases that aim at managing the flow of a discourse. They can express various types of relationships, such as addition, contrast, reason, cause and result, order, summary, etc.

a. What does *although* express?

_____

b. Which discourse marker could replace *although* with no significant difference in meaning? Read sentences *a*, *b*, and *c* in activity 2 and choose one of the discourse connectors in bold.

_____

2. What do the discourse markers in bold express in the sentences below? Read, identify, and complete the chart.

a. Even though she didn't want to buy products affected by toxic herbicides, she didn't have any other option.

b. She has lived in four other countries **besides** India.

c. Since most users canceled their subscriptions, our company has decided to shut down this service.

d. The agricultural expansion and, **consequently**, natural resources degradation can cause a massive impact on the environment.

e. There have been discussions about the exaggerated use of pesticides. **Along with this**, new laws are expected to be created.

f. Due to decades of studies and research, scientists are believed to have been able to create herbicides that are harmless to human beings.

g. Most companies say that they are no longer producing and selling toxic herbicides. Some companies, **however**, don't seem to mind the political and social pressures.

h. The pesticides used by farmers were inappropriate for this type of plantation. **For this reason**, crops were severely damaged.

Addition	Cause and result	Contrast	Reason

3. Complete the following statements with your own ideas. Pay attention to the discourse markers used.

a. Besides soil, other important agricultural resources are _____

_____ .

b. Although pesticides can cause harm to people and the environment, _____

_____ .

c. Many trees are planted every year. Consequently, _____

_____ .

LISTENING COMPREHENSION

1. **You are going to listen to some news about Brazil's position as an agricultural powerhouse. Before you listen, talk to a classmate and guess if the following statements are true (T) or false (F). Then listen and check.**

   a. (   ) When the text was published, Brazil was the world's sixth largest economy.
   _____

   b. (   ) Although the agribusiness in Brazil has been growing, the country is not a key player in the international arena yet.
   _____

   c. (   ) At the time the news was published, Brazil had the second largest reserves of farmable and not cultivated land in the world.
   _____

   d. (   ) At the time the news was published, Brazilian bioethanol production was the second largest worldwide.
   _____

   e. (   ) In 2009, agribusiness accounted for more than 3 percent of the labor force.
   _____

2. **Listen again and correct the false statements from activity 1.**

3. **Read the extract below from the audio and answer the question: What does the underlined word mean in this context?**

   "Blessed with the world's largest reserves of farmable and not cultivated land, Brazil has carved out its regional and international rank thanks to strong exporting agricultural activities, radical economic reforms, and an <u>aggressive</u> trade and influence policy."
   _____

4. **In your opinion, will the agribusiness grow in the next few years in Brazil? Why (not)? How could agroforestry be encouraged in order to occupy some of the land which is not cultivated yet? Exchange your ideas with your classmates.**

>> EXPAND YOUR HORIZONS >>>>

Check (✓) the column that best describes your opinion about each statement. Then discuss your answers with your classmates and teacher, justifying your point of view.

	I agree.	I'm not sure.	I disagree.
a. Every farmer should be motivated to use part of their land to plant trees.			
b. Agroforestry should not be considered a responsibility of small farmers.			
c. Although pesticides can cause harm to people, they are necessary to protect the food and commercial products.			

REVIEW 3

Units 5 and 6

1. Skim the text and identify its target audience. *Skimming to identify target audience*

---

http://time.com/money/4982643/6-future-jobs/

The 6 Jobs Everyone Will Want in 2040

If you're a new parent, or **prone to** abstract theorizing, you've probably spent some late nights wondering what the future holds for job **seekers**.

In 2040, the babies born today will be at the start of their careers. Will the job market they face look anything like now?

Maybe, maybe not. Automation has already eliminated millions of manufacturing, foodservice, and **retail** jobs, and there's little doubt it will eventually reshape every other industry.

Some good news: Research from Oxford University shows there are hundreds of roles that aren't going anywhere – like occupational therapy, choreography, environmental engineering, and mental health counseling, among others.

Some better news: While some jobs will disappear, **loads** more will be created.

In fact, according to a forecast from the Institute for the Future (IFTF), 85% of the jobs in 2030 haven't even been invented yet. Ten years after that, the workforce may be totally **unrecognizable**.

Here's what the hottest jobs for 2040 could look like:

Virtual Store Manager

More consumers are shopping online, but they still **crave** human connection. [...]

Robot Mediator

Sure, robots are **disrupting** some industries. But in others, they're actually just making humans better at their jobs. [...]

Robot Trainer

Machine learning, which uses algorithms to train computers to, say, make a Spotify playlist, was once a skill known by an elite few. [...]

Drone Traffic Controller

[...] With Amazon and Google testing ways to deliver packages by drone, corporate job openings in this field are an inevitability (future drone pilots are already enrolling at "Unmanned Vehicle" specialty schools). [...]

Augmented Reality Designer

Some industries, like marketing and retail, have already tapped AR designers to create interactive experiences for consumers. [...]

Micro Gig Agents

As the gig economy expands, independent consultants will work alongside a growing number of independent contractors, says Christie Lindor, a management consultant and host of the MECE Muse Unplugged podcast. [...]

Adapted from http://time.com/money/4982643/6-future-jobs/. Accessed on October 12, 2018.

---

2. Check (✓) the statements that are true according to the text. *Understanding details*

a. (   ) Roles in occupational therapy, choreography, environmental engineering, and mental health counseling, will be extinct in the next 10 years.

b. (   ) In 2040 the job market will be very different from what it is today.

c. (   ) Automation will continue to reshape the job market. One example of its impact is the drone delivery service that it is being tested by Google and Amazon.

d. (   ) Undoubtedly, all industries and businesses are being disrupted by robots.

3. Which extracts from the text correct the false statements from the previous activity? Write them on the lines below. *Understanding details*

_____
_____
_____
_____

4. Read two extracts from the text on page 61, paying attention to the parts in bold, and check (✓) the alternative that states what they indicate.

> In 2040, the babies born today **will be** at the start of their careers.

> Automation has already eliminated millions of manufacturing, foodservice, and retail jobs, and there's little doubt it **will** eventually **reshape** every other industry.

a. (   ) Promises
b. (   ) Plans
c. (   ) Predictions
d. (   ) Decisions made at the moment of speaking

5. Scan the text on page 61 to find passive voice statements and underline them.

6. Change the extracts below into the passive voice.

a. "Sure, robots are disrupting some industries."

_____

b. "Machine learning […] uses algorithms to train computers."

_____

c. "[…] consumers […] still crave human connection."

_____

7. Choose the correct alternative to complete the statements below.

a. They were on vacation at the time of the strike, so they _____ be at the factory when it all happened.

b. Due to the advances in technology, by 2040 the job market _____ have as many openings as it does today.

c. Because of technology, companies _____ change the way they hire employees in the future.

(   ) may / might not / could
(   ) couldn't / might not / may
(   ) couldn't / might / may not

8. Read the text and use the connectors from the box to fill in the blanks. There is an extra connector. Then talk to a classmate about the main points of the text.

> Consequently   Moreover   Since   Yet

Argentina and Brazil are already agricultural giants. But the best local companies are far more advanced than the rest.

Rising wealth, changing diets, and increased food consumption across the developing world, along with a growing global population, are fueling a steady rise in demand for agricultural commodities such as sugar, soybeans, and meat. _____, the prospects for growers, ranchers, processors, and other agribusinesses are blossoming – and perhaps nowhere more so than in Brazil and to a certain extent in Argentina, already agricultural giants that accounted for $73 billion in exports last year.

The opportunities are considerable. Historically fragmented businesses such as livestock and sugar, for instance, are beginning to consolidate, offering companies the benefits of increased scale. New sources of financing allow players to overcome historically underdeveloped capital markets. Increased demand for affordable and clean energy is creating nontraditional opportunities, such as the production and export of biofuels. (Brazil is already the world's largest producer of ethanol; its exports rose by more than 65 percent in 2006.)

_____ some domestic companies (including local ones and local units of multinationals) aren't benefiting fully, because they aren't as efficient as they could be or aren't getting as much as they could from technology. Smaller enterprises often lack the sophistication to use new financing options to pay for their growth. _____, in some cases, complex or rigid organizational structures promote duplication and inefficiency, which prevent agribusinesses from taking full advantage of a changing commercial environment.

Still, a few companies are moving to address these and related issues and thereby positioning themselves to be leaders in the sector. A look at the practices of these companies – a mix of global powerhouses and smaller players – can show others how to confront some of Latin America's perennial challenges, shed light on the evolution of agribusiness in Argentina and Brazil, and offer insights into the skills and strategies competitors will need in the coming years.

[…]

Adapted from https://industrytoday.com/article/harvesting-latin-americas-agribusiness-opportunity. Accessed on October 12, 2018.

UNIT 7
The Economic Effects of Globalization

▶ IN THIS UNIT YOU WILL...

- talk about how globalization might affect economic growth;
- learn about the rise of new economies;
- use the present perfect tense with *for* and *since*;
- compare the present perfect and the simple past.

LEAD OFF

- What does the picture represent? How does it relate to the title of the unit?
- Have you heard the expression *global village*? If so, what does it mean?
- How might globalization affect the prosperity and economic growth of a country?

READING

BEFORE READING

Look at the text you are about to read. Where was it probably extracted from? *Identifying the source of the text*

a. ( ) An encyclopedia.

b. ( ) An online magazine.

c. ( ) An atlas.

WHILE READING

Read the text and classify the author's tone as mocking, apprehensive, vindictive, or humorous. Underline the fragments that support your answer. *Identifying the author's tone*

The 1914 effect
The globalization counter-reaction
Globalization is a highly disruptive force. It provoked a reaction in the early 20th century. Are we seeing a repeat?

Buttonwood's notebook
Jun 14th, 2017 | by Buttonwood

[…]
Globalization was one of the forces that helped to create the First World War because it has profoundly **destabilizing** effects, effects we are also seeing today. In large part globalization is about the more efficient allocation of resources—labor, capital, even land—and that creates losers. People don't like change, especially when they lose from it. […]

5   Globalization **disrupted** both international power structures and domestic ones. This rapid change caused a reaction that was often violent. World War I was not inevitable, but it was unsurprising.

So let us move to the current era of globalization, during which the export share of global **GDP** has more than doubled since the 1960s. New economic powers have emerged to challenge American dominance; first, Japan, and now China and potentially India. Imperial **overstretch threatens** America as it did Edwardian Britain. The ability and,
10   more recently, **willingness** of America to act as global sheriff policeman has been **eroded**. […]

Migration has increased again, not quite to pre-1914 levels but in another direction: from the developing world to the developed. This has led to cultural and economic resentment among voters and imported the **quarrels** of other countries. […] Economic integration means that financial crises can quickly spread; just as American **subprime mortgages** hit the world in 2008, Chinese bad debt may do so in future.

15   Within the economy two big changes have occurred. Manufacturing capacity has moved from the developed world to Asia. Technology has rewarded skilled workers and **widened pay gaps**. Voters have rebelled by turning to parties that reject globalization. This didn't happen in France, but generally it has made life more difficult for **center-left parties** and turned center-right parties more **nativist**. America's Republicans used to be enthusiasts for **free trade**. Now they have elected Donald Trump.

20   Just as in the first era, globalization has disrupted international and domestic power structures. Thankfully this does not mean that another world war is inevitable. But it is easy to imagine regional conflicts: Iran against Saudi Arabia, or an American attack on North Korea that provokes a Chinese reaction.
[…]
The real danger is that this is a zero-sum game. Governments will appear to **grab** a larger share of global trade for their own countries. In doing so, they will cause trade to **shrink**. That might make voters even angrier. From the early
25   1980s to 2008, most companies could count on a business-friendly political environment in the developed world. But it looks as if that era has ended with the financial crisis. Globalization has caused another counter-reaction.

The best hope is that technology can deliver the economic **growth** and rising prosperity voters want. If that happens, these threats will not disappear, but they will be much reduced. But for all the **hype** about new technology, productivity has been **sluggish**. The **omens** are not great.

Adapted from www.economist.com/buttonwoods-notebook/2017/06/14/the-globalisation-counter-reaction?zid=295&ah=0bca374e65f2354d553956ea65f756e0".
Accessed on July 23, 2018.

›› AFTER READING

1. What's the main idea of the text? Explain it in your own words.   `Stating the main idea of the text`

_____

_____

2. Decide if the sentences are true (T) or false (F). If necessary, go back to the text.   `Understanding details`

   a. (   ) Globalization has improved domestic and international power structures.

   b. (   ) Fortunately, there is some expectation of economic growth and rising prosperity in the face of globalization.

   c. (   ) Due to globalization, China and Japan have **come out** as new economic powers that **threaten** American supremacy.

   d. (   ) The movement of manufacturing capacity from the developed world to Asia was one of the forces that **triggered** World War I.

   e. (   ) Because of the advances in technology, workers are more skilled and payments are quite similar around the world.

3. The author ends the text in a pessimistic tone in "The omens are not great." Do you share the same feeling? Talk to a classmate and justify your opinion relating the author's views to your reality.

EXPAND YOUR VOCABULARY

1. Scan the text on page 64 for the words or expressions from the box and infer their meanings. Then insert them in the headlines that follow.

> developing world   GDP
> economic growth   mortgage
> free trade   threatens

a.
> The Rise of China and the Fall of the '_____' Myth
>
> By PANKAJ MISHRA FEB. 7, 2018
>
> 查看简体中文版　查看繁體中文版

Extracted from www.nytimes.com. Accessed on July 24, 2018.

b.
> The circular economy in the _____
>
> BY JEREMY WILLIAMS
>
> September 6, 2016

Extracted from https://makewealthhistory.org. Accessed on July 24, 2018.

c.
> BUSINESS
> April 25 2018 - 17:04
>
> World Cup Generates All of Russia's _____ – Deputy PM

Extracted from https://themoscowtimes.com. Accessed on July 24, 2018.

d.
> Japan's _____ market slammed by higher rates
> Consumers shun increased borrowing costs
>
> January 19, 2017 04:07 JST

Extracted from https://asia.nikkei.com. Accessed on July 24, 2018.

e.
> TRADE TENSIONSu
>
> Trump's China trade war _____ world economy
> Risks grow of dangerous economic divorce despite Beijing's efforts to stop it
>
> Minxin Pei
> March 25, 2018 11:00 JST

Extracted from https://asia.nikkei.com. Accessed on July 24, 2018.

f.
> Brazil sees one-percent _____ growth in 2017
>
> Source: Xinhua 2018-03-02 06:19:55

Extracted from www.xinhuanet.com/english/2018-03/02/c_137009512.htm. Accessed on July 24, 2018.

2. How does the economic status of a country affect its people's behavior? How does it affect you in particular? Exchange ideas with a partner. Then report your opinions to the class.

VOCABULARY IN USE

1. Reread these excerpts from the text on page 64.

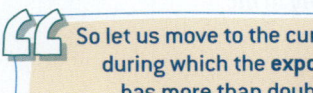

   > So let us move to the current era of **globalization**, during which the **export share** of global GDP has more than doubled since the 1960s.

   > In large part globalization is about the more efficient allocation of **resources**—**labor**, **capital**, even **land**.

   The words in bold are part of a word group about economy. Go back to the text and circle other words or expressions related to the same word group.

2. Below are other words or expressions that belong to the same word group mentioned in activity 1. Match them with their definitions.

   a. inflation
   b. interest rate
   c. budget deficit
   d. bond
   e. recession
   f. capital market
   g. depreciation

   ( ) a market where companies can get capital in the form of shares or bonds, etc.

   ( ) the amount by which what a government spends is more than it receives in taxes or other income, during a particular period of time

   ( ) a continuing increase in prices, or the rate at which prices increase

   ( ) an official document promising that a government or company will pay back money that it has borrowed, often with interest

   ( ) the percentage amount charged by a bank, etc. when you borrow money, or paid to you by a bank when you keep money in an account there

   ( ) a difficult time when there is less trade, business activity, etc. in a country than usual

   ( ) a reduction in the value or price of something

   Extracted from www.ldoceonline.com. Accessed on July 24, 2018.

3. Use the words from the box to complete the text. If necessary, refer back to the definitions in activity 2.

   > bonds   budget deficits   depreciations
   > inflation   interest rates

Is the next global financial crisis brewing?

By Robert J. Samuelson Columnist May 13

The world is not ready for another financial crisis, but another financial crisis may be ready for the world.
[…]
Think Thailand in 1997; a run against the Thai baht ultimately led to crises in South Korea, Indonesia, Russia, and Brazil. Or consider U.S. subprime mortgages; in 2008, they triggered a collapse of global credit markets. Or recall Greece in 2010; its debt threatened the very existence of the euro.

The action these days involves Argentina. It has suffered a sudden loss of confidence. Since mid-April, its currency, the peso, has lost about 12 percent of its value against the dollar. To stem the panic — that is, to persuade investors not to sell pesos for dollars — Argentina's central bank has raised _____ on pesos to 40 percent from 27.25 percent.
[…]
The present president, Mauricio Macri, who took office in late 2015, inherited a doleful legacy of economic mismanagement: high _____, unemployment, and _____ after 12 years of leftish economic policies.
[…]
What is to be feared is the possibility that what's happening to Argentina could happen to other nations. For the past two years or so, international investors have poured money into "emerging market" countries, such as Argentina, Brazil, Mexico, India, China, and Indonesia.
[…]
If these inflows slowed significantly—or stopped altogether—there would be negative consequences for the wider world economy. Countries might have to raise interest rates to defend their currencies against crippling _____. At some point, herd behavior might take over: Investors would buy or sell financial instruments (stocks, _____, currencies, and the like), mainly because they thought that others were going to buy or sell the same instruments.
[…] We may or may not be on the edge of another financial crisis, but regardless of what you think, there's plenty of room for self-doubt. One way or another, Argentina matters.

Extracted from www.washingtonpost.com/opinions/why-the-financial-crisis-in-argentina-matters/2018/05/13/ee84f270-553f-11e8-a551-5b648abe29ef_story.html?utm_term=.2a90fdcf29c8. Accessed on July 24, 2018.

4. Work in pairs to answer the question from the title of the text. Use the words and expressions from the previous activities.

LANGUAGE IN USE 1

Unit 7

PRESENT PERFECT – *SINCE / FOR*

1. Read an excerpt from the text on page 64 and check (✓) the correct alternative to complete the sentence.

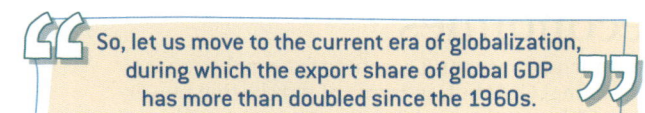

> So, let us move to the current era of globalization, during which the export share of global GDP has more than doubled since the 1960s.

The expression "since the 1960s" refers to…

a. ( ) a period of time.

b. ( ) a starting point.

2. Now read the quote and check (✓) the correct alternative to complete the statement about it.

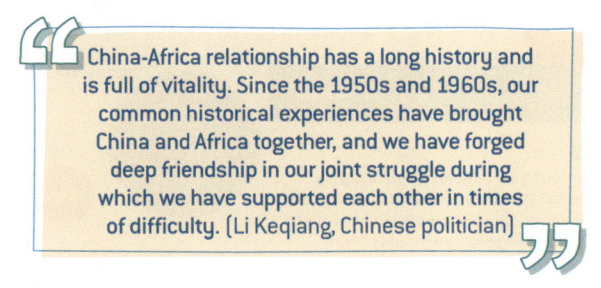

> China-Africa relationship has a long history and is full of vitality. Since the 1950s and 1960s, our common historical experiences have brought China and Africa together, and we have forged deep friendship in our joint struggle during which we have supported each other in times of difficulty. (Li Keqiang, Chinese politician)

Extracted from www.brainyquote.com/quotes/li_keqiang_690958. Accessed on July 24, 2018.

According to Li Keqiang, China and Africa have had friendship bonds for…

a. ( ) the 1950s and 1960s.

b. ( ) more than 60 years.

3. The present perfect is often used with time expressions preceded by *for* and *since*. Use those words to complete the sentences below.

a. We use _____ to talk about the time when an action started.

b. We use _____ to talk about the duration of an action.

4. Why is the present perfect tense used in the sentences in activities 1 and 2?

_____

5. Read the texts and fill in the blanks with the verbs from the box in the present perfect tense, as well as *for* or *since* when needed. Then exchange ideas about the texts in small groups.

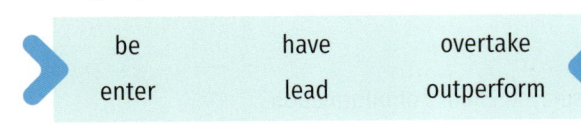

be	have	overtake
enter	lead	outperform

a. China shines a bright light on the **path** ahead

[…]

In his keynote address to a high-level meeting on July 26, Xi Jinping, general secretary of the Central Committee of the Communist Party of China, said socialism with Chinese characteristics _____ a new development stage _____ the 18th National Congress of the CPC.

[…]

Extracted from www.telegraph.co.uk/news/world/china-watch/politics/china-socialism-new-dawn. Accessed on July 24, 2018.

b. China vs. United States: A Tale of Two Economies

[…]

The United States _____ the world's largest economy _____ about 140 years, and it **roughly** accounts for 22% of global GDP. However, in recent times China _____ the U.S. by at least one measure of total economic strength, which is GDP based on purchasing power parity (PPP).

Either way you slice it, the economies are the two strongest globally in absolute terms.

[…]

Extracted from www.visualcapitalist.com/china-vs-united-states-a-tale-of-two-economies. Accessed on July 24, 2018.

c. The Next Global Financial Crisis is Inevitable (Pt 1/2)

July 22, 2018

It _____ ten years _____ the last major financial crisis. With systemic **deregulation undoing** the safeguards, we are due for another crisis very soon. Thomas Hanna, research director of the Democracy Collaborative's Next System Project, says it is almost guaranteed.

[…]

Adapted from https://therealnews.com/stories/the-next-global-financial-crisis-is-inevitable-pt-1-2. Accessed on July 24, 2018.

d. China is the world's new science and technology powerhouse

[…]

While the U.S. _____ the world in the production of scientific knowledge for decades, in terms of both quantity and quality, and the EU as a bloc (still including the UK) _____ the US in numbers of scientific publications _____ 1994, China now publishes more than any other country apart from the U.S. China's scientific priorities are shown by a particularly big increase in its share of published papers in the fields of computer sciences and engineering. While China—for now—is making modest **inroads** into the top-quality segment of publications, it is already on par with Japan.

Extracted from http://bruegel.org/2017/08/china-is-the-worlds-new-science-and-technology-powerhouse. Accessed on July 24, 2018.

EXPAND YOUR READING

1. Skim the text and answer: What's the purpose of this infographic?

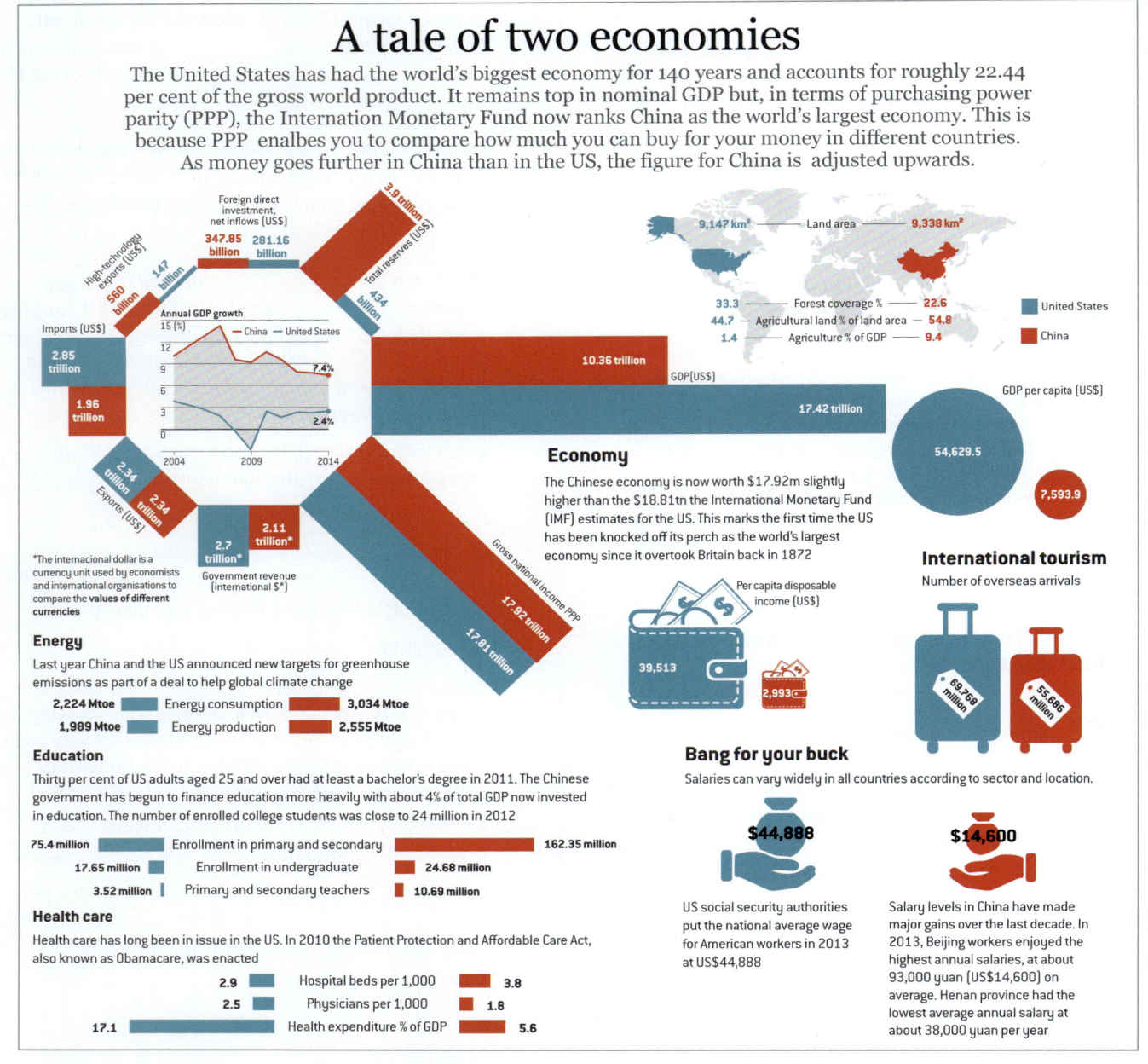

A tale of two economies

The United States has had the world's biggest economy for 140 years and accounts for roughly 22.44 per cent of the gross world product. It remains top in nominal GDP but, in terms of purchasing power parity (PPP), the Internation Monetary Fund now ranks China as the world's largest economy. This is because PPP enalbes you to compare how much you can buy for your money in different countries. As money goes further in China than in the US, the figure for China is adjusted upwards.

High-technology exports (US$): 147 billion / 560 billion
Foreign direct investment, net inflows (US$): 347.85 billion / 281.16 billion
Total reserves (US$): 434 billion / 3.9 trillion
Imports (US$): 2.85 trillion / 1.96 trillion
Exports (US$): 2.34 trillion / 2.34 trillion
Government revenue (international $*): 2.7 trillion* / 2.11 trillion*

*The internacional dollar is a currency unit used by economists and international organisations to compare the **values of different currencies**.

Annual GDP growth (%): China 7.4% / United States 2.4% (2004–2014)

Land area: 9,147 km² / 9,338 km²
Forest coverage %: 33.3 / 22.6
Agricultural land % of land area: 44.7 / 54.8
Agriculture % of GDP: 1.4 / 9.4

GDP (US$): 10.36 trillion / 17.42 trillion
Gross national income PPP: 17.92 trillion / 17.81 trillion

Economy
The Chinese economy is now worth $17.92m slightly higher than the $18.81tn the International Monetary Fund (IMF) estimates for the US. This marks the first time the US has been knocked off its perch as the world's largest economy since it overtook Britain back in 1872

GDP per capita (US$): 54,629.5 / 7,593.9
Per capita disposable income (US$): 39,513 / 2,993

International tourism
Number of overseas arrivals: 69,768 million / 55,686 million

Energy
Last year China and the US announced new targets for greenhouse emissions as part of a deal to help global climate change
- Energy consumption: 2,224 Mtoe / 3,034 Mtoe
- Energy production: 1,989 Mtoe / 2,555 Mtoe

Education
Thirty per cent of US adults aged 25 and over had at least a bachelor's degree in 2011. The Chinese government has begun to finance education more heavily with about 4% of total GDP now invested in education. The number of enrolled college students was close to 24 million in 2012
- Enrollment in primary and secondary: 75.4 million / 162.35 million
- Enrollment in undergraduate: 17.65 million / 24.68 million
- Primary and secondary teachers: 3.52 million / 10.69 million

Bang for your buck
Salaries can vary widely in all countries according to sector and location.
$44,888 — US social security authorities put the national average wage for American workers in 2013 at US$44,888
$14,600 — Salary levels in China have made major gains over the last decade. In 2013, Beijing workers enjoyed the highest annual salaries, at about 93,000 yuan (US$14,600) on average. Henan province had the lowest average annual salary at about 38,000 yuan per year

Health care
Health care has long been in issue in the US. In 2010 the Patient Protection and Affordable Care Act, also known as Obamacare, was enacted
- Hospital beds per 1,000: 2.9 / 3.8
- Physicians per 1,000: 2.5 / 1.8
- Health expenditure % of GDP: 17.1 / 5.6

Adapted from www.visualcapitalist.com/wp-content/uploads/2015/10/tale-of-two-economies2.html. Accessed on May 26, 2018.

2. Read the infographic and check (✓) the correct alternative about its content.
   a. ( ) A larger amount of money from other countries is invested in the USA, when compared to China.
   b. ( ) Both the USA and China have developed policies that address global warming and its effects.

3. Underline the only statement that is <u>not</u> true about infographics.
   a. They are visual representations of complex information.
   b. They present often brightly colored messages with small, clearly-displayed chunks of information.
   c. They are divided into acts and scenes and the use of direct speech is predominant.
   d. Their format includes timelines, flow charts, annotated maps, graphs, Venn diagrams, etc.

LANGUAGE IN USE 2

Unit 7

PRESENT PERFECT vs. SIMPLE PAST

1. Below you will find some extracts from the infographic on page 68. Read them, paying attention to the verb forms in bold, and then use these to complete the chart.

> Salary levels in China **have made** major gains over the last decade. In 2013, Beijing workers **enjoyed** the highest annual salaries, at about 93,000 yuan (US$14,600) on average.

> Thirty per cent of U.S. adults aged 25 and over **had** at least a bachelor's degree in 2011. The Chinese government **has begun** to finance education more heavily with about 4% of the total GDP now invested in education.

Actions or events that started and finished at a specified time in the past	Actions or events that started in the past and continue in the present

2. Go back to the infographic on page 68 and look for another extract that contrasts the use of the present perfect and the simple past. Write it on the lines below, highlighting the verb tenses.

_____
_____
_____
_____

3. Now, based on activities 1 and 2, complete the following explanations with present perfect or simple past.

  a. We use the _____ for actions or events that happened at unspecific times in the past and for actions that started in the past and continue in the present or have consequences in the present.

  b. We use the _____ for actions or events that happened at definite times in the past, actions or events that started and finished in the past, and actions or events that are part of a list of complete actions in the past.

  c. We use expressions such as *yet, since,* and *for* with the _____ and expressions such as *yesterday, two months ago,* and *last week* with the _____.

4. Complete the following text with the verbs in parentheses. Use the present perfect or the simple past.

> New Economy
> […]
> Are We in the New Economy?
> The question ever since the bursting of the tech bubble is, of course, whether or not the new economy is here or still on the horizon. Since the tech boom of the 90s, we _____ (see) the growth of many new and exciting subsectors in tech. These include the sharing economy, the streaming economy, the **gig** economy, cloud computing, big data, and artificial intelligence. The companies involved in tech, particularly Google, Facebook, and Apple, _____ (overtake) most companies in the world in terms of **market cap**. More and more of the traditional manufacturing economy is being automated using innovations coming out of the tech sector. Of course, we still buy and sell products, but the service economy – again enabled by technology – is becoming an ever growing part of the global economy.
>
> So, we are definitely living in an economy that is qualitatively different from the one in the 1980s. Less people are employed in direct manufacturing, we are more anxious about being replaced by a machine than outsourced and data _____ (become) a currency of its own. Now that the new economy is here, we're not as confident that it _____ (be) the one we _____ (want) after all.

Adapted from www.investopedia.com/terms/n/neweconomy.asp#ixzz5MGNDNcwj.
Accessed on July 25, 2018.

5. Use your own words to explain the two economies mentioned in the infographic on page 68. Contrast the present perfect and the simple past in your answer.

_____
_____
_____
_____
_____

6. Talk to a classmate about what you know regarding economic changes of your country. Use the present perfect and the simple past.

69

LISTENING COMPREHENSION

1. **Answer in small groups:** What's a financial crisis? Are we due for another one soon? Explain your views.

2. **Listen to Sharmini Peries, from *The Real News Network*, and check (✓) the correct alternatives to complete the sentences.**

   1. According to a report issued by the Next Systems Project, another major financial crisis is...
      a. ( ) certain.   b. ( ) doubtful.

   2. The report is entitled...
      a. ( ) "Will there be another financial crisis, or even another great recession like that of 2007 and 2008?"
      b. ( ) "The Crisis Next Time: Planning for public ownership as an alternative to corporate bank bailouts."

   3. The report estimates that the next financial crisis could be...
      a. ( ) less severe than the last one we experienced.
      b. ( ) worse than the last one we experienced.

   4. The report recommends the creation of a public banking sector...
      a. ( ) to cope with the next crisis and prevent future crises.
      b. ( ) to banish upcoming crisis for good.

3. **Listen to Thomas Hanna and Sharmini Peries in the second part of the recording and choose the correct segments from the box to complete the transcript. Note that there are three extra alternatives.**

10 years	corporate bank bailouts	neoliberal period
70 years	deregulation	taxpayer-funded rescue
addressing or changing	financial crisis	
average	Great Depression	

THOMAS HANNA: Thank you very much for having me.
SHARMINI PERIES: Thank you for joining us here. […] Let's start with the first issue, which is you went back _____, and you took a look at the history of crises. And so, based on that, tell us why there's another crisis pending.
THOMAS HANNA: Well, I think the first thing that we need to understand is that we are exactly _____ from the last major financial crisis, which was essentially the biggest financial crisis in this country in 70 years, since the _____. And if you look at history in the post-1970 period, what we call the _____, crises happen on _____ about once every 10 years. So, 10 years from the financial crisis, we're looking at a time when there should, or probably would be, another _____ just based on history alone. That's not taking into account what has happened in the intervening 10 years since the financial crisis. And essentially what has happened is nothing. We've had very little movement on _____ any of the underlying basis of the financial sector that caused the crisis. […]

Extracted from https://therealnews.com/stories/the-next-global-financial-crisis-is-inevitable-pt-1-2. Accessed on May 20, 2018.

4. **Work with a partner to answer the questions:** In what ways would Brazil be affected if a new financial crisis erupted in the USA? In your opinion, what's the best way out of a crisis? How could growing economic inequality be addressed in middle-income countries like Brazil, for example? Report your opinions to the class.

>> EXPAND YOUR HORIZONS >>>

Check (✓) the column that best describes your opinion about each statement. Then discuss your answers with your classmates and teacher, justifying your point of view.

	I agree.	I'm not sure.	I disagree.
a. Globalization is beneficial to the world economy because it allows countries to interact and cooperate, enables the development of new technologies, and improves citizens' lives.			
b. China has become a leading manufacturer of goods without being ready to take over so much and at such low costs.			
c. Everyone should prepare for the worst financial crisis since the 2008 crisis that started in the United States and spread across the world.			

UNIT 8
Spotting Fake News among the Real Stories

FACTS
FAKE NEWS

▶ IN THIS UNIT YOU WILL...
- talk about the importance of distinguishing fake from real stories;
- understand what can be done to check if news is fake or not;
- review some verb tenses;
- learn what embedded questions are and how they are formed.

LEAD OFF
- What does the image mean to you?
- How can you relate the image to the title of the unit?
- In your opinion, why do people fabricate fake news?

READING

BEFORE READING

Check (✓) the statements that are true about you. *Thinking about personal experience*

a. (   ) I get my news from print newspapers.
b. (   ) I listen to the news on the radio.
c. (   ) I watch the news on TV.
d. (   ) I read the news online.

WHILE READING

Read the news article below and find the answer to the following question: Why does Facebook have a fake news "war room"? *Scanning*

---

www.theguardian.com/technology/2018/oct/18/facebook-war-room-social-media-fake-news-politics

Facebook has a fake news "war room" — but is it really working?

Corporation shows off room of engineers, data scientists and other experts but offers reporters few new specifics

Facebook is promoting a new "war room" as a part of its solution to election interference, unveiling a team of specialists working to stop the spread of *misinformation* and propaganda.

It's unclear how well it's working.

The Silicon Valley company, which has faced intensifying *scrutiny* over its role in amplifying malicious
5 political content, opened its doors to reporters to tour a new workspace at its Menlo Park **headquarters** on Wednesday. Engineers, data scientists, **threat** investigators and other Facebook experts from 20 teams recently began collaborating inside the so-called "war room", a term that political campaigns typically use to describe operation centers.

The press **briefing** provided minimal new information about Facebook's specific strategies and impacts
10 when it comes to combatting foreign interference and false news. The corporation has been **eager** to publicly demonstrate that it is taking abuses on its platforms seriously *amid* an avalanche of scandals. That includes a vast data **breach**, government *inquiries* across the globe, new ad fraud allegations, and the continuing stream of viral fake content and hate speech.

[…] WhatsApp, the Facebook-owned messaging service, has also been linked to widespread false news stories
15 that have led to violence and mob lynchings in India. The platform has further struggled to mitigate harms it is causing in Myanmar, where an explosion of social media hate speech has contributed to violence and genocide. American hate groups and far-right activists have also weaponized the site.

On Wednesday morning, a group of journalists **crowded** outside a windowless room, *snapping* iPhone photos of a closed door with a small sign stuck to it that said "WAR ROOM" in red letters. Inside, digital
20 dashboards displayed real-time information about activity on the platform. CNN played in the background, and the wall displayed a large American flag and motivational posters saying "Focus on impact" and "Bring the world closer together".

Some screens were "off the record" and could not be photographed, Facebook communications representatives said. The names of employees inside the room could not be published.

[…]

25 Samidh Chakrabarti, Facebook's director of elections and civic engagement, said WhatsApp had been "doing quite a bit of work to try to stay ahead of any sort of emerging issues", adding: "They've been **cracking down** on *spamming* accounts on WhatsApp – and they've removed hundreds of thousands."

Facebook […] noted that it has a fact-checking partnership with the Associated Press in all 50 states for the midterms. The continuing collaborations with **third-party** factcheckers, however, have been controversial, with
30 some partner journalists expressing frustration over the **seemingly** minimal impact.

Asked how Facebook has been measuring the success of the factchecking and if the company had new data on its effectiveness, Harbath told the Guardian that it was "one piece of the puzzle" and cited "automated work" to reduce the reach of "clickbait" and "ad farms".

[…]

Adapted from www.theguardian.com/technology/2018/oct/18/facebook-war-room-social-media-fake-news-politics Accessed on November 20, 2018.

Unit 8

» AFTER READING

1. Read the text and complete the chart below with the information presented in it. *Understanding details*

a. What Facebook is trying to combat together with the press:	
b. The name of the operation center Facebook uses to meet with journalists:	
c. Characteristics of the war room:	
d. Kind of partnership that Facebook has with Associated Press:	
e. Examples of abuses taking place on the Facebook platform:	

2. Read the statements below and check (✓) the one that describes the main purpose of the text. *Identify the main purpose of a text*

a. ( ) To present the main companies involved in spreading false news.

b. ( ) To present Facebook and what kind of false news it may spread.

c. ( ) To inform readers about the existence and the meaning of a term used to describe the fighting of false news.

d. ( ) To inform readers about an action Facebook is taking in order to avoid the spread of false news.

3. Read the questions below and discuss them with a classmate. Then share your ideas with the rest of the class.

a. What negative effects can you think of regarding the spread of fake news?

b. Do you think that social media companies have an obligation to prevent people from being exposed to fake news?

c. What do you think makes some fake news go viral? Do you think that people are aware of the fact that some pieces of news are false when they share them? Justify your answer.

d. Do you think that fake news is more likely to be spread by bots (web robots) than by people? Justify your answer.

EXPAND YOUR VOCABULARY

Refer to the text on page 72 and find the words in italics that correspond to the definitions below.

a. _____ : careful and thorough examination of someone or something

b. _____ : while noisy, busy, or confused events are happening – used in writing or news reports

c. _____ : incorrect information, especially when deliberately intended to deceive people

d. _____ : questions you ask in order to get information

e. _____ : taking a photograph

f. _____ : email accounts that send the same message to many different people, usually as a way of advertising something – used to show disapproval

Adapted from www.ldoceonline.com. Accessed on November 20, 2018.

73

VOCABULARY IN USE

1. **Read a fragment extracted from the article on page 72 and choose the most appropriate explanation for "clickbait."**

   > [...] Asked how Facebook has been measuring the success of the factchecking and if the company had new data on its effectiveness, Harbath told the Guardian that it was "one piece of the puzzle" and cited "automated work" to reduce the reach of "**clickbait**" and "ad farms".

   a. ( ) Online tool developed to keep users online for the longest time possible in order to make them interact with people from different locations without displaying their identity.
   b. ( ) Social media tool that allows people to create content on the web and spread it as fake news.
   c. ( ) Online content intended to attract users and encourage them to click on a link to access a certain webpage.

2. **The following words are commonly used when talking about fake news. In pairs, match them with their meanings.**

   a. sham
   b. slander
   c. hoax
   d. bot
   e. web crawler

   ( ) a false warning about something dangerous
   ( ) a computer program that finds information on the Internet, especially so that this information can be used by a search engine
   ( ) a false spoken statement about someone, intended to damage the good opinion that people have of that person
   ( ) someone or something that is not what they are claimed to be – used to show disapproval
   ( ) a computer program that continuously performs the same operation, such as searching for specific information online

   Extracted from https://www.ldoceonline.com/. Accessed on October 05, 2018.

3. **Still in pairs, read the following extract and decide which word from the previous activity it refers to.**

   > In 2011, Katie Holmes settled a lawsuit against celebrity gossip rag, *The Star*, for $50 million. The suit was over an article that claimed that Holmes was a drug addict. The magazine issued an apology and even said that they would donate a "substantial donation" to one of Holmes's favorite non-profits. [...]

   Extracted from www.ranker.com/list/celebrities-who-sued-for-defamation/jacob-shelton. Accessed on October 7, 2018.

4. **How is it possible to tell a fake from a real story? Are you able to identify a fake story? How important is this? Work in small groups and figure out which of the statements below are real and which are fake. Then exchange ideas with your classmates.**

   a. (_____) There are more tigers in captivity in the U.S. than in the wild worldwide.
   b. (_____) Queen Elizabeth II removed Barack and Michelle Obama from royal wedding guest list.
   c. (_____) Between 2011 and 2013, China used more cement in three years than the U.S. did in the entire 20th century.
   d. (_____) A woman named Violet Jessop survived the sinking of both the Titanic and its sister ship, the Britannic.
   e. (_____) Scientists who work with cockroaches often become addicted to pre-ground coffee.
   f. (_____) England intends to forbid Canadians to use expressions created by Shakespeare.

LANGUAGE IN USE 1

Unit 8

VERB TENSE REVIEW

1. Work in pairs. Read the fragments below, extracted from the article on page 72, paying attention to the underlined parts. Then match them with what they express.

> a. The corporation <u>has been</u> eager to publicly demonstrate that it is taking abuses on its platforms seriously amid an avalanche of scandals.

> b. The Silicon Valley company, which has faced intensifying scrutiny over its role in amplifying malicious political content, <u>opened</u> its doors to reporters to tour a new workspace at its Menlo Park headquarters on Wednesday.

> c. Facebook <u>is promoting</u> a new "war room" as a part of its solution to election interference, unveiling a team of specialists working to stop the spread of misinformation and propaganda.

> d. [...] "war room", a term that political campaigns typically <u>use</u> to describe operation centers

( ) a finished action in the past
( ) an action in progress at the moment
( ) an action that started at an indefinite time in the past and is still true in the present
( ) a fact

2. Use *will* or *be going to* and the verbs from the box to complete the extracts below.

> end up   happen   miss

a. "That is, if we take the current culturally liberal consensus of what is fake news as our decider, then we _____ entirely _____ that news which is speaking truth to the power of that consensus, aren't we? Which is rather to miss the point of the speaking truth part."

b. "Any system which suppresses the news _____ also _____ enforcing, not challenging, current misconceptions that are widely believed."

Extracted from www.washingtonexaminer.com/opinion/youtube-is-going-to-fight-fake-news-but-how-do-you-define-fake-news. Accessed on October 8, 2018.

c. "Throughout the history of the 20th century, whether in Soviet-era Russia or Nazi Germany, regimes based on lies have ultimately collapsed because reality catches up with them. In today's more open societies, this reality check _____ more quickly."

Extracted from www.ft.com/content/a352f9a6-99f4-11e8-ab77-f854c65a4465. Accessed on October 8, 2018.

EXPAND YOUR READING

1. Read the title of the following essay and answer: What kind of information do you expect to find in the text?

_____

_____

_____

EXPERIENCE: I WRITE FAKE NEWS
by AMLE - Association for Middle Level Education

I've been writing articles for **far-right** websites in the US for a year now. I didn't **set out** to do this; it started in October 2016, when I was finishing my PhD in London. My **funding ran out**, and I
5 started writing content to pay the rent. I found clients through websites that allow potential writers to **bid** for work, and then build a portfolio of reviews from clients. There is an enormous amount of work available – everything from
10 writing product copy to ghost-writing novels.

The first jobs I got were pretty **shady**. I was writing fake Amazon reviews and descriptions of perfume that had yet to be produced. A **reliable** client put me in touch with a colleague
15 who runs a number of websites, one of which focuses on news about, and reviews of, guns. I have never seen a gun, let alone used one, but I took the job. The site carries reviews of handgun accessories, and for each product there is a link
20 to Amazon. My client gets paid for every click-through he generates through Amazon's affiliate scheme. There are vast numbers of such sites: I've written fake reviews of amplifiers, baby products, printers, [...].

[...]

25 Recently, we've tried to **boost** the site **up** the Google rankings. This involves writing for other sites that are visited by gun enthusiasts, a lot of them pretty extreme, and **sneaking in** a link to our own site. This is against their rules, so you
30 have to hide the link deep in the middle of a dense paragraph, so no one notices.

[...]

But I don't have a moral problem with it. I wish I had some **snappy** argument about why what I'm doing is not wrong. I'm furthering ignorance,
35 certainly, and perhaps contributing to an atmosphere of **hatred**. But I don't think people have died as a result of my work. [...]

I have never made up a statistic, invented a story, or been racist. I think I would refuse to do so. I
40 see my role as providing an extreme **right-wing** interpretation of breaking news. Though I do not believe the stories I write, I don't count this as lying.

I suppose the articles I write would be regarded as fake news. Though that has got a lot of
45 attention recently, I think it is merely a new term for an old phenomenon. This type of ideologically driven journalism pre-dates the Internet and perhaps even the printing press. [...]

My friends know what I do for a living, and
50 find it **amusing**. There is an absurd humor in a young(ish), left(ish), British arts student pretending to be a far-right, middle-aged, American gun enthusiast. They recognize that my **earnings** give me the freedom to live and
55 work where I want.

I'll continue to work for this client for at least another six months, by which time I will have finished my PhD and saved enough to go traveling. Then I'll get my first proper job in five
60 years. If my rate continues to increase, though, I'll continue to write for this client. It's easy money.

Adapted from www.theguardian.com/lifeandstyle/2018/jan/26/experience-i-write-fake-news. Accessed on October 8, 2018.

2. Were your guesses in activity 1 correct? Why or why not? Talk to your classmates.

3. What kind of essay is this? Check (✓). Then justify your choice.

a. ( ) exposition

b. ( ) description

c. ( ) argument

d. ( ) narrative

LANGUAGE IN USE 2

Unit 8

EMBEDDED QUESTIONS

1. Read the sentences below, paying attention to the parts in bold, and check (✓) the appropriate alternatives.

> **Can you tell** which news story is real and which one is fake?
> (Which news story is real and which one is fake?)

> **I wonder if** fake news might actually be a good thing for real journalism.
> (Might fake news actually be a good thing for real journalism?)

> **Do you know** how to spot fact from fiction?
> (How do you spot fact from fiction?)

> **We need to find out** whether he is a victim of fake news or not.
> (Is he a victim of fake news or not?)

a. ( ) The sentences above are questions, but they are not direct questions. They are inside another question or statement.

b. ( ) The parts in bold are introductory phrases to these questions.

c. ( ) The structure of these questions is the same as the one used in direct questions.

In English, a question that appears in a declarative statement or in another question is called an *embedded question*.

Embedded questions are used when we don't want to be too direct. Below you'll find some other common introductory phrases used in embedded questions:

> Could you tell me...?   The question is...
> I wanted to know...   Who knows...?

2. Transform the direct questions below into embedded questions. Use the introductory phrases from the box. Make sure you do not repeat them in two different questions.

> I wonder...
> I can't understand...
> What I need to know is...
> Would you mind telling...
> We need to find out...
> I'd like to know...

a. Where does she live?

_____

_____

b. Why do people post fake content on social media?

_____

_____

c. Is this post real or fake?

_____

_____

d. What does this news report mean?

_____

_____

e. Where do her friends live?

_____

_____

f. Did she order this package online?

_____

_____

LISTENING COMPREHENSION

1. **You are going to listen to a teacher talk about what he does to help students identify real news. Listen and answer the following questions.**

   a. In how many steps can real news be confirmed?
   _____

   b. What are these steps?
   _____
   _____

2. **Match the columns according to what the teacher says about each step. Then listen again and check.**

   a. argument   c. language
   b. evidence   d. reliability

   (   ) "determine if a source is trustworthy"
   (   ) "check sources, citations, and facts"
   (   ) "identify the two sides in every story"
   (   ) "show how words and tone matter"

3. **Read the extracts from the text and identify which step from activity 2 each of them corresponds to.**

   a. _____ "The final step of identifying real news is to evaluate the tone and level of sensationalism of an article. Incorporate analysis of word choice in evaluating the reliability of a news source."

   b. _____ "As students learn to discern real from fake news, it is important to remember that there is a difference between fake news and inaccurate information. Reliable news sources will include links to professional sources, fact-based evidence, and will present multiple sides of an issue. Train students to check the evidence within the article they are reading."

   c. _____ "We now know that there are intentional efforts to widely disseminate false content on social media channels, blogs, and other websites. Making sure students know how to measure the reliability of a source is a critical first step to helping them spot fake news."

   d. _____ "This step can be tricky, as even the most factual news outlets can still have a bias or unique perspective on a topic. A biased article does not inherently imply that it's fake news; rather, it's part of the overall formula (along with reliability and evidence) that can help students. A well-written article is balanced, representing many sides of a story. Recognizing that there are, more often than not, multiple perspectives of an event or a political issue, can lead students to better understand their community and the world as a whole."

4. **Do you usually follow these four steps to check if the news is true? Why or why not? Are you going to follow them from now on? Justify.**

>> EXPAND YOUR HORIZONS >>>>

Check (✓) the column that best describes your opinion about each quote below. Then discuss your answers with your classmates and teacher, justifying your point of view.

	I agree.	I'm not sure.	I disagree.
a. The source of information might affect its credibility and authenticity; that's why it's always important to check our sources and references.			
b. Trends demonstrate that people are changing the way they access the news or access information. In a few years, TV will not be as relevant as it is today.			
c. The rise of fake news has brought a new set of worries to the spotlight. We are now subject to many threats when surfing the web, and it's our responsibility to make sure we spread only relevant and real content.			

REVIEW 4

Units 7 and 8

1. Look at the text below. Where do you think it is from? *Identifying the source of the text*

   a. ( ) An online encyclopedia   b. ( ) A print newspaper   c. ( ) A news website

---

Are people becoming less reliant on Facebook for their news?

Paul Chadwick

Two new surveys suggest the public still values traditional news publishers

When you try to imagine a media diet consisting only of retweets, random blogs or the Facebook posts of family and friends, you grasp the value of journalism created by professional media organizations. Traditional news organizations aren't perfect, but they are not fake. Nor are they as readily manipulated as we know social media can be. Professional journalism's longstanding skills of access to sources, verification, presentation and dependable distribution remain an essential element of what **nourishes** democratic societies.

That insight, sharply conveyed in images accompanying this column, informs a new campaign to promote the well-regarded Columbia Journalism Review (CJR), a not-for-profit magazine based at the graduate school of journalism at Columbia University, New York. The campaign's assertion of the importance to a healthy democracy of the public sphere – alongside the private, of course – coincides with two new reports that, in different ways, affirm the same. However, the emerging picture is not clear yet.

"Americans and the news media: what they do – and don't – understand about each other" **broadly** finds that journalists and the public have similar aims, but that to maintain trust journalists have to better explain what they do. The American Press Institute and the Associated Press-Norc Center for Public Affairs Research at the University of Chicago surveyed 2,019 adult Americans and 1,127 journalists, and analyzed their expectations. Both groups strongly valued accuracy and fairness. Journalists rated their role as watchdogs who scrutinize the powerful far more highly (93%) than did the public (54%). Both groups saw transparency and trust as linked. The CJR has been casting a critical eye over journalism for almost 60 years, and its editor and publisher, Kyle Pope, told me demands on CJR from the public have been growing as US media organizations dispense with their public editors, who are in-house but independent contacts/critics known elsewhere as news **ombudsmen** or readers' editors.

[…]

Looking beyond the US, the 2018 digital news report of the UK-based Reuters Institute for the study of journalism tends to support the notion that the public understands that "real journalism matters", although the authors' optimism is cautious. Reliance on Facebook for news is falling, they report, and **willingness** to pay for professionally produced journalism seems to be increasing. But a majority prefer "side-door access" to news through search and social media, rather than going direct to the traditional news publishers. Use of messaging apps is rising "as news consumers look for more private (and less confrontational) spaces to communicate", the report says.

Adapted from www.theguardian.com/commentisfree/2018/jun/17/facebook-news-publishers-accuracy Accessed on November 20, 2018.

---

2. Find what each of these numbers refer to in the text and match them with the alternatives. *Understanding details*

   a. 1,127   b. 93   c. 54

   ( ) the percentage of journalists who value accuracy and fairness in news
   ( ) the number of journalists interviewed in the survey
   ( ) the percentage of random people who value accuracy and fairness in news

3. From your point of view, does "real journalism" matter? Is most news on Facebook and other social media reliable? Justify your answer.

_____
_____
_____

4. Read the text and fill in the blanks with the verbs from the box.

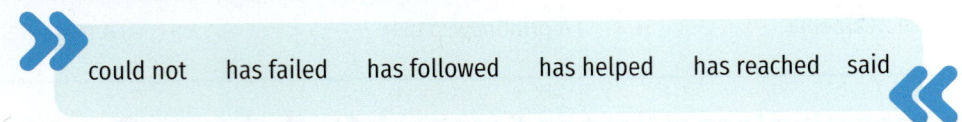

> could not   has failed   has followed   has helped   has reached   said

[…]
China faces certain social challenges, and creative measures are needed to overcome them.
[…]
Two key words, transcendence and rejuvenation, best describe this new era. Here transcendence means going beyond the two preceding stages. Mr. Xi _____ a major conclusion — that the two previous stages _____ negate each other. The new stage will help deepen reform and opening-up under the socialist system. […]
Transcendence also means going beyond the Western mode of development, which _____ only a small number of countries with a cumulative population of about 1 billion to lead comfortable lives but _____ to realize common prosperity. […]
China _____ its own path of economic development and become the largest and fastest-growing developing country. As Mr. Xi _____, socialism with Chinese characteristics has widened the path of modernization for developing countries […].

Adapted from www.telegraph.co.uk/news/world/china-watch/politics/china-socialism-new-dawn. Accessed on October 14, 2018.

5. Read the extracts from the previous text and write whether the verb forms in bold indicate a prediction for the future, an action that started in the past and continues up to the moment, or a fact.

a. "China **faces** certain social challenges":
   _____

b. "The new stage **will help** deepen reform and opening-up under the socialist system":
   _____

c. "As Mr. Xi said, socialism with Chinese characteristics **has widened** the path of modernization for developing countries":
   _____

6 Check (✓) the text that contains an embedded question. Then underline that question.

a.
( ) **Will Facebook Decide Which News Is Fake?** 
Facebook, a site from which a substantial number of people acquire their daily news, has decided that pages that post fake stories will be banned from advertising. That's a perfectly fine decision, but it raises a bigger and more profound question: Who decides which news is fake? Mark Zuckerberg?
Read more

b.
( ) **Apparently, CNBC Is Now A PR Firm** 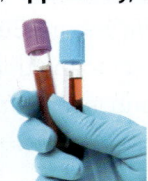
Wonder why "fake news" is taking hold as a concept and a description? Look no further than a recent CNBC article and its accompanying video, showcasing a new blood collection product.
Read more

c.
( ) **An Object Lesson In Fake 'News' Sites** 
"Fake news" has become a meme — and it's all over the Internet. For example, take a look at a site that claims to provide real evidence that aspartame is carcinogenic in humans. Not only does it cite old data, it has picked a study whose authors don't agree with them. Can you get much more fake than that?
Read more

Extracted from www.acsh.org/tags/fake-news. Accessed on October 14, 2018.

GRAMMAR OVERVIEW

Verb tenses

Tense	Use(s)	Example(s) – affirmative	Example(s) – negative	Example(s) – interrogative
Simple past	• Completed action in the past. When used with the past continuous, refers to an action that interrupts an action in progress in the past.	She was sleeping when I **arrived** home.	When their boss **came** in, everything was a mess.	Were you studying when she **called** you?
Past continuous	• An action in progress in the past.	While the students **were doing** the activities, the teacher **was correcting** their tests.	Debbie **was not** / **wasn't talking**, so I **was not** / **wasn't** talking either.	What **were** you **doing** while I **was doing** my homework?
Present perfect	• Past experiences when time is not mentioned; • Actions that started in the past and are still going on in the present; • Finished actions that influenced the present; • When someone has gone to a place and returned (been); • When someone has gone to a place and has not returned yet (gone).	I **have** / **'ve lived** in Canada since 2009. She **has started** a new job. Sue is tired. She **has studied** hard all day. I **have** / **'ve been** to Spain once. The kids **have gone** to the beach and they will be back by Sunday.	She **has not** / **hasn't lost** her tickets. He **has not** / **hasn't finished** his homework yet. I'm hopeless. I **have not** / **haven't done** my chores lately. I **have** / **'ve** never **been** to China. Dad **has not** / **hasn't returned** from France.	**Have** you **met** the new neighbor? **Have** you **started** planning your trip? You look exhausted. **Have** you **worked** hard today? **Have** you ever **been** to Greece? Where is Grace? **Has** she **returned** from work?
Present perfect (adverbs) Just Already Always Since For Never Yet	• *just*: an action that happened very recently; • *already*: an action that is not a new experience; • *always*: something that has been true for a lifetime; • *since*: a previous point in time; • *for*: indicates how long something lasts; • *never*: something that has not ever happened; • *yet*: an activity that has not happened, but is expected to happen soon;	I've **just** finished work. He has **already** bought the tickets. We have **always** loved this house. I've lived in NY **since** 2015. We've been traveling **for** two weeks. They have **never** been to China.	I haven't met him **yet**.	Have you read this book **yet**?

Modal verbs

Modal verb	Use(s)	Example(s) – affirmative	Example(s) – negative	Example(s) – interrogative
Can	• Ability; • Permission; • Possibility; • Requests; • Offers; • General truths; • Prohibition (can't).	I **can drive** your car. You **can come** here anytime you'd like.	I **cannot** / **can't read** without my glasses. You **cannot** / **can't dive** in this pool.	**Can** you play the drums? **Can** you give me some information, please?
Could	• Ability in the past; • Formal requests; • Suggestions; • Possibility.	He **could go** camping.	Susan **could not** / **couldn't run** that fast before; now she's beating everyone in the race.	**Could** I **take** your order?
Be able to*	• Ability (in all tenses); • To use the infinitive.	He **was able to** pay for his own food. I would love to **be able to** travel to Greece.	He's **not able to** drive at this age. I **won't be able to** finish this game today.	Are you **able to** walk that far? Do you think he **would be able to** take me home after school?

* It is not a modal verb, but sometimes it replaces *can* and *could*.

GRAMMAR OVERVIEW

Need to vs. Have to

Verb	Use(s)	Example(s) – affirmative	Example(s) – negative	Example(s) – interrogative
Need to	· To talk about something that is / isn't necessary for someone to do.	She **needs to pick up** her luggage before she checks out.	I **don't need to worry** about her.	**Do** I **need to dress up** for the party?
Have to	· To express obligation; something we are committed to; · Something that cannot be postponed; · To express no obligation or necessity to do something (*not have to*).	Flight attendants **have to wear** uniforms. You can't miss this plane. You **have to be** on time for your next flight.	They **don't have to worry** about it anymore.	**Do** you **have to tell** him our secret?

Phrasal verbs

Kind of phrasal verb	Use	Examples
Separable	· With the object between the verb and the particle.	I have to **take back** the book I lent you. I have to **take** it **back**.
Inseparable	· Cannot separate the verb from the particle.	I just **came across** this new app. It's awesome!

Conditional sentences

Conditional	Use	Form	Examples
Zero	· To talk about things that are always true; · To talk about general habits.	If + simple present, → simple present	**If** you **add** one and one, you **get** two. **If** you **exercise** daily, you **stay** in shape.
First	· To talk about results that are likely to happen in the future.	If + simple present, → future with *will*	**If** I **study** hard, I **will** pass the test.

Tag questions

Verb tense	Examples – affirmative	Examples – negative
Simple present	I am coming with you, **aren't I**? You have some news for us, **don't you?**	You are never late, **are you**? There are no leftovers from lunch, **are there**?
Simple past	He was late again, **wasn't he**?	They weren't very nice to us, **were they**?
Present perfect	You have traveled to Europe many times, **haven't you**?	Mary has never been to England, **has she**?

Make vs. do

Verb	Common collocations	Examples
Do	do research	The teacher told us to **do** some **research** on sea animals.
Do	do the shopping	Mom is responsible for **doing the shopping** on Saturdays.
Make	make plans	I would like us to **make plans** for the summer.
Make	make a reservation	Don't forget to **make a reservation** at the Plaza.

Relative clauses

Relative pronoun	Use	Example(s)
Who	• People (Defining and non-defining)	I don't know the girl **who** called you yesterday.
Which	• Animals and things (Defining and non-defining)	This is the rarest species **which** can only be found in Africa.
That	• People, animals, and things; • Informal situations. (Defining only)	The man **that** spoke at the meeting was very wise.
Whom	• Formal style or written form; as the object of the relative clause. (Defining and non-defining)	There was only one person to **whom** the boy spoke frequently.
Whose	• People and animals; • Possessive situations. (Defining and non-defining)	I have a friend **whose** brother is annoying.
Where	• Places (Defining and non-defining)	I want to live in a place **where** there are plenty of trees.
No pronoun	• When the object of the clause is defined by the relative pronoun. (Defining only)	I'm sorry, but that is all (**that**) I have to say. The people (**who / whom / that**) we talked to were very happy.

Set vs. *get*

Verb	Common collocations	Examples
Set	set a tone	Her speech today **set the tone** for the group meeting.
Get	get a call	I didn't **get a call** from anyone.

Word categories

Category	Use	Examples
Idioms related to technology	• To talk about technology.	Being part of a **well-oiled machine** makes things work smoothly! His new car has all the **bells and whistles** he could dream of.
Expressions about travel	• To talk about different and modern ways of traveling.	We often go **couchsurfing** on our vacation. Ann goes **glamping** every year with her boyfriend in beautiful nature and modern luxury. I can't wait to read the chronicles of a **solivagant** journey through Asia.
-ly adverbs	• To show us how someone does something. Adverbs can modify verbs, adjectives, or other adverbs. They occur in different types such as: manner, time, frequency, degree, focusing, and evaluative.	George spoke **softly** to his wife. We watch the news **daily**. I come to this coffee shop **regularly**. This class starts at **precisely** 8 o'clock. **Honestly**, I could watch another episode. *Exceptions*: Look, it's raining **hard**! They are running very **fast**.
Terms related to fake news	• To talk about fake news.	The **anonymous group** was asked to apologize for spreading **fake news**. Salespeople often use **confirmation bias** to state only the positive aspects of their product. They used digital **misinformation** to turn the public against the president.

GRAMMAR OVERVIEW

Passive voice

Verb tense	Form	Examples
Simple present	am / is / are + past participle	The housework **is done** by everyone at home.
Present continuous	am / is / are + being + past participle	A poem **is being written** by a famous poet.
Simple past	was / were + past participle	A very nice song **was sung** by the group.
Modal verbs: *can, must, will, should, may, might, could.*	modal verb + be + past participle	Pancakes **can be made** here in the kitchen. Employees **must be paid** in the first week of the month. The contract **will be signed** by the manager. This car **should be repaired** by Friday. The book **may be read** by the teacher.

Discourse markers

Use	Discourse markers	Examples
Addition	*furthermore*	The boys were cold and tired, and, **furthermore**, they were starving.
Cause / reaction / effect	*therefore*	It's raining. **Therefore**, they need their umbrellas.
Comparison	*unlike*	**Unlike** her brother, she cannot swim.
Consequence / result	*so*	**So**, we'll see you at the party, Michael.
Contrast	*however*	They are lost. **However**, we still have hope.
Emphasis	*as a matter of fact*	I'm not a child. **As a matter of fact**, I'm sixteen years old.
Condition	*as long as*	You will pass the test **as long as** you study.
Illustrating	*for instance*	What would you do, **for instance**, if you found some money in the train?
Ordering	*now*	**Now**, let's welcome Kate to our show!
Purpose	*in order (not) to*	We never forget the homework **in order not to** upset the teacher.

Embedded / Indirect questions

Use	Common beginnings	Example(s)
A question that is included inside another question or statement in order to sound more polite. The word order in the main question doesn't change.	Can you remember...? Can you tell / show me...? Do you have any idea...? Do you know...? I wonder if you would mind telling / showing me...? Let's ask... We need to find out... Would you mind explaining...? Would you mind telling / showing me...?	**Can you remember** what he said? **Can you tell me** if we are almost there? **Do you have any idea** if he is the doctor? **I wonder if you would mind telling** me what to do? **Let's ask** what time the bus arrives. **We need to find out** where we should go next. **Would you mind explaining** why she decided not to come? **Would you mind telling me** where he is?

LANGUAGE REFERENCE

UNIT 1
PRESENT PERFECT
Usage Notes

The present perfect is often used to refer to:

- our past experiences.

  Have you ever **tried** Thai food?

- actions that started at an unspecific time in the past and continue up to the present.

  They **have started** making their honeymoon plans.

- actions that happened in the past but are important at the time of speaking.

  I'm exhausted. I**'ve worked** hard all day long.

  We**'ve missed** the bus. Let's take a cab.

- actions that refer to a time that is not yet finished.

  Has she **been** to the club **this week**?

  We **haven't had** time to talk **today**.

- When someone has gone to a place and returned, we use the present perfect of the verb *be*.

  A: **Have** you ever **been** to the new mall by the bay?

  B: No, I haven't. Is it nice?

- When someone has gone to a place but has not returned, we use the present perfect of the verb *go*.

  A: Where's Grandma? She hasn't visited us lately.

  B: She**'s gone** to your aunt's farm and won't be back until the end of the month.

PAST CONTINUOUS – SIMPLE PAST
Usage Notes

- The past continuous is used to talk about actions in progress in the past.

  I **was working** in the morning.

- In general, the action described by the simple past interrupts the situation described by the past continuous.

  Leo **was taking** a shower when the lights **went out**.

  Where **were you going** when I **called** you?

- Use only the past continuous for multiple actions happening at the same time in the past.

  While Claire **was getting dressed** for work, her brother **was doing the dishes**.

  What **were you doing** while I **was having** lunch?

- The conjunctions *when* and *while* are used to indicate "during the time that" and to connect two situations happening at the same time.

  They took lots of pictures **when** they were traveling.

  While he was watching his favorite TV show, he preferred to remain silent.

SEPARABLE AND INSEPARABLE PHRASAL VERBS

Many phrasal verbs are transitive, which means that they take an object, while others are intransitive and don't take an object.

Transitive phrasal verbs can be used in different ways: in some <u>the verb and the particle can be separated</u> (these are called **separable phrasal verbs**) and the object can be positioned in the middle, between the verb and the particle, or at the end; while in others the object must come at the end because <u>the verb and the particle can't be separated</u> (these are called **inseparable phrasal verbs**).

When **separable phrasal verbs** are used with a pronoun, the pronoun must be placed between the verb and the particle.

Can you repeat that old saying? I want to **write it down**.

I want to **write down that old saying**. Can you repeat it?

Here are some separable and inseparable phrasal verbs.

Separable phrasal verbs	Inseparable phrasal verbs
throw away	catch up
turn on / off	check in
look up	come across
call off	drop by
figure out	grow up
make up	put up with
pick up	run into
put on	look after
turn down	run out of
get on / off*	write down

*can be both separable and inseparable depending on the context of the sentence.

85

LANGUAGE REFERENCE

IDIOMS

Idiom	Meaning	Example
a well-oiled machine	something that works very smoothly and effectively	If you're trained correctly you become like **a well-oiled machine**.
bells and whistles	extra things that are offered with a product or system to make it more attractive to buyers	The basic rule about computer memory is this: Buy as much as you can afford, even if it means sacrificing other **bells and whistles**.
get your wires crossed	to become confused about what someone is saying because you think they are talking about something else	We **got our wires crossed** and I waited for an hour in the wrong place.
leading edge	the area of activity where the most modern and advanced equipment and methods are used	Software companies are on the **leading edge** of technology in very competitive markets.
press / push the panic button	to do something quickly without thinking enough about it, because something unexpected or dangerous has suddenly happened	Why haven't governments in the region **pushed the panic button?**
silver surfer	an old person who uses the Internet	Many **silver surfers** use the Internet to keep in touch with their grandchildren.

Extracted from www.ldoceonline.com/dictionary. Accessed on August 2, 2018.

▶ UNIT 2

CAN vs. COULD BE ABLE TO

Usage Notes

We sometimes use *be able to* instead of *can* and *could*. Although *be able to* sometimes replaces *can* and *could*, it is not a modal verb. The expression consists of the verb *be* followed by the adjective *able* and a verb in the infinitive form.

- *Be able to* replaces *can* and *could* to express ability.

  I **am** not **able** to drive.

  Are you **able to** read without your glasses?

- We can use *be able to* for abilities in all tenses, while *can* and *could* are used for present and past abilities, respectively.

  They **will be able to** swim backstroke if they practice hard.

  She **has been able to** speak Spanish fluently since she was 14.

- As *can* and *could* have no infinitive form, we use *be able* to when we want to use the infinitive.

  I **would like to be able to** windsurf.

  Do you think you **would be able to** hand in the report by Monday?

ZERO AND FIRST CONDITIONALS

Usage Notes

Conditions are expressed mainly by the word *if* in English. To make a condition, two clauses are necessary: an <u>*if* clause</u>, in which <u>the condition is stated</u>, and a <u>main clause</u>, which <u>states the results of the successful completion of the condition</u>.

You can make a condition about a situation or a fact in the present, in the past, or in the future (a hypothetical situation), and that condition can have its result in the past, in the present, or in the future. In order to identify the time in which your condition and results are going to be in, you need to observe the verb tense of the clauses.

	Idea	*If* clause	Main clause
Zero Conditional	The result always happens if the condition is met.	present	present
		If you leave ice cream out of the freezer for too long,	it melts.
First Conditional	The result is likely to happen in the future because of a condition in the present	present	will
		If you meet Claire on your way home,	she will ask you for a ride.

- Note that in the zero conditional, *if* can be replaced with *whenever*.

  Whenever you leave ice cream out of the freezer for too long, it melts.

  Whenever red and blue are mixed, you get purple.

- In the first conditional, it is possible to use *can*, *may*, *might*, or *could* instead of *will* to indicate that something is a possible consequence, and not a certainty, in the future.

  If it is rainy, I **may** stay indoors on the weekend.

  If they beat their next opponent, they **might** win the championship.

  Could she flunk math if she doesn't take the finals?

- It's sometimes possible to vary the tenses in conditionals. In the first conditional, for example, the present continuous or the present perfect might be used, depending on the context.

    If she **is working**, I won't disturb her.

    If you **have called** a cab, you will have to wait right here.

- The imperative can also be used in the result clause in the first conditional to indicate an instruction.

    If you finish your assignment, **turn** to page 20 for the reading passage.

    Ask me for help if you think you can't do the activity by yourself.

UNIT 3
RELATIVE CLAUSES

Relative clauses can be either defining or non-defining. Defining relative clauses add important information and non-defining relative clauses provide additional information.

> The man **whose** son was awarded the first prize is a famous chef.

> The movie **that I watched last week** was nominated for the Oscar.

In non-defining relative clauses, the relative pronoun can't be omitted and *that* can never be used. Non-defining clauses are more frequent in written English and they are separated by commas.

> Lucy, **who is a sports fan**, was invited to host the prom dance.

> My dog, **which is a bull terrier**, is 3 years old.

Usage Notes

- In relative clauses, we can use the relative pronoun *whom* instead of *who* when it's the object of the verb or the object of a preposition in the dependent clause, preferably in formal styles and in writing.

    The cashier **whom** I gave my credit card to warned me it had expired.

    The girl with **whom** I spoke at the party was very polite.

- Relative clauses can be reduced to shorter forms if the relative clause modifies the subject of a sentence. They might be reduced to an adjective phrase, a prepositional phrase, a past participle phrase, a past participle, and a present participle.

Full: The people **who were tall** had to sit at the back of the auditorium.

Reduced: The **tall people** had to sit at the back auditorium.

Full: The children, **who seemed to be afraid of the animals**, were accompanied by their parents.

Reduced: The children, **afraid of the animals**, were accompanied by their parents.

Full: The worker **who was promoted** is very well-known.

Reduced: The **promoted worker** is very well-known.

Full: The man **who was elected** was very popular.

Reduced: The **elected man** was very popular.

Full: The lady **who lives near my store** takes the subway every day.

Reduced: The lady **living near my store** takes the subway every day.

SO
Usage Notes

In sentences showing cause and effect, *so* is used to show the effect while *as, since, because,* and other connectors may be used to show the cause.

> Most guests have arrived, **so** we will start serving dinner.

> **As** most guests have arrived, we will start serving dinner.

> **Since** most guests have arrived, we will start serving dinner.

> **Because** most guests have arrived, we will start serving dinner.

COLLOCATIONS WITH *DO* AND *MAKE*

Collocation	Example
do a course	I decided to **do a course** in gardening this summer.
do homework	I never go out before **doing** my **homework**.
do one's best	Kelly **did her best** but it wasn't enough to get a good grade.

LANGUAGE REFERENCE

do research	You should **do** some **research** before you buy a new car.
do the housework	He spent all day **doing the housework**.
do the laundry	We **did the laundry** and hung it out to dry early in the morning.
do the shopping	I prefer to **do the shopping** on weekdays.
make a joke	The **jokes** he **makes** aren't funny at all.
make a mess	They **made a mess** of their lives. But it's never too late to start all over.
make a mistake	I can't **make** such **a mistake** in my calculations!
make a reservation	At that restaurant, you should **make** table **reservations** in advance.
make plans	Have you **made** any **plans** for the weekend?
make time	The doctor told me to **make time** for exercise in my life.
make sure	He just called to **make sure** I was all right.

▶ UNIT 4

NEED TO / DON'T NEED TO / HAVE TO / DON'T HAVE TO

Usage Notes

- We use *need to* or the negative form *don't / doesn't need to* when we want to talk about something that is / isn't necessary for someone to do. In this context, we often mention who is going to do it.

  We **need to** go over our notes before the test.

  (It's necessary for us to go over our notes before the test.)

  I **don't need to** reread the text to answer the questions.

  (It's not necessary for me to reread the text to answer the questions.)

  We use *have* to express an obligation, something we are committed to, or a situation that can't be postponed.

  Do students **have to** wear a uniform in your school?

  Lydia can't answer phone calls because she **has to** keep her phone in her bag when she's teaching.

- We use *don't have to* when there is no obligation or necessity to do something.

  You **didn't have to** take care of your little brother last night because his babysitter was here.

  She **doesn't have to** call me every time there's something to be resolved at the office! She can make her own decisions.

- Unlike *don't have to*, *must not* is used when we want to say that something is not allowed.

  You **must** not use your cellphones if you're attending classes in my school.

  You **must not** turn right on Oak Avenue. Look at the prohibition sign!

TAG QUESTIONS

Tag questions are often used as confirmation questions at the end of a sentence.

Usage Notes

- For question tags with "I am", the question tag "aren't I" is used.

  I'm your best friend, **aren't I**?

  I'm calling the right phone number, **aren't I**?

- When we use the *there be* structure, it is reflected in the question tag.

  There's a little sugar left, **isn't there**?

  There weren't other alternatives to choose from, **were there**?

- When *nothing, nobody, somebody, something,* or other similar compounds are the subject in the statement, we use *it* in the question tag to refer to *something* or *nothing* and *they* in the question tag to refer to *someone* or *nobody*.

  Something should be done to solve the problem, shouldn't **it**?

  No one agreed to work late on Fridays, did **they**?

- When we want to express surprise or some particular interest, we can use a positive question tag with a positive statement.

  So you're celebrating your promotion, **are you**? Congratulations!

  Oh, you've passed the finals, **have you**? Great news!

MODERN WORDS / EXPRESSIONS ABOUT TRAVEL

Word / Expression	Meaning
couchsurfing	the practice of moving from one friend's house to the other, often sleeping on the couch or floor while you are temporarily of no fixed abode

staycation	a vacation that is spent at home enjoying time to relax and exploring your local area
flashpacker	not to be confused with a naked backpacker, flashpackers are usually a little bit older than the standard beer-swilling, party hostel staying backpacker
ratpacker	their priority is usually drinking copious amounts of beer or buckets full of the local alcohol
mancation	a vacation for men only, where women are banned and the guys do some sort of "manly" activity like go spear fishing, play poker in Vegas, or head to a rowdy sports game final
glamping	camping in luxury and can be in house-like tents or something creative like a yurt
grey nomad	a mature aged traveler with a keen sense of adventure who travels around a country staying in a campervan, caravan, or tent for a reasonably long time
solivagant	solitary wanderer
wayfarer	a person who travels from place to place, usually on foot
fernweh	a German word that means a craving for travel or distant places

Extracted from www.huffingtonpost.com/shanti-burton/10-modern-travel-words_b_9001326.html. Accessed on October 15, 2018.

UNIT 5

WILL VS. BE GOING TO
MODAL VERBS: MAY, MIGHT, COULD

Usage Notes

- We often use *will* for prediction with the following verbs and phrases: *be sure, be afraid, believe, expect, hope, think, wonder*, etc.

  I'm sure my classmates **will get** good grades.
  I'm afraid I **won't be** able to help you this time.
  He hopes she **will** never **leave** her job.
  Do you think we **will make** it to the top?

- We often use *will* (and not *be going to*) with adverbs of certainty such as *certainly, perhaps*, and *probably*.

  Jennifer **will certainly run** for class representative this year.
  Perhaps Claude **will invite** you to join him at the party tonight.
  We **will probably travel** together again next time.

- In question tags after imperatives, we use *will* (and not *be going to*).

  Take those heavy boxes upstairs, **will** you?
  Don't pretend you forgot to sign the list, **will** you?

- For threats, we also use *will*.

  Pay what you owe me, or I **won't** lend you any more money.
  Listen carefully or you **will** miss important details.

OTHER COMMON EXPRESSIONS USED TO TALK ABOUT THE FUTURE

- *Be about to*: to talk about things that we expect to happen very soon.

  Hurry up! Our bus **is about to** leave.

- *Be due to*: to refer to things that are scheduled.

  My guests **are due to** arrive after 10 P.M.

- *Be to*: to refer to obligations and commands or instructions.

  Helen **is to** visit Grandma tomorrow.
  You **are to** hand in your tests by 11:30 A.M.

- *May, might,* and *could* can be used to talk about future possibility:

  She **may** come to the party, but she depends on a ride.
  We **might** travel abroad, but we haven't decided yet.

TYPES OF -LY ADVERBS

Depending on the aspects of modification, *-ly* adverbs have different types such as manner, time, frequency, degree, focusing, evaluative, etc.

- <u>Manner adverbs</u> indicate the way something happens or is done.
- <u>Time adverbs</u> indicate when something happens.
- <u>Frequency adverbs</u> indicate how often or how many times something occurs.
- <u>Degree adverbs</u> indicate the degrees of qualities, properties, states, conditions, and relations.
- <u>Focusing adverbs</u> point to something.
- <u>Evaluative adverbs</u> comment or give an opinion about something.

Manner	Time	Frequency	Degree	Focusing	Evaluative
cautiously	lately	usually	completely	especially	surprisingly
quickly	recently	frequently	slightly	mainly	obviously
professionally	early	occasionally	absolutely	particularly	frankly
anxiously	finally	generally	totally	largely	hopefully

LANGUAGE REFERENCE

UNIT 6

PASSIVE VOICE

Usage Notes

The passive voice is used when we are more interested in the action than in the agent (or doer of the action), when we are more interested in the receiver of the action than in the agent, or when the agent is not important, not known, or obvious.

Formation chart

Passive forms are composed of an appropriate form of the verb *be* followed by the past participle form of the main verb.

Verb Tense	Passive Voice
Simple present	am / is / are + past participle
Present continuous	am / is / are + being + past participle
Simple past	was / were + past participle
Modal verbs (present)	can / must / should / could / may / might + be + past participle

Usage Notes

- In non-standard English, *get* is sometimes used instead of *be* in passives.

  Henry **got promoted** last week.

  Sandra **got stood up** this morning. She was waiting for the guy, but he never showed up.

- When verbs have two objects, a direct and an indirect object, we can use two different formations.

  (Active voice)   The students **gave** a present to the teacher.

  (Passive voice)   A present **was given** to the teacher (by the students).

  (Passive voice)   The teacher **was given** a present (by the students).

DISCOURSE MARKERS

Discourse markers (or connectors) have distinct functions such as showing turns, joining ideas, changing a topic, adding information, contrasting information, ordering speech, expressing reason and effect, concluding, etc.

Some common discourse markers are listed in the following chart.

Addition	Cause, Reason, or Effect	Comparison	Consequence or Result	Contrast
and	because	like	consequently	but
moreover	for	as	as a result	however
furthermore	as	unlike	so	even though
in addition	since	similarly	thus	nevertheless
also	therefore	in the same way	hence	yet
besides	given that	just as	in conclusion	whereas
along with this	due to	in comparison	because (of)	on the contrary

Emphasis	Condition	Illustrating	Ordering	Purpose
in fact	if	for example	first	so that
as a matter of fact	whether	for instance	second	to
indeed	as long as	in some cases	then	not to
actually	provided that	such as	next	in order to
in reality	assuming that	like	now	in order not to
essentially	unless	let's say	continuing	so as to
fortunately	now that	be it	finally	so as not to

COLLOCATIONS WITH *GET* AND *SET*

Collocation	Example
get dressed	It takes her half an hour to **get dressed** in the morning.
get drunk	Lisa **got drunk** last night and had to take a taxi home
get lost	Without your help, I would **get lost**. Thank you!
get sick	Gosh, this is the second time I've **gotten sick** this month!
set a precedent	What you have done will **set a** legal **precedent**.
set an example	Parents and teachers should **set an example**.
set the date and time	Have you **set the date and time** for Jason's farewell party?
set the table	She hasn't **set the table** yet. How can I serve dinner?

UNIT 7
PRESENT PERFECT – ADVERBS

Some adverbs are often used with the present perfect tense.

Example	Form	Meaning
He's **just left** for work.	subject + have/has + **just** + past participle	*Just* indicates the fact that the activity has been completed very recently.
I **have already made** up my mind about college.	subject + have/has + **already** + past participle	*Already* indicates the fact that the activity is not a new experience.
They **have always liked** the country.	subject + have/has + **always** + past participle	*Always* indicates something that has been true for a lifetime.
She**'s lived** in LA **since** 2010.	subject + have/has + past participle + **since** + time phrase	*Since* indicates a previous point in time.
We**'ve been** here **for** 15 minutes.	subject + have/has + past participle + **for** + time phrase	*For* indicates how long something lasts.
We**'ve never been** friends.	subject + have/has + **never** + past participle	*Never* indicates a situation that has not happened ever.
You **haven't had** lunch **yet**.	subject + have/has + not + past participle + object + **yet**	*Yet* indicates an activity that has not happened but will hopefully happen soon.
Have you **been** to the new Italian restaurant **yet**?	have / has + subject + past participle + object + **yet**	*Yet* indicates an activity that we expected to be completed but we are still waiting for it to be done.
Have you **ever bought** any pieces of clothes and never worn them? This is the best pizza I **have ever eaten**!	have / has + subject + **ever** + past participle	*Ever* is used in questions to indicate "at any time" or "at all times". It is commonly used in interrogative forms or superlative sentences.

PHRASAL VERBS RELATED TO BUSINESS AND ECONOMY

Phrasal Verb	Meaning
cash in	to make a profit from a situation in a way that other people think is wrong or unfair
contract out	to arrange to have a job done by a person or company outside your own organization
draw up	to prepare a written document, such as a list or contract
hire out	to allow someone to borrow something for a short time in exchange for money
lay off	to stop employing someone because there is no work for them to do
pencil in	to make an arrangement for a meeting or other event, knowing that it might have to be changed later
put back	delay or postpone
rip off	to charge someone too much money for something, or sell someone a product that is faulty
sell out	to sell your business or your share in a business
set up	to start a company, organization, committee etc
stock up	to buy a lot of something in order to keep it for when you need to use it later
take over	to take control of something
write off	to write a letter to a company or organization asking them to send you goods or information

Extracted from www.ldoceonline.com/dictionary/. Accessed on August 05, 2018.

LANGUAGE REFERENCE

UNIT 8
EMBEDDED QUESTIONS

Embedded or indirect questions are more formal than regular questions and they don't need a change in word order in the main question. With embedded questions, we make our requests or questions in a softer and more polite way.

Usage Notes

- Embedded questions can be used as part of other questions or as part of statements.

  (Regular question) — Where does he live?

  (Embedded question as part of a question) — Could you tell me where he lives?

  (Embedded question as part of a statement) — I don't know where he lives.

- Other common introductory phrases used in embedded questions are:

  Can you remember…?
  Can you tell / show me…?
  Do you have any idea…?
  Do you know…?
  I wonder if you would mind telling / showing me…?
  Let's ask…
  We need to find out…
  Would you mind explaining…?
  Would you mind telling / showing me…?

TERMS RELATED TO FAKE NEWS

Term	Meaning
anonymous	of unknown authorship; not revealing one's identity
bogus	false; counterfeit; fake; fraudulent
confirmation bias	the tendency to seek information that supports one's decisions and beliefs while ignoring information that does not match one's decisions and beliefs.
distortion	an exaggeration or stretching of the truth to achieve a desired effect.
fabricated	made up; false; made to deceive
falsehood	a lie
gatekeeper	media executives, news editors, and prominent reporters who decide what news to present and how it will be presented
legitimate	lawful; authentic; genuine
misinformation	creation of fictitious (fake) memories by providing misleading information about an event after it takes place
partisan	biased; one-sided; committed to one group
rumor	a piece of information or a story passed from one person to another without any proof that it is true
reputable	respectable; well thought of considered to be honest and to provide a good service
vetting	checking or investigating. In journalism, internally double- or triple-checking everything in a news report for accuracy, fairness and context.

Extracted from https://quizlet.com/200280714/fake-news-vocabulary-flash-cards/. Accessed on October 15, 2018.

READING STRATEGIES

Ao longo da coleção, estamos sinalizando algumas estratégias de leitura voltadas à melhora na compreensão de textos. O principal objetivo dessas estratégias é fazer com que você, aluno, torne-se um aprendiz mais eficaz e alcance resultados positivos nos exames e vestibulares a serem realizados ao final do Ensino Médio.

A seguir você encontrará uma breve explicação sobre as estratégias mais comumente abordadas antes e durante a leitura dos textos.

Activating or using previous knowledge – Esta estratégia consiste em acionar, quando preciso, o conhecimento que você tem guardado em sua mente. Quando falamos em conhecimento prévio na leitura, estamos nos referindo às informações que você precisa ter para ler um texto sem muita dificuldade para compreendê-lo.

Brainstorming – O termo foi criado a partir da junção das palavras *brain* (cérebro) e *storm* (tempestade), portanto, significa "tempestade cerebral" ou "tempestade de ideias". A estratégia propõe que você e seus colegas de sala explorem sua capacidade criativa, na medida em que trocam ideias a respeito do assunto que será abordado no texto.

Bridging – O termo vem da palavra *bridge*, que significa "ponte". A estratégia consiste, então, em "fazer uma ponte", isto é, em estabelecer uma relação entre o seu conhecimento prévio sobre o assunto que será explorado no texto e o texto propriamente.

Finding organizational patterns or understanding text structure – A estrutura de um texto diz respeito à forma como as informações estão nele organizadas. Artigos, por exemplo, contam com uma introdução, um desenvolvimento e uma conclusão; as informações nas biografias são, em geral, organizadas em sequência cronológica; as receitas, na maioria das vezes, são divididas em duas partes – ingredientes e modo de preparo. Assim, estar atento aos padrões de organização de um texto ajuda-o a identificar seu gênero e, consequentemente, sua função social.

Predicting – A palavra *predict* significa "prever". Ao lermos o título de um texto ou observarmos as imagens que o acompanham, por exemplo, podemos prever ou deduzir seu conteúdo. Quanto mais conhecimento geral você tiver, mais facilmente vai prever o assunto de um texto. Em algumas atividades, você é convidado especificamente a prever o tema e o gênero do texto (*predicting the theme and the genre*).

Recognizing or identifying – Reconhecer significa identificar algo que se conhece. Portanto, reconhecer ou identificar o tipo textual (*textual type*), a voz, ou seja, quem está falando no texto (*voice in a text*), a perspectiva do autor (*the author's perspective*), a fonte do texto (*the source of the text*), o público ao qual o texto se destina (*the target audience*), o propósito principal do texto (*the main purpose*) etc. ajuda-o a antecipar o que está por vir no texto a ser lido.

Skimming – Consiste em observar o texto rapidamente para detectar o assunto geral ou o seu propósito geral (*skimming to identify the main purpose*), por exemplo. Nesse momento, não há nenhuma preocupação em se atentar aos detalhes. É importante que você observe o *layout* do texto, seu título e sub-títulos, cognatos, primeiras e últimas linhas de cada parágrafo, bem como as imagens, gráficos e tabelas que o acompanham.

Scanning - É uma técnica de leitura que consiste em correr rapidamente os olhos pelo texto até localizar a informação específica desejada. O *scanning* é prática rotineira na vida das pessoas. Alguns exemplos típicos são o uso do dicionário para obter informação sobre o significado de palavras ou a utilização do índice de um livro para encontrar um artigo ou capítulo de interesse.

Há, também, estratégias que são trabalhadas após a leitura dos textos. Observe:

Making inferences or inferring – A estratégia de inferência tem como objetivo fazê-lo capturar aquilo que não está dito no texto de forma explícita. Essas adivinhações podem ter como base as pistas dadas pelo próprio texto ou o seu próprio conhecimento. Trata-se de uma estratégia de leitura extremamente importante, pois um texto só terá sentido se você puder estabelecer relações entre as partes, ou seja, entre as palavras, frases, parágrafos etc.

Selecting a good title – Muitas vezes o título de um texto resume sua ideia central. Para selecionar o título mais apropriado para o texto que você acabou de ler, leia-o novamente e anote os pontos que mais chamaram sua atenção. O mesmo se aplica para quando você tiver que afirmar ou declarar a ideia ou o propósito principal do texto lido (*stating the main idea or the main purpose of the text*).

Understanding details – Para entender os detalhes de um texto é preciso fazer uma leitura lenta e concentrar-se durante essa leitura, isto é, ficar longe de qualquer coisa que possa distraí-lo. Recorrer a um dicionário para consultar as palavras e expressões desconhecidas e anotar seu significado, bem como fazer paráfrases durante a leitura, são algumas das ações que contribuem para a compreensão detalhada do texto. Podem contribuir, também, para as atividades que pedem que você resuma o texto lido (*summarizing*).

Understanding main ideas – Para realizar atividades que têm esta estratégia sinalizada, não é necessário fazer uma leitura tão detalhada, nem mesmo procurar todas as palavras desconhecidas em um dicionário. Basta fazer uma leitura geral do texto com atenção e compreender sua mensagem principal.

IRREGULAR VERBS

Base form	Past form	Past participle	Translation
awake	awoke	awoken	acordar
be	was, were	been	ser, estar
become	became	become	tornar-se
begin	began	begun	começar
bend	bent	bent	dobrar
bet	bet	bet	apostar
bite	bit	bitten	morder
blow	blew	blown	soprar
break	broke	broken	quebrar
bring	brought	brought	trazer
build	built	built	construir
burn	burnt/burned	burnt/burned	queimar
buy	bought	bought	comprar
catch	caught	caught	pegar
choose	chose	chosen	escolher
come	came	come	vir
cut	cut	cut	cortar
do	did	done	fazer
draw	drew	drawn	desenhar
dream	dreamed/dreamt	dreamed/dreamt	sonhar
drink	drank	drunk	beber
drive	drove	driven	dirigir
eat	ate	eaten	comer
fall	fell	fallen	cair
feed	fed	fed	alimentar
feel	felt	felt	sentir
fight	fought	fought	lutar
find	found	found	achar
fly	flew	flown	voar
forget	forgot	forgotten	esquecer
forgive	forgave	forgiven	perdoar
get	got	got/gotten	conseguir
get up	got up	got up/gotten up	levantar-se
give	gave	given	dar
go	went	gone	ir
grow	grew	grown	crescer
hang out	hung out	hung out	passar tempo
have	had	had	ter
hear	heard	heard	ouvir
hide	hid	hidden	esconder
hit	hit	hit	atingir
hold	held	held	segurar
hurt	hurt	hurt	machucar
keep	kept	kept	manter

Base form	Past form	Past participle	Translation
know	knew	known	saber, conhecer
lean	leant/leaned	leant/leaned	inclinar-se
learn	learnt/learned	learnt/learned	aprender
leave	left	left	deixar, sair
lend	lent	lent	emprestar
let	let	let	deixar
lose	lost	lost	perder
make	made	made	fazer
mean	meant	meant	significar
meet	met	met	encontrar, conhecer
overcome	overcame	overcome	superar
pay	paid	paid	pagar
put	put	put	colocar
read	read	read	ler
ride	rode	ridden	andar de
ring	rang	rung	tocar
rise	rose	risen	subir, aumentar
run	ran	run	correr
say	said	said	dizer
see	saw	seen	ver
sell	sold	sold	vender
send	sent	sent	enviar
set	set	set	estabelecer
show	showed	shown	mostrar
sing	sang	sung	cantar
sit	sat	sat	sentar
sleep	slept	slept	dormir
speak	spoke	spoken	falar
spell	spelled/spelt	spelled/spelt	soletrar
spend	spent	spent	gastar, passar tempo
split	split	split	dividir
stand up	stood up	stood up	ficar de pé
steal	stole	stolen	roubar
swim	swam	swum	nadar
take	took	taken	pegar, tomar
teach	taught	taught	ensinar
tell	told	told	contar
think	thought	thought	pensar
throw	threw	thrown	jogar
understand	understood	understood	entender
wake up	woke up	woken up	acordar
wear	wore	worn	vestir
win	won	won	ganhar
write	wrote	written	escrever

COMMON MISTAKES

Speakers of Portuguese are more likely to make certain mistakes in English because of interference from Portuguese. Let's take a look at some common mistakes:

TOPIC	COMMON MISTAKE	RIGHT FORM	SOME EXPLANATION
USING PAST TIME EXPRESSIONS WITH PRESENT PERFECT	I have been to the supermarket ~~yesterday~~, that's why the fridge is full.	I have been to the supermarket, that's why the fridge is full. OR I went to the supermarket yesterday, that's why the fridge is full.	In Portuguese, a past form is usually used to indicate that something happened in a recent or unknown past, and therefore, we can use past time expressions. However, in English you can only use time expressions such as since, for, or today with the present perfect.
ASKING QUESTIONS WITH *DID*	Did she work~~ed~~ last weekend?	Did she work last weekend?	When asking a question with the auxiliary *did* or making a negative statement with *did not* or *didn't*, the main verb is in the infinitive form.
NON-ACTION VERBS	I ~~am not seeing~~ you. Are you here in the party, too?	I can't see you. Are you at the party, too? OR I don't see you. Are you at the party, too?	Non-action verbs, such as *see*, *be*, *know*, and *like can't* be used in the continuous tenses.
TALKING ABOUT FUTURE ABILITY OR POSSIBILITY	He will ~~can~~ buy a motorcycle after he gets a job.	He will be able to buy a motorcycle after he gets a job. OR He can buy a motorcycle after he gets a job.	The modal verb *can* refers to present and future, but it can't be used with any other modal verbs (e.g. *will*, *should*, *must*, etc.). When using another modal verb or a perfect tense, we use *be able to* instead of *can*.
USING *THAT* AS A RELATIVE PRONOUN IN NON-DEFINING RELATIVE CLAUSES	The cake, ~~that~~ I made all by myself, was a success at the party.	The cake, which I made all by myself, was a success at the party.	The pronoun *that* cannot be used in non-defining relative clauses (when the information is not essential, and is separated from the rest of the sentence by commas). Beware! *That* can only be used in defining relative clauses in the place of *who* and *which*.
HAVE TO IN NEGATIVE STATEMENTS AND QUESTIONS	We ~~haven't~~ to pay. It's free! AND ~~Have~~ we to pay?	We don't have to pay. It's free! AND Do we have to pay?	Although *have to* performs the function of a modal verb, it is a verb phrase that needs an auxiliary verb in negative statements and questions.
TAG QUESTIONS WITH *I AM*	I'm a good student, ~~am not I?~~	I'm a good student, aren't I?	There are some exceptions to form tag questions, such as using the tag *aren't I?* when the affirmative statement starts with *I am* OR the use of *shall we?* when the statement starts with *Let's*.

TOPIC	COMMON MISTAKE	RIGHT FORM	SOME EXPLANATION
ELLIPSIS OF THE VERB AFTER *WILL*	I will go to your house and she too.	I will go to your house, and she will [go] too.	The modal verb *will* in Portuguese can be translated as "*vou (fazer algo)*" or "*vai (fazer algo)*", depending on the context. However, it is necessary to use *go* when we want to say, for example: "*Eu irei para a sua casa.*" *Will* can come without another verb in short answers or ellipsis.
THE FORM OF THE VERB AFTER MODAL VERBS	I may ~~to~~ see a movie tonight.	I may see a movie tonight.	The verb that follows a modal verb is never conjugated, nor is it an infinitive with *to*. With modal verbs, we use the infinitive <u>without</u> *to*.
ADDING AN AGENT TO A SENTENCE IN THE PASSIVE VOICE	This house was built ~~for~~ my great-grandfather.	This house was built by my great-grandfather.	When referring to the agent of a passive sentence, the preposition we use to mean "*por*" is *by*. We would use *for* if we wanted to say "*Esta casa foi construída <u>para</u> meu bisavô.*"
GET VS. *STAY*	I don't go to class when I ~~stay~~ sick.	I don't go to class when I get sick.	Both *get* and *stay* can be translated into "*ficar*". However, *stay* conveys the idea of "*permanecer*" while *get* refers to starting having a feeling or an idea.
ALREADY VS. *EVER* IN QUESTIONS	Have you ~~already~~ been to Canada?	Have you ever been to Canada?	Both words can mean "*já*". The use of the adverb *ever* refers to a question about an experience in someone's life, while *already* refers to something that we expect to happen or have happened and we want to ask about its conclusion up to the time of speaking.
USING OBJECT PRONOUNS WITH SEPARABLE PHRASAL VERBS	Is the heater working? Let's turn on ~~it~~!	Is the heater working? Let's turn it on!	When using separable phrasal verbs, such as *turn on / off, pick up,* and *give up* with an object pronoun, the pronoun must come between the verb and the particle. If there is a noun instead of a pronoun, it can go both between the verb and the particle and after the particle (e.g. *turn the TV off / turn off the TV*).
REMOVAL OF *DO / DOES / DID* IN THE FORMATION OF EMBEDDED QUESTIONS	She asked Marco where ~~did~~ he ~~go~~ on Saturdays.	She asked Marco where he went on Saturdays.	When forming an embedded question, it is important to remember that the structure changes. We can't keep the question structure, so the auxiliaries *do, does,* and *did* aren't used anymore and the main verb is conjugated.

FALSE FRIENDS

False friends are similar-sounding words with different meanings. When we look at the word *actually*, for example, we immediately associate it with the Portuguese word "*atualmente*", because of its similarity. However, *actually* means "*na realidade*" as in "It **actually** costs three thousand dollars, not three hundred." Let's take a look at some other examples.

English	Portuguese translation	Example	Don't get confused with...	Which in English is...
alias	pseudônimo, nome falso	He used to work under an **alias**.	aliás	by the way
anthem	hino	Are you able to sing the American national **anthem**?	antena	antenna
appoint	nomear	Tom Leary was **appointed** to a new position.	apontar	point
assist	ajudar	Who is going to **assist** the new judge?	assistir (a um programa)	watch
college	faculdade	I can't believe you are not excited about going to **college**!	colégio	school
comprehensive	abrangente, amplo	It was a very **comprehensive** report.	compreensível	understandable
convict	condenado(a)	The **convict** had to be handcuffed.	convicto(a)	certain
costume	fantasia	How much is the vampire **costume**?	costume	habit
data	dados	We have gathered a lot of **data** on the subject.	data	date
exit	saída	Where is the **exit** door?	êxito	success
fabric	tecido	Silk is a very expensive **fabric**.	fábrica	factory
hazard	risco	This medicine presents no **hazard** to your health.	azar	bad luck
inhabited	habitado(a)	It is an **inhabited** island.	inabitado(a)	uninhabited
journal	revista especializada, diário	Tom is the editor of a very important medical **journal**.	jornal	newspaper
lecture	palestra	The **lecture** had a very young audience.	leitura	reading
legend	lenda	Have you heard of the **legend** of Billy Jack?	legenda	subtitle
library	biblioteca	Is there a **library** around here where I can borrow some comics?	livraria	bookstore
novel	romance	*My Brilliant Friend* is a **novel** written by Elena Ferrante, a mysterious Italian writer.	novela	soap opera
notice	notar, observar	Have you **noticed** the new furniture in the Study Hall?	notícia	news
parents	pais	My **parents** got married in the early nineties.	parentes	relatives
physician	médico	He is a respected **physician** who is looking after the president's health.	físico	physicist
prejudice	preconceito	We must always fight against all kinds of **prejudice**.	prejuízo	harm
pretend	fingir	Stop **pretending**! I know you are not telling the truth.	pretender	intend
realize	perceber	Have you **realized** how far we are from our goal?	realizar	accomplish
resume	recomeçar	After a long break they **resumed** the session.	resumir	summarize
sensible	sensato(a)	Choosing to cross the river in such a small boat is not a **sensible** option.	sensível	sensitive
support	apoiar	The homeless shelter is **supported** by a group of volunteers.	suportar	bear

GLOSSARY

Unit 1

acronym – acrônimo, abreviatura
angst – angústia
diehard – persistente
glazed – olhou fixo (infinitivo: *glaze*)
go cold turkey – parar um hábito de maneira abrupta
hindsight – em retrospecto
landscapes – paisagens
lead to – levar a
littered – repleto(a) (conotação negativa)
omertà – código de honra
pundits – especialistas
refrain – abster-se
remarks – comentários
shorthand – forma curta
somehow – de alguma forma
supposedly – supostamente

Unit 2

acquired – adquiriu (infinitivo: *acquire*)
ameliorate – aperfeiçoar, melhorar
beyond – além de
commutes – deslocamentos
core – principal
currently – atualmente
fill up – encher
fossil fuels – combustíveis fósseis
garbage – lixo
greenhouse gas – gás de efeito estufa
hip pockets – bolsos traseiros (termo financeiro)
income – renda
lavish – extravagante
missing – perder (infinitivo: *miss*)

narrowed – estreitado (infinitivo: *narrow*)
near-miss – quase (acidente)
peer-to-peer – entre pares
P.E.I. – Prince Edward Island, província canadense
poisoning – envenenando (infinitivo: *poison*)
rather – um tanto
ride-hailing – chama-carona
seek – buscar
sheer – completo
slewing – deslizando (infinitivo: *slew*)
stakeholders – investidores
tailored – customizado (infinitivo: *tailor*)
through – através
transitioning – transitando

Review 1

amounted – somou (infinitivo: *amount*)
canons – cânones, padrões aceitos
oversee – supervisionar
path – caminho
remain – permanecer
safeguard – proteger
spread – espalhado(a)
standing at – posicionando-se em (infinitivo: *stand*)
tiny – pequenino
viability – viabilidade

Unit 3

cohort – tropa
disrupt – perturbar
do harm – prejudicar
entrepreneurial – empreendedor
floods – inundações
instead – ao invés disso

GLOSSARY

loneliness – solidão
polls – pesquisas (de opinião)
pragmatic – pragmático, prático
shelf-life – vida útil
short-term – a curto prazo
therefore – portanto
trend – tendência
unrealistically – de modo não realístico
upbringing – criação (de pessoa)
willing – disposto
witnessed – testemunhou (infinitivo: *witness*)

Unit 4

're (are) all geared up – estamos todos preparados (infinitivo: *be geared up*)
carry-on sized backpack – mochila de tamanho pequeno, possível de carregar
Commonwealth – com políticas e economia em comum
daunting – assustador(a)
facet – faceta
featured – destacado(a)
figure – número(s)
flavor – sabor
flocks – rebanhos
freeing – libertador
gap-year – ano sabático
intrepid – intrépido, sem medo
issued – emitido(a) (infinitivo: *issue*)
itch – comichão
laborers – trabalhadores
lesser known – menos conhecido(a)
look forward to – esperar ansiosamente
perhaps – talvez
preach – pregar
pristine – limpo(a)
rookie – novato
spread – espalhar

tailor-made trip – viagem feita sob encomenda com uma agência
tall order – exigência absurda
tempting – tentador
terrain – terreno
understatement – narração incompleta
whetted – aguçado(a) (infinitivo: *whet*)

Review 2

approaches – abordagens
believably – crivelmente
breadwinners – ganha-pão
embracing – acolhendo (infinitivo: *embrace*)
off the beaten track – fora da área turística
reminisce – relembrar
threshold – limite

Unit 5

available – disponível
bendy – flexível
block grant – concessão
bursaries – bolsas de estudos
catchy – cativante
CEO – *Chief Executive Officer*, diretor(a) executivo(a)
cheerful – animado(a)
coding – codificação
crackpot – excêntrico, ruim
developable – possível de desenvolver
diminished – diminuiu (infinitivo: *diminish*)
dive – mergulho
enhancers – potenciadores
fiend – monstro
fools – bobos(as)
future-proof – preparar para o futuro
hoodies – jovens vestidos de moletom (usado para mostrar desaprovação)
midst – meio

misled – enganado(a) (infinitivo: *mislead*)
off-putting – desagradável
on the fly – com pressa
patches – remendos
pigeon – pombo
pulped – destruído (infinitivo: *pulp*)
relieving – aliviando (infinitivo: *relieve*)
school leaver – alguém que para de estudar após a educação básica
stand out – destacar-se
stealing – roubar (infinitivo: *steal*)
STEM skills – habilidades STEM (ciência, tecnologia, engenharia e matemática)
tackle – resolver, lidar com
trading – trocando (infinitivo: *trade*)
whether – se

Unit 6

amid – no meio de
bleak – desanimador(a)
buffer – amortecer
carried out – conduziu (infinitivo: *carry out*)
crops – colheitas
damage – dano
deaths – mortes
droughts – períodos de seca
hedges – cercas vivas
intractable – intratável
lack of – falta de
laid out – disposto(a)
landscape – paisagem
lawn – gramado
livestock – criação
mitigate – atenuar
mitigation – suavização
niche – nicho
output – saída

overworked – sobrecarregado(a)
partnerships – parcerias
pillar support – apoio
plot – terreno
poisonings – envenenamentos
rather than – ao invés de
reap – colher
rodents – roedores
seeks – busca (infinitivo: *seek*)
showcased – apresentado(a)
shrubs – arbustos
the latter – o último
timber – madeira
toughest – mais difícil
waste – lixo
water tables – lençóis freáticos
weeds – ervas daninhas
whilst – enquanto
woody perennials – arbustos lenhosos
yields – produções

Review 3

augmented – aumentado(a)
crave – ansiar
disrupting – perturbando (infinitivo: *disrupt*)
loads – muitos
prone to – inclinado(a) a
retail – varejo
seekers – buscadores
unrecognizable – irreconhecível

Unit 7

center-left parties – partidos de centro-esquerda
come out – surgir
counter-reaction – reações adversas
deregulation – desregulamentação

GLOSSARY

destabilizing – desestabilizador
disruptive – desordeiro(a)
eroded – desgastado(a) (infinitivo: *erode*)
free trade – comércio livre
GDP – *Gross Domestic Product,* Produto Interno Bruto
gig – bico, trabalho informal
grab – apanhar
growth – crescimento
hype – propaganda
inroads – invasões
market cap – valor de mercado
nativist – nativista
omens – presságios
outweighed – superado(a) (infinitivo: *outweigh*)
overstretch – alongamento demasiado
path – caminho
pay gaps – brechas de pagamento
plank – princípio
quarrels – discussões
roughly – aproximadamente
shrink – diminuir
sluggish – lento(a)
subprime mortgages – hipotecas de segunda categoria
survey – pesquisa
threat – ameaça
threatens – ameaça (infinitivo: *threaten*)
triggered – provocou (infinitivo: *trigger*)
undoing – desfazendo (infinitivo: *undo*)
unemployment – desemprego
widened – amplificado(a)
willingness – vontade

Unit 8

abiding commitment – comprometimento duradouro
amusing – divertido
bid – fazer um lance
boost (the site) up – alavancar

breach – violação
briefing – resumo
cracking down – fechando o cerco (infinitivo: *crack down*)
crowded – amontoaram-se (infinitivo: *crowd*)
eager – ansioso(a)
earnings – ganhos
far-right – extrema direita
forefront – frente
funding – fundo
groundbreaking – revolucionário
hatred – ódio
headquarters – sede principal
held – realizado(a) (infinitivo: *hold*)
provide – fornecer
pursuing – buscando (infinitivo: *pursue*)
ran out – acabou (infinitivo: *run out*)
reach – alcance
reliable – confiável
right-wing – de direita
seemingly – aparente
set out – pretender
shady – sombrio(a)
snappy – rápido(a)
sneaking in – esgueirando-se (infinitivo: *sneak in*)
third-party – terceirizado(a)
tough – duro(a)
threat – ameaça
weaponization – armamento

Review 4

broadly – amplamente
enhances – acentua (infinitivo: *enhance*)
fairness – justiça
flaws – falhas
nourishes – nutri (infinitivo: *nourish*)
ombudsmen – mediadores
willingness – desejo

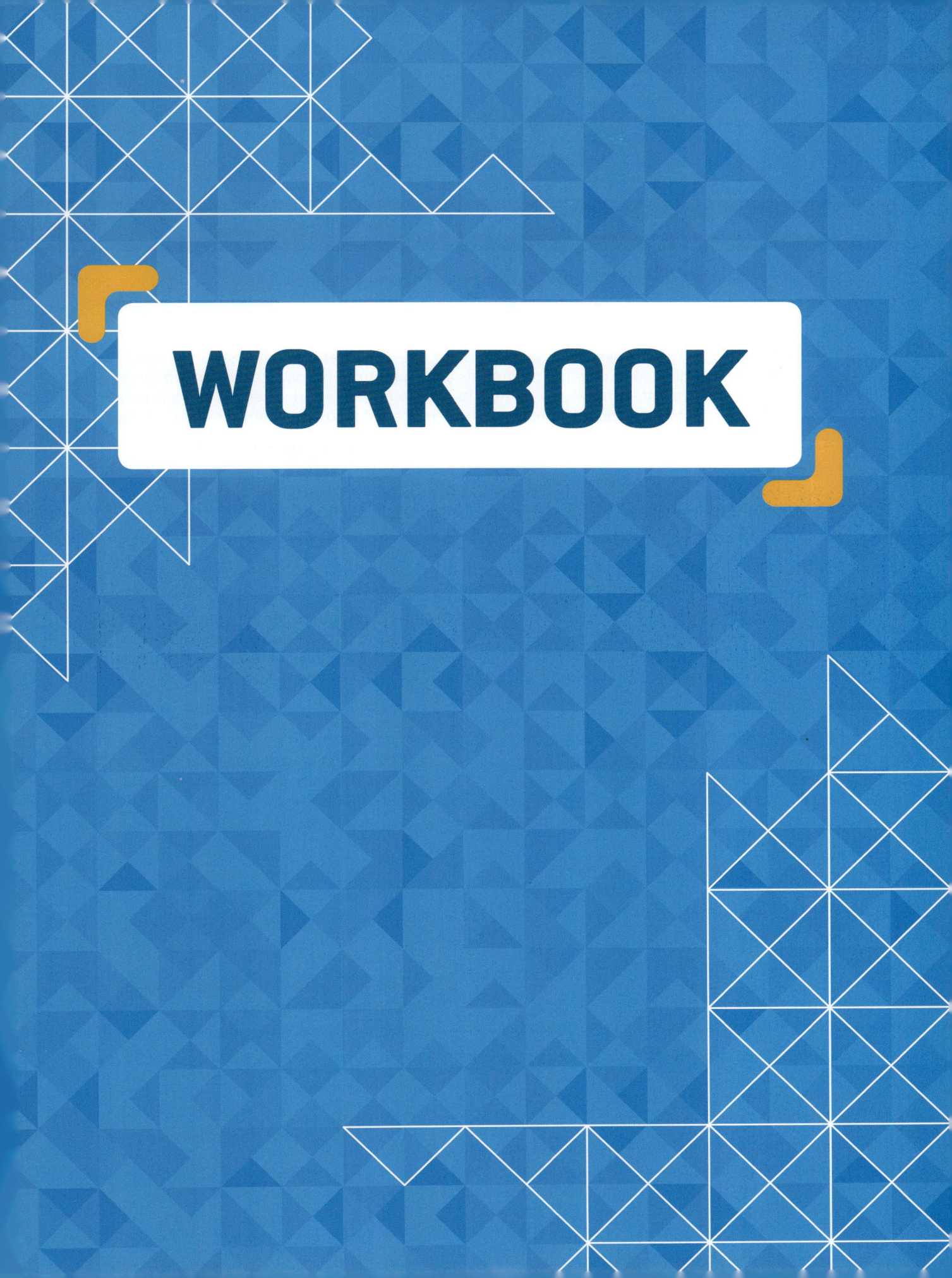

WORKBOOK

Unit 1 — Hooked on Social Media

1. Read the excerpt below and choose the extract that best summarizes it. *Skimming*

`www.theguardian.com/media/2018/jan/23/never-get-high-on-your-own-supply-why-social-media-bosses-dont-use-social-media`

WHY SOCIAL MEDIA BOSSES DON'T USE SOCIAL MEDIA

Developers of platforms such as Facebook have admitted that they were designed to be addictive. Should we be following the executives' example and **go cold turkey** – and is it even possible for mere mortals?

by **Alex Hern**

Mark Zuckerberg doesn't use Facebook like you or me. The chief executive has a team of 12 moderators dedicated to deleting comments and spam from his page, according to Bloomberg. He has a "handful" of employees who help him write his posts and speeches and a number of professional photographers who take perfectly stage-managed pictures of him meeting veterans in Kentucky, small-business owners in Missouri, or cheesesteak vendors in Philadelphia.

[…]

It is a pattern that holds true across the sector. For all the industry's focus on "eating your own dog food", the most **diehard** users of social media are rarely those sitting in a position of power.

[…]

Sean Parker, the founding president of Facebook, broke the **omertà** in October last year, telling a conference in Philadelphia that he was "something of a conscientious objector" to social media.

"The thought process that went into building these applications, Facebook being the first of them, was all about: 'How do we consume as much of your time and conscious attention as possible?' That means that we need to sort of give you a little dopamine hit every once in a while, because someone liked or commented on a photo or a post or whatever. And that's going to get you to contribute more content and that's going to get you more likes and comments," he said.

Adapted from www.theguardian.com/media/2018/jan/23/never-get-high-on-your-own-supply-why-social-media-bosses-dont-use-social-media. Accessed on July 18, 2018.

a. Since social media was intentionally developed to be addictive and time consuming, developers of these platforms recommend people not to use it regularly and only occasionally check the amount of likes and comments they get on their posts.

b. The author suggests that social media users should not be worried about social media executives' behavior, since it has never been proved that social media may have negative effects on people's lives.

c. Social media developers never meant to design a platform for their own amusement, but they were looking for alternatives to intentionally take as much of our time as they possibly could. And they succeeded.

d. Sean Parker, the founding president of Facebook, is also an advocate for social media relevance when he admits to building something that would entertain people for the longest amount of time possible.

e. Sean Parker claims that social media is able to control the amount of dopamine a person can experience in one day by sharing or withholding comments directed to them on their social media profile.

2. Read the excerpt again and underline the verb in the present perfect form. In the context given, the use of the present perfect shows…

a. something that happened in a non-specific moment in the past, but is still relevant at the present time.

b. a situation that started in the past and is still happening in the present.

c. something that happened in a specific moment in the past and has no influence on events taking place now.

3. Read the sentences below and write the appropriate question for each of them. Use *ever*.

a. Yes, I have already been to the USA.

_____

b. No, Chloe has never seen any of the Star Wars movies.

_____

Unit 1

4. Complete the sentences below using the present perfect form of the verbs given.

a. Although I have already seen your brother, I _____ (never talk) to him in person.

b. Shonda _____ (live) in Atlanta for over a decade now. The last time I saw her we had a farewell party.

c. My sister started looking for a new job months ago. She _____ (apply) to a lot of positions on LinkedIn, but she _____ (not hear) from any headhunters yet.

d. I _____ (live) in this house since my parents moved to Chicago.

e. _____ you _____ (ever spend) more than five hours in a row on social media?

5. Read the sentences and say if they are in the simple past (SP), past continuous (PC), or present perfect (PP).

a. (   ) Jason has already traveled to the Hamptons with his girlfriend.

b. (   ) My father didn't go to the west coast with us last year.

c. (   ) We haven't spoken in years. What have you done lately?

d. (   ) Did you apply for the Mandarin class like I told you to?

e. (   ) She wasn't calling you, she was texting you.

6. Read the sentences in activity 5 again and identify whether the verbs used in the sentences are regular or irregular.

a. _____

b. _____

c. _____

d. _____

e. _____

7. Read the statements below and complete them with the simple past or past continuous form of the verbs in parentheses.

a. I _____ (not go) to the movies yesterday. I _____ (stay) home with my father.

b. Alicia _____ (do) the dishes when Peter _____ (call).

c. Marcus _____ (visit) his girlfriend yesterday. That's why he _____ (not come) to your house.

d. _____ you _____ (invite) my sister to your party?

e. Sorry, but I _____ (not feel) very well.

f. I _____ (not check) my Instagram again. I _____ just _____ (send) my friend a message.

g. Diana _____ (create) a new email account when Carlton _____ (arrive).

105

8. Read the excerpt below and underline the phrasal verb in it.

Livia Weinstein didn't know what to expect when she created a Facebook account almost 10 years ago. The now 79-year-old from Washington, D.C., said her reason for joining the online world was due to her desire to **keep up** with the times, more than it was a means for socialization. For the former school counselor, nothing could replace the value of face-to-face communication with all its inflections and tones, a characteristic absent from instant messaging and texting. [...] Older adults across the United States are adjusting to a world of advancing technology. Not only are they accepting the changes, but some, like Weinstein, are actively implementing technology in their daily lives.

Adapted from www.deseretnews.com/article/865685302/How-social-media-and-technology-are-changing-the-lives-of-the-elderly.html. Accessed on July 21, 2017.

9. Use the phrasal verbs in the box to fill in the blanks.

> log on   come up with   run out of   filter out   sign up

a. Morgan hasn't _____ an idea for her new book yet. She has no idea what to write about.

b. If you want more privacy, you must _____ the unwanted contacts from your social media profile.

c. I think my account has been hacked. I keep getting an error message every time I try to _____.

d. If you want to get our weekly newsletter, _____ at the end of this article.

e. We need to go to the supermarket. I have totally _____ paper towels.

10. Read the excerpt from activity 8 again and circle the adjective followed by the preposition *to*. Then complete the sentences with the adjectives from the box and the preposition *to*.

> committed   generous   engaged   dedicated   accustomed

a. She's _____ a certain lifestyle and she doesn't want to lower her standards.

b. Peter is _____ Taylor, but he hasn't told his parents about their engagement yet.

c. Teachers are _____ helping students get ready for the exams.

d. This project is _____ supporting small businesses survive competition.

e. Your mother has been _____ me whenever I need her.

11. Read the following statement. Which alternative best completes it?

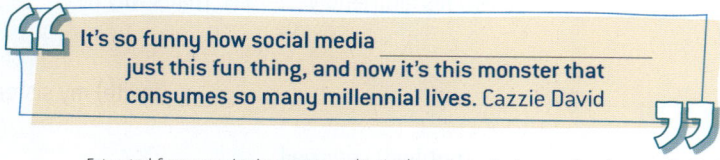

> "It's so funny how social media _____ just this fun thing, and now it's this monster that consumes so many millennial lives." Cazzie David

Extracted from www.brainyquote.com/topics/social_media. Accessed on January 15, 2019.

a. was

b. was being

c. has been

12. Rewrite the sentences below in the simple past, adding a time expression at the end. Follow the example.

My friends don't have English class.
My friends didn't have English class (yesterday).

a. My mother cooks chicken and pasta.
___

b. Do you play soccer?
___

c. Steve doesn't swim, and he doesn't play video games.
___

d. Miranda speaks English and Spanish fluently.
___

e. Does William drive automatic cars?
___

AN EYE ON ENEM

ENEM 2015 – Prova Rosa
Questão 92

Na tira da série *For better or for worse*, a comunicação entre as personagens fica comprometida em um determinado momento porque

a. as duas amigas divergem de opinião sobre futebol.
b. uma das amigas desconsidera as preferências da outra.
c. uma das amigas ignora que o outono é temporada de futebol.
d. uma das amigas desconhece a razão pela qual a outra a maltrata.
e. as duas amigas atribuem sentidos diferentes à palavra *season*.

Unit 2 — The Rocky Road of Good Urban Transportation

1. **Read part of a news report and check (✓) the correct statement.** *Identifying the purpose of a text*

   a. ( ) The news report aims to present research on the effects of commuting on people's time for breakfast in Britain.

   b. ( ) The news report aims to discuss the unhealthy content of breakfasts around Britain.

   c. ( ) The news report provides a detailed report on breakfasts in Britain.

---

www.dailymail.co.uk/news/article-2207637/One-busy-commuting-doing-school-run-eat-breakfast.html

One in three of us is too busy commuting or doing the school run to eat breakfast

- **Survey of 2,000 adults was commissioned by electrical goods firm Philips**
- **Dutch firm claim breakfast takes an average eight and a half minutes to eat**

By BEN SPENCER FOR THE DAILY MAIL
PUBLISHED: 00:04 GMT, 24 September 2012 | UPDATED: 22:14 GMT, 24 September 2012

It is, the old saying goes, the most important meal of the day. But it seems millions of Britons are far too busy for breakfast (and old sayings) these days.

One in three adults never eats breakfast at all, research suggests, with the school run and daily commute forcing us to **fill up** on unhealthy snacks later in the day. Another 30 percent of Britons said they ate their food during their commute. Researchers also found that the majority of families – 70 percent – never sit down together to eat breakfast.

The survey of 2,000 adults was commissioned by electrical goods firm Philips. The results said it takes an average eight and a half minutes to make and eat breakfast.

[…]

The survey revealed the people in Birmingham were the best beakfasters, with 73 per cent regularly sitting down for a morning meal. London was ninth on the list, with 63 percent eating breakfast regularly.

Dr. Ollie Hart, a family GP in Meersbrook, Sheffield, said: 'The danger with **missing** breakfast is that you get low blood sugar midway **through** the morning and then you snack.

'If people have breakfast they tend to eat slow-release food such as toast or cereal, which sustains them. But if people miss that meal and get hungry they will probably eat **garbage**.'

Adapted from www.dailymail.co.uk/news/article-2207637/One-busy-commuting-doing-school-run-eat-breakfast.html. Accessed on November 20, 2018.

---

2. **Find the following information in the article.** *Scanning*

   a. Number of adults who never eat breakfast at all. _____

   b. Percentage of British families who never have breakfast together. _____

   c. Percentage of Britons who eat their breakfast while they are going to work or school. _____

   d. City in Britain where people most eat breakfast regularly. _____

   e. City in Britain which was the ninth best breakfast eaters. _____

3. **Read the text again and underline all the statements that are implied by the author.** *Understanding main ideas*

   a. Britons don't give importance to breakfast, but they find old sayings important.

   b. It is worrying that so few Britons eat breakfast regularly.

   c. Not having breakfast leads people to eating unhealthy snacks.

   d. The time it takes to make and eat breakfast is considerably long.

   e. Dr. Ollie is concerned about what people end up eating if they skip breakfast.

4. **Read the article again. Identify and underline two sentences using a conditional structure. Then read the statements below and circle the correct alternatives.**
   a. One sentence shows an example of zero conditional and the other shows an example of first conditional.
   b. The first conditional is used when a situation is generally true, and both verb forms are supposed to be the same.
   c. The zero conditional is used when a situation is generally true, and both verb forms are supposed to be the same.
   d. In the first conditional, the result is likely to happen in the future, but it always depends on a situation that must happen in the present.
   e. A good example of first conditional is: *"Whenever my children come home early from school, they do their homework before dinner."*
   f. In the zero conditional, the result is likely to happen in the future, but it always depends on a situation that must happen in the present.

5. **Use the prompts to write sentences in the first or the zero conditional.**
   a. it / rain / we / take an umbrella (first conditional)

   _____

   b. my parents / come over / we / take them to the mall (zero conditional)

   _____

   c. we / work overtime / we / come home late (zero conditional)

   _____

   d. I / go to France / I / need a translation app (first conditional)

   _____

   e. she / need to take two trains / she / not come to the meeting (first conditional)

   _____

   f. he / arrive at the company earlier / I / let you know (first conditional)

   _____

6. **Read an extract about commuting in New York and underline the correct alternative.**

   > "Carson Tate, a productivity consultant who heads Working Simply, a Charlotte, NC-based firm, observes that New Yorkers, despite their long commutes, '**can take trains or subways and actually get some work done or recharge**.'"
   >
   > Extracted from www.nypost.com/2017/11/04/new-yorkers-have-one-of-the-worst-commutes-survey-says. Accessed on July 24, 2018.

   a. The modal verb *can* in the statement conveys the idea of...
      a. having an obligation.
      b. being able to (ability).
      c. possibility.
      d. willing to.
      e. enjoying.
      f. suggesting.

   b. The verb *recharge* is formed with the prefix *re-* followed by the verb *charge*. What does the prefix *re-* mean?
      a. not
      b. again or back to a former state
      c. do something with someone else
      d. without
      e. more
      f. less

Unit 2

109

7. Read the sentences below and check (✓) the statement that best describes each of them according to the use of the modal verbs *can* and *could*.

  a. I can't remember where I put my keys.
   ( ) inability in the present
   ( ) inability in the past

  b. Before she had her second baby, Monica could cycle 10 miles to work.
   ( ) possibility in the past
   ( ) ability in the past

  c. My mother says that I can't go out with you guys until she has arrived from work.
   ( ) impossibility in the present
   ( ) prohibition in the present

  d. OK, Lily. You can drive my car to school, but be back by 10!
   ( ) permission in the present
   ( ) ability in the present

  e. Sorry I couldn't come earlier. I had an important meeting at work.
   ( ) impossibility in the past
   ( ) prohibition in the past

  f. I can't go by bus because I have no cash with me.
   ( ) impossibility in the past
   ( ) impossibility in the present

8. Complete the sentences with *can*, *can't*, *could*, or *couldn't*.

  a. Patrick _____ walk to school because he lives too far!

  b. When she was younger, Molly _____ speak Spanish very well. Nowadays, not only is she fluent in Spanish, but she _____ also speak French, German, and Portuguese.

  c. Sorry, I _____ hear you. Please speak louder.

  d. When I was younger I _____ run 5 miles in 40 minutes.

  e. My sister _____ play the piano. She's practiced it for years! She has a concert next Wednesday.

  f. Do you want to go to a restaurant nearby? If so, you _____ take Sarah to *La Pasta*.

9. Read the following statement and underline the words with prefixes. What do the prefixes in these words mean?

> "Problems involving traffic jams and lack of parking spaces are making it impossible to drive in big cities. More and more people are shifting to public transportation encouraged by the possibility of reaching destinations faster and safer."

_____

_____

10. Read the explanations about prefixes in the box on page 20 of your Student's Book. Then use the words in the box to fill in the blanks adding the appropriate prefix to each of them.

> legal   gain   wanted   experienced   responsible

  a. He is very _____. We can't keep him in our company anymore.

  b. After losing his job, he had to _____ control of his life.

  c. Although she's a wonderful cook, she's _____ in running a restaurant.

  d. You can donate your _____ presents to charity.

  e. Some countries believe that _____ immigration leads to higher levels of unemployment, crime rates, and poverty.

Unit 2

11. Read the quotes below and underline the words with prefixes. What do the words mean? Complete the chart.

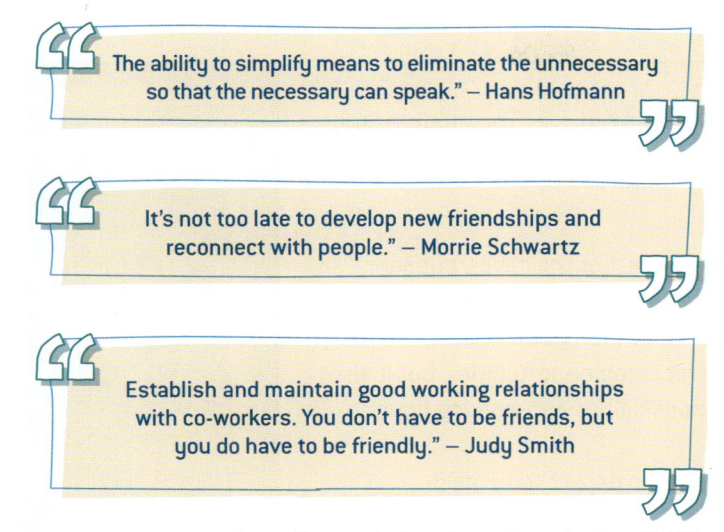

> "The ability to simplify means to eliminate the unnecessary so that the necessary can speak." — Hans Hofmann

> "It's not too late to develop new friendships and reconnect with people." — Morrie Schwartz

> "Establish and maintain good working relationships with co-workers. You don't have to be friends, but you do have to be friendly." — Judy Smith

Extracted from www.brainyquote.com. Accessed on August 2, 2018.

word with prefix	meaning

AN EYE ON VESTIBULAR

UNICAMP 2017 – Provas Q e Y
Questão 87

Ranking Universities by 'Greenness'

Universities these days are working hard to improve their sustainability credentials, with efforts that include wind power, organic food and competitions to save energy. They are also adding courses related to sustainability and energy. But which university is the greenest?

Several ranking systems have emerged to offer their take. The Princeton Review recently came out with its second annual green ratings. Fifteen colleges earned the highest possible score — including Harvard, Yale and the University of California, Berkeley.

Another group, the Sustainable Endowment Institute's GreenReportCard.org, rates colleges on several different areas of green compliance, such as recycling, student involvement and green building. Its top grade for overall excellence, an A-, was earned by 15 schools.

(Adaptado de http://green.blogs.nytimes.com/2009/08/20/ranking-universities-bygreenness/?_r=0. Acessado em 31/08/2016.)

Conforme o texto, universidades norte-americanas estão se empenhando para

a. oferecer mais cursos sobre ecologia.

b. melhorar sua posição em um ranking que define as instituições mais "verdes".

c. oferecer os melhores cursos sobre preservação ambiental.

d. participar de uma competição que define os *campi* com maior área verde.

Unit 3 — Generation Z: Conservative or Liberal?

1. Read part of an online article and mark the statements true (T) or false (F). *Understanding details*

> […] The labor market of modern society has greatly changed. […] The modern labor market is more exciting, vibrant, diverse, and personal, welcoming Millennials and their talents.
>
> **Short-term jobs**
> […] Millennials no longer commit to a single job for the rest of their lives, but are always looking for something better, more exciting, and promising. […] Millennials are turning to freelancing and **short-term** projects rather than traditional employment. Not only does this provide them with more job opportunities, but it also gives them more flexibility both in terms of job responsibilities and working hours.
>
> **Value and purpose before money**
> Millennials are well aware of their personal worth and do expect to be paid accordingly, but they don't mind putting other perks of a job, such as opportunities for job advancement, personal growth, and fun working environment, before compensation.
>
> **Organizations with personalities**
> Millennials don't want to work for a company where they would be just another face in the crowd. This is why they are looking for positions in organizations with a clear personality. […]
>
> **Dynamic workplace**
> Millennials don't want to work in cubicles isolated from the rest of their colleagues. **Instead**, they are looking for a fun and informal workplace where their creativity will be valued and encouraged. […]
>
> Adapted from www.chelseakrost.com/millennials-changing-job-market. Accessed on July 30, 2018.

Inside This Issue
What are Millenials' greatest talents?
The Job Market then and now.
Who are the so called Millennials?

a. (   ) Millennials value long term jobs, that will get them recognition and provide them with opportunities to advance in their careers the fastest way possible.

b. (   ) The difference between Millennials and past generations has changed the way the labor market deals with career and professional priorities.

c. (   ) Millennials are likely to have several jobs throughout their lives and that's because they are always looking for better opportunities and they are not afraid of change.

d. (   ) Millennials really care about their compensation package. So, recruiters need to be aware that, besides demanding high salaries, Millennials are also looking for fun and informal workplaces.

e. (   ) When choosing their jobs, Millennials take into account the company's position in the job market. They want to work at a place where they'll be noticed, in a company with personality.

f. (   ) Being able to express their creativity is not so relevant for Millennials. They are willing to give up working in groups if they feel their creativity is encouraged by the company.

2. Read the titles below and choose the one that best fits the article in activity 1. *Skimming*

a. Job Market: Baby Boomers and Millennials being confronted

b. Are the changes in the job market affecting the new generations?

c. How Millennials are changing the job market

d. Dynamic workplaces: how Millennials deal with careers and the job market

e. Four reasons why Millennials won't go to work

Unit 3

3. Using your previous knowledge and the information provided in the article and on page 28 of your Student's Book, write some similarities we can notice between Millennials and the Generation Z.

_____

_____

4. Read the following statement extracted from the article and complete the tasks that follow:

*"Millennials don't want to work for a company **where** they would be just another face in the crowd."*

  a. The author used the relative pronoun _____ in the sentence above to provide specific information about the kind of place Millennials wouldn't like to work at.

  b. What's the name of the structure used in this sentence? _____.

  c. The subject pronoun *they* refers to _____.

  d. The relative pronoun *where* refers to _____.

5. Match the clauses using one of the relative pronouns given. Then write the sentences you come up with.

She lives in a neighborhood	whose	showed up at my house yesterday
I'm not sure if I know the boy	where	boss refuses to pay double for overtime
Here at our company, we use a computer program	when	explains how the job market is impacted by Millennials
We are the employees	which	we must come together to fight prejudice
This is a time	that	people barely know each other
HR executives are looking for research	who	detects and blocks spyware

a. _____

b. _____

c. _____

d. _____

e. _____

f. _____

6. Fill in the blanks with the relative pronouns in the box. Then underline the three sentences where the relative pronoun can be omitted.

> when   where   whose   which   who

  a. Not a day goes by _____ I don't think about moving to Canada.
  b. Caleb usually travels to the same place _____ he first met his wife.
  c. These are the pictures _____ Louise took during her trip to Morocco.
  d. I have a friend _____ parents moved to an island in the Pacific.
  e. Tania was the first person _____ I met when I joined this company.

113

7. Read the comic strip below and complete the tasks that follow.

> **Panel 1:** HEY, GARFIELD, WHAT SAY WE GO ON A DIET TOGETHER? — SURE!
> **Panel 2:** I'LL _____ SURE YOU ONLY EAT WHAT YOU'RE SUPPOSED TO! — OF COURSE!
> **Panel 3:** I'LL WATCH YOU EVERY WAKING MINUTE! — AND I'LL SNEAK FOOD WHILE YOU'RE SLEEPING!

Extracted from www.garfield.com/comic/2018/05/18. Accessed on July 28, 2018.

a. Which word best fills in the blank in the conversation, *do* or *make*?

b. Read the statements below and check (✓) the ones that are correct about the use of *do* and *make*. Then rewrite the incorrect ones.

( ) With phrases such as *the homework* and *a favor*, we use *do*.

_____

( ) With phrases such as *a phone call* and *lunch*, we use *make*.

_____

( ) With phrases such as *the homework* and *a favor*, we use *make*.

_____

( ) With phrases such as *the bed* and *an offer*, we use *do*.

_____

8. Read the sentences below and write *make* or *do* in the correct form to complete the collocations in bold.

a. She's been so thoughtful to me. It really _____ **a difference** when someone shows their support through hard times.

b. After several interviews and a formal presentation, the company has finally _____ me **an offer**.

c. Would you please _____ me **a favor**? I need you to pick up the kids from school this afternoon.

d. Louise was really sorry to have hurt your feelings. I'm convinced she never meant to _____ you **harm**.

e. She's trying to _____ some **money** and pay for her trip herself. She doesn't want her parents to pay for anything.

f. I love going out to parties. It's a nice opportunity to have a great time and _____ new **friends**.

g. She needs to _____ **well** on the exams if she wants to pass.

9. Complete the sentences with *so... that...* and a word from the box.

> little   cool   handsome   many   happy   big   much   high

a. Prices were _____ clients refused to buy their products.

b. There is _____ to be decided _____ we'll work overtime until we have everything figured out.

c. Their house is _____ they won't have it renovated in time for the holidays.

d. They looked _____ in that picture _____ you wouldn't believe the problems they were dealing with.

e. There was just _____ space in the room _____ most of the people had to wait outside.

f. He looked _____ in that suit _____ no one recognized him.

g. We had _____ friends over to our party _____ we had to pay extra for the catering service.

h. The movie Andrew and I watched yesterday was _____ we ended up getting tickets to watch it again next Wednesday evening. Do you want to come with us?

10. Write sentences connecting the clauses in the two columns with the conjunction *so*.

a. Sonja called in sick,
b. We decided to stay home tonight,
c. The local farmer's market has been shut down,
d. Mark's on a diet,
e. I had to ask my mom to move her head,
f. The criminal didn't want to leave the house,
g. Alex was in a hurry when he left,

now we have to drive to the city whenever we need to buy groceries.
she won't come to work today.
we could watch the season finale of our favorite show.
I could see the TV screen better.
he needs to stop eating chocolate.
the police had to call for backup.
he didn't realize he'd left his suitcase at home.

a. ___
b. ___
c. ___
d. ___
e. ___
f. ___
g. ___

AN EYE ON ENEM

ENEM 2011 – Prova Rosa
Questão 93

Na fase escolar, é prática comum que os professores passem atividades extraclasse e marquem uma data para que as mesmas sejam entregues para correção. No caso da cena da charge, a professora ouve uma estudante apresentando argumentos para:

a. discutir sobre o conteúdo do seu trabalho já entregue.
b. elogiar o tema proposto para o relatório solicitado.
c. sugerir temas para novas pesquisas e relatórios.
d. reclamar do curto prazo de entrega do trabalho.
e. convencer de que fez o relatório solicitado.

REPORTS DUE TODAY!

"My report is about how important it is to save paper, electricity, and other resources. I'll send it to you telepathically."

©Glasbergen

Unit 4 What's going abroad like?

1. Read the fragment below, extracted from the blog post "How to find work overseas: 15 ways to earn money when you travel," and find the information that follows. *Understanding details*

Under 30? Get a working holiday visa!

Working holiday schemes allow people under the age of 30 to work abroad. These programs tend to be used mostly by **gap-year** travelers, students, or young adult backpackers. Most of the countries that offer these programs are English-speaking **Commonwealth** countries such as Canada, England, New Zealand, and Australia (under 35 now). The visa application process is pretty simple, and the visas are usually **issued** for one year. Typically, the visa comes with the stipulation that you can't work in one place for more than six months.

Most of the working holiday jobs you can find are typically service or low-wage office jobs. Most people become office assistants, **laborers**, bartenders, or waiters. The pay is not always great, but it's enough to live off of and usually will give you a little extra money to save for traveling.

For these jobs, you'll need to bite the bullet, fly to these countries, and look for work when you land. While sites like Gumtree have some listings, you'll find the majority of work when you land. Many companies specialize in placing travelers. And hostels usually have job boards and can offer a lot of assistance in finding work!

Extracted from www.nomadicmatt.com/travel-blogs/working-overseas. Accessed on August 19, 2018.

a. the types of work offered to people under 30 in the circumstances described: _____

b. the country that accepts people older than 30 years old: _____

c. how difficult it is to apply for this type of visa: _____

d. the maximum amount of time people can spend in the country with this type of visa: _____

e. places where job boards are available: _____

2. Read the extract again and circle the correct alternatives. *Understanding main ideas*

a. You **have to** / **don't have to** be on a gap year to apply for these jobs.

b. You **have to** / **don't have to** be under 30 to apply for these jobs in England.

c. You **need to** / **don't need to** be under 30 to apply for these jobs in Australia.

d. You **will have to** / **won't have to** fly to these countries and look for work when you land.

e. Visas usually stipulate that you **can** / **can't** work for one place for more than six months.

3. According to the text, certain jobs are more popular among travelers. If you were moving to a foreign country, which of those jobs would you choose? Justify your answer.

_____
_____
_____

4. Look at the words in the box. Then choose one of them to complete the extract below.

> off-road   mainstream   overcrowded

> When you hear that China is _____, that's an understatement. I was shocked at the number of people. Even in the rural areas. I was also shocked at the poverty and at the living conditions. - Rosemary Mahoney.

Extracted from www.brainyquote.com/search_results?q=overcrowded+abroad. Accessed on January 15, 2019.

5. Complete the tag questions with one word.

a. She is studying for her test right now, _____ she?

b. Tina and Bob were working when their house was broken into, weren't _____?

c. She always tells you to eat slowly, _____ she?

d. You didn't tell Mom and Dad about me being fired, _____ you?

e. You were driving the car when the accident happened, _____ you?

f. Why are you reading this book now? The test is only three weeks from now, _____ it?

g. Paul was a very good student in high school, _____ he?

h. Pete and Gloria are writing an Italian travel guide for foreign students, _____ they?

6. Look at the pictures below and write a sentence using *need to* or *have to* for each of them.

a.

b.

c.

d.

e.

f.

7. The three tips below were extracted from "Travel tips: 11 mistakes every first-time traveler makes." Read them carefully and complete with *have to* or *don't have to*.

www.traveller.com.au/travel-tips-11-mistakes-every-firsttime-traveller-makes-1mlb2g

You're excited, obviously. You're about to head off for your first overseas trip, and it's an amazing feeling. It's inevitable that you'll make mistakes the first time you travel, just the same as you'd make mistakes in any other **facet** of life. These are the common ones that **rookie** adventurers make.

Overbooking

It's **tempting**, on that first **daunting** trip away, to get everything locked in — every hostel, every transfer, every breakfast, lunch, and dinner. That way you _____ worry about anything, right? But you'll soon come to realize that it pays to have some flexibility. Book in the big things, sure. But also leave yourself space to change your itinerary and take opportunities as they present themselves.

Using a travel agent… for everything

While it's now easy for you to book an entire trip yourself over the Internet, I can understand the wish to have the safety net of a travel agent. But that doesn't mean you _____ use them for everything. Book your flights, and maybe an accommodation package. But you'll generally save money if you look after everything else yourself.

Trying to see everything

This is why the group tours are popular, why people see things like "seven countries in 12 days" and think that's a good thing. This is your big overseas trip and you want to see as much as possible — you want to check as many boxes as you physically can. But that's a mistake. You _____ trust that you'll travel again. Instead of trying to see everywhere at once, slow down, get to know one country, or maybe two, and your appetite will be **whetted** for a lifetime of similar adventures.

Adapted from www.traveller.com.au/travel-tips-11-mistakes-every-firsttime-traveller-makes-1mlb2g. Accessed on August 21, 2018.

8. Read the sentences and complete the idioms with the words from the box.

> beaten   wheel   back   suitcase

a. OK, Dylan. I'll go with you, but only if I am the one at the _____. I drive way better than you.

b. Let's go together. Just please, don't be a _____ seat driver. I hate it when you tell me how to drive.

c. We're changing plans. I'm tired of traveling to these busy places where everyone goes. Let's travel somewhere off the _____ track.

d. My plan is to live out of a _____ for the next six months, just traveling around and getting to know new places.

9. Read the extract below and choose an idiom from activity 8 to complete it with.

> Ferðafélag Íslands (the Iceland Touring Association) runs 40 mountain huts around Iceland. Some are on popular hiking routes, such as the Laugavegur trail, while others are more _____.

Extracted from www.theguardian.com/travel/2018/oct/06/europe-hut-cabin-hostel-stay-accommodation-bothy-bothies-mountain-lake-wild-remote-free-hiking-trail. Accessed on August 30, 2018.

10. Use the tag questions from the box to complete the dialogue. There is an extra alternative which you do not need to use.

> are you?   will you?   won't you?   do you?   aren't you?   don't I?

Jake: Wow, that's a big suitcase, Liz. You are not taking too many things, _____
Liz: Of course I am! I'm spending a year in Australia, so I have to take everything I need for a year, _____
Jake: Well, yes, but you can buy some things when you get there, too. Clothes are quite cheap in Australia. You don't want to pay an extra fee for luggage when you come back, _____
Liz: Well...
Jake: And you are planning to bring everything back home, _____
Liz: You're probably right. Help me choose between these things then, _____
Jake: OK. Let's make a list of what you need first. Then we can check the items we have already placed into your suitcase.

11. Complete the sentences below with the appropriate tag question.

a. Gloria is always talking about her amazing trips, _____ ?
b. I wasn't invited to Morgan's birthday party, _____ ?
c. Travis and Brianna didn't travel to London again, _____ ?
d. I am the only person to have access to this account, _____ ?
e. Georgia lives in the country with her husband and four kids, _____ ?
f. Malcolm would help me if I needed some money, _____ ?
g. Morty and Paula aren't taking a gap year in London anymore, _____ ?
h. Solange can speak four different languages, _____ ?
i. You shouldn't be driving your dad's car, _____ ?
j. Your mom wouldn't mind if I spent the night on your couch, _____ ?

AN EYE ON VESTIBULAR

UNESP 2017 (1º Fase)
Questão 30

Observe o cartum.

A alternativa que completa corretamente a lacuna do número 4 do cartum, sem prejuízo de sentido, é:

a. It's too hot in here.
b. I don't want to be tired all day.
c. Otherwise, I'll miss the bus.
d. I'm quite hungry.
e. Breakfast smells good.

Reasons to sleep through your alarm
1. I was having a really good dream.
2. Still so sleepy!
3. It's not even daylight yet.
4. _____
5. I've just gotten comfortable.
6. It's cold out there but warm in bed.

Reasons not to sleep through the alarm
1. I don't want to be late for work.

(www.systemcomic.com. Adaptado.)

Unit 5 — What the Future Holds

1. Read part of an article by *The Atlantic* and choose the correct alternative about the content of the text.

Understanding main ideas

> www.theatlantic.com/business/archive/2016/09/how-can-todays-college-students-futureproof-their-careers/499244
>
> ## The Atlantic
>
> **Ask an Economist: How Can Today's College Students Future-Proof Their Careers?**
>
> **Julia Kirby**, a contributing editor at Harvard Business Review and the co-author of *Only Humans Need Apply: Winners and Loser in the Age of Smart Machines*.
>
> Studies are famously declaring that, with the encroachment of smart machines into knowledge work, something like 40 percent of U.S. jobs will go the way of the passenger **pigeon**. The implication: You'd better find a robot-proof line of work. Don't be **misled**. Virtually every kind of work will be affected – but every kind will still be **available**. **Whether** you're an actuary or an activist, a scientist or a soldier, you'll work in an augmented way, with software **relieving** you of a lot of cognitive heavy lifting and tedium, and you doubling down on the human strengths that will still be the key to moving your enterprise forward. So, the thing to focus on in college is gaining experience in working with smart machines – learning what they're capable of and what you're capable of. Choose your class projects with an eye to this. Ask: What problem could I solve in this field if I had a tireless, number-crunching **fiend** as a teammate? What if I had a partner capable of retrieving from memory instantly, and discerning patterns in seemingly chaotic information? When you arrive in the workplace, that's exactly what you'll have. And you'll rise fast if you know how to do big things with it.
>
> Extracted from www.theatlantic.com/business/archive/2016/09/how-can-todays-college-students-futureproof-their-careers/499244. Accessed on August 1, 2018.

a. Julia Kirby provides educators with helpful information to guide them through the process of helping students make their career choices in the world of technology.

b. The author discusses the future of the labor market, gives companies advice on what to do to be ready for the new generation of employees, and tells students to focus primarily on technology.

c. Besides informing that all types of jobs will be affected by technology, Julia Kirby goes on to tell students what they should do during college to be ready for the new labor market.

d. Julia Kirby talks about the importance of technology and smart machines in the process of changing the labor market structure and tells students that most current jobs will not be available in the near future.

e. The author is not sure of how technology will impact the labor market as it is, but she's concerned by the fact that it will take away 40 percent of U.S. jobs within the next few years.

2. Read the article again and do the following tasks.

a. Underline all structures in the future tense you can find in the text.

b. In the sentences you found, what auxiliary or modal verb is used to express future? _____

c. What is the contracted form of the auxiliary or modal verb you marked in *b*? _____

3. Read the sentences below and complete with the structures that express future from the box.

> will be   is going to move   am going to visit   won't pick   will try

a. I don't know which dress to wear to my sister's wedding tonight, but I _____ a white one. She'd be really upset.

b. As soon as she retires, Meghan _____ to Miami. She wants to live by the ocean.

c. Grace brought cookies to the meeting and they look delicious. I think I _____ one.

d. I _____ a friend from college today after work. We've been planning to see each other for months, and I miss her so much.

e. Don't worry about your brother's reaction. I'm sure everything _____ all right.

4. Unscramble the words to form sentences.

a. his wife / move to / Mr. Packer / going / is / Oregon / to / with / .

_____

b. James / call / will / soon / as / I / get / as / home / I think / I / .

_____

c. to / you / Michigan / when / visit / sister / are / going / in / your / you're / ?

_____

d. Thailand / to charity / will donate / Bob / his money / all / move to / and / .

_____

e. give Janet / a call / and thank / for / her / I'll / maybe / the gifts / .

_____

5. The fragments below were extracted from original publications. To express future predictions, one of them is using *will* and the other is using *be going to*. Can you guess which fragment is using each form? Complete with your guesses.

> a. It is by now close to certain that there are millions of people currently in high school and college who are fine-tuning their skills for steady-looking careers that _____, following technological breakthroughs, dissipate by the time they retire.

Extracted from www.theatlantic.com/business/archive/2016/09/how-can-todays-college-students-futureproof-their-careers/499244. Accessed on August 1, 2018.

> b. Professor Richard Susskind, author of "The Future of the Professions and Tomorrow's Lawyers", echoes this distinction. "What you _____ see for a lot of jobs is a churn of different tasks," he explains.

Extracted from www.theguardian.com/us-news/2017/jun/26/jobs-future-automation-robots-skills-creative-health. Accessed on August 2, 2018.

6. Read the fragment below, extracted from the article "What to study in college to score the jobs of the future". Then read the tasks and check (✔) the correct alternatives.

> One field of study that **might** seem a stretch for a list of majors that, in the future, will yield great jobs with growing salaries is Architecture. Data shows that only 9,144 students graduated with such degrees in the United States in 2014.

Extracted from www.forbes.com/sites/karstenstrauss/2016/08/19/what-to-study-in-college-to-score-the-jobs-of-the-future/#1ef075c4567f. Accessed on August 01, 2018.

a. In the context given, the verb *might* is used by the author to express that...

( ) there's a possibility his prediction will come true.
( ) he is sure that his prediction will come true.
( ) there's no possibility of his prediction coming true.
( ) he doesn't believe his prediction will come true.
( ) he wants his prediction to come true.

b. In the fragment, the verb *might* can be replaced by other verbs without changing the main idea of the paragraph. Choose the alternative with the verbs that would best replace *might*.

( ) *could* and *must*
( ) *may* and *could*
( ) *should* and *could*
( ) *may* and *must*
( ) *can* and *should*

7. Choose the modal verbs that best complete the sentences below.

a. I'm calling, but Mary won't answer the phone. She _____ (may not / couldn't) be home.

b. She left about an hour ago. She _____ (may be / couldn't be) home now. Thirty minutes is more than enough to get home.

c. You're running out of alternatives. Place an order by the end of the day because these tickets _____ (might not / couldn't) be available tomorrow.

d. He _____ (couldn't be / might) Brazilian. He didn't understand a word I said.

e. Our boss _____ (couldn't / might not) be happy about it, but we are all taking the day off tomorrow.

8. Read the fragment below and complete the tasks that follow.

> **Joel Mokyr**, a professor of economics at Northwestern University and the author of *A Culture of Growth: The Origins of the Modern Economy*.
>
> There are three skills that will count in the future. One is to learn how to access information. Because no set of skills will be unaffected by continued and probably accelerating technological progress, it is important to be able to find out that what you know is obsolete, and keep updating. To do that you have to know where to find that information quickly, cheaply, and effectively, sorting the reliable from the **crackpot** websites.

Extracted from www.theatlantic.com/business/archive/2016/09/how-can-todays-college-students-futureproof-their-careers/499244/. Accessed on August 01, 2018.

a. Underline the *-ly* adverbs you find in the paragraph above.

b. Write the adjectives for the adverbs you found. _____

9. Read the definitions below and complete with the adverbs you underlined in activity 8.

a. _____ : in a way that produces the result that was intended.

b. _____ : with speed, very soon.

c. _____ : for a low price or cost.

d. _____ : likely to happen or be true.

10. Complete the sentences below with the adverbs from the box.

> academically   automatically   especially   financially   hopefully   primarily   probably   really

a. Please tell visitors not to touch the doors at our offices. They are set to open and close _____.

b. With the advances in technology, _____ in Artificial Intelligence, most low-paid workers will lose their jobs and be replaced by robots.

c. We see this agreement _____ as an alternative to reduce costs and save jobs.

d. Although he was not _____ involved in his studies, Peter was a tremendous addition to our college's baseball team.

e. Technology will _____ change the course of education and labor market within the next 10 years.

f. Diane didn't know her decision would cost hundreds of jobs in the long run, but as soon as she realized the negative impacts of her decision, she felt _____ sorry.

g. I know we don't see eye to eye when it comes to politics, but _____ we can find a solution that's best for everyone.

h. Although her plan to prevent employees from leaving the company for the competition was very impressive, her boss told her it was not _____ viable.

11. **Complete the sentences with your own information.**

a. I'd really like to _____
_____ when I finish school.

b. I am extremely worried about _____
_____.

c. Next year, I will probably _____
_____.

d. Hopefully, by the end of this year I _____
_____.

e. If I practice really hard, I might learn how to _____
_____ well.

AN EYE ON VESTIBULAR

2018 PUC-SP – Verão
Questão 63

Man in the mirror
Escrita por Siedah Garrett e Glen Ballard.
Gravada por Michael Jackson.

I'm gonna make a change, for once in my life
It's gonna feel real good, gonna make a difference
Gonna make it right…
I'm starting with the man in the mirror
I'm asking him to change his ways
And no message could have been any clearer
If you wanna make the world a better place
(If you wanna make the world a better place)
Take a look at yourself, and then make a change…

Esse trecho da música "Man in the Mirror" sugere que

a. qualquer pessoa consegue mudar, basta querer.

b. se queremos tornar o mundo um lugar melhor, devemos olhar para o próximo.

c. melhorar o mundo começa com nossa própria mudança.

d. fazer o bem ao próximo nos muda para melhor.

Extracted from https://vestibular.brasilescola.uol.com.br/downloads/pontificia-universidade-catolica-sao-paulo.htm. Accessed on August 3, 2018.

Unit 6 — It's Time We Reforested the Agribusiness

1. Read the title of the article below. What benefits of agroforestry do you think the article might mention? *Predicting*

HOME / BIODIVERSITY / KNOWLEDGE / AGROFORESTRY AND ITS BENEFITS

Agroforestry and its Benefits

Agroforestry is the management and integration of trees, **crops**, and/or livestock on the same **plot** of land and can be an integral component of productive agriculture. It may include existing native forests and forests established by landholders. It is a flexible concept, involving both small and large-sized land holdings.

Scientifically speaking, agroforestry is derived from ecology and is one of the three principal land-use sciences, the other two being agriculture and forestry. Agroforestry differs from **the latter** two principles by placing an emphasis on integration of and interactions among a combination of elements **rather than** just focusing on each element individually.

Agroforestry has a lot in common with intercropping (the practice of planting two or more crops on the same plot) with both practices placing an emphasis on interaction between different plant species. **Generally speaking**, both agroforestry and intercropping can result in higher overall **yields** and reduced operational costs.

[…]

Over the past two decades, a number of studies have been **carried out** analyzing the viability of agroforestry. The combined research has highlighted that agroforestry can **reap** substantial benefits both economically and environmentally, producing more output and proving to be more sustainable than forestry or agricultural monocultures. Agroforestry systems have already been adopted in many parts of the world.

[…]

As well as building on practices used in forestry and agriculture, agroforestry also works towards land protection and conservation through more effective protection of stock, control of soil erosion, salinity, and **water tables** and a higher quality control of **timber**.

Extracted from https://en.reset.org/knowledge/agroforestry-and-its-benefits. Accessed on August 29, 2018.

---

2. Read the statements below and check (✓) the ones mentioned in the article. *Understanding main ideas*

   a. ( ) Agroforestry is practiced in many countries around the world.

   b. ( ) Agroforestry integrates and combines different elements to achieve best results in the field, which is the same principle as in agriculture.

   c. ( ) Intercropping and agroforestry have many similarities.

   d. ( ) Agroforestry, agriculture, and forestry are the three main land-use sciences.

   e. ( ) Intercropping consists of planting the same crops in different areas.

3. According to the text, what's the main difference between agroforestry and agriculture and forestry? *Understanding details*

_____
_____
_____
_____
_____

4. Read the text once again and underline two sentences in the passive voice.

Unit 6

5. Read the extracts below. Then look at the words in bold and check (✓) the correct alternatives.

a. "[...] efficiency in agriculture **is needed** now more than ever."

Extracted from www.gamaya.com/blog-post/how-ai-in-agriculture-is-being-used/. Accessed on September 3, 2018.

( ) It shows an active voice structure.
( ) It shows a passive voice structure.
( ) It mentions the necessity of efficiency in agriculture.
( ) it mentions that to achieve efficiency in agriculture something else is needed.

b. "The world's population **is growing** at an increasing rate and there need to be enough resources to continue to support that growth [...]."

Extracted from www.gamaya.com/blog-post/how-ai-in-agriculture-is-being-used/. Accessed on September 3, 2018.

( ) It shows an active voice structure.
( ) It shows a passive voice structure.
( ) It talks about the effect the growth of the world's population is having on something else.
( ) It talks about the growth in the world's population.

c. "When there are robots [...] helping with farms and satellites in the sky scanning farms every day, a lot of data **is being collected**."

Extracted from https://gamaya.com/blog-post/how-ai-in-agriculture-is-being-used/. Accessed on September 3, 2018.

( ) It shows an active voice structure.
( ) It shows a passive voice structure.
( ) It says that robots and satellites are collecting a lot of data.
( ) It says that a lot of data is collecting robots and satellites.

6. Rearrange the words below to form sentences in the passive voice.

a. used / robots / been / have / in agribusiness / .

_____

b. conducted / were / a lot of studies / of the century / at the beginning / on agroforestry / .

_____

c. needed / to support / resources / the population growth / are / .

_____

d. in agroforestry / is / the land / protected and conserved / .

_____

e. agroforestry techniques / improved / will / we expect that / in the near future / be / .

_____

f. banned / been / has / deforestation / countries / in many / .

_____

7. Read the sentences below and cross out the verb that **can't** be used to complete it.

a. A book is being _____ on the use of Artificial Intelligence in the agribusiness.

published / written / reading

b. This location is _____ by hundreds of researchers every year.

visited / saw / accessed

c. The tractor was _____ in Gina's fields when no one was watching.

stolen / hit / driving

d. A movie about the importance of agroforestry is being _____ by critics all over the world.

watching / watched / analyzed

e. What questions _____ be asked by the speakers during the National Environmental Monitoring Conference?

could / will / are

f. Planting techniques _____ be improved.

can / could / was

125

8. Look at the phrases in bold in the article on page 124. Which of them means that the author's statement…

   a. describes a common feeling or opinion? _____
   b. describes an expert's point of view? _____
   c. is adding information to the subject being discussed? _____

9. Read the following fragments and underline the discourse markers. Then identify the idea conveyed by each discourse marker.

   a.
   > Major obstacles to the spread of agroforestry strategies are the **lack of** support for such systems through public policies, which often take little notice of tree-based farming systems. Consequently, agroforestry is often absent from recommendations for ensuring food security under climate change, even though many practices have been shown to deliver benefits for rural development, **buffer** against climate variability, help rural populations adapt to climate change, and contribute to climate change **mitigation**.

   Extracted from www.sciencedirect.com/science/article/pii/S1877343513001449. Accessed on August 30, 2018.

   _____
   _____

   b.
   > The world-wide **deaths** and chronic diseases due to pesticide poisoning number about 1 million per year (Environews Forum, 1999).

   Extracted from www.ncbi.nlm.nih.gov/pmc/articles/PMC2984095/. Accessed on August 30, 2018.

   _____

   c.
   > However, despite these high costs, farmers continue to use pesticides and in most countries in increasing quantities.

   Extracted from www.sciencedirect.com/science/article/pii/S0921800901002385. Accessed on August 30, 2018.

   _____

10. Complete the sentences below with the discourse markers from the box.

> due to   since   in addition   consequently   thanks to   however

   a. She was hired to help during the harvest. _____, I don't think she has any experience in the agribusiness.
   b. _____ the agribusiness has been growing, a lot of Artificial Intelligence tools are being produced.
   c. We are hiring people to support us during peak season. _____, every employee will get a bonus for working overtime in this period.
   d. _____ a lot of hard work, our country has achieved great improvements in the agroforestry field.
   e. In the last century, a lot of trees were cut down. _____, the importance of planting new trees is greater than ever.
   f. Excuse me, Ma'am. I would like to inform you that, _____ the weather conditions, your visit to the gardens must be canceled. We apologize for that.

11. Complete the extracts below with the correct form of the verbs *get* or *set*.

   a. "[…] As agroforestry tries to _____ closer to the way nature works, it is intrinsically related with agroecology."

   Extracted from www.fcrn.org.uk/interviews/perspectives-agroforestry-model-sustainable-intensification-agriculture. Accessed on September 3, 2018.

   b. "The Rainforest Alliance _____ standards for sustainability that conserve wildlife and wildlands and promote the well-being of workers and their communities. […]"

   Extracted from www.rainforest-alliance.org/business/climate/documents/coffee_carbon_guidance.pdf. Accessed on September 3, 2018.

   c. "Small employers need to _____ ready for super payment changes in the agribusiness."

   Extracted from www.sheepcentral.com/agribusiness-small-employers-need-to-get-ready-for-super-payment-changes/. Accessed on September 3, 2018.

12. Complete the questions using the verbs *get* and *set* in the correct form. Then answer them with your own opinion.

   a. What could the government in your country do to make sure people _____ the message about the importance of agroforestry and ecology?

   _____
   _____
   _____

   b. Do you know how someone in your country can _____ permission to cut down trees?

   _____
   _____
   _____

   c. Do you think your school _____ an example on sustainable habits? If so, what does it do? If not, how could this be changed?

   _____
   _____
   _____
   _____

AN EYE ON VESTIBULAR

FUVEST 2015 – 1º fase (Prova V)
Questão 43

Between now and 2050 the number of people living in cities will grow from 3.9 billion to 6.3 billion. The proportion of urban dwellers will swell from 54% to 67% of the world's population, according to the UN. In other words, for the next 36 years the world's cities will expand by the equivalent of six São Paulos every year. This growth will largely occur in developing countries. But most governments there are ignoring the problem, says William Cobbett of the Cities Alliance, an NGO that supports initiatives such as the one launched by New York University to help cities make long term preparations for their growth. "Whether we want it or not, urbanization is inevitable," say specialists. "The real question is: how can we improve its quality?"

The Economist, June 21st 2014. Adaptado.

De acordo com o texto

   a. A população rural crescerá na mesma proporção que a população urbana nos próximos 20 anos.

   b. A população, nas cidades, chegará a mais de 6 bilhões de pessoas até 2050.

   c. A expansão de cidades como São Paulo é um exemplo do crescimento global.

   d. A cidade de São Paulo cresceu seis vezes mais, na última década, do que o previsto por especialistas.

   e. O crescimento maior da população em centros urbanos ocorrerá em países desenvolvidos.

Unit 7 — The Economic Effects of Globalization

1. Read part of a news report and check (✔) the most appropriate headline. *Skimming*

> Business leaders around the globe have said the rise of economic nationalism **triggered** by Brexit, Donald Trump, and populist politics poses the greatest **threat** to their growth.
>
> According to a **survey** of 1,300 chief executives from some of the world's biggest companies, carried out by the accountancy company KPMG, British business leaders are notably more pessimistic than their peers.
>
> Two-thirds of U.K. CEOs said they were most worried about the growing use of protectionism, which includes measures such as tariffs and quotas on imports, compared with just over half of their international counterparts.
>
> Such barriers have the potential to protect jobs in the countries that put up trade barriers, but business leaders argue the benefits are **outweighed** by higher prices for consumers.
>
> Extracted from www.theguardian.com/business/2018/may/22/economic-nationalism-biggest-threat-growth-business-leaders-poll-political-populism. Accessed on August 4, 2018.

a. ( ) Donald Trump's election and its impact on global economy.

b. ( ) Business leaders say Brexit might affect economic growth.

c. ( ) Business leaders blame politics for global economic problems.

d. ( ) Why isn't the economy getting better?

e. ( ) Business leaders say economic nationalism is the biggest threat to growth.

2. Find the following information in the article. *Scanning*

a. the nationality of the business leaders who took part in the survey: _____

b. the number of CEOs who took part in the survey: _____

c. ratio of British chief executives worried about the growing use of protectionism: _____

d. protectionism measures: _____

3. Read the fragment below, extracted from the article in activity 1. Circle the verb tense of the phrase in bold.

> Business leaders around the globe **have said** the rise of economic nationalism triggered by Brexit, Donald Trump, and populist politics poses the greatest threat to their growth.

a. simple present

b. simple past

c. present continuous

d. present perfect

e. past perfect

f. past continuous

4. Check (✓) the alternative that completes the sentence below.

The _____ in the affirmative form is formed using the auxiliary verb _____ and the main verb in the _____ form.

a. ( ) present perfect / have / past participle
b. ( ) simple present / be / infinitive
c. ( ) present perfect / be / past participle
d. ( ) simple present / have / present participle

5. Read the fragment below and underline the statements in the simple past and in the present perfect. Then read the sentences that follow and mark SP for simple past and PP for present perfect.

> [...]
> In declaring that the U.S. economy has entered a new era of faster growth, President Donald Trump is dismissing signals from financial markets and the outlook of economists from Wall Street to the Federal Reserve.
>
> Flanked by his top economic advisers, Trump delivered remarks on the South Lawn of the White House on Friday to celebrate a report that the economy expanded in the second quarter at the fastest pace in four years. He said the economy is on track to reach an annual growth rate of more than 3 percent.
> [...]
>
> Extracted from www.chicagotribune.com/business/ct-biz-trump-gdp-economists-20180727-story.html#.
> Accessed on August 05, 2018.

a. ( ) The U.S. economy has entered a new era.
b. ( ) Donald Trump won the presidential elections in 2016.
c. ( ) President Trump delivered remarks on the South Lawn of the White House on Friday.
d. ( ) It is believed that the economy has already expanded substantially.
e. ( ) He said the economy is on track to reach a 3% annual growth rate.

6. Complete the sentences below with the words from the box in the simple past or present perfect.

> be   tell   apply   discuss   not be

a. _____ for that job yesterday? When I saw the job post, I knew you would consider filling in an application.
b. I _____ her not to come in before dinner time because I would be studying.
c. _____ she able to explain the economic situation during the meeting?
d. _____ these topics with your classmates?
e. I _____ to your house in years. The last time I was there was in 2011.

7. Read the statements below and complete them with *for* or *since*. Then complete the rule about the use of *for* and *since*.

   a. I've had this car _____ two years.

   b. We've lived alone _____ our parents moved to the countryside.

   We use _____ to stress the idea that something started at a given point in time in the past and still takes place in the present, whereas _____ is used to stress the duration of an activity or situation.

8. Read the extract below and complete with *for* and *since*.

   All of that slower growth last year, then, means that the economy is probably chugging along at the same 2 to 2.5 percent annual pace that it has been _____ most of the recovery. That makes sense when you consider that job growth hasn't sped up _____ Trump took office but has slowed a little.

   Extracted from www.washingtonpost.com/news/wonk/wp/2018/05/02/trump-has-not-made-the-economy-great-again/?utm_term=.9a35dfa98ff8. Accessed on August 5, 2018.

9. Complete the sentences below with *just*, *for*, or *since*.

   a. Joshua and Miranda have lived in this house _____ five years now. They want to sell it and move to a penthouse.

   b. What have you done for Anna _____ she lost her job? Maybe she needs some extra help finding something new.

   c. I have seen a lot of people going through customs _____ the last plane landed.

   d. She had been looking for a job for months, but she has _____ found one now.

   e. I've worked at the same company _____ 32 years.

   f. Our economical welfare has been at stake _____ 2016.

   g. Louise has _____ arrived! She arrived about five minutes ago.

10. Answer the questions with your own information. You can use *for* and *since*.

   a. How long have you studied at this school?
   _____

   b. How long have you lived in your house / apartment?
   _____

   c. How many English tests have you had this year?
   _____

   d. Have you written in your book today?
   _____

   e. Can you think of an activity you have just done? Write about it.
   _____

11. The fragment below analyzes the economic growth in the USA during Trump's election campaign for president of the United States. Complete it with the verb *be* in the simple past or present perfect.

www.macleans.ca/economy/economicanalysis/trumps-economy-looks-just-like-obamas-except-for-one-important-thing/

"I will be the greatest jobs producer that God ever created" - Donald Trump, Jan. 11, 2017

Jobs might _____ the dominant **plank** in Trump's election campaign, but employment _____ growing at a slightly quicker pace by this point in Obama's second term. The challenge for Trump going forward is that **unemployment** in the USA is already at such a low level, at just 4.1 percent, that the easy gains have been had. On the campaign trail Trump regularly stated that 96 million American workers _____ shut out of the economy. But while there _____ indeed 96.2 million people not in the labor force in December – a new all-time high – that figure includes retirees, students, people with family responsibilities, and people with disabilities.

Adapted from www.macleans.ca/economy/economicanalysis/trumps-economy-looks-just-like-obamas-except-for-one-important-thing/. Accessed on August 7, 2018.

AN EYE ON VESTIBULAR

2018 – UNICAMP
Vestibular de Verão
Questão 33

ZOMBIE NEUROSCIENCE
I don't know if cockroaches dream, but I imagine if they do, jewel wasps feature prominently in their nightmares. These small, solitary tropical wasps are of little concern to us humans; after all, they don't manipulate our minds so that they can serve us up as willing, living meals to their newborns, as they do to unsuspecting cockroaches. The story is simple, if grotesque: the female wasp controls the minds of the cockroaches she feeds to her offspring, taking away their sense of fear or will to escape their fate. What turns a once healthy cockroach into a mindless zombie is its venom. Not just any venom, either: a specific venom that acts like a drug, targeting the cockroach's brain.

(Adaptado de Christie Wilcox, Zombie Neuroscience. Scientific American, New York, v. 315, n. 2, p. 70–73, 2016.)

De acordo com o autor,
a. certas baratas conseguem escapar de ataques de vespas comportando-se como zumbis.
b. baratas são capazes de ações predatórias que mal podemos imaginar.
c. vespas fêmeas de uma certa espécie podem controlar a mente das baratas.
d. uma barata pode inocular um veneno que transforma uma outra barata em um zumbi.

Unit 8 — Spotting Fake News Among the Real Stories

1. **Read part of a news report by the National Democratic Institute (NDI). Check (✓) the alternative that describes its main purpose.**

    Identifying the main purpose of a text

    a. (   ) To discuss the problems caused by incorrect reporting of facts in politics.

    b. (   ) To present the topics of an NDI's annual dinner concerning false news and the reasons why this is an issue.

    c. (   ) To present NDI and its fight against false news together with three other organizations.

---

https://www.ndi.org/our-stories/disinformation-vs-democracy-fighting-facts

DISINFORMATION VS. DEMOCRACY: FIGHTING FOR FACTS

TWEET   SHARE   +

Thursday, October 26, 2017

NDI's annual Democracy Dinner will be **held** November 2nd at the Fairmont Hotel in Washington, DC. This year, NDI will honor three organizations on the front lines of fighting the global challenge of disinformation and false news. In addition, Senator Chris Murphy will provide a perspective from the U.S. Congress on this important topic and efforts that are being taken to counter disinformation. [...]

The global **reach** of social media platforms, coupled with the rise of artificial intelligence and machine learning, has provided a powerful suite of new tools that are increasingly used by autocratic regimes seeking to control the information space. While control of information has long been a key feature of autocracies at home, the rise of social media platforms and online political discourse now **provide** new opportunities for autocracies to manipulate public opinion abroad and disrupt domestic politics in geopolitical adversaries. The **weaponization** of social media is a global challenge, both during and between elections. Emerging democracies have often been used to "weapons test" new approaches to computational propaganda and disinformation, and the work being done to counter it is critical to the future of democracy.

At the dinner, NDI will recognize three organizations that have demonstrated a deep and **abiding commitment** to democracy and human rights:

- **StopFake.org** – StopFake.org in Ukraine works with journalists and citizen groups to monitor and uncover false news sources, and has created tools on "how to identify a fake" on its website. It checks facts and verifies information in media to help consumers obtain objective news that is free from distorted information, specifically on events in Ukraine. Long before most were aware of the use of false media to manipulate public opinion, StopFake was on the front lines exposing these tactics in a very **tough** neighborhood in which Ukraine is facing lots of outside pressure. One of the challenges of "fact checking" approaches to disinformation is that in correcting the record, after the fact, it is difficult to displace opinions or ideas that have already been formed or reinforced by disinformation. [...]

- **Rappler** – Rappler is an online social news network based in the Philippines. It holds public and private sectors accountable, **pursuing** truth and transparency for the people served. It encourages its readership to be aware of the spread of disinformation and propaganda, and exposes the hidden social media "machines" or bots that distort the truth. [...]

- **The Oxford Internet Institute's Project on Computational Propaganda** – The Oxford Internet Institute (OII), a multi-disciplinary research teaching department of the University of Oxford, has been at the **forefront** of research in the field of disinformation. In early 2017, OII's Project on Computational Propaganda issued a **groundbreaking** study on the use of social media and computational propaganda to manipulate public opinion in nine countries. [...]

Extracted from www.ndi.org/our-stories/disinformation-vs-democracy-fighting-facts. Accessed on September 18, 2018.

Unit 8

2. Read the news report again and answer the questions. *Understanding details*

a. How many organizations will be honored in this NDI meeting? What are they?
_____

b. Who is going to talk about the efforts being made to fight misinformation?
_____

c. What is considered a global challenge in election times?
_____

d. Which organization has a tool to identify false news?
_____

e. Which organization works with research and has recently conducted a study on the use of social media to manipulate opinions?
_____

3. Read the extracts below and check (✓) the correct alternative regarding the verb tenses of the words in bold.

a. "'Fake news' **was not** a term many people used two years ago, but it **is** now seen as one of the greatest threats to democracy, free debate, and the Western order. […]

Governments and powerful individuals **have used** information as a weapon for millennia, to boost their support and quash dissidence. […]"

Extracted from www.telegraph.co.uk/technology/0/fake-news-exactly-has-really-had-influence. Accessed on September 18, 2018.

( ) simple past – present perfect – simple present
( ) simple past – simple present – present perfect

b. "Students often look to teachers for information about how the Internet **works**. 'If they **don't get** it from teachers, they**'re not getting** it anywhere else,' **said** Matthew Johnson, director of education at MediaSmarts, an Ottawa-based organization that provides media literacy resources. […]"

Extracted from http://teachmag.com/archives/9860. Accessed on September 18, 2018.

( ) simple present – present continuous – simple present – simple past

( ) simple present – simple present – present continuous – simple past

4. Complete the sentences with the verbs from the box in the correct form. Pay attention to the verb tense used in each sentence.

> convince   access   realize   tell   be   check   try   share   visit

a. I am not _____ that website. Almost 50% of the information on it is fake news!

b. Margaret is sure that you _____ that web page yesterday. She was just _____ me that she saw your navigation history this morning.

c. Don has _____ online for too long. Could you ask him to be careful about what he reads on the Internet?

d. She didn't _____ me this is real news. I'm sure she's _____ to pass on fake news.

e. When I was _____ my Facebook page I _____ that my friend was _____ a lot of news from an unreliable website.

5. Complete the questions below with one word.

a. _____ you ever shared news without checking its veracity?
b. _____ you try to send me a link by WhatsApp yesterday? I couldn't open it.
c. _____ you still want to report that piece of news you got yesterday by e-mail?
d. _____ you telling me that I should just stop reading online news?
e. _____ you at the lecture about spreading false news yesterday? I didn't see you there.
f. _____ Sarah know that people are saying things about her? I really don't think they are true.

6. Complete the following sentences with the affirmative or negative form of *will* or *be going to*.

a. I _____ tell anyone about your secret. You can trust me.

b. Louise _____ report that fake news to Facebook. She is already writing an e-mail to them.

c. Maybe the president _____ show his support to our commission against spreading false information during the annual meeting.

d. I can't find any information about yesterday's accident in the newspaper. I think I _____ check online.

e. Apparently, the conservative candidate _____ win the election. Polls show that 54% of voters prefer him over the other candidate.

7. Read the excerpts below and check (✔) the alternative that best completes them. Then write the missing word in the blank.

a. "NEW DELHI: Under fire over fake and provocative messages being circulated on its platform, WhatsApp on Tuesday began an awareness campaign to help users identify and prevent the spread of false information, _____ and fake news. [...]"

Extracted from http://timesofindia.indiatimes.com/articleshow/64930914.cms?utm_source=contentofinterest&utm_medium=text&utm_campaign=cppst. Accessed on September 18, 2018.

( ) web crawler ( ) hoax ( ) bot

b. "Use a mobile antivirus – Keep a proactive defense on your Android so that if any malware, ransomware, adware, or _____ try to infiltrate, it'll be blocked and rejected. [...]"

Extracted from https://blog.avast.com/fake-apps-android-spyware. Accessed on September 18, 2018.

( ) spyware ( ) bot ( ) slander

c. "The production values are high and the message is compelling. In an 11-minute mini-documentary, Facebook acknowledges its mistakes and pledges to 'fight against _____.' [...]"

Extracted from www.theguardian.com/commentisfree/2018/jul/20/facebook-pledge-to-eliminate-false-information-is-itself-fake-news. Accessed on September 18, 2018.

( ) misinformation ( ) bot ( ) spyware

d. "_____ have become one of the biggest threats to security systems today. Their growing popularity among cybercriminals comes from their ability to infiltrate almost any internet-connected device [...]."

Extracted from www.pandasecurity.com/mediacenter/security/what-is-a-botnet/. Accessed on October 10, 2018.

( ) Spyware ( ) Botnets ( ) Misinformation

8. Unscramble the words to form embedded questions.

a. news / fake / ? / how to / know / do / you / identify

_____

b. tell / ? / can / me / you / what / is / a web crawler

_____

c. if / do / know / you / this antivirus / the phone / protects / ? / from spyware

_____

d. this website / I / is / wonder / reliable / . / if

_____

9. Match the parts of sentences to form embedded questions.

a. Can anybody tell me… ( ) the information on this website is reliable.

b. What I really need to know is if… ( ) where the bathroom is?

c. Could you tell us when… ( ) her students can't use reliable sources in their school projects.

d. Do you think you can figure out what… ( ) the information will be available for students?

e. She wonders why… ( ) Anna ever checks before passing on news?

f. Do you know if… ( ) we must do to put the system back in place?

10. Read the direct questions and complete the questions and sentences that follow.

a. Is this the most expensive ring in this jewelry store?

Do you know _____?

b. Where do you want to go on your vacation?

Can you tell _____?

c. When is Mona's birthday?

Can you remember _____?

d. What's the most important thing about this project?

I wonder _____.

e. Did Anthony tell anyone about the false information on this link?

Does anybody know _____?

11. After everything you read throughout this unit, can you summarize what fake news is and what problems it can cause?

_____

_____

_____

AN EYE ON ENEM

ENEM 2010 – Prova Azul
Questão 91

The record industry

The record industry is undoubtedly in crisis, with labels laying off employees in continuation. This is because CD sales are plummeting as youngsters prefer to download their music from the Internet, usually free of charge. And yet it´s not all gloom and doom. Some labels are in fact thriving. Putumayo World Music, for example, is growing, thanks to its catalogue of ethnic compilation albums, featuring work by largely unknown artists from around the planet.

Putumayo, which takes its name from a valley in Colombia, was founded in New York in 1993. It began life as an alternative clothing company, but soon decided to concentrate on music. Indeed its growth appears to have coincided with that of world music as a genre.

Speak Up. Ano XXIII, nº 275 (fragmento).

A indústria fonográfica passou por várias mudanças no século XX e, como consequência, as empresas enfrentaram crises. Entre as causas, o texto da revista *Speak Up* aponta

a. o baixo interesse dos jovens por alguns gêneros musicais.

b. o acesso a músicas, geralmente sem custo, pela Internet.

c. a compilação de álbuns com diferentes estilos musicais.

d. a ausência de artistas populares entre as pessoas mais jovens.

e. o aumento do número de cantores desconhecidos.

AUDIO SCRIPTS

Unit 1

Track 02 – Activity 2

Five apps to help social media addicts fight Fomo

Some teens are glued to social media feeds, and research suggests it's causing anxiety and sleeplessness, but there are ways of taking back control.

Fomo (Fear Of Missing Out) may sound like a silly acronym, but it can drive people to spend excessive time staring at social media feeds, anxious that they may miss a social opportunity or be left out.

The advent of Facebook in 2004 followed by other big social networks over the past decade means the amount of time children spend online has skyrocketed.

[...]

Extracted from www.theguardian.com/sustainable-business/2016/may/18/five-apps-help-smartphone-addicts-fight-fomo. Accessed on November 19, 2018.

Track 03 – Activity 3

"Research clearly shows that the amount of time British children and adolescents spend on social media has more than doubled in the past 10 years," says Dr Andrew Przybylski, research fellow at the Oxford Internet Institute. While in the USA, a quarter of teens are online "almost constantly", according to the Pew Research Centre, with 71% using multiple social networks.

Research suggests there are negative impacts to this increase in young people's time spent online. The Australian Psychological Society surveyed teens aged 13 to 17 at the end of last year and reported that half suffer from FOMO and feel anxious because of it.

Alongside potentially increasing the risk of anxiety and depression, a University of Glasgow study found using social media late at night could lead to less, and lower-quality, sleep. This result chimes with research from the University of Pittsburgh on young adults, which found that participants who were on social media the most had three times the level of sleep disturbance compared with those who checked least frequently.

[..]

But it's not all bad news: the teens surveyed by the Australian researchers said social media helped them to build stronger relationships, set better goals, seek help and guidance, and feel "part of a global community".

Adapted from www.theguardian.com/sustainable-business/2016/may/18/five-apps-help-smartphone-addicts-fight-fomo. Accessed on November 19, 2018.

Unit 2

Tracks 04 and 05 – Activities 1 and 2

A self-driving car has killed a pedestrian for the first time ever.

The autonomous car, operated by Uber, struck a pedestrian and killed them in what is thought to be the first death of its kind. The autonomous taxi was operating as part of a trial that Uber hoped would represent the future, but has now been suspended.

At the time of the accident, the car was driving itself in autonomous mode, Tempe police said. There was a vehicle operator behind the wheel, but they weren't in control of the car at the time of the crash.

[...]

A spokesman for Uber Technologies Inc. said the company was suspending its North American tests.

People have died in crashes involving vehicles that are driving themselves before. But this is thought to be the first time that a pedestrian has died after being hit by a self-driving vehicle.

Uber's autonomous taxis, like the self-driving cars made by other companies, use a series of sensors built into the car to spot pedestrians, cyclists, and other cars, feeding that into a computer that is able to steer and accelerate. Until recently, they have required a real person to be sat in the front of the car and ready to take over – but recently California officials approved the testing of such vehicles without humans in the front seats.

[...]

The cars have also been involved in smaller issues, such as running red lights.

Extracted from www.independent.co.uk/life-style/gadgets-and-tech/news/uber-self-driving-car-killed-pedestrian-death-tempe-arizona-autonomous-vehicle-a8263921.html. Accessed on September 20, 2018.

Unit 3

Tracks 06 and 07 – Activities 2 and 3

Gen Z, Gen Y, baby boomers – a guide to the generations

As a new report says Generation Z is smarter and more prudent than Gen Y, here's a guide to all those complex generational labels.

[...]

Generation Z

[...]

They have grown up in a world in political and financial turmoil. As a result, they are keen to look after their money, and make the world a better place. A report by Sparks & Honey, a U.S. advertising agency [...], describes this generation as the "first tribe of true digital natives" or "screenagers". But unlike the older Gen Y, they are smarter, safer, more mature, and want to change the world.

Generation Y

Also known as Millennials, born between about 1980 and 2000.

Born between the advent of the Walkman and the founding of Google, the members of Gen Y are unsurprisingly shaped by technology. Some have made fortunes from it. [...]

Generation X

Gen X are those born between the early 1960s and the early 1980s. [...]

This generation has been characterized as being saddled with permanent cynicism. Too young to have fought in any major war, old enough to have enjoyed a free education – they have spent too much of their adulthood sitting around in coffee shops trying to set the world to rights. And failing.

[...]

Adapted from www.telegraph.co.uk/news/features/11002767/Gen-Z-Gen-Y-baby-boomers-a-guide-to-the-generations.html. Accessed on November 19, 2018.

Unit 4
Track 08 – Activity 1

Jason: Very excited to welcome Tim Leffel to the show. Tim, welcome to the "Zero to Travel" podcast my friend.

Tim: Thank you so much for having me, Jason. It's good to talk with you again.

Jason: No problem. When we connected for the first time you were part of the "Paradise Pack" and this book that we're talking about today – "A better life for half the price" was one of the books in the pack. I'm really blown away by the content in here and I just want to preface this whole conversation by letting you, the listener, know that Tim is from the U.S.A. so, we're coming from, the perspective, I guess, but Tim would you say that maybe this perspective applies to all sort of Western cultures?

Tim: Yeah, I think I tried to cover that in the book too, by interviewing a lot of people that were from England, or Australia, or New Zealand. Basically, whenever you move from a really expensive country, to a much cheaper country you're going to get that benefit of a lower cost of living, so while the specifics may vary from, you know, place to place, depending on where you came from, the visa situation might be different. In general if you move from a more developed country to a less developed country, you're just going to be able to cut your expenses in half pretty easily if you do it right.

Jason: So, what prompted you to move abroad at first and why is this something somebody should consider?

Tim: Well, I actually lived abroad when I was back in my backpacking days and traveling around the world we actually lived in Turkey for a while, and we lived for more than a year in Seoul, South Korea. I say we – it was my wife and I, and we were teaching English as second language teachers. [fade out]

Adapted from http://zerototravel.com/podcast/living-abroad-tim-leffel/. Accessed on October 2, 2018.

Unit 5
Track 09 – Activity 2

Hi. I'm Josh, I am a third year primary education student here at Macquarie and I'm here today to talk to you a little bit about a gap year. You might ask what is a gap year and it's, um, it's just time between school and college, where usually you go away or some people work for the year, but it's a time when you kind of you learn more about what you wanna do in your career, what you wanna do once you leave school, university life, those kinds of things.

Adapted from www.youtube.com/watch?v=oJTwlOHk9Ro. Accessed on July 20, 2018.

Track 10 – Activity 3

So, I finished school, I was only 17 at the time, I was under age and I was really young. I had no idea what I wanted to do for a career. I went away for a year, I worked in a school in England just south of Manchester, a place called Alderley Edge, so we were living there, we were working there and then we were able to go into Manchester and the local towns. I started off being the music gap student, so that meant working in the music department filing music, running classes, being involved in the choir and the orchestra, which I was really keen on doing because I was big singing, big on singing. My mate here in Sydney, they decided to put him in the office and so what we figured out really quite early on and what the teachers and the headmaster of the school figured out was that I wasn't so good at the music and my mate wasn't so good at the office and so that was a bonus of a gap year: learning what your strengths are, where they are. Later on in the year I decided that, you know, what I would like to have a bit of a go at was some teaching and I was able to teach a computer class, so we were teaching them you know Word, PowerPoint, those skills and these kids we knew too so they were like seven or eight and they'd never done anything like that, so it was a great experience because I was teaching them something that they had never done before, they hadn't got at school before and it was something that they were really going to use and they were able to go home and show their parents, "Hey, guess what I can do". So I came back and I had deferred a Bachelor of Arts here at Macquarie University and so I am, I switched my degree into a Bachelor of Arts with the Diploma of Education, which is the degree to become a primary school teacher. In your third year here at Macquarie University you get to go to a school and so I went up to school in Pennant Hills and it was an incredible experience. I had a year three and they were fantastic. I feel that Macquarie did support me through my gap year because I was able to defer my course, I felt a lot more comfortable about, about going away knowing that I had a position still here.

Transcribed from www.youtube.com/watch?v=oJTwlOHk9Ro. Accessed on July 20, 2018.

Track 11 – Activity 4

So, guys, a gap, a gap year is good because it teaches you more about yourself, you develop a self-understanding and a self-awareness, you learn what your strengths are and through that understanding you're able to kind of figure out what you want to do with the rest of your life. So that's why I chose a gap year and if it's right for you that's why you should too.

Transcribed from www.youtube.com/watch?v=oJTwlOHk9Ro. Accessed on July 20, 2018.

Unit 6

Tracks 12 and 13 – Activities 1 and 2

Brazil has progressively emerged as a major agricultural powerhouse during the past few years: A net importer of agricultural products in the 1970s, the country now ranks among the world's five largest agricultural producers and exporters. The world's largest country in terms of land size and South America's largest nation in terms of land and population size, Brazil is currently a key player in the international arena and a great power among emerging countries.

As the world's sixth largest economy, Brazil ranks third among the world's major agricultural exporters and fourth for food products. With 25 percent of global investment, the country is the principal recipient and source of foreign direct investment in Latin America and fifth recipient nation in the world. Thanks to its agricultural and oil resources, Brazil also ranks second worldwide for bioethanol production.

Blessed with the world's largest reserves of farmable and not cultivated land, Brazil has carved out its regional and international rank thanks to strong exporting agricultural activities, radical economic reforms, and an aggressive trade and influence policy.

Even while manufacturing and services are showing a steep growth, agriculture is still a driving force of the Brazilian economy with 5.8 percent of GDP (against 2 percent in France), and with the agribusiness share reaching 23 percent. In 2009, agriculture accounted for 19.3 percent of the labor force, or 19 million people, thus strongly contributing to poverty reduction. Agribusiness employment accounted for 2.7 percent of the labor force.

Extracted from www.momagri.org/UK/focus-on-issues/Agriculture-a-strategic-sector-for-Brazil-s-economic-growth_1089.html. Accessed on August 31, 2018.

Unit 7

Track 14 – Activity 2

SHARMINI PERIES: It's The Real News Network. I'm Sharmini Peries, coming to you from Baltimore. Will there be another financial crisis, or even another great recession like that of 2007 and 2008? A new report issued by the Next Systems Project argues that it is almost inevitable that there will be another major financial crisis. The report, titled "The Crisis Next Time: Planning for public ownership as an alternative to corporate bank bailouts," looks at the history of financial crises over the past 70 years, and it predicts that another major crisis is very likely. Secondly, the report outlines a plan for how to deal with the next crisis. The calculated guess is that the next financial crisis could even be worse than the last one we experienced. And the report's main recommendation is to create a public banking sector not only to cope with the next crisis when it happens, but also to prevent future crises.

Joining me now here in our Baltimore studio is the report's author, Thomas Hanna. And Thomas is the research director at the Democracy Collaborative, to which the Next Systems Project belongs.

Extracted from https://therealnews.com/stories/the-next-global-financial-crisis-is-inevitable-pt-1-2;. Accessed on July 24, 2018.

Track 15 – Activity 3

THOMAS HANNA: Thank you very much for having me.

SHARMINI PERIES: Thank you for joining us here. All right, Thomas, let's take up this very important issue, because it is very solution-oriented. But let's step back a bit and first, in our first segment, discuss, looking at history, why you think that there is a next crisis pending, and what are the indicators, what does history tell us. And then in the second segment we'll take up what the potential solution that you're proposing is here, which is public banking. But let's start with the first issue, which is you went back 70 years, and you took a look at the history of crises. And so, based on that, tell us why there's another crisis pending.

THOMAS HANNA: Well, I think the first thing that we need to understand is that we are exactly 10 years from the last major financial crisis, which was essentially the biggest financial crisis in this country in 70 years, since the Great Depression. And if you look at history in the post-1970 period, what we call the neoliberal period, crises happen on average about once every 10 years. So, 10 years from the financial crisis, we're looking at a time when there should, or probably would be, another financial crisis just based on history alone. That's not taking into account what has happened in the intervening 10 years since the financial crisis. And essentially what has happened is nothing. We've had very little movement on addressing or changing any of the underlying basis of the financial sector that caused the crisis.

[...]

Extracted from https://therealnews.com/stories/the-next-global-financial-crisis-is-inevitable-pt-1-2. Accessed on July 24, 2018.

Unit 8

Tracks 16 and 17 – Activities 1 and 2

Real News Can be Confirmed in Four Steps

Teaching with current events has always been a vital way to help students become informed and engaged citizens. But the importance of news literacy has perhaps never been as critical as it is today, with the pronounced rise of deliberately misleading and patently fake news.

[...]

As educators, we have a role to play in equipping our young adults with the critical thinking skills necessary to assess the credibility of news reports as they make their own informed opinions about the day's topics.

Reliability: Determine if a source is trustworthy

We now know that there are intentional efforts to widely disseminate false content on social media channels, blogs, and other websites. Making sure students know how to measure the reliability of a source is a critical first step to helping them spot fake news.

[...]

Evidence: Check sources, citations, and facts

As students learn to discern real from fake news, it is important to remember that there is a difference between fake news and inaccurate information. Reliable news sources will include links to professional sources, fact-based evidence, and will present multiple sides of an issue. Train students to check the evidence within the article they are reading.

[...]

Argument: Identify the two sides in every story

This step can be tricky, as even the most factual news outlets can still have a bias or unique perspective on a topic. A biased article does not inherently imply that it's fake news; rather, it's part of the overall formula (along with reliability and evidence) that can help students. A well-written article is balanced, representing many sides of a story. Recognizing that there are, more often than not, multiple perspectives of an event or a political issue, can lead students to better understand their community and the world as a whole.

[...]

Language: Show how words and tone matter

The final step of identifying real news is to evaluate the tone and level of sensationalism of an article. Incorporate analysis of word choice in evaluating the reliability of a news source.

[...]

Extracted from www.amle.org/BrowsebyTopic/WhatsNew/WNDet/TabId/270/ArtMID/888/ArticleID/878/Fight-Fake-News.aspx. Accessed on October 8, 2018.

NOTES

NOTES

NOTES

EXPAND 3

STUDENT'S BOOK & WORKBOOK

Carla Maurício Vianna
Luciana Santos Pinheiro

Pearson

Pearson

Head of Product - Pearson Brasil	Juliano de Melo Costa
Product Manager - Pearson Brasil	Marjorie Robles
Product Coordinator - ELT	Mônica Bicalho
Authors	Carla Maurício Vianna
Teacher's Guide	Carla Maurício Vianna
Workbook	Luciana Santos Pinheiro (Allya Assessoria Linguística)
Extra content	Carla Maurício Vianna Luciana Santos Pinheiro (Allya Assessoria Linguística)
Editors - ELT	Gisele Aga Renata S. C. Victor Simara H. Dal'Alba (Allya Assessoria Linguística)
Editors (Teacher's Book)	Gisele Aga Simara H. Dal'Alba (Allya Assessoria Linguística)
Proofreader (English)	Silva Serviços de Educação
Proofreader (Portuguese)	Fernanda R. Braga Simon
Copyeditor	Maria Estela Alcântara
Pedagogical Reviewer	Najin Lima
Quality Control	Viviane Kirmeliene
Art and Design Coordinator	Rafael Lino
Art Editor - ELT	Emily Andrade
Acquisitions and permissions Manager	Maiti Salla
Acquisitions and permissions team	Andrea Bolanho Cristiane Gameiro Heraldo Colon Maricy Queiroz Paula Quirino Sandra Sebastião Shirlei Sebastião
Graphic design	Mirella Della Maggiore Armentano MRS Consultoria Editorial
Graphic design (cover)	Mirella Della Maggiore Armentano MRS Consultoria Editorial
Media Development	Estação Gráfica
Audio	Maximal Studio
Audiovisual Editor	Tatiane Almeida
Audiovisual	Desenrolados

The publisher would like to thank the following for their kind permission to reproduce their photographs:

Alamy Stock: p. 24, 40, 46. **Always/ Leo Burnett:** p. 12. **Cartoonstock:** p.48. **Getty Images:** p. 43. **iStock:** capa, p. 9, 17, 18, 24, 27, 34, 38, 45, 53, 63, 64, 68, 71, 72, 79. **Jennifer Siebel Newsom:** p. 16. **King Vidor (Warner Home Video):** p. 16. **Los Angeles Times:** p. 32. **Mark Andrews (Pixar Animation Studios):** p. 16. **Shutterstock:** p. 35, 41, 52, 57, 70, 73. **Sustain:** p. 43. **The Penguin Press:** p. 28.

Every effort has been made to trace the copyright holders and we apologize in advance for any unintentional omissions. We would be pleased to insert the appropriate acknowledgement in any subsequent edition of this publication.

Dados Internacionais de Catalogação na Publicação (CIP)
(Câmara Brasileira do Livro, SP, Brasil)

Expand 3: Student's Book / Carla Maurício Vianna, Luciana Santos Pinheiro. -- São Paulo: Pearson Education do Brasil, 2019.

ISBN 978-65-50110-36-9

1. Inglês (Ensino Médio) I. Pinheiro, Luciana Santos. II. Título.

19-25487   CDD-420.7

Índices para catálogo sistemático:
1. Inglês: Ensino Médio 420.7
Maria Alice Ferreira - Bibliotecária - CRB-8/7964

ISBN 978-65-50110-36-9 (Student's Book & Workbook)
ISBN 978-65-50110-37-6 (Teacher's Book)

EXPAND 3

» **Unit 1**	**9**
» **Unit 2**	**17**
» Review 1	25
» **Unit 3**	**27**
» **Unit 4**	**35**
» Review 2	43
» **Unit 5**	**45**
» **Unit 6**	**53**
» Review 3	61
» **Unit 7**	**63**
» **Unit 8**	**71**
» Review 4	79
Grammar Overview	81
Language Reference	85
Reading Strategies	93
Irregular Verbs	94
Common Mistakes	96
False Friends	98
Glossary	99
Workbook	103
Audio Scripts	136

CONTENTS

	READING	VOCABULARY IN USE	LANGUAGE IN USE 1	EXPAND YOUR READING	LANGUAGE IN USE 2	LISTENING COMPREHENSION
UNIT 1 Gender Equality is for Everybody page 9	Research article: Working women: Key facts and trends in female labor force participation	Expressions for gender parity and inequality	Present perfect continuous	Position article: Boys do cry: one man's experience of depression	Present perfect simple vs. present perfect continuous	A talk about an interview with a documentary director
UNIT 2 Technology in the School Curriculum page 17	Informative article: Coding In Education: Why It's Important & How It's Being Implemented	Coding language	Subject-verb agreement	Curriculum: Junior Computer Curriculum	Compound adjectives	An interview with students who built a robot

Review 1 (Units 1-2)
Page 25

	READING	VOCABULARY IN USE	LANGUAGE IN USE 1	EXPAND YOUR READING	LANGUAGE IN USE 2	LISTENING COMPREHENSION
UNIT 3 Can We Eat with a Clear Conscience? page 27	Book excerpt: Omnivore's dilemma	Words derived from Latin	Second conditional	Book review: No Accounting for Mouthfeel	Zero, first, and second conditionals	A lecture about agriculture and the environment
UNIT 4 Extreme Weather Events Affecting the Planet page 35	News stories: 4 People Who Faced Disaster – And How They Made It out Alive	Weather-related phrasal verbs and idioms	Past perfect	Expository essay: Widespread impacts	Adverbs of degree	A testimonial about being caught in an avalanche

Review 2 (Units 3-4)
Page 43

Grammar Review page 81

Language Reference page 85

Reading Strategies page 93

Irregular Verbs page 94

	READING	VOCABULARY IN USE	LANGUAGE IN USE 1	EXPAND YOUR READING	LANGUAGE IN USE 2	LISTENING COMPREHENSION
UNIT 5 **In the Limelight** page 45	Entertainment news: What would have happened next if these TV characters hadn't died?	Homonyms, homophones, and homographs	Third conditional	List: TV Shows You Wish You Were a Character On	*Wish*	Results of research on binge-watching TV shows
UNIT 6 **Uncovering Blockchain and the Dark Web** page 53	Opinion article: Forget Bitcoin, It's All About The Blockchain	Technology and financial nouns and phrasal verbs	*Some, any, no, every*	Information report: The dark web and how to access it	Direct and indirect speech	A talk about Bitcoin and the Dark Web

Review 3 (Units 5-6)
Page 61

	READING	VOCABULARY IN USE	LANGUAGE IN USE 1	EXPAND YOUR READING	LANGUAGE IN USE 2	LISTENING COMPREHENSION
UNIT 7 **Digital Influencing** page 63	Blog post: Under the Influence: The Power of Social Media Influencers	Adjectives ending in *-ed* and *–ing*	Modal verbs for assumption: *must* and *can*	Guide: How to make it as an Instagram influencer	Passive voice	A talk about what makes a real influencer
UNIT 8 **The End of a Journey** page 71	News article: Too many graduates are mismatched to their jobs. What's going wrong?	Collocations with *have* and *take*	Future continuous and future perfect	Advice letter: How do I deal with the post-university blues?	Verb tense review	A graduation speech

Review 4 (Units 7-8)
page 79

Common Mistakes	**False Friends**	**Glossary**	**Workbook**	**Audio Scripts**
page 96	page 98	page 99	page 103	page 136

PRESENTATION

STUDENT'S BOOK

Welcome to the *Expand* collection! *Expand* prepares students for the English part of Brazilian exams ENEM and vestibular, which are aimed at testing students' ability to read a wide variety of authentic texts of different genres. *Expand* provides students with listening, speaking, and writing activities that help them to develop their overall knowledge of the language. Each thematic unit contains two reading sections that introduce grammar and vocabulary topics, as well as listening comprehension activities that give students contact with oral text genres.

OPENING PAGE

Each unit starts with an opening page containing:

IN THIS UNIT YOU WILL…

This shows the main objectives for the unit.

> **IN THIS UNIT YOU WILL…**
> - take part in discussions about coding in education;
> - talk about a technology curriculum and robotics;
> - learn about subject-verb agreement;
> - identify and use compound adjectives.

LEAD OFF

This section presents three to four questions for content contextualization.

> **LEAD OFF**
> - What situation does the picture represent? Are you familiar with that situation?
> - Do you know what *coding* means? Explain.
> - What do you think about the integration of technological projects in school curriculums?

READING PAGES

This two-page section contains the first reading text and activities of the unit. It develops reading strategies and is subdivided into the following stages:

BEFORE READING

This section contains one or two activities that help students to prepare for the text topic, which is presented in the section WHILE READING.

> **READING**
> **▸▸ BEFORE READING**
> You are going to read a text about the implementation of computer programming in education. Is this a reality in your country or school? How do you think students could benefit from having computer programming lessons? Exchange ideas with your classmates.

WHILE READING

In this section students read a text and answer a question related to it. Texts are in a variety of different genres and aimed at developing several reading strategies.

> **▸▸ WHILE READING** *Selecting a good title*
> Read the whole text and check (✓) the best title for it.
> a. ( ) The YouTube Phenomenon: a disruptive force
> b. ( ) Globalization: Concepts, Causes, and Consequences
> c. ( ) Under the Influence: The Power of Social Media Influencers

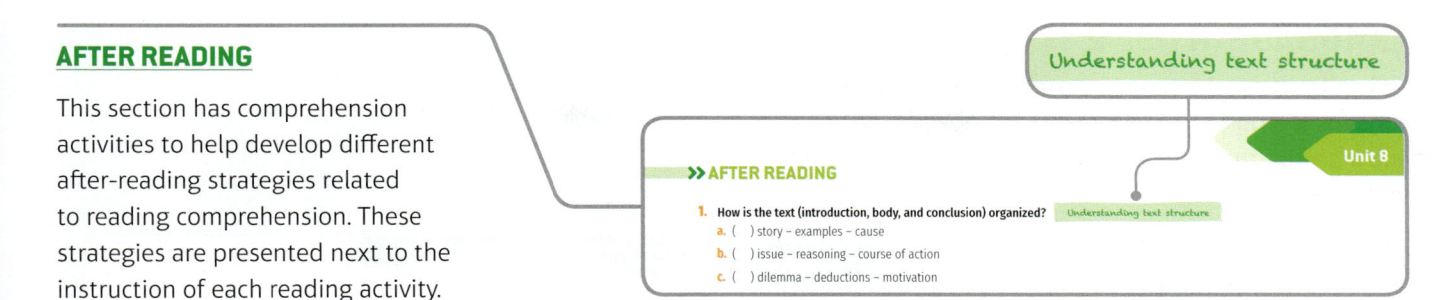

AFTER READING

This section has comprehension activities to help develop different after-reading strategies related to reading comprehension. These strategies are presented next to the instruction of each reading activity.

> **AFTER READING**
>
> 1. How is the text (introduction, body, and conclusion) organized?   *Understanding text structure*
>   a. ( ) story – examples – cause
>   b. ( ) issue – reasoning – course of action
>   c. ( ) dilemma – deductions – motivation
>
> *Understanding text structure* — Unit 8

VOCABULARY PAGES

This stage develops students' vocabulary through activities containing vocabulary from the text and related to the topic of the unit.

EXPAND YOUR VOCABULARY

This section contains one to three activities related to the vocabulary presented in the text. It also prompts students to engage in conversational topics based on the text students have read.

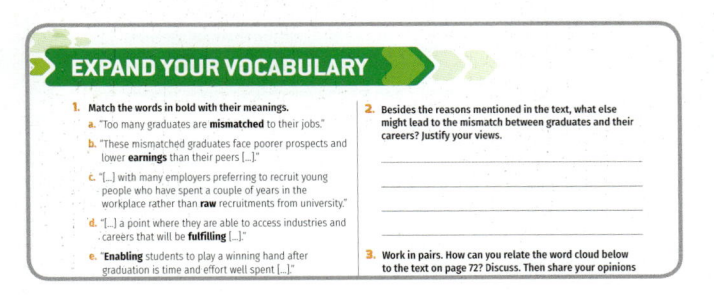

> **EXPAND YOUR VOCABULARY**
>
> 1. Match the words in bold with their meanings.
>   a. "Too many graduates are **mismatched** to their jobs."
>   b. "These mismatched graduates face poorer prospects and lower **earnings** than their peers […]"
>   c. "[…] with many employers preferring to recruit young people who have spent a couple of years in the workplace rather than **raw** recruitments from university."
>   d. "[…] a point where they are able to access industries and careers that will be **fulfilling** […]"
>   e. "**Enabling** students to play a winning hand after graduation is time and effort well spent […]"
>
> 2. Besides the reasons mentioned in the text, what else might lead to the mismatch between graduates and their careers? Justify your views.
>
> 3. Work in pairs. How can you relate the word cloud below to the text on page 72? Discuss. Then share your opinions

VOCABULARY IN USE

Here students are presented with an example of the target vocabulary taken from the main reading text and do activities to develop their vocabulary knowledge.

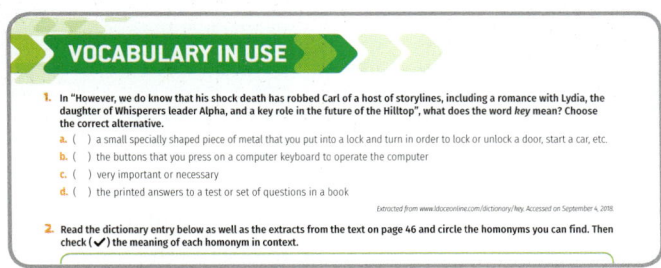

> **VOCABULARY IN USE**
>
> 1. In "However, we do know that his shock death has robbed Carl of a host of storylines, including a romance with Lydia, the daughter of Whisperers leader Alpha, and a key role in the future of the Hilltop", what does the word **key** mean? Choose the correct alternative.
>   a. ( ) a small specially shaped piece of metal that you put into a lock and turn in order to lock or unlock a door, start a car, etc.
>   b. ( ) the buttons that you press on a computer keyboard to operate the computer
>   c. ( ) very important or necessary
>   d. ( ) the printed answers to a test or set of questions in a book
>
> Extracted from www.ldoceonline.com/dictionary/key. Accessed on September 4, 2018.
>
> 2. Read the dictionary entry below as well as the extracts from the text on page 46 and circle the homonyms you can find. Then check (✓) the meaning of each homonym in context.

LANGUAGE IN USE 1

This page shows the first grammar topic of the unit. It contains examples from the text and activities that develop students' grammar knowledge in the target language.

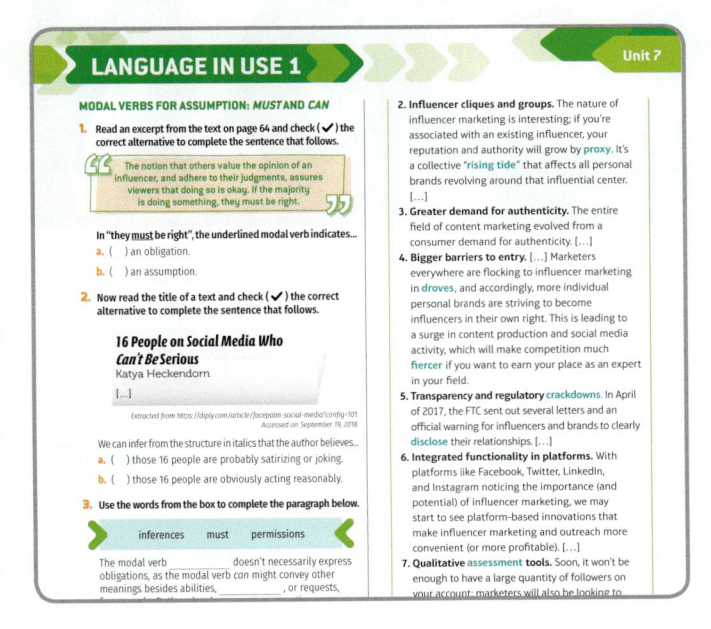

> **LANGUAGE IN USE 1** — Unit 7
>
> MODAL VERBS FOR ASSUMPTION: *MUST* AND *CAN*
>
> 1. Read an excerpt from the text on page 64 and check (✓) the correct alternative to complete the sentence that follows.
>
> > "The notion that others value the opinion of an influencer, and adhere to their judgments, assures viewers that doing so is okay. If the majority is doing something, they must be right."
>
> In "they **must be right**", the underlined modal verb indicates…
>   a. ( ) an obligation.
>   b. ( ) an assumption.
>
> 2. Now read the title of a text and check (✓) the correct alternative to complete the sentence that follows.
>
> **16 People on Social Media Who Can't Be Serious**
> Katya Heckendorn
> […]
>
> Extracted from https://dlply.com/article/facepalm-social-media/config-101. Accessed on September 19, 2018.
>
> We can infer from the structure in italics that the author believes…
>   a. ( ) those 16 people are probably satirizing or joking.
>   b. ( ) those 16 people are obviously acting reasonably.
>
> 3. Use the words from the box to complete the paragraph below.
>
> | inferences | must | permissions |
>
> The modal verb _____ doesn't necessarily express obligations, as the modal verb *can* might convey other meanings besides abilities, _____, or requests,
>
> 2. **Influencer cliques and groups.** The nature of influencer marketing is interesting; if you're associated with an existing influencer, your reputation and authority will grow by **proxy**. It's a collective "**rising tide**" that affects all personal brands revolving around that influential center. […]
>
> 3. **Greater demand for authenticity.** The entire field of content marketing evolved from a consumer demand for authenticity. […]
>
> 4. **Bigger barriers to entry.** […] Marketers everywhere are flocking to influencer marketing in **droves**, and accordingly, more individual personal brands are striving to become influencers in their own right. This is leading to a surge in content production and social media activity, which will make competition much **fiercer** if you want to earn your place as an expert in your field.
>
> 5. **Transparency and regulatory crackdowns.** In April of 2017, the FTC sent out several letters and an official warning for influencers and brands to clearly **disclose** their relationships. […]
>
> 6. **Integrated functionality in platforms.** With platforms like Facebook, Twitter, LinkedIn, and Instagram noticing the importance (and potential) of influencer marketing, we may start to see platform-based innovations that make influencer marketing and outreach more convenient (or more profitable). […]
>
> 7. **Qualitative assessment tools.** Soon, it won't be enough to have a large quantity of followers on your account; marketers will also be looking to

EXPAND YOUR READING

This section contains another text for students to work on both the text genre and comprehension.

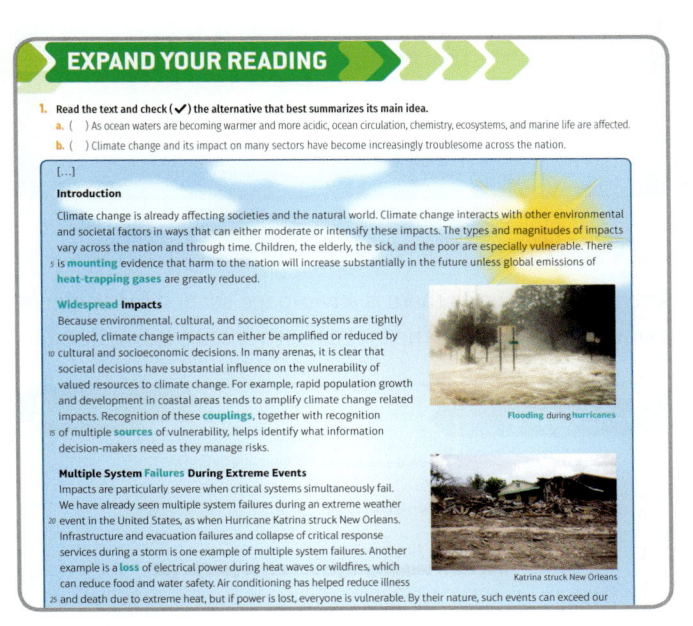

> **EXPAND YOUR READING**
>
> 1. Read the text and check (✓) the alternative that best summarizes its main idea.
>   a. ( ) As ocean waters are becoming warmer and more acidic, ocean circulation, chemistry, ecosystems, and marine life are affected.
>   b. ( ) Climate change and its impact on many sectors have become increasingly troublesome across the nation.
>
> […]
>
> **Introduction**
>
> Climate change is already affecting societies and the natural world. Climate change interacts with other environmental and societal factors in ways that can either moderate or intensify these impacts. The types and magnitudes of impacts vary across the nation and through time. Children, the elderly, the sick, and the poor are especially vulnerable. There
> 5 is **mounting** evidence that harm to the nation will increase substantially in the future unless global emissions of **heat-trapping gases** are greatly reduced.
>
> **Widespread Impacts**
> Because environmental, cultural, and socioeconomic systems are tightly coupled, climate change impacts can either be amplified or reduced by
> 10 cultural and socioeconomic decisions. In many arenas, it is clear that societal decisions have substantial influence on the vulnerability of valued resources to climate change. For example, rapid population growth and development in coastal areas tends to amplify climate change related impacts. Recognition of these **couplings**, together with recognition
> 15 of multiple **sources** of vulnerability, helps identify what information decision-makers need as they manage risks.
>
> *Flooding during hurricanes*
>
> **Multiple System Failures During Extreme Events**
> Impacts are particularly severe when critical systems simultaneously fail. We have already seen multiple system failures during an extreme weather
> 20 event in the United States, as when Hurricane Katrina struck New Orleans. Infrastructure and evacuation failures and collapse of critical response services during a storm is one example of multiple system failures. Another example is a **loss** of electrical power during heat waves or wildfires, which can reduce food and water safety. Air conditioning has helped reduce illness
> 25 and death due to extreme heat, but if power is lost, everyone is vulnerable. By their nature, such events can exceed our
>
> *Katrina struck New Orleans*

PRESENTATION

LANGUAGE IN USE 2

This page shows the second grammar topic of the unit. It contains examples from the text in *Expand your reading* and activities that develop students' grammar knowledge in the target language.

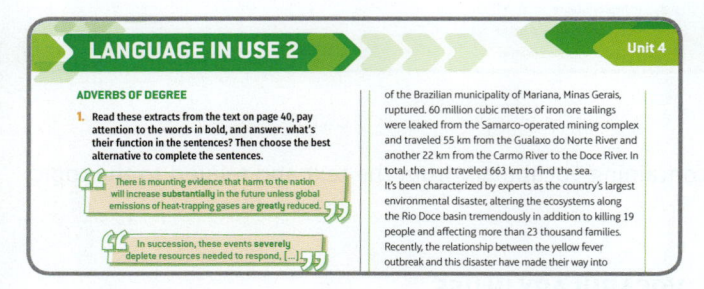

LISTENING COMPREHENSION

This section contains listening activities with authentic texts aimed at developing students' listening skills.

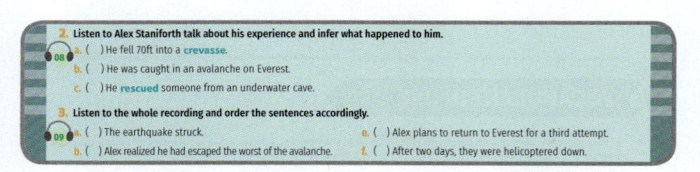

EXPAND YOUR HORIZONS

In this end-of-unit section students are presented with three statements that allow them to discuss the topic in the listening comprehension section and think critically about it while using the target language.

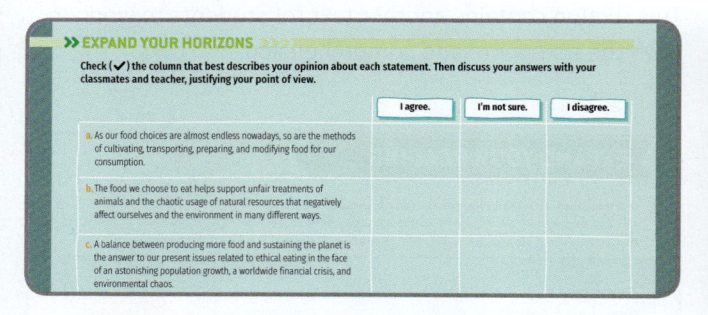

REVIEW

After every two units there is a two-page section for students to review and practice the language they have learned so far.

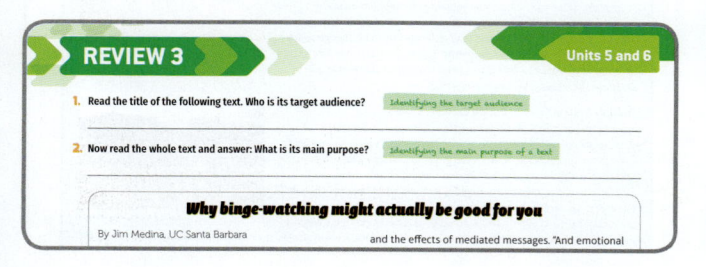

WORKBOOK

Each unit has four pages of reading, vocabulary, and grammar activities. It also has an ENEM or vestibular question in the section AN EYE ON ENEM / VESTIBULAR.

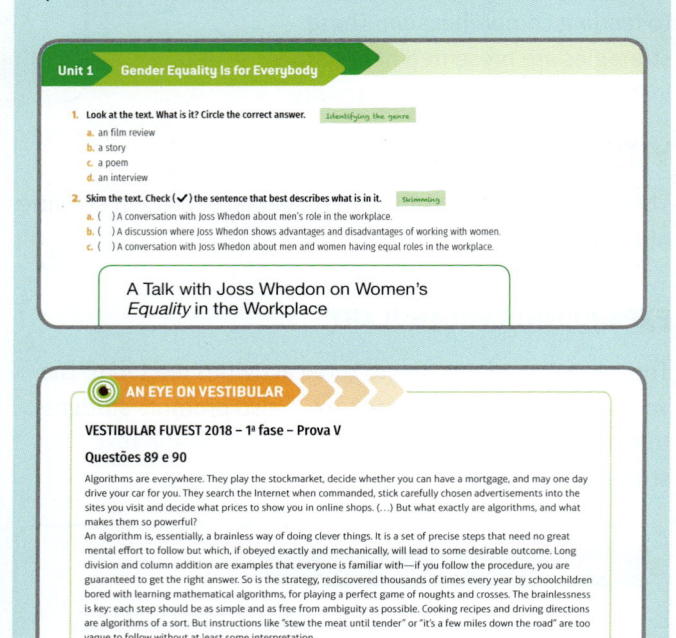

DIGITAL COMPONENTS

Video lessons for all *Language in Use* and *Vocabulary in Use* sections and for exam practice.

Mock test generator with major Brazilian *Vestibular* and ENEM questions to prepare students for these exams.

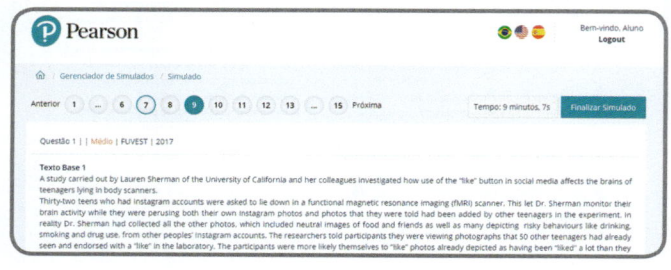

UNIT 1
Gender Equality is for Everybody

▶ IN THIS UNIT YOU WILL...

- reflect on gender equality;
- talk about gender stereotypes and modern masculinity;
- learn how to use the present perfect continuous for actions or states that started in the past and are still going on in the present;
- compare the uses of the present perfect simple and the present perfect continuous.

LEAD OFF

- ▶ Do you agree with the title of this unit? How can you relate it to the picture?
- ▶ Do women and men have equal opportunities in Brazil? What about in other parts of the world?
- ▶ What are some stereotypes about men and women? Do you think that any of them are true?

READING

›› BEFORE READING

Work in pairs. What do you understand from the quotes below? *Bridging and relating to the topic*

> " My message to girls everywhere in this world: believe in yourself and trust yourself, because if you don't believe in yourself, no one else will.
> (Marta Vieira da Silva, Brazilian – FIFA Women's World Player of the Year 2006, 2010, and 2018) "

> " Speak without shame and stand up with love for women's equality, and bring about the change we all want to see.
> (Ram Devineni, Indian-American – co-creator of comic book superhero Priya, who fights gender-based violence) "

Extracted from www.unwomen.org. Accessed on January 27, 2019.

›› WHILE READING

Skim the text. What is it about? *Skimming to identify the main topic*

Working women: Key facts and trends in female labor force participation

In almost every country in the world, men are more likely to participate in labor markets than women. However, these gender differences in participation rates have been narrowing substantially in recent decades. [...]
- All over the world, labor force participation among women of working age increased substantially in the last century.
- In some parts of the world, the historical increase in female labor force participation has slowed down or even regressed slightly in recent years.
- Women all over the world allocate a substantial amount of time to activities that are not typically recorded as "economic activities". **Hence**, female participation in labor markets tends to increase when the time-cost of unpaid care work is reduced, shared equally with men, and/or made more compatible with market work.

[...]

The following visualization provides a picture of how men and women compare today in terms of participation in labor markets, country by country. Shown is the female-to-male **ratio** in labor force participation rates (expressed in percent). These **figures** show estimates from the International Labor Organization (ILO). These are "modelled estimates" in the sense that the ILO produces them after harmonizing various data sources to improve comparability across countries.

As we can see, the numbers for most countries are well below 100%, which means that the participation of women tends to be lower than that of men. Yet differences are **outstanding**: in countries such as Syria or Algeria, the ratio is below 25%. In contrast, in Laos, Mozambique, Rwanda, Malawi, and Togo, the relationship is close to, or even slightly above 100% (i.e. there is gender parity in labor force participation or even a higher share of women participating in the labor market than men).
[...]

Ratio of female to male labor force participation rates (%), 2015

The female-to-male ratio of labor force participation rates is calculated by dividing the labor force participation rate among women, by the corresponding rate for men. The labor force participation rate is defined as the proportion of the population ages 15+ that is economically active. All figures correspond to 'modeled ILO estimates' (see source for details).

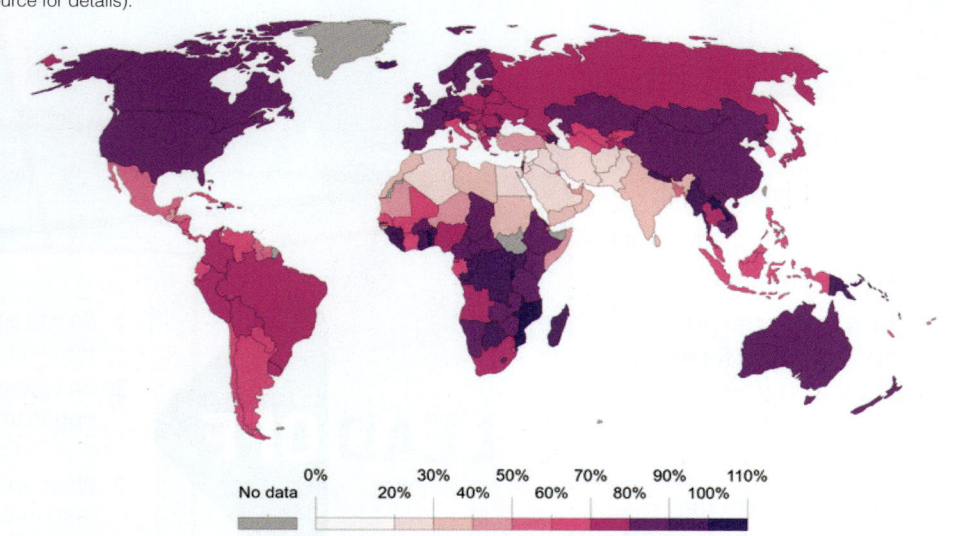

Source: World Bank – WDI

Extracted from https://ourworldindata.org/female-labor-force-participation-key-facts. Accessed on August 7, 2018.

>> AFTER READING

1. Check (✓) the statement that best summarizes the text. *Summarizing*
  a. ( ) Men and women participate equally in labor markets around the world.
  b. ( ) In most countries men tend to take part in job markets more than women.
  c. ( ) All around the world, women participate in job markets more than men.

2. Decide if the sentences are true (T) or false (F). Use fragments from the text to correct the false ones. *Understanding details*
  a. ( ) Women's participation in the job market has declined around the world in this century.
  _____
  _____

  b. ( ) The ratio of female to male labor force participation is similar in Syria and Mozambique.
  _____
  _____

  c. ( ) All over the world, some activities performed by women are not considered economic activities.
  _____
  _____

EXPAND YOUR VOCABULARY

1. Refer to the text on page 10 to infer the meaning of these words and match the columns to find their synonyms. Then use some of them to complete the headlines that follow.

  a. parity   ( ) assign
  b. labor   ( ) equality
  c. slow down   ( ) work
  d. allocate   ( ) portion
  e. share   ( ) reduce

  a. "In many countries, at least four-in-ten in the _____ force are women"
  Extracted from www.pewresearch.org Accessed on August 8, 2018.

  b. "Gender _____ in the Workplace Is Possible. We Did It; You Can, Too"
  Extracted from www.workforce.com Accessed on August 8, 2018.

  c. Women make up nearly half of the labor force; _____ will remain steady in coming decades
  Extracted from www.pewresearch.org Accessed on August 8, 2018.

2. Work in pairs. Discuss the headlines from activity 1. Relate them to the text on page 10 and to your previous knowledge on the subject. Then answer the question: What does women's labor force participation actually tell us about gender equality?
_____
_____
_____

VOCABULARY IN USE

1. Read an extract from the text on page 10 and pay attention to the part in bold. Then use other expressions from the same word group to complete the diagrams below. Use the suggestions from the box.

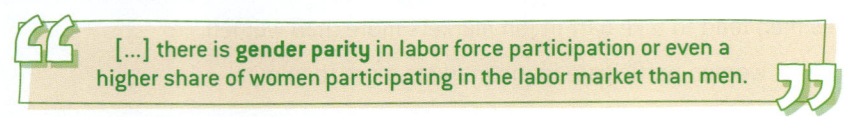

> [...] there is **gender parity** in labor force participation or even a higher share of women participating in the labor market than men.

biased stereotypes	call for change	diversity appreciation	equal pay
human rights	imbalance of power	sexual harassment	social awareness
social exclusion	unequal salaries	women's empowerment	workplace discrimination

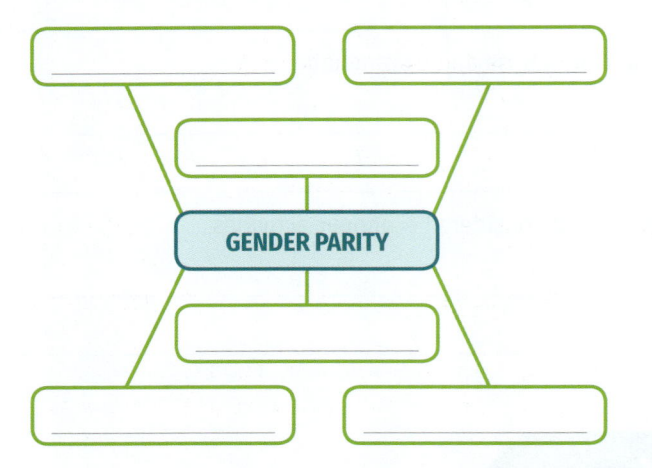

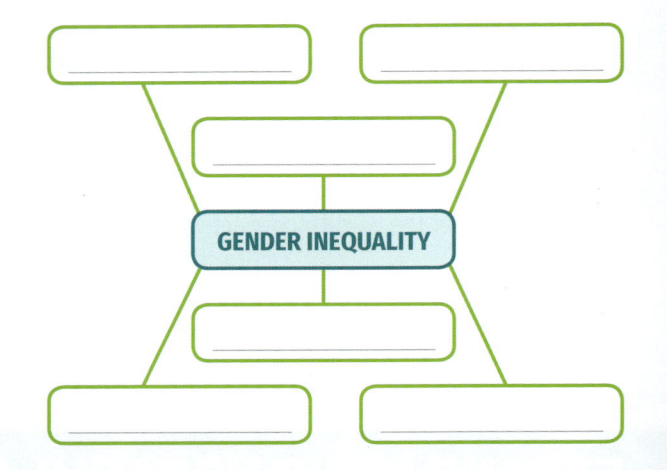

GENDER PARITY

GENDER INEQUALITY

2. The campaign ad below is part of the feminine hygiene products line Always initiative "#LikeAGirl", which aims at ensuring girls' self-confidence by showing them that doing things like a girl is great. Exchange ideas about it with your classmates.

You are incredible. You are unstoppable. And you do things #LikeAGirl.

Rewrite the Rules.

3. Look at the ad again and answer: What is the function of the hashtag in this context?
   a. (   ) It expresses humor by referring to a famous internet meme.
   b. (   ) It encourages people to share and support the campaign.

4. Match the hashtags with the corresponding initiatives.
   a. #GeenaOnGender   **b.** #ItsOnUs   **c.** #girlsCHARGE

   (   ) To back the movement to abolish sexual assault on college campuses, saying that all of us have the responsibility to stop it.

   (   ) Created by Geena Davis, it aims to modify how women and girls are portrayed in media, film, and entertainment.

   (   ) To promote the effort to safely educate and raise ambition for more girls globally.

Based on https://mashable.com/2014/10/01/women-hashtags/#ol0EvZdAysqp. Accessed on August 8, 2018.

LANGUAGE IN USE 1

Unit 1

PRESENT PERFECT CONTINUOUS

1. The excerpt below was extracted from the text on page 10. Read it, pay special attention to the part in bold, and answer the questions.

> However, these gender differences in participation rates **have been narrowing** substantially in recent decades.

a. When did gender differences start narrowing?
_____

b. Are they still narrowing nowadays?
_____

2. Considering the extract and your answers in activity 1, check (✓) the correct alternatives to complete the sentences below.

a. The structure *have been narrowing* was used to

( ) talk about an action that was in progress in the past.
( ) talk about an action that started in the past and is still in progress.

b. The verb tense used in the structure is the present perfect continuous. It is formed by

( ) have/has + been + verb + *-ing*.
( ) have/has + been + verb in the past participle.

3. Use the verbs *consider*, *fight*, and *go* in the present perfect continuous to complete the text fragments that follow.

a. **How the Fight for Gender Equality Is Changing in 2018**

[…]

Women _____ for equal rights for generations, for the right to vote, the right to control our bodies, and the right to equality in the workplace. And these battles have been hard fought, but we still have a long way to go, and our victories are under threat. Equality in the workplace – women in a **range** of fields from domestic work to the entertainment industry can tell you – it's still just a dream.

[…]

The message is loud and clear: We'll take over from here, thanks. The rate things _____, we're certain we'll do a better job. When Lev Grossman wrote the feature for TIME's Person of the Year in 2006, he said, "It's about the many **wresting** power from the few and helping one another for nothing and how that will not only change the world, but also change the way the world changes." The same is true of the power shift we are witnessing with women.

[…]

Extracted from http://time.com/5191419/women-leading-fight-equality-sexual-harassment. Accessed on August 9, 2018.

b. **Eurimages and gender equality**

Since 2012, Eurimages _____ the issue of gender equality in the film industry. A Gender Equality Working Group composed of representatives from a number of member states has been set up and meets quarterly, with the aim of:

- studying the current situation of the presence of women in the cinema sector at national and international level in co-operation with other national and international bodies;
- analyzing the current situation of Eurimages with regards to gender equality in the selection of projects;

[…]

Adapted from www.coe.int/en/web/eurimages/gender-equality. Accessed on August 9, 2018.

4. Work in pairs and answer these questions. If possible, use the present perfect continuous in your answers. Then report your opinions to the class.

a. What other aspects concerning gender equality have we been neglecting nowadays?
_____
_____

b. Have gender stereotypes been showing boys and girls in your country what the culture expects?
_____
_____

c. Have gender roles been changing in your community? Provide examples.
_____
_____

EXPAND YOUR READING

1. **Read the text and check (✓) the correct alternative to answer the question: What's the author's purpose?**
   a. ( ) To teach or provide information.
   b. ( ) To tell his story and convince the reader that his position is valid.
   c. ( ) To hold the attention of the reader through entertainment.

Men do cry: one man's experience of depression
By Matt Heig - Canongate Books

I can remember the day the old me died. It started with a thought. Something was going wrong. That was the start. Before I realized what it was. And then, a second or so later, there was a strange sensation inside my head. Some biological activity in the **rear** of my **skull**, not far above my neck. The cerebellum. A pulsing or intense flickering, as though a butterfly was trapped inside, and a **tingling** sensation. I did not yet know of the strange physical effects depression and anxiety would create.

[...]

Anyway, I was 24. I was living in Spain – in one of the more sedate and beautiful corners of the island of Ibiza. It was September. Within a **fortnight**, I would have to return to London, and reality. After six years of student life and summer jobs. I had put off being an adult for as long as I could, and it had loomed like a cloud. A cloud that was now breaking and raining down on me. [...] I didn't want to die. Death was something that scared me. And death only happens to people who have been living. [...]

When you are trapped inside something that feels so unreal, you look for anything that can give you a sense of your bearings. I **craved** knowledge. I craved facts.

A lot of people still believe that depression is about chemical imbalance. "Incipient insanity was mainly a matter of chemicals," wrote Kurt Vonnegut, in Breakfast of Champions. "Dwayne Hoover's body was manufacturing certain chemicals which unbalanced his mind." It is an attractive idea. And one that has, over the years, been supported by numerous scientific studies. A lot of research into the scientific causes of depression has focused on chemicals such as dopamine and, more often, serotonin. Serotonin is a neurotransmitter, a type of chemical that sends signals from one area of the brain to the other. The theory goes that an imbalance in serotonin levels – caused by low brain cell production of serotonin – equates to depression. So it is no surprise that some of the most common antidepressants, from Prozac down, are SSRIs – selective serotonin reuptake inhibitors – which raise serotonin levels in your brain.

However, the serotonin theory of depression looks a bit wobbly. The problem has been highlighted by the emergence of antidepressants that have no effect on serotonin, and some that do the exact opposite of an SSRI (namely, selective serotonin reuptake **enhancers**, such as tianeptine) which have been shown to be as effective at treating depression. Add to this the fact that serotonin in an active living human brain is a hard thing to measure and you have a very inconclusive picture indeed.

[...]

For me, the moment of recovery came in April 2000. It was totally inconsequential. In fact, there is not much to write about. That was the whole point. It was a moment of nothingness, of absent-mindedness, of spending almost 10 seconds awake but not actively thinking of my depression or anxiety. I was thinking about work. About trying to get an article published in a newspaper. It wasn't a happy thought, but a neutral one. But it was a break in the clouds, a sign that the sun was still there, somewhere. It was over not much after it began, but when those clouds came back there was hope. There would be a time when those painless seconds would become minutes and hours and maybe even days.

[...]

So what should we do? Talk. Listen. Encourage talking. Encourage listening. Keep adding to the conversation. Stay on the lookout for those wanting to join in the conversation. Keep **reiterating**, again and again, that depression is not something you "admit to", it is not something you have to blush about, it is a human experience. It is not you. It is simply something that happens to you. And something that can often be eased by talking. Words. Comfort. Support. It took me more than a decade to be able to talk openly, properly, to everyone, about my experience. I soon discovered the act of talking is in itself a therapy. Where talk exists, so does hope.

Adapted from www.theguardian.com/society/2015/feb/22/men-do-cry-depression-matt-haig-reasons-to-stay-alive. Accessed on February 5, 2019.

2. **What is the author's assumed position in the article?**
   _____

3. **Underline the correct statements about position articles such as the one above.**
   a. They focus on topics that need or call for discussion or reconsideration.
   b. They shouldn't report a clear position on the target topic.
   c. They should suggest a call for action or a proposal regarding the target topic.
   d. They present a balanced and logical view of an issue.
   e. They are short pieces of fiction that present the following parts: introduction, rising action, climax, falling action, and resolution.

LANGUAGE IN USE 2

Unit 1

PRESENT PERFECT SIMPLE vs. PRESENT PERFECT CONTINUOUS

1. Read the extracts from the text on page 14 and choose the correct words in parentheses to complete the information about the present perfect simple and the present perfect continuous.

> And death only happens to people who **have been living**.

> A lot of research into the scientific causes of depression **has focused** on chemicals such as dopamine [...].

a. Both the present perfect simple and the present perfect continuous are used to indicate that an action started in the past and is _____ (not / still) going on or has just finished.

b. In some cases, both tenses are correct, but there is often a difference in meaning. Besides meaning that an action is still in progress in the present, we use the present perfect simple mainly to emphasize the _____ (completion / progress) or the result of an action and the present perfect continuous focuses on the _____ (conclusion / duration) or continuous course of an action.

2. Refer back to the extracts in activity 1 and complete the chart below with the structures in bold.

Focus on the result or completion	Focus on the duration

3. Use the verb forms from the box to complete the text.

> has been   has found   have captured
> have changed   've been trying

Modern masculinity: Are we in crisis? 06 March 2017
In recent years, female **empowerment** _____ a hot topic in marketing and broader culture – from the 3% Conference (and their mission to support female creative **leadership** in agencies) to the lyrics of Beyoncé. But while we _____ to address female stereotypes, have we been blind to the stereotypes around masculinity? Our view on what it is to be 'a man' still remains limited. [...]
In just three generations, our ideas about masculinity _____ dramatically. A recent UK YouGov survey highlighted this divide, with 56% of 65+ men describing themselves as 'completely masculine', opposed to only 2% of 18-24s. [...]
The psychologist Geert Hofstede applied 'masculine' and 'feminine' traits to countries, examining how a society's culture influenced its values and behavior. More 'masculine' countries favor ambition, wealth, and differentiated gender roles, while more 'feminine' countries **overlap** gender roles, and place value on things like modesty and quality of life. In Mexico, a machismo culture is associated with masculine **pride** and power. This _____ negative expression in sexual violence and abuse, to the point that many women and men have tired of this norm and are protesting against it in an effort to promote change.
By contrast, in South Korea, many men use **skincare** products and makeup as a part of their daily routine. The perfectly **kohl-lined eyes** of the country's **K-Pop bands** _____ the hearts of fans worldwide.
[...]

Adapted from www.iris-worldwide.com/news/modern-masculinity-are-we-in-crisis. Accessed on August 9, 2018.

4. Discuss the quote below in small groups. Then come up with your own definition of gender injustice.

> Gender injustice is a social impairment and therefore has to be corrected in social attitudes and behavior.
> (Mohammad Hamid Ansari)

Extracted from www.brainyquote.com/quotes Accessed on August 9, 2018.

_____
_____
_____
_____
_____

15

LISTENING COMPREHENSION

1. What do you think the movies in these posters have in common?

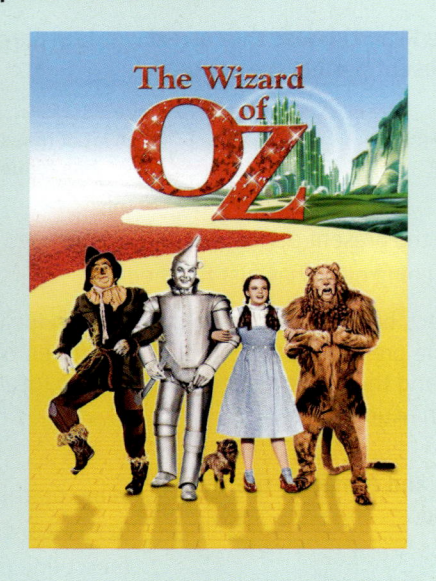

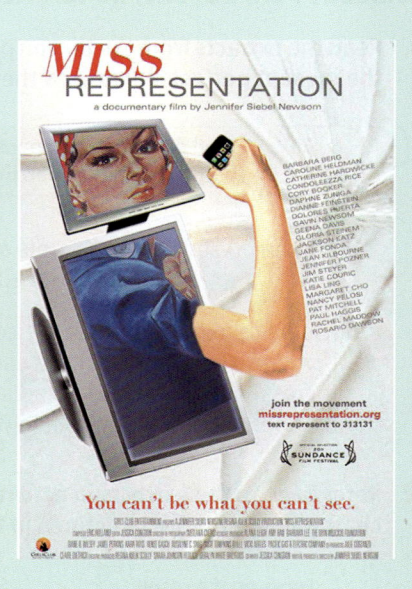

2. Listen to part of a talk on an interview with Jennifer Siebel Newsom. Which movie listed in activity 1 is it about?

02 _____

3. Listen to another part of the talk that explains what the movie is about and fill in the blanks.

03

[…]
Her film was originally shown at Sundance and broadcast in the US in 2011. It features an impressive line-up of _____ women, including Nancy Pelosi, Condoleezza Rice, Katie Couric, and Gloria Steinem, as well as academics and activists who all flesh out the idea that the demeaning and _____ representation of women in the media is a significant contributor in holding women back from positions of power. This, in turn, _____ the lives of all women, from the _____ pay gap and career opportunities after _____, to mental health issues and the rise of cosmetic surgery.
[…]

Extracted from www.theguardian.com/lifeandstyle/2014/mar/03/feminist-film-maker-taking-on-hollywood. Accessed on October 4, 2018.

4. Work with a partner. Refer to the texts you have read in this unit and to the transcript on page 136. Then answer: How has the way media portrays women and men been changing over the past years? What other changes do you think should happen in the future? Share your opinions and experiences with the class.

❯❯ EXPAND YOUR HORIZONS ❯❯❯

Check (✓) the column that best describes your opinion about each statement. Then discuss your answers with your classmates and teacher, justifying your point of view.

	I agree.	I'm not sure.	I disagree.
a. The growth of the number of women in the workforce is unquestionably the most significant change in the economy in the past century.			
b. Gender stereotypes sustain gender-specific behaviors that can harm everybody.			
c. Gender roles and expectations are still deep-rooted into our culture although a lot of progress has been made towards gender equality.			

UNIT 2
Technology in the School Curriculum

▶ IN THIS UNIT YOU WILL…
- take part in discussions about coding in education;
- talk about a technology curriculum and robotics;
- learn about subject-verb agreement;
- identify and use compound adjectives.

LEAD OFF

- What situation does the picture represent? Are you familiar with that situation?
- Do you know what *coding* means? If so, explain.
- What do you think about the integration of technological projects into school curriculums?

READING

BEFORE READING

Contextualizing

You are going to read a text about the implementation of computer programming in education. Is this a reality in your country or school? How do you think students could benefit from having computer programming lessons? Exchange ideas with your classmates.

WHILE READING

Predicting

Look at the picture and read the title of the text. Then write down two reasons for coding in education that you think will be mentioned in the text. Finally, read the whole text.

_____

_____

Coding In Education: Why It's Important & How It's Being Implemented

By Marianne Stenger

Although computer *programming* was once seen as a skill reserved for **geeks** and computer nerds, it's now regarded as an essential ability for 21st century learners and is becoming a key component of many curriculums, even in elementary schools. So, what's the benefit of teaching kids as young as five years old how to code?

For starters, basic coding courses in schools provide students with the know-how to develop their own websites, apps, and computer software.

LinkedIn data shows that skills like mobile development and user **interface** design will be in high demand in the coming years, and a 2016 Gallup report found that 40% of American schools now offer coding classes, compared to just 25% a few years ago.

In Australia, the government has been investing in **STEM** initiatives in recent years, and coding classes will soon be mandatory in Queensland schools. Meanwhile in the UK, kids aged five and over have been learning the fundamentals of coding since 2014.

But coding education can also be beneficial for students who aren't necessarily interested in **pursuing** computer programming, but would like to gain a better understanding of technology and how it's shaping our world.

At its most basic, learning how to code is learning to tell machines what to do. But this requires the **mastery** of a problem-solving skill known as computational *thinking*, which involves breaking larger tasks into a logical sequence of smaller steps, diagnosing errors, and coming up with new **approaches** when necessary.

So, what exactly does coding look like in schools and learning institutions throughout the world and why does it matter? We talked to a few teachers and EdTech experts about some of the ways coding is being implemented in education.

Coding Bootcamps

[...]

Coding to Transition into the Workforce

[...]

Coding For Cyber Security

[...]

Coding to Build Logic and Persistence

[...]

Coding For Early *Literacy* Development

[...]

An Informal Approach to Learning How to Code

Former software engineer and co-founder of the Holberton School of *Software* Engineering Sylvain Kalache says coding is important because it's all around us.

"From the smartphone in our pocket, to the smartwatch on our wrist, it's also launching rockets in space or controlling our fridge," says Kalache. "All industries are disrupted by software and even if not all of us will become Software Engineers, all of us will be interacting with it, so it's important to understand the foundations of it."

[...]

Adapted from www.opencolleges.edu.au/informed/features/coding-education-important-implemented. Accessed on August 11, 2018.

Unit 2

» AFTER READING

1. Go back to the text and underline the reasons why coding is important. Do the reasons mentioned match the ones you wrote down in the While Reading task? `Scanning to check predictions`

2. What's the main purpose of the text? Use your own words to state it. `Stating the main purpose of the text`

_____

_____

3. Underline the correct statements about the text. `Understanding details`
   a. Computer programming is still considered a skill reserved for computer experts.
   b. The number of schools using coding in their curriculum in North America has increased by 15% in the last few years.
   c. The introduction of coding in classrooms prepares students for real-life situations such as entering the job market.
   d. Computational thinking is the ability to master the concepts to work with word processing and spreadsheets.

EXPAND YOUR VOCABULARY

1. Use the words in italics in the text on page 18 to complete the text below.

   _____ in Coding is an advantage in this technology-driven economy.
   [...]
   _____ and computers are taking over the world. Almost everything we do requires some form of programming and almost every student has access to computers, tablets, and smart cell phones. Are we doing enough in our schools to encourage computer science and prepare our students for this future? More than half of projected STEM (science, technology, engineering, and mathematic) jobs are in computing occupations. There is more demand for people who can write computer programs than there is supply.
   In the United States, there will be 1.4 million jobs in computer science over the next 10 years but only 400,000 will qualify for it.
   Coding is the new **buzz language** of today's **tech-savvy** world. No matter what the occupation is, it would surely **coincide** with using technology, and those who know how to code, which is the basis of computer science _____ language, would surely be at an advantage.
   Computer science develops students' computational and critical thinking skills and shows them how to create, and not simply use, new technologies.
   This fundamental knowledge is needed to prepare students for the 21st century. Perhaps incorporating computer science studies in lessons will help improve the desired critical _____ in our students.
   [...]

   Adapted from https://bambooinnovator.com/2013/11/30/steve-jobs-everybody-in-this-country-should-learn-to-program-a-computer-because-it-teaches-you-how-to-think. Accessed on August 11, 2018.

2. Discuss the quote below in small groups. Refer to the texts you have read and to your own experience and expectations. If possible, use some of the words and expressions from activity 1 to develop your arguments.

   > I think everybody in this country should learn how to program a computer, should learn a computer language, because it teaches you how to think. I view computer science as a liberal art. It should be something that everyone takes.
   > (Steve Jobs, American entrepreneur)

   Extracted from https://bambooinnovator.com/2013/11/30/steve-jobs-everybody-in-this-country-should-learn-to-program-a-computer-because-it-teaches-you-how-to-think. Accessed on August 11, 2018.

VOCABULARY IN USE

1. Read an extract from the text on page 18 and check (✔) the statement that mentions probable aims of basic coding courses.

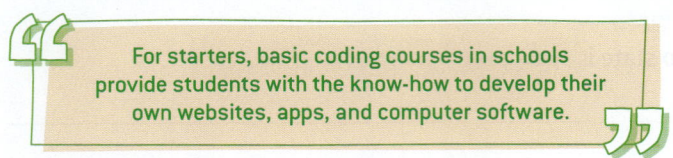

   > For starters, basic coding courses in schools provide students with the know-how to develop their own websites, apps, and computer software.

   a. (   ) To master dynamic programming and to start diving into understanding algorithms.

   b. (   ) To learn common terminology, working practices, and software tools.

2. When a person sets out to learn the science and art of computer programming, he/she is learning a whole new language to write the code in. Some basic coding language is listed below. Match the words or expressions with their definitions.

   > algorithm   compiler   GUI   Iteration   JSON   loop
   > markup language   run time   sandbox   variable

   a. _____: a program which takes the code you have written and translates it into the binary ones and zeros of actual machine code

   b. _____: a set of logical or mathematical procedures to solve a problem

   c. _____: a piece of code which keeps running until a certain condition is fulfilled, or isn't fulfilled in the case of an 'infinite loop', which will crash the system running it

   d. _____: a way to store a piece of data which can then be modified at any time

   e. _____: a place to run a program for testing, and for experimenting

   f. _____: the time during which a program is running

   g. _____: a relatively simple language used to format pages, such as HTML

   h. _____: General User Interface, refers to the "front end" of a piece of software which the end user actually sees and interacts with

   i. _____: a sequence of instructions which are repeated

   j. _____: a format for transmitting information between locations which is based on JavaScript

   Adapted from https://owlcation.com/stem/Programming-Basics-for-Beginners. Accessed on August 11, 2018.

3. Work in pairs. Read the infographic below and discuss whether you agree or not with the reasons mentioned to teach coding. Justify your answer.

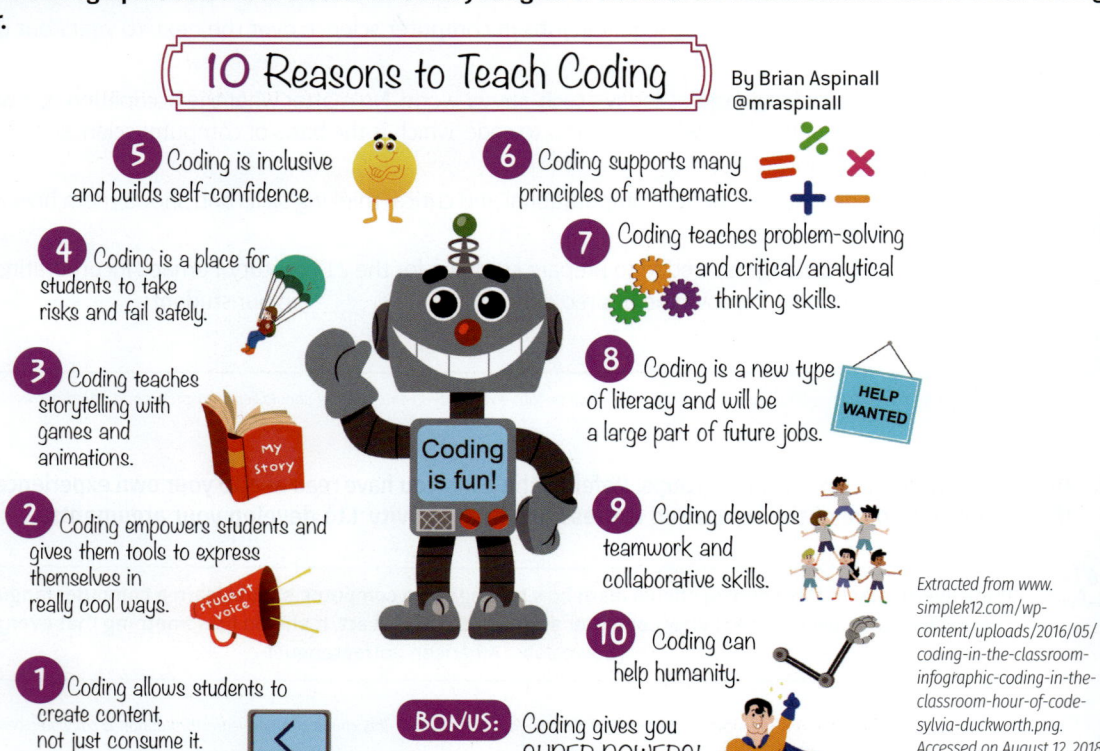

   ## 10 Reasons to Teach Coding
   By Brian Aspinall @mraspinall

   5. Coding is inclusive and builds self-confidence.
   6. Coding supports many principles of mathematics.
   4. Coding is a place for students to take risks and fail safely.
   7. Coding teaches problem-solving and critical/analytical thinking skills.
   3. Coding teaches storytelling with games and animations.
   8. Coding is a new type of literacy and will be a large part of future jobs.
   2. Coding empowers students and gives them tools to express themselves in really cool ways.
   9. Coding develops teamwork and collaborative skills.
   1. Coding allows students to create content, not just consume it.
   10. Coding can help humanity.

   BONUS: Coding gives you SUPER POWERS!

   Extracted from www.simplek12.com/wp-content/uploads/2016/05/coding-in-the-classroom-infographic-coding-in-the-classroom-hour-of-code-sylvia-duckworth.png. Accessed on August 12, 2018.

LANGUAGE IN USE 1

Unit 2

SUBJECT-VERB AGREEMENT

1. The excerpts below were extracted from the text on page 18. Underline the subjects and circle the verbs. Then complete the sentences.

> **I.** For starters, basic coding courses in schools provide students with the know-how to develop their own websites, apps, and computer software.

> **II.** In Australia, the government has been investing in STEM initiatives in recent years.

> **III.** Meanwhile in the UK, kids aged five and over have been learning the fundamentals of coding since 2014.

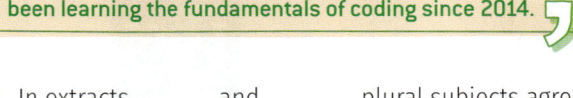

a. In extracts _____ and _____, plural subjects agree with plural verbs and in extract _____, a singular verb agrees with a singular noun.

b. If you have a noun phrase, such as "basic coding courses in schools" in extract I, the verb agrees with the head of the noun, which is *courses*. As *courses* is a plural subject, it agrees with a plural verb. In extract III, the head of the noun phrase is _____.

2. Read other extracts from the texts on pages 18 and 19 and pay attention to the parts in bold to complete the explanations.

> **I.** "More than **half** of projected STEM... jobs are in computing occupations."

> **II.** "[…] a 2016 Gallup report found that **40%** of American schools now offer coding classes."

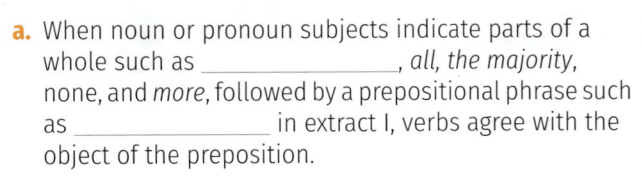

a. When noun or pronoun subjects indicate parts of a whole such as _____, *all*, *the majority*, *none*, and *more*, followed by a prepositional phrase such as _____ in extract I, verbs agree with the object of the preposition.

b. Percentages and fractions require a plural verb form when the object of the preposition is plural, such as _____ in extract II, and a singular verb form when the object of the preposition is singular.

3. Check (✓) the statement that explains the subject-verb agreement in the following quotes.

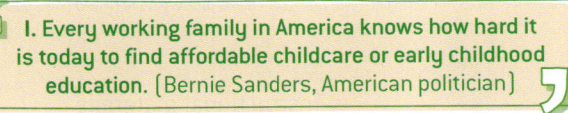

> **I.** Every working family in America knows how hard it is today to find affordable childcare or early childhood education. (Bernie Sanders, American politician)

Extracted from www.brainyquote.com/quotes/bernie_sanders_714833. Accessed on September 3, 2018.

> **II.** Each country thinks its school is in a specific crisis, without ever linking the school's crisis to that of the society around it. (Daniel Pennac, French writer)

Extracted from www.brainyquote.com/quotes/daniel_pennac_522388. Accessed on September 3, 2018.

a. (   ) When words such as *every* and *each* are used as subjects, they take plural verb forms.

b. (   ) When words such as *every* and *each* are used as subjects, they take singular verb forms.

4. Choose between the singular or plural verb forms in parentheses to fill in the blanks.

> **Why are there so few girls in computer science? And how can we change that?**
>
> In September 2015, New York City Mayor Bill de Blasio announced that within 10 years every child in the city would be able to study computer science in a public school. The **decree** came as no surprise. Nationwide, educators _____ (is coming / are coming) to the consensus that computer science literacy _____ (is / are) beneficial – even necessary – for students to succeed in a digitized world. Writer Alison Derbenwick Miller on the technology blog TechCrunch: "With the shift to data-based decision-making for everything from traditional business marketing to local government and health care, a basic understanding of how computers work and process information, as well as a basic literacy in computer programming and data analysis, _____ rapidly _____ (is… becoming / are… becoming) workplace essentials."
> Unfortunately, these essentials _____ (is / are) harder to come by for some students than for others. Low-income communities are more likely to be technology deserts, **disproportionately** leaving behind students of color and English language learners. And, **despite** the growing number of computer science programs in public schools (including traditional classes and coding "boot camps"), another group of students _____ (is / are) **conspicuously** absent: girls.
> The disconnect between girls and computer science _____ (doesn't improve / don't improve) after high school. In the last two decades, the percentage of U.S. computer science bachelor's degrees awarded to women has fallen from 28 to just 18. According to the National Science Foundation, only 25 percent of computer and math scientists _____ (is / are) women.
> […]

Extracted from www.tolerance.org/magazine/spring-2016/cracking-the-code. Accessed on August 12, 2018.

EXPAND YOUR READING

1. **Read part of a curriculum and check (✓) the correct alternative. A curriculum refers to...**
   a. ( ) the days and times of classes taught in a school or in a specific course or program.
   b. ( ) the subjects that are taught by a school, college, etc., or the things that are studied in a particular subject.

Junior Computer Curriculum

Project-Based Learning and Elementary Students

TechnoKids Junior Computer Curriculum is a collection of technology projects. Each project includes a teacher guide, workbook, and customizable resource files. Computer lessons are project based and have students apply technology to make learning meaningful.

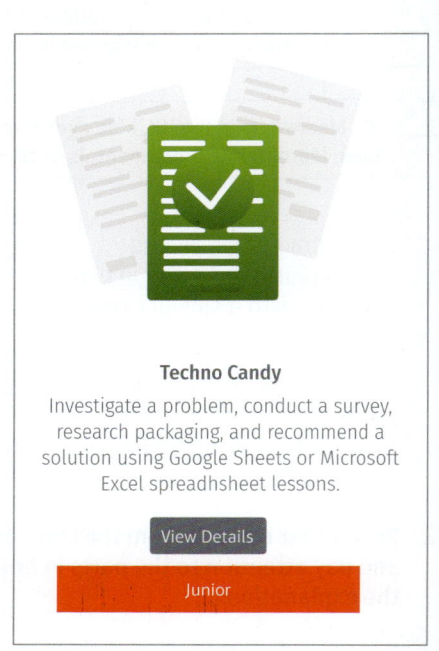

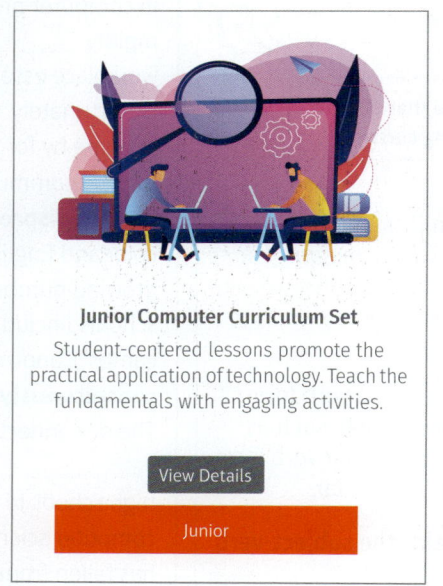

Techno Research
Lessons for teaching essential research skills. Create a Fun Fact Card in Google Docs or Word using word processing lessons.
View Details
Junior

Techno Toon
Create a graphic story that looks like a cartoon or animated comic strip using Google Slides or PowerPoint. Integrate creative writing with technology using digital storytelling lessons.
View Details
Junior

Techno Candy
Investigate a problem, conduct a survey, research packaging, and recommend a solution using Google Sheets or Microsoft Excel spreadsheet lessons.
View Details
Junior

Spanish Bundle Google Apps
Spanish resources for immersion classrooms or English language learners. Instructional materials that integrate technology into learning.
View Details
Junior

Junior Computer Curriculum Set
Student-centered lessons promote the practical application of technology. Teach the fundamentals with engaging activities.
View Details
Junior

Techno Internet
Lessons provide a thorough introduction to the Internet. Studentes apply search strategies, access digital resources, practice Internet safety, and communicate electronically.
View Details
Junior

Extracted from www.technokids.com/computer-curriculum/junior.aspx. Accessed on August 12, 2018.

2. **Cross out the item that is not part of the curriculum in activity 1.**
   a. web protection tools
   b. word processing software
   c. nanotechnology
   d. animated stories
   e. instructional materials

LANGUAGE IN USE 2

Unit 2

COMPOUND ADJECTIVES

1. Read these extracts from the texts on pages 22 and 18, paying attention to the parts in bold, and answer: What's their function in the sentences? Then check (✔) the correct alternative to complete the paragraph.

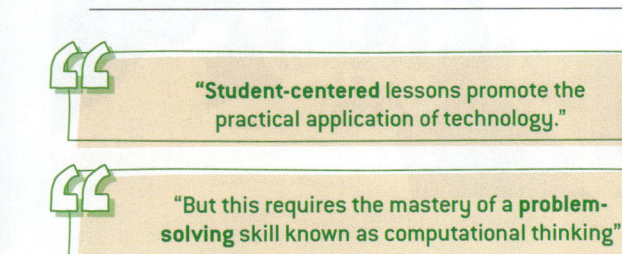

_____

> "**Student-centered** lessons promote the practical application of technology."

> "But this requires the mastery of a **problem-solving** skill known as computational thinking"

The adjectives *student-centered* and *problem-solving* are called _____ adjectives because they are formed by two or more words. They can be formed by different word classes such as _____, verbs, nouns, and adverbs, for example. A _____ is often used between the words to indicate they act as a single idea.

a. (   ) defining – articles – apostrophe
b. (   ) compound – adjectives – hyphen

2. Use the two compound adjectives from the extracts above and others from the box to complete the chart. Then read the sentences and fill in the blanks with some of them.

bottom-left	old-fashioned
good-looking	real-life
highly-respected	smoke-free

adjective + adjective	
adjective + noun	
adjective + verb + -ing	
adjective + verb (past participle)	
verb + adjective	
noun + verb + -ing	
noun + verb (past participle)	
adverb + verb (past participle)	

a. Unfortunately, most students found the computing course material boring and _____.
b. Computer programming tutorials are likely to be devoted to _____ skills.
c. Carnegie-Mellon University is one of the most _____ universities in the USA due to their Robotics Systems Development program.
d. Coding classes are mainly _____ as the focus of instruction is on the student.

3. Finish the paragraph below. Use at least one compound adjective in your answer.

In my opinion, the biggest challenges of implementing a technology curriculum in schools throughout Brazil is...

_____
_____
_____
_____

4. Now read the definitions below and match them with a compound adjective from the box. There is an extra option which you will not use. Then look up the other compound adjective and write a definition for it.

well-known	narrow-minded
absent-minded	five-star
kind-hearted	well-behaved
hard-working	open-minded

a. _____: someone who performs a task with a lot of effort
b. _____: notorious, known by a lot of people
c. _____: likely to forget things, especially because you are thinking about something else
d. _____: the characteristic of a place that has been judged to be of the highest standard
e. _____: generous
f. _____: willing to consider and accept other people's ideas and opinions
g. _____: not being rude or violent

Based on www.ldoceonline.com. Accessed on October 22, 2018.

_____
_____
_____

LISTENING COMPREHENSION

1. Read the dictionary entry and discuss the questions below.

   > **robotics**
   > ro‧bo‧tics /rəʊˈbɒtɪks $ ˈroʊbɑː-/
   > **noun** [uncountable]
   > the study of how robots are made and used

   Extracted from www.ldoceonline.com/dictionary/robotics. Accessed on August 13, 2018.

   a. What is the connection between robotics and coding?
   b. How is robotics used nowadays?
   c. What might be the downsides of robotics?
   d. How can robotics be useful in education?

2. You are going to learn about a robot built by ten students from Berwick Lodge, Glendal, and Mount View elementary schools in Australia. Listen to the first part of the recording, pay attention to what that robot can do, and check (✔) the picture that illustrates it.

   04

   a. (   )

   Extracted from www.pocket-lint.com/gadgets/news/134820-real-life-robots-that-will-make-you-think-the-future-is-now. Accessed on August 13, 2018.

   b. (   )

   Extracted from http://education.abc.net.au. Accessed on August 13, 2018.

3. Now listen to the whole recording and answer the questions.

   05

   a. What's the name of the robot?
   _____

   b. According to the reporter, why isn't robotics popular in many Australian schools?
   _____

   c. What's stopping the students from competing at the World Robotics Championships in Spain?
   _____

   d. What institutions have approved the initiative?
   _____

4. What kind of robot could help you with your studies? Talk to a classmate and justify your answer.

»EXPAND YOUR HORIZONS »»»

Check (✔) the column that best describes your opinion about each statement. Then discuss your answers with your classmates and teacher, justifying your point of view.

	I agree.	I'm not sure.	I disagree.
a. The benefits of learning to code aren't limited to knowing how to create an app or develop a website, for example. They involve skills that can be applied to different areas of our lives.			
b. We use coding skills every day when we program our microwave oven, our phones, our TVs, etc.			
c. The advantages of robotics in our lives are unquestionable, but there may also be downsides to it. The more prepared we are to deal with both the advantages and disadvantages, the more we'll be able to integrate robotics successfully into our everyday lives.			

REVIEW 1

Units 1 and 2

1. Skim the text. What is it about? *Skimming*

INTERNATIONAL EDUCATION

Adding Coding to the Curriculum

By Beth Gardiner

March 23, 2014

LONDON — Estonia is teaching first graders how to create their own computer games and offering scholarships to **entice** more **undergraduates** into technology-driven disciplines. In England, an updated national curriculum will soon expose every child in the public school system to computer programming, starting at age five. The American "Hour of Code" effort says it has already **persuaded** 28 million people to give programming a try.

5 Around the world, students from elementary school to PhD. level are increasingly getting **acquainted** with the basics of coding, as computer programming is also known. From Singapore to Tallinn, governments, educators, and advocates from the tech industry argue that it has become crucial to hold at least a basic understanding of how the devices that play such a large role in modern life actually work.

10 Such knowledge, the advocates say, is important not only to individual students' future career prospects, but also for their countries' economic competitiveness and the technology industry's ability to find qualified workers.
Exposing students to coding from an early age helps to **demystify** an area that can be intimidating. It also breaks down stereotypes of computer scientists as boring geeks, supporters argue. Plus, they say, programming is highly creative: studying it can help to develop problem-solving abilities, as well as equip students for a world transformed by technology.

[…]

Adapted from www.nytimes.com/2014/03/24/world/europe/adding-coding-to-the-curriculum.html. Accessed on August 22, 2018.

2. Read the fragment below and find out which initiative mentioned in the text in activity 1 it describes. Then exchange ideas about that project with a classmate. *Understanding details*

> […]
> The _____ is an attempt to teach people the basics of computer programming in 60 minutes in a fun, simple way. It is part of a campaign that Code.org, a non-profit organization, launched in the U.S. with the goal of introducing coding into the U.S. curriculum and **raising awareness** around what coding is. The idea was to show that it's not just about the geek in the basement or the super-tech-savvy person but that it actually plays a role in everything we do and everybody should have access to it. And 20 million kids signed up to it.
> […]
>
> *Adapted from www.theguardian.com/technology/2014/mar/02/hour-of-code-get-with-program-try-coding. Accessed on August 22, 2018.*

3. Now read the text carefully and decide if the sentences are true (T) or false (F). *Understanding details*
   a. ( ) Computer scientists are often thought to be boring geeks.
   b. ( ) According to the modern national curriculum in England, every child in the public school system should be exposed to computer programming from the age of five.
   c. ( ) In Singapore, the government argues that it is not yet time for children to be learning the basics of computer programming.
   d. ( ) Teaching students how to program means providing them with means to become more creative and better at problem-solving.

4. **Read the extract below and answer the question: Does the verb form in italics focus on the result or on the duration of a situation that started in the past and continues up to the present?**

> "From Singapore to Tallinn, governments, educators, and advocates from the tech industry argue that it *has become* crucial to hold at least a basic understanding of how the devices that play such a large role in modern life actually work."

_____
_____

5. **Read a fragment from a text entitled "The hour of code: why we should get with the program... and try coding" and fill in the blanks with the verbs *build*, *get into*, and *work on* in the present perfect continuous.**

> [...]
> **Nicki Cooper**, *computing teacher at Northfleet School for Girls, Kent, and a Computing at School master teacher* [...] I've found working in an all-girls school very different from a mixed school because here the girls are really free to express themselves. They're quite happy that they're into Minecraft or _____ computer games. That's what we _____ in lessons, and they _____ really _____ it. Whereas when I was in a mixed school, the girls took a back seat and it was the boys that would be shouting out and getting enthusiastic.
> They saw it as a boys' thing. [...]
>
> Extracted from www.theguardian.com/technology/2014/mar/02/hour-of-code-get-with-program-try-coding. Accessed on August 22, 2018.

6. **Choose between singular or plural verb forms to make subject-verb agreements and complete the quotes.**
   a. "Computer science _____ (is not / are not) just for smart 'nerds' in hoodies coding in basements. Coding is extremely creative and is an integral part of almost every industry." (Reshma Saujani)
   b. "From building robots and video games to coding apps that solve a problem in your community, or 3D printing in fashion tech, it is important that we _____ (explores / explore) different ways to engage girls in STEAM and also ensure that _____ (there is / there are) many, and different, women role models that will inspire our girls to pursue STEAM careers." (Rana el Kaliouby)
   c. "Coding is like writing, and we live in a time of the new industrial revolution. What's happened is that maybe everybody _____ (knows / know) how to use computers, like they know how to read, but they _____ (doesn't know / don't know) how to write." (Susan Wojcicki)

7. **Read the last quote in activity 6 again. The author uses an analogy to talk about people's ability to code. How does she do this? Do you agree with her views? Justify your answer.**

_____
_____
_____
_____
_____
_____
_____

UNIT 3
Can We Eat with a Clear Conscience?

IN THIS UNIT YOU WILL...
- reflect on making ethical food choices;
- talk about the impacts of food choices;
- learn how to use the second conditional for unreal and impossible situations;
- compare the uses of the zero, first, and second conditionals.

LEAD OFF

- What can you see in the picture? How is it linked to the question in the title of the unit?
- Which issues are involved in making food choices?
- Where does the food you eat come from? Do you care about its origin?

READING

›› BEFORE READING

Discussion and brainstorming

Read and discuss the comic strip below in pairs. Then list ideas relating to the topic of the text you are about to read.

Comic strip:
- Panel 1: "SIR, HERE'S YOUR FOOD, BUT I CAN'T HELP BUT NOTICE YOUR T-SHIRT."
- Panel 2: T-shirt reads "I THINK OF MY BODY AS A TEMPLE"
- Panel 3: "IF YOU FEEL THAT WAY, HOW CAN YOU INGEST FAST FOOD?"
- Panel 4: "I'M NON-PRACTICING."

Extracted from www.gocomics.com/luckycow/2004/10/21. Accessed on August 17, 2018.

›› WHILE READING

Skim the text and check (✓) the correct alternative to complete the sentence.

Skimming to identify the text genre

The text is a…

a. ( ) cookbook recipe.   b. ( ) book description.   c. ( ) book excerpt.

The Omnivore's Dilemma
A NATURAL HISTORY of FOUR MEALS
MICHAEL POLLAN
Author of THE BOTANY OF DESIRE

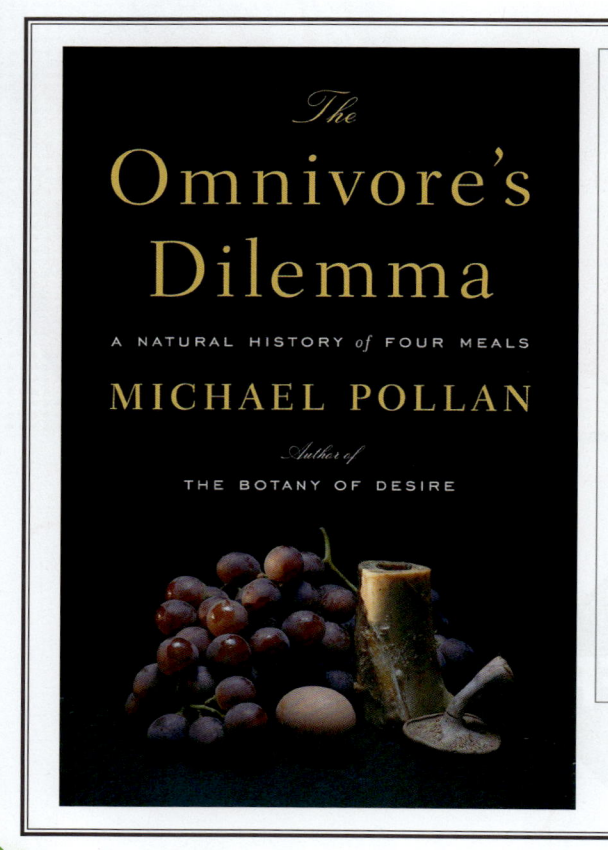

"Imagine if we had a food system that actually produced wholesome food. Imagine if it produced that food in a way that restored the land. Imagine if we could eat every meal knowing these few simple things: What it is we're eating. Where it came from. How it found its way to our table. And what it really cost. If that was the reality, then every meal would have the potential to be a perfect meal. We would not need to go hunting for our connection to our food and the web of life that produces it. We would no longer need any reminding that we eat by the grace of nature, not industry, and that what we're eating is never anything more or less than the body of the world. I don't want to have to forage every meal. Most people don't want to learn to garden or hunt. But we can change the way we make and get our food so that it becomes food again – something that feeds our bodies and our souls. Imagine it: Every meal would connect us to the joy of living and the **wonder** of nature. Every meal would be like **saying grace**." – Michael Pollan, The Omnivore's Dilemma: A Natural History of Four Meals.

Extracted from www.goodreads.com/work/quotes/3287769-the-omnivore-s-dilemma. Accessed on August 17, 2018.

>> AFTER READING

1. Read the text carefully. Check (✓) the statement that best summarizes the main idea of the book excerpt you have read.   `Summarizing the main idea`
   a. (   ) The implications people's food choices have on the economy of the planet are shocking.
   b. (   ) How perfect our meals would be if we were really aware of where our food came from.
   c. (   ) The importance of gardening and hunting to restore the sacred value of eating and how we can contribute to that.

2. Underline the correct statements about the book cover and excerpt on page 28.   `Understanding details`
   a. *The Botany of Desire* is the title of another book written by Michael Pollen.
   b. Many people are eager to learn the basics of gardening and hunting.
   c. Changing the way we get our food and how we make it is unlikely to happen.
   d. Knowing simple things like what we are eating and where the food came from would reestablish our connection to our food.
   e. Ideally, our daily meals should connect us to the joy of living and the wonder of nature.

EXPAND YOUR VOCABULARY

1. Refer to the text on page 28 to infer the meaning of the words from the box. Then match them with the definitions below.

> forage   hunt   omnivore
> restore   soul   wholesome

   a. _____ : likely to make you healthy
   b. _____ : to go around searching for food or other supplies
   c. _____ : the part of a person that is not physical, and that contains their character, thoughts, and feelings
   d. _____ : to chase animals and birds in order to kill or catch them
   e. _____ : to make something return to its former state or condition
   f. _____ : an animal that eats both meat and plants

   Extracted from www.ldoceonline.com. Accessed on August 18, 2018.

2. Use three words from activity 1 to complete the quotes below. Make any necessary adjustments.
   a. "Elsewhere the paper notes that vegetarians and vegans (including athletes) 'meet and exceed requirements' for protein. And, to render the whole we-should-worry-about-getting-enough-protein-and-therefore-eat-meat idea even more useless, other data suggests that excess animal protein intake is linked with osteoporosis, **kidney** disease, calcium stones in the urinary **tract**, and some cancers. Despite some persistent confusion, it is clear that vegetarians and vegans tend to have more optimal protein consumption than _____." – Jonathan Safran Foer, Eating Animals

   Extracted from www.goodreads.com/work/quotes/3149322-eating-animals. Accessed on August 18, 2018.

   b. "If you have a significant **layer** of fat around your **waist**, it means you have regularly consumed food in response to toxic hunger or have eaten recreationally. The body does not store large amounts of fat when fed a _____ natural diet and given only the amount of food demanded by true hunger." – Joel Fuhrman, Eat to Live: The Revolutionary Formula for Fast and Sustained Weight Loss

   Extracted from www.goodreads.com/work/quotes/389572-eat-to-live. Accessed on August 18, 2018.

   c. "Food should not only satisfy hunger, it should feed the _____, **nourish** the body, and **delight** the senses." – Karista Bennett

   Extracted from www.goodreads.com/quotes/search?commit=Search&page=3&q=food+to+feed+the+soul&utf8=%E2%9C%93. Accessed on August 18, 2018.

3. What should be people's primary concern when choosing their food?

   _____
   _____
   _____
   _____

Unit 3

29

VOCABULARY IN USE

1. Look at the book cover on page 28 again. Read the title of the book once more and complete the sentence.

> The word _____ derives from the Latin **omnis** (which means **all**), and **vora** (which means **eat** or **devour**). Common examples of English words derived from Latin include the words **agriculture**, **digital**, **picture**, and **school**.

2. Now come up with other English words you already know to complete the chart. The words must be derived from the Latin ones listed in the first column.

Latin word	Meaning	English word
antiqua	old	
aqua	water	
divus	god	
domus	house	
finis	end, limit	
genus	birth, creation	

Latin word	Meaning	English word
lac	milk	
longa	long	
nominare	to name	
obscura	dark	
prima	first	
terra	land, earth	

3. The examples from the box below are also common words derived from Latin. Use them to complete the text.

> progress   consecutive   items   percentage   organic

Supermarket sales of organic food and drink continue to rise

[...]

Supermarket sales of organic food and drink in the UK have risen by 4% this year, new figures reveal, marking seven _____ years of growth.

[...]

Supermarket shoppers spent £1.5bn on _____ food and drink, including baby products, in the 52 weeks to the end of June, according to new independent data.

That represents sales through "British retail outlets" – predominantly the big supermarkets but with a small _____ from chains such as Nisa and Costcutter. It does not include independent organic retailers or vegetable box schemes. The figures provide a half-year '_____ report' before publication of the sector's detailed Organic Market Report and full breakdown in February.

Sales of fresh organic fruit and vegetables sales grew by 5.3% in the year to the end of June, while dairy – the largest overall market sector for organic – saw a sales increase of 3.5%.

Other areas seeing strong growth are organic delicatessen _____ – including many chilled vegetarian and plant-based products – up 27.8% year on year, while sales of organic beer, wine and spirits were up by 8.7%.

[...]

Extracted from www.theguardian.com/environment/2018/sep/04/supermarket-sales-of-organic-food-and-drink-continue-to-rise. Accessed on December 4, 2018.

4. Why do you think people have been buying more organic food? Why is organic food considered better for you? Use at least three words derived from Latin in your answer.

_____
_____
_____
_____
_____

LANGUAGE IN USE 1

Unit 3

SECOND CONDITIONAL

1. **The excerpt below was extracted from the text on page 28. Read it and underline the statement that best describes it.**

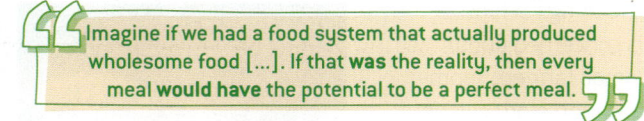

   > Imagine if we had a food system that actually produced wholesome food [...]. If that **was** the reality, then every meal **would have** the potential to be a perfect meal.

   a. The speaker is talking about an impossible situation in the past.

   b. The speaker is imagining what would happen in case a certain circumstance changed.

   c. The speaker is describing what happens every time a specific situation occurs.

2. **Choose the correct alternatives in parentheses to complete the sentences about the second conditional in English.**

   a. The second conditional is used to refer to _____ (hypothetical / definite) or unreal situations.

   b. We form the second conditional with *if* + subject + _____ (simple present / simple past) + *would / could / might* + base form of the main verb.

   c. It is possible to use *were* instead of _____ (is / was) in the second conditional.

3. **Use the second conditional to fill in the blanks in the comic strips below. Then work in pairs to explain the humor in both of them.**

   a. care about; buy (contraction)

   Extracted from www.gocomics.com/thatababy/2010/12/30. Accessed on August 19, 2018.

   b. cut out; start; not have (contraction)

   Extracted from https://licensing.andrewsmcmeel.com/features/bu?date=2018-01-21. Accessed on August 19, 2018.

4. **Complete the sentences below. If necessary, refer to activity 2 again.**

   a. If I were an advocate of animal rights, _____.

   b. Teenagers would be more worried about eating ethically if _____.

EXPAND YOUR READING

1. **Skim the book cover, read the text title and subtitle, and answer: Is the author's position for or against fast food?**

   _____

   ## No Accounting for Mouthfeel
   Fast food is an inescapable part of the modern world, and the author thinks that's a very bad thing.

   Related Links
   - An Audio Interview With Eric Schlosser
   - First Chapter: 'Fast Food Nation'

   By ROB WALKER - January 21, 2001

   [...]

   Fast-food restaurants evolved from the drive-in eateries **spawned** by the post-World War II car culture of Southern California. The men who built the new industry were **rugged** individualists, but their insights all revolved around
   5 **relentless** homogeneity – in the food they offered and in the way they acquired, produced and served it. [...] Schlosser also calls on "the flavor industry" – labs where the taste of foods that are frozen and **otherwise** processed is **devised**. In what seems like an **outtake** from "Sleeper,"
   10 scientists called "flavorists," wearing lab coats, **cobble** together chemicals to recreate the flavor of fresh cherries or grilled hamburgers, always keeping "mouthfeel" in mind. And then there's the hamburger itself, which has traveled a long road from being "a food for the poor" at the start of the
   15 20th century to the down-home meal of choice for capitalist royalty at the start of the 21st. It was drive-ins and fast-food places that made hamburgers a national favorite, especially when the easy-to-eat burger was positioned as a great choice for kids. More recently, **cattle** raising and meatpacking
   20 have been industrialized just like the potato business, flavor science, and fast-food outlets themselves. [...] While the things Schlosser is concerned about (small farmers, mom-
   25 and-pop store owners, low-skilled immigrant workers, child-focused marketing, the political **clout** of big business)
   30 and the solutions he suggests (mostly better government regulation) will seem like predictable liberal **carping** to some,
   35 the book manages to avoid **shrillness**. This is a fine piece of **muckraking**, alarming without being alarmist. At the very least, Schlosser makes it hard to go on eating
   40 fast food in **blissful** ignorance. [...] At one point, Schlosser quotes a scientist who specializes in food safety. This man is discussing the meat industry's **reluctance** to perform certain tests on its products, but he could be talking about almost any of the questions Schlosser raises about the fast-food
   45 business – or, come to think of it, about the culture that **takes** that business **for granted**. "If you don't know about a problem," the man observes, "then you don't have to deal with it."
   Rob Walker, a contributing writer for Money and Slate, lives in
   50 New Orleans.

   Extracted from https://archive.nytimes.com/www.nytimes.com/books/01/01/21/reviews/010121.21walkert.html. Accessed on August 20, 2018.

2. **Read the text and underline the incorrect information in the sentences below. Then rewrite them with the correct information.**

   a. Rob Walker is worried about issues related to small farmers, low-skilled immigrant workers, child-focused marketing, etc.

   _____

   _____

   b. Being classified as an excellent choice for parents made hamburgers a national favorite.

   _____

   _____

   c. "The Fast Food Nation" labs are, in Schlosser's opinion, places where the taste of processed and frozen foods is conceived.

   _____

   _____

3. **Check (✓) the sentences that describe book reviews.**

   a. (   ) They are always in informal language and written in the first person singular.

   b. (   ) They offer a critical assessment of the book.

   c. (   ) They may provide the reader with a concise summary of the content.

   d. (   ) They are written in chronological order and never include a personal judgment.

   e. (   ) They might suggest whether the reader would enjoy the book.

LANGUAGE IN USE 2

Unit 3

ZERO, FIRST, AND SECOND CONDITIONALS

1. Read these extracts from the texts on pages 28 and 32. Then use the suggestions from the box to complete the sentences and review what you have studied about the conditionals in English.

> I. If you feel that way, how can you ingest fast food?

> II. If that was the reality, then every meal would have the potential to be a perfect meal.

> III. 'If you don't know about a problem,' the man observes, 'then you don't have to deal with it.'

future	hypothetical	I	II	III
not	possible	result	second	
when	will	zero		

a. The zero conditional used in extract _____ indicates that the _____ of the condition always happens or is always true. In this case, *if* can be replaced by _____ with no change in meaning.

b. The first conditional used in extract _____ indicates things that might happen in the future or results of imagined situations in the future. In the first conditional, the main clause may have any modal verb with _____ meaning, e.g., _____, *can, may*, or the imperative.

c. While the _____ conditional describes what happens in general, the first conditional describes a particular situation.

d. The second conditional used in extract _____ indicates the _____ result of an unreal or _____ situation in the present or in the future.

e. While the first conditional describes things that will probably happen in the future, the _____ conditional describes things that are _____ likely to happen.

2. Use the correct conditional form to complete the quotes below. Then take some time to read them again and check (✓) the ones you agree with. Share your opinions with a classmate.

a. ( ) "If we _____ (give up) eating beef, we **would have** roughly 20 to 30 times more land for food than we have now." – James Lovelock, English scientist

Extracted from www.brainyquote.com/quotes/james_lovelock_314096. Accessed on August 20, 2018.

b. ( ) "If we _____ (pursue) organic farming as our healthy food style, we **can bring down** cost of treatment to a great extent." – Sulaiman Abdul Aziz Al Rajhi, Saudi Arabian businessman

Extracted from www.brainyquote.com/quotes/sulaiman_abdul_aziz_al_ra_732605. Accessed on August 20, 2018.

c. ( ) "If you truly _____ (get) in touch with a piece of carrot, you get in touch with the soil, the rain, the sunshine. You **get** in touch with Mother Earth and eating in such a way, you feel in touch with true life, your roots, and that is meditation. If we _____ (chew) every **morsel** of our food in that way, we **become** grateful and when you are grateful, you are happy." – Thich Nhat Hanh, Vietnamese clergyman

Extracted from www.brainyquote.com/quotes/thich_nhat_hanh_531558. Accessed on August 20, 2018.

d. ( ) "I'm an animal rights activist because I believe we _____ (have) a planet if we **continue** to behave toward other species the way we do." – James Cromwell, American actor

Extracted from www.brainyquote.com/quotes/james_cromwell_523948. Accessed on August 20, 2018.

e. ( ) "If everybody _____ (switch) to organic farming, we **couldn't support** the earth's current population - maybe half ." – Nina Fedoroff, American scientist

Extracted from www.brainyquote.com/quotes/nina_fedoroff_512796. Accessed on August 20, 2018.

3. Answer the questions below. Then report your views to the class. If possible, use conditionals in your arguments.

a. Can you, as a consumer, be considered an accomplice in animal exploitation? Why (not)?

_____

_____

b. Have you heard of organic farming? If so, what is it?

_____

_____

c. What do you think would happen if people stopped eating beef?

_____

_____

d. Why do you think fast food is cheaper than fruits and vegetables in so many countries?

_____

_____

LISTENING COMPREHENSION

1. **In pairs, describe the photos below. Then match them with their corresponding captions.**

   a.

   b.

   ( ) At Granja Mantiqueira in Brazil eight million hens lay 5.4 million eggs a day. **Conveyor belts whisk** the eggs to a packaging facility. Demand for meat has tripled in the developing world in four decades, while egg consumption has increased **sevenfold**, driving a huge expansion of large-scale animal operations.

   ( ) On the Vulgamore farm near Scott City, Kansas, each combine can **harvest** up to 25 **acres** of wheat an hour – as well as provide real-time data on crop **yields**.

   Most of the food Americans eat is now produced on such large-scale, mechanized farms, which grow row after row of a single crop, allowing farmers to cover more ground with less labor.

   Extracted from www.nationalgeographic.com/foodfeatures/feeding-9-billion. Accessed on August 21, 2018.

2. **Listen to the first part of a talk on threats to the planet and complete the sentences accordingly.**

   06

   a. One of the biggest dangers to the planet is our need for _____.

   b. _____ contributes to global warming and accelerates the loss of biodiversity.

   c. If the spread of prosperity across the world continues, the amount of _____ will need to be doubled by _____.

   d. The debate over how to address the global food challenge has been polarized by those who favor _____ agriculture and proponents of local and _____ farms.

   e. As we try to meet the _____ for food worldwide, the _____ challenges posed by agriculture will become more urgent.

3. **Listen to the last part of the text and rephrase the speaker's conclusion using your own words. Then share your answer with your classmates.**

   07

   _____

   _____

» EXPAND YOUR HORIZONS »»»

Check (✓) the column that best describes your opinion about each statement. Then discuss your answers with your classmates and teacher, justifying your point of view.

	I agree.	I'm not sure.	I disagree.
a. As our food choices are almost endless nowadays, so are the methods of cultivating, transporting, preparing, and modifying food for our consumption.			
b. The food we choose to eat helps support unfair treatments of animals and the chaotic usage of natural resources that negatively affect ourselves and the environment in many different ways.			
c. A balance between producing more food and sustaining the planet is the answer to our present issues related to ethical eating in the face of an astonishing population growth, a worldwide financial crisis, and environmental chaos.			

UNIT 4
Extreme Weather Events Affecting the Planet

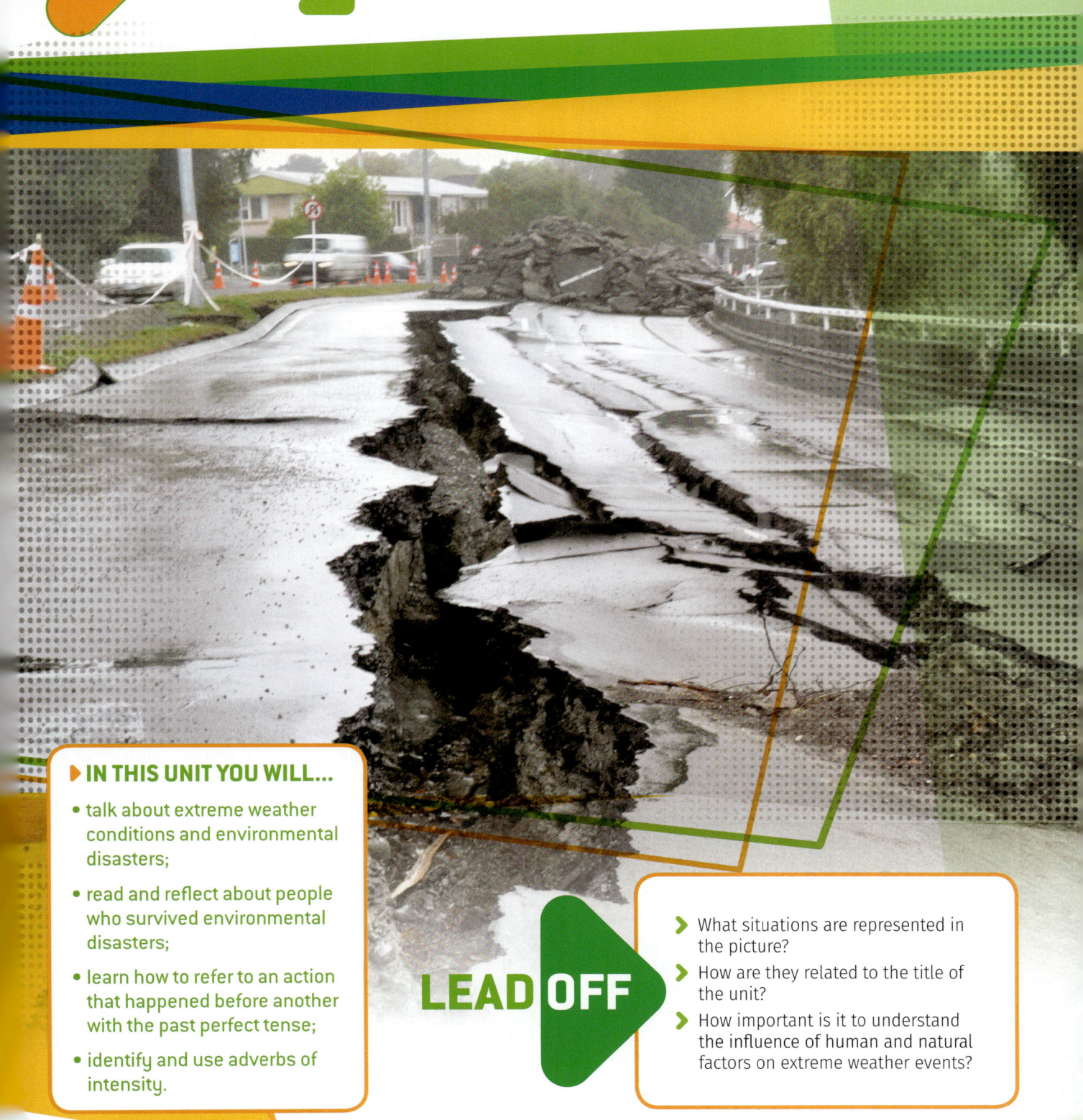

IN THIS UNIT YOU WILL...
- talk about extreme weather conditions and environmental disasters;
- read and reflect about people who survived environmental disasters;
- learn how to refer to an action that happened before another with the past perfect tense;
- identify and use adverbs of intensity.

LEAD OFF
- What situations are represented in the picture?
- How are they related to the title of the unit?
- How important is it to understand the influence of human and natural factors on extreme weather events?

READING

BEFORE READING

Mention a natural disaster or an extreme weather condition that happened in the region where you live and explain its impact on your community. *Contextualizing*

_____

_____

_____

WHILE READING

Read the title of the text carefully. Does the author say that those people survived the disasters they faced? Justify your answer. *Locating key words*

_____

_____

4 People Who Faced Disaster – And How They Made It out Alive

Some disasters are simply not survivable. But most are, and research on human behavior suggests that the difference between life and death often comes down to the simple – yet surprisingly difficult – task of recognizing
5 **threats** before they **overwhelm** you, then working through them as discrete challenges. The people who survive disasters tend to be better prepared and more capable of making smart decisions under pressure. Not everyone is born with these traits, but almost anyone can learn them.
10 […]

Rule 1:

It was early, 9:00 A.M., and **eerily** dark in Poway, Calif., as 75-**mph** winds drove **chaparral** *embers* through the air and **shook** the bones of Frank Vaplon's house. One ember
15 **lodged** in his woodpile and set it **ablaze**. Most of his neighbors had evacuated, but Vaplon had decided to stay and fight the wildfire that was closing in on his property.

Geared up in a mail-order *firefighter*'s outfit – helmet, **bunker coat**, respirator, the whole thing – Vaplon began
20 his *assault* by shooting a high-pressure stream of water at the flames, but it just blew back against him in a hot *mist*. "It was like **pissing into** the *wind*," Vaplon says. "So I turned around and started spraying down the house."

The Witch Creek fire was the fourth largest on record in
25 California. A reported 1,800 firefighters battled the *blaze* and several others nearby; more than 250,000 people in San Diego County were evacuated. Conventional wisdom says that when a wildfire is burning down your neighborhood, you shouldn't stick around. And, for most
30 homeowners, evacuation was certainly the smartest option. But Vaplon stayed and fought back against the fire. What did he know that everyone who followed the conventional **wisdom** didn't?

"The last thing I want from my story is for people to risk
35 their lives," Vaplon says. "But I'd thought about protecting my home, and I felt comfortable with my decision to stay." The day before the fire swept through his 2.5-acre spread, he woke up early to the distant smell of smoke. He immediately broke out 500 feet of fire **hose** and attached it
40 to a *standpipe* hooked up to a 10,000-gallon water tank. "I started watering down everything that I could," Vaplon says. "The roof, my lawn, everything."

[…]

"The brain is an engineering system," says John Leach, a
45 former Royal Air Force combat survival instructor who now works with the Norwegian military on survival training and research. "Like any engineering system, it has limits in terms of what it can process and how fast it can do so. We cope by taking in information about our environment,
50 and then building a model of that environment. We don't respond to our environment, but to the model of our environment." If there's no model, the brain tries to create one, but there's not enough time for that during an emergency. Operating on an inadequate mental model,
55 disaster victims often **fail** to take the actions needed to save their own lives.

Not Vaplon. As the firestorm approached, he stayed calm and **clearheaded**. He had done so much advance work that he had created a model for his brain to act on when
60 disaster came. […]

Extracted from www.popularmechanics.com/adventure/outdoors/a4623/4331486.
Accessed on August 24, 2018.

>> AFTER READING

1. Read the text carefully. Why was Vaplon able to survive the firestorm? `Understanding main ideas`

_____

_____

2. Check (✓) the correct alternative to complete the statements about the text. `Understanding details`

a. More than 250,000 people left San Diego County because of _____.

( ) Frank Vaplon ( ) the Witch Creek fire

b. When Vaplon _____, he decided to start watering down the roof, the lawn, and everything he could.

( ) woke up to the smell of smoke

( ) got dressed in a firefighter's outfit

c. Vaplon challenged conventional wisdom when he _____.

( ) stayed and fought back against the fire

( ) did a lot of work in advance

EXPAND YOUR VOCABULARY

1. Look for the words and expressions listed below in the text and infer their meanings. Underline the one that does not belong in each group below. Then talk to a classmate about why the word is not part of the group.

a. helmet, hose, bunker coat

b. firestorm, wildfire, wisdom

c. property, house, chaparral

d. sweep through, water down, spray down

2. Write the words in italics in the text next to their corresponding definitions below.

a. _____ : someone whose job is to stop fires burning

b. _____ : a light cloud low over the ground that makes it difficult for you to see very far

c. _____ : a piece of wood or coal that stays red and very hot after a fire has stopped burning

d. _____ : an attempt to achieve something difficult, especially using physical force

e. _____ : a big dangerous fire – used especially in news reports

f. _____ : a pipe that provides water in a public place in the street

g. _____ : moving air, especially when it moves strongly or quickly in a current

Extracted from www.ldoceonline.com. Accessed on August 24, 2018.

3. Choose words from activity 2 to complete the text. Make any necessary adjustments.

Brazil's worst month ever for forest fires blamed on human activity

Brazil has seen more forest fires in September than in any single month since records began, and authorities have warned that 2017 could surpass the worst year on record if action is not taken soon.

Experts say that the _____ are almost exclusively due to human activity, and they attribute the uptick to the expansion of agriculture and a reduction of oversight and surveillance. Lower than average rainfall in this year's dry season is also an exacerbating factor.

[…]

Burning is illegal and carries heavy fines, but fire is often used to clear land for pasture or crops and hunting or results from land conflicts.

[…]

In September, after a month-long battle, _____ gave up on a fire in Tocantins state park, believed to have been lit by local fishermen and carried by strong _____ during an intense dry period. An area three times the size of São Paulo was destroyed, according to local media.

Extracted from www.theguardian.com/world/2017/sep/28/brazil-forest-fires-deforestation-september-record-amazon. Accessed on August 24, 2018.

4. Do you agree that human activity is responsible for some disasters and extreme weather conditions we face around the world? Share your opinion with a classmate.

VOCABULARY IN USE

1. **Pay attention to an extract from the text on page 36 and check (✓) the correct meaning for the phrasal verb in bold.**

   > Conventional wisdom says that when a wildfire is **burning down** your neighborhood, you shouldn't stick around.

   a. ( ) to become weaker and produce less heat
   b. ( ) to destroy by fire

2. **Read some examples with other phrasal verbs related to weather conditions or environmental disasters. Match them with their corresponding meanings.**

   a. The storm **had blown** itself **out**, leaving the sky pearly.
   b. By late fall, Mediterranean islands have **cooled off** and can have rainy days.
   c. Once the weather **warms up**, you can move the plants outdoors.
   d. I can't see where I'm going with the windows all **misted up** like this.

   ( ) becomes warm, or to make someone or something warm
   ( ) had ended
   ( ) became covered with very small drops of water
   ( ) returned to a normal temperature after being hot

   Adapted from www.ldoceonline.com. Accessed on August 26, 2018.

3. **Circle the correct alternative to complete the explanation of the weather-related idiom pictured below.**

   When someone says "it's raining cats and dogs", he/she means…
   a. it's raining a lot.
   b. it's raining pets.
   c. there are lots of cats and dogs walking around.
   d. cats and dogs are fighting.
   e. it's raining, but it's a very light rain.

4. **The idioms in bold in the sentences have weather-related words. Infer their meaning and use them to fill in the blanks.**

   > There is no need to make **a storm in a teacup**! It's just a small problem.
   >
   > Anna was **on cloud nine** after she got an A+ on her biology exam.
   >
   > Young man, you are going to the dentist's today **come rain or shine**, do you understand?
   >
   > We can't let the press **get wind of** the mayor's illness.
   >
   > Joshua is still a little **under the weather**, so he will stay home and rest.

   a. _____: to hear or find out about something secret or private
   b. _____: whatever happens or whatever the weather is like
   c. _____: to be very happy about something
   d. _____: slightly ill
   e. _____: an unnecessary expression of strong feelings about something that is very unimportant

   Extracted from www.ldoceonline.com. Accessed on August 26, 2018.

5. **Choose two idioms from activity 4 and contextualize them in a paragraph or dialogue. Then share your answer with your classmates.**

LANGUAGE IN USE 1

Unit 4

PAST PERFECT

1. The excerpt below was extracted from the text on page 36. Read it, pay attention to the parts in bold, and underline the correct alternatives to complete the sentences about the past perfect tense.

> He **had done** so much advance work that he **had created** a model for his brain to act on when disaster came.

a. To form the past perfect tense, we use the auxiliary verb **has / had** + the main verb in its past **simple / participle** form.

b. The past perfect tense is used to refer to an action that occurred **before / after** another action in the **past / future**.

c. Besides the verb tense, some words or expressions might also help identify which action happened first, such as **now / before**, *after*, and *previously*, for example.

2. Refer back to the text on page 36 and underline other past perfect occurrences.

3. In the extract "But I'd thought about protecting my home, and I felt comfortable with my decision to stay," what happened first: Vaplon's feeling comfortable with his decision or Vaplon's thinking about protecting his home?

_____

4. Below you will find two other stories about people who survived disasters. Use the past perfect tense of the verbs from the box to fill in the blanks.

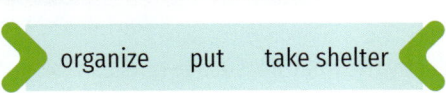

> organize   put   take shelter

[…]
Rule 2:
The tornado siren sounded at the Little Sioux Scout Ranch in western Iowa just before the power went out on June 11, 2008. Scout Leader Fred Ullrich, an IT manager at the University of Nebraska Medical Center, opened the door of the building where he and 65 Boy Scouts _____. […]
Ullrich didn't know what he and his scouts were in for that day, but mental preparedness and responsibility are central to the Boy Scout philosophy. The night before the tornado, Ullrich _____ the boys through a first-aid drill. When emergency responders arrived after the tornado, what they saw was devastating – four scouts were dead or mortally wounded. Scores were suffering from broken pelvises, dislocated shoulders, lacerations and punctured lungs. Yet, amazingly, the rescue crew also saw that Ullrich and the uninjured scouts were putting their training to work. They _____ an on-the-spot triage center, helping to prepare the most seriously injured for their journey to the hospital.
[…]

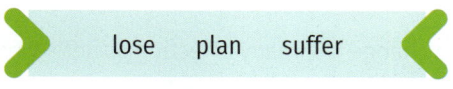

> lose   plan   suffer

Rule 3:
On Saturday, Nov. 18, 2007, Daryl Jané left his cottage on Bainbridge Island in Washington State to head for an overnight sky-watching event 190 miles southeast at Trout Lake. He _____ to be back the next day to watch a Seattle Seahawks game. Jané never made it to Trout Lake. Instead he became the prisoner of a tremendous late fall snowstorm. Jané was driving on a widely used – at least in good conditions – forest service road as the snow began to pile up. He became stuck 35 miles from his destination when the tires of his '93 Jeep Cherokee sank into deep snow.
[…]
In the end, Jané was stuck for 14 days before a local snowmobile club found him. He _____ 10 pounds but _____ from neither frostbite nor hypothermia.
[…]

Extracted from www.popularmechanics.com/adventure/outdoors/a4623/4331486. Accessed on August 27, 2018.

5. Read and discuss the excerpt below in small groups. If possible, use the past perfect in your argumentation.

> **Why Save the Amazon?**
> For one, the Amazon is on the **frontlines** of the fight against global warming.
> Currently, the Amazon is a **carbon sink**, meaning it stores carbon dioxide and prevents it from entering the atmosphere and **fueling** climate change. Deforestation, on the other hand, releases that carbon into the air, making global warming worse. Because of this, deforestation accounts for about 10 to 15 percent of global greenhouse gas emissions. Losing the Amazon means more carbon emissions and a warmer world.
> No matter how far from the region you live, the Amazon plays an important role in all of our lives, and we all play a role in protecting the homes of thousands of people and some of the world's rarest wildlife.
> […]

Extracted from www.greenpeace.org/usa/forests/amazon-rainforest. Accessed on August 27, 2018.

EXPAND YOUR READING

1. **Read the text and check (✓) the alternative that best summarizes its main idea.**
   a. (   ) As ocean waters are becoming warmer and more acidic, ocean circulation, chemistry, ecosystems, and marine life are affected.
   b. (   ) Climate change and its impact on many sectors have become increasingly troublesome across the nation.

[…]

Introduction

Climate change is already affecting societies and the natural world. Climate change interacts with other environmental and societal factors in ways that can either moderate or intensify these impacts. The types and magnitudes of impacts vary across the nation and through time. Children, the elderly, the sick, and the poor are especially vulnerable. There
5 is **mounting** evidence that harm to the nation will increase substantially in the future unless global emissions of **heat-trapping gases** are greatly reduced.

Widespread Impacts

Because environmental, cultural, and socioeconomic systems are tightly coupled, climate change impacts can either be amplified or reduced by
10 cultural and socioeconomic decisions. In many arenas, it is clear that societal decisions have substantial influence on the vulnerability of valued resources to climate change. For example, rapid population growth and development in coastal areas tends to amplify climate change related impacts. Recognition of these **couplings**, together with recognition
15 of multiple **sources** of vulnerability, helps identify what information decision-makers need as they manage risks.

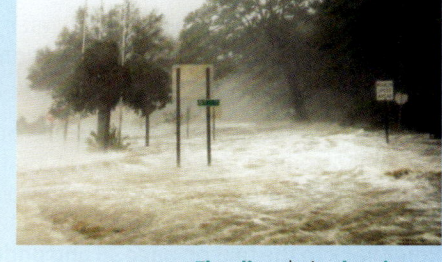

Flooding during **hurricanes**

Multiple System Failures During Extreme Events

Impacts are particularly severe when critical systems simultaneously fail. We have already seen multiple system failures during an extreme weather
20 event in the United States, as when Hurricane Katrina struck New Orleans. Infrastructure and evacuation failures and collapse of critical response services during a storm is one example of multiple system failures. Another example is a **loss** of electrical power during heat waves or wildfires, which can reduce food and water safety. Air conditioning has helped reduce illness
25 and death due to extreme heat, but if power is lost, everyone is vulnerable. By their nature, such events can exceed our capacity to respond. In succession, these events severely **deplete** resources needed to respond, from the individual to the national scale, but disproportionately affect the most vulnerable populations.
[…]

Katrina struck New Orleans

Cascading Effects Across Sectors

Agriculture, water, energy, transportation, and more are all affected by climate change. These sectors of our economy
30 do not exist in isolation and are linked in increasingly complex ways. For example, water supply and energy use are completely **intertwined**, since water is used to generate energy, and energy is required to pump, treat, and deliver water – which means that irrigation-dependent farmers and urban dwellers are linked as well.
[…]

Extracted from https://nca2014.globalchange.gov/highlights/report-findings/widespread-impacts. Accessed on August 27, 2018.

2. **Underline the alternative that best describes expository essays.**
   a. They are a mostly oral genre. They aim at convincing the reader to understand and accept the writer's point of view.
   b. They are a mostly written genre. They present facts, statistics, and definitions to inform the reader about a given topic.

LANGUAGE IN USE 2

Unit 4

ADVERBS OF DEGREE

1. Read these extracts from the text on page 40, pay attention to the words in bold, and answer: what's their function in the sentences? Then choose the best alternative to complete the sentences.

> There is mounting evidence that harm to the nation will increase **substantially** in the future unless global emissions of heat-trapping gases are **greatly** reduced.

> In succession, these events **severely** deplete resources needed to respond, [...]

a. Adverbs of degree tell us about the _____ of an action, an adjective, or another adverb. These include *almost*, *enough*, *too*, _____, etc.

( ) manner / quickly   ( ) intensity / very

b. Many adverbs of degree end in _____, for example: _____ and *intensely*.

( ) -ly / extremely   ( ) -ing / intensifying

c. Adverbs of degree are usually positioned _____ the adjective, adverb, or _____ that they modify.

( ) after / pronoun   ( ) before / verb

2. Read part of a text about the Mariana mining disaster effects and underline the adverb of degree. Then answer: what word does it modify?

_____

How Brazil's Worst Environmental Disaster Is Still Affecting Thousands of People

[...]
What could possibly be worse than one socio-environmental catastrophe?
Two of them.
On November 5, 2015, the Fundão dam, located in the sub-district of Bento Rodrigues, 35 km from the center of the Brazilian municipality of Mariana, Minas Gerais, ruptured. 60 million cubic meters of iron ore tailings were leaked from the Samarco-operated mining complex and traveled 55 km from the Gualaxo do Norte River and another 22 km from the Carmo River to the Doce River. In total, the mud traveled 663 km to find the sea.
It's been characterized by experts as the country's largest environmental disaster, altering the ecosystems along the Rio Doce basin tremendously in addition to killing 19 people and affecting more than 23 thousand families. Recently, the relationship between the yellow fever outbreak and this disaster have made their way into the mainstream media's narrative, just as biologist and environmentalist Augusto Ruschi predicted two years ago. [...]

Extracted from www.theinertia.com/environment/how-brazils-worst-environmental-disaster-is-still-affecting-thousands-of-people. Accessed on August 28, 2018.

3. Form *-ly* adverbs of degree to complete the chart below.

Adjectives	Adverbs of Degree
entire	
high	
huge	
moderate	
partial	
strong	
total	

4. In your notebook, summarize the text excerpt below using your own words. Insert two adverbs of degree from the previous activities.

Thailand cave: How the rescue operation unfolded
After a soccer practice on Saturday 23 June, 12 young players and their "Wild Boars" team coach entered the 10km (6 mile) Tham Luang cave complex in Chiang Rai province, northern Thailand.
When they failed to return home, a huge search operation was launched, with rescuers facing a race against time to find them as heavy rain battered the region and flooded parts of the cave.
After 10 days, they were found weak but alive. [...]

Extracted from https://news.sky.com/story/thailand-cave-rescue-how-the-boys-were-found-11424201. Accessed on August 28, 2018.

LISTENING COMPREHENSION

1. **Look at the magazine covers and answer: what do they have in common? Then work in small groups to discuss the issues shown on these covers.**

Extracted from http://content.time.com/time/covers/europe/0,16641,20051003,00.html. Accessed on August 28, 2018.

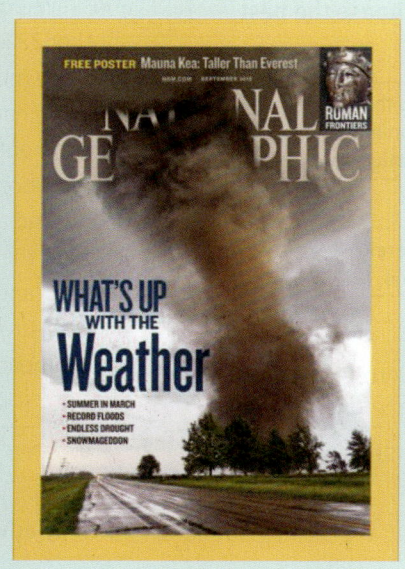

Extracted from www.nationalgeographic.com. Accessed on August 28, 2018.

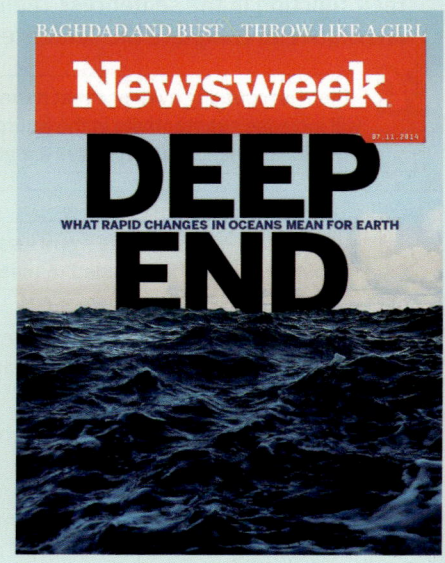

Extracted from www.newsweek.com/archive/2014. Accessed on August 28, 2018.

2. **Listen to Alex Staniforth talk about his experience and infer what happened to him.**
   - a. (   ) He fell 70ft into a **crevasse**.
   - b. (   ) He was almost caught in an avalanche on Everest.
   - c. (   ) He **rescued** someone from an underwater cave.

3. **Listen to the whole recording and order the sentences accordingly.**
   - a. (   ) The earthquake struck.
   - b. (   ) Alex realized he had escaped the worst of the avalanche.
   - c. (   ) An avalanche killed 16 Sherpa guides on Mount Everest.
   - d. (   ) Alex thought of his family and imagined the headlines announcing his death.
   - e. (   ) Alex plans to return to Everest for a third attempt.
   - f. (   ) After two days, they were helicoptered down.
   - g. (   ) Twelve months later, Alex was ready to venture back.
   - h. (   ) The avalanche hit Alex like an express train.

>> EXPAND YOUR HORIZONS >>>

Check (✓) the column that best describes your opinion about each statement. Then discuss your answers with your classmates and teacher, justifying your point of view.

	I agree.	I'm not sure.	I disagree.
a. Disaster survivors are often more prepared and capable of making smart decisions when they are under pressure in future events.			
b. Although natural disasters are apparently caused by nature, they are usually at least partly caused or made worse by human decisions.			
c. Nations across the world must address issues related to global warming, climate change, and carbon emissions to reduce the risks of environmental disasters.			

REVIEW 2

Units 3 and 4

1. Read the title of the text carefully. Then list words or expressions relating to the theme you are going to read about. `Brainstorming`

_____

_____

_____

2. Work in pairs. Discuss some of the things you think the author of the text says you can do to help make our food and farming system better for the future. `Discussing and Predicting`

3. Now read the whole text and check your predictions.

What you can do — and ask others to do — to help make our food and farming system fit for the future

The Sustain Guide to Good Food

sustain
the alliance for better food and farming

[...]

*Please consider adopting a Good Food at Work policy, **committing** your organisation to improve the food you buy and serve to staff, visitors, clients and the public, and to help communicate Good Food principles. If you do adopt a Good Food Policy, tell us. Share your story and inspire more organisations to get involved.*

[...]

Good food

What we mean by good food can be summed up by our seven principles:

1) Aiming to be waste-free

Reducing food waste (and packaging) saves the energy, effort, and natural resources used to produce and dispose of it, as well as money.

2) Eating better, and less meat and dairy

Consuming more vegetables and fruit, grains and pulses, and smaller amounts of animal products produced to high-welfare and environmental **standards** helps reduce health risks and greenhouse gases.

3) Buying local, seasonal, and environmentally friendly food

This benefits wildlife and the countryside, minimises the energy used in food production, transport, and storage, and helps protect the local economy.

4) Choosing Fairtrade-certified products

This scheme for food and drinks imported from poorer countries ensures a fair deal for disadvantaged producers.

5) Selecting fish only from sustainable sources

Future generations will be able to eat fish and seafood if we act now to protect our rivers and seas and the creatures living there.

6) Getting the balance right

We need to cut down on sugar, salt, and fat, and most of us want to avoid questionable ingredients and processes such as genetic modification (GM) and some additives.

7) Growing our own, and buying the rest from a wide range of outlets

Fresh out of the garden or **allotment** is **unbeatable**, and a vibrant mix of local markets, small shops and cafés, and other retailers provides choice, variety, and good **livelihoods**.

Extracted from www.sustainweb.org/sustainablefood/. Accessed on November 12, 2018.

4. Read the text and decide if the statements are true (T) or false (F).

a. (   ) The author defends that we should reduce the amount of meat that we eat.

b. (   ) You should give preference to imported food rather than local food.

c. (   ) If you buy imported food, you should give preference to smaller producers.

d. (   ) Even though we should eat less or avoid sugar, the same is not true for additives.

5. Read the text again and underline two first conditional sentences.

6. Now read these other sentences, paying close attention to the parts in bold, and match them with their use.

a. If we **reduce** packaging, we **will save** natural resources.

b. If we **want** to get a good eating balance, we **need** to reduce our consumption of sugar, salt, and fat.

c. We **would help** disadvantaged farmers **if** we **bought** more Fairtrade-certified products.

(   ) It describes a hypothetical situation and its hypothetical result.

(   ) It describes a general truth.

(   ) It describes a possible situation and its possible result.

43

7. Use the verbs in parentheses in the past perfect to complete the text.

Thai cave soccer players tell of how they tried to dig their way out

[…]
The press conference was a jovial affair. The boys, dressed in their matching Wild Boars soccer shirts, entered the packed hall dribbling soccer balls to loud cheers. They smiled, some widely, some more **shyly**, at the audience of hundreds who _____ (gather) to hear their account of the drama for the first time.
A video played at the beginning of the press conference showed the boys openly **weeping** as they thanked the medical
5 staff at the hospital who _____ (help) in their recovery over the past week.
[…]
Ekaphol, 25, said they _____ (decide) to make the trip to the Tham Luang cave complex on June 23 as a fun activity because none of them _____ (be) inside before.
They cycled there after soccer practice and planned to spend an hour in the caves but as they reached a junction on
10 the way out, they saw the water rising.
[…]
It was only after ten days, when many _____ almost _____ (lose) hope of finding them, that two British divers finally came across the boys sheltered on a shelf deep in the cave.
[…]
One of the first questions the boys had for the divers was how many days they had been there, since they had lost all track of the time. "Our brains were very slow," said Adul. "We _____ (forget) everything about mathematics."
15 They also revealed that the eventual decision about who should leave the cave first was not based on strength, but decided by the boys themselves. It was based on who lived furthest away from the cave and therefore would have the longest cycle back home.
[…]

Adapted from www.theguardian.com/news/2018/jul/18/thai-cave-rescue-footballers-and-coach-describe-ordeal. Accessed on August 29, 2018.

8. There are different types of adverbs in the following cartoon strip. Circle only the ones that indicate degree or intensity. Then work in pairs to discuss the writer's tone: is it serious or sarcastic? Justify your view.

The Boondocks by Aaron McGruder

TODAY A GOVERNMENT SPOKESMAN SAID THAT AMERICANS SHOULD FEEL ABSOLUTELY, POSITIVELY AND DEFINITELY CERTAIN …

BEYOND THE SHADOW OF ANY DOUBT THAT THE AMERICAN BEEF SUPPLY IS COMPLETELY, TOTALLY AND UNQUESTIONABLY …

… NOT GONNA GIVE YOU A FATAL BRAIN-EATING DISEASE, PROBABLY. THANK YOU, AND EAT WELL.

Extracted from www.gocomics.com/boondocks/2006/01/18. Accessed on August 29, 2018.

UNIT 5
In the Limelight

▶ IN THIS UNIT YOU WILL...
- talk about TV characters and shows;
- exchange ideas about binge-watching;
- learn how to talk about hypothetical situations in the past using the third conditional;
- learn how to express wishes and regrets.

LEAD OFF

- What does the idiom *in the limelight* mean? How does it connect to the picture?
- What are your favorite TV shows and characters of all time? Justify your answer.
- Do you agree that excessive watching of TV shows has become widespread across the world due to online streaming? Has it affected your daily life? If so, how?

READING

›› BEFORE READING

Read the title of the text below. In your opinion, who is its target audience? *Identifying the target audience*

_____

_____

›› WHILE READING

Read the whole text and answer: What is its main purpose? *Identifying the main purpose of a text*

What would have happened next if these TV characters hadn't died?

BY IAN SANDWELL   31 AUGUST 2018

We've already told you what your favorite TV characters are up to nowadays, but **spare** a thought for those characters killed off before their time.

So many storylines unfulfilled and promising futures **dashed** with one **tap** of the writer's keyboard, although if we're lucky, we'll get a **hint** of what they would have been *getting up to* if they hadn't been killed off.

Here are seven such occasions where we can fill in the 'what if?' question surrounding some major TV characters.

1. Poussey – Orange Is the New Black

Just in case you weren't devastated enough by Poussey's tragic death in Orange Is the New Black season four, writer Lauren Morelli revealed that if Poussey had survived, she would have *gone on* to get out of Litchfield and live a happy life.

[...]

2. Doyle – Angel

The sacrificial death of Angel's loveable psychic **sidekick** Doyle just nine episodes in wasn't originally planned, but it potentially wasn't going to be the end of Doyle – Joss Whedon wanted to bring the character back as a Big Bad in season three or four.

[...]

3. Professor Arturo – Sliders

In the season two episode "Post Traumatic Slide Syndrome" of cult sci-fi Sliders, Professor Arturo and his **double** have a battle. As the **vortex** opens, one Arturo *knocks* the other *down* and goes with the group to the next world.

[...]

4. Tara – Buffy the Vampire Slayer

There were actually two opportunities for Tara to come back in Buffy the Vampire **Slayer** after her cruel death in season six. [...] We don't know why it never happened, but maybe it's something to do with the choice not making sense in light of Buffy's traumatic return from the dead.

5. Tony Almeida – 24

We know that Tony Almeida eventually came back to life in 24 season seven and had turned **evil**, but before his "death" in season five, we were robbed of an exciting storyline for him – the writers had planned for him to go on a **revenge** mission after the death of his wife Michelle.

[...]

6. David Tennant – Doctor Who

When Steven Moffat took over as the Doctor Who **showrunner**, he almost persuaded David Tennant to *stick around* for one more season as the Doctor, before Tennant decided to leave and Matt Smith *took over* the iconic role for season five. The Tennant version of season five would have started off in similar fashion with the Doctor crashing into Amelia Pond's garden.

[...]

7. Carl – The Walking Dead

We're being a bit cheeky here as there's no guarantee that The Walking Dead would have followed the comic books with Carl's storylines. However, we do know that his shock death has robbed Carl of a host of storylines, including a romance with Lydia, the daughter of Whisperers leader Alpha, and a key role in the future of the Hilltop.

[...]

Adapted from www.digitalspy.com/tv/feature/a865204/dead-tv-characters-scrapped-storylines. Accessed on September 1, 2018..

>> AFTER READING

1. Which other TV characters would you add to the list on page 46? Work in pairs and justify your choices. *Discussing*

_____

_____

_____

2. Decide if the sentences are true (T) or false (F). *Understanding details*

a. ( ) According to Lauren Morelli, if Poussey hadn't died, she would have led a happy life.

b. ( ) In *The Walking Dead*, Lydia's death prevented her from having an affair with Carl.

c. ( ) Steven Moffat played the doctor in *Doctor Who*.

d. ( ) The writers of *24* had planned for Tony Almeida to seek revenge for Michelle's death.

e. ( ) Joss Whedon had decided to kill Doyle right at the beginning of season 3 or 4, but the character ended up dying in season 1.

3. What reasons might make a writer decide to kill off certain promising characters? Talk to your classmates.

EXPAND YOUR VOCABULARY

1. Scan the text to find the phrasal verbs in italics that match the definitions below. Write them in the base form.

a. _____ : to hit or push someone so that they fall to the ground

b. _____ : to stay in a place a little longer, waiting for something to happen

c. _____ : to take control of something

d. _____ : to continue doing something or being in a situation

e. _____ : to do something, especially something slightly bad

Extracted from www.ldoceonline.com. Accessed on September 3, 2018.

2. Read these extracts from the text on page 46 and check (✓) the word that best replaces the one in italics.

a. "We're being a bit cheeky here as there's no guarantee that The Walking Dead would have followed the comic books with Carl's *storylines*."

( ) climax   ( ) plot

b. "(...) Tennant to stick around for one more season as the Doctor, before Tennant decided to leave and Matt Smith took over the iconic *role* for season five."

( ) situation   ( ) part

c. "We know that Tony Almeida *eventually* came back to life in 24 season seven and had turned evil,"

( ) finally   ( ) soon

d. "We're being a bit *cheeky* here as there's no guarantee that The Walking Dead would have followed the comic books with Carl's storylines."

( ) audacious   ( ) entertaining

3. Read the proverb below and answer the questions: Do you think it might apply to television programs as well? Can the shows you watch say anything about who you are or affect your behavior? Use some words from the previous activity in your answers. Then report your opinions to the class.

> "You are what you eat."

_____

_____

_____

Unit 5

47

VOCABULARY IN USE

1. In "However, we do know that his shock death has robbed Carl of a host of storylines, including a romance with Lydia, the daughter of Whisperers leader Alpha, and a key role in the future of the Hilltop", what does the word *key* mean? Choose the correct alternative.

   a. ( ) a small specially shaped piece of metal that you put into a lock and turn in order to lock or unlock a door, start a car, etc.
   b. ( ) the buttons that you press on a computer keyboard to operate the computer
   c. ( ) very important or necessary
   d. ( ) the printed answers to a test or set of questions in a book

   Extracted from www.ldoceonline.com/dictionary/key. Accessed on September 4, 2018.

2. Read the dictionary entry below as well as the extracts from the text on page 46, paying special attention to the words in bold. Then check (✔) the meaning of each homonym in context.

   > **hom·o·nym** / **noun** [**countable**] *technical* a word that is spelled the same and sounds the same as another, but is different in meaning or origin. For example, the noun 'bear' and the verb 'bear' are homonyms.

   Extracted from www.ldoceonline.com/dictionary/homonym. Accessed on September 4, 2018.

   a. "So many storylines unfulfilled and promising futures dashed with one **tap** of the writer's keyboard, although if we're lucky, we'll get a hint of what they would have been getting up to if they hadn't been killed off."

   ( ) a piece of equipment for controlling the flow of water, gas etc. from a pipe or container
   ( ) an act of hitting something lightly, especially to get someone's attention

   b. "There were actually two opportunities for Tara to come back in Buffy the Vampire Slayer after her cruel death in **season** six."

   ( ) a series of films, plays, television programs, etc. that are shown during a particular period of time
   ( ) to add salt, pepper, etc. to food you are cooking

   Extracted from www.ldoceonline.com. Accessed on September 4, 2018.

3. Homonyms can be subdivided into homophones and homographs. Study the word clouds and match them with their corresponding categories.

   a. BYE FOUR BY BUY HERE HEAR HOUR NO FLOUR KNOW FLOWER FOR MEAT SON WHERE SUN OUR WEAR

   b. BAT WOUND WIND OBJECT BOW LEAD TEAR SECOND DESERT SUBJECT FINE BASS ROW

   ( ) **hom·o·graph** / **noun** [**countable**] *technical* a word that is spelled the same as another, but is different in meaning, origin, grammar, or pronunciation. For example, the noun 'record' is a homograph of the verb 'record'.

   Extracted from www.ldoceonline.com/dictionary/homograph. Accessed on September 4, 2018.

   ( ) **hom·o·phone** / **noun** [**countable**] *technical* a word that sounds the same as another but is different in spelling, meaning, or origin. For example, 'knew' and 'new' are homophones.

   Extracted from www.ldoceonline.com/dictionary/homophone. Accessed on September 4, 2018.

4. Use one homograph or homophone from the word clouds above to complete the cartoon. Then explain your choice to a classmate.

   I SAW YOU THROW THAT PAPER DOWN!
   LOOK, IT'S OK.
   FOR LITTERING

   Extracted from www.cartoonstock.com/directory/f/fining.asp. Accessed on September 4, 2018.

LANGUAGE IN USE 1

Unit 5

THIRD CONDITIONAL

1. Read the extracts from the text on page 46 and underline the correct alternatives to complete the sentences.

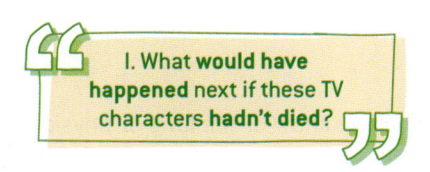

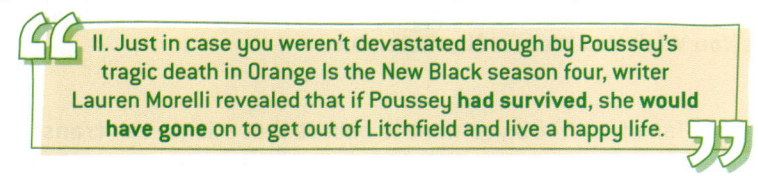

> I. What **would have happened** next if these TV characters **hadn't died**?

> II. Just in case you weren't devastated enough by Poussey's tragic death in Orange Is the New Black season four, writer Lauren Morelli revealed that if Poussey **had survived**, she **would have gone** on to get out of Litchfield and live a happy life.

About extract I, it is correct to say that…
- a. the TV characters died.
- b. the TV characters might not have died.

About extract II, it is correct to say that…
- a. it talks about a real possibility in the future.
- b. it talks about a hypothetical situation in the past.

We use the third conditional to refer to…
- a. an unlikely situation that probably won't be fulfilled, but we imagine its possible result.
- b. a situation that didn't happen and won't happen, but we imagine its hypothetical result.

2. Read the extracts again and fill in the blanks about the formation of the third conditional.

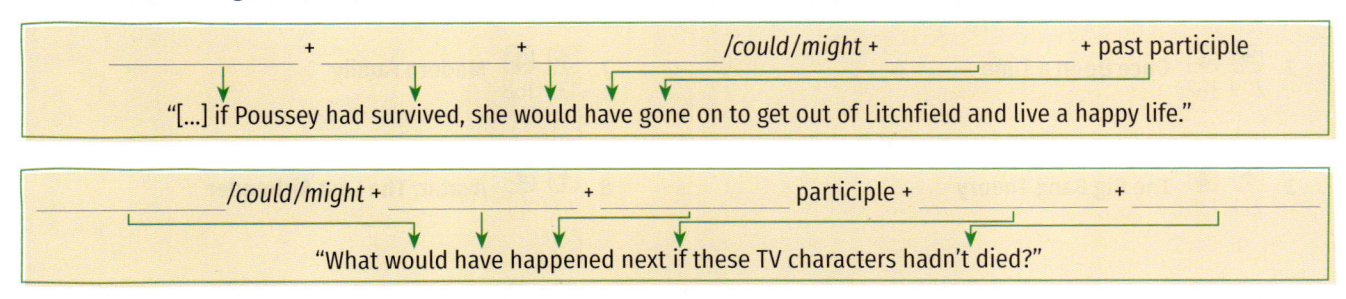

_____ + _____ + _____ /could/might + _____ + past participle

"[…] if Poussey had survived, she would have gone on to get out of Litchfield and live a happy life."

_____ /could/might + _____ + _____ participle + _____ + _____

"What would have happened next if these TV characters hadn't died?"

3. Use the verbs from the box to complete the extracts below. Remember to follow the rule for the third conditional.

> be   do   happen (x2)   have

What if TV Had Never Been Invented?

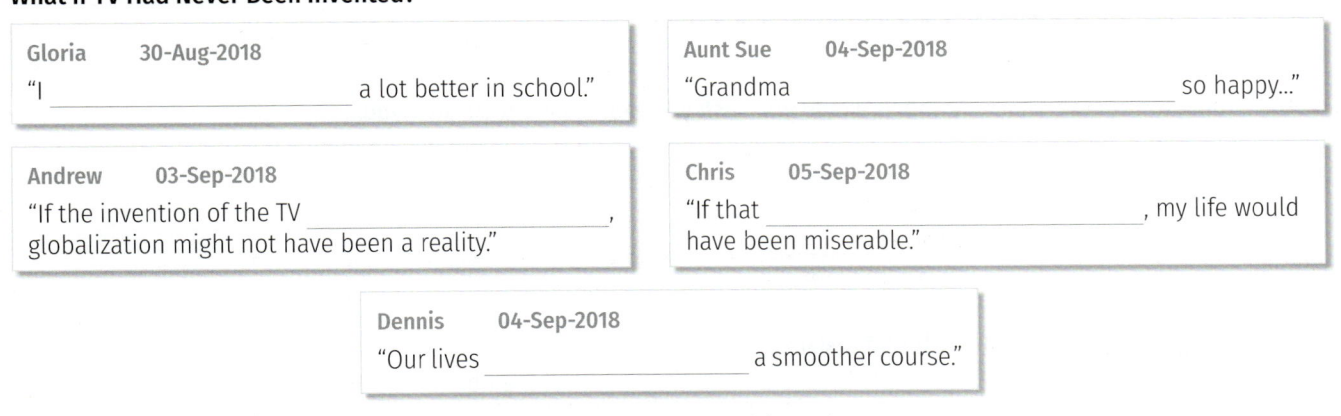

Gloria   30-Aug-2018
"I _____ a lot better in school."

Aunt Sue   04-Sep-2018
"Grandma _____ so happy…"

Andrew   03-Sep-2018
"If the invention of the TV _____, globalization might not have been a reality."

Chris   05-Sep-2018
"If that _____, my life would have been miserable."

Dennis   04-Sep-2018
"Our lives _____ a smoother course."

4. Answer the questions below. Use the correct form of the third conditional in your answers.

- a. What TV show would you have watched until the end if it hadn't been canceled prematurely? Why?

- b. Which viewing habits might you have changed if you had been asked to?

EXPAND YOUR READING

1. Skim the text to find out its predominant genre. Then choose the correct alternative to complete the sentence.
   The text is a/an _____ (advice letter / joke / list / song).

> **TV Shows You Wish You Were a Character On**
> […]
>
> Are you a huge fan of sci-fi? Do you want to believe that science can **transcend** what we know of the laws of physics? Perhaps joining the crew of Battlestar Galactica is your **jam**. Do you want to hang out with a bunch of crazy classmates in a Spanish study group that does anything but study? Hey, *Community's* probably your style. Or perhaps you want to **boldly** go where no one has gone before? *Star Trek: The Next Generation* has to be your choice. Whether you want to join the great big *Modern Family*, or you want to time travel with the **cast** of *Doctor Who*, there are plenty of awesome television worlds and TV shows you'd like to be part of.
>
> So vote up the television series you wish you were a character on and maybe the *Happy Endings* gang will invite you to sit with them, or you'll get a job in the Pawnee Parks Department. Even if the show is off the air, if you think it would be fun to have been a character on the series, vote it up!
>
> 1 ↑↓ **Friends**
> 221 135
> […]
>
> 2 ↑↓ **Once Upon a Time**
> 209 162
> […]
>
> 3 ↑↓ **The Big Bang Theory**
> 221 135
> […]
>
> 4 ↑↓ **How I Met Your Mother**
> 176 170
> […]
>
> 5 ↑↓ **Doctor Who**
> 155 165
> […]
>
> 6 ↑↓ **Sherlock**
> 70 59
> […]
>
> 7 ↑↓ **Modern Family**
> 137 168
> […]
>
> 8 ↑↓ **Avatar: The Last Airbender**
> 47 45
> […]
>
> 9 ↑↓ **When Calls the Heart**
> 47 49
> […]
>
> 10 ↑↓ **The Office**
> 120 156
> […]

Extracted from www.ranker.com/list/tv-shows-you-wish-you-were-on/ranker-tv. Accessed on September 3, 2018.

2. According to the text, which TV shows would you wish you were a character on if you…
   a. were a sci-fi addict? _____
   b. wanted to travel through time? _____
   c. intended to visit unexplored places? _____
   d. wanted to hang out with a group of mad classmates? _____

3. Check (✔) the items commonly found in lists.
   a. ( ) standard language
   b. ( ) complex questions
   c. ( ) a set of items
   d. ( ) a title for the list
   e. ( ) organized information
   f. ( ) the results of a research

4. Where do you often come across lists? Do you write lists yourself? What for? Exchange ideas with a partner.

LANGUAGE IN USE 2

Unit 5

WISH

1. Read an extract from the text on page 50, paying attention to the verb structures in bold, and circle the correct alternatives to complete the sentences.

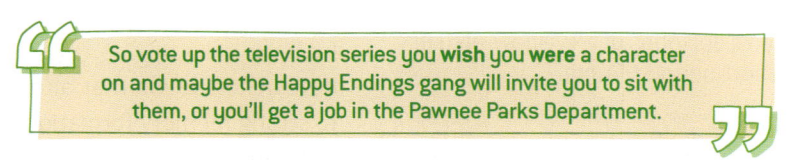

> "So vote up the television series you **wish** you **were** a character on and maybe the Happy Endings gang will invite you to sit with them, or you'll get a job in the Pawnee Parks Department."

a. The readers who are invited to vote **are** / **aren't** TV characters.
b. The structure in bold expresses a present wish that **is contrary to reality** / **might come true**.
c. We should use the subjunctive form **did** / **were** instead of *was* when expressing wishes with the verb *be*.

2. Now read a question from a question-and-answer website called Quora and underline the correct statements about it.

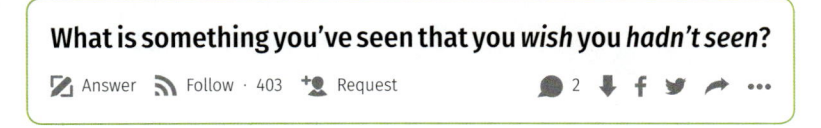

> What is something you've seen that you *wish* you *hadn't seen*?
> Answer Follow · 403 Request   2

Extracted from https://www.quora.com. Accessed on February 8, 2019.

a. The author of the question assumes the reader has already seen something and disliked it.
b. The question indicates that the reader might want to see that again.
c. The verb structure in italics in the question expresses a regret about the past.

3. Based on activities 1 and 2, complete the chart below with either *past perfect* or *simple past*.

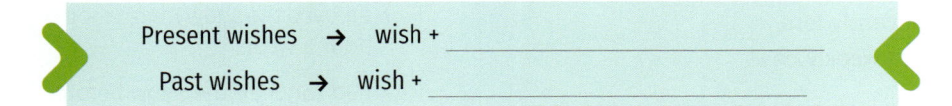

Present wishes	→	wish + _____
Past wishes	→	wish + _____

4. Read the cartoon strip below and check (✓) the correct alternative to complete the sentence. Then discuss the strip content with a classmate. Try to use present and past wishes in your discussion.

In "When you're old, you'll **wish** you **had** more than memories of this tripe to look back on", the structure in bold…

a. ( ) expresses a regret or a desire for a situation in the past to be different.
b. ( ) indicates a wish for a situation in the present or future to be different.

5. Work in pairs. Think of possible answers for the question posed in activity 2 and complete the sentence:

I wish I hadn't seen _____

Extracted from https://licensing.andrewsmcmeel.com/features/ch?date=1991-05-05. Accessed on September 5, 2018.

LISTENING COMPREHENSION

1. Look at the picture and infer what *binge-watching* means. Then underline the best definition for the expression.
   a. to transfer or transmit (data) in such a way that it is processed in a steady and continuous stream
   b. to watch (multiple videos, episodes of a TV show, etc.) in one sitting or over a short period of time

   Extracted from www.dictionary.com. Accessed on September 5, 2018.

2. Listen to the first part of a news program that talks about the results of a research on binge-watching TV shows and complete the transcript below.

   Cancel your Netflix session: Binge watching TV makes it LESS enjoyable as you're more likely to forget plot details

   Binge watching television series like Game of Thrones could make it significantly less _____ than watching it on a weekly basis.

   New research found watching too much television in one go diminishes the _____ of the show with viewers getting 'significantly less' enjoyment than those who paced themselves.

   Research led by the University of Melbourne found how people watch television _____ affects how much enjoyment they get out of it.

   'Binge watching via video-on-demand services is now considered the new 'normal' way to consume television programs', _____, wrote in their paper in peer-reviewed journal First Monday.

   […]
   Researchers found that 'although binge watching leads to strong memory formation _____ following program viewing, these memories decay more _____ than memories formed after daily- or weekly-episode viewing schedules.'
   […]

   Extracted from www.dailymail.co.uk/sciencetech/article-4861672/Binge-watching-TV-makes-enjoyable-study-claims.html. Accessed on December 11, 2018.

3. Listen to the second part of the video and match the columns accordingly.
   a. A total of 51 students…
   b. Three groups of participants…
   c. None of the participants of this study…
   d. One of the tasks included…
   e. The results of the research showed that viewers…

   ( ) filling out a questionnaire with questions about the show.
   ( ) enjoyed the show more when they watched it only one hour a week.
   ( ) had watched the show before.
   ( ) watched *Cold War* for different periods of time.
   ( ) participated in the study.

4. How much TV watching is too much? Are viewing habits different for older and younger generations? In what ways might binge-watching harm your health? Exchange ideas with your classmates.

›› EXPAND YOUR HORIZONS ›››

Check (✓) the column that best describes your opinion about each statement. Then discuss your answers with your classmates and teacher, justifying your point of view.

	I agree.	I'm not sure.	I disagree.
a. Undoubtedly, everyone has dreamed of being a character in his/her favorite TV show.			
b. The old days when we needed to tune in live or buy expensive discs to watch our favorite shows and movies are gone. Streaming services are here to stay.			
c. Binge-watching has turned out to be a worldwide phenomenon, if not a disease.			

UNIT 6
Uncovering Blockchain and the Dark Web

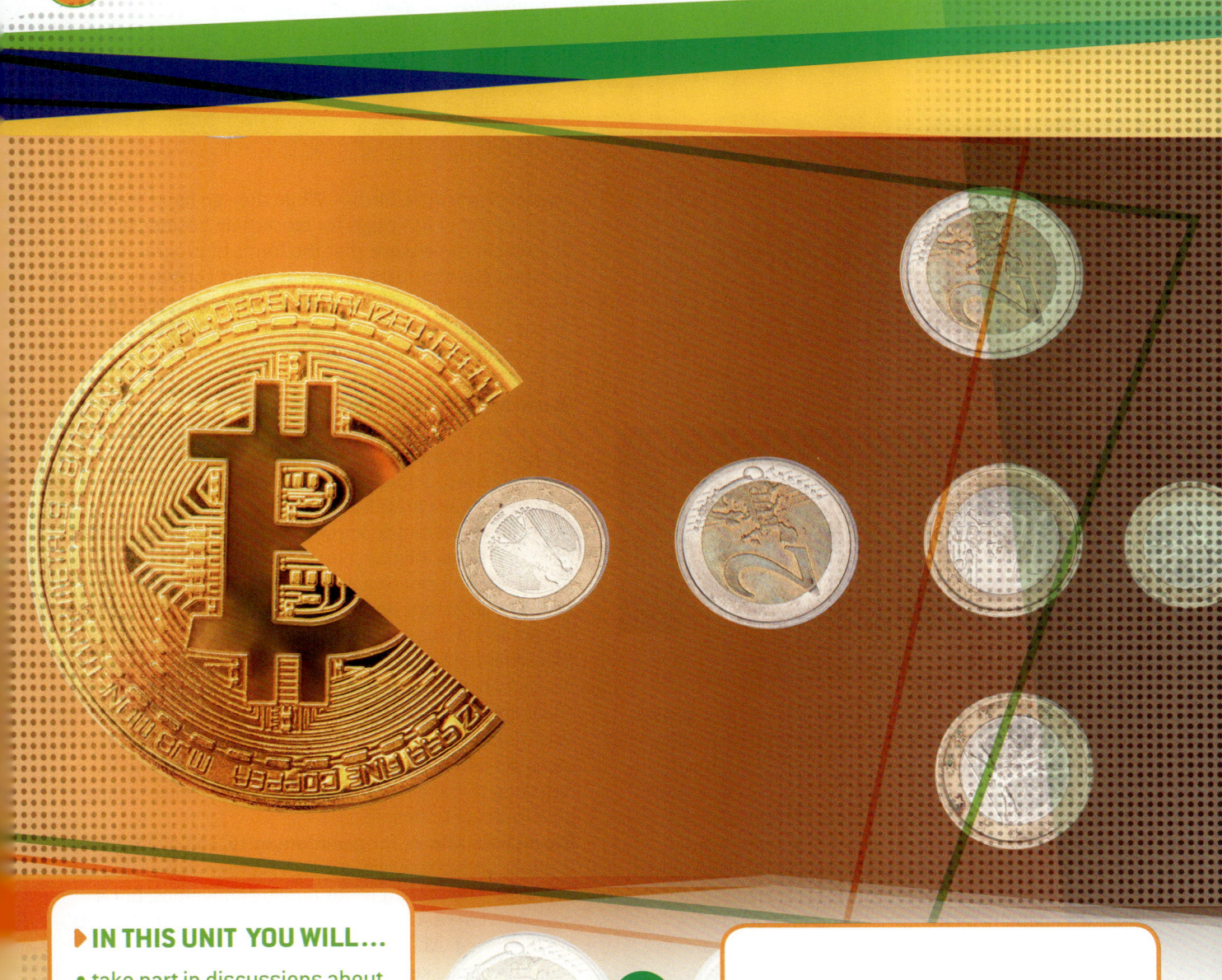

▶ IN THIS UNIT YOU WILL…

- take part in discussions about bitcoins and blockchain;
- talk about the dark web;
- identify and use the determiners *some*, *any*, *no*, and *every*;
- learn how to use direct and indirect speech.

LEAD OFF

- Are you familiar with the situation represented in the picture? What does it refer to?
- What do you know about digital currencies? What about blockchain?
- Have you heard of the Internet's evil twin? Share what you know with your classmates.

BEFORE READING — Identifying the source of the text

Scan the text you are about to read. What kind of publication was it extracted from?

WHILE READING — Identifying the author's tone

Read the text and classify the author's tone as *regretful*, *nostalgic*, *objective*, or *ironic*. Justify your answer.

---

www.forbes.com/sites/jamiemoy/2018/02/22/forget-bitcoin-its-all-about-the-blockchain/#3028c50b5f6b

20,092 views | Feb 22, 2018, 06:33am

Forget Bitcoin, It's All About The Blockchain

Jamie Moy

[…]

Illustration of the blockchain network.
PHOTO COURTESY OF GERD ALTMANN VIA PIXABAY.

Bitcoin gets headlines. I see them too. I admit it **grabs** attention, but the substance is blockchain technology. That's why it's critical to get familiar with blockchain technology. To do so, start here:

5 **Blockchain is a public distributed *ledger*.** Throughout most of history, we've been living in a centralized world. We have governments, financial institutions, big tech companies, and credit bureaus as "**trusted**" third parties enabling us to transact and interact. These
10 intermediaries control and have access to our money and data and are occasionally hacked. Blockchain technology allows for decentralization. It is essentially a **database** managed by a peer-to-peer *network* of computers. Blockchain facilitates the transfer and
15 payment of digital money without the need for a trusted entity, such as a bank. The data it holds is public and **immutable**.

Blockchain is not bitcoin. Bitcoin is digital money, a virtual currency that was the first successful blockchain
20 product. Blockchain is the technology that enables *cryptocurrency* like bitcoin. While they go hand-in-hand, there are other use cases for blockchain besides bitcoin. Blockchain can **ensure** that the terms of programmable autonomous contracts, known as smart contracts, are met.
25 It can be used for online voting to address voter **fraud**. It can be used to secure identity and many other situations where transparency and security is lacking.
[…]

Blockchain is secure and safe. Security is a big topic
30 and everyone should fully understand. Maybe you've heard about **hacks** of centralized **exchanges**. And you've probably heard about a person going "dumpster diving" to find an old hard drive because their private key was stored there. It's important to know that virtually all the **losses**
35 were due to hacking of centralized exchanges, losing private key information and gaining control of private keys by bad actors, and not some security vulnerability in Bitcoin technology.
Blockchains, like Bitcoin and Ethereum, have not yet been
40 hacked. They are considered to be very secure. It is very challenging, almost impossible, to change any *transaction* information once it is validated and becomes part of a block. Bitcoin is commonly referred to as digital gold. Referring to bitcoin as insecure or unsafe is like calling
45 gold insecure or unsafe.

Blockchain allows for pseudonymity. The blockchain is public where transactions are recorded and visible to everyone, therefore it is not purely anonymous. But it does provide pseudonymity. For example, digital wallets
50 are identified via the wallet's public address (aka public key). The public key is not connected to a person's other personal information such as name or address. This allows participants to transact privately and **reputably** with *data* remaining secure.
55 Blockchain technology has been referred to as the next revolution and although it's only in the early stages, it is here to stay.
[…]

Adapted from www.forbes.com/sites/jamiemoy/2018/02/22/forget-bitcoin-its-all-about-the-blockchain/#3028c50b5f6b. Accessed on September 8, 2018.

» AFTER READING

1. What's the author's purpose? Use your own words to state it and justify your answer. *Stating the author's purpose*

_____
_____
_____

2. Based on the information provided by the author, check (✔) the correct definition for *blockchain*. *Understanding the main idea*

a. (   ) It's a crypto-currency allowing for anonymous transactions and using a decentralized architecture.

b. (   ) It's a digitized, decentralized, and continuously growing public ledger that consists of records called blocks, which are linked and secured using cryptography.

Adapted from www.urbandictionary.com. Accessed on September 9, 2018.

3. Underline the true statements according to the text. *Understanding details*

a. Blockchain allows digital information to be distributed, but not copied.
b. Blockchain deals with cryptocurrency, contracts, or other data.
c. Since blockchain's transactions are visible to everybody, one's personal information such as name and address is made public.
d. Despite their popularity, bitcoins are proven to be unsafe.

EXPAND YOUR VOCABULARY

1. Read the text again, find the words in italics to fit each definition below, and use them to complete the infographic.

a. _____ : a book in which a business, bank etc. records how much money it receives and spends

b. _____ : a business deal or action, such as buying or selling something

c. _____ : a set of computers that are connected to each other so that they can share information

d. _____ : digital system or type of money

e. _____ : information in a form that can be stored and used, especially on a computer

Adapted from www.ldoceonline.com. Accessed on September 9, 2018.

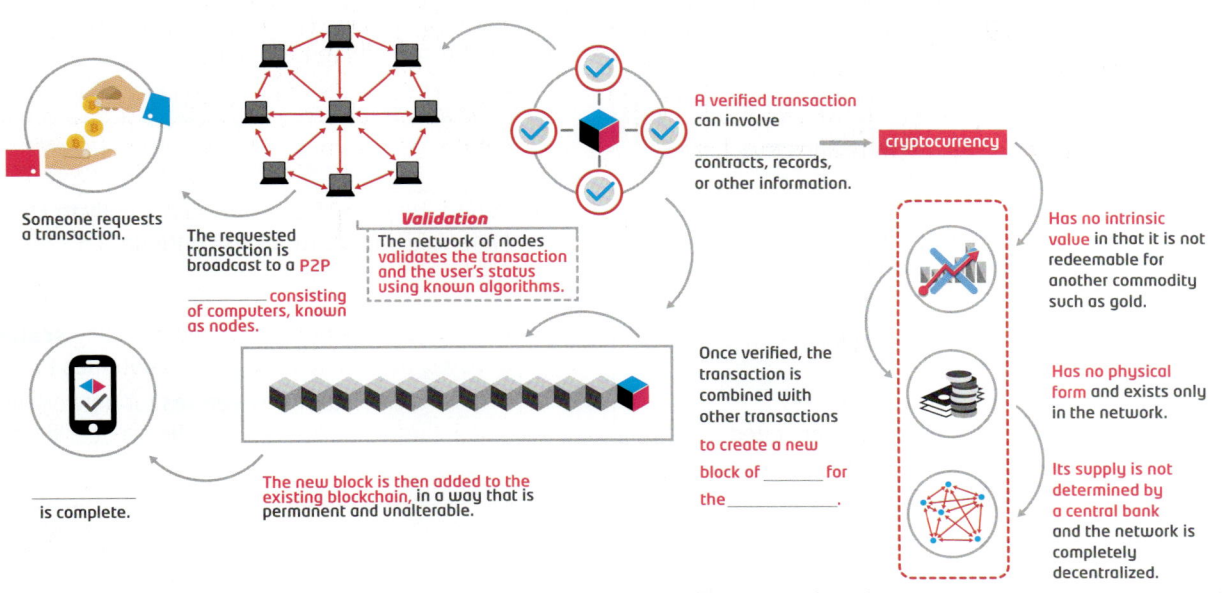

Someone requests a transaction.

The requested transaction is broadcast to a P2P _____ consisting of computers, known as nodes.

Validation
The network of nodes validates the transaction and the user's status using known algorithms.

A verified transaction can involve contracts, records, or other information. → **cryptocurrency**

Once verified, the transaction is combined with other transactions to create a new block of _____ for the _____.

The new block is then added to the existing blockchain, in a way that is permanent and unalterable.

_____ is complete.

Has no intrinsic value in that it is not redeemable for another commodity such as gold.

Has no physical form and exists only in the network.

Its supply is not determined by a central bank and the network is completely decentralized.

Adapted from https://blockgeeks.com/guides/what-is-blockchain-technology. Accessed on September 9, 2018.

2. Read the last paragraph of the text again and answer: Do you agree that blockchain technology is revolutionary? Why or why not?

_____
_____

VOCABULARY IN USE

1. Read an extract from the text on page 54 and check the alternative that explains the expression in bold.

   > And you've probably heard about a person going **'dumpster diving'** to find an old hard drive because their private key was stored there.

   a. ( ) the sport of jumping from a plane and falling through the sky before opening a parachute

   b. ( ) the activity of looking through a large metal container for clothes, food, furniture, etc. that other people have thrown away

   Adapted from www.ldoceonline.com. Accessed on September 9, 2018.

2. Like the Internet or your bike, for example, you don't need to know everything about blockchain technology to use it. However, having some knowledge of this new technology language is useful. Use the terms related to blockchain technology listed below to complete their descriptions.

block explorers	mining	node
private key	proof-of-stake	smart contracts

   a. _____ are computer protocols that facilitate, verify, or enforce the negotiation or performance of a contract, or that obviate the need for a contractual clause. [...]

   b. [...] _____ can serve as blockchain analysis and provide information such as total network hash rate, coin supply, transaction growth, etc.

   c. _____ (PoS) is a method by which a cryptocurrency blockchain network aims to achieve distributed consensus. [...]

   d. _____ is the process of adding transaction records to Bitcoin's public ledger of past transactions or blockchain. [...]

   e. Any computer that connects to the blockchain network is called a _____. [...]

   f. [...] The _____ is a randomly generated number which allows users to transact over the blockchain. It is locally stored and kept secret. [...]

   Extracted from https://blockchainhub.net/blockchain-glossary. Accessed on September 10, 2018.

3. The phrasal verbs below also have to do with business, finance, or economy matters. Match them with their corresponding meanings.

   a. bail out   b. buy out   c. rake in
   d. shell out   e. go under   f. take over

   ( ) to spend a lot of money on something, often when you do not really want to

   ( ) to take control of a company by buying more than 50% of its shares

   ( ) to provide money to get a person or organization out of financial trouble

   ( ) to earn a lot of money without trying very hard

   ( ) to stop operating because of financial problems

   ( ) to buy someone's share of a business or property that you previously owned together, so that you have complete control

   Adapted from www.ldoceonline.com/dictionary. Accessed on September 10, 2018.

4. Choose two phrasal verbs from activity 3 to complete the text fragments that follow.

   a. Missed out on the bitcoin boom? Try these virtual currencies instead

      [...]

      Several alternative currencies have also seen significant movement in the past year, rising anywhere from 600 to 37,000 percent. But before you buy, do your research.

      The first thing to remember is that you can buy a fractional piece of almost any cryptocoin for just a few bucks – no need to _____ thousands of dollars for a full bitcoin, for example.

      [...]

      Extracted from www.euronews.com/2018/01/03/missed-bitcoin-boom-check-out-these-five-rising-cryptocurrencies-n834436. Accessed on September 10, 2018.

   b. Report: Nearly $2.5 Billion Paid Annually to Ethereum Miners, ETH Issuance Woes Continue

      [...]

      Despite **waning** prices and never-ending **scalability** debates, the Ethereum protocol continues to _____ massive **revenues** for network miners, with figures confirming $2.5 billion-a-year payouts.

      [...]

      Extracted from https://cryptoslate.com/report-nearly-2-5-billion-paid-annually-to-ethereum-miners-eth-issuance-woes-continue. Accessed on September 10, 2018.

5. Will blockchain technology have a huge impact on society? Exchange ideas with a classmate, justifying your point of view. Then report the main insights of your discussion to the rest of the class.

LANGUAGE IN USE 1

Unit 6

SOME, ANY, NO, EVERY

1. The excerpts below were extracted from the text on page 54. Read them and check (✔) the correct alternative to complete the sentence that follows.

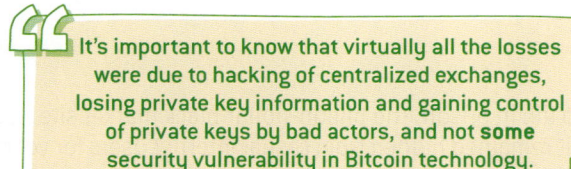

> It's important to know that virtually all the losses were due to hacking of centralized exchanges, losing private key information and gaining control of private keys by bad actors, and not **some** security vulnerability in Bitcoin technology.

> It is very challenging, almost impossible, to change **any** transaction information once it is validated and becomes part of a block.

We use *some* and *any* to
a. (　) talk about an indefinite quantity or number.
b. (　) ask questions about number or quantity.

2. Pay attention to the words in bold in the quotes below. Then use the words from the box to complete the statements.

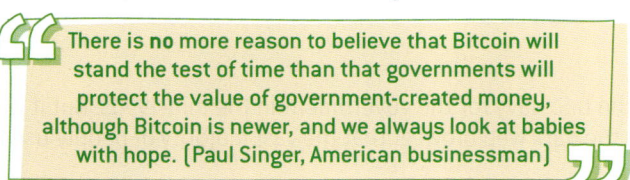

> There is **no** more reason to believe that Bitcoin will stand the test of time than that governments will protect the value of government-created money, although Bitcoin is newer, and we always look at babies with hope. (Paul Singer, American businessman)

Extracted from www.brainyquote.com/quotes/paul_singer_680170. Accessed on September 10, 2018.

> Assess Bitcoins? All you can do is examine the trading patterns, which do not provide a real analysis of **any** underlying economic value. The economics of investments are not solely based on supply and demand, and that is all that goes into Bitcoin prices. (Kurt Eichenwald, American editor)

Extracted from www.brainyquote.com/quotes/kurt_eichenwald_711317. Accessed on September 10, 2018.

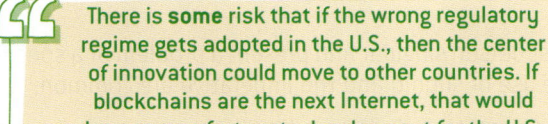

> There is **some** risk that if the wrong regulatory regime gets adopted in the U.S., then the center of innovation could move to other countries. If blockchains are the next Internet, that would be a very unfortunate development for the U.S. (David O. Sacks, South African businessman)

Extracted from www.brainyquote.com/quotes/david_o_sacks_851308. Accessed on September 10, 2018.

> Bitcoin was created with security in mind. The Blockchain is Bitcoin's public ledger that records **every** transaction in the Bitcoin economy. (Perianne Boring, American businesswoman)

Extracted from www.brainyquote.com/quotes/perianne_boring_850612. Accessed on September 10, 2018.

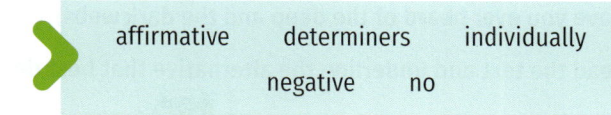

| affirmative | determiners | individually |
| negative | no | |

a. In these extracts, the words *no*, *any*, *some*, and *every* are _____. They are used to express quantities.

b. We use *some* in _____ sentences and in questions (often expecting a positive answer).

c. We use *any* in questions, _____ sentences, and to mean "it does not matter which or what".

d. We use *every* to refer _____ to all the members of a complete group and _____ to indicate *not any*. *Every* is always followed by a singular noun.

3. Choose the correct determiner in parentheses to complete the text below.

> _____ (Every / Some) things you need to know
>
> If you're getting started with Bitcoin, there are a few things you should know. Bitcoin lets you exchange money and transact in a different way than you normally do. As such, you should take time to inform yourself before using Bitcoin for _____ (any / no) serious transaction. Bitcoin should be treated with the same care as your regular wallet, or even more in _____ (any / some) cases!
> […]

Extracted from https://bitcoin.org/en/you-need-to-know. Accessed on September 10, 2018.

4. Complete the meme with a determiner. Then exchange ideas with a classmate about what you understand from the text.

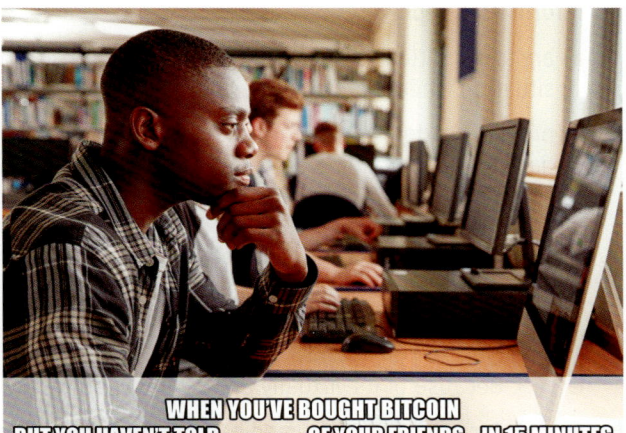

WHEN YOU'VE BOUGHT BITCOIN BUT YOU HAVEN'T TOLD _____ OF YOUR FRIENDS... IN 15 MINUTES

EXPAND YOUR READING

1. Have you ever heard of the deep and the dark webs? What are they? Exchange ideas with a classmate.
2. Read the text and underline the alternative that best describes its genre.

THE DARK WEB

MacKenzie Sigalos   Published 10:00 A.M. ET Sat, 14 April 2018
Updated 11:40 PM ET Sat, 14 April 2018

In 2015, the founder of a website called the Silk Road was sentenced to life in prison. The billion-dollar black market site was once the premiere online **bazaar** for drugs and other contraband, but it remained hidden from casual internet users for years because of something called the dark web.

Here's how that dark side of the Internet actually works.

Anatomy of the Internet

If you think of the web like an iceberg, you have the surface web up top. It's the Internet you see and use every day and consists of all the websites indexed by traditional search engines like Google. It's where you shop on Amazon and listen to music on Spotify.

What's submerged is the deep web – an anonymous online space only accessible with specific software. Then there's the dark web, which is the part of the deep web that hides your identity and location.

It's basically just "a series of encrypted networks that serve to **anonymize** peoples' use of the Internet," said Matthew Swensen, a Special Agent for the Department of Homeland Security with an expertise in cybercrimes.

[...]

Swensen said the most common dark web networks are Tor, I2P, and Freenet, but "Tor is, by far and away, the most popular."

Tor

Tor stands for "the onion routing project." It was developed by the U.S. Navy for the government in the mid-1990s. But it was open-sourced in 2004, and that's when it went public. Tor is now the dark web browser that the vast majority of people use to anonymously surf the Internet.

[...]

For some users – like journalists or **whistleblowers** – the dark web is about identity protection. It's where individuals can share anonymous tips with the press on secure drop sites. But more often than not, it's tied to the world of cybercrime. Special agents like Swensen are looking for the kinds of users who want this full cloak of anonymity in order to mask their illegal activity.

Putting a stop to this kind of crime has been described as a "never-ending game of whack-a-mole" for law enforcement. But even with the odds seemingly stacked against it, the anonymity of the dark web can sometimes play to the law's advantage. No ID and no location means you never really know who's communicating with you.

— CNBC's Ylan Mui and Karen James contributed to this report.

Adapted from www.cnbc.com/2018/04/13/the-dark-web-and-how-to-access-it.html. Accessed on September 10, 2018.

Information reports...

a) are texts written as requests for help. They are often written in the first person singular and present a problem or a specific situation. There are generally answers offering some advice and the use of should and the imperative are common.

b) provide readers with information on a chosen topic by presenting facts. They often give details about that topic and hardly ever contain personal views. These reports generally fall into three main categories: scientific, technological, and social studies.

3. Decide if the sentences are true (T) or false (F) according to the text.
   a. (   ) The dark web is part of the deep web.
   b. (   ) Being on the dark web makes it easier for someone to discover your true identity.
   c. (   ) Because of its virtually untraceable nature, the dark web is a center for criminal activity.
   d. (   ) Tor is a paid social media app that enables communication among peers on the Internet.

LANGUAGE IN USE 2

Unit 6

DIRECT AND INDIRECT SPEECH

1. Read these extracts from the text on page 58 and answer the questions.

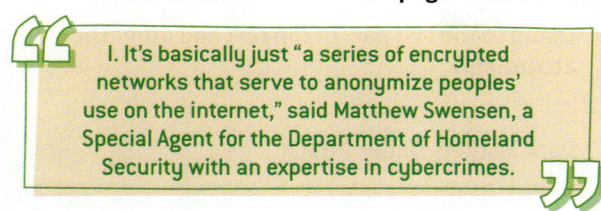

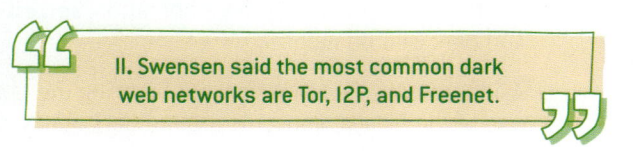

> I. It's basically just "a series of encrypted networks that serve to anonymize peoples' use on the internet," said Matthew Swensen, a Special Agent for the Department of Homeland Security with an expertise in cybercrimes.

> II. Swensen said the most common dark web networks are Tor, I2P, and Freenet.

a. Which extract contains Swensen's own words?
_____

b. Which extract reports what Swensen said?
_____

c. Which punctuation is used to indicate Swensen's exact words?
_____

d. Which verb is used to indicate Swensen's words?
_____

2. Based on the extracts and on your answers in activity 1, complete the statements with the words *direct* or *indirect*.

a. In _____ (or reported) speech, we report what the speaker says, but we don't use his/her exact words.

b. In _____ speech, we quote the speaker's exact words and use quotation marks.

3. Read the text carefully. Then look at the sentences extracted from it and complete the indirect speech sentences. Write two words in each blank.

> When a scam is targeted at a person it can be carried out via email, over the phone, via text, in person or without he or she knowing anything about it until something suspicious shows up on a statement or credit report.
> Married IT security consultant Tom Chantler […] discovered in May that contracts for top-end mobile phones had been taken out in his name.
> Tom says: "When I phoned the bank to ask if the account details matched one in my name, it became clear they were somebody else's. I am very careful with my personal information and always shred sensitive documents."
> […]
> He adds: "This can happen to anybody, even if they haven't done anything wrong."

Adapted from www.thisismoney.co.uk/money/bills/article-3287561/I-m-careful-phone-contracts-signed-cyber-attacks-sophisticated-look-protect-DARK-WEB.html. Accessed on April 5, 2019.

a. "I am very careful with my personal information."

Tom said that _____ very careful _____ personal information.

b. "This can happen to anybody, even if they haven't done anything wrong."

Tom explained _____ happen to anybody, even if they _____ anything wrong.

4. Work in pairs. Based on the previous activities, use the words or expressions from the box to complete the statements about direct and indirect speech.

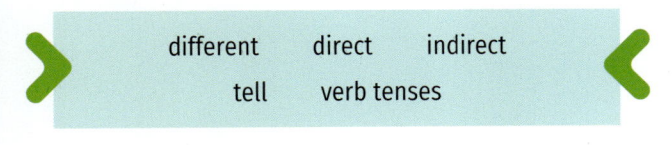

> different   direct   indirect
> tell   verb tenses

a. To report a person's words, we can use _____ or indirect speech.

b. In direct speech, a speaker's exact words are used. However, in indirect speech, the _____, pronouns, as well as place and time expressions may be _____ from those in the original sentence.

c. If we are reporting something that is a general truth, we keep the simple present in _____ speech.

d. Common reporting verbs are: *say*, _____, *ask*, *answer*, *warn*, *announce*, *add*, *argue*, and *urge*, among others.

LISTENING COMPREHENSION

1. **You are going to listen to a text entitled *The Illicit World of Bitcoin and the Dark Web*. What comes to your mind when you read the title? How might bitcoins be related to the dark web? Exchange ideas in pairs.**

2. **Listen to the first part of the text and answer the questions.**

   🎧 12

   a. Is Silk Road a digital currency or a dark market?

   _____

   b. Are dark markets inevitably illegal?

   _____

   c. Why do dark markets accept bitcoins as a method of payment?

   _____

   d. What kinds of products do most dark markets allow vendors to sell?

   _____

3. **Listen to the second part of the text and decide if the sentences below are true (T) or false (F).**

   🎧 13

   a. ( ) Created by Ross Ulbricht, Silk Road was a digital marketplace that connected vendors of illegal drugs with potential buyers.

   b. ( ) Customers buying drugs from vendors who listed on Silk Road would send their funds to Silk Road through bank deposits.

   c. ( ) Because Silk Road ran on Tor, it was an unprotected marketplace.

   d. ( ) The FBI arrested Ulbricht but many more dark markets have sprung up.

4. **Listen to the last part of the text and order the sentences accordingly.**

   🎧 14

   [...]

   Dark Markets Under Attack

   ( ) In November 2014, Operation Onymous, an international law enforcement operation, **seized** over 400 dark web domains.

   ( ) Aside from the fact that they are breaking the law, one of the biggest concerns around dark markets is trustworthiness.

   ( ) Law enforcement is also getting better at targeting these dark markets and taking them down.

   ( ) Dark markets including CannabisRoad, Blue Sky, and Hydra have been taken down.

   ( ) Law enforcement says that it has found a way to target sites using Tor, although it has refused to reveal how.

   ( ) In several cases, dark markets have suddenly vanished with millions of dollars in escrow funds, leaving customers robbed of their funds.

   ( ) Dark markets continue to operate, and law enforcement continues to take them down in a continuous game of cat and mouse.

   Adapted from www.thebalance.com/what-is-a-dark-market-391289.
   Accessed on September 11, 2018.

›› EXPAND YOUR HORIZONS ›››

Check (✓) the column that best describes your opinion about each statement. Then discuss your answers with your classmates and teacher, justifying your point of view.

	I agree.	I'm not sure.	I disagree.
a. Bitcoin has turned out to be a lot more than just digital money because it tackles issues related to equality, access, and a more open framework for our society.			
b. Changing our passwords frequently and not using the same password on every site is enough for one to be protected against the dangers of the dark web.			
c. Although some products for sale on dark markets are legal, the offer of illicit goods such as drugs, stolen information, and weapons turns people who get involved with those dark websites into potential criminals.			

REVIEW 3

Units 5 and 6

1. Read the title of the following text. Who is its target audience? *Identifying the target audience*

2. Now read the whole text and answer: What is its main purpose? *Identifying the main purpose of a text*

Why binge-watching might actually be good for you

By Jim Medina, UC Santa Barbara

Tuesday, May 30, 2017

Joe Smith (not his real name) cheated on his wife. Up late one night alone, he watched half a season of "Game of Thrones" without her. Not cool, Joe.

Turns out Joe is not alone, though. In a recent Netflix survey, 46 percent of all respondents admitted to such infidelity. Worse, 81 percent admitted to being repeat offenders, and 45 percent never confess their betrayal at all.

[…]

Relationship issues aside, what benefits, if any, does binge-watching offer? Is it really just a waste of valuable time? According to UC Santa Barbara communication professor Robin Nabi, people are fascinated by a drama-filled series – from "Orange Is the New Black" to "Downtown Abbey" – and use them to escape daily stresses through what she described as "narrative transportation," in which they engage in a story world that seems "real."

"Typically, these shows are far more dramatic than our daily lives and the combination of the **plot**, the acting, and the music – all that combines to create this very strong emotional experience," said Nabi, whose research focuses on the interplay between emotion and the effects of mediated messages. "And emotional experiences keep our attention and we engage with them. We think about them. We talk about them. And then we look forward to having those emotions again."

[…]

Though research has been conducted on the value of media consumption, Nabi disagrees with critics who argue that TV watching is a waste of time. "They say you're ignoring your spouse, you're ignoring your work, and you're staying up too late, not getting enough sleep – and there's some truth to that," she said. "But another way of looking at this is there are times you just really need to do something for yourself to calm down."

For example, Nabi's media research with breast cancer survivors showed that people can watch TV to block out their concerns – from talking about illness, from engaging with others – and just be someplace where they're not dealing with that major stressor. "It can be very functional," she said, adding that people rely on TV for a range of psychological needs: **surveillance** (to be informed about what's happening in our environment), social connection, and diversion.

[…]

Adapted from www.universityofcalifornia.edu/news/binge-watching-healthy-diversion-or-waste-time. Accessed on September 12, 2018.

---

3. Underline the correct statements about the text. *Understanding details*

   a. In a recent survey, more than half of all respondents said that they cheated on their partners by watching TV series episodes without them.

   b. Nabi disagrees entirely with critics who say that TV watching is a waste of time.

   c. Nabi's media research showed that binge-watching can be beneficial for people who need to block out things that are worrying them.

   d. Binge-watchers are captivated by the drama in some TV series and tend to use them as a way out of the stress from their routine.

4. Work in pairs. Can you name other benefits to binge-watching?

5. Refer to the text again and find a sentence that shows both direct and indirect speech.

6. Read these comic strips and complete the sentences about them. Pay attention to the parts in bold.

Grand Avenue – November 10, 2015

Extracted from https://assets.amuniversal.com/28fe05c063f00133182a005056a9545dw. Accessed on September 12, 2018.

If Grandma **hadn't told** Michael to always finish what he starts, _____
_____.

Grand Avenue – November 13, 2015

Extracted from https://assets.amuniversal.com/2cdb9b4063f00133182a005056a9545dw. Accessed on September 12, 2018.

Grandma **wishes** technology _____.

7. Check (✓) the correct alternative to complete the text.

> [...]
> Google uses different methods to find new webpages. Among them are following links from known webpages to new ones, checking sitemaps, or receiving tips from one of our best web hosting providers about a new webpage.
>
> **Indexing content on the web**
>
> When a page is found, Google decides what it's about through indexing. This process includes studying and categorizing _____ the content, images, and video embedded on the webpage. The goal is to guess the intended topic so that a search for how to knit a llama sweater doesn't yield _____ webpages on how to make a pig fly.
>
> Google knows that it will stay the world's most popular search engine only by getting this stuff right, so it's sort of a big deal. After indexing, _____ webpage lands in the Google Index, which is a massive database stored across a huge computer network.
>
> [...]

Adapted from www.cloudwards.net/the-deep-web/. Accessed on April 7, 2019.

a. ( ) all / every / any   **b.** ( ) every / any / all   **c.** ( ) all / any / every

62

UNIT 7
Digital Influencing

▶ IN THIS UNIT YOU WILL...
- talk about digital influencers;
- discuss issues related to influencer marketing;
- use the modal verbs *must* and *can* for assumptions;
- use the passive voice.

LEAD OFF

- What does the picture represent?
- Have you ever heard the expression *influencer marketing*? What do you think it means?
- In your opinion, what are some of the characteristics of an online influencer?

READING

▶▶ BEFORE READING

Look at the picture that accompanies the text and read the two first paragraphs. What do you think it is about? Read the first paragraph and check your answer.

Predicting the topic of the text

▶▶ WHILE READING

Read the whole text and check (✓) the best title for it.   *Selecting a good title*

a. (   ) The YouTube Phenomenon: a disruptive force

b. (   ) Under the Influence: The Power of Social Media Influencers

In the darkly comical Ingrid Goes West, a small-budget **indie-flick** that flew under the radar of many moviegoers last year, a young woman by the name of Ingrid becomes **morbidly** obsessed by Instagram-
5 famous blogger Taylor.
Ingrid becomes **infatuated** by Taylor's seemingly perfect life and starts **mimicking** her every move. Taylor posts a picture of her breakfast at her favorite **bagel** place, Ingrid stops by for lunch the same day. Taylor
10 quotes a passage from her favorite book, Ingrid orders it online right away.
While the events depicted in the film might be a little over-exaggerated for cinematic purposes, they are, in fact, closer to reality than you might think.
15 Promoting products via social media influencers can be categorized as a form of subconscious marketing. For ages, brands and advertisers have been seeking to shape consumers' thoughts, attitudes, and behavior, without us even being aware of it. […]
20 **Why are social media influencers so influential?**
[…]
Credibility and social proof
[…]
According to French and Raven's (1960) **framework**
25 of power bases, one of the key elements to perceived power lies in expertise. A blogger that focuses on one particular subject, let's say cooking, will be perceived to have more authority when it comes to a particular brand of food (as opposed to a technology or sport blogger).
30 This authoritative position is further strengthened by a game of **sheer** numbers: a large number of followers, shares, and likes will provide viewers with a form of social proof. The notion that others value the opinion of an influencer, and adhere to their
35 judgments, assures viewers that doing so is okay. If the majority is doing something, they must be right.
Attractiveness
[…]
As humans are susceptible to attractiveness **bias**, we
40 subconsciously attribute attractive or charismatic people with many other qualities simply because they are good looking. Furthermore, this could lead to positive associations between the person and the brand as well. These opinions influence the
45 subconscious of the viewer, potentially priming them when faced with a product-related decision.
Relatability and the millennial crowd
But, what really sets social media influencers apart from other types of **endorsers** is their relatability.
50 Despite having a large popularity and internet following, influencers are still perceived as mostly normal, down-to-earth people.
[…]
More importantly, most influencers belong to the
55 younger age group of millennials, a demographic that is **notoriously** difficult to reach for marketers. They're a group that places strong value on forming their own identity, one of the most important parts of growing up. To do so, teens often look up to role models to
60 shape their own behavior. Having a role model that is relatable and easy to identify with makes it all the more likely that teens will copy their behavior.
[…]

Extracted from https://medium.com/crobox/under-the-influence-the-power-of-social-media-influencers-5192571083c3. Accessed on September 18, 2018.

64

>> AFTER READING

1. Read the text again. Underline the correct endings to the phrase below.

Understanding main ideas

The author of the text states that...

a. consumers' thoughts, attitudes, and behavior have been modeled by brands and advertisers without our conscious acknowledgement.

b. when teens have a role model with whom they identify, it makes them more inclined to imitate that behavior.

c. the credibility of a peer depends only on expertise and attractiveness.

2. What makes social media influencers so attractive for brands? Read the fragments and write *1* for credibility and social proof, *2* for attractiveness, and *3* for relatability and the millennial crowd.

Understanding details

a. ( ) "[...] This is a strategy that marketers have already been using for ages—I'm sure you can think of numerous examples of advertisements featuring some handsome Hollywood actor recommending a certain luxury product. [...]"

b. ( ) "[...] They post about their everyday life, stay connected with their followers, and are able to interact directly with them. Plus, they often share the same age group, demographics, interests, and behaviors of their target audience. [...]"

c. ( ) "[...] Studies have shown that the credibility of a peer endorser depends on the factors of **trustworthiness**, expertise, attractiveness, and similarity. Taking the first two into account, we can note that the degree of influence a person possesses depends on his degree of perceived power. [...]"

Extracted from https://medium.com/crobox/under-the-influence-the-power-of-social-media-influencers-5192571083c3. Accessed on September 18, 2018.

3. Work in small groups. Reread the questions in activity 2: What other reasons would you add to the ones listed?

_____

_____

EXPAND YOUR VOCABULARY

1. Scan the text on page 64 for the words or expressions from the box and infer their meanings. Then insert them in the text fragments that follow.

| brand | expertise | followers |
| marketing | relatability | social proof |

a. "[...] Social media influencers are people who have large audiences of _____ on their social media accounts, and they **leverage** this to influence or persuade this following to buy certain products or services. [...]

Perhaps the most interesting aspect of this relatively new concept is that social media influencers do not necessarily have to be well-known celebrities or famous athletes. Instead, ordinary people have risen up the ranks of social media to **amass** hundreds, thousands, or even millions of followers due to their charisma, business **savvy**, and _____ on a given subject.. [...]"

Adapted from www.forbes.com/sites/forbesagencycouncil/2018/08/21/are-social-media-influencers-worth-the-investment/#3dded9e8f452. Accessed on September 18, 2018.

b. "[...] One of the other important factors in influencer _____ is relatability. Even the most **sleek** and sophisticated social media personality will resonate better with their audience than a page-turning celeb. Micro-influencers and mid-range targets work well because they **max out** that _____ factor, offering a 'real-people' vibe. This shows your audience that, yes, this product is something that they can look fantastic in; it isn't just for elite 'fashion model' types. [...]"

Extracted from https://jobs.sacbee.com/article/how-influencer-marketing-can-bolster-your-fashion-brand/7447. Accessed on September 18, 2018.

c. "[...] Whether you're familiar with social proof or not, chances are it has influenced decisions—both big and small—throughout your life.

_____ makes people pause to check out a social media post because it's **buzzing** with high engagement numbers. It gets them to take a chance on an unknown _____ because of the good things others are saying about it. [...]"

Extracted from www.shopify.com/blog/social-proof. Accessed on September 18, 2018.

2. Some people say influencer marketing affects the way we feel toward a product or service. Do you believe that is true? How are you and your friends affected by influencer marketing? Exchange ideas with a partner.

VOCABULARY IN USE

1. Reread these excerpts from the texts on pages 64 and 65, paying attention to the words in bold, and answer the questions.

   > "In the darkly comical Ingrid Goes West, a small-budget indie-flick that flew under the radar of many moviegoers last year, a young woman by the name of Ingrid becomes morbidly **obsessed** by Instagram-famous blogger Taylor."

   > "Perhaps the most **interesting** aspect of this relatively new concept is that social media influencers do not necessarily have to be well-known celebrities or famous athletes."

   a. Which adjective in bold describes an emotion, how someone feels?

   _____

   b. Which adjective in bold describes a situation or what causes an emotion?

   _____

   Adjectives ending in -ed, such as *bored*, describe how someone feels, while adjectives ending in -ing, such as *boring*, describe a situation that leads to a feeling. Therefore, if something is boring, it causes someone to feel bored.

2. Many adjectives end in *-ed* and *-ing* in English, and these are often based on verbs. Complete the chart below accordingly.

Verbs	-ed adjectives	-ing adjectives
annoy		
challenge		
confuse		
disappoint		
entertain		
exhaust		
frighten		
inspire		
interest		
relax		
satisfy		
shock		
tire		
touch		
worry		

3. Discuss the comic strip below in pairs. Then write sentences about it using at least two adjectives from each column in activity 2.

   Extracted from www.gocomics.com/thatababy/2018/11/09. Accessed on January 8, 2019.

4. Work in pairs. List characteristics you think good digital influencers have. Then report your ideas to the class.

LANGUAGE IN USE 1

Unit 7

MODAL VERBS FOR ASSUMPTION: *MUST* AND *CAN*

1. Read an excerpt from the text on page 64 and check (✔) the correct alternative to complete the sentence that follows.

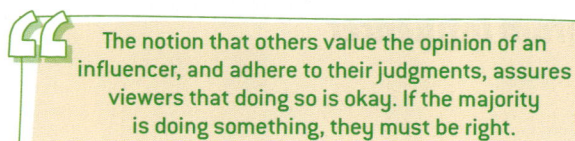

> The notion that others value the opinion of an influencer, and adhere to their judgments, assures viewers that doing so is okay. If the majority is doing something, they must be right.

In "they <u>must</u> be right", the underlined modal verb indicates...

a. ( ) an obligation.
b. ( ) an assumption.

2. Now read the title of a text and check (✔) the correct alternative to complete the sentence that follows.

16 People on Social Media Who Can't Be Serious
Katya Heckendorn
[...]

Extracted from https://diply.com/article/facepalm-social-media?config=101. Accessed on September 19, 2018.

We can infer from the structure in italics that the author believes...

a. ( ) those 16 people are probably satirizing or joking.
b. ( ) those 16 people are obviously acting reasonably.

3. Use the words from the box to complete the paragraph below.

| inferences | must | permissions |

The modal verb _____ doesn't necessarily express obligations, as the modal verb *can* might convey other meanings besides abilities, _____, or requests, for example. Both verbs also express assumptions, _____, possibilities, or certainties.

4. Based on the text below, use the modal verbs *must* and *can* to come up with 2 assumptions about influencer marketing.

> **7 Predictions On The Future Of Influencer Marketing**
> [...]
> **1. Status diversity.** Today, if you want to get in touch with an influencer and have them advocate for your brand, most companies start targeting people with 100,000 followers or more. They gravitate toward the biggest names in the industry, and understandably so; the more powerful an influencer is, the more valuable their advocacy will be. [...]
>
> **2. Influencer cliques and groups.** The nature of influencer marketing is interesting; if you're associated with an existing influencer, your reputation and authority will grow by **proxy**. It's a collective "**rising tide**" that affects all personal brands revolving around that influential center. [...]
>
> **3. Greater demand for authenticity.** The entire field of content marketing evolved from a consumer demand for authenticity. [...]
>
> **4. Bigger barriers to entry.** [...] Marketers everywhere are flocking to influencer marketing in **droves**, and accordingly, more individual personal brands are striving to become influencers in their own right. This is leading to a surge in content production and social media activity, which will make competition much **fiercer** if you want to earn your place as an expert in your field.
>
> **5. Transparency and regulatory crackdowns.** In April of 2017, the FTC sent out several letters and an official warning for influencers and brands to clearly **disclose** their relationships. [...]
>
> **6. Integrated functionality in platforms.** With platforms like Facebook, Twitter, LinkedIn, and Instagram noticing the importance (and potential) of influencer marketing, we may start to see platform-based innovations that make influencer marketing and outreach more convenient (or more profitable). [...]
>
> **7. Qualitative assessment tools.** Soon, it won't be enough to have a large quantity of followers on your account; marketers will also be looking to see how you engage with your followers, and what types of followers you have. [...]

Adapted from www.forbes.com/sites/jaysondemers/2018/04/19/7-predictions-on-the-future-of-influencer-marketing/#b4742d6581df. Accessed on September 19, 2018.

_____
_____
_____
_____

5. From your point of view, can brands survive without influencer marketing? Share your opinions with a classmate. Use *must* and *can* for assumptions in your argumentation.

EXPAND YOUR READING

1. Skim the text to find out its genre.
   a. ( ) a survey report
   b. ( ) a testimonial
   c. ( ) a guide
   d. ( ) an essay

How to make it as an Instagram influencer

From boosting your following to acing the **lingo**

The first influencer species evolved from the millennial. They were discovered around seven years ago on YouTube, where they spent their days vlogging about their pets and how many avocados they ate for lunch. They then briefly migrated to Twitter and Facebook, where they were bored and did nothing, before settling in their millions on the glossy plains of Instagram, where they now post selfies wearing **athleisure** and drinking **turmeric** lattes in an attempt to **lure** their primary source of sustenance: followers. Between followers, the influencer snacks on good lighting, symmetry and **modishly shabby** Shoreditch rooftops. The influencer's special treat is a juicy "paid-for-partnership".
[…]
So, who is part of this new breed? What do they want? How do they live? And, more importantly, what exactly is their game? Welcome to GQ's guide to influencers, where we put this strange creature under the microscope…

[…]
How to talk Influencer
[…]
Know your hashtags
[…]
Anatomy of a post
[…]
Three things you should never say as an influencer
[…]
How to buy friends and influence people
[…]
How to spot a bot buyer in three easy steps
[…]
Finally: know the law
Become an LAI: Law **Abiding** Influencer
[…]
1. Get your facts straight
"If promoting health products, it must be an authorized **claim**."
2. And the hashtag right
"Ads must be identifiable and therefore must be labelled with #Ad or Ad. #Sp or #Spon [sponsored] are unacceptable."
3. But don't be sneaky
"The word 'ad' must be one of the first words in the comment section. It cannot be lost under the 'view more' tab."
[…]

Adapted from www.gq-magazine.co.uk/article/how-to-be-an-instagram-influencer. Accessed on September 20, 2018.

2. What is the purpose of the text?
   _____
   _____

3. Underline the best definition for guides.
   a. They are short pieces that give brief instructions without detailing the steps to do something.
   b. They are testimonials of people who have done something and want to tell others how they did it.
   c. They are pieces of writing that provide information on a particular subject or explain how to do something.

Adapted from www.ldoceonline.com. Accessed on September 19, 2018.

LANGUAGE IN USE 2

Unit 7

PASSIVE VOICE II

1. Read the following extracts from the texts on pages 68 and 64, circle the verb forms, and write AV for active voice or PV for passive voice.

> Ads [...] must be labelled with #Ad or Ad. (   )

> Three things you should never say as an influencer. (   )

> Promoting products via social media influencers can be categorized as a form of subconscious marketing. (   )

> For ages, brands, and advertisers have been seeking to shape consumers' thoughts, attitudes, and behavior, without us even being aware of it. (   )

2. Now read a short fragment from a text entitled "Influencer Marketing Guide: How To Find And Verify Influencers For Your Next Campaign", paying attention to the part in bold. Then use the words from the box to complete the rules about the passive voice.

> When managed correctly, it [influencer marketing] can deliver wonders – A recent Collective Bias study proved that 60% of consumers **had been influenced** by a social media post or a blog review while shopping offline. It naturally has an enormous impact on purchasing online as well.

Adapted from https://wersm.com/influencer-marketing-guide-how-to-find-and-verify-influencers-for-your-next-campaign. Accessed on September 19, 2018.

| action | be | by | past participle | who |

a. We use the passive voice when we want to focus on the _____ rather than on _____ or what causes that action, or when it's not really important to mention the doer of that action.

b. To form the passive voice, we use the auxiliary verb _____ and the main verb in the _____.

c. In the passive voice, to indicate who or what is responsible for the action, we use the particle _____ before the doer of that action.

3. Choose the appropriate verb form in parentheses to complete the first two paragraphs of this text.

Will fake social media followers derail the booming influencer marketing business?

August 22, 2018 by Christine Regan Davi, Northeastern University

Celebrities, social media stars, and other online personalities have taken a hit to their credibility in recent months, as millions of their followers _____ (have exposed / have been exposed) as fake or bought. This _____ (has created / has been created) a bigger problem for advertisers and consumers, who no longer can trust in high follower numbers as a measure of influence and credibility. Now, a machine-learning algorithm developed by Northeastern graduates is giving marketers a way to keep their advertising real—and rebuild consumer trust. Brands have always sought celebrity endorsements, but the mass adoption of social media _____ (has given / has been given) rise to a new kind of endorser: the influencer, an online personality with a large number of followers. [...]

Extracted from https://phys.org/news/2018-08-fake-social-media-derail-booming.html. Accessed on September 19, 2018.

4. Answer the question posed in the title of the text in activity 3. Use one passive structure in your answer. Then share your opinion with a partner.

_____
_____
_____
_____
_____
_____
_____
_____
_____
_____

LISTENING COMPREHENSION

1. **What makes someone an influencer? What types of online influencers have you heard of? Look at the picture and debate in small groups.**

2. **Listen to Dan Knowlton, from the agency KPS Digital Marketing, in Kent, England, and check (✓) the alternative that indicates what he's going to talk about.**
   - a. ( ) generating more leads and sales
   - b. ( ) real influencers and fake influencers
   - c. ( ) drone video businesses

3. **Listen to the whole recording, read the sentences below, and underline the one that is incorrect.**
   - a. Dan Knowlton has been featured as an influencer.
   - b. It's common to find lists of influencers on credible articles.
   - c. There is always certified data to back up the identification of influencers and their naming on lists.
   - d. When you see a list of influencers, question the methodology behind how the influencers were identified.

4. **What was Dan's main purpose in recording the video?**
   _____
   _____
   _____
   _____

5. **Should we really question those lists or are they perfect? Is it important to be a critical consumer of information derived from all sources? Why (not)? Exchange ideas with a classmate and then report your views to the class.**
   _____
   _____
   _____

» EXPAND YOUR HORIZONS »

Check (✓) the column that best describes your opinion about each statement. Then discuss your answers with your classmates and teacher, justifying your point of view.

	I agree.	I'm not sure.	I disagree.
a. Digital influencers make my world go round. I dedicate a good part of my time to consuming media content on digital platforms such as YouTube, Twitter, and Instagram.			
b. Influencer marketing is not going to disappear. It has evolved quickly and keeps up with changeable demands and rules of the existing and future social media platforms.			
c. A lot of people can be fooled by fake influencers and their messages; that's one of the reasons why it's important to be a critical information consumer.			

UNIT 8
The End of a Journey

▶ IN THIS UNIT YOU WILL...

- take part in discussions about career preparation;
- exchange ideas about high school graduates' expectations;
- learn how to use the future continuous and the future perfect;
- review verb tenses.

LEAD OFF

> Which situation is represented in the picture?
> What are the causes and consequences of the so-called mismatch between education and occupation?
> Are you aware of your own skills and experiences? How ready are you to face the challenges that will come when high school ends?

READING

›› BEFORE READING — Discussion and Brainstorming

Work in pairs. Look at the picture that accompanies the text, read its caption, and share your opinions about it. Then list ideas to answer the question posed in the title of the text.

›› WHILE READING — Recognizing textual types

Read the whole text. Is it a technical, procedural, or expository writing? Justify your answer.

Too many graduates are mismatched to their jobs. What's going wrong?

Students often aren't aware of their own skills and experience, or what different jobs require. They need more meaningful careers advice.

Advice about the art of interview preparation and how to **craft** the perfect CV isn't enough to put every student on a **path** to a career they want. About one in three graduates
5 end up being "mismatched" to the jobs they find after leaving college, research by Universities UK suggests. These mismatched graduates face poorer prospects and lower earnings than their peers who embark on careers
10 that are a better fit for the knowledge and skills they have acquired through three or four years of study. It suggests that traditional careers advice isn't working.

Are students taking the wrong courses?
The problem isn't necessarily that too many students are taking the wrong course. There is little evidence that
15 graduates are studying the "wrong" subjects, according to the U.K. research, since most are on courses that offer subject knowledge and employability skills that are very much **in demand**.
Instead, students need better careers advice that will help
20 them define their skills and attributes – and understand how these match different career options. Students also need help finding out which skills they'll need to break into certain industries – particularly in sectors that aren't good at diversifying their recruitment, or when they have no family
25 or social network of contacts to call on for help and advice. Politicians complain of a skills **gap**, but graduates face an "experience gap" – with many employers preferring to recruit young people who have spent a couple of years in the workplace rather than raw recruitments from college.
30 Yet graduates have often picked up at university many of the soft skills that employers are looking for in more experienced recruits – they just don't know it yet.

"Students need better careers advice to help them define their skills and attributes – and understand how these match different career options." Photograph: Alamy

How can universities help?
To help graduates find the right jobs for them, lots of
35 universities are experimenting with new ways to make their career advice more accessible and meaningful.
[…]
At Norwich University of the Arts, we are gamifying career support. We've developed a career card game called
40 Profile, which provides students with a deck of cards in which half describe skills and attributes, and the other half describe workplace scenarios which require different tactics to resolve them.
Students are asked to match skills cards to the scenarios
45 – and think about how that applies to them and the best approach to overcome practical problems. It makes them aware of the skills they already have, and the ones they'll need in the workplace.
[…]
50 We should measure our success as universities by the extent to which we help students develop their talents and skills to a point where they are able to access industries and careers that will be fulfilling. Enabling students to play a **winning hand** after graduation is time
55 and effort well spent.

Adapted from www.theguardian.com/higher-education-network/2018/jan/25/
too-many-graduates-are-mismatched-to-their-jobs-whats-going-wrong.
Accessed on September 24, 2018.

>> AFTER READING

1. How is the text (introduction, body, and conclusion) organized? `Understanding text structure`
   a. ( ) story – examples – cause
   b. ( ) issue – reasoning – course of action
   c. ( ) dilemma – deductions – motivation

2. Refer back to the text and underline the topic sentences in each chunk. `Understanding main ideas`

3. Decide if the sentences are true (T) or false (F) according to the text. `Understanding details`
   a. ( ) The author thinks that universities shouldn't interfere with the students' choices because they need to be made by the students themselves.
   b. ( ) Graduates who are matched incorrectly to their careers have lower incomes than those who make a well-adjusted choice.
   c. ( ) Graduates are unaware of their skills and assume that employers are looking for more experienced recruits.
   d. ( ) Most employers tend to hire young people who have just left university instead of recruiting those that have spent a couple of years in the workplace.

EXPAND YOUR VOCABULARY

1. Match the words in bold with their meanings.
   a. "Too many graduates are **mismatched** to their jobs."
   b. "These mismatched graduates face poorer prospects and lower **earnings** than their peers […]."
   c. "[…] with many employers preferring to recruit young people who have spent a couple of years in the workplace rather than **raw** recruitments from college."
   d. "[…] a point where they are able to access industries and careers that will be **fulfilling** […]."
   e. "**Enabling** students to play a winning hand after graduation is time and effort well spent […]."
   f. "At Norwich University of the Arts, we are **gamifying** career support."

   ( ) not experienced or not fully trained
   ( ) to combine things or people that do not work well together or are not suitable for each other
   ( ) making it possible for someone to do something, or for something to happen
   ( ) to design an activity such as learning, solving a problem, or being a customer so that it is like a game
   ( ) the money that you receive for the work that you do
   ( ) making you feel happy and satisfied because you are doing interesting, useful, or important things

   Adapted from www.ldoceonline.com/dictionary/mismatch. Accessed on September 24, 2018.

2. Besides the reasons mentioned in the text, what else might lead to the mismatch between graduates and their careers? Justify your views.
   _____
   _____
   _____

3. Work in pairs. How can you relate the word cloud below to the text on page 72? Discuss. Then share your opinions with your classmates.

   Word cloud: SKILLS, SATISFACTION, THINKING, LIFE, FUTURE, KEY, WORK, DREAMS, EXPECTATIONS, MAKE, IDENTIFY, NEED, CHALLENGE, ATTITUDE, CAREER, JOB, OPPORTUNITIES, THINGS

   _____
   _____
   _____

VOCABULARY IN USE

1. Pay attention to the subheading extracted from the text on page 72. Observe that the part in bold shows a collocation with the verb *take*. Check the correct meaning conveyed by that combination.

> Are students **taking** the wrong **courses**?

a. (   ) to do something that involves risks

b. (   ) to do a series of lessons in a particular subject

c. (   ) to do something to deal with a problem

Adapted from www.ldoceonline.com. Accessed on September 24, 2018.

2. Choose the correct words in parentheses to complete the paragraph.

The verb _____ (be / take), as well as the verbs *have*, *make*, *do*, and *set*, for example, can often be confusing in English because they are delexical verbs. These are common verbs which have _____ (little / much) meaning of their own if used with particular nouns. In these collocations, most of the meaning is found in the _____ (noun / verb), not in the _____ (noun / verb) itself.

3. Can you figure out new collocations with the verbs *take* and *have*? Complete the chart with the words from the box. Then use one collocation from each column to complete the texts. Make changes, if needed.

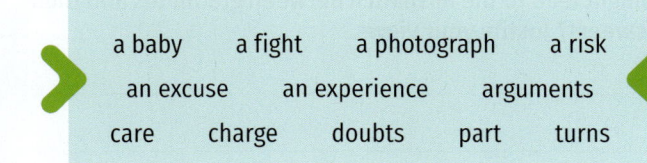

a baby	a fight	a photograph	a risk
an excuse	an experience	arguments	
care	charge	doubts	part	turns

Take	Have

a.
Survey reveals parental influence on students' career choices

The majority of students say their parents play a major role in their decision-making about careers and study, according to a report published last week. More than half (54%) of the students who _____ said that their parents tried to exert influence over their choice of course or career, while 69% said their parents had tried to influence their choice of university.

[...]

Extracted from https://targetjobs.co.uk/news/ 421008-survey-reveals-parental-influence-on-students-career-choices. Accessed on September 24, 2018.

b.
Doubting your career choice

It is not uncommon to _____ about your career choice at some point in your studies. We give some insight into how to overcome career doubts.

There can be a lot of excitement when starting a new qualification and taking your first class; however, after time it is not uncommon for feelings of doubt, restlessness, or uncertainty over your career choices to creep up.

[...]

Extracted from https://graduate.accaglobal.com/global/home/ maximise-your-employability/doubting-your-career-choice.html. Accessed on September 25, 2018.

4. Discuss the texts from activity 3 with a classmate. Try to use at least one collocation with *take* or *have* in your argumentation.

LANGUAGE IN USE 1

Unit 8

FUTURE CONTINUOUS AND FUTURE PERFECT

1. Based on the fragment from the text on page 72, underline what you can infer about students' search for fulfilling careers.

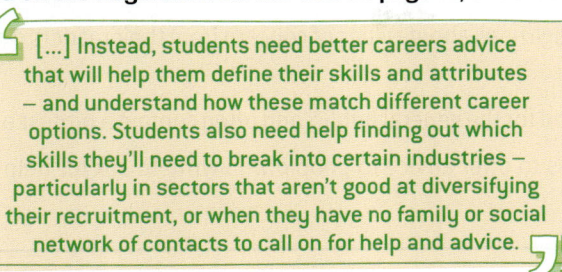

   > [...] Instead, students need better careers advice that will help them define their skills and attributes – and understand how these match different career options. Students also need help finding out which skills they'll need to break into certain industries – particularly in sectors that aren't good at diversifying their recruitment, or when they have no family or social network of contacts to call on for help and advice.

   a. Students will be able to define their abilities more effectively once they get better career advice.

   b. By the time students understand how their expertise matches distinct career alternatives, they will have already identified their skills and attributes.

   c. Students who don't have a short network of contacts won't need to search for help to enter some industries.

2. How do we form the future continuous and the future perfect in English? Underline their forms in the examples below and fill in the blanks accordingly.

Future continuous	Future perfect
Students will be defining their abilities more effectively once they get better career advice.	By the time students understand how their expertise matches distinct career alternatives, they will have found what it takes to get the right job.
will + _____ + main verb in the _____ form	will + _____ + main verb in the _____ form

3. Now reread the chart in activity 2 and complete the sentences about the usage of the future continuous and the future perfect tenses. Use the words from the box.

   > finished   progress   planned   time

   a. We use the future continuous to talk about something that will be in _____ at or around a time in the future and to talk about future actions that are already _____.

   b. We use the future perfect to talk about something that will be _____ or completed before a particular _____ in the future.

4. Read and complete the comic strips below. Use the verbs *drift* and *go* either in the future continuous or in the future perfect tense.

   Lucky Cow – June 22, 2005

   Extracted from https://licensing.andrewsmcmeel.com/features/luc?date=2005-06-22. Accessed on September 24, 2018.

   Grand Avenue for August 31, 2017

   Extracted from www.gocomics.com/grand-avenue/2017/08/31. Accessed on September 24, 2018.

5. Answer the questions with a classmate: What will you be doing one year after high school finishes? What goals will you have accomplished by then?

   _____
   _____
   _____
   _____
   _____
   _____
   _____
   _____
   _____

EXPAND YOUR READING

1. **Read the text and the genre descriptions that follow and write *A* if the description refers to advice letters, *E* if it refers to letters to the editor, or *O* if it refers to open letters.**

   a. (   ) They are sent to publications such as newspapers and magazines about issues of concern from their readers. They often rely on facts and opinions to try to persuade the reader.

   b. (   ) These are usually addressed to an individual, but intended for the general public, and often contain a protest or appeal.

   c. (   ) These letters are published in newspapers or magazines to offer advice to people who write to ask for help with a certain problem.

   ---

   www.theguardian.com/education/2011/jul/17/graduate-jobs-advice-experts

   ### "How do I deal with the post-university blues?"

   It's normal to feel low just after graduation. For some, it's because the energy they needed is still flowing but now it has no **outlet**, so they feel anxious. For others, it's because they've realized how much effort they've expended, and they feel exhausted. Whatever the reason, here are three tips to help you feel more positive again:

   1. Pay attention to the words you use. Graduation represents an ending, it's true – but it also represents new beginnings. It's more energizing to speak of new beginnings.
   2. The key here lies in the word "beginnings" as opposed to "beginning". Instead of saying, "I need to start my career," break the task ahead into smaller steps and frame each step in a way that allows you to measure progress. So, for example, instead of expecting to "sort myself out", ask yourself to "prepare my CV", "find two **referees**", and "register with an employment agency". Put these goals in chronological order and focus on one at a time until you have **achieved** it.
   3. In the long run you will almost certainly conclude that the most treasured aspect of your university experience wasn't your academic education or any career advice, but rather the friends you made. Make it a priority to stay in touch with those who **mattered** most to you during your university career.

   Linda Blair, clinical psychologist

   Adapted from www.theguardian.com/education/2011/jul/17/graduate-jobs-advice-experts. Accessed on February 5, 2019.

2. **Answer these questions about the advice letter in activity 1.**

   a. Why do some people feel anxious after graduating from college or university?

   _____
   _____
   _____
   _____

   b. Why does Linda Blair advise people to have "new beginnings" instead of "a new beginning"?

   _____
   _____
   _____
   _____

   c. What does Linda Blair say is the most valuable aspect of someone's university experience?

   _____
   _____
   _____
   _____

LANGUAGE IN USE 2

Unit 8

VERB TENSES REVIEW

1. Read a few extracts from the advice letter on page 76, paying attention to the verb forms in bold, and match them with their corresponding usage.

> a. [...] they **feel** anxious.

> b. [...] they**'ve realized** how much effort they**'ve expended** [...].

> c. [...] the most treasured aspect of your university experience **wasn't** your academic education or any career advice, but rather the friends you **made**.

> d. In the long run you **will** almost certainly **conclude** that the most treasured aspect of your university experience [...].

( ) Finished actions or states in the past
( ) Habits or generalizations in the present
( ) An action that happened at an indefinite time in the past
( ) A prediction based on an opinion

2. Scan the text below and provide the requested information.

Dear Graduate,
Congratulations, you have crossed the finish line. As you know, your route here was filled with tears of joy and sorrow, dreams shattered and fulfilled, moments that dispatched you to the arms of a beloved, remarkable beginnings, and ends sealed with generous promises.
Closing this chapter in your life offers a time of reflection on you. In fact, the day you were born, the world became more luminous. Chances are along the way you forgot this truth. At times it was overshadowed by fear or dismissed as insecurity, but I am here to remind you that it is still present. It is something that is uniquely yours, and can't be outsourced. In fact, there is no end to your luminosity. It is there amidst the lump in your throat and misty eyes. It is there in your sweaty palms and confused mind. It is there deep in your belly and lined in your heart. It is there.
[...]
Kristin

Extracted from www.huffpost.com/entry/an-open-letter-to-all-gra_b_9986202. Accessed on January 13, 2019.

a. An extract that indicates the action happened recently.
_____
_____

b. Three extracts that indicate a past action at a specific time.
_____
_____
_____

c. What is the difference in use between the verb tense from question *a* and the verb tense from question *b*?
_____
_____
_____

3. Read the text and choose the correct alternatives from the box to fill in the blanks.

> 's having / 'll have had
> had / 'll have   have worked / had worked
> is providing / provides

Letter to the editor: Congratulations, graduates.

[...] So here you are, a high school graduate. [...] Whether you're going to Princeton or Penn, Rutgers or Rowan, higher education _____ unimaginable opportunities. Your parents _____ hard and saved long to give you this opportunity for a better life that they might never have had, but there really is no better life than a parent's selfless sacrifice for their child's future.
For the next four years you'll be tested many times, but the most difficult test you _____ to take isn't one of essays or multiple choice but a test of will.
[...] As you listen to the commencement speaker's inspiring words, there are many serious things to consider, but for now, the only things to consider are who _____ the parties, whose parties you are going to, who'll be there and what kind of fun might develop. [...]
Savor your very special day.
George DeGeorge

Extracted from https://washingtontownshipsun.com/letter-to-the-editor-congratulations-graduates-ef1bfc0cfb0a. Accessed on September 25, 2018.

4. Based on the discussions throughout this unit and on the letter in activity 3, in your notebook, write a short message to your graduating high school classmates. Use mixed verb tenses in your writing.

LISTENING COMPREHENSION

1. Graduation speeches often aim at entertaining the audience. But what other functions might graduation speeches, whether delivered by students, school staff members, or even celebrities have?

   _____
   _____
   _____

2. Listen to the first part of the graduation speech given by Chase Dahl at the Weber High School graduation for the Class of 2015. Then complete the sentences.

   17

   a. To ensure clear communication with the "_____ generation," Chase uses _____ and pop-culture references in his speech.

   b. **Ebola**, **ISIS**, _____, and facial acne are among the _____ that **plague** the world in Chase's opinion.

   c. Chase compares Weber High _____ to the changing _____ of Hogwarts.

3. Listen carefully, read the statements below, and decide if they are true (T) or false (F).

   18

   a. ( ) In real life, we must count on being born great, or we'll never achieve greatness at all.

   b. ( ) Being recognized by the world is mandatory for one to reach greatness in his/her life.

   c. ( ) The legacies we must leave are the ones that are related to the kind of people we were.

4. Quotations are often used at graduation speeches to inspire the audience. Read the quote below, part of which was mentioned by Chase in his speech, and relate it to your reality as high school graduates. Share your opinion with a classmate.

   > It was the best of times, it was the worst of times, it was the age of wisdom, it was the age of foolishness, it was the epoch of belief, it was the epoch of incredulity, it was the season of light, it was the season of darkness, it was the spring of hope, it was the winter of despair. — Charles Dickens, *A Tale of Two Cities*

   Extracted from www.goodreads.com/quotes/341391-it-was-the-best-of-times-it-was-the-worst. Accessed on September 25, 2018.

» EXPAND YOUR HORIZONS »»»

Check (✓) the column that best describes your opinion about each statement. Then discuss your answers with your classmates and teacher, justifying your point of view.

	I agree.	I'm not sure.	I disagree.
a. We don't need to be the wisest people in the world to be successful in finding a satisfying career. But we must know ourselves really well.			
b. Skills, communication and work styles, learning preferences, payment models, passions, and personal priorities altogether should be taken into account in the choice of a career.			
c. High school years are all about managing all kinds of conflicts, overcoming obstacles, and setting the goals we are to reach.			

REVIEW 4

Units 7 and 8

1. **Work in pairs. Look at the picture, read its caption, and come up with an answer to the question raised. Then list ideas related to the content of the text.** *Discussion and Brainstorming*

_____

_____

2. **Read the whole text and check (✓) the best title for it.** *Selecting a good title*

   a. (   ) It's time to address the elephant in the room: Influencers don't really influence anything or anyone!

   b. (   ) Brand Communities & Community Marketing: everything you need to know at once!

[…]
I think it's time we addressed the elephant in the room: Who really are these "influencers" and who do they "influence", if at all?

The concept of an "influencer" is pretty clear. An individual who can reach many people through various communication channels and can therefore, potentially, influence them to like or dislike, to adopt or ban, to buy or skip buying, products and services.

The more people the "influencer" can reach (read: the more "followers" they have), the better, stronger, and more of an "influence" he or she has. There is a whole marketing strategy called "influencer marketing" or "influencer outreach". There is even a concept called "micro influencer" to describe people with less following who are still considered "important" in their **niche**.

Who are these people "influencing"?

But let's consider a few of questions:

1. What do numbers of followers mean in an age where buying likes and follows and YouTube video watches is easier than ever? […]
2. What does "coverage" even mean in a culture of multiple social media and new trends born daily? […]
3. Speaking of measuring and monitoring – how can you really tell that new business was generated by a particular collaboration with a specific influencer? […]

Let's face it, the concept of becoming an influencer is mostly appealing as a "job" to younger people who don't have many other options. When you look at the beauty segment, for instance, you can clearly see that the biggest YouTube channels with millions of followers, are usually ones that were built with hard work over years and years… and… the YouTubers are actually refusing "collabs" and sponsored content. Most of the time they pay for the products on their own, full price and they state so.

But, since Instagram and Snapchat, more and more "web influencers" have popped up, especially in the lifestyle (beauty, fashion, travel) niche and in technology (consumer electronics) and they have been enjoying the **gullibility** of brands that think they can actually generate real business by working with them.

Adapted from https://medium.com/21st-century-marketing/its-time-to-address-the-elephant-in-the-room-influencers-don-t-really-influence-anything-or-ee036b4abbb. Accessed on September 25, 2018.

---

3. **Read the text and write its main idea using your own words.** *Understanding main ideas*

_____

_____

4. **Read the extract below. Does the modal verb in italics indicate an assumption or a possibility?**

> An individual who *can* reach many people through various communication channels and *can* therefore, potentially, influence them to like or dislike, to adopt or ban, to buy or to skip buying, products and services.

Now read these other examples. What do the modal verbs in italics indicate?
a. Harriet is an online influencer. She *must* know a lot about media contents.
b. Today is your prom. You *can't* be so calm!

5. **Scan the text below and find…**
a. an action in progress in the present.

b. three actions that happened at an indefinite time in the past.

c. a prediction based on an opinion:

Today's letters: Readers' sage advice for high school graduates
[…]
Be kind to others
— You are entering a world of challenges. Look at the big picture. Humanity has reached the limits to growth. Work with others to conserve what you value most. Natural ecosystems, which support all life on earth, must be protected. […] Nurture positive relationships with those you love.
Lyn Adamson, Toronto.
[…]
Never give up
[…]
— Progressive employers look for individuals who have experienced a significant setback and whether they have grown and learned from it. Failure, not success, is the best teacher. Find an intelligent way to include this as part of your qualifications and experience; don't hide it. And buy the best mattress you can't afford. You will spend more than one-third of your life on it.
Jim Sanders, Guelph, Ont.
[…]

Adapted from https://nationalpost.com/opinion/todays-letters-readers-sage-advice-for-highschool-graduates. Accessed on September 25, 2018.

6. **Check (✓) the only extract from the text that is in the passive voice.**
a. ( ) "And buy the best mattress you can't afford."
b. ( ) "Work with others to conserve what you value most."
c. ( ) "Natural ecosystems, […], must be protected."
d. ( ) "Failure, not success, is the best teacher."

7. **Read the text and underline the verb form used to talk about something that will be in progress in the future. Then answer: Which verb tense is it?**

Overcoming Social Anxiety

So you've done it. You have survived several years of exam pressure and of dealing with stressful social situations, and you have graduated. And now "they" want you to stand up in front of a crowd and be the center of attention in a graduation ceremony? "Is there no end to the ways the world will torture me?", you may be thinking!
[…]
If you suffered from social anxiety at your high school graduation, chances are that you will be dreading your college graduation. However, remember what the ceremony is really about. It won't be like prom and its expectations of "performance" on the day. You have already done the work and you don't have to do anything except collect your symbolic reward – and standing up in front of everybody of course! The only response you will get from the audience is applause and congratulations.
[…]

Extracted from http://overcomingsocialanxiety.com/social-anxiety-college-graduation-tips. Accessed on September 25, 2018.

GRAMMAR OVERVIEW

Verb tenses

Tense	Use(s)	Example(s) – affirmative	Example(s) – negative	Example(s) – interrogative
Present perfect simple	To refer to actions that focus on length of time, achievements and results.	We **have eaten** all our meal at lunch.	They **haven't drunk** their milk during breakfast.	How long **have** you **had** this car?
Present perfect continuous	To refer to actions that started in the past and continue up to the present time; To refer to actions that started in the past and ended recently.	We **have been waiting** for you all day. It**'s been raining**. (the floor outside is wet)	Mary **hasn't been watching** TV for so long. I **haven't been eating** your cookies!	How **have** you **been coming** to work lately? How long **have** you **been living** here?
Past perfect	To indicate that an action was completed at some point in the past before something else happened.	The bus **had gone** before I reached the bus stop.	You **had not met** me when I was at school.	**Had** she **cooked** some food for the kids?
Future perfect	To refer to actions that will be completed before some other point in the future, or within a period of time.	Don't worry. By ten o'clock I **will have left** already.	We **will not have eaten** breakfast before we get to the game tomorrow morning.	**Will** you **have finished** your homework in an hour, so we can go to the movies?
Future continuous	To refer to an action that will occur in the future and continue for an expected length of time.	I **will be watching** the game with you.	When Mike gets home, I **won't be cooking** dinner.	What **will** you **be doing** next weekend?

Modal verbs

Modal verb	Use / meaning	Example(s) – affirmative	Example(s) – negative	Example(s) – interrogative
Wish	To refer to a situation that they want to be different; As an alternative to conditional sentences; As a formal alternative to refer to present and future wish situations; To criticize and talk about things we don't like and want to change.	I **wish** you **could** be here at the beach with me. I **wish** we **had met** before. I **wish to speak** to Ms. Smith, please. I **wish** I **were** there to help you with the project. I **wish** this rain **would** stop! I want to go out.	I **do not wish to** complain, but you are always late! I **do not wish to** do this, unless I'm forced to. I **wish** he **wasn't** so selfish.	**Do** you **wish** you **could** be someone else for a day? **Do** you **wish** you **had studied** more?
Will	To express assumptions with reference to present and future time; When followed by the perfect infinitive, it is used to express assumptions about past events.	They are calling out the numbers again. I **will be** next. I'm sure you **will have seen** me before.	I'm not repeating myself. You **won't** understand. Most of you **won't have seen** this yet.	
Should	To express assumptions with reference to present and future time; When followed by the perfect infinitive, it is used to express assumptions about past events.	I **should exercise** more often. I feel a little out of shape. We **should have worked** harder on the project.	You **shouldn't speak** to your teacher that way. Mike **should not have lied** about that.	The phone is ringing. **Should** that **be** for me? **Should** we **have studied** harder for the exams?
Ought to	When followed by the perfect infinitive, it is used to express assumptions about past events.	I **ought to have studied** harder for the test. Now, I'll have to take it again.	You **ought not to have told** her about the incident.	Questions with **ought to** are very formal. We use **should** instead.

81

GRAMMAR OVERVIEW

Homonyms

Category	Explanation	Examples
Homonyms	A word that is spelled the same and sounds the same as another, but is different in meaning or origin.	What's your e-mail **address**? This letter is **addressed** to Carl.
Homophones	A word that sounds the same as another, but is different in spelling, meaning, or origin.	Can I talk **to** you now? It's half past **two**. It's not **too** late to change your mind.
Homographs	A word that is spelled the same as another, but is different in meaning, origin, grammar, or pronunciation.	Don't forget to **wave** her goodbye. The **waves** are high today!

Extracted from www.ldoceonline.com/dictionary. Accessed on Dec. 29, 2018.

Conditional sentences

Conditional	Use	Form	Examples
Zero	To talk about things that are always true or always happen.	*If* + simple present → simple present	**If** babies **are** hungry, they cry.
First	To talk about real and possible situations.	*If* + simple present → *will* + infinitive	**If** you don't **leave** soon, you **will miss** the train.
Second	To talk about unreal or impossible situations.	*If* + simple past → *would* + infinitive	**If** I **won** the lottery, I **would travel** around the world!
Third	To talk about things that didn't happen.	*If* + past perfect → *would / could / might have* + main verb (past participle)	**If** they **had studied**, they **would have passed** the exams.

Some, any, no, every

Pronoun	Use	Examples
Someone Somebody Something Somewhere	Affirmative and interrogative sentences; When they mean invitation or when we expect an affirmative answer.	**Someone** is calling you outside. **Somebody** ate my sandwich. There is **something** missing in this room. Doesn't he live **somewhere** around here?
Anyone Anybody Anything Anywhere	Negative and interrogative sentences; Affirmative sentences meaning *every*.	I don't know **anyone** (**anybody**) in this room. He can do **anything** he wants to. They can be **anywhere** around town.
No one Nobody Nothing Nowhere	Affirmative sentences that have a negative meaning.	There is **no one** here to help us. She thinks that **nobody** likes her work. There is **nothing** here for you to see. This road will get us **nowhere**.
Everyone Everybody Everything Everywhere	Affirmative, interrogative, or negative sentences; When referring to a total number of people, things, or places.	Not **everyone** finished their work. **Everybody** loves chocolate! Is **everything** all right? **Everywhere** we go, people are so friendly!

Indirect / Reported speech

Verb tense in direct speech	Verb tense in indirect / reported speech	Example – direct speech	Example – indirect / reported speech
Simple present	Simple past	He said, "I always **drink** black coffee."	He said (that) he always **drank** black coffee.
Present continuous	Past continuous	"I'**m studying** for the math test," Mark said.	Mark said (that) he **was studying** for the math test.
Present perfect	Past perfect	She said to me, "I **have been** to the beach twice **this** year."	She told me (that) she **had been** to the beach twice **that** year.
Simple past	Past perfect	Sam said, "I **bought** a big new house."	Sam said (that) he **had bought** a big new house.
Will	Would	"We **will** do our homework," they said.	They said (that) they **would** do their homework.
Can / May	Could / Might	We explained, "It **can** be difficult to find a parking space **here**."	We explained that it **could** be difficult to find a parking space **there**.
Must	Had to	He said, "You **must** listen to me."	He told us (that) we **had to** listen to him.
Imperative	Infinitive	Lucy said, "**Be quiet**, please!"	Lucy told us **to be quiet**.

Compound adjectives

Form	Examples of compound adjectives	Examples in a sentence
Adjective + adjective	fat-free	I got a delicious **fat-free** yogurt.
Adjective + noun	last-minute	Joe was doing some **last-minute** revision.
adjective + verb –ing	long-lasting	I hope this is a **long-lasting** summer.
Adjective + verb (past participle)	absent-minded	She is such an **absent-minded** girl.
Noun + adjective	world-famous	Picasso is a **world-famous** painter.
Noun + verb + –ing	time-consuming	This is a **time-consuming** project.
Noun + verb (past participle)	sun-dried	I love **sun-dried** tomatoes.
Adverb + verb (past participle)	well-known	J. K. Rowling is a **well-known** writer.

Word categories

Category	Use / meaning	Examples
Expressions related to men and women	To say that you are related to that person; To say that a group of people do something together, at the same time; It is a traditional belief that is spread from one person to the other, over time.	We are **kissing cousins**. Let's all sing the song **as one man**. There are no werewolves. That's just **an old wives' tale**.
Types of technology	Scientific advanced technology; Scientific studies that involve transforming matter and developing gadgets on an atomic, or molecular scale.	This city has become the new **high technology** center of studies. They have been using **nanotechnology** in their field for some years.
Computer science abbreviations	Artificial Intelligence; Gigabytes.	**AI** is an area of computer science that develops intelligent machines. This cellphone has only 64 **GB** of storage.
English words derived from Latin	*Postpone* means *after*; *Campus* means *the land and buildings of a university or college*.	He has **postponed** the meeting again. Don't be scared. The college **campus** is very safe.
Idioms containing weather-related words	If someone has a face like thunder, they are very angry. Used to say that a problem is much bigger than is apparent.	She burst into the store with **a face like thunder**! Oh! This is just **the tip of the iceberg**. You know nothing.

GRAMMAR OVERVIEW

Category	Use / meaning	Examples
Adverbs of degree	To describe the intensity, degree, or extent of the verb, adjective, or adverb being modified; They can be mild, medium, strong, or absolute.	The pool was **extremely** cold today. This dress is **quite** expensive! The coffee is **somewhat** warm. She is swimming well **enough**. She can get into the pool.
-ed and –ing adjectives	-ed ending describes emotions; -ing ending describes what causes the emotion.	I'm **depressed** after watching that **depressing** movie. We are **thrilled** about our next vacation. It is a **thrilling** trip to Peru.

Passive voice

Verb tense	Form	Examples
Simple present	*am / is / are* + past participle	The library **is used** by the students.
Present continuous	*am / is / are* + *being* + past participle	The car **is being repaired**.
Simple past	*was / were* + past participle	The card **was sent** on time.
Modal verbs (present)	*can / must / should / could / may / might* + *be* + past participle	It **might be finished** by the end of the day.
Past continuous	*was / were* + *being* + past participle	The room **was being cleaned** yesterday.
Present perfect	*has / have* + *been* + past participle	The house **has been painted** since he left.
Past perfect	*had* + *been* + past participle	The chair **had been fixed** before you arrived.
Simple future	*will* + *be* + past participle	It **will be washed** tomorrow.
Imperative	*let* + object + *be / get* + past participle	**Let** the truth **be told**.
Modal verbs (past)	*can / must / should / could / may / might* + *have been* + past participle	This task **could have been done** this morning.

Subject-verb agreement

Use	Discourse markers	Examples
Use the verb form (singular or plural) that agrees with the subject closer to the verb.	or, nor	**The boys or the girls are** going to give the correct answer. Just wait. **The boy or the girls are** going to give the correct answer. Just wait. **The boys or the girl is** going to give the correct answer. Just wait. Neither **the boys nor the girl gets** the bus to school.
When group nouns are considered as a single unit, they take a singular verb. (AmE)	government, group, family, team, etc.	The **government decides** about the taxes we pay. The **group was** very happy with the results.
When some nouns end in -s, but are considered singular, they take a singular verb.	news, politics, mathematics, athletics, etc.	I think that **mathematics is** a very interesting subject. **Politics was** his favorite subject.
The indefinite pronouns take plural verbs.	both, few, many, several, others.	**Several are** often late. Just **a few are** here today.
Prepositional phrases between subject and verb don't change the conjugation.		**The bag** with toys **is** mine. **The cars** with a turbo **are** faster.

LANGUAGE REFERENCE

UNIT 1
PRESENT PERFECT CONTINUOUS
Usage Notes
The present perfect continuous is often used to refer to:
- actions that started in the past and continue up to the present time.

  I'm tired because I **haven't been sleeping** well at night.
- actions that started in the past and stopped recently.

  Why are you soaking wet? **Have** you **been walking** in the rain?

As not all verbs are compatible with continuous actions, they cannot be used in the present perfect continuous. A few examples are the verbs *be*, *arrive*, and *own*.

  I **have owned** a house at the beach since 2015.

NOT ~~I have been owning a house at the beach since 2015.~~

  They **have been** tired lately.

NOT ~~They have been being tired lately.~~

PRESENT PERFECT SIMPLE VS. PRESENT PERFECT CONTINUOUS
Usage Notes
- We use the present perfect continuous when we want to emphasize the length of time that an action has lasted or stress the fact that it is continuous. We use the present perfect simple when we want to focus more on achievements and results.

  I'**ve been studying** for this test for three days.

  (This focuses on the length of time.)

  I'**ve completed** my geography homework, but I **haven't started** my math assignment yet.

  (This focuses on the achievements and results.)
- We don't use the present perfect continuous when we are talking about amounts (*how much*) or quantities (*how many*). In these cases, we use the present perfect simple.

  The babies **have drunk** a lot of milk this afternoon.

NOT ~~The babies have been drinking a lot of milk this afternoon.~~

  I **have eaten** two donuts today.

NOT ~~I have been eating two doughnuts today.~~

- While the present perfect simple often focuses on the fact that the action is completed, the present perfect continuous focuses on the action itself.

  Sue'**s been watching** the TV series about vampires.

  (She hasn't finished watching the TV series.)

  Sue'**s watched** the TV series about vampires.

  (She's finished watching the TV series.)
- The present perfect continuous can also be used to emphasize that something is momentary.

  I'**ve been working** full-time this month.

  (I don't often do this.)

  They'**ve been coming** to school by bus recently.

  (They usually come by car.)

EXPRESSIONS RELATED TO MEN AND WOMEN

Expression	Meaning	Example
the poor man's something	used to say that something can be used for the same purpose as something else, and is much cheaper	Herring is **the poor man's salmon**.
as one	if a group of people do something as one, they do it together	The audience rose **as one** to applaud the singers.
it's every man for himself	used to say that people will not help each other	In journalism **it's every man for himself**.
father figure	an older man who you trust and respect	Ken was a **father figure** to all of us.
grandfather clause	a clause in a new rule stating that a person or business already doing the activity covered by the rule does not have to follow it	The new rule has a good chance of winning approval because it has a generous **grandfather clause**.
a man of his word	a man you can trust, who will do what he has promised to do	He had promised to help, and Sally knew that Dr. Neil was **a man of his word**.
man/woman of many parts	someone who is able to do many different things	He was a **man of many parts**: writer, literary critic, and historian.
old wives' tale	a belief based on old ideas that are now considered to be untrue	I think it's an **old wives' tale** that make-up ruins the skin.

Adapted from www.ldoceonline.com/dictionary. Accessed on October 16, 2018.

LANGUAGE REFERENCE

UNIT 2

SUBJECT–VERB AGREEMENT

Usage Notes

- When two or more singular subjects are joined by *or* or *nor*, use the verb form (singular or plural) that agrees with the subject closer to the verb.

  The teacher or the director is going to hand out the diplomas.

  The teachers or the director is going to hand out the diplomas.

  The teacher or the directors are going to hand out the diplomas.

- In American English, when group nouns such as *government*, *group*, *family*, *team*, etc. are considered as a single unit, they take a singular verb.

  My family makes the decisions over dinners.

  Their team wins all the games!

- Although some nouns such as *news*, *politics*, *mathematics*, *athletics*, etc. end in *s*, they are considered singular. So, they take a singular verb.

  Good news doesn't travel fast.

  Is mathematics your favorite school subject?

- The indefinite pronouns *both*, *few*, *many*, *several*, and *others* always take plural verbs.

  Many are joining us for Tom's party tonight.

  Both want to get married in December.

- When a prepositional phrase is placed between the subject and verb, it does not interfere in the agreement. To make the correct agreement, we address the subject and choose a verb that agrees with it.

  The woman at the counter **is** the cashier.

  The students with the best performance **are** going to be graded.

COMPOUND ADJECTIVES

Some compound adjectives in English:

adjective + adjective	fat-free
	dark-blue
adjective + noun	last-minute
	full-length
adjective + verb + -ing	long-lasting
	slow-moving
adjective + verb (past participle)	kind-hearted
	absent-minded
verb + adjective	smoke-free
	world-famous
noun + verb + -ing	mouth-watering
	time-consuming
noun + verb (past participle)	wind-powered
	sun-dried
adverb + verb (past participle)	brightly-lit
	well-known

Usage Notes

- For compound adjectives showing a number + a time period, the word referring to a time period takes the singular form.

  When will you take your **two-week** vacation?

  That was a **five-minute** delay.

COMPUTER SCIENCE ABBREVIATIONS

Abbreviation	Stands for
AI	Artificial Intelligence
ALGOL	Algorithmic Language
BASIC	Beginners All-purpose Symbolic Instruction Code
BIOS	Basic Input Output System
CASE	Computer Aided Software Engineering
CL	Command Language
CPU	Central Processing Unit
DDS	Digital Data Storage
DSN	Distributed Systems Network
EPG	Electronic Programming Guide
FM	Frequency Modulation
GB	Gigabytes
HTML	HyperText Markup Language
HTTP	HyperText Transport Protocol
ISDN	Integrated Services Digital Network
LAN	Local Area Network
MS-DOS	Microsoft Disk Operating System
NOS	Network Operating System
URL	Uniform Resource Locator
VoIP	Voice over Internet Protocol

Adapted from www.tutorialspoint.com/basics_of_computer_science/basics_of_computer_science_abbreviations.htm. Accessed on October 17, 2018.

UNIT 3
SECOND CONDITIONAL
Usage Notes

- The second conditional is used when we want to talk about the results of unreal or hypothetical situations or things we don't think will happen.

  If I **had** more time, I **would take up** gardening.

  We **would invite** Lenny and George for a drink if they **arrived** early.

- When the imaginary situation comes first in the sentence, we need to insert a comma between the clauses that indicate the situation and the result.

  If Lydia **didn't know** how to drive, it **would be** more difficult for her to keep her job.

- *Were* might be used instead of *was* to indicate the imaginary clause of a second conditional sentence. There is no change in meaning; however, *were* sounds more formal than *was*.

  If I **were** taller, I wouldn't sit in the front seats in the classroom.

- Although most conditional sentences use *if*, other words such as *when, in case, unless, if only, supposing*, etc. might be used as well.

  If only I had more money, I would be able to afford my son's college tuition.

  Unless students' parents signed the contract, they wouldn't be allowed to join us for the field trip.

ZERO, FIRST, AND SECOND CONDITIONALS
Usage Notes

- The zero conditional is used to talk about things that are always true or always happen. The simple present is used in both clauses.

  If you **heat** metals, they **expand**.

  If anyone **leans** against that wall, the alarm **goes off**.

- The first conditional is used to talk about real and possible situations. The structure is usually *if* + simple present + *will / can / may / might* + infinitive.

  I'll help you with the housework if I **have** time.

  If Dennis **doesn't come**, we **may call** him.

- The second conditional is used to talk about unreal or impossible things. The structure is usually *if* + simple past + *would / could / might* + infinitive.

  If you **weren't** so sedentary, you **wouldn't feel** so tired every time you do some physical activity.

  Where **would** you **travel** to if you **won** the lottery?

ENGLISH WORDS DERIVED FROM LATIN

Latin Word	Definition	English Derivatives
amicabilis	kind (friendly)	amiable
annus	year	annual, annually, annuity
arma	arms (weapons)	arms, armed, armament, army
desidare	to want	desire, desirable, desirability
docere	teach	docent, doctrine, document, documentary
grata	pleasing	grateful, gratitude, gratuity
janua	door	January, janitor, janitress
libera	free	liberal, liberator, liberate
locus	place	locus, location, locate
magister	teacher	magistrate, magisterial, magistracy
morbus	disease	morbid, morbidity, morbific
mortuus	dead	mortuary, mortician, mortality
mutare	to change	mutation, commute, transmute
occupare	to occupy	occupy, occupation, occupational
patria	native country	patriotic, expatriate, patriotism
populus	people	populous, population, popular
post	after	postmortem, postnatal, postpone
temptare	to try	tempt, temptation, attempt
territa	frightened	terrified, terrific
trans	across	transport, transmit, transact
umbra	shade, ghost	umbrella, penumbra, umbra, umbrage
vitare	to avoid	inevitable, inevitably, inevitability
vulnerare	to wound	vulnerable, invulnerable, vulnerary

Extracted from www.enhancemyvocabulary.com/word-roots_latin_2.html.
Accessed on October 19, 2018.

LANGUAGE REFERENCE

UNIT 4

PAST PERFECT

Usage Notes

- We use the past perfect when we want to refer to a past that is earlier than another past time in the narrative. Using the past perfect, we convey a sequence of the events.

  We **had seen** the weather forecast when you told us it was going to be a rainy weekend.

  (First we saw the forecast, then you told us it was going to be a rainy weekend.)

  When the ambulance arrived, the woman **had** already **died**.

  (First the woman died, then the ambulance arrived.)

- Don't use the past perfect tense if you aren't trying to convey some sequence of events. As the past perfect implies an action that occurred before another, when you don't say what that something else is (or if it's not inferred by context), the past perfect doesn't make sense.

- To distinguish the uses of the simple past and the past perfect, keep in mind that the past perfect is used to sequence events in the past and show which event happened first, whereas the simple past usually indicates a stronger connection between the time of the two events.

  When he **stepped** on the stage, everyone **applauded** wildly.

  (Everyone started applauding at the time he stepped on the stage.)

  The temperature **had fallen** when it **started** snowing.

  (It started snowing as soon as the temperature fell.)

ADVERBS OF DEGREE

Usage Notes

- To describe the intensity, degree, or extent of the verb, adjective, or adverb they are modifying, adverbs of degree can be mild, medium, strong, or absolute.

  She was **undoubtedly** the most beautiful girl at the party. (absolute degree)

  I'm **very** sorry for not being here for you guys when you needed me. (strong degree)

  The books you bought were **pretty** expensive. (medium degree)

  It'll take them **a little** longer to finish the task. (mild degree)

- Some adverbs of degree are easily identified because they end in -*ly*. However, many other adverbs of degree do not have the same ending. Some of them are: *enough, less, almost, even, just, most, quite, so, altogether, least, rather, somewhat, too, very*.

- When the word *enough* is used as an adverb of degree, it can only modify adverbs and adjectives and it is always positioned after the word it is describing.

  My students couldn't finish reading the text quickly **enough**.

  The movie was funny **enough**, but I wouldn't watch it twice.

IDIOMS CONTAINING WEATHER-RELATED WORDS

Idiom	Meaning
a face like thunder	if someone has a face like thunder, they look very angry
a ray of hope/light	something that provides a small amount of hope or happiness in a difficult situation
any port in a storm	used to say that you should take whatever help you can when you are in trouble, even if it has some disadvantages
ask for the moon	to ask for something that is difficult or impossible to obtain
keep/put something on ice	to do nothing about a plan or suggestion for a period of time
like greased lightning	extremely fast
shoot the bull/breeze	to have an informal conversation about unimportant things
the tip of the iceberg	a small sign of a problem that is much larger
under a cloud (of suspicion)	if someone is under a cloud, people have a bad opinion of them because they think they have done something wrong
windbag	someone who talks too much

Extracted from www.ldoceonline.com/dictionary. Accessed on October 19, 2018.

UNIT 5

THIRD CONDITIONAL

Usage Notes

- The third conditional is used to describe something that didn't happen. The structure is usually *if + past perfect + would / could / might have + main verb in the past participle form.*

  If it **had rained**, I **wouldn't have traveled** to the beach.

  (But it rained.)

  They **would have had** better grades if they **had studied** harder.

  (But they didn't study harder.)

- Third conditionals may be used in mixed conditional sentences, which combine two different types of conditional patterns. The two most common mixed conditionals combine the third and the second conditionals.

- The mixed third / second conditional (a type 3 conditional in the *if-* clause – past perfect – followed by a type 2 conditional in the main clause – *would / could / might* + main verb in the base form) contrasts an imagined or real event in the past with its present result. This condition is used when we regret past action or inaction.

  If they**'d told** me they would be late, I **wouldn't** still **be** here waiting for them.

  If I **had followed** a balanced diet, I **would feel** healthier.

- The mixed second / third conditional (a type 2 conditional in the *if-* clause – If + past simple – followed by a type 3 conditional in the main clause – *would / could / might have* + main verb in the past participle form) describes ongoing circumstances in relation to a previous past event.

  If you **weren't** a good professional, I **wouldn't have hired** you for such an important position in my company.

  If you **didn't cover** up all his lies, he **would've realized** that he needed help much sooner than he did.

WISH

Usage Notes

- The use of *wish + simple past* or *wish + past perfect* is an alternative to conditional sentences.

  I **wish** you **could** spend Christmas with me this year.

  (If you could spend Christmas with me this year, that would be great.)

  We **wish** we **had studied** more before the test.

  (If only we had studied more before the test, our grades would've been better.)

- The structure *wish + infinitive* can also be used as a more formal alternative to *want* or *would like* when we refer to present and future wish situations.

  He **wishes to talk** to the admissions dean, but he hasn't scheduled an appointment.

  I **do not wish to sound** rude, but I'm running out of time here. Could you please go straight to the point?

- For present wishes with *wish +* simple past of verb *be*, *was* and *were* are interchangeable with first, second, and third person pronouns, singular and plural, although *were* sounds more formal than *was*.

  I **wish** I **weren't** here to witness the bankruptcy of our company.

  Chris **wishes** she **were** more hardworking.

- We often use *wish + would* to criticize and to talk about things that we don't like and want to change. It's not usually used to talk about ourselves, though.

  I **wish** my neighbors **would stop** making all that noise late at night.

  I **wish** you **wouldn't wake up** early so frequently!

HOMONYMS: HOMOPHONES AND HOMOGRAPHS

- Homophones are words that sound alike, whether they are spelled differently or not.

  pear (fruit) – pare (cut off) – pair (two of a kind)

  bear (carry) – bear (animal)

- Homographs are words that are spelled identically but may or may not share the same pronunciation.

  wind (an air current or to twist)

  fair (pleasing in appearance or a market)

- Homographs that are spelled the same but sound different are called heteronyms.

  tear (in the eye) – tear (rip)

  lead (to guide) – lead (metal)

LANGUAGE REFERENCE

UNIT 6

SOME, ANY, NO, EVERY — COMPOUNDS

Compounds

PEOPLE	somebody / someone	anybody / anyone	nobody / no one	everybody / everyone
THINGS	something	anything	nothing	everything
PLACES	somewhere	anywhere	nowhere	everywhere

Usages

Examples

Someone / Somebody / Something / Somewhere	Affirmative sentences; Interrogative sentences when they show invitation or when we expect an affirmative answer.	**Someone** (**Somebody**) has to answer the phone. There's **something** under the mattress. Would you like to go **somewhere** special this Sunday?
Anyone / Anybody / Anything / Anywhere	Negative and interrogative sentences; Affirmative sentences meaning *every*.	I don't know **anyone** (**anybody**) in this picture. I didn't do **anything** interesting last night. Does she intend to travel **anywhere** in July? You can buy **anything** you want on the Internet.
No one / Nobody / Nothing / Nowhere	Affirmative sentences which have a negative meaning.	**No one** (**Nobody**) told me to keep quiet. I could do **nothing** to prevent her from falling. There's **nowhere** like home.
Everyone / Everybody / Everything / Everywhere	Affirmative, negative, or interrogative sentences.	**Everyone** (**Everybody**) can be assigned for the role. He told us **everything** he remembered about the accident. I've looked **everywhere** but my socks are still missing.

INDIRECT / REPORTED SPEECH

Observe the changes in verb tenses.

Direct speech	Indirect / reported speech
Simple present He said, "I **want** to get home before noon."	Simple past He said (that) he **wanted** to get home before noon.
Present continuous She said, "I'**m doing** the laundry."	Past continuous She said (that) she **was doing** the laundry.
Present perfect They said, "We **haven't worked** together before."	Past perfect They said (that) they **hadn't worked** together before.
Simple past You said, "I **didn't forget** to do the homework."	Past perfect You said (that) you **hadn't forgotten** to do the homework.
Will We said, "We **will** arrive late."	Would We said (that) we **would** arrive late.
Can / May I said, "I **can't** control his attitude." He said, "I **may** need some help."	Could / Might I said (that) I **couldn't** control his attitude. He said (that) he **might** need some help.
Must She said, "I **must** check the attendance every class."	Had to She said (that) she **had to** check the attendance every class.
Imperative They said to us, "**Slow down**."	Infinitive They told us **to slow down**.

Observe the changes in time and place expressions.

Direct speech	Indirect / reported speech
a week / a month / a year ago	a week / a month / a year before
last week / month / year	the week / month / year before
next	the following
now	then / at that time
today	that day
tomorrow	the next day / the following day
tonight	that night
yesterday	the day before / the previous day
here	there

Usage Notes

- Note that *could, might, would,* and *should* don't show any changes.

  He said, "I **could** contact a lawyer." (Direct speech)

  He said (that) he **could** contact a lawyer. (Indirect / reported speech)

  She said, "It **might** take a little time." (Direct speech)

  She said (that) it **might** take a little time. (Indirect / reported speech)

- To change a *yes/no* question from direct to indirect speech, we use if + the affirmative form and make all the necessary changes in verbs, time, and place expressions.

  Louis asked her sister, "**Will you invite** Joan to the party?"

  Louis asked her sister **if she would invite** Joan to the party.

- To change a *wh-* question from direct to indirect speech, we repeat *the question word* + the affirmative form and make all the necessary changes in verbs, time, and place expressions.

  The teacher asked, "Where **are you** going?"

  The teacher asked where **we were** going.

- The demonstrative pronouns *this* and *these* are often changed to *that* and *those* in indirect speech.

  Lucca said, "I can't work with **this** old computer."

  Lucca said (that) he couldn't work with **that** old computer.

TYPES OF TECHNOLOGY

Collocation	Meaning
assistive technology	technology which helps people who have a disability
biotechnology	the use of living things such as cells, bacteria, etc. to make drugs, destroy waste matter, etc.
high technology	the use of the most modern machines and methods in industry, business, etc.
information technology	the study or use of electronic processes for gathering and storing information and making it available using computers
nanotechnology	a science which involves developing and making extremely small but very powerful machines
niche technology	technological products that are designed for a particular small area of a market

Extracted from www.ldoceonline.com/dictionary. Accessed on October 22, 2018.

▶ **UNIT 7**

EXPRESSING ASSUMPTIONS

Besides *must* and *can,* there are other modal verbs that might be used to express assumptions.

- *Will* and *should* are used when we want to express assumptions with reference to present and future time. Note that assumptions with *will* are more probable.

  There's someone at the door. That**'ll** be the mailman.

  I have never gone skiing, but it **shouldn't** be too difficult.

- *Will, should,* and *ought to* followed by the perfect infinitive can be used to express assumptions about past events.

  Most of the students **will have seen** me around before.

  Mark **should have arrived** home by now.

PASSIVE VOICE

Formation chart

Passive forms are composed by an appropriate form of the verb *be* followed by the past participle form of the main verb.

Verb tense	Passive voice
Simple present	*am / is / are* + past participle
Present continuous	*am / is / are* + *being* + past participle
Simple past	*was / were* + past participle
Modal verbs (present)	*can / must / should / could / may / might* + *be* + past participle
Past continuous	*was / were* + *being* + past participle
Present perfect	*has / have* + *been* + past participle
Past perfect	*had* + *been* + past participle
Simple future	*will* + *be* + past participle
Modal verbs (past)	*can / must / should / could / may / might* + *have been* + past participle

Usage Notes

- When we have a whole sentence as the object of the active voice, there are two possibilities to make the passive voice.

  They say (that) she is British. (active)

  It is said that she is British. (passive)

  She is said to be British*. (passive)

- With verbs of opinion like *say, think, expect, know, believe, understand, consider, find,* etc., there are also two possible options to make the passive.

  They thought (that) I was stupid. (active)

  It was thought (that) I was stupid. (passive)

  I was thought to be stupid*. (passive)

- When we want to change an imperative form into the passive voice, we use the structure: *let* + object + *be/get* + past participle.

  Play the best music. (active)

  Let the best music be played. (passive)

LANGUAGE REFERENCE

Don't change the subject. (active)

Let the subject not be changed. (passive)

* Most frequent option.

OTHER -ED AND -ING ADJECTIVES

-ed adjectives	Meanings	-ing adjectives	Meanings
alarmed	worried or frightened	alarming	making you feel worried or frightened
charmed	have / lead a charmed life	charming	very pleasing or attractive
convinced	feeling certain that something is true	convincing	making you believe that something is true or right
depressed	very unhappy	depressing	making you feel very sad
disturbed	worried or upset	disturbing	worrying or upsetting
embarrassed	feeling uncomfortable or nervous and worrying about what people think of you	embarrassing	making you feel ashamed, nervous, or uncomfortable
fascinated	extremely interested by something or someone	fascinating	extremely interesting
surprised	having a feeling of surprise	surprising	unusual or unexpected
thrilled	very excited, happy, and pleased	thrilling	interesting and exciting
troubled	worried or anxious	troubling	worrying

Extracted from www.ldoceonline.com/dictionary. Accessed on October 22, 2018.

▶ UNIT 8

FUTURE PERFECT AND FUTURE CONTINUOUS

Usage Notes

- We can also use the future continuous to talk about what we assume is happening at the moment.

  The students' behavior seems very suspicious to me. They**'ll be doing** something wrong, for sure!

  Give Gabriel a call. He**'ll be having** dinner already.

- We usually use the future perfect with *by* or *in*. *By* indicates *not later than a specific time* and *in* indicates *within a period of time*.

  I think technology **will have taken** control of school curricula by the year 2030.

  Will you **have finished** your work in one hour, so we can talk?

FIGURES OF SPEECH

Term	Definition
alliteration	the commencement of two or more words of a word group with the same letter, as in "apt alliteration's artful aid"
anaphora	the use of a word as a regular grammatical substitute for a preceding word or group of words, as in the use of *it* and *do* in "I know it and he does too."
antithesis	the placing of a sentence or one of its parts against another to which it is opposed to form a balanced contrast of ideas, as in "Give me liberty or give me death."
euphemism	the substitution of a mild, indirect, or vague expression for one thought to be offensive, harsh, or blunt. […] "To pass away" is a euphemism for "to die"
hyperbole	an extravagant statement or figure of speech not intended to be taken literally, as in "to wait an eternity"
irony	the use of words to convey a meaning that is the opposite of its literal meaning: the irony of her reply, "How nice!" when I said I had to work all weekend
metaphor	a figure of speech in which a term or phrase is applied to something to which it is not literally applicable in order to suggest a resemblance, as in "A mighty fortress is our God."
metonymy	a figure of speech that consists of the use of the name of one object or concept for that of another to which it is related, or of which it is a part, as "scepter" for "sovereignty," or "the bottle" for "strong drink," or "count heads (or noses)" for "count people"
onomatopoeia	the use of words that sound like the thing that they are describing, for example "hiss" or "boom"
simile	a figure of speech in which two unlike things are explicitly compared, as in "She is like a rose."

Based on www.ldoceonline.com and www.dictionary.com. Accessed on October 23, 2018.

READING STRATEGIES

Ao longo da coleção, estamos sinalizando algumas estratégias de leitura voltadas à melhora na compreensão de textos.. O principal objetivo dessas estratégias é fazer com que você, aluno, torne-se um aprendiz mais eficaz e alcance resultados positivos nos exames e vestibulares a serem realizados ao final do Ensino Médio.

A seguir você encontrará uma breve explicação sobre as estratégias mais comumente abordadas antes e durante a leitura dos textos.

Activating or using previous knowledge – Esta estratégia consiste em acionar, quando preciso, o conhecimento que você tem guardado em sua mente. Quando falamos em conhecimento prévio na leitura, estamos nos referindo às informações que você precisa ter para ler um texto sem muita dificuldade para compreendê-lo.

Brainstorming – O termo foi criado a partir da junção das palavras *brain* (cérebro) e *storm* (tempestade), portanto, significa "tempestade cerebral" ou "tempestade de ideias". A estratégia propõe que você e seus colegas de sala explorem sua capacidade criativa, na medida em que trocam ideias a respeito do assunto que será abordado no texto.

Bridging – O termo vem da palavra *bridge*, que significa "ponte". A estratégia consiste, então, em "fazer uma ponte", isto é, em estabelecer uma relação entre o seu conhecimento prévio sobre o assunto que será explorado no texto e o texto propriamente.

Finding organizational patterns or understanding text structure – A estrutura de um texto diz respeito à forma como as informações estão nele organizadas. Artigos, por exemplo, contam com uma introdução, um desenvolvimento e uma conclusão; as informações nas biografias são, em geral, organizadas em sequência cronológica; as receitas, na maioria das vezes, são divididas em duas partes – ingredientes e modo de preparo. Assim, estar atento aos padrões de organização de um texto ajuda-o a identificar seu gênero e, consequentemente, sua função social.

Predicting – A palavra *predict* significa "prever". Ao lermos o título de um texto ou observarmos as imagens que o acompanham, por exemplo, podemos prever ou deduzir seu conteúdo. Quanto mais conhecimento geral você tiver, mais facilmente vai prever o assunto de um texto. Em algumas atividades, você é convidado especificamente a prever o tema e o gênero do texto (*predicting the theme and the genre*).

Recognizing or identifying – Reconhecer significa identificar algo que se conhece. Portanto, reconhecer ou identificar o tipo textual (*textual type*), a voz, ou seja, quem está falando no texto (*voice in a text*), a perspectiva do autor (*the author's perspective*), a fonte do texto (*the source of the text*), o público ao qual o texto se destina (*the target audience*), o propósito principal do texto (*the main purpose*) etc. ajuda-o a antecipar o que está por vir no texto a ser lido.

Skimming – Consiste em observar o texto rapidamente para detectar o assunto geral ou o seu propósito geral (*skimming to identify the main purpose*), por exemplo. Nesse momento, não há nenhuma preocupação em se atentar aos detalhes. É importante que você observe o *layout* do texto, seu título e sub-títulos, cognatos, primeiras e últimas linhas de cada parágrafo, bem como as imagens, gráficos e tabelas que o acompanham.

Scanning – É uma técnica de leitura que consiste em correr rapidamente os olhos pelo texto até localizar a informação específica desejada. O *scanning* é prática rotineira na vida das pessoas. Alguns exemplos típicos pode. Alguns exemplos típicos são o uso do dicionário para obter informação sobre o significado de palavras ou a utilização do índice de um livro para encontrar um artigo ou capítulo de interesse.

Há, também, estratégias que são trabalhadas após a leitura dos textos. Observe:

Making inferences or inferring – A estratégia de inferência tem como objetivo fazê-lo capturar aquilo que não está dito no texto de forma explícita. Essas adivinhações podem ter como base as pistas dadas pelo próprio texto ou o seu próprio conhecimento. Trata-se de uma estratégia de leitura extremamente importante, pois um texto só terá sentido se você puder estabelecer relações entre as partes, ou seja, entre as palavras, frases, parágrafos etc.

Selecting a good title – Muitas vezes o título de um texto resume sua ideia central. Para selecionar o título mais apropriado para o texto que você acabou de ler, leia-o novamente e anote os pontos que mais chamaram sua atenção. O mesmo se aplica para quando você tiver que afirmar ou declarar a ideia ou o propósito principal do texto lido (*stating the main idea or the main purpose of the text*).

Understanding details – Para entender os detalhes de um texto é preciso fazer uma leitura lenta e concentrar-se durante essa leitura, isto é, ficar longe de qualquer coisa que possa distraí-lo. Recorrer a um dicionário para consultar as palavras e expressões desconhecidas e anotar seu significado, bem como fazer paráfrases durante a leitura, são algumas das ações que contribuem para a compreensão detalhada do texto. Podem contribuir, também, para as atividades que pedem que você resuma o texto lido (*summarizing*).

Understanding main ideas – Para realizar atividades que têm esta estratégia sinalizada, não é necessário fazer uma leitura tão detalhada, nem mesmo procurar todas as palavras desconhecidas em um dicionário. Basta fazer uma leitura geral do texto com atenção e compreender sua mensagem principal.

IRREGULAR VERBS

Base form	Past form	Past participle	Translation
awake	awoke	awoken	acordar
be	was, were	been	ser, estar
become	became	become	tornar-se
begin	began	begun	começar
bend	bent	bent	dobrar
bet	bet	bet	apostar
bite	bit	bitten	morder
blow	blew	blown	soprar
break	broke	broken	quebrar
bring	brought	brought	trazer
build	built	built	construir
burn	burnt/burned	burnt/burned	queimar
buy	bought	bought	comprar
catch	caught	caught	pegar
choose	chose	chosen	escolher
come	came	come	vir
cut	cut	cut	cortar
do	did	done	fazer
draw	drew	drawn	desenhar
dream	dreamed/dreamt	dreamed/dreamt	sonhar
drink	drank	drunk	beber
drive	drove	driven	dirigir
eat	ate	eaten	comer
fall	fell	fallen	cair
feed	fed	fed	alimentar
feel	felt	felt	sentir
fight	fought	fought	lutar
find	found	found	achar
fly	flew	flown	voar
forget	forgot	forgotten	esquecer
forgive	forgave	forgiven	perdoar
get	got	got/gotten	conseguir
get up	got up	got up/gotten up	levantar-se
give	gave	given	dar
go	went	gone	ir
grow	grew	grown	crescer
hang out	hung out	hung out	passar tempo
have	had	had	ter
hear	heard	heard	ouvir
hide	hid	hidden	esconder
hit	hit	hit	atingir
hold	held	held	segurar
hurt	hurt	hurt	machucar
keep	kept	kept	manter

Base form	Past form	Past participle	Translation
know	knew	known	saber, conhecer
lean	leant/leaned	leant/leaned	inclinar-se
learn	learnt/learned	learnt/learned	aprender
leave	left	left	deixar, sair
lend	lent	lent	emprestar
let	let	let	deixar
lose	lost	lost	perder
make	made	made	fazer
mean	meant	meant	significar
meet	met	met	encontrar, conhecer
overcome	overcame	overcome	superar
pay	paid	paid	pagar
put	put	put	colocar
read	read	read	ler
ride	rode	ridden	andar de
ring	rang	rung	tocar
rise	rose	risen	subir, aumentar
run	ran	run	correr
say	said	said	dizer
see	saw	seen	ver
sell	sold	sold	vender
send	sent	sent	enviar
set	set	set	estabelecer
show	showed	shown	mostrar
sing	sang	sung	cantar
sit	sat	sat	sentar
sleep	slept	slept	dormir
speak	spoke	spoken	falar
spell	spelled/spelt	spelled/spelt	soletrar
spend	spent	spent	gastar, passar tempo
split	split	split	dividir
stand up	stood up	stood up	ficar de pé
steal	stole	stolen	roubar
swim	swam	swum	nadar
take	took	taken	pegar, tomar
teach	taught	taught	ensinar
tell	told	told	contar
think	thought	thought	pensar
throw	threw	thrown	jogar
understand	understood	understood	entender
wake up	woke up	woken up	acordar
wear	wore	worn	vestir
win	won	won	ganhar
write	wrote	written	escrever

COMMON MISTAKES

Speakers of Portuguese are more likely to make certain mistakes in English because of interference from Portuguese. Let's take a look at some common mistakes:

TOPIC	COMMON MISTAKE	RIGHT FORM	SOME EXPLANATION
BEEN VS. *BEING*	I have ~~being~~ abroad twice in my life. My car is ~~been~~ washed.	I **have been** abroad twice in my life. My car **is being washed**.	With both the present perfect simple and the present perfect continuous, the verb that comes after *have / has* is in the past participle (i.e., *been*), not in the present participle (i.e., *being*). The words *been* and *being* differ in use, spelling, and pronunciation.
COUMPOUND SUBJECT: USING *I*	Jenny and ~~me~~ are from South Africa.	Jenny and **I** are from South Africa.	*I* is a subject pronoun so it comes before the verb.
AGE AS AN ADJECTIVE BEFORE A NOUN	Two-year~~s~~-old children are still learning to speak.	**Two-year-old** children are still learning to speak.	When we place someone's age before the noun, we are using it as an adjective, and adjectives don't have a plural form in English, so we can't use any of the words that are part of the compound adjective in the plural form.
WOULD IN SECOND CONDITIONAL SENTENCES	If I ~~would have~~ more money, I would travel all over the world.	If I **had** more money, I would travel all over the world.	In second conditional sentences, the *if* clause is in the simple past, and *would* can only be used in the result clause.
THE FORMATION OF PAST PERFECT	When my parents got home, I had already ~~did~~ my homework.	When my parents got home, I had already **done** my homework.	Making mistakes with past participles is common. In the past perfect tense, we always use the past participle as the conjugation of the main verb.
ADVERBS OF DEGREE AND GRADABLE / UNGRADABLE ADJECTIVES	This house is ~~very~~ enormous!	This house is **enormous**! OR This house is **very big**!	Gradable adjectives are those that you can use an adverb of degree with, such as *big* and *good*. With ungradable adverbs we can use only a few adverbs: *absolutely, really, completely, totally, utterly*.
FORMATION OF SENTENCES WITH *WISH*	I wish ~~that~~ I ~~have~~ a brother.	I wish **I had** a brother.	When expressing wishes in the present, we use a past verb; when expressing a past wish, the main verb is in the past perfect.

TOPIC	COMMON MISTAKE	RIGHT FORM	SOME EXPLANATION
USING THE DETERMINER *EVERY*	Every ~~people~~ in my school must wear a uniform, students, teachers, and even the principal.	**Every member** of my school must wear a uniform, students, teachers, and even the principal.	We use the determiner *every* with a singular noun, even though it refers to more than one of the nouns.
TIME EXPRESSIONS IN INDIRECT / REPORTED SPEECH	He said (that) he ~~will~~ buy a car ~~today~~.	He said (that) he **would** buy a car **that day**.	Although the use of *will* and *today* in the first example can be accepted when the sentence is reported on the same day, the same is not true when the sentence is reported some time after it was first said.
TOLD VS. *SAID*	She said ~~me~~ that her name was Emma.	**She said that** her name was Emma. OR **She told me that** her name was Emma.	The verb *tell* usually requires an object, we *tell someone something*; the verb *said* can only have an object if we add the preposition *to* after the verb: *we say something to someone*.
MODAL VERBS FOR ASSUMPTION	You ~~mustn't~~ be serious!	You **can't** be serious!	When we are making an assumption and we are sure of something, we use the modal verb *must*; however, the negative assumption uses a different modal verb, *can't. Mustn't*, or *must not*, is not possible when referring to assumptions.
FUTURE PERFECT AND FUTURE CONTINUOUS	At 10:25 my plane will ~~have landing~~.	At 10:25 my plane **will be landing**. OR At 10:25 my plane **will have landed**.	Portuguese speakers sometimes make mistakes in verb conjugation when there is more than one verb in a structure. Beware! Continuous tenses always have the main verb in the *–ing* form, while perfect tenses have the main verb in the past participle.
PRESENT SIMPLE VS. PRESENT PERFECT	I ~~live~~ in this town since my childhood.	I **have lived** in this town since my childhood.	In English, we can't use the present simple if we are also talking about the past. If you want to say *"Eu moro nesta cidade desde minha infância."* you need to use the present perfect, as the activity started ten years ago (past) and is still true now (present).

FALSE FRIENDS

False friends are similar-sounding words with different meanings. When we look at the word *actually*, for example, we immediately associate it with the Portuguese word "*atualmente*", because of its similarity. However, *actually* means "*na realidade*" as in "It **actually** costs three thousand dollars, not three hundred." Let's take a look at some other examples.

English	Portuguese translation	Example	Don't get confused with...	Which in English is...
alias	pseudônimo, nome falso	He used to work under an **alias**.	aliás	by the way
anthem	hino	Are you able to sing the American national **anthem**?	antena	antenna
appoint	nomear	Tom Leary was **appointed** to a new position.	apontar	point
assist	ajudar	Who is going to **assist** the new judge?	assistir	watch
college	faculdade	I can't believe you are not excited about going to **college**!	colégio	school
comprehensive	abrangente, amplo	It was a very **comprehensive** report.	compreensível	understandable
convict	condenado(a)	The **convict** had to be handcuffed.	convicto(a)	certain
costume	fantasia	How much is the vampire **costume**?	costume	habit
data	dados	We have gathered a lot of **data** on the subject.	data	date
exit	saída	Where is the **exit** door?	êxito	success
fabric	tecido	Silk is a very expensive **fabric**.	fábrica	factory
hazard	risco	This medicine presents no **hazard** to your health.	azar	bad luck
inhabited	habitado(a)	It is an **inhabited** island.	inabitado(a)	uninhabited
journal	revista especializada, diário	Tom is the editor of a very important medical **journal**.	jornal	newspaper
lecture	palestra	The **lecture** had a very young audience.	leitura	reading
legend	lenda	Have you heard of the **legend** of Billy Jack?	legenda	subtitle
library	biblioteca	Is there a **library** around here where I can take out some comics?	livraria	bookstore
novel	romance	*My Brilliant Friend* is a **novel** written by Elena Ferrante, a mysterious Italian writer.	novela	soap opera
notice	notar, observar	Have you **noticed** the new furniture in the Study Hall?	notícia	news
parents	pais	My **parents** got married in the early nineties.	parentes	relatives
physician	médico	He is a respected **physician** who is looking after the president's health.	físico	physicist
prejudice	preconceito	We must always fight against all kinds of **prejudice**.	prejuízo	harm
pretend	fingir	Stop **pretending**! I know you are not telling the truth.	pretender	intend
realize	perceber	Have you **realized** how far we are from our goal?	realizar	accomplish
resume	recomeçar	After a long break they **resumed** the session.	resumir	summarize
sensible	sensato(a)	Choosing to cross the river in such a small boat is not a **sensible** option.	sensível	sensitive
support	apoiar	The homeless shelter is **supported** by a group of volunteers.	suportar	bear

GLOSSARY

Unit 1

craved – ansiar (infinitivo: *crave*)
empowerment – empoderamento
enhancers – potenciadores
figures – estimativas
fortnight – período de 14 dias
hence – logo, por isso
Kohl-lined eyes – olhos delineados
K-pop bands – bandas de música pop coreana
leadership – liderança
outstanding – excepcional
overlap – sobrepõe
pride – orgulho
range – variedade
ratio – proporção
rear – traseira
reiterating – repetindo, reiterando (infinitivo: *reiterate*)
roles – papéis
skincare – cuidados com a pele
skull – crânio
speed up – acelerar
targeted – direcionado(a)
tingling – formigamento
wresting – obtido à força

Unit 2

approaches – abordagens
bootcamps – campo de treino de recrutas
buzz language – linguagem do momento
coincide – coincidir
conspicuously – visivelmente
decree – decreto
despite – apesar de
disproportionately – desproporcionalmente
disrupted – perturbado(a)
fire up – entusiasmar
geeks – nerds
interface – interface fronteira
mastery – domínio
offspring – prole
pattern – padrão
pursuing – buscar (infinitivo: *pursue*)
STEM – sigla em inglês para *science, technology, engineering, and mathematics*
tech-savvy – inteligência tecnológica

Review 1

acquainted – familiarizado
awareness – consciência
demystify – desmistificar
entice – convencer
persuaded – persuadiu (infinitivo: *persuade*)
raising – aumentando (infinitivo: *raise*)
shatter – estilhaçar-se
stuck to – preso a
undergraduates – não-graduados(as)

Unit 3

acres – medida para terrenos
as a whole – como um todo
available – disponível
behavior – comportamento
blissful – feliz
carping – resmungo
cattle – gado
clout – golpe
cobble – remendar
conveyor belts – esteiras rolantes
delight – agradar
devised – criado(a) (infinitivo: *devise*)
harvest – colheita
herds – rebanhos
kidney – rim
layer – camada
leap – salto

GLOSSARY

morsel – bocado
muckraking – sensacionalismo
nourish – nutrir
nurture – educar
offsetting – compensação
otherwise – de outra forma
outcome – resultado
outtake – corte
regardless of – independente de
relentless – implacável
reluctance – relutância
rugged – bruto(a)
saying grace – orando (infinitivo: *say grace*)
sevenfold – sete vezes
shrillness – estridor
spawned – gerado(a) (infinitivo: *spawn*)
standpoints – posições
sticking with – aderindo a (infinitivo: *stick with*)
takes […] for granted – tem como certo (infinitivo: *take […] for granted*)
tract – trato (intestinal)
waist – cintura
weight – peso
whisk – bater
wonder – maravilha
yields – produções

Unit 4

ablaze – ao fogo
attics – sotãos
bunker coat – casaco de bombeiro
chaparral – tipo de vegetação chamada chaparral
clearheaded – lúcido(a)
couplings – acoplamentos
crevasse – fenda
deplete – esgotam
drizzle – garoa
eerily – sinistramente
embroidered – bordado
fail – falhar
failures – falhas
floodings – alagamentos
frontlines – linhas de frente
fueling – alimentando (infinitivo: *fuel*)
geared up – preparado(a)
hazardous – perigoso
heat-trapping gases – gases retentores de calor
hose – mangueira
hurricanes – furacões
intertwined – entrelaçado(a)
lightweight – leve (em peso)
lodged – alojou-se (infinitivo: *lodge*)
loose-fitting – folgado(a)
loss – perda
mounting – organizando (infinitivo: *mount*)
mph – abreviação para *miles per hour*, milhas por hora
overwhelm – sobrecarregar
pissing into – urinando em (infinitivo: *piss into*)
rags – trapos
replenished – reabastecido (infinitivo: *replenish*)
rescued – resgatou (infinitivo: *rescue*)
scramble – engatinhar
shook – sacudiu (infinitivo: *shake*)
sources – fontes
spinning – rodando
thaw – descongelamento
threats – ameaças
tremendously – tremendamente
widespread – generalizado(a)
wisdom – sabedoria
yelling – gritando (infinitivo: *yell*)

Review 2

aiming – objetivando (infinitivo: *aim*)
allotment – lote
committing – comprometendo (infinitivo: *commit*)

livelihoods – subsistências
range – extensão
shyly – timidamente
standards – padrões
unbeatable – invencível
weeping – chorando (infinitivo: *weep*)

Unit 5

abducts – sequestra (infinitivo: *abduct*)
airbender – controlador de ar
boldly – corajosamente
cast – elenco
concoct – fabricar
dashed – arruinado(a) (infinitivo: *dash*)
doomed – condenado(a) (infinitivo: *doom*)
double – dupla
hint – dica, ideia
jam – favorito (gíria)
kidnapping – sequestrando (infinitivo: *kidnap*)
mayhem – desordem
measly – miserável
misunderstood – mal-compreendido(a)
preying – predando (infinitivo: *predar*)
revenge – vingança
sequel – sequência
showrunner – produtor do programa
sidekick – aliado(a)
slayer – assassino(a)
spare – reservar
starvation – fome
tap – batida
transcend – ultrapassar
vortex – vórtice
wasteland – terreno baldio

Unit 6

aided – ajudava (infinitivo: *aid*)
anonymize – ocultar
assets – bens
bazaar – bazar

censorship – censura
credentials – credenciais
database – base de dados
downtime – tempo de inatividade
ensure – assegurar
exchanges – trocas
fraud – fraude
grabs – chama (infinitivo: *grab*)
grants – garante (infinitvo: *grant*)
hacks – alterações
harvested – colhido(a) (infinitivo: *harvest*)
immutable – imutável
litany – ladainha
losses – perdas
pseudonymity – estado de identidade disfarçada
redress - retificação
reputably – respeitavelmente
revenues – receitas
scalability – escalabilidade
scammers – fraudador
scoured – corroeu (infinitivo: *scour*)
seized – confiscou (infinitivo: *seize*)
trusted – confiável
volatility – volubilidade
waning – decrescente
whistleblowers – informantes

Review 3

cheated – traiu (infinitivo: *cheat*)
plot – narrativa
surveillance – vigilância

Unit 7

abiding – durável
albeit – embora
amass – aglomerar
assessment – avaliação
athleisure – roupas de ginástica para outras ocasiões
bagel – rosca (alimento)
bias – inclinação, propensão

GLOSSARY

buzzing – zunindo (infinitivo: *buzz*)

claim – afirmação

crackdowns – medidas enérgicas

creepy – assustador

derail – descarrilhar

disclose – revelar

droves – bandos

endorsers – endossadores

fiercer – mais feroz

framework – estrutura

increase – aumento

indie-flick – filme independente (gíria)

infatuated – obcecado(a)

leverage – influenciar

lingo – jargão

lure – atrair

max out – estourar

measure – medida

mimicking – fazendo mímica, copiando (infinitivo: *mimick*)

modishly – de acordo com o padrão da moda

morbidly – morbidamente

notoriously – infamemente

nutshell – casca de noz

proxy – procuração

rising tide – maré crescente

savvy – habilidade

shabby – esfarrapado

sheer – total

sleek – elegante

smutty – manchado(a)

sneaky – ordinário

theft – roubo

trustworthiness - confiança

turmeric – cúrcuma (tempero)

ubiquitous – onipresente

wannabes – que querem ser (gíria)

whether – se

Unit 8

achieved – alcançou (infinitivo: *achieve*)

billboard – outdoor de propaganda

biohackers – pessoa que mistura biologia com ética hacker

blues – tristeza

counseling – orientação

craft – produzir

depletion – esgotamento

earnings – ganhos

ebola – doença por vírus, ebola

enabling – possibilitando (infinitivo: *enable*)

gap – brecha

in demand – desejado(a)

ISIS – Sigla para Estado Islâmica do Iraque e da Síria

mattered – importou, deu importância (infinitivo: *importar*)

mismatched – mal combinado

outlets – saídas

path – caminho

plague – praga

raw – cru

referees – referências

sift – peneirar

stunning – deslumbrante

triggering – provocando (infinitivo: *trigger*)

whooping – gritando (infinitivo: *whoop*)

winning hand – mão vitoriosa (termo usado em poker)

Review 4

niche – nicho

gullibility – ingenuidade

sage – sábio

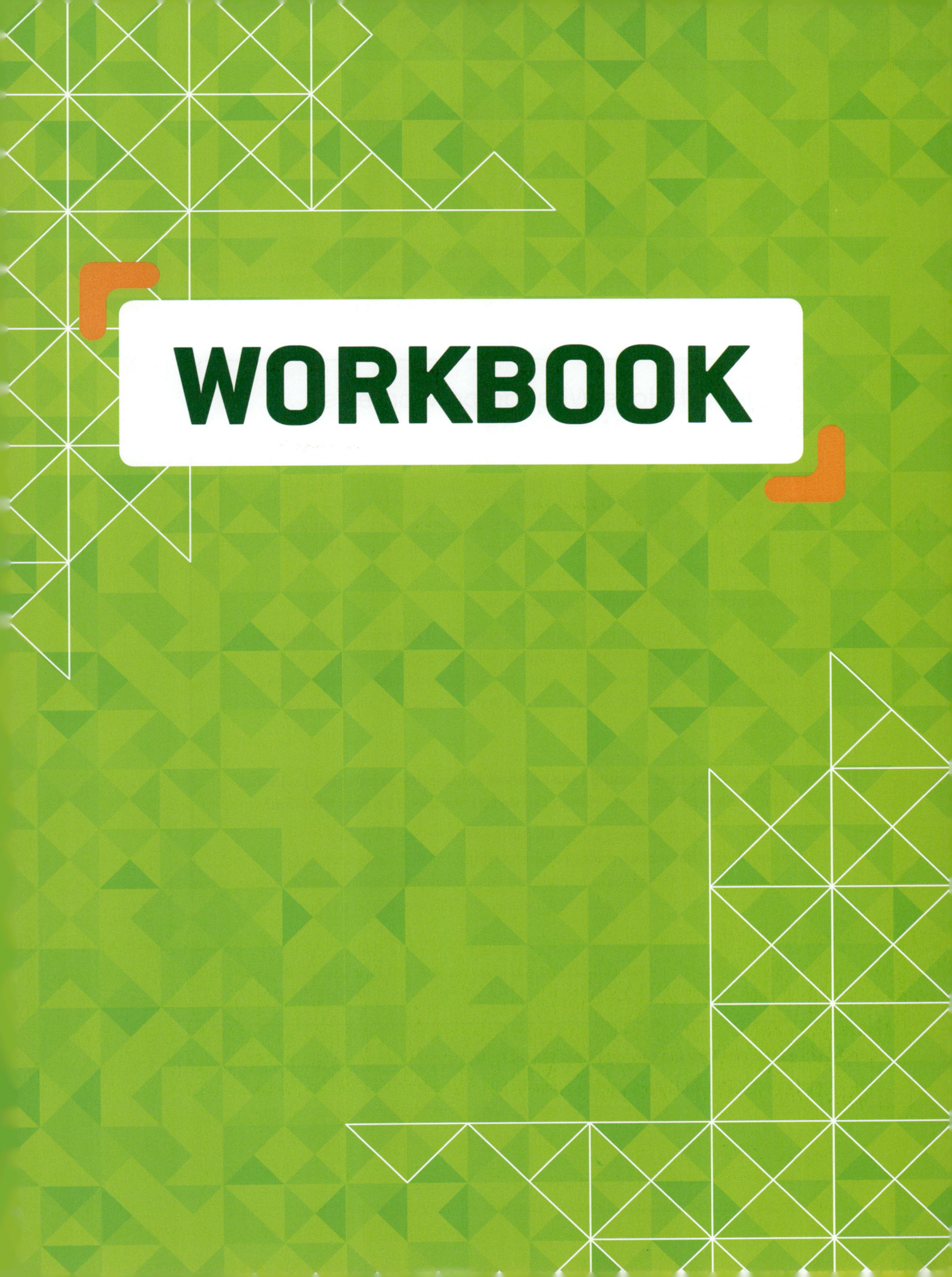

WORKBOOK

Unit 1 — Gender Equality Is for Everybody

1. **Look at the text. What is it? Circle the correct answer.** *Identifying the genre*
   a. an film review
   b. a story
   c. a poem
   d. an interview

2. **Skim the text. Check (✓) the sentence that best describes what is in it.** *Skimming*
   a. ( ) A conversation with Joss Whedon about men's role in the workplace.
   b. ( ) A discussion where Joss Whedon shows advantages and disadvantages of working with women.
   c. ( ) A conversation with Joss Whedon about men and women having equal roles in the workplace.

A Talk with Joss Whedon on Women's *Equality* in the Workplace

[…]

Joss Whedon is a perfect example of a man *stepping forward* to fight the battle for *equal pay*. He has consistently pushed strong female **roles** to become an unremarkable standard. Whedon told us why we must pay more attention than ever to elevating women in media. […]

What does the word "feminist" mean to you?

"It's someone who's just trying to restore a *balance* that **has missed / has been missing** from our culture for far too long. It means understanding the effect you have on the people around you, and what a certain amount of respect can *accomplish* in your daily life — as much as the more *tangible* things like, 'People should get paid.'"

[…]

I read a statistic that it would take 44 years for the pay to be equal […] What do you think both men and women can do to help speed up that timeline?

"We need to overcompensate a little bit for the fact that **we've under compensated / have been under compensating** forever. Things have to be pushed to be even. People have to make decisions that may seem *counterintuitive* to a businessman every now and then, because they'll pay as little as they can to everyone.

[…]

Adapted from https://businesscollective.com/an-interview-with-joss-whedon-on-womens-equality-in-the-workplace/index.html.
Accessed on September 17, 2018.

---

3. **Check (✓) the statements you can infer from the text.** *Inferring*
   a. ( ) Women are all underpaid.
   b. ( ) Feminists believe that women should have the same rights and opportunities as men.
   c. ( ) It may take a long time for both men and women to have equal pay.
   d. ( ) The text is all about men valuing women.
   e. ( ) Men have the best salaries and positions in the jobs market.
   f. ( ) #HeForShe is a movement that promotes economic equality within the local communities.

Unit 1

4. Read the text again. Think of the rules about present perfect simple and present perfect continuous and underline the correct alternative to complete the sentences in the interview on page 104. Then write the form of each of these verb tenses.

_____

_____

5. Reread these sentences from the interview on page 104 and circle the correct alternative.

  a. The sentence "It's someone who's just trying to restore a balance that has been missing from our culture for far too long" focuses on the **completion** / **duration** of an action.

  b. The sentence "We need to overcompensate a little bit for the fact that we have been under compensating forever" focuses on the **completion** / **duration** of an action.

6. Look at the words in italics in the interview on page 104. Use them to complete the dictionary entries below.

_____ (noun): a state in which opposite forces or influences exist in equal or the correct amounts, in a way that is good

_____ (adjective): clear enough to be easily seen or noticed

_____ (phrasal verb): to come and offer help, information, etc.

_____ (adjective): not based on a feeling

_____ (noun): the principle that men and women should have the same salary if they do the same work

_____ (noun): a situation in which people have the same rights, advantages, etc.

_____ (verb): to succeed in doing something, especially after trying very hard

Adapted from www.ldoceonline.com. Accessed on September 18, 2018.

7. Read the testimonials below. What are the people talking about? Check (✔) the correct alternative.

  a. "In my job both men and women are treated the same way. Women are respected and can also take leading posts. In fact, my boss is a woman, and she is one of the best managers in our factory." - Dylan, 28
  ( ) unequal pay   ( ) balance of power   ( ) equal pay

  b. "I have been working at my current job for about six years. Last month I found out my male colleague, who has been working with me for less than a year, gets around 15% more than me and does the same job. It is so unfair!" - Sonia, 33
  ( ) unequal pay   ( ) equal pay   ( ) balance of power

  c. "I work for a clothing store. Sometimes I feel that my boss comments on our appearance way too much. Just last week he told me to stand by the front door because I was pretty and I would attract lots of customers. I have more qualities than just being pretty! I'm a good salesperson!" - Vivian, 24
  ( ) unequal pay   ( ) sexual harassment   ( ) women's empowerment

8. Complete the sentences with the verbs in brackets in the present perfect continuous.

a. My mom _____ (read) a lot of articles about feminist movements lately.
b. You have a lot of good ideas. _____ you _____ (study) about the subject recently?
c. We _____ (wait) here for over an hour.
d. Women _____ (fight) for gender equality for a very long time.
e. I _____ (do) research for a new article on equal pay.
f. Mark _____ (work) for us for a year now.

9. Read the quotes about gender equality. Complete the sentences with the verbs from the box to form present perfect simple or present perfect continuous sentences.

> be (x2)   reach   show   succeed   try   write

a. Women's value _____ under-recognized for far too long. (Sidney Sheldon)

b. The failure of women to _____ positions of leadership has been due in large part to social and professional discrimination. In the past, few women _____, and even fewer _____. (Rosalyn Sussman Yalow)

c. Some of the greatest survivors have been women. Look at the courage so many women _____ after surviving earthquakes in the rubble for days on end. (Bear Grylls)

d. Women's progress _____ a collective effort. (Gloria Steinem)

e. I'm just one voice, but there are many others like me. Women _____ strong women characters for a long time – hello, Maxine Hong Kingston! – it's just taken mainstream comics a really long while to catch up. (Marjorie Liu)

Extracted from www.brainyquote.com. Accessed on September 18, 2018.

10. Refer back to the quotes in activity 9. Identify and write two time expressions that focused on the duration of the action.

_____

Unit 1

11. Answer the questions with your own information.

　a. How long have you been living in this town/city? What do you like most about it?

　_____
　_____
　_____

　b. How long have you been studying English? In your opinion, is it important to learn a foreign language? Justify your answer.

　_____
　_____
　_____

　c. Do women in your family work outside of the home? If so, how long have they had a job? Did your great-grandmother have a job or was she a housewife?

　_____
　_____
　_____

　d. How long have women in your country been allowed to vote?

　_____
　_____
　_____

AN EYE ON VESTIBULAR

VESTIBULAR UNICAMP 2016 – Provas Q e Z
1ª Fase – Questões 36 e 37

Advice for new students from those who know (old students)

"The first day of college I was a ball of nerves. I remember walking into my first class and running to the first seat I found, thinking everyone would be staring at me. But nobody seemed to notice and then it hit me: The fact that nobody knew me meant nobody would judge, which, upon reflection, was what I was scared of the most. I told myself to let go. All throughout the year, I forced myself into situations that were uncomfortable for me — for example, auditioning for a dance piece. Believe it or not, that performance was a highlight of my freshman year. My advice: challenge yourself to try something new, something you couldn't have done in high school."

– *Ria Jagasia, Vanderbilt University, '18.*

(Adaptado de www.nytimes.com/2015/08/02/ education/edlife/advice-for-new-students-from-those-who-know-old-students.html?ref=edlife.)

No primeiro dia de faculdade, Ria ficou muito nervosa
　a. por não conhecer ninguém.
　b. por achar que seria julgada pelos colegas.
　c. porque ninguém olhou para ela.
　d. porque não sabia dançar.

Para lidar com a situação, a estratégia adotada foi deixar de se preocupar e
　a. fazer coisas que nunca fez antes.
　b. fazer novos amigos.
　c. fazer um curso de dança como ouvinte.
　d. abandonar o curso.

Unit 2 — Technology in the School Curriculum

1. Read the article and answer: What's the main purpose of the text? *Understanding the purpose of a text*

_____

_____

10 signs a career in coding and software development might be right for you

[…]
To help present the skills needed for computer programming in a different light, here are 10 signs coding could be right for you; signs that aren't always accounted for in academic tests.

1. You're a problem-solving pro
Lots of people will simply tolerate problems without looking for a proactive way to solve them, particularly if tolerating the problem is easier. If you don't take this approach, but actually enjoy the challenge of solving problems of all kinds, then that's a great sign that you could be **suited to** software development. If, in your desire to solve problems, you also take into account realistic **constraints** – such as timeframes and budgets – then this could be a real **asset** in your search for a career.

2. You have a passion for strategy games
Yes, it can be true that gaming is good for you, particularly where strategy games are concerned. These help **hone** your ability to make decisions based on a number of relevant factors, taking into account both short and long-term consequences. As well as computer games, those who enjoy offline games like chess, bridge or risk, could also have an underlying aptitude for programming. […]

3. _____
While the evidence for the correlation between music and maths is still in debate, it seems commonplace for those with musical talent to have mathematical abilities too. […]

4. You have a talent for winning arguments
No, we're not talking about **full-blown** shouting matches. But if your logical approach to arguing your points in a structured way means that you frequently win over your opponents, this could be a sign that you have the systematic thinking needed for software development.

5. _____
You can get the same sense of satisfaction from making something in the virtual world as you can in the physical world. Indeed, in the digital world, you aren't constrained by practicalities like materials and space, so imagination is your only limit. Having a natural curiosity for how things work, and how to make them work better, is a good indication of a nascent software developer.

6. You're a people person
Contrary to the stereotype of the IT team **hidden away** from the rest of the company, working as a developer can actually involve a great deal of interaction with others across the business. This means that an enjoyment of communicating and an ability to explain things in a way that is easily understood by others are both really important.

7. You'd like to know more about the theory of computer science
While you may not have digested the full history of computer science, an interest in the theory behind software engineering is an important aspect of a coder's skillset. You don't want to spend your time re-inventing the wheel, so being interested in what others have discovered, and being prepared to build on those foundations, will fast-track your potential **achievements**.

8. _____
Coding itself is a very collaborative process; continuously reviewing and redefining code with others helps you to shake out bugs, makes your work more likely to meet users' needs and is one of the best ways to learn. Developers therefore need to enjoy working together and should be prepared to study, critique, and improve one another's work.

9. You are intrinsically motivated
Putting some amateur psychology to use, it seems to be true that the best developers are intrinsically motivated. This means they take their reward and motivation from the process of finding a solution to a problem, or creating something innovative in itself. In other words, developers often do what they do for the love of doing it, rather than just being paid to do it.

10. _____
This is fairly obvious, but it is worth re-iterating that if you want to work in software engineering, you need to have an appreciation for the amazing possibilities that technology brings to the world. Being interested in how you can **harness** the potential of technology, for whichever company you want to work in, will definitely stand you in good **stead**, and is a sure sign you are on the right career track for success in coding.

Adapted from www.theguardian.com/careers/ten-signs-career-coding-software-development-right-for-you. Accessed on December 5, 2018.

2. Complete the text with the headings from the box. *Understanding details*

> You're a team player
> You have a musical mind
> You love technology
> You love making things

3. Match some words from the article with their meanings.

a. problem-solving ( ) abilities to do something well, talents
b. systematic ( ) when you find ways of doing things, or answers to problems
c. skills ( ) someone who you think is not very skilled at something
d. bugs ( ) faults in the system of instructions that operates a computer
e. critique ( ) to say how good or bad a book, play, painting, or set of ideas is
f. amateur ( ) organized carefully and done thoroughly

Adapted from www.ldoceonline.com. Accessed on December 5, 2018.

4. Read this summary from the text on page 108 and underline the correct alternative.

The article "10 signs a career in coding and software development might be right for you" **present /presents** ten characteristics people may have that could help them to pursue a career in coding. **Most / Few** skills are simple personality traits that many people have. If you **like /likes** technology, music, making things, and solving problems, for instance, it **mean / means** that you could start thinking about working with coding in the future. A surprising factor that is presented in the text **is / are** the ability to interact with others from your team.

5. Which of the characteristics presented in the text in activity 1 do you think you have? Would you like to pursue a career in coding? Justify your answer.

_____
_____
_____
_____
_____
_____

6. Circle the correct option to complete the sentences.

a. I believe that _____ (each / all) skills presented in the text may be important for someone who wants to learn to code.
b. When I read the article, I noticed that I have more than _____ (half of / all of) the skills needed.
c. I believe that we can learn to do things if we practice _____ (every / each) day.
d. If you think you have _____ (all of / none of) the skills presented in the article, don't worry. You can learn new skills.

7. Complete the extracts with the words from the box. There are two extra words.

> algorithm   variable   iteration   sandbox

a. "Is Facebook's advertising _____ sexist? That's what Tobias Dengel, CEO of WillowTree is claiming after a job advertisement was rejected because of the use of the term 'equal pay' in a job announcement run on November 5, 2018. [...]"

Extracted from www.forbes.com. Accessed on December 5, 2018.

b. "Fortnite is getting a major new _____ mode, separate from battle royale."

Extracted from www.eurogamer.net. Accessed on December 5, 2018.

Unit 2

109

8. Read an excerpt from another article about coding. Then identify and circle the compound adjectives you find.

https://www.theguardian.com/technology/2016/sep/11/make-computer-coding-childs-play-programming-apps

HOW TO MAKE COMPUTER CODING CHILD'S PLAY

With *programming* lessons now part of the school day, can parents help their **offspring** get top grades? Fear not – toys, gadgets, and *apps* are all available to make *coding* a fun part of growing up. [...]

Nowadays there's a renewed wave of interest in the topic, thanks partly to programming being part of England's national curriculum starting at five-year-old children. [...] There are inevitably apps for that, but also some inventive hardware. For children wanting to get in some extracurricular practice, these *gadgets*, programs, and books could be just the thing.

Gadgets
Kano
Billed as "an easy-to-build computer", Kano arrives in its constituent parts, which children put together as the first step in their journey towards programming. [...]

Fisher-Price Code-a-pillar
Aimed at pre-school children, this certainly looks the part as a Fisher-Price toy: a characterful plastic caterpillar with bold, bright colours. It's one of the most accessible introductions to computational thinking in the guise of fun play. [...]

Osmo coding kit
Osmo is an iPad *accessory*, that functions as a stand-up base for your tablet, and a mirror that clips on to its top, enabling the camera to "see" what's in front of the device.
[...]

LittleBits Arduino coding kit
With this kit children can build their own Etch-a-Sketch toy or a version of arcade game Pong. It uses the Arduino computer, an alternative to the Raspberry Pi, and is aimed at children aged 14 and older to hack together their own inventions, including *hardware* and software.
[...]

PROGRAMMING READS
A selection of old-fashioned printed books that could **fire up** children's interest in coding.

Hello Ruby: Adventures in Coding [...]
Coding for Beginners: Using Scratch [...]
Computer Coding for Kids [...]

Adapted from www.theguardian.com/technology/2016/sep/11/make-computer-coding-childs-play-programming-apps. Accessed on September 21, 2018.

9. The words in italics in the excerpt are related to education and technology. Read and complete the definitions below.

a. _____ are small, useful, and cleverly-designed machines or tools.

b. _____ is the activity of writing programs for computers, or something written by a programmer.

c. _____ are some pieces of software for a particular use or job.

d. _____ is the activity of writing computer programs.

e. An _____ is something such as a piece of equipment or a decoration that is not necessary, but that makes a machine more useful or more attractive.

f. _____ is computer machinery and equipment, as opposed to the programs that make computers work.

Adapted from www.ldoceonline.com. Accessed on September 24, 2018.

10. Now choose three of the compound adjectives from activity 8 and write sentences that are true for you.

_____
_____
_____

11. Complete the sentences with the correct compound adjective from the box.

> well-known   state-of-the-art   two-year-old
> time-saving   20-page   fastest-growing

a. Let's buy it. It's a _____ gadget. We can spend more time on other things then.

b. Do you know what the _____ programming language is? I need to have these figures for my coding class.

c. The municipality is building a new _____ hospital, where only the latest devices are going to be used.

d. Mark Zuckerberg is one of the most _____ programmers in the world.

e. Mike has just submitted a _____ project. He will only get his grade on it next week, as it will take his teacher some time to read it all.

f. This is Simba. He's my _____ dog.

AN EYE ON VESTIBULAR

VESTIBULAR FUVEST 2018 – Prova V

1ª Fase – Questões 89 e 90

Algorithms are everywhere. They play the stockmarket, decide whether you can have a mortgage, and may one day drive your car for you. They search the Internet when commanded, stick carefully chosen advertisements into the sites you visit, and decide what prices to show you in online shops. (…) But what exactly are algorithms, and what makes them so powerful?

An algorithm is, essentially, a brainless way of doing clever things. It is a set of precise steps that need no great mental effort to follow but which, if obeyed exactly and mechanically, will lead to some desirable outcome. Long division and column addition are examples that everyone is familiar with—if you follow the procedure, you are guaranteed to get the right answer. So is the strategy, rediscovered thousands of times every year by schoolchildren bored with learning mathematical algorithms, for playing a perfect game of tic-tac-toe. The brainlessness is key: each step should be as simple and as free from ambiguity as possible. Cooking recipes and driving directions are algorithms of a sort. But instructions like "stew the meat until tender" or "it's a few miles down the road" are too vague to follow without at least some interpretation.

(…)

The Economist, August 30, 2017.

No texto, um exemplo associado ao fato de algoritmos estarem por toda parte é

a. o cartão de crédito.
b. o livre mercado.
c. a dieta.
d. o jogo de xadrez.
e. o comércio eletrônico.

Segundo o texto, a execução de um algoritmo consiste em um processo que

a. prevê a memorização de tabelas e fórmulas.
b. envolve mecanismos de seleção e detecção de erros.
c. se apoia em um número infinito de etapas.
d. é incompatível com análises subjetivas e imprecisas.
e. alterna níveis altos e baixos de esforço intelectual.

Unit 3 — Can We Eat with a Clear Conscience?

1. Read the title of the blog post. What can you infer from it? Check (✓) all the possible answers. *Inferring*

   a. ( ) All unhealthy food is expensive.
   b. ( ) Some healthy foods are cheap.
   c. ( ) Healthy food is not cheap.
   d. ( ) Unhealthy food is cheaper than healthy food.

2. Read the whole text. What is the author's purpose? *Identifying the purpose of the text*

---

www.huffingtonpost.com/deane-waldman/what-if-healthy-food-were_b_323831.html

THE BLOG

What if healthy food were cheaper?

By Deane Waldman

Choose!

Everyone knows that obesity is a major health problem in the USA. One estimate suggests that 30% of *health care* costs (actually the cost of sickness care) can be attributed to the consequences of obesity.

Obesity clearly reduces productivity. Thus, from the national commercial standpoint, obesity produces a *double whammy*: it both reduces *revenue* and at the same time increases costs.

While there are some endocrine conditions and genetic disorders that predispose to obesity, the vast majority of obesity is culturally driven and over-eating is under conscious control.

If we ate properly, most obese people would not be obese. Unfortunately, unhealthy foods are generally cheaper and much more available. Worst of all, people are programmed to think they taste better.

The production and distribution of unhealthy foods is very big business and highly *profitable*. Big food, like big pharma, is politically active and quite effective at defending their profitable position.

Consider obesity from the **standpoints** of three different people: provider, taxpayer, and President. The health care provider doesn't care about your weight other than the medical complications. It is part of their moral code to provide services to sick people **regardless of** all other factors.

Both healthy-sized people and super-sized people pay the same amount into the healthcare system. Yet the super-sized take more out because they require more health care services. The healthy-eating taxpayer feels this is unfair.

Finally, imagine yourself the CEO of Corporation USA, also known as the President of the USA. Your primary goal is to protect and **nurture** the nation **as a whole**. In contrast to either the provider or the taxpayer, you have power. You can encourage passage of laws, rules, and regulations. You have influence over the tax code.

You cannot legislate morality or **behavior** in the national best interest or even behavior in the individual's best interest. Intellectually, people know they should eat "healthy" but the bad stuff tastes sooooo good and besides, it's cheaper.

So, Mr. CEO of Corporation U.S.A., what can you do? You can change *incentives*. You know that incentives affect behavior and behavior determines **outcome**. If the people ate more healthy foods, they would be less obese. Health care would cost less, and productivity would increase (the reverse of the double whammy above).

Finally, Mr. CEO, you know that carrots work better than sticks. It is always better to offer a positive incentive to encourage the behavior you want than to punish the behavior you do not want.

If you want to reduce obesity, instead of punishing super-sized persons, *subsidize* healthy foods. Make them cheaper and more **available**. What if apples and vegetables were easier to come by than coke, French fries, and cheetos?

Imagine diverting 10% of what we spend now on obesity-care – say $60 billion – to subsidize healthy foods. How much less might we spend later on obesity-care – $100 billion, $300 billion? Then add the gains in productivity. Sounds to me like a win-win scenario.

Adapted from www.huffingtonpost.com/deane-waldman/what-if-healthy-food-were_b_323831.html. Accessed on September 23, 2018.

3. Read the blog post on page 112 again. Underline two problems that can be attributed to obesity. `Understanding details`

4. Scan the text. Circle the healthy food and cross out the unhealthy food you find. `Scanning`

5. Scan the text on page 112 to find the words in italics that match the definitions below. Then complete the paragraph that follows with one of the words.

a. _____ : things that encourage you to work harder, start a new activity, etc.
b. _____ : producing a profit or a useful result
c. _____ : money that a business or organization receives over a period of time, especially from selling goods or services
d. _____ : two bad things that happen together or one after the other
e. _____ : if a government or organization does it, it pays part of the cost
f. _____ : the services that are provided for looking after people's health, or the activity of doing this

Adapted from www.ldoceonline.com. Accessed on September 26, 2018.

> "Can thoughtful legislation help tackle the challenge of food recovery? Italy is optimistic that it will, hoping to reduce its 5.6 million tons in annual food waste by 20 percent through a law that rewards positive behaviors in the marketplace. The measure includes _____ for donating food, in addition to removing restrictions that have stood in the way of such benevolent actions. [...]"

Extracted from http://blog.ifco.com/how-incentives-could-reduce-food-waste. Accessed on November 26, 2018.

6. Match the columns to form second conditional sentences.

a. If we had a better diet, ...   (   ) people would eat in restaurants that offer healthy food.
b. We would buy those pears...   (   ) if he went to a nutritionist.
c. If the government invested more in health care, ...   (   ) if they were cheaper.
d. If there weren't so many fast-food franchises, ...   (   ) the people in that country would be healthier.
e. Daniel wouldn't have stomachaches so often...   (   ) obesity wouldn't be a problem for us.

7. Look at some sentences extracted from the text on page 112. Then complete the sentences that follow with your own ideas using the second conditional form.

a. "What if healthy food were cheaper?"
If healthy food were cheaper, _____
_____
_____

b. What if "10% of what we spend now on obesity-care – say $60 billion – were diverted to subsidize healthy foods"?
If _____
_____

c. "What if apples and vegetables were easier to come by than coke, French fries, and cheetos?"
If _____
_____

d. What if "super-sized people paid a different amount to the healthcare system"?
If _____
_____

8. Read the two first paragraphs of an article about changing your eating habits and underline a first and a second conditional sentence.

Changing Your Habits for Better Health

Are you thinking about being more active? Have you been trying to cut back on less healthy foods? Are you starting to eat better and move more but having a hard time **sticking with** these changes?

Old habits die hard. Changing your habits is a process that involves several stages. Sometimes it takes a while before changes become new habits. And you may face roadblocks along the way.

Adopting new, healthier habits may protect you from serious health problems like obesity and diabetes. New habits, like healthy eating and regular physical activity, may also help you manage your **weight** and have more energy. After a while, if you stick with these changes, they will probably become part of your daily routine.
[…]

Contemplation: Are you thinking of making changes?

Making the **leap** from thinking about change to taking action can be hard and may take time. Asking yourself about the pros (benefits) and cons (things that get in the way) of changing your habits may be helpful. How would life be better if you made some changes?

Think about how the benefits of healthy eating or regular physical activity might relate to your overall health. […]

You may learn more about the benefits of changing your eating and physical activity habits from a health care professional. This knowledge may help you take action.

Look at the list of pros and cons below. Find the items you believe are true for you. Think about factors that are important to you.

If you eat more healthily, you...	
Pros	**Cons**
• will have more energy	• will probably spend more money and time on food
• will improve your health	• will probably need to cook more often at home
• will lower your risk of health problems	• will probably need to eat less of foods you love
• will maintain a healthy weight	• will probably need to buy different foods
• will feel proud of yourself	• will probably need to convince your family that you all have to eat healthier foods
• will set an example for friends and family	

Adapted from www.niddk.nih.gov/health-information/diet-nutrition/changing-habits-better-health. Accessed on September 26, 2018.

9. Read the pros and cons list in the chart in activity 8. Think of two more pros and cons for the list in the text in activity 8. Then complete the chart below with them.

If I eat more healthily...	
Pros:	**Cons:**
a. _____	c. _____
b. _____	d. _____

10. Read again a question from the text and write your own answer for it. Use the second conditional in your answer.

"How would life be better if you made some changes?"

_____

_____

Unit 3

11. Complete the zero and first conditional sentences with the verbs in parentheses.

   a. If you don't eat any vegetables, you _____ (develop) nutrient deficiencies.
   b. People usually have constipation if they _____ (not drink) water every day.
   c. If you eat bananas before going to the gym tomorrow, you _____ (probably avoid) having muscle cramps.
   d. If Ana _____ (never drink) water, she will end up having some severe symptoms, such as increased blood sugar.
   e. You _____ (get) more vitamin A into your body if you eat carrots.
   f. What _____ (happen) if someone eats too much sugar?

12. Complete the conditional sentences with your own ideas using the correct conditional form.

   a. If someone eats too much chocolate, _____
   _____.

   b. If you stop having breakfast, _____
   _____.

   c. If you stopped eating at fast-food restaurants, _____
   _____.

   d. If you don't eat dessert every day, _____
   _____.

   e. If you could grow your own vegetables, _____
   _____.

AN EYE ON ENEM

ENEM 2014 - 2º dia Caderno Cinza
Questão 91

If you can't read it, why eat it?

Know what you're putting in your body. If it doesn't sound like food, think twice. Many packaged and over-processed foods and snacks are loaded with fillers and preservatives. That means less of the good stuff your body needs.

Food Label Illiteracy. It's just not natural.

Disponível em: http://1.bp.blogspot.com. Acesso em: 30 jul. 2012.

Implementar políticas adequadas de alimentação e nutrição é uma meta prioritária em vários países do mundo. A partir da campanha *If you can't read it, why eat it?*, os leitores são alertados para o perigo de

   a. acessarem informações equivocadas sobre a formulação química de alimentos empacotados.
   b. consumirem alimentos industrializados sem o interesse em conhecer a sua composição.
   c. desenvolverem problemas de saúde pela falta de conhecimento a respeito do teor dos alimentos.
   d. incentivarem crianças a ingerirem grande quantidade de alimentos processados e com conservantes.
   e. ignorarem o aumento constante da obesidade causada pela má alimentação na fase de desenvolvimento da criança.

Unit 4   **Extreme Weather Events Affecting the Planet**

1. Look at the title, headings, and pictograms in the text in activity 2. What is it about? List some ideas of what you expect to find in the text. *Predicting and taking notes*

   _____

   _____

2. Read some safety guidelines from "Winter Storm Safety," by redcross.org. Underline the words related to the weather. Then infer their meaning by context or look them up on a dictionary, if necessary. *Scanning*

Winter Storm Safety

Learn how to stay safe during a blizzard and how to prevent or **thaw** frozen pipes.

About

Each year, hundreds of Americans are injured or killed by exposure to cold, vehicle accidents on wintry roads, and fires caused by the improper use of heaters. Learn what to do to keep your loved ones safe during blizzards and other winter storms!

Take immediate precautions if you hear these words on the news:

Winter Storm WARNING: Life-threatening, severe winter conditions have begun or will begin within 24 hours.

Blizzard WARNING: Sustained winds or frequent gusts of 35 miles per hour or greater, plus considerable falling or blowing snow reducing visibility to less than a quarter mile, expected to prevail for three hours or longer. […]

Staying Safe During a Winter Storm or Blizzard

- Stay indoors and wear warm clothes. Layers of **loose-fitting**, **lightweight**, warm clothing will keep you warmer than a bulky sweater. If you feel too warm, remove layers to avoid sweating; if you feel chilled, add layers. […]
- Bring your companion animals inside before the storm begins.
- Move other animals to sheltered areas with a supply of non-frozen water. Most animal deaths in winter storms are caused by dehydration.
- Eat regularly. Food provides the body with energy for producing its own heat.
- Keep the body **replenished** with fluids to prevent dehydration. […]
- Conserve fuel. Winter storms can last for several days, placing great demand on electric, gas, and other fuel distribution systems (fuel oil, propane, etc.). Lower the thermostat to 65° F (18° C) during the day and to 55° F (13° C) at night. Close off unused rooms, and stuff towels or **rags** in cracks under the doors. Cover the windows at night.
- Check on relatives, neighbors, and friends, particularly if they are elderly or if they live alone.

Driving in Winter Conditions

- Check your vehicle emergency supplies kit and replenish it if necessary. […]
- Let someone know your destination, your route, and when you expect to arrive. If your vehicle gets stuck along the way, help can be sent along your predetermined route.
- Before leaving, listen to weather reports for your area and the areas you will be passing through, or call the state highway patrol for the latest road conditions.
- Be on the lookout for sleet, freezing rain, freezing **drizzle**, and dense fog, which can make driving very **hazardous**. […]

If You Become Stranded

- Stay in the vehicle and wait for help. Do not leave the vehicle to search for assistance unless help is visible within 100 yards (91 meters). You can quickly become disoriented and confused in blowing snow. […]
- Run the engine occasionally to keep warm. Turn on the engine for about 10 minutes each hour (or five minutes every half hour). Running the engine for only short periods reduces the risk of carbon monoxide poisoning and conserves fuel. Use the heater while the engine is running. Keep the exhaust pipe clear of snow, and slightly open a downwind window for ventilation.
- Do light exercises to keep up circulation. Clap your hands and move your arms and legs occasionally. Try not to stay in one position for too long. […]

Extracted from www.redcross.org/get-help/how-to-prepare-for-emergencies/types-of-emergencies/winter-storm.html. Accessed on September 27, 2018.

3. Now that you have read the text, were your predictions in activity 1 correct? Write a comparison between your predictions and what is in the text.

_____

_____

_____

_____

4. Complete the statements below using the idioms containing weather-related words from the box.

> be on cloud nine
> a storm in a teacup
> to be under the weather
> it's raining cats and dogs
> take a rain check
> come rain or shine

a. Oh, no! Look outside, _____.
b. Susan has _____ since she heard how well she did on her final papers.
c. I couldn't understand why he was so angry. His protest was nothing but _____.
d. I'm feeling a little _____ today, so I won't be able to come to your party.
e. Put on your sweater and let's go. The concert is happening _____.
f. I can't meet you guys today. Sorry, I'll _____.

5. Now use the words from the box to complete these other idioms containing weather-related words. Read the definitions to help you.

> break   storm   cloud   pours   rainy

a. *every _____ has a silver lining*: used to say that there is something good even in a situation that seems very sad or difficult
b. *it never rains but it _____*: used to say that as soon as one thing goes wrong, a lot of other things go wrong as well
c. *_____ the ice*: to make people feel more friendly and willing to talk to each other
d. *save something for a _____ day*: to save something, especially money, for a time when you will need it
e. *the calm before the _____*: a calm, peaceful situation that will not continue because a big argument, problem, etc. is coming

Adapted from www.ldoceonline.com. Accessed on September 28, 2018.

6. Read the extracts from page 116. Underline the adverbs of intensity that best convey the ideas of the words in bold.

a. "If you feel **too** (nearly / extremely) warm, remove layers to avoid sweating."
b. "Be on the lookout for sleet, freezing rain, freezing drizzle, and dense fog, which can make driving **very** (extremely / moderately) hazardous."
c. "Run the engine **as much as needed** (a lot / enough) to keep warm."
d. "Running the engine for **a short** (a lot / a little) while reduces the risk of carbon monoxide poisoning and conserves fuel."
e. "Keep the exhaust pipe clear of snow, and **slightly** (a little / totally) open a downwind window for ventilation."

7. Read part of a Katrina survivor's tale. Then complete the blanks with a verb from the box in the past perfect.

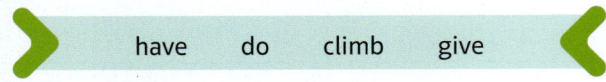

> have   do   climb   give

[…]
We _____ ourselves the luxury of ordering two new chairs after discarding both our storm-damaged sofas.
The deliveryman was already on the front porch when I came around from the back of the house. He was a head taller than me, a bit over six feet, with short hair, an engaging smile, and a shirt **embroidered** with the store logo and his name: Andre.
I asked how he _____ in the storm, a standard opening to conversation in those days.
"Not too bad," he said, with only the slightest hesitation. "Well, we lost our house, but we're all here and OK now. I got a picture here," he said as he pulled out a wallet and began searching the various pockets, "a picture of my wife and baby."
[…]
"We stayed," he continued. "My fault. Gotta say that first. We got a solid two-story brick house out in Gentilly. […] The levees broke, then the water started coming up so fast we had to **scramble** upstairs from the first floor.
The water was running by my house just below the balcony railings, and I could see this black, oily surface going all around the block, filling streets and yards. People was (*sic*) **yelling**, banging on the roofs of houses from the inside. They _____ to get away from the water and got themselves stuck in their **attics** with no way to break out. […]
"I couldn't tell where exactly the yelling was coming from, because everything was echoing off the water and **spinning** from every which way. I went inside. […] We drunk some water out of the upstairs bathroom sink, figuring the water _____ time to get bad yet."
[…]
"About a week later we all got evacuated to Charlotte, North Carolina, and I got no complaints about that." […]

Extracted from www.theguardian.com/us-news/2015/aug/27/katrina-survivors-tale-they-up-and-forgot-us. Accessed on September 28, 2018.

8. Read the extract in activity 7 again and order the events 1-5.

a. ( ) The author bought a chair.
b. ( ) The water started coming up Andre's house.
c. ( ) People climbed up the attics of their houses.
d. ( ) The delivery man arrived.
e. ( ) Andre and his family went to Charlotte, North Carolina.

9. Reorder the words to form sentences.

a. had already / the volcano / erupted / when / left town / they / .
_____

b. the supplies / had bought / tragedy struck / before / Diana / .
_____

c. to change / started / the weather / we / after / had arrived / .
_____

d. was / because / scared / Tom / had never seen / he / before / such horrible weather / .
_____

e. her family / when / arrived home / Sarah / to bed / had already gone / .
_____

f. saw that / a lot of people / Andre / the roofs / had climbed up / .
_____

10. Complete the sentences below with the verbs in parentheses in the simple past or past perfect.

a. Alan didn't want to watch the news with us because he _____ (read) about the hurricane in the morning.
b. Lizzy hadn't seen a snowstorm before, so she _____ (get) very interested in the pictures.
c. By the time Terry arrived, we _____ (finish) the research on natural disasters.
d. We _____ (not say) anything until she had finished talking.
e. I _____ (help) people who _____ (be) through natural disasters before, so I knew I could help them, too.
f. After Cindy _____ (move out), I found her notes.

11. Read the paragraph below. Then write two things Collin had done before the school bus arrived.

> I woke up at 6:30. Then I put on my school uniform and went to the kitchen. I ate my breakfast, cereal with fruit and milk. Then I brushed my teeth and heard the school bus stopping in front of my house.

Before the bus arrived, Colin _____.

AN EYE ON VESTIBULAR

VESTIBULAR PUC-RJ – 2015
1º dia – Questão 12

Tsunami Science:
advances since the 2004 Indian ocean tragedy

The Indian Ocean tsunami was one of the worst natural disasters in history. Enormous waves struck countries in South Asia and East Africa with the little to no warning, killing 243,000 people. The destruction played out on television screens around the world, fed by shaky home videos. The outpouring of aid in response to the devastation in Indonesia, Sri Lanka, Thailand and elsewhere was unprecedented.

The disaster raised awareness of tsunamis and prompted nations to pump money into research and warning systems. Today (Dec. 26), on the 10th anniversary of the deadly tsunami, greatly expanded networks of seismic monitors and ocean buoys are on alert for the next killer wave in the Indian Ocean, the Pacific, and the Caribbean. (…)

By Becky Oskin, Senior Writer. Adapted from htttp://www.livescience.com/49262-indian-ocean-tsunami-anniversary.html. December 26, 2014.

In the sentence "The disaster raised awareness of tsunamis and prompted nations to pump money into research and warning systems", the word *prompted* means

a. motivated.
b. persuaded.
c. suggested.
d. restricted.
e. impeded.

Unit 5 — In the Limelight

1. Skim the text and check (✓) the correct alternative to complete the sentence. *Skimming and identifying the genre*

   The text is from...
   a. ( ) a TV guide.
   b. ( ) a comic strip.
   c. ( ) an interview.
   d. (✓) a blog.
   e. ( ) an advertisement campaign.

Two post-apocalyptic movie endings that were changed by audience opinions

Companies selling products aren't the only businesses using paid surveys to increase sales. There are other industries that collect opinions in different ways and use them to drastically change projects and outcomes.

The movie industry is well-known for using test audiences to alter your favorite movies. In fact, oftentimes a crowd's reaction to a rough cut can change the way a movie ends, which is essentially the most important part of many
5 cinematic adventures.

For better or worse, studio executives weren't happy with the way audiences reacted to the original endings of these movies, so viewers got something drastically different than what was first intended. Read on if you don't mind spoilers.

'I Am Legend'

This 2007 post-apocalyptic film starred Will Smith as Doctor Robert "Legend" Neville. He's perhaps the only survivor
10 of a plague that has turned the citizens of New York City – and maybe the world – into vampires, and he's frantically working to **concoct** a cure using his natural immunity and vampire test subjects he **abducts**.

The movie is an adaptation based on a novella by Richard Matheson of the same name. However, the two end quite differently because the original was disliked by test audiences. The original cut of the movie and the book end with Neville realizing that he is the monster **preying** on the **misunderstood** vampires. The vampires reveal themselves as
15 intelligent, organized, and caring creatures. Meanwhile, Neville has been **kidnapping** them to experiment on.

Instead, the movie adaptation ends with Neville sacrificing himself and killing a group of vampires before they can rescue their kidnapped member. The original moral of the story is lost, but audiences preferred the change.

'28 Days Later'

20 Danny Boyle's cult classic movie '28 Days Later' was never predicted to earn such a popular following. But despite having a **measly** $8 million budget, according to the Internet Movie Database, the movie attracted so much attention that producers followed up with a **sequel**. That may be because the original ending was changed.

"28 Days Later" follows Jim, a delivery man who fell into a coma after a bike accident. During his time in the hospital, Great Britain spiraled into zombie **mayhem**. When Jim awakens, he finds some remaining survivors and they leave the
25 city in search of others.

At the climax of both movies, the original one and the sequel, Jim is shot in the stomach while escaping from an army compound with two of his surviving female friends. In the original version, the two frantically try to revive Jim but fail. They're left to confront the zombie **wasteland** alone.

Test audiences got the impression that the two women were **doomed** after Jim's death, so the movie was given a
30 brighter new ending. Jim is successfully revived after escaping the compound and the movie picks up with him waking up the same way he did in the hospital at the beginning. However, now the three survivors have successfully outlived most of the undead, who are now dying of **starvation**. The movie ends with the three catching the attention of a passing fighter jet.

Your opinion has a lot of power. It can be used to change your favorite products for the better with paid surveys, or it
35 can even save characters from a zombie wasteland.

Adapted from www.opinionoutpost.com/en/blog/2-postapocalyptic-movie-endings-that-were-changed-by-audience-opinions#.W6w1NmhKjIU. Accessed on October 1, 2018.

Unit 5

2. Scan the text. What does this information relate to? `Scanning`
   a. 2007: _____
   b. Will Smith: _____
   c. New York City: _____
   d. Richard Matheson: _____
   e. $8 million: _____
   f. Great Britain: _____

3. Look at the title of the text on page 120 again. Do you agree with changing movie endings according to the audience's opinion? Justify.

_____
_____
_____

4. Read the text again and decide if the sentences are true (T) or false (F). `Understanding details`
   a. ( ) The movie industry doesn't usually use test audiences to change movies from their original plot.
   b. ( ) The movie industry was comfortable with the original endings of these movies.
   c. ( ) Many movies are adaptations based on novels. These two movies are an example of this.
   d. ( ) Neville kills himself at the end of *I Am Legend*.
   e. ( ) Test audiences wanted Jim to be killed at the end of *28 Days Later*.
   f. ( ) The viewer's opinion doesn't have any impact on the movie industry.

5. Read these extracts from the text, paying special attention to the homographs in bold. Then check (✓) the correct meaning in context.

   a. "[…] he's frantically working to concoct a cure using his natural immunity and vampire test **subjects** he abducts."
   ( ) the thing you are talking about or considering in a conversation, discussion, book, movie, etc.
   (✓) a person or animal that is used in a test or experiment
   ( ) an area of knowledge that you study at a school or university

   b. "They're **left** to confront the zombie wasteland alone."
   ( ) the side of your body that contains your heart
   ( ) the opposite direction of right
   (✓) the past tense and past participle of leave

   c. "The original cut of the movie and the **book** end with Neville realizing that he is the monster preying on the misunderstood vampires."
   ( ) to make arrangements to stay in a place, eat in a restaurant, go to a theater, etc. at a particular time in the future
   ( ) to put someone's name officially in police records, along with the charge made against them
   (✓) a set of printed pages that are held together in a cover so that you can read them

   Adapted from www.ldoceonline.com. Accessed on October 2, 2018.

6. Which of the words in activity 5 can be pronounced in two different ways? Underline the stressed syllable in each of the cases. Use a dictionary if necessary.

_____

7. Use the third conditional to complete the statements related to the text.

   a. If the producers of *I Am Legend* _____ (keep) the original ending, Neville _____ (be) kidnapping creatures to experiment on them forever.
   b. If the producers of *28 Days Later* _____ (stick) to the original ending from the book, Jim's gunshot wound _____ (kill) him.

121

8. Complete the sentences so that they are true for you. Use the third conditional.

a. If I had gone to bed earlier, _____
_____ .

b. If I'd known that _____
_____ .

c. If I'd studied _____
_____ .

d. I would have been on time _____
_____ .

e. Last year, I would have gotten better grades in _____
_____ .

f. I wouldn't have missed _____
_____ .

9. Read the comic strip. Complete the blanks with the verbs from the box.

> tell   need   have   send

Panel 1: I WISH I _____ A SECRET ADMIRER...
Panel 2: SOMEONE WHO WOULD _____ ME FLOWERS AND LITTLE NOTES AND THINGS LIKE THAT...
Panel 3: AND THEN, ALL OF A SUDDEN, HE WOULD _____ ME WHO HE WAS...
Panel 4: THEN YOU'D _____ ANOTHER SECRET ADMIRER

Adapted from www.gocomics.com/peanuts/2003/06/20. Accessed on September 1, 2018.

10. Read the situations below. Then check (✓) the best past regret for them.

a. I stayed up late watching a movie last night. I'm so tired today.
   ( ) I wish I had watched one more movie last night.
   (✓) I wish I hadn't watched that movie last night.

b. I went to Suzy's house on Sunday and I missed the latest episode of *The Walking Dead*. Now my friends are all giving spoilers.
   (✓) I wish I had stayed at home on Sunday.
   ( ) I wish I had gone to Suzy's house.

c. I woke up late this morning and missed my bus.
   ( ) I wish I had slept in today.
   (✓) I wish I had set my alarm clock.

d. We went to the movies on Friday to watch a horror movie. I had horrible nightmares that night.
   (✓) I wish I had seen a comedy instead.
   ( ) I wish I had seen that horror movie twice.

Unit 5

11. Look at the pictures. Guess what these people are wishing for and complete the blanks.

a.

I wish _____ _____ to Paris.

b.

We wish _____ _____ that beautiful car.

c.

They wish _____ _____ famous singers.

d.

She wishes _____ _____ more money to pay for her studies.

AN EYE ON VESTIBULAR

VESTIBULAR DE VERÃO PUC SP 2017 – Prova V

1ª fase – Questão 40

The Heyday of the Silents
GEOFFREY NOWELL-SMITH

By the middle of the 1920s the cinema had reached a peak of splendour which in certain respects it would never again surpass. It is true that there was not synchronized sound, nor Technicolor, except at a very experimental stage. Synchronized sound was to be introduced at the end of the decade, while Technicolor came into use only in the mid-1930s and beyond. Nor, except in isolated cases like Abel Gance's Napoléon (1927), was there anything approaching the wide screen that audiences were to be accustomed to from the 1950s onwards. It is also the case that viewing conditions in many parts of the world, particularly in rural areas, remained makeshift and primitive.

Source: The Oxford History of World Cinema EDITED BY GEOFFREY NOWELL-SMITH OXFORD UNIVERSITY PRESS 1996

De acordo com o texto,

a. no início da década de 20, a indústria cinematográfica não contava com som nem com tecnicolor.
b. de acordo com Nowell-Smith, recursos cinematográficos como som sincronizado e tecnicolor foram introduzidos no final da década de 20.
c. a leitura do texto permite inferir que a palavra "heyday", encontrada no título, representa algo positivo.
d. o esplendor da indústria cinematográfica, atingido na década de 20, só se repetiu com a introdução de efeitos especiais, principalmente em algumas partes do mundo.

Unit 6 — Uncovering Blockchain and the Dark Web

1. **Look at the text in activity 2. What is the genre of the text? Who wrote it?** *Identifying the genre and the author of the text*

2. **Read the text that follows and answer the questions.** *Reading for specific information*
   a. What sells on the dark web for just $5.20?
   b. What is described as "the shadowy corner of the Internet"?
   c. What is Fractl?
   d. What's the number of Facebook users hacked by the dark web?
   e. Name a special network used by the dark web.
   f. What are vampire apps?

---

www.dailymail.co.uk/sciencetech/article-5533871/How-Facebook-data-worth-Hackers-sell-dollars.html

How much is YOUR data worth? In wake of Facebook's massive privacy scandal, experts say login details sell for just $5.20 on the dark web

- A study of dark web marketplaces show that Facebook logins sell for just $5.20
- By comparison, hacked financial details are in high demand from **scammers**
- The price of user privacy has been in focus in the wake of Facebook's massive data scandal, which led to 50 million users' data being compromised

By ANNIE PALMER FOR DAILYMAIL.COM
PUBLISHED: 22:25 BST, 22 March 2018 | UPDATED: 22:59 BST, 22 March 2018

If most people were asked how much their privacy is worth, they'd likely say it's priceless.

Unfortunately, hackers and identity thieves aren't so generous.

User logins for many of the most popular apps sell for next to nothing on the dark web, a shadowy corner of the Internet that's frequented by criminals, drug users, arms dealers and is often the grounds for all kinds of illicit activities.

Now, a recent report from content marketing agency Fractl has **found out** just how much your data is worth on the dark web.

The price of user privacy has been cast into the spotlight in the wake of Facebook's massive data scandal, which led to 50 million users' data being **harvested** without their knowledge.

Facebook has since announced that it would notify all users whose data was misused by British research firm Cambridge Analytica or any app developers who are found to have mismanaged users' personal information.

This addresses the issue of user information being sold to advertisers, research firms and the like, but it doesn't **touch upon** one of the Internet's busiest marketplaces – the dark web.

For the study, Fractl **scoured** all the fraud-related listings on the three biggest dark web marketplaces – Dream, Point, and Wall Street Market – last month, according to MarketWatch.

[…]

To do this, they downloaded a Tor client, or a network that **grants** anonymity to Internet browsers, which is required in order to access the dark web.

There, they discovered that Facebook logins are sold for just $5.20 each.

Obtaining someone's Facebook **credentials** can serve as a gateway into hundreds of other apps they've also granted access.

That's because Facebook allows thousands of third-party 'vampire apps' to **plug in** to its social network and **siphon off** data from its users.

This means anything from popular services like Airbnb and Spotify, to dodgy quiz apps or online games like Farmville.

Many users may use their Facebook account to **log in** to these apps, which means that if a hacker has your credentials for the social media platform, they can easily get into many other accounts.

Meanwhile, credentials for other popular services like Gmail, Uber, and Grubhub are just as cheap.

Your Gmail username and password is a bargain at just $1, while Uber account logins go for $7 and Grubhub logins sell for $9.

By comparison, the most expensive logins are for PayPal, which can demand up to $247, according to Fractl.

According to experts, the reason why some credentials sell for cheap is because hackers can so easily obtain it nowadays.

It's a classic case of supply and demand: With so much data available on the Internet, hackers can easily obtain it, sell it and **move on**.

Similarly, a separate study by security research firm Top 10 VPN revealed that your entire online identity can be sold for approximately $1,200.

Top 10 VPN also found that Facebook logins would sell for $5.20 on the dark web.

Extracted from www.dailymail.co.uk/sciencetech/article-5533871/How-Facebook-data-worth-Hackers-sell-dollars.html. Accessed on September 03, 2018.

3. Read the text on page 124 again. Check (✓) all the alternatives that apply. The author's tone is...   *Identifying the author's tone*

    a. ( ) optimistic.
    b. ( ) factual.
    c. ( ) entertaining.
    d. ( ) frank.
    e. ( ) supportive.
    f. ( ) critical.

4. Read the text on page 124 again and find the phrasal verbs in bold to fit each definition below.

    a. _____ : to dishonestly take money or goods from a business, account, etc. to use it for a purpose for which it was not intended.
    b. _____ : to connect a piece of electrical equipment to the main supply of electricity, or to another piece of electrical equipment.
    c. _____ : to get information after trying to discover it or by chance.
    d. _____ : to do the necessary actions on a computer system that will allow you to begin using it.
    e. _____ : to leave your present job, class, or activity and start doing another one.
    f. _____ : to mention a particular subject when talking or writing.

Adapted from www.ldoceonline.com. Accessed on September 04, 2018.

5. Complete the sentences below using the phrasal verbs from activity 4 in the correct form.

    a. The FBI _____ that Facebook's logins were stolen by people on the dark web.
    b. The report _____ the issue of the anonymity of dark web users.
    c. You need to _____ the cord before turning the computer on.
    d. They illegally _____ secret information from other people's bank accounts.
    e. It's time for a change, let's _____ .
    f. Don't forget to _____ to your new account to change your password.

6. Read these two extracts from the text on page 124. Check (✓) all the information that describes the uses of *some* and *any* in the sentences.

"According to experts, the reason why **some** credentials sell for cheap is because hackers can so easily obtain it nowadays."
"Facebook has since announced that it would notify all users whose data was misused by British research firm Cambridge Analytica or **any** app developers who are found to have mismanaged users' personal information."

    ( ) These determiners are being used before a noun.
    ( ) *Some* is being used with an exact quantity or number.
    ( ) *Any* refers to specific app developers.
    ( ) *Some* and *any* refer to unspecified quantities or numbers.

7. Complete the sentences below with *some, any, no,* or *every*.

    a. _____ of the information we find online is not reliable.
    b. She said that she would appreciate _____ tip she could get to learn about how she could benefit from buying bitcoin, even the basic ones.
    c. Have you ever read _____ articles about cryptocurrency?
    d. We have _____ words to express how much we appreciate your help.
    e. I really have _____ desire whatsoever to access the dark web. I think I will never want to know it.

8. Read the text below about the use of bitcoin in the UK. Then answer the question: Who did the journalist talk to in order to obtain the information for this news report?

_____

> ### Time to regulate bitcoin, says Treasury committee report
> #### MPs in U.K. say 'wild west' cryptocurrency industry is leaving investors vulnerable
>
> Bitcoin and other cryptocurrencies are "wild west" **assets** that expose investors to a **litany** of risks and are in urgent need of regulation, MPs on the Treasury select committee have said.
>
> ⁵ The committee said in a report that consumers were left unprotected from an unregulated industry that **aided** money laundering, while the government and regulators "bumble along" and fail to take action.
>
> The Conservative MP Nicky Morgan, the chair of the committee, said the current situation was unsustainable. "Bitcoin and other crypto-assets exist in the wild west industry of crypto-assets. This unregulated industry leaves investors facing numerous risks," Morgan said. "Given the high price **volatility**, the hacking vulnerability of exchanges, and the
>
> ¹⁰ potential role in money laundering, the Treasury committee strongly believes that regulation should be introduced." Crypto-assets are not covered by the City regulator, the Financial Conduct Authority (FCA), and there are no formal mechanisms for consumer **redress** or investor compensation.
>
> The committee argues in the report that at a minimum, regulation should be introduced to add consumer protection and counter money laundering.
>
> ¹⁵ It said that as things stood, the price of crypto-assets was so volatile that while potential gains were large, so too were potential losses. "Accordingly, investors should be prepared to lose all their money," the committee said.
>
> The FCA said: "The FCA agrees with the committee's conclusion that bitcoin and similar crypto-assets are ill-suited to retail investors, and as we have warned in the past, investors in this type of crypto-asset should be prepared to lose all their money."
>
> ²⁰ [...]
>
> In 2017, the price of a bitcoin soared by more than 900%, hitting a peak of almost $20,000 in December. Its popularity has since waned, with one bitcoin now priced at around $6,270.
>
> The digital currency emerged after the financial crisis. It allows people to bypass banks and usual payment processes to pay for goods and services.
>
> ²⁵ [...]
>
> The Treasury committee said cryptocurrency exchanges were at increased risk of cyber-attacks, and some retail investors who lost their passwords had found themselves locked out of their accounts permanently. However, it said that if regulated and dealt with properly, the industry could be an opportunity for Britain.
>
> [...]
>
> Extracted from www.theguardian.com/technology/2018/sep/19/time-to-regulate-bitcoin-says-treasury-committee-report. Accessed on September 03, 2018.

9. Read the extracts from the text above and decide if they are direct speech (D) or indirect speech (I).

a. (   ) "The committee said in a report that consumers were left unprotected from an unregulated industry that aided money laundering [...]."

b. (   ) "He said: 'The currency isn't going to work. [...]'."

c. (   ) "'As an industry we have been calling for the introduction of proportionate regulation to improve standards and encourage growth,' said Iqbal Gandham, the chair of CryptoUK."

d. (   ) "The committee argues in the report that at a minimum, regulation should be introduced to add consumer protection and counter money laundering."

10. Rewrite the direct speech sentences from activity 9 into indirect speech.

_____

_____

_____

Unit 6

11. Read the pairs of sentences below and circle all the mistakes you can find in the second sentence, considering that they are not true in the present. Then rewrite the sentences.

a. "Cryptocurrency exchanges are at high risk of cyber-attacks", said the experts.

The experts said that cryptocurrency exchanges are at high risk of cyber-attacks.

_____

_____

b. "I've invested a lot of money in Bitcoin," said Marie.

Marie said that I had invested a lot of money in Bitcoin.

_____

_____

c. The president said, "we need regulation, so the money laundering can stop."

The president said that we needed regulation, so the money laundering can stop.

_____

_____

d. "John must stop throwing his money around" said his mother.

John's mother said that she must stop throwing his money around.

_____

_____

AN EYE ON ENEM

ENEM 2012 - 2º dia - Prova Amarela

Questão 93

Cartuns são produzidos com o intuito de satirizar comportamentos humanos e assim oportunizam a reflexão sobre nossos próprios comportamentos e atitudes. Nesse cartum, a linguagem utilizada pelos personagens em uma conversa em inglês evidencia a

a. predominância do uso da linguagem informal sobre a língua padrão.
b. dificuldade de reconhecer a existência de diferentes usos da linguagem.
c. aceitação dos regionalismos utilizados por pessoas de diferentes lugares.
d. necessidade de estudo da língua inglesa por parte dos personagens.

Unit 7 — Digital Influencing

1. Read the text. Then read the titles below and check (✓) the one that best fits the text. *Selecting a good title*

a. (   ) The Top 10 Digital Influencers
b. (   ) Good Influence in Digital Social Media
c. (   ) How to Spot the Fakers in Social Media Influencing
d. (   ) The Top 5 Worst Influencers In Digital Media

www.collabary.com/blog/bad-influence-how-to-spot-the-fakers-in-social-media-influencing

Bad influence –

Team Collabary | 4 August 2017

(   ) **Beyond the filter**

Being a social media influencer, unlike being an Olympic sprinter or an astronaut, is worryingly easy to fake.

From being **sneaky** with the stuff you show in your pictures, to artificially inflating your follower count, there are plenty of ways to make you look more influential than you actually are.

Or at least, that's what these Insta-fakers tell themselves. The reality is that giving a false impression about your real social influence is a) amazingly easy to see through and b) will kill off any hopes you had about making a living from influencer marketing.

Some of the more obvious tricks are about creating a picture of your amazing, inspiring life that simply isn't true. For example, if a travel blogger constantly shares pictures of themselves in amazing hotels – but only ever shows public spaces, like the lobby – the chances are they're really staying in a caravan down the road.

More sinister than this is the outright **theft** of someone else's creativity. Weirdly, even some of the biggest (so-called) influencers out there are just as guilty as the **wannabes**.

[...]

(   ) **Never trust a bot**

Much worse (and much stupider) is the practice of buying Instagram followers or automating interactions.

Hootsuite recently did a fabulous study into the benefits (there were none) of each of these shady social media practices.

In a **nutshell**, they created a dummy account and clicked one of those **ubiquitous** 'get followers now!!' buttons. The results were a definite **increase** in followers – **albeit** ones that didn't offer a single engagement to any post.

Their test for automatic interaction is even more revealing (and funnier). Signing up for a bot to automatically target selected hashtags with generic comments like 'great job!' or 'love this!', Hootsuite's experimenter quickly realized auto-commenting this way is, at best, a bit pointless and at worst can make you look weird, irrelevant, and **creepy**.

(   ) **Keep it real**

But if we now know a bit more about how these people fake their credentials as content creators, it's still hard to understand *why* they do it.

Admittedly, some platform users (and even some brands) still regard someone's follower number as a **measure** of their authority. But, given how simple it is to determine **whether** someone's following is filled with fake accounts and **smutty** bots, that first impression of authority can be quickly and irrevocably broken.

We can't deny that some of the methods above are a cheap way to inflate your audience numbers – you can probably buy around 100 new 'followers' for just a few dollars.

But given that any brand who is serious about social media influencing would sooner give their Twitter password to a monkey than work with someone so shifty, you've potentially lost way more money than you've saved.

The reassuring truth is that there are guaranteed ways to boost your audience numbers and interactions – but these don't come from being sneaky about who you really are. They come from truly knowing and engaging with an audience and from being a specialist, who shares what you know generously and creatively.

Adapted from www.collabary.com/blog/bad-influence-how-to-spot-the-fakers-in-social-media-influencing. Accessed on October 6, 2018.

Unit 7

2. Read the subtitles of the blog post on page 128 and mark the boxes according to the content below.   *Skimming*
   a. How to guarantee ways of raising your audience number without lying about who you are.
   b. How fake social media influencers give false impressions to their audiences.
   c. How the research in getting followers was conducted and its results.

3. A blog is a webpage containing information or opinions from a particular person or about a particular subject. People who read a blog can add their opinion about what it contains. Add your own opinion about the blog you just read.   *Giving opinion*

_____
_____
_____
_____

4. The words in the box below were taken from the text on page 128. Match them with their definitions.

> sneaky   outright   fake   dummy   bot   share

   a. _____ : a computer program that performs the same operation many times in a row, for example one that searches for information on the Internet as part of a search engine
   b. _____ : doing things in a secret and often dishonest or unfair way
   c. _____ : to have or use something with other people
   d. _____ : clear and direct
   e. _____ : a product made to look like a real one and is used for tests, getting people's opinions, etc.
   f. _____ : someone who is not what they claim to be or does not have the skills they say they have

   Adapted from www.ldoceonline.com. Accessed on October 6, 2018.

5. Look at the extracts taken from the text on page 128 and check (✓) the alternatives that best apply.
   a. "Some of the more obvious tricks are about creating a picture of your **amazing**, **inspiring** life that simply isn't true."
      ( ) The adjectives in bold are used to describe the characteristics of something.
      ( ) The adjectives in bold are used to describe the way someone feels.
   b. "The **reassuring** truth is that there are guaranteed ways to boost your audience numbers and interactions – but these don't come from being sneaky about who you really are."
      ( ) The adjective in bold is used to describe the characteristics of something.
      ( ) The adjective in bold is used to describe the way someone feels.

6. Now read the quote below and pay close attention to the adjectives in bold. Then check (✓) the alternative that best applies.

> "No matter how **frustrated**, **disappointed** and **discouraged** we may feel in the face of our failures, it's only temporary. And the faster you can stop wallowing in guilt, blame or resentment, the faster you can put it behind you." – Fabrizio Moreira
>
> *Extracted from www.brainyquote.com. Accessed on October 11, 2018.*

   a. ( ) The adjectives in bold are used to describe the characteristics of something.
   b. ( ) The adjectives in bold are used to describe the way someone feels.

129

7. Read the sentences below and circle the correct alternative.

a. Some influencers live very **exciting** / **excited** lives.
b. They worked hard all weekend long. They must be **tiring** / **tired**.
c. Some of the comments I read on the blog were quite **insulting** / **insulted**.
d. My sister loves your blog! She is absolutely **thrilling** / **thrilled**!
e. That YouTuber is so **boring** / **bored**! I can't watch her videos without falling asleep.
f. His methods to expand his audience numbers are definitely **confusing** / **confused**.

8. Read the quotes of some top media influencers of 2018 according to cbsnews.com. Then read the sentences and underline *must* or *can't*.

a. He **must** / **can't** be a very skilled and methodical actor and comedian.

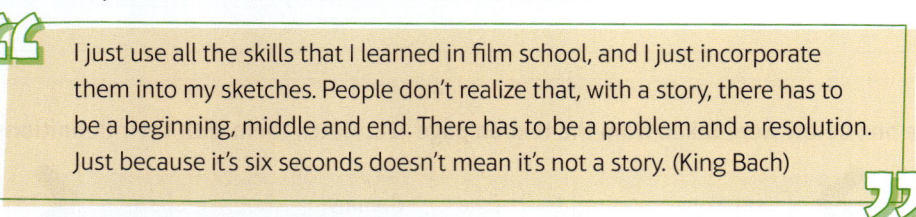

> I just use all the skills that I learned in film school, and I just incorporate them into my sketches. People don't realize that, with a story, there has to be a beginning, middle and end. There has to be a problem and a resolution. Just because it's six seconds doesn't mean it's not a story. (King Bach)

b. She **must** / **can't** be very worried about what people think of her.

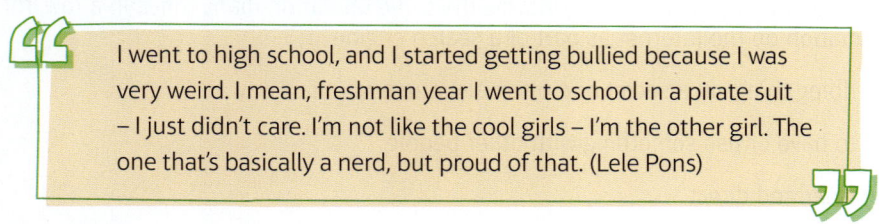

> I went to high school, and I started getting bullied because I was very weird. I mean, freshman year I went to school in a pirate suit – I just didn't care. I'm not like the cool girls – I'm the other girl. The one that's basically a nerd, but proud of that. (Lele Pons)

c. He **must** / **can't** have made mistakes when he was younger.

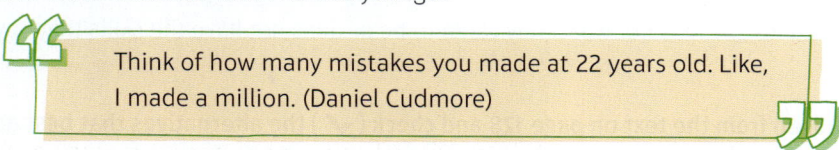

> Think of how many mistakes you made at 22 years old. Like, I made a million. (Daniel Cudmore)

d. She **must** / **can't** have been through difficult moments in her life.

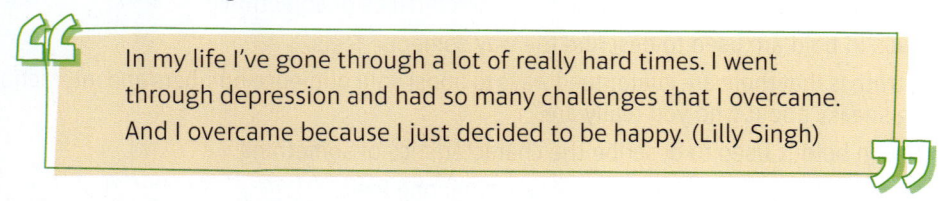

> In my life I've gone through a lot of really hard times. I went through depression and had so many challenges that I overcame. And I overcame because I just decided to be happy. (Lilly Singh)

Extracted from www.brainyquote.com. Accessed on October 6, 2018.

9. Read an extract from the text on page 128. Circle the correct alternatives about the rules for the passive voice.

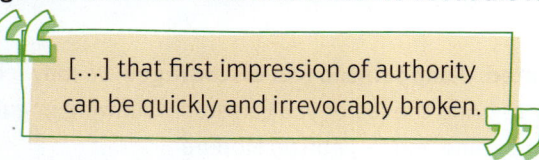

> […] that first impression of authority can be quickly and irrevocably broken.

a. We form the passive voice using the verb *be* + past participle.
b. We use the passive voice using the verb *be* + the infinitive.
c. We form the passive voice with modal verbs using a modal verb + *be* + past participle.
d. We always use *to* after a modal verb.

10. Rewrite the sentences using passive voice. Add *by* when necessary.

a. They should organize the event in the park.

b. The researchers handed in the reports about the bad influencers.

c. Claire has washed John's car three times this month.

d. You must read the blog messages before she gets here.

e. Cameron Dallas may produce a new movie soon.

f. They are going to build a new factory in my neighborhood.

AN EYE ON VESTIBULAR

VESTIBULAR UNESP - 2017

Questão 29

"One never builds something finished": the brilliance of architect Paulo Mendes da Rocha

Oliver Wainwright
February 4, 2017

"All space is public," says Paulo Mendes da Rocha. "The only private space that you can imagine is in the human mind." It is an optimistic statement from the 88-year-old Brazilian architect, given he is a resident of São Paulo, a city where the triumph of the private realm over the public could not be more stark. The sprawling megalopolis is a place of such marked inequality that its superrich hop between their rooftop helipads because they are too scared of street crime to come down from the clouds.

But for Mendes da Rocha, who received the 2017 gold medal from the Royal Institute of British Architects this week – an accolade previously bestowed on such luminaries as Le Corbusier and Frank Lloyd Wright – the ground is everything. He has spent his 60-year career lifting his massive concrete buildings up, in gravity-defying balancing acts, or else burying them below ground in an attempt to liberate the Earth's surface as a continuous democratic public realm. "The city has to be for everybody," he says, "not just for the very few."

(www.theguardian.com. Adaptado.)

No trecho do primeiro parágrafo "the triumph of the private realm over the public could not be more **stark**", o termo em destaque tem sentido equivalente, em português, a

a. gritante.
b. purificado.
c. vazio.
d. simples.
e. disfarçado.

Unit 8 — The End of a Journey

1. **Look at the article. What do you think are some new jobs that graduates will be doing from 2026? Read the article and check your predictions.** *Predicting and skimming*

10 jobs graduates **will be applying / will have applied** for from 2026

Rachael Pells @rachaelpells | Tuesday 9 August 2016 00:12

Tomorrow's graduates **will be applying / will have applied** for jobs working in virtual worlds and outer space, experts claim, following the release of a new report predicting career trends for the next ten years. [...]

The report highlights that 65 per cent of school students in university today will take up jobs that don't exist yet. [...]

Ten jobs of the future

1) Virtual Habitat Designer

Required skills/qualifications: _____, editing, psychology

Researchers predict tens of millions of us **will be spending / will have spent** hours each day working and learning in virtual reality environments by the year 2026. The role of a Virtual Habitat Designer will be to design these worlds, creating suitable environments for virtual meetings to take place, or VR galleries for artists to display their work.

2) Ethical Technology Advocate

Required skills/qualifications: _____, philosophy, ethics

An Ethical Technology Advocate will act as a go-between for humans, robots and AI, setting the moral and ethical rules under which the machines operate and exist. [...]

3) Digital Cultural Commentator

Required skills/qualifications: _____, business studies, PR and marketing

In ten years' time, visual communication will dominate social media. [...]

Frances Morris, director of Tate Modern, believes skilled workers such as digital culture commentators will be key to enabling art institutes such as her own to attract visitor spending power and guarantee future commercial success.

4) Freelance Biohacker

Required skills/qualifications: Biosciences, medical methodology, _____

Science has long been dominated by professional teams working in universities, corporate research and development departments – but the rise of open source software platforms will democratise this sector, say researchers.

Freelance **biohackers** will work remotely on open-source software platforms along with thousands of others in virtual teams connected online. [...]

5) IoT (Internet of Things) Data Creative

Required skills/qualifications: Engineering, problem solving, _____ and entrepreneurship

IoT Data Creatives will **sift** through the waves of data being generated each day by devices in our clothes, our homes, our cars and our offices and find meaningful and useful ways to tell us what all that information is saying. [...]

6) Space Tour Guide

Already on the horizon thanks to the likes of Virgin Galactic, Earth orbit will become the new frontier for adventurous travellers by 2026.

7) Personal Content Curator

By the late 2020s, software-brain interfaces, pioneered by teams of neuroscientists, **will be starting / will have started** to enter the mainstream, allowing mass audiences to read and capture thoughts, memories, and dreams. [...]

8) Rewilding Strategist

By 2025, the planet will struggle to cope with nine billion humans and the resources they require, and traditional conservation won't be enough. [...]

9) Sustainable Power Innovator

By the mid-2020s, resource **depletion** will mean a shift to sustainable energy. The main struggle here **will be storing / will have stored** power for the days when the wind doesn't blow or the sun doesn't shine. [...]

10) Human Body Designer

Engineering advances will extend the average healthy human life as the growth of replacement tissues and organs becomes an everyday and affordable proposition.

Adapted from www.independent.co.uk/news/education/education-news/10-jobs-graduates-will-be-applying-for-from-2026-a7179316.html. Accessed on October 9, 2018.

Unit 8

2. Read the first five jobs of the future in the article on page 132. Then complete the required skills / qualifications of these with the words from the box below. *Understanding main ideas*

> communications   data analytics
> architectural design
> art history   communications

3. Look at the article on page 132 again and pay close attention to the sentences using future perfect and future continuous. Then underline the correct alternative.

4. What do you think you will be doing ten years from now? Write your answer using future continuous.

_____
_____
_____

5. Look at these two extracts taken from the article. You will see two phrasal verbs using *take*. Check (✓) the correct meaning for each one.

a. "The report highlights that 65 per cent of school students in university today will **take up** jobs that don't exist yet."
- ( ) to fill a particular amount of time or space
- ( ) to start something new or have a new responsibility
- ( ) to make a piece of clothing shorter
- ( ) to do something about an idea or suggestion that you have been considering

b. "[...] creating suitable environments for virtual meetings to **take place**, or VR galleries for artists to display their work."
- ( ) to suddenly start being successful
- ( ) to let people know the true facts about a bad or shocking situation
- ( ) to make something better, stronger, etc.
- ( ) to happen, especially after being planned or arranged

Adapted from www.ldoceonline.com. Accessed on October 10, 2018.

6. Look at the words in the box below. Circle the words that collocate with *take* and underline the words that collocate with *have*.

> the lead   a dream   a plan
> responsibility   action   questions
> a rest   a chance   notes   a bus

7. Use some collocations from activity 6 to complete the sentences below. Make sure to use the correct form of the verb.

a. We need to write a report. Did you _____ during the seminar?
b. Today you _____ to talk to her about your problems.
c. That's not fair. You must do something about it. Let's _____!
d. Our country _____ in the environmental discussions last week.
e. Sarah has been working a lot to solve that problem. I'm sure she _____.
f. If you _____ any _____, just ask your teacher for some help.

133

8. Read an excerpt from a blog post and complete it with the verbs from the box in the form indicated in parentheses.

> give   choose   offer   thank   identify
> fit   change   head   choose

https://zety.com/blog/how-to-choose-a-major

HOW TO CHOOSE A MAJOR - A COMPLETE GUIDE

By Christian Eilers – Resumé expert at Zety

There are literally thousands of majors to choose from, and each university and college program will vary on their offerings. You need to pick one that your future self _____ (future simple) you for.
[…]
As with relationships and the latest **billboard** hits, you may decide that the major you _____ (past simple) is not right for you anymore.

Don't worry about this – you're not alone. According to the NY Times, a **whopping** 61% of the students at the University of Florida _____ (simple present) their minds about their major by the end of their sophomore year. So, you'd be in the minority if you *didn't* second-guess yourself.

One thing to keep in mind is to make sure that you don't just pick the easiest program out there. Choose a path that _____ (simple future) you a degree that you'll be proud of and that at least fits somewhat with the idea of the direction you _____ (present continuous).

One quick thing to mention before we end – the reality check. Before pulling the trigger on the major of your choice, ask yourself:

1. What kind of job is right for me in the future as a career?
2. Will this major _____ (present perfect) help me with this?
3. What college is right for me for my undergraduate studies?
4. _____ this college _____ (simple present) a great program for my chosen major?
5. _____ my chosen major _____ (simple present) my abilities, values, interests, and passions?
6. _____ I _____ (present perfect) all the downsides and disadvantages of my chosen major?

Adapted from https://zety.com/blog/how-to-choose-a-major. Accessed on October 9, 2018.

9. Read the six questions at the end of the post in activity 8 again. How would you answer these questions?

1. _____
2. _____
3. _____
4. _____
5. _____
6. _____

10. Reorder the words to form sentences.

a. take / will / a year off / choosing / before / a major / I / .
_____

b. last train / the / will / arriving / be / soon / .
_____

c. already / has / Samantha / several / vocational tests / taken / .
_____

d. working / really / is / hard / his final / Kevin / exams / to pass / .
_____

e. already / gone over / three first pages / the / when arrived / she had / we / .
_____

f. been / preparing / have / we / all week / for / test / this / .
_____

g. before / graduated / will / I / have / Christmas / .
_____

AN EYE ON VESTIBULAR

VESTIBULAR PUC-SP 2017-1

Questão 43

COMMENTS (4) (Please sing in to comment)

> **orinoco womble said**, *22 days ago*
> Good things: Living in the dorms, far from parental supervision, you can get up to all sorts of trouble and they won't know if you don't tell 'em. Pizza parlours and takeaways occupy a whole street near campus. You could eat pizza every night and your parents couldn't say a word (I realize I'm showing my age, I'm before the junkfood generation).
> You get to make your own mistakes. No helicopter parents around. Some of those mistakes are a lot of fun at the time! Everyone around you likes your music or something even crazier. You can experiment with life.
>
> *http://www.gocomics.com/JustinBoyed*
> *Acessado em 22/08/2016*

O comentário [...] foi postado após um artigo sobre

a. o uso de helicópteros por pais para supervisionar jovens adultos que moram em universidades.
b. algumas das novas experiências que a vida no campus universitário propicia.
c. o saudável controle dos pais sobre a vida universitária dos filhos.
d. o crescimento do comércio ao redor dos campi universitários.

AUDIO SCRIPTS

Unit 1

Track 02 – Activity 2

Jennifer Siebel Newsom wasn't even planning to direct her documentary, Miss Representation. She first approached some established female directors to take on her film about how women are portrayed in the mainstream media, but every one declined to do it, saying nobody would hire them afterwards – a stark illustration of who runs the entertainment industry even before you get to the hard-hitting statistics and appalling examples of sexism in her film.

Extracted from www.theguardian.com/lifeandstyle/2014/mar/03/feminist-film-maker-taking-on-hollywood. Accessed on October 4, 2018.

Track 03 – Activity 3

Her film was originally shown at Sundance and broadcast in the US in 2011. It features an impressive line-up of powerful women, including Nancy Pelosi, Condoleezza Rice, Katie Couric, and Gloria Steinem, as well as academics and activists who all flesh out the idea that the demeaning and stereotypical representation of women in the media is a significant contributor in holding women back from positions of power. This, in turn, affects the lives of all women, from the gender pay gap and career opportunities after motherhood, to mental health issues and the rise of cosmetic surgery.

[...]

Extracted from www.theguardian.com/lifeandstyle/2014/mar/03/feminist-film-maker-taking-on-hollywood. Accessed on October 4, 2018.

Unit 2

Track 04 – Activity 2

REPORTER: Their team name is Ctrl Alt Delete, and they know a lot about robots.

STUDENT: It's really nice how you can program them to do whatever you want.

REPORTER: The ten students from Berwick Lodge, Glendal, and Mount View primary schools won the National Robotics Championships in Sydney with this creation – the HotSpot Spotter robot. Fitted with a heat sensor, the robot can identify trees which don't appear burned, but are likely to explode in coming weeks. Currently, firefighters do the checks manually with handheld detectors. It's unsafe and inefficient.

STUDENT 2: It senses the obstacles in its path, so all the trees, and it looks at each of them one by one, and then whichever one of the trees have combustion, it sends the coordinates back to base, so the CFA can adjust the tree and take it down.

Extracted from http://education.abc.net.au/home#!/media/1453656/hotspot-spotter-wins-top-robot-prize. Accessed on August 13, 2018.

Track 05 – Activity 3

REPORTER: Their team name is Ctrl Alt Delete, and they know a lot about robots.

STUDENT: It's really nice how you can program them to do whatever you want.

REPORTER: The ten students from Berwick Lodge, Glendal, and Mount View primary schools won the National Robotics Championships in Sydney with this creation—the HotSpot Spotter robot. Fitted with a heat sensor, the robot can identify trees which don't appear burned, but are likely to explode in coming weeks. Currently, firefighters do the checks manually with handheld detectors. It's unsafe and inefficient.

STUDENT 2: It senses the obstacles in its path, so all the trees, and it looks at each of them one by one, and then whichever one of the trees have combustion, it sends the coordinates back to base, so the CFA can adjust the tree and take it down.

REPORTER: Robotics is slowly gaining popularity, but many schools still put it in the too-hard-and-too expensive basket.

TEACHER: Look, education's about many things. One of them is preparing children for the workforce of the future. Robotics in Asia, America, Europe is big. In Australia, we use robots, but it's undertaught in our schools.

REPORTER: And there's also the gender imbalance to address.

STUDENT 3: It's nice to have another girl, Zoe, on our team. It would be cool to have maybe, like, one or two more girls.

REPORTER: The team wants to compete at World Robotics Championships in Spain next year, but they need a sponsor. Their teachers say they're a good investment. There's no way they could have come up with the HotSpot Spotter.

TEACHER 2: Oh, no.

TEACHER 3: I'm not that clever, no.

TEACHER 2: No, it's the children's...

TEACHER 3: It's the children's idea.

REPORTER: The teachers say the CFA and the Royal Fire Service have given it the thumbs up, and have encouraged the kids to explore commercial opportunities. Kerri Ritchie, ABC News, Melbourne.

Extracted from http://education.abc.net.au/home#!/media/1453656/hotspot-spotter-wins-top-robot-prize. Accessed on August 13, 2018.

Unit 3

Track 06 – Activity 2

[...]

When we think about threats to the environment, we tend to picture cars and smokestacks, not dinner. But the truth is, our need for food poses one of the biggest dangers to the planet.

Agriculture is among the greatest contributors to global warming, emitting more greenhouse gases than all our cars, trucks, trains, and airplanes combined—largely from methane released by cattle and rice farms, nitrous oxide from fertilized fields, and carbon dioxide from the cutting of rain forests to grow crops or raise livestock. Farming is the thirstiest user of our precious water supplies and a major polluter, as runoff from fertilizers and manure disrupts fragile lakes, rivers, and coastal ecosystems across the globe. Agriculture also accelerates the loss of biodiversity. As we've cleared areas of grassland and forest for farms, we've lost crucial habitat, making agriculture a major driver of wildlife extinction.

The environmental challenges posed by agriculture are huge, and they'll only become more pressing as we try to meet the growing need for food worldwide. We'll likely have two billion more mouths to feed by mid-century—more than nine billion people. But sheer population growth isn't the only reason we'll need more food. The spread of prosperity across the world, especially in China and India, is driving an increased demand for meat, eggs, and dairy, boosting pressure to grow more corn and soybeans to feed more cattle, pigs, and chickens. If these trends continue, the double whammy of population growth and richer diets will require us to roughly double the amount of crops we grow by 2050.

Unfortunately, the debate over how to address the global food challenge has become polarized, pitting conventional agriculture and global commerce against local food systems and organic farms. The arguments can be fierce, and like our politics, we seem to be getting more divided rather than finding common ground. Those who favor conventional agriculture talk about how modern mechanization, irrigation, fertilizers, and improved genetics can increase yields to help meet demand. And they're right. Meanwhile proponents of local and organic farms counter that the world's small farmers could increase yields plenty—and help themselves out of poverty—by adopting techniques that improve fertility without synthetic fertilizers and pesticides. They're right too.

[...]

Extracted from www.nationalgeographic.com/foodfeatures/feeding-9-billion/>. Accessed on August 21, 2018.

Track 07 – Activity 3

[...] We need to find a balance between producing more food and sustaining the planet for future generations.

This is a pivotal moment when we face unprecedented challenges to food security and the preservation of our global environment. The good news is that we already know what we have to do; we just need to figure out how to do it. Addressing our global food challenges demands that all of us become more thoughtful about the food we put on our plates. We need to make connections between our food and the farmers who grow it, and between our food and the land, watersheds, and climate that sustain us. As we steer our grocery carts down the aisles of our supermarkets, the choices we make will help decide the future.

Extracted from www.nationalgeographic.com/foodfeatures/feeding-9-billion/. Accessed on August 21, 2018.

Unit 4
Track 08 – Activity 2

[...]

I was 14 when I asked a friend's stepdad where Mount Everest was. We were on a hill-walking trip and the sense of achievement at scaling those Lake District crags awakened a thirst for adventure. Bullied mercilessly at school, I suffered attacks of anxiety and was reluctant to be away from home. But once the idea struck, there was no stopping me – having asked where to find the world's highest peak, it would be only four years until I first set foot on it.

[...]

At 18, I would have been the youngest British climber ever to reach the top of Everest on the south route, but it was not to be. After weeks of trekking, my team arrived at base camp on 19 April 2014, the day after an avalanche killed 16 Sherpa guides. It was, at that time, the worst human tragedy in Everest's history, and all climbing on the mountain was abandoned for the rest of the season.

[...]

Extracted from www.theguardian.com/lifeandstyle/2016/may/13/experience-caught-in-avalanche-everest. Accessed on August 28, 2018.

Track 09 – Activity 3

[...]

I was 14 when I asked a friend's stepdad where Mount Everest was. We were on a hill-walking trip and the sense of achievement at scaling those Lake District crags awakened a thirst for adventure. Bullied mercilessly at school, I suffered attacks of anxiety and was reluctant to be away from home. But once the idea struck, there was no stopping me – having asked where to find the world's highest peak, it would be only four years until I first set foot on it.

[...]

At 18, I would have been the youngest British climber ever to reach the top of Everest on the south route, but it was not to be. After weeks of trekking, my team arrived at base camp on 19 April 2014, the day after an avalanche killed 16 Sherpa guides. It was, at that time, the worst human tragedy in Everest's history, and all climbing on the mountain was abandoned for the rest of the season.

It would be 12 months until I was able to venture back. An extra year's training left me feeling much more prepared and I started to feel excited about the prospect of some real climbing. The morning we set out to climb to camp one from base camp was grim, stormy, and turbulent. [...]

We passed towering columns, crumbling ledges, and yawning crevasses; but as thick fog obscured the route, I kept my head down, focusing on one step at a time. After several tough hours, I was past the most technical section of the climb, on some big, open ice blocks. I was close to camp one but completely alone – Tim, the team leader, and Ellis, another climber, were perhaps 20 minutes behind me. Most other members were already at the camp when the earthquake struck.

I'll never forget the cracking noise that echoed through the valley. I looked up, startled, knowing it was ice breaking away from the mountain, but was unable to see more than a few meters ahead. There was nowhere to run; I barely had time to wonder whether I'd be better off unclipping myself from my climbing rope before the avalanche hit me like an express train.

It just kept coming, forcing snow into my nose and mouth. [...] I thought of my family back home and imagined the headlines announcing my death – I had no expectation of surviving.

Abruptly, the wind subsided and the mountain fell silent. I'd only been hit by powder snow and had escaped the worst of the avalanche, but knew a further collapse could be on the way. There was no response when I tried to radio ahead, and I wondered if everyone above and below me had been swept away: was I the only team member left alive? Crying, I pressed on, eventually reuniting with Tim, Ellis, and two more members of the team; alive, but overwhelmed. [...]

When we radioed base camp, we realized how lucky we'd been. The whole area had been hit by a much bigger avalanche and completely destroyed. It was two days before we could be helicoptered down, and the camp still looked like the site of a plane crash. [...]

Nearly 9,000 people were killed by that earthquake. Since then, I've focused on raising funds to help rebuild Nepal. I plan to return to Everest for a third attempt one day. Like the bullying at school, it's something I need to overcome before I can move on.

Adapted from www.theguardian.com/lifeandstyle/2016/may/13/experience-caught-in-avalanche-everest. Accessed on August 28, 2018.

Unit 5

Track 10 – Activity 2

Cancel your Netflix session: Binge watching TV makes it LESS enjoyable as you're more likely to forget plot details.

Binge watching television series like Game of Thrones could make it significantly less enjoyable than watching it on a weekly basis.

New research found watching too much television in one go diminishes the quality of the show with viewers getting 'significantly less' enjoyment than those who paced themselves.

Research led by the University of Melbourne found how people watch television significantly affects how much enjoyment they get out of it.

'Binge watching via video-on-demand services is now considered the new 'normal' way to consume television programs', researchers wrote in their paper in peer-reviewed journal First Monday.

[...]

Researchers found that 'although binge watching leads to strong memory formation immediately following program viewing, these memories decay more rapidly than memories formed after daily or weekly episode viewing schedules.'

[...]

Extracted from www.dailymail.co.uk/sciencetech/article-4861672/Binge-watching-TV-makes-enjoyable-study-claims.html. Accessed on December 11, 2018.

Track 11 – Activity 3

The team took 51 students from the university and split them into groups of 17 to watch the BBC Cold War drama The Game over different periods of time.

One group watched one-hour weekly another watched it daily and the other group watched the whole season (six hours) in one sitting [...].

No participants had previously watched the show and they all watched it in the lab.

Any time a character lit a cigarette or poured a drink they had to press a keyboard to prove that they were concentrating.

They filled out a questionnaire straight after finishing the show, then 24 hours later, and then twice a week until 140 days had passed.

Questions included things like 'In episode four, what was delivered to Arkady's secret mailbox?'

People who binge-watched had the best memory the day after the show but this declined sharply from then on.

People who viewed the show weekly remembered the least after 24 hours but then could retain the most information over time.

Weekly viewers also reported enjoying the show more than any of the other groups.

[...]

Extracted from www.dailymail.co.uk/sciencetech/article-4861672/Binge-watching-TV-makes-enjoyable-study-claims.html. Accessed on December 11, 2018.

Unit 6

Track 12 – Activity 2

The Illicit World of Bitcoin and the Dark Web

Two words will be indelibly etched on the minds of many people following bitcoin: Silk Road. This was the original dark market, and it became notorious for enabling people to sell drugs and other illegal items online. But, what is a dark market, and how does one work?

By themselves, dark markets aren't necessarily illegal. They are simply digital marketplaces, created using the same kinds of technologies that typically underpin bitcoin. At the very least, they will accept bitcoin as a method of payment because of its quasi-anonymous characteristics.

Having said that, most dark markets quickly become illegal because of the kinds of products that they allow vendors to sell. As soon as a digital marketplace allows for the trafficking of drugs, weapons, or other illegal items, then it is breaking the law, and law enforcement officials will quickly get interested.

[...]

Extracted from www.thebalance.com/what-is-a-dark-market-391289. Accessed on September 11, 2018.

Track 13 – Activity 3

[...]

Silk Road

That's what happened to Silk Road, which was one of the first – if not the first – dark markets on the web. Created by Ross

Ulbricht, it was a digital marketplace that connected vendors of illegal drugs with potential buyers. Vendors would advertise their wares on listings maintained by Silk Road, which was similar to the kinds of listings you might find on any legitimate e-commerce marketplace.

When someone decided to buy drugs via the website, they generally wouldn't want to send money directly to that person. Drug peddling isn't exactly a trustworthy business, and everyone who advertised and purchased using Silk Road was anonymous. This would have made it very easy for crooks to make off with customers' money without sending any goods in return.

To solve this problem, Silk Road provided an escrow service. Customers buying drugs from vendors who listed on Silk Road would send their funds to Silk Road, instead of the vendor. The website would then hold these funds until the customer confirmed that they had received what they had ordered. Then, Silk Road would release the funds to the vendor.

The funds were always sent in bitcoin, rather than fiat currency, because when used correctly, the network can provide a great degree of anonymity.

[...]

Silk Road wasn't a decentralized marketplace, though. It ran on a computer controlled by Ulbricht. It was protected, though, because it ran on Tor, which is a communications protocol designed to offer anonymity to those who use it. Originally developed by the U.S. Navy, Tor has become popular among those wanting to protect their identities online.

The FBI eventually arrested Ulbricht by piecing together clues that they gathered from various places outside the Tor network. Now, though, many more dark markets have sprung up, most of them dealing with drugs.

[...]

Extracted from www.thebalance.com/what-is-a-dark-market-391289. Accessed on September 11, 2018.

Track 14 – Activity 4

Dark Markets Under Attack

Aside from the fact that they are breaking the law, one of the biggest concerns around dark markets is trustworthiness. In several cases, dark markets have suddenly vanished with millions of dollars in escrow funds, leaving customers robbed of their funds. Law enforcement is also getting better at targeting these dark markets and taking them down. In November 2014, Operation Onymous, an international law enforcement operation, seized over 400 dark web domains. Dark markets including CannabisRoad, Blue Sky, and Hydra have been taken down.

Law enforcement says that it has found a way to target sites using Tor, although has refused to reveal how.

Dark markets continue to operate, and law enforcement continues to take them down in a continuous game of cat and mouse. Anyone considering engaging in illegal activities through these marketplaces should be aware of the risks.

Extracted from www.thebalance.com/what-is-a-dark-market-391289. Accessed on September 11, 2018.

Unit 7

Track 15 – Activity 2

Next time you see someone calling themselves an influencer, next time you see a list of influencers on a very credible article think to yourself: how was this made? Influencers are everywhere, everyone's calling themselves an influencer, even I'm guilty of calling myself an influencer when I was featured as an influencer last year. But what actually makes a real influencer? What makes a fake influencer? Should you be calling yourself an influencer? Should I be calling myself an influencer? These are all questions I've been thinking a lot about lately and in this short talk I wanna share with you some of my thoughts and I wanna hear from you.

Transcribed from www.youtube.com/watch?time_continue=10&v=bN5HYYZd_Fk. Accessed on September 20, 2018.

Track 16 – Activity 3

Next time you see someone calling themselves an influencer, next time you see a list of influencers on a very credible article think to yourself: how was this made? Influencers are everywhere, everyone's calling themselves an influencer, even I'm guilty of calling myself an influencer when I was featured as an influencer last year. But what actually makes a real influencer? What makes a fake influencer? Should you be calling yourself an influencer? Should I be calling myself an influencer? These are all questions I've been thinking a lot about lately and in this short talk I wanna share with you some of my thoughts and I wanna hear from you.

Just before we start, I wanna just say that this isn't about calling anyone out, this isn't like I've seen something, I've got annoyed, and I want to dig someone out, this is literally me trying to shed some light on the whole influence of space for you and share some of the insights that I've found that I was quite shocked by, and just to kind of, put us all on a level playing field when it comes to understanding what an influencer is and how these influences are being identified. One of the main points that this talk is all about is about lists of influencers. I'm sure you've all seen on very credible articles, "The top 20 snapchatters of 2017", "The top 10 social media experts", "The top 10 LinkedIn experts". We've all seen these lists, I've been named on a few of them as well myself, but what actually is the methodology behind creating those lists? What is the data backed up to actually identify those people and those featured influencers as the most influential in that space? In a lot of cases there's no data, there's literally like no data to back this stuff up. It's all the opinions of the contributor who's writing that article. It's just someone's opinions. It's literally someone's opinions on who they think the top influencers are in that certain field and people are pulling the wool over your eyes! Every time you read these articles... Why are they choosing these people as the top 20? Why are they choosing them? I honestly think one of the big things they're doing it for is to do favors for people they wanna do favors for. [...]

So what I want you all to think about next time you see

someone calling themselves an influencer, next time you see a list of influencers on a very credible article, think to yourself: how was this made? And it will change the way you think about things. [...]

*Transcribed from www.youtube.com/watch?time_continue=10&v=bN5HYYZd_Fk.
Accessed on September 20, 2018.*

Unit 8

Track 17 — Activity 2

You know, I've never understood how, um, imagining the audience naked was supposed to make you less nervous. Honestly, I'm just uncomfortable right now. Especially with Mr. Wardle. Um, okay. To ensure clear communication with this "social media generation", hashtags and pop-culture references will be used. #you'rewelcome. Good afternoon, ladies and gentlemen. Today is an exciting day: today I'm gonna give you a speech. Now, graduates, I don't know if you know me, but I'm Chase. We went to High School together. That was good times, follow me on Twitter.

And I want to give a big congratulations to everyone --including myself-- for being here today. The world we live in is plagued with dangers: Ebola, ISIS, Global Warming, facial acne. And despite all the odds, we still managed to graduate, so let's give us a big round of applause.

[Applause]

It was only three years ago that we came to the labyrinth known as Weber High. As young, timid sophomores we found ourselves lost in its halls like they were the changing staircases of Hogwarts.

[...]

*Transcribed from www.youtube.com/watch?v=DRiV4KZBoIY.
Accessed on September 25, 2018.*

Track 18 — Activity 3

And now, here we are: done with high school!

As Charles Dickens put it, "It was the best of times, it was the worst of times."

[...]

Now, at the end of our careers as students, we have an opportunity: now is our time to take on the world, and to find and pursue our passions; to quote unquote, "Leave a Legacy." William Shakespeare, and also Channing Tatum, once said, "Some are born great, some achieve greatness, and some have greatness thrust upon them." In life, we can't always count on being born great, or having greatness thrust upon us, but always, always remember that the opportunity to achieve greatness is within our grasp. Keep in mind that many of our social and political leaders and heroes started their lives as an average person; as just one of you and me. Despite the failures and mistakes we will make, and although we may be "average", we find that the average can achieve greatness, whether recognized by the world or just a few. Greatness comes from our friends reaching out to us, those who go out of their way to be thoughtful; the "unsung heroes".

If there's anything you take from today, remember that to "leave a legacy" and to "achieve greatness" is not to get money and recognition, it's to leave those with whom you cross paths with a little more happiness and hope. Our time here together as a senior class will not be remembered by grades, popularity, likes, or favorites, but by our relationships. The kind of person you were. These are legacies, the kind we must leave.

Class of 2015, it's been a #splendid three years with you, and from the bottom of my heart, I wish you all the very, very, very best. Thank you.

[Applause]

*Transcribed from www.youtube.com/watch?v=DRiV4KZBoIY.
Accessed on September 25, 2018.*

NOTES

NOTES

NOTES

NOTES

NOTES

NOTES

NOTES